Hewitt Family

of Maryland, Pennsylvania and Ohio

and Allied Families

Cochran, Davis,
Durham, Edwards, Fisher,
Gulick, Hall, Hull, Jacks,
Kennedy, Kenny, Kyle, Morrison,
Piersol, Schmidt, Terhune,
Williamson and Wood

Marilyn Schmidt

HERITAGE BOOKS
2015

HERITAGE BOOKS

AN IMPRINT OF HERITAGE BOOKS, INC.

Books, CDs, and more—Worldwide

For our listing of thousands of titles see our website
at
www.HeritageBooks.com

Published 2015 by
HERITAGE BOOKS, INC.
Publishing Division
5810 Ruatan Street
Berwyn Heights, Md. 20740

International Standard Book Numbers
Paperbound: 978-0-7884-4124-0
Clothbound: 978-0-7884-6250-4

Francese Vesta Hewitt (1889-1910), ca. 1900

❖

IN MEMORY

This book is lovingly dedicated to

FRANCESE VESTA HEWITT,
my grandmother

❖

Before she reached her 21st birthday,
her life was shortened
by tuberculosis

Never having truly lived,
it is my hope
that the richness
of her family's history
will lend weight and significance
to her brief
but intense life

❖

CONTENTS

CONTENTS (continued)

ILLUSTRATIONS

PREFACE

I never intended to write this book. At first I was merely curious about the family Dad left behind in Ohio, but as our conversations continued stories began to unfold. He talked about his friends and how eight year-old boys amused themselves on long summer days, about skating on frozen creeks and ponds in the winter and about his grandmother's cooking. Raised by his father's family, he knew a lot about them, but he was also observant and interested in their lives. Eventually our conversations lead me to ask about his mother, Vesta, because he did not talk about her or her family. What at first seemed like a closely held secret, I later came to realize was that he did not know them because his mother died when he was very young, his father remarried, and he was raised by his grandparents. One day after a bit of probing I learned that Dad knew a lot about both sides of his family, including naming three generations of the male line on his mother's side. So that I could understand the relationships, I began framing what he told me as a family tree. As he talked he threw in intriguing tidbits, saying that although his was an Ohio family his grandfather lived in Tennessee and that one of his grandparents was Dutch. Just to add spice to the tale he said that the sword that hung in the tree for so many years belonged to his great-grandfather who had fought in the Civil War.

After that I was off and running. Who could this Dutch ancestor be? Why did his mother's uncle have a stable of horses and what was the story behind the sad little Christmas card she mailed from Boulder, Colorado, when I knew she lived in Cincinnati? I love a mystery, be it in a novel or a family, and was intrigued by the clues my father gave me. With a public library nearby, I soon began unlocking the answers to my personal history. What began as a challenge soon grew into a passion. I soon learned that one branch of my grandmother's family was English and the other Dutch, and the more I looked the greater the number of clues. It was just one giant jigsaw puzzle and I wanted to find every piece. At one point, I realized I had my fifth grade history teacher to thank for his patience in meting out little bits of history to a mostly uninterested group of ten year-olds. He persevered and I must have remembered, because the cobwebs soon fell out of those long ago lectures when I placed my ancestors in the historical context I had grudgingly learned so many years before. Just like the dramas that played large in the movie theater I frequented as a kid, my ancestors were a part of America's development in a long running adventure story that played across the screen of history. Yet they mostly turned out to be ordinary people, although in some ways more adventurous, often living life more on the edge than we do today. Their problems and challenges were different than ours and yet they were the same. My ancestors worked, tended sick children and wondered how they would pay the mortgage. They got bored and raged at injustice, but mostly they kept going, facing life day by day as it was meted out to them, just like us, just like me.

WITH GRATITUDE

The search for my family history took me on a journey to places I might otherwise never have visited. I connected with lives that now seem as familiar to me as my living kin. Along the way I discovered surprising, and sometimes humbling revelations about those who came before me. Most of all, the pathway back in time led me to wonderful people who helped and encouraged me. Some I never met, but got to know through letters, via Internet correspondence and on the phone. Some exchanges lasted for years, while others were brief but productive.

Occasionally a bit of luck chanced upon this venture and filled in a large chunk of the puzzle. In 1995 I discovered a handwritten reproduction of a page from an early Hewitt Bible included in an unpublished manuscript by William Buckner McGroarty who lived in the Cincinnati area. I am exceptionally grateful to him for interviews he began about 1912 with relatives who lived in nearby Georgetown, Ohio. He discovered that an elderly aunt had the Jacob Hewitt Family Bible containing birth dates beginning in 1697 and continuing through four generations to 1809. Mr. McGroarty had the Bible rebound, copied the records from it, and gave it back to its owner. The book I have written is the second time this record has served as the keystone for Hewitt history. Sometime before 1940, Mr. McGroarty documented his grandmother's story, titled *Hewitt Family, the Ancestry of Mrs. Sophia Hewitt Buckner, wife of Dr. Philip Johnson Buckner*, now in the Cincinnati and Hamilton County Public Library. That Mr. McGroarty's history contained an exact copy of the original Bible record is a small miracle, but its re-emergence supporting my years of research has been invaluable. I am indebted to his discovery and inclusion in his manuscript of this precious family record.

I am grateful to Arcilee Frost and Doris Harker of the Salt Lake City area, and to Rudy Heath of Cincinnati who shared research and helped me on Hall family connections.

I thank my friend Frances Williamson Smith, with whom I spent many hours at the Denver Public Library piecing together our Williamson families, and to Sandra Wamsley of Windsor, Colorado, who also shares Williamson ancestors. Warren McBride graciously shared his research linking two generations of Fisher and Cochran family connections. Many others shared research, photographs and personal history, and to them, I am both indebted and grateful.

To my friends Dorla and Don Johnson, I do not have adequate words to say thank you for the many ways they assisted me in searching for family in southern Ohio and northern Kentucky where Dorla and I share Kyle and Kenny ancestors. They not only shared their home, but drove me down many miles of country roads, waited patiently while I walked and photographed the countryside. They tramped cemeteries and pored through courthouse records with me. One day they cheerfully donned white "Haz-Mat" suits to look at county records, which after years of exposure to bird droppings, dust and mildew, had been moved to archival storage and were in a decontamination process. On the last visit, just before driving me to the airport, they took me to the river where I walked to the middle of the suspension bridge spanning the Ohio River, linking Cincinnati to its smaller neighbor, Covington, Kentucky. It had rained hard that afternoon, and as I stood looking down into its misty depths, I was filled with the spirit of my ancestors. On fragile flatboats, this mighty river carried them safely to their destination. They built homes and businesses nearby, but the river is a living thing demanding respect. Those living along its bank quickly learn that the Ohio River can be raging, unpredictable and pleasurable in it calmer moods, but it will never be tamed.

INTRODUCTION

Long before tall ships breached the horizon or axes broke the silence, the tide lapped the shores of an earthly paradise. Thick reeds and grasses bordered Chesapeake Bay marking the rivers and estuaries, home to duck, geese and other waterfowl. Disturbed by a presence on the water, a half dozen mallards broke from the protective mists, moving up and away, their echoing cries marking their destination. Undulating beneath dark waters were bass, bluefish, sturgeon and catfish, creatures that flourished in the perfect mixture of fresh and saltwater. The bottoms held clam and oyster beds, and a blue crab that loses its shell in summertime. Beyond and behind the water's border lay the forest, thick and green. In a densely packed mixture, oak and ash shared space with hickory and maple, and numerous other varieties of trees and shrubs. Beneath this overhanging mantle of green, fox and bear ruled at will, keeping the deer, rabbit and squirrel population in balance. Above them all, keeping watch, were scores of birds lending song to an otherwise silent world.

While mist held silence hostage in the woodlands, it was broken on the water by the cry of a heron as it escaped from the rushes. A man glided by in a canoe, silent except for the slap of an oar as it dipped beneath the water; across his lap a bow and arrow lay ready. He was native to the bay in the same way as the geese and fox who shared the wilderness. He might be Powhatan, Nanticoke or Susquehannock, a warring tribe feared by all the others. On that day, nature was alive in its magnificence, in the cry of an animal caught by its prey, and in the watchfulness of a man listening for his enemy. This was the cycle of life on the Chesapeake before the Europeans landed on its shores. Unknowing, and with little understanding of what they encountered, they brought with them the means to change the naturally symbiotic relationship between earth, man and beast into surroundings more familiar to them and to the world they left.

By the 1640s, it was the height of adventure for the European upper class to explore the "new world." However, until the founding of Jamestown Colony in 1607, early forays were not particularly successful, and even that experiment initially failed. A few years later, with survival in Jamestown nearly guaranteed, another colony was established in Massachusetts Bay. Others quickly followed. When Captain John Smith, one of Jamestown's founders, first approached the Virginia coastline to establish a colony there, he was unprepared for what he saw. To him the land seemed overgrown with trees, in contrast to England, a long settled island green with fields and pastures, interlaced with roads and pathways leading to towns and marketplaces.

A quarter of a century after Jamestown, in 1634, the English king gave George Calvert, Lord Baltimore, a grant to form a colony north of the Potomac River where he was charged with the power to appoint a governor, establish laws and collect rents. From its earliest settlement, the Maryland Colony tolerated other religions, and even though the Anglican Church eventually held sway, initially it was home to Puritans, Quakers, and a group of Catholics who settled St. Mary's County. In the beginning, Maryland had an uneasy alliance with its Virginia neighbor because of boundary disputes between the two colonies. Most vocal of all was William Claiborne, the secretary of Virginia, who relentlessly waged war against Lord Baltimore's men from his plantation on Kent Island. Although clearly operating within the Maryland patent, Claiborne refused to acknowledge Baltimore's jurisdiction, and was replaced.

The settlers of Maryland learned from the mistakes made at Jamestown, and brought slips of fruit trees to plant, as well as corn and tobacco, one to help them survive the first difficult year and the other to plant for export. The settler's first job was to clear land for crops and build a rude cabin, but he had an additional challenge, to survive the "seasoning," a period of adjustment needed to become immune to native diseases, a time when death claimed children, and men and women at the peak of life. Each year more than a third of the new arrivals died, a mortality rate higher than in most of the other colonies. Before 1700, most immigrants died from typhus or malaria, but also from dysentery and influenza. Once weakened, they were susceptible to any of the region's diseases, be it native or those introduced by man.

While basic survival was of primary concern, the immigrants shared land with a native population. Initially friendly, the Indians grew wary as settlers moved up the coastline, further encroaching on their land. When raids began, Lord Baltimore's solution was to enlarge the English population so that eventually they outnumbered the natives. Most disturbing to the peace was the Susquehannock tribe, called the "people of the Muddy River." Sometimes noble and heroic, they were also warlike and aggressive. Feared by other more peaceful tribes, they were bitter enemies of the Iroquois. When the Europeans first encountered them, the Susquehannock were one of the most formidable of the mid-Atlantic tribes, dominating the area from the Susquehanna River to the Chesapeake Bay, and from Pennsylvania to southern New York. They lived inland most of the year, in fortified villages surrounded by fields of maize, beans, and squash, but in the summer, they moved south to fish on Chesapeake Bay. Initially they traded with the settlers but by 1642, Maryland's governor was weary of their aggression, declared them enemies of the colony, and ordered them shot on sight. Hostilities continued until they signed a treaty giving up their lands between the Choptank and Patuxent Rivers. A century later, with the Europeans in control, the tribe was gone, wiped from the earth along with much of their history.

New settlers were vital to the growth and success of Maryland's colony, and throughout the seventeenth century, hopeful young men and women came for land or to marry and begin a family. Others, desperate to leave a bad life behind, were more than willing to accept the privations that awaited them in the new world. The trip across the ocean lasted about six weeks, and with little to do, there was time to think, even to regret their decision. While traversing a dangerous ocean they stood on deck in calm weather, but when rough seas tossed the precarious ship in every direction, they hid below in a cramped and dirty hold. Eager for a new life they confronted crowded conditions, bad food, illness and sometimes death, only to end up in the wilds of a vast and uninviting land. It was an environment that tested character and courage, and many of those who lacked encouragement did not make it.

The colonists came from diverse backgrounds, beginning with the adventurers who were mostly upper class Englishmen. Following them were young men mostly of good character, without land but with the means to obtain it. Accompanying them were men and women, sometimes families, whose passage they paid in return for four years service. Some indentured servants were of the same class with goals similar to their temporary masters, while many from the lower classes moved from farms into cities like London or Bristol, but left to escape crowded conditions, low wages and even fewer jobs. The adventurous ones found a sponsor and shipped to America.

The voyage overseas was grueling, with days of calm followed by fierce storms, then periods of unrelenting heat. After weeks spent on the endless ocean, someone spotted land, and those on deck craned their necks to see the speck on the horizon. Wordlessly they watched as it grew larger and took form. Up close, the newcomer gazed in wonder at the more than three thousand miles of shore lining the edges of a vast bay. Drawing nearer, they passed the capes, entrance to the waters of the great Chesapeake Bay. Moving deeper into its embrace, on the west they passed the James, the York and the Rappahannock Rivers before entering the Potomac, a river so vast it took their breath away.

As startling as the land mass was to their hungry eyes, the sight of abundant waterfowl nesting in the low-lying grasses was welcoming. However, the swampy tidewater also brought hordes of mosquitoes to feast on new flesh. The climate and the weather were a surprise to the Englishman accustomed to the sameness of cloudy gray skies and ongoing drizzle. The wind, then as now, determines Chesapeake weather, bringing rain from April to September and frost that seeps in by mid-October. The southern winds of summer can boost temperatures to ninety degrees, creating a sultry humidity difficult for those accustomed to the milder English climate. More troubling to the settlers were the intense squalls and gale force winds that accompanied it. Winter winds carry snow or clear, crisp, but freezing temperatures when they shift, creating ice on the rivers and in the bay. Heavy spring rains and snowmelt from the mountains cause flooding, but they also enrich the soil and nourish the land, boosting the promise of natural abundance.

The Charter of Maryland provided the means for the earliest settlers to get land and sometimes wealth. Some arrived with families and servants, with tools to work and clothing for a year. In exchange, a man received one hundred acres for himself, the same for his wife and each sponsored servant, and for each child under sixteen he received fifty acres. These few men and women became the landed gentry, and their children the next generation's merchants and businessmen, who intermarried creating political and social connections that along with a strong identity nourished their common interests. Most, however, were indentured servants, and in the beginning, once their service was completed they received freedom dues of fifty acres and were free to marry. After 1681, a man no longer got land, and often worked for wages or leased land from the planter who had just freed him, creating a landlord class whose social rank and wealth was above that of ordinary planters. By the 1690s there were more native births than there were immigrants, and twenty years later the proportion of men to women was nearly equal. Life expectancy had also increased so that for the first time in the colonies, a man could reasonably anticipate that he would live to see his son grow up. The colonial experiment was a success and tobacco was king, the coin of the realm, used exclusively to pay taxes, fees and debts. Maryland was essentially an English colony and thus the Church of England became its established religion, a faith that provided spiritual sustenance to its members and education for their children.

For many years, the greater number of those who came to this colony were indentured servants, and men outnumbered women four to one. They were uneducated and only about half of the freemen, regardless of class, could sign their names. Most of them were the younger sons of farmers, artisans, tradesmen and laborers who came to be planters, an English euphemism for one who "planted a colony overseas." In Maryland, it came to mean one who planted tobacco.

Chapter One

THE BEGINNING
The Hewitt Family in Early Maryland (1680-1730)

Maryland records show traces of the Hewitt name in St. Mary's, the original and most southern county in Maryland. It was also found in records from there north, up the coastline to Anne Arundel and Baltimore Counties as well as on the Kent County side of Chesapeake Bay. This study focuses on the northern counties, as they appear to be where this branch of the family settled. Prior to living in Maryland, their origins are unknown, but can likely be traced back to England. Several men with this surname lived in Anne Arundel and Baltimore Counties in the late seventeenth century, and while probably related to one another, the immigrant ancestor of this family has yet to be discovered. What follows are probable ancestors but because proof is lacking, their profiles are drawn without conclusion.

In an early record from Anne Arundel County, Henry Hewitt witnessed the will of Benjamin Lawrence of West River in 1684.[1] Other records indicated that Hewitt served in the Anne Arundel County militia. When Philip Calvert became governor of Maryland, he directed each county to organize a militia of horse and foot soldiers, and over the years, it became a tradition for the heads of leading families to serve as officers while private soldiers came from the yeoman class. In 1696 Hewitt was among those men[2] of "the gentry [who] were chosen because they were most able to meet the requirements that an officer supply his own equipment and transportation to do the job. With a wide territory to cover and few men to do it, the ranger's job was to scout the countryside checking for hostilities between the settlers and its Native population. "In the early days the frontier extended from Georgetown, through the woods to Laurel, then across Howard County territory to Fort Garrison in Baltimore County and thence to the Gunpowder River." From a string of small stone forts and blockhouses, it was this area that the rangers patrolled and protected.[3] A few years later in 1701/2, Henry Hewitt witnessed the will of William Cotter[4] a housekeeper for All Hallows Parish Church. Hewitt worked for Cotter as an overseer and when he died on 5 Apr 1702 a few days after Cotter, both men were buried in the parish church.[5] If Hewitt had a wife and family, no records have been located confirming their identity.

Robert Hewitt

A man named Robert Hewett was issued a warrant in Baltimore County in 1705 for 200 acres of *The Range*, located at the head of the Bush River and sometimes referred to as *Hewits Range*.[6] That year and the next Robert Hewitt paid taxes on his land located on the north side of the Patapsco River.[7] While he owned property in Baltimore County, Hewitt probably lived in Anne Arundel County where many court records attest to it.

Beginning with a summons in January 1705, he went to court because of a judgment against him for trespassing.[8] He was a witness in a lawsuit in 1708 brought by Henry Pinckney of Anne Arundel County who sued to recover legacies due him.[9] In 1709 he both witnessed a will,[10] and was sued in an action that turned out agreeably.[11] In 1710 Hewitt witnessed the will of Charles Greenberry.[12] These men were his neighbors and some were his friends, all lived near enough to assist each other with various civic and familial duties.

Amos Garrett was a wealthy Annapolis merchant and banker who bought property from planters who were deep in debt. In 1711 Robert Hewitt and his wife, Elizabeth sold *The Range* to Garrett for £12.[13] Garrett died sometime after making his will in 1714 in which he indicated that after buying his land, he had allowed Hewitt to continue living there as an overseer. The will described the land's location on Wyatt's Ridge near William McCubbin's property, placing Hewitt's home between the Severn and South Rivers in the Parish of St. Anne.[14] Hewitt's financial problems continued and in November 1714 Rachel Greenberry brought suit for £8 he owed.[15]

In 1722 Robert Hewitt was about 60 years old when he was asked to recollect some of the county's old boundaries, indicating he had lived in Anne Arundel County for many years. Others who attested to the county's growth and its changes over the years were large landowners, namely Richard Warfield who was the same age as Hewitt.[16] In 1724 Hewitt and other, mostly wealthy Anne Arundel County landowners, appeared on the Maryland Proprietors list for taxes owed to the Crown. He owed £86, more than most of the others, an indication that while no longer a landowner he continued to accumulate large debts.[17] Robert was a contemporary of Henry Hewitt who died in 1702 and they were probably related, perhaps brothers. By 1737 Robert Hewitt was no longer living on Wyatt's Ridge and may have died.

Richard Hewitt

In 1711 Richard Huett, was among others who witnessed a deed for an Anne Arundel County gentleman who sold a lot to Amos Garrett.[18] Hewitt became an innkeeper after marrying the widow, Elizabeth Frazier on 28 Jul 1722 at St. Anne's Church, Middle Neck Parish in Anne Arundel County.[19] Her former husband, Alexander Frazier, had a tavern at Whetstone Point in Baltimore and after they married it is where Hewitt set up shop.[20] Richard and Elizabeth lived there at least by 1726 because he was listed as a debtor in an estate inventory.[21] A year later his occupation was given as innkeeper when he purchased Lot 19 on Church Street in the newly laid out town of Joppa.[22]

In 1729 the fates of Richard Hewitt, innkeeper of Baltimore and Robert Hewitt, overseer of Anne Arundel County came together. Sometime before 19 Aug 1729, Robert Hewitt died and Richard Hewitt became his administrator, an indication he was a relative, likely his son. After paying a £50 sterling bond,

Charles Ridgely became the co-administrator.[23] Often pursued by his neighbors for debts he owed, it was no surprise that after Garrett bought his land, Robert Hewitt's worldly good were worth no more than £15.[24]

Even as he accepted the estate's probate, Richard Hewitt was ill, and perhaps it was the reason Ridgely assisted him. Two months later Hewitt made his will leaving his entire estate except legacies to his daughter, Mary.[25] He died on 20 Feb 1729/1730 and was buried at St. Paul's Parish, Baltimore where Ridgely was a vestryman.[26] Knowing he was unable to conclude his responsibility towards Robert Hewitt's estate, he asked Ridgely to serve as co-administrator of both estates. His will was problematic and his widow contested it, demanding her thirds. She also knew that if she married again, she would no longer be co-executor.[27] That Ridgely agreed to act as accountant and caretaker of both estates suggested some kind of a relationship between Hewitt or his wife, either as businessmen or kin. In his will Richard gave his mother, Elizabeth Hewitt, her choice of any property except that which his wife wanted, and with Ridgely's assistance, Hewitt was assured that his mother had a place to live. In 1731, an Elizabeth Hewitt donated money to St. Paul's Parish to build a new church. She was probably Richard's mother, because his wife Elizabeth upon receiving her widow's thirds, married Benjamin Price four months after Richard died.[28]

Hewitt was grateful for Ridgely's help, and he thanked him by designating two of Ridgely's children as benefactors should his daughter die without issue. While their true relationship is unknown, they were not of the same class. Ridgely's family was among the very wealthy original settlers of Anne Arundel County. He and his brother inherited from their grandfather, John Dorsey, a vast estate of more than 2,000 acres called *White Wine and Claret*.[29] While Charles chose to live north of Baltimore on a tract called *Hampton*,[30] his brother lived on their inheritance on the Severn River. By profession Ridgely was a merchant and he either knew Hewitt through the inn or from previous years when both lived in Anne Arundel County.

Ridgely and Hewitt both purchased lots in the new town of Joppa in early 1730, just prior to Hewitt's death.[31] Because he died suddenly, Hewitt lost the lot by forfeit although it was eventually purchased in 1742 by the pastor of St. Paul's Church.[32] Only a good friend and a dedicated accountant would spend more than seven years collecting money and paying bills, especially since many were small and difficult to collect. Hewitt left small personal gifts to his stepchildren, John and Elizabeth Frazier, as well as Ridgely's children, John and Pleasance, who he wanted to have "one pistol each to buy them a ring each."[33] Whatever the relationship between Hewitt and Ridgely, his administrator served him ably until 1730 when he brought the last tiresome detail to its final close.

Hewitt's inventory showed how an eighteenth century innkeeper lived and because it contained everything he owned, down to his gloves and wigs, it revealed much about the man. His personal property not including land was valued at £179, a respectable but not a large estate, and since his debts and assets were about equal, there was no need for an estate sale.

In homes of this period, the best bed included a bedstead and furnishings, which were the sheets and blankets, pillows, mattress and coverlet plus the side hangings. Apart from livestock, they were often the most valuable possessions.

Hewitt's house had eleven beds, a confirmation that he was an innkeeper. He and his wife had the best bed and the children used two or three of the others, leaving five or six on the upper floor, or in another wing of the house, including two feather beds, to let out to guests. His was a small hotel or boarding house with a manservant to do heavy work and repairs and a woman who helped Elizabeth with cooking and serving, cleaning and laundry, leaving Richard Hewitt to tend to their guests, do the accounts and tend bar.

The inventory provided a fair description of how Hewitt looked when he greeted a visitor who came to his establishment. Depending on the importance of the occasion, Richard pulled out a shirt he stored in a trunk and put it on, then wrapped a muslin stock around his neck letting it fall in a loose bow. He put on cotton stockings, then breeches reaching to the knee. Depending upon the weather and his duties that day he chose from several pair of shoes. A razor suggested he was clean-shaven and perhaps even shaved his head before donning his wig.[34] Worn by most merchants, he had three of them all periwigs styled with curls just above the ears and covering the back of the head just to the neck. Although there were longer wigs reaching to the shoulders, judges wore them as a mark of their profession, but occasionally the gentry wore them.

To ward off the winter cold Hewitt wore a Roqueloe, a short cloak with a cape that fit around the shoulders creating the effect of a double coat, after which he donned his "fine new hatt." Important occasions called for Richard to wear silk stockings and his best-embroidered oiled buck breeches. After placing a silver buckled belt around his waist, he inserted silver buttons into his shirt and cuffs and a "stone ring" upon his finger. Last, he donned a cape and gloves and upon leaving, picked up his silver cane as he walked out the door. Should Hewitt be going any distance, he mounted a gelding valued at £5 whose saddle was worth £3.10. The man must have looked the picture of prosperity as he rode down the street, the outer statement of a successful and solid citizen of early Baltimore. In all, his personal effects, clothing, silver and jewelry were worth £20, a considerable lot then. When compared to his father, who died with an estate of no more than £15, he was a rousing success. Hewitt was literate and possessed both a Bible and a prayer book. He used a writing box or secretary for his accounts, had £2.9 in cash in a moneybox and about £4 in safekeeping with the sheriff. There was a scale and weights for tobacco payments, a brass mortar and pestle to grind powders and somewhere in the house he kept an old gun.

A picture of the inn's interior and furnishings can be determined based on the description of the contents of each room. Beginning with the entry, when a guest arrived and rang the house bell, Richard or Elizabeth answered his call and brought him into a sitting room where a black walnut tea table was set with pots, cups and saucers, and nearby a high-standing candlestick lit up the room meant for relaxing, reading or chatting. Before turning in for the evening on chilly nights, a guest's bed was heated with a warming pan. In the dining area meals were served on linen-covered tables around which benches were placed. Most of the table wear was pewter but Hewitt also had about £5 worth of silver spoons. Alcohol was plentiful, with 27 gallons of rum and 70 gallons of cider available served from a glass punch bowl into drinking glasses. There was a vast kitchen inventory used in food preparation, cooking and serving. Hewitt had lots of livestock including cows and calves, pigs, sheep and lambs.[35] In all his estate was valued well above the average man and while he was not rich, he was comfortable and prosperous.

The name Caleb was common in the Hewitt family, and in 1717, a man by that name witnessed a will in Baltimore, signing his name with a mark.[36] It appeared again in Kent County in 1737, that time as the recipient of an estate debt, perhaps the same man, or his son, mentioned twenty years earlier.[37] As late as 1740, a soldier named Richard Hewitt served Anne Arundel County and was perhaps a descendant of Henry Hewitt the militia officer introduced in 1684.[38] While there were other men by this surname living in this county and in Baltimore, those profiled had something in their history, either in naming patterns, their occupation, a known neighbor or a marriage partner whose name was akin to those ancestors who are of proven lineage to this family.

Chapter Two

ROBERT AND ELIZABETH HEWITT
Anne Arundel County, Maryland (1700-1736)

Tobacco Colony

To understand early eighteenth century Maryland, it is helpful to know two things. First, it was an English royal colony and subject to the king and his governors in all things. Second that it, along with the colony of Virginia, was the largest producer of tobacco in the New World, a product that ultimately tied it to Europe and particularly to England. Even during the years when prices on the English market dropped so low that planters barely survived, the colony continued to grow. For those who weighed a perilous journey across the seas and an unsure future in a distant land, it often seemed a better choice than remaining in England under conditions that included religious intolerance and a system of inheritance favoring elder sons. Driving others to seek refuge in the colonies was omni-present poverty, especially in the cities, but they went even though it meant binding oneself for seven years as an indentured servant.

The colony established in the seventeenth century grew but changes, while providing order in governance, also bound the planters more tightly to its owners, the Calvert family and their appointed overseers. By an Act of Assembly in 1683, the commissioners of Lord Baltimore's Royal Colony began laying towns into "hundreds." Further division into parishes was made by the end of the century, all supported by tobacco tithes payable to the governor. Anne Arundel County, where Robert and Elizabeth Hewitt lived, had four parishes each separated from its neighbor by a river running into Chesapeake Bay. A church was within a ten-mile radius of any other and most people were no further than five miles from any one of them.[1] When a boundary line changed it sometimes appeared that families moved from one county into another. This happened in 1727 when boundary realignments caused those living on the south side of the Severn River to become a part of Anne Arundel County whereas previously they were residents of Baltimore County.

Tobacco was the mainstay of the planter's livelihood. Its long growing season required more than a year to bring it from seed to a product ready for shipping. Further requirements were good soil, lots of space to grow and a ready water source to ship the product to market. Maryland had all of the essentials. Thus, early settlers lived as close to the rivers as possible spending nearly all their waking hours engaged in raising and preparing their crops for shipment to England. In the early 1700's, tobacco plantations of varying sizes were all along the Anne Arundel coastline, each supported by navigable rivers that flowed from the land into the Bay. It is reasonable to think that Robert Hewitt, like nearly everyone in the county, was involved with tobacco in some capacity and was probably a planter. There is no evidence he owned land, and so he probably worked for someone else, perhaps as a caretaker on a plantation. However, he made his living, without property his life and that of his family was modest. Not only was tobacco their livelihood, it permeated everyone's life as a common means for exchange of all goods. Used to pay taxes and private debts or to purchase goods, it was the coin of the realm. So whether Robert tended the fields, worked in the shipyards or when he bartered tobacco for goods, he and his neighbors were immersed in the planter's life in every way.[2]

Tobacco's success in the southern colonies of the New World was due to the rich soil and amenable climate of Virginia and Maryland, but it was also inextricably tied to the social habits of Western Europe. The consumption of tobacco in England was greater than in any other part of Europe at that time, and the planter's financial prosperity was determined by the Englishman's demand for it.[3] However, while the English may have depended on their tobacco, the colonists on the other hand were vastly more reliant upon England for nearly everything else. Nearly all of their clothing, and household furnishings were imported, creating a dependence on the motherland, which England used to control them. This yoke held into the late eighteenth century, until colonial desire for self-reliance reached revolutionary fervor and allowed them to break away.[4]

Maryland had a ready market for product overseas but the intensive labor needed to grow tobacco meant that unlike other crops, its production was an all-consuming way of life for planters large and small.[5] Families lived near the rivers but because tobacco required ample space to grow, few towns emerged and the population, rather than converging, spread thinly over the landscape. This discouraged an organized social life that fed the natural inclination for community and instead caused isolation from both neighbor and friend. Consequently the church, which traditionally supported other needs, played an even more important role in bringing people together for the only social interaction a planter was likely to experience. The church was important in other ways too. Although the people legislated for their churches and initiated laws to educate their children, including in 1723 creating a school and board of visitors in each county, colonial interest never met the level of education supported by the New England colonies.[6] Thus without a formal system of education the poor and middle level planters depended upon the church to instruct their children, particularly if they were not literate themselves.[7] Parents often died young, contributing to a less than well-educated society, regardless of class, and an orphan was less likely to receive even the rudiments of education since a guardian had less motivation than a parent did to teach a child to read and write. Other than the church, home education was the rule in Maryland and the Bible, often the only book the family possessed, was the main instrument of instruction. While these skills were not considered a necessity for success within one's community, literacy was then as now, the key to upward mobility, and in the upper class it was the means to greater power.[8]

Robert and Elizabeth Hewitt were married at St. Anne's Episcopal Church in a parish lying between the Severn and the South Rivers in Anne Arundel County. On 9 Jan 1723 the record shows that "Robert Hewytt married Elisabeth Chandler."[9] Their son Robert was born on 2 Jul 1726, and recorded at St. Margaret's Church, Westminster Parish. Jacob was born next on 17 Aug 1728 followed by Edward on 2 Mar 1830.[10] Their youngest child was Hannah, born on 10 Oct 1732. Each child was born, like the average, about two years apart. However, there was more than three years between their wedding and Robert's birth, suggesting the death of a child born before him. Little else is known about this couple, but they were probably like other planters in early eighteenth century Maryland.

The Chandler family arrived in Maryland before 1651 and settled in Port Tobacco, Charles County.[11] Much later, the name turned up in an Anne Arundel County deed in 1723 when William Chandler sold land on the "north side of Ridgely's Run on the Patuxent River," and Richard Warfield was his witness.[12] There were perhaps two Chandler families living in the county when Elizabeth married Robert Hewitt. Two men, perhaps brothers, were married in St. Anne's Parish in 1713.[13] One was Robert Chandler who married Elizabeth Bryon and the other William Chandler whose wife was Ann Laswell. Elizabeth may have been either their younger sister or a cousin.

St. Anne's Parish boundaries tell us where Robert and Elizabeth lived, but it also suggests that rather than a planter, Robert may have been a seaman, since both the South River and the Severn, where Annapolis is located, were important eighteenth century shipping ports. A sea voyage to England and back took from a year up to eighteen months, and depending on the ice floes, ships arrived in Chesapeake Bay in February and March and activity continued until November or December.[14] All Chesapeake freighters were required to file a record when shipping tobacco to London, and on 24 May 1722, Captain Robert Hewitt was "riding at anchor in South River in Anne Arundel County," waiting to load cargo on board at the charge of £7 sterling per ton.[15] With time on his hands he was free to engage in other business, or to begin the courtship of a special lady with the hope of marriage before he shipped out again for England. There is no proof this man married Elizabeth Chandler although the circumstances were timely, and there was clearly a season when seamen were present in the colony. He may be the Hewitt children's father but there are reasons why he probably was not. Few Maryland planters were engaged in international shipping or had seaworthy vessels, and of those who did, most were men of wealth. In addition, most seamen who came to the Chesapeake were British citizens, working for an owner or agency in London or Liverpool.[16] If Robert the mariner was Jacob Hewitt's father, perhaps he lost command of his vessel after 1722 and settled in the colony.

Robert Hewitt died sometime between January 1732 and spring 1736. Perhaps he perished in a storm while crossing the ocean, but he may have died from accident or disease while stripping tobacco or pushing hogsheads down to the loading docks. Neither his death, nor that of his wife Elizabeth were found in Maryland records. They had nothing and left nothing behind but their children. No land, no inventory of even the most meager estate has been discovered. Jacob Hewitt's father may have been a mariner, but he was more likely a planter. Three of the children were baptized at St. Margaret's Church, Westminster Parish, indicating that the family lived between the Severn and the Magothy Rivers and near the northern border of Baltimore town.[17]

A Planter's Life

The child Robert was sixteen months old in November 1727 when his mother became pregnant with Jacob and stopped nursing him. As she cared for the child and prepared for the upcoming birth, Elizabeth's thoughts were on the seasonal preparations beginning with the observance of Christmas. Down at the landing, her husband and his neighbors prepared tobacco for shipment to England.

With harvest completed, planters spent the early fall drying the mature product on racks in their barns. Preparation was critical because in this climate, if tobacco was not properly dried it would rot. Fires were lit to force drying if it was unseasonably wet, but because tobacco is flammable the process was carefully monitored. Once dried the leaves were stacked into large piles, covered and left to sweat, a process that increased the flavor and made the leaf pliable for packing. After curing, the stems were removed and the leaves were transferred to a barrel, called a hogshead, where they were packed and compressed as tightly as possible. Full hogsheads weighed between 700 and 1,000 pounds each, while barrels of sweet scented tobacco sometimes weighed 1,400 pounds. When filled, the hogsheads were rolled down to the docks and either placed on a ship or stored until one came into port. Departing fully laden, the ship's captain moved his cargo out of the harbor and began the dangerous journey across the waters to England.[18] Open to anything from piracy, bad weather and illness it was a trip that, no matter how many times a man crossed the ocean, was never made without serious consideration for the perils of the journey.

Even before the last of his product was on its way to England, the planter was deep into the next season's process. Sometime between January and February planting began anew. Whatever position Robert held on a plantation, the first work began with a small seedbed that was covered with branches for protection against the frost. On most plantations the land was partially cleared for planting, leaving stumps around which tobacco was planted. About June Hewitt transplanted the seedlings into a larger field, and within a month the plant was a foot high, requiring hoeing and worming daily until it was ripe. Ground leaves were removed as it grew and the plant was topped out to prevent flowering. The decision about when to cut the tobacco was critical to proper curing, and required experience and a critical eye to know just when to do it. A good eye and better instincts set one planter apart from his neighbor giving him an edge in the market and a better price for his crops. For an individual planter or an overseer on a plantation, a good crop meant the difference between a hand to mouth existence and the ability to meet one's obligations from one year to the next.

Jacob was born in August when the tall tobacco plants were reaching toward the sky. They were cut in September and placed in the barns to dry, a critical time because an early frost could wipe out a year's work in a few days. Knowing this, the experienced planter developed a keen sense of timing. Thus Jacob's arrival after his brother's second birthday and before the harvest was perhaps the only lull of the planting season and thus a much-celebrated affair.

Elizabeth gave birth at home, perhaps with a midwife from the neighborhood or a relative who helped her through the process. Robert probably left the fields for the day to remain nearby to alert neighbors and family that another son was born into the family.

Parents closely attended their children in the eighteenth century until about age three, often allowing the child to sleep with them at night. Until then babies were susceptible to illness and many died before then. Once he reached the magical age of three, Jacob's parents treated him more like a little adult, consigning him to the loft with his brother Robert who was five. Funds permitting, both children received new clothes and shoes each spring when goods from England were in and plentiful.[19] Prior to 1700, Maryland had few spinning wheels or looms, and those who did were from upper class households where there was time to learn these skills and the tools to make them. Even then, local wool was not of high quality so it had to be imported. Consequently, those least able to afford it purchased cloth from abroad, even more reason for a family to anticipate the arrival of ships in the spring.

Edward Hewitt was born in the early spring of 1730, a critical time for the tobacco market and all those supporting it. With a family of five to feed and clothe, Robert labored to provide and Elizabeth struggled to make ends meet. He owed rent and the year's food and clothing bills were due then. Subtracting the debts he owed, Hewitt based the next year's spending on the projected price of the new tobacco crop in London's market. Nearly everyone used tobacco as payment, regardless of status, and they charged merchandise throughout the year hoping to pay up in the spring. Even in good times, some had large debts that were never fully paid off.[20] However, 1730 was not a good year. In London prices dropped and planters got far less for their product than they had spent that year. Hard times visited the colony, and even as Edward was welcomed into the family, his father struggled to support them. When ships arrived in the harbor that year and creditors clamored for payment, those who ordinarily lined up to see what new goods were in from London did without instead. Families living at a marginal level suffered even greater privation, and many barely survived.[21]

In October, just prior to a record-breaking cold winter, Robert and Elizabeth's only daughter Hannah was born. Hard times continued for Maryland's planters in late 1732 and into the following year. Afterward it was remembered as one of the most severe winters in Chesapeake history, when all the rivers of Maryland were frozen and ships were imprisoned in the ice until spring.[22] Hannah must have been a hardy child because she survived the winter, but her mother may have died in childbirth or soon after.

Economic change was to blame for some poverty, but some lived extravagantly, were poor managers and accumulated large debts. Many lost their property to ever-watchful individuals who grew rich by taking advantage of those in desperate situations.[23] However, bad times helped planters discover new ways to make money. Some diversified their crops, trading tobacco for grain or livestock they sold or used to get through the hard times. Others slaughtered hogs, salted and packed them for sale overseas, while some men selected fine woods from the forest and turned trees into furniture that they shipped to the European markets.

A young physically fit man could clear, plant and hoe about three acres of land each year, and with several people working the land, even a small plantation could yield a living for a family. However, tobacco eventually depleted the soil and if a planter had no other land to turn, he changed to other crops, planting corn, wheat or barley instead. Whatever the crop, there was a continuous cycle of clearing new land and returning old fields to woods so that the land might be enriched and renewed. The reward for diversification was discovering that other crops were less labor intensive than growing tobacco.[24]

Annapolis was the largest town in Anne Arundel County, and with few recognizable settlements other than at crossroads where plantations met, that area remained a frontier nearly a hundred years after settlement. A boat or ship was about the only means to get from one place to another, so that when Hewitt had visitors they used the Severn River. The land was flat with great stretches of uncleared wilderness between tobacco plantations and depleted land left to grow back to its natural state. Every plantation whether large or small had a landing with a boat tied to it.[25] Upon docking a visitor trekked through stomped down grasses to the house. Many were built for temporary living because once tobacco could no longer be grown there, the family moved out leaving the house and its outbuildings to fall down on their own. Like most planters' houses, Hewitt's was simple, square and unpainted, with perhaps two rooms. Robert cut each tree by hand, splitting the wood with an ax in a rough-cut fashion. It may have had a loft under its peaked roof, with a planked floor, and below it a single room with a dirt floor. Used more for ventilation than light, the first floor had windows on opposite walls that were covered in the winter with paper or cloth and perhaps shutters. Some houses had a brick chimney and glass in their windows, but all classes had some kind of outbuilding. The gentry may have had more outbuildings on their property, but only the upper third of society had more than three rooms in their house, consisting usually of a separate kitchen with a washing area and perhaps a dairy and slave quarters. Once split and dried, Hewitt used green wood for the walls and plastered over the gaps. He assembled this boxy structure using split boards in five or six foot lengths, overlapping the ends and notching them to hold. Later he might add shingles. However, once the soil was depleted and the house in need of repair, it was time to move to another part of the plantation and build a new one. This process was repeated many times because the land was in a state of constant change, and the longer previously cleared land was left vacant the more nature covered up the leavings of habitation. Rotting tree stumps made it hazardous to walk on any but a beaten path, and the eerie landscape of fallen buildings poking up through the vegetation created an effect of neglect and disarray. A stranger from any other place might see its untidy and haphazard appearance as that of a primitive existence within a lushly endowed natural environment.[26]

The Orphaned Children

It was a summer's day in August 1736 when young Jacob Hewitt walked into court at Annapolis, Maryland. It was unlikely he understood how much his life was going to change. Frightened, he grasped ten-year old Robert's hand. Or perhaps he stood between Edward who was six and their little sister Hannah not yet four years old, holding onto them as a protective older brother. Jacob was turning eight years old that month, but try as he might he did not understand some of the words the judge was saying. Standing next to the children and speaking for them were Thomas and Elizabeth Jacks with whom they had been living. Two months earlier, in June 1736, the Jackses took the children into court for the first time and began proceedings that would legally bind them as indentured servants. The boys were to retain that status until age 21 and Hannah until she was sixteen. What was most difficult for Jacob to face was that he would not see his mother and father again.[27] Both had died and he missed them. Looking at his brothers and then his little sister, he knew they did too. He had a birthday coming soon but it was not going to be like any of the others. Nothing was going to be like it had been, ever again. Somehow he knew that.

The spring and summer of 1736 was pivotal in the children's lives. While Jacob might look to Robert for guidance, the youngest and most vulnerable was Hannah who at three years old was little more than a baby. Two orphan's court records are all that remain of a complex family story that might have revealed how and why their parents died, and which of them died first. The children were placed, for their guidance and welfare, in the hands of Thomas and Elizabeth Jacks. Their charge was the usual definition of safekeeping, "to find them sufficient meat, drink, washing of clothing and lodging and to give each of them a good suit of clothes at the expiration of their servitude, also to use their endeavor to learn them to read and write." This spare court ruling could not be amended as long as the children were reasonably cared for in their new life.

There may have been a relationship between Elizabeth or Thomas Jacks and the Hewitt children either by blood or through marriage, but there is no proof of it. Their daughter Elisabeth was eighteen in 1726 and old enough to be young Robert's mother. Marriage to Robert Hewitt would also explain why her parents brought the Hewitt orphans into their home ten years later.[28] However, there is no proof that Elizabeth ever married. Eighteenth century law regarding orphans was a harsh reality because it meant a life of servitude, an accepted practice at the time.[29] That period of Maryland history contained many records of young orphans, and when their parents died it was customary that "children whose property provided insufficient income to pay their keep were to be bound out as servants, according to a law of 1663."[30] Often they became lost in a culture that supported both indentured servitude and slavery, and so there was little regard for orphaned youth. Legal recourse was available, but the courts supported the system by relegating children as chattel when life left them impoverished in this way. These circumstances were no more unusual for the Hewitt orphans than they were for others left in similar circumstances. However, factors regarding their lives are more or less dramatic depending upon who Thomas and Elizabeth Jacks were to them. Rather than grandparents, one of them may have been aunt or uncle to the children. The argument for some degree of family tie rings true, particularly when looked at from one aspect, that rather than being bound out individually as might be expected, the children were all brought into their household—a heavy responsibility considering they were aged ten and under. Theirs was an act of courage regardless of the relationship between them, and a rather remarkable undertaking for an older couple.

Thomas and Elizabeth Jacks

To understand how the orphaned children lived during their childhood, it is important to know more about this couple. Thomas Jacks lived in Anne Arundel County when he married Elizabeth Powell Walters on 9 Oct 1704, a twice-widowed woman whose maiden name is unknown. In 1706 Elizabeth bore a son they named Thomas.[31] Prior to his marriage Jacks owned property near St. Anne's Parish Church where he and Elizabeth were wed. By 1717 he also had a 100-acre tract on the South River, but he sold *Elk Thicket* to William Nicholson that year.[32] Theirs was a complex match because Elizabeth brought three older children, John and Joseph Powell and Christopher Walters (Watters), to their marriage. Her elder children sought to protect and provide for their mother and her younger children, because in 1715, John Powell made a will giving his mother 125 acres of *Powell's Inheritance* during her life, and if she died, it went to his brother, Joseph. Should Joseph have no heirs the land went to Richard Jacks, Elizabeth's second son by Thomas. In his will Powell called Thomas Jacks Junior, "Thomas Jacks Senior's sole heir," and wanted assurances that Richard and his mother were similarly endowed. Powell's will named all of Elizabeth's children born by that time, including daughters, Barbara and Elizabeth who were three and seven years old to whom he gave a cow each.[33]

In 1719 Thomas Jacks Senior bought *Jacks Peacock*, a 300-acre grant in the northern section of Anne Arundel County near the future town of Baltimore.[34] Richard Jacks was thirteen years old in August 1726 when Joseph Powell, who had no children, fulfilled his brother's will by conveying a deed to his brother Richard for "love and affection.[35]

In 1724 Thomas Jacks was deeply in debt and with Elizabeth's permission, he sold 200 acres of *Jacks Peacock* to clear his name and avoid jail. The family lived on the remaining 100 acres while Jacks struggled to remain solvent. Thomas never recovered and the next four years was a long and troublesome slide into debt, which probably began initially with his creditors attempting to collect arrears through payment in crops rather than in tobacco.[36] The plunge began on 14 Nov 1728 when Thomas sold their home and the remaining 100 acres of the plantation to an Anne Arundel County merchant he owed.[37]

This sacrifice was not enough to stave off the family's downfall because when a man's debts were more than his assets he landed in jail. In June 1730, Thomas Jacks and several others were escorted to the Annapolis jail. Angered by imprisonment, they petitioned the legislature for release but were rejected. Undeterred, they sent repeated petitions to the high court with complaints that while in prison, they could not work to pay their bills. Not only that, conditions at the Annapolis jail were unbearable, and an historical document attested to what the prisoners endured. The first privilege lost upon incarceration was privacy, as both men and women were held in the same quarters. The facility had two rooms, one above the other and it was supplied with the crudest sanitary facilities imaginable. One simply used a pipe that began in the upper room, and then passed down to the ground level and into a pit below them. The stench was always offensive but in the summer many became ill from it. The odor was so bad that passersby complained of it. Lack of proper sanitation was not only a serious health risk but reportedly the cause of death as well. Cold was another problem and there was such urgency one winter from lack of heat that some of the prisoners were driven to cut down the ceiling joists and burn them to keep from freezing.[38]

Identified as a shoemaker, Thomas Jacks languished in this place of torment nearly two years while his creditors were beating down the door at home. When the governor finally gave them a reprieve in 1730, he and the other prisoners had to "surrender to the sheriff in their district all real and personal estate either in their possession...in trust or in which they have any claim or interest whatsoever."[39] In other words, everything! To pay his debts Jacks relinquished the remainder of his children's legacy, *Powell's Inheritance*, even though technically it belonged to Elizabeth and then to their son Richard. As long as Thomas Jacks Senior was alive, it all belonged to him, and thus the courts could demand its surrender. Elizabeth did not sign its release, so perhaps she did not have the right of refusal before it was turned over to the sheriff. As he surrendered the last of his family's legacy to his creditors, Jacks must have felt a sense of fatality. He was free, but at what cost. Attached to the deed was a list of his meager possessions while in jail. They were an old hammock, a flock bed and a three-gallon iron pot, which he left behind in prison. In May of 1730, he was among others who owed money to the estate of a deceased man. It seemed he was released from jail just in time for the administrator to attempt collection.[40]

While the Jacks family no longer owned property, they probably paid rent so they could live there. *Jacks Peacock* was on the border between Baltimore and Anne Arundel Counties "on the south side about one mile from the main falls of the Patapsco River." In 1783 Rezin Hammond owned a portion that was on the west side of Elkridge Hundred.[41] Part of the grant was south of Baltimore Highlands near Cabin Creek. Jacks was sometimes described as a planter, or as a cordwainer, one who made fine leather boots and shoes.[42] Jacks probably continued making boots for the gentry and repairing shoes for others who like him owned no property. Perhaps he taught those skills to Jacob Hewitt.

The events described above happened prior to the Hewitt children coming into their family but the scene was set for their entry into a household of much reduced circumstances. Debt and jail time with its accompanying loss of esteem within the community affected everyone, including the children. The Hewitt children not only endured poverty, but conditions mandated by the courts were not met. Although required to teach the children to read and write, neither of them was literate, and records prove that their charges received no instruction. Under better circumstances they might have had a tutor. Jacob Hewitt signed his will in 1790 with a mark, a clear indication that this responsibility had been overlooked during his youth.

Children's education in the early eighteenth century bears little resemblance to contemporary schooling. Throughout history, the philosophy of educators was that children should be educated as befitted their circumstances.

In New England, children of widowed mothers were often apprenticed to an adult so they might learn a trade, and so they earned their food and clothing. Maryland's primary economy was tobacco, and most young boys labored in the fields along with the men, and that was their education. Servants and young girls of the lower classes also worked in the fields when necessary while most young women helped perform endless house chores. In families of modest means, children were expected to work a large part of their day. A child laborer was viewed differently than those within the family, although it was often more a matter of attitude rather than actual mistreatment. Without financial status an orphan was at the whim of his master to grow up kindly or harshly. If the Jacks family had retained their property, the children might have lived separately in outbuildings meant for servants. As this was not the case, Jacob and his siblings became fully integrated into family life, sharing meals and sleeping together under the same roof with the Jacks children, perhaps even in the same bed. If there was anything fortunate in being an orphan, it was that the Hewitt children were raised together; creating a bond in adversity that was as strong as their familial relationship. It served as protection when needed and helped them to speak up for each other when necessary. There were no records of complaint from the children, as was their right, or that they ran away from the Jacks household. This proves nothing either way, and without records from their childhood, how they fared can only be interpreting by looking at the way they lived as adults.[43]

About 1900, Jacob Hewitt's direct descendant, Katie B. McGoon, wrote a short story about her grandfather, Richard Hewitt Junior, who was Jacob's grandson. Passed down in her memoirs was a long remembered impression, told with seeming overtones of either sadness or anger about an ancestor who "was an orphan ... taken [in] by an uncle and given no education."[44] While Richard Junior may have told other stories about his family, by the time Katie wrote about Jacob it seemed to be the only fact remembered about him. McGoon's remembrances of his ancestors lend support to the suggestion that there was a biological connection between Jacob, his siblings, and the Jacks family. If they were indeed "raised by an uncle," then the Hewitt children were related in some way either to Thomas Jacks or to his wife Elizabeth. While evidence may never surface to explain the relationship between these two families, taking the orphans into their home also suggested familial bonds. The courts made every attempt to place children with relatives whenever possible, regardless of their financial means. Perhaps the language of the heart spoke loudest that day in 1736 when they all appeared together in court, and Elizabeth Jacks looked down at those four young children and knew she was doing the right thing.

This conclusion suggests that Jacob Hewitt's mother was Elisabeth Jacks Junior, rather than Elizabeth Chandler. With few available records, neither scenario can be proved. There remains also the question about which parent died first, Robert or Elizabeth. Apart from the court record with her date of birth, there are no other records for the child, Hannah. The most likely course of events was that Elizabeth assumed the responsibility for her children's baptisms, and that she died before Hannah's could take place. Thus Robert died about three years later or shortly before Hannah turned four and they were placed with the Jacks family. Had it been the reverse, without other means of support,

Elizabeth would have bound her children to a neighbor or a family member much sooner. Women with property married again quickly to support their children, but those without means had to give their children over to anyone who would take them. The Jacks were responsible for court costs, suggesting the children were left with no means of support.

The last event affecting the Hewitt-Jacks relationship happened in 1751 when Jacob was probably living elsewhere. That year Edward turned 21, and he may also have moved from the Jacks household. The following episode, while not conclusive, indicates the household's turmoil. William Hall was an Elkridge merchant who sued Thomas for non-payment of a bill. On the day in question, Jacks went to Hall's store and bought twenty pounds of sugar, three gallons and five pints of rum, a package of tea and another item that he carried home in a bag.[45] Perhaps there was food in the cupboard at home and his purchases were for a social occasion. If his intent was a solitary celebration, the likely result was a powerful headache, and tea an inducement to get up in the morning to minister to his aches and pains. However, while Jacks may have liked his rum, a jury acquitted him of all charges and Hall had to pay court costs for "false clamor."

Although Thomas Jacks and his son shared the same name, it was the elder man who died in 1754 having lived a full, if not altogether happy life. His son was alive then and in 1767 when he witnessed a man's will in Baltimore County.[46] Thomas Senior was about 75 years old when he died and his son, Richard posted bond as his administrator on 20 Jan 1755. The co-administrators were Nicholas Peddicord[47] and Luke Mercier, husbands of Ann and Barbara Jacks, called next of kin, and proof that Thomas Senior was the man who died rather than his son.[48] The final distribution was on October 1756 showing assets of about £85 and a "distribution to representatives unknown to this office."[49] The "unknown" were probably other relatives, but the final record left nothing more than an ambiguous and puzzling statement. The children endured so much during the difficult years they lived with the Jacks family, and it would have been fitting if a small legacy was left to them. And perhaps it was.

Chapter Three

JACOB HEWITT IN MARYLAND
Anne Arundel and Baltimore Counties, Maryland (1728-1775)

Ruth Davis's Ancestors

As the summer of 1736 waned and the days turned into weeks, the Hewitt children adjusted to their new life in the Jacks household. Observing the similarities to their home gave them balance but learning the differences gave them the strength and resilience to adapt to a new life. Fate created Jacob's status as an orphaned servant, a condition under which some of his younger siblings labored for nearly fifteen years. They grew from childhood to adults as servants, laboring to learn skills that would serve them in the future. To survive Jacob had to be spirited and resourceful since fate made him older than his actual years. Losing his parents, particularly his father, made him independent, but it also helped his resolve to stand up for his rights. Growing up he learned that patience and perseverance would help him achieve his goals, and he learned every skill available to him. At the same time, his desire for freedom was at odds with the obligations that held him bound to the Jacks family, at times causing anger and resentment to boil up inside. Meanwhile, others observed that he was an affable and friendly young man, with a questioning and curious mind.

By the summer of 1749 when he turned 21, Jacob Hewitt had spent nearly half his life with the Jacks family. It was a long time to be a servant, and whether the years were kind to him or not, he counted the days until his birthday and the walk away to freedom. Life was a struggle for an orphan but he and his brothers learned how to make do growing up, and if nothing else, they shared both good times and bad. He thought about the years they had stood side by side as they tilled the fields and when it was harvest time, had helped bring in the corn and tobacco crops. In August he walked away from those memories without looking back. It must have been with a certain degree of exhilaration when, for the first time, he offered his skills for payment to an overseer on a neighboring plantation. With the energy of youthful zeal, Jacob was ready to step into the world and begin life on his terms even though it meant leaving Edward, who turned nineteen that spring, behind with two years' service remaining. If their brother Robert lived, he would have been 23 that summer, but nothing suggests he survived those early years.

One of the most significant events in Jacob's adult life occurred during the first five years thereafter. Sometime between 1750 and 1755 he met and courted a young widow named Ruth Davis Elder. They were not married in church and had no formal arrangement other than a promise, but a family Bible recognized their union. In it were three generations of birth records for the Davis and Hewitt families, collected and passed down from family to family. In 1913, after tracking down the owner of the original Bible, a descendant copied the records from the "Hewitt Family Bible," as it will be called in further references. He, William B. McGroarty, copied everything on those pages into a manuscript he wrote on his branch of this family.[1] The current location of the original Bible is unknown. As such, the author has relied upon the handwritten copy as an authentic reproduction of the original record.

The first names and dates are those of Ruth Davis's parents, an indication that it may have been a wedding present from Ruth's mother.[2] Entered first was "Richard Davis born 26 Oct 1697," also confirmed by church records for All Hallows Church, Anne Arundel County.[3] The second was for Ruth's mother, called Ruth Davis in the Bible, although born a Warfield. Her birthday was 28 December 1700.

Church records identified Richard's parents as Thomas and Mary Davis, but she was Mary Pierpont, daughter of Henry and Elizabeth Pierpont. Although Mary was born in Maryland her father was from Hertfordshire England, the son of Amos Parpoynt a tailor, who in 1665 immigrated to Maryland with his family.[4] In all there were nine children; the four youngest were born in Maryland.[5] Although Henry did not leave a will, there was one for Jabez Pierpont, Mary's brother. In 1720 he left specific bequests of a pound each to his five sisters, among them was Mary Davis.[6] She grew up in Middle Neck Hundred of All Hallows Parish where over time her father acquired several properties. Beginning on 1 Nov 1665 he obtained a warrant for 350 acres called *Pierpont's Lot* in Middle Neck Hundred, then 80 acres known as *Pierpont's Rocks*, surveyed on 15 Dec 1665. The last property was surveyed on 4 Feb 1665, 40 acres called *Pierpont's Branch*.[7] These tracts are near the present Crownsville in Anne Arundel County.[8]

Ruth Warfield was eighteen years old when on 15 Sep 1719 she married Richard Davis, eldest son of Thomas and Mary, at St. Anne's Church South River, a part of Middle Neck Parish. Ruth's mother, also named Ruth, was a widow. On 17 Jun 1719, just three months before her daughter's marriage, Ruth Warfield wed Daniel Carter.[9] The younger Ruth's father, John Warfield, died about a year before both events. His death must have occurred suddenly as he did not leave a will. Whether from an accident or sudden illness, his death occurred between 24 June 1718 when he was a testator for Amos Pierpont's will and July 29 of that year when Thomas Davis and a neighbor inventoried his estate.[10] Warfield's estate was large, over £500, not including property left to him by his father Richard in 1703.[11] In his will, Richard Warfield the immigrant ancestor of this family divided the property between his six children, leaving *Warfield's Plains* and 180 acres of *Warfield's Forest* to John.[12] Brought over from England as a servant to John Sisson about 1659, Richard Warfield served out his time with Cornelius Howard after Sisson's death. With Edward Gardner in 1669, Richard Warfield purchased his first parcel of land, called *Gardner's Warfield*. By the time he died, he had accrued well over two thousand acres. Elinor, the daughter of John Brown a planter on the Severn River, may have been his wife but his will does not name her.[13]

On 16 Feb 1696 at All Hallows Church, John Warfield married Ruth Gaither. She was the eldest daughter of Ruth and John Gaither of South River[14] who was born 8 Sep 1679.[15] The Warfields and their nine children, including Ruth who married Richard Davis, lived on *Warfield's Plains*, land near the present Millersville about halfway between Waterbury and Indian Landing. Then, it was the westernmost part of St. Anne's Parish,[16] not far from where Ruth Gaither grew up. Although John Gaither died without a will, his personal estate was worth more than £550 including a large quantity of pewter, books, several slaves, an indentured servant and numerous livestock.[17] He also left a great deal of land to his eldest son, John. Among the personal legacies he gave his heirs, including Ruth, was £35 paid directly to his son-in-law, John Warfield. Ruth's mother married again on 13 Jan 1703/4 to Francis Hardisty who lived in South River Hundred,[18] and it was he who raised the younger children of Ruth and John Gaither.[19]

The Davis Family

Ruth Davis was also from a large family. Although she was the eldest daughter, she had three older brothers, Thomas, Richard and John. There were also two brothers and sisters younger than she was.[20] Named after both her mother and grandmother, future generations bore both her first and last names, not only as a measure of respect but also to remember the important Maryland family from which they descended.

Thomas Davis's family origins are unknown. There were men of the same name who lived in Somerset County, Maryland and even earlier in Virginia. If related, there is no direct proof connecting them to Thomas Davis, a prosperous Anne Arundel County planter. He was born in 1668[21] and about 1696 he married Mary Pierpont. In 1704 Thomas bought *Davistone,* a 240-acre tract at the head of the Severn River near Highland in Anne Arundel County. He was by then a married man with several children, a tobacco planter who invested in land to secure his and his children's future.[22] In 1709 he bought *Diamond,* a 115-acre parcel, from Mary's brother, Amos Pierpont.[23] He acquired a sizeable fortune in land, more than 1,500 acres during his lifetime. Thomas and Mary raised a family of eleven children at *Davistone,* and then married them to other prominent families in the area, namely Warfield mentioned before, but also the Marriott, Riggs, Gaither and Hammond families of the county. Prior to his death in 1749, Thomas made a will leaving specific bequests of land and personal items to each of his children.

Richard Davis died before his father, at a time when he and Ruth were living on *Duvall's Delight.* He left a will, and when viewed together, they not only prove relationships, but also provide insight into how wealth was distributed in that age. Thomas wrote his will on 20 Jan 1743, six years before he died but only a few months before the death of his eldest son, Richard, who was obviously ill and not expected to live.[24] He designated legacies to all his children and their heirs, but he specifically noted what land he wanted his grandchildren to have after Richard's death. He named his wife Mary as one of the executors as well as their sons, John and Francis. To his grandson Caleb, he gave two hundred acres of *Duvall's Delight* "whereon his mother now dwells" and that she, Ruth Davis, "shall possess said tract without any interruption." The will's language not only indicated where the family homestead was, it connected three generations of this family. When Thomas Davis died on 11 Apr 1749 and his wife, Mary Pierpont Davis, followed shortly thereafter on 13 May 1749, their sons had to dispense this large estate.[25]   Thomas Davis's identification of Caleb Davis as his grandson verified the family lineage but at the same time, naming Caleb's mother as Ruth Davis identified her as the Ruth Warfield who married Richard Davis in St. Anne's Parish in 1719. The legacies of father and son, as expressed through their wills and other documents, also connected Ruth Davis to her brother, Caleb, thus naming her parents and grandparents as well.

Ruth Davis

Richard Davis wrote a will in 1743, naming his wife Ruth as executor and apportioning his children their legacies. To his sons he left land. After his debts were paid, he divided the remaining part of his personal estate between his three daughters, Ruth, Mary and Elizabeth and his youngest son, Joshua.[26]

Ruth Davis, born 12 Jan 1728/1729, was approximately fifteen years old when her father died.[27] On adjacent property but also a part of *Duvall's Delight*, lived John Elder and his family, one of them was a son named Charles. As neighbors, the two families knew each other socially and attended the same church, and so their children were acquainted. 1736 records for Christ Church in Queen Caroline Parish, indicated that both families were members, and that Richard and Thomas Davis were assigned pew number seven while John Elder and his son, John Junior were in pew number twenty-five.[28] For Charles and Ruth, these neighborly links lead to an even closer relationship. Sometime after her father died, around 1745-1747 when she was between eighteen and twenty years of age, Ruth Davis married or at least lived in a married state with Charles, son of John Elder Senior. It may have come about during one of those mother-daughter chats over spinning that Ruth announced she was pregnant. On the other hand, perhaps her canny mother observed it and helped her plan the wedding. If so, Ruth Davis initiated an arrangement between the families for a private ceremony between the couple. Charles Elder had property because his father's will of 29 Dec 1740 stated that John Elder gave Charles 100 acres of the *Addition to Huntingtown Quarter*. He gave similar gifts to sons, Alexander and James, but John Junior was not named because he received his inheritance earlier.   Richard Davis, Ruth's father, witnessed Elder's will, providing additional proof they were neighbors and friends, but also related through their children's marriage.[29]

Charles Elder was baptized at All Hallows Parish on 2 Sep 1716, so he was about 24 years old when his father died and about 30 when he and Ruth united.[30] Although Ruth and Charles Elder had no marriage record, the same was not true of their daughter Delilah. In 1913 her birth date was no longer legible in the Hewitt Family Bible, but her name was, and it came immediately after those of Ruth Davis and Jacob Hewitt, which was then followed by their eight children. Since the Bible held only the names of the Davis and Hewitt family, Delilah's placement before her siblings indicated she was Ruth's daughter and their half-sister. She was surely born by the time her father died on 4 Nov 1751 and when Ruth, as estate administrator, produced sureties of £60 to begin probate.[31]   As the story unfolds, other clues will emerge showing that Ruth married Charles Elder and that Delilah Elder was her daughter.

Ruth was nineteen and Charles was 32 when Delilah was born about 1748. She was not more than three or four years old when her father died and her mother took over probate.[32]   Davis family influence weighed heavily in the estate settlement, probably because of Ruth's youthfulness and inexperience in these matters. Her brothers, Caleb and Richard Davis, assisted her by posting bond.   Many neighbors attended the estate sale, including Joshua Warfield, Ruth's uncle by marriage, and Henry Griffith, the brother of Lucretia who later married Caleb Davis.[33]   Representing the Elder family were James and Alexander who witnessed the inventory. Immediately following their signatures were those of Elder's creditors, Philip Hammond and William Hall of Elk Ridge, names that will appear again in this story.

The couple lived near Ruth's mother, and she likely returned home after Charles died. Some of the furniture described in the inventory she inherited from her father, or her mother gave it to her, and when she married again, she took it with her. Ruth made some of their clothing using sheep's wool from their stock that she spun into thread on her wheel. They had little more than a pound in cash but their clothing, valued at over £8, was of good quality. Among the most prized items in a household of this period were their beds and bedding, including bolsters, pillows and the curtains and valances that enclosed the bed. This family had three beds valued at £5 each, adequate but not fancy, especially when contrasted with that of their slave whose bedding was valued at less than a pound. Two additional beds indicated others were living with them, probably family members.   In many homes slaves were the single most valued "possession," and "Sambo" who was valued at £30 was probably a young field worker. The estate showed a harvest of twelve bushels of oats, two of wheat, ten of beans and fifteen bushels of corn, an inventory suggesting their crops were grown solely to feed the family. They had two horses worth £10 and other livestock that included hogs and cattle. Charles may not have grown tobacco because none was listed in the inventory, or it was past harvest time and new crops had not yet planted.

Ruth's personal items were a smoothing iron for pressing clothes and a looking glass. To grind corn she used a mortar and pestle and they sat and ate upon boxes. Ruth set her table with a cloth and they ate using both earthen and glass tableware. She had "old knives and forks" and "old pewter" which she likely inherited from her family. It included ale tankards, plates, cups and bowls, common service for a planter of their social status. However, the clearest indicators were the inclusion of an iron and a mirror, and that they used a tablecloth, and pewter tableware. These implements did not appear in the households of poorer planters. In one last note of interest and contrast, there were several old books in Charles' inventory indicating he was literate and a man of some education. Ruth signed with an "X," not because she was of low social status, but because even in the upper classes, girls in colonial society were not taught to read. The Elders' estate was worth £107, suggesting this young, self-supporting farmer had potential, and if he had lived, his family would have been comfortably secure.

Although the Elder family was of equal status with the Davises, Charles Elder died too young to achieve the economic bounty of his widow's family. On their rung of society, the position an individual enjoyed within the community was partially determined by how much land he had and how it was managed. The description following of a middling and an affluent planter illustrates the subtle but important differences between classes.

> When we compare the living conditions and material goods of the middling planters with those more affluent, the principal differences are two: clearer separation of the family from the rest of the people on the plantation, and clearer distinction between master and servant, mistress and maid. No great divide marks off the boundary between the upper tier of estates from those below, and no single style of living characterized the well to do. Some lived as gentlemen who never soiled their hands with fieldwork, but many were as adept at the ax and hoe as any of their men. The principal distinction of this ascendant class lay in the managerial nature of their daily round of duties, the need for them to keep careful accounts, and to plan ahead not only in order to maintain their good credit but to acquire stocks of necessaries for the coming year. Most importantly, they had to anticipate and provide for contingencies because of the large numbers of people dependent upon them. Many were also called upon to furnish their time and labor to the offices and duties of local government and parish, acting as justices of the peace, militia officers, and vestrymen.[34]

Whereas Charles Elder had potential, his father-in-law was in his prime when he died at the age of 46. By 1743 Richard Davis had accomplished much of what the paragraph above expected of a man of his station. An elder of Queen Caroline Parish, he was also a large landholder connected to other important Anne Arundel County families by birth and marriage. He left a large family and expectations that would connect them even more closely to the families of neighboring planters. Richard's father, sensing his son's days were getting shorter, made provisions for his grandchildren in his will. Thus, Richard Davis's estate of about 600 acres, along with his father's bequest, adequately provided land and personal property enough for all of his children. Ruth's elder brothers each received about 200 acres. Thomas received 194 acres of *Davis' Purchase* and Richard 200 of *Dear Bought* in Prince George's County. Because Ruth was the eldest daughter, her name appeared before those of her sisters.

One of Richard Davis's most remarkable choices was that he appointed his wife, Ruth Warfield, his sole executor. He left a large estate, one that required a skilled manager as well as an astute accountant. She must have been a woman of formidable talents and capabilities because he did not appoint a friend to assist her in these duties. Hers was a daunting task, one that required not only managerial skills, but also the grace to cajole those who owed the estate while holding off her creditors at the same time. Perhaps Ruth had learned these skills alongside her husband, and thus experienced she was able to take over when he died. This responsibility aside, Ruth had to manage the plantation as well as mother a large brood of children approaching marriageable ages. Daniel Dulany, the Commissary General of Maryland, may have been a friend of her late husband, and as the accountant for the estate, her reports went directly to him. This process took until 1750, fully seven years after her husband died, and at times Ruth had to beg off paying Dulany until she was able to collect from her debtors. At some point, she asked for help from her nephew Alexander, son of Richard Warfield, her brother. He helped her collect the last "desperate debts" from her husband's estate."[35]

An example of the tasks Ruth had to carry out occurred in 1745. She had to collect money due from two London merchants with whom her husband had consigned a shipment of three hogsheads of tobacco. After paying several bills she bought a barrel of corn to feed her family until the harvest was in. Then with the balance, she paid her lawyer and the accountant his administrative fees. At times it was necessary to draw money from the estate for living expenses. In another instance Ruth submitted a bill for killing a cow, a sheep and a hog for the "use of the deceased's family before the appraisal of the estate" showing that as they were assets of the estate, she wanted reimbursement for their loss. In 1745, she ordered four hogsheads to pack up the tobacco crop. Then she paid to have the barrels rolled down to the wharf for shipment to London. Loans were costly, some were at sixteen percent, payable after the tobacco harvest, but the Davis family did not have a lot of debt. However, like other planters, they paid their bills after harvest and ordered goods with what remained. Ruth's management skills helped her to hold off her lenders until she collected what was due the estate. In that way she avoided having to sell any part of the estate. This was a daunting task because in some cases it took up to five years for some creditors to receive satisfaction. This ability was an indication of the status and perhaps even the power held by the family within the community. Those she owed knew Ruth Davis could pay her debts.

Davis's inventory aptly determined that part of their land was a working plantation meant to feed their family, and Ruth's success at estate administration decided her family's future. Undoubtedly, they had an overseer who maintained daily oversight of the farm. They also had six slaves, one a man who worked in the fields, and two women who helped in the house caring for the children, including three of their own. They had four horses, one to ride worth £10, the others a colt and two plough horses. There was a large stock of farm animals including eighteen head of cattle, 38 pigs and twenty sheep all together valued at £78. Some of the working tools for the plantation included three ploughs plus hoes, axes and spades, as well as carpenter and coopers tools. The year's harvest included 42 barrels of corn, 18 bushels of beans, 59 bushels of oats and eight bushels of wheat, all of which was meant to be consumed by the family. Davis had a large apple orchard and a distillery on his property that produced 860 gallons of "cyder" valued at £17 that he sold locally. On part of his plantation Davis grew tobacco, and this is known because London merchants owed his estate money for product shipped to them.

The inventory was conducted in about eight sections, an indication the house was large and had several rooms. The kitchen was separate, and there were additional outbuildings probably including a milk-house, cellar, a buttery, and several sheds or storerooms. After completing a survey of crops, livestock, tools and storage items, they moved indoors to continue their count. They began in the main living area then moved into an adjacent loft or two to three smaller rooms where the family slept and kept their clothing and storage trunks.

The main living area was probably the largest, and it was where the family ate and worked. Here was Richard's writing desk and a rush bottomed chair where he worked on estate accounts. Next to him was a worn copy of Cole's Dictionary plus an ink holder. On the top of the desk were his money weight and scales, and one of the steelyards used to measure tobacco and perhaps several of his books. He hung his violin on a wall peg and nearby was his hunting gun. The desk's cubbyholes held the paper of ink powder for his pen, and perhaps the flints, shot and gunpowder for his gun. There was room for his old razors and penknives as well. He shaved using a small mirror tacked to the wall next to his desk. In the same area Ruth stored her trunks of sewing fabrics, which could be used for seating when needed.

There were several trunks with family linens, but Richard stored his tools, including hinges, hasps, staples, sheep sheers and other devices he used on the plantation. The family ate at an oval table surrounded by seven rush-bottomed chairs. Adding Richard's chair provided seating for eight people. They had additional eating and working space at two smaller oval tables, plus a leather chair and a trunk. Imagine Ruth and Richard sitting down on an evening with their family. Their children of all ages gathered around the large table, as many boys as girls ready to feast on the bounty of the land. Afterwards Richard brought a candle to his desk and retired to his paperwork while Ruth sat with her daughters to spin until it became too dark to see the thread. By today's standards, the room's description seems ordinary, even crowded and lacking in essentials of daily use, but in eighteenth century Maryland, it was the comfortable setting of a successful planter, repeated in nearby households across the landscape of Anne Arundel County.

Among her tools for making clothes, Ruth had four wheels, two each for spinning wool and linen, a skill she undoubtedly taught her daughters. Spinning brought the women together and allowed ample time for conversation and lessons, but also a time to memorize the rules of conduct. Young Ruth and her sisters were decidedly interested in some topics more than in others. One they probably fell into easily was whom among the young men of the neighborhood they liked and which they did not. Having listened carefully to her daughters chatter together, if she heard a certain young man's name brought up and thought him a suitable husband, she might interject his name into the conversation to see if any of her daughters reacted. If one did, she took note and depending upon the response, she may or may not proceed with further discussion. Had Richard been living when his daughters reached the age of eighteen or so, he and Ruth would have had further conversations, and if agreed between them, he would have approached the father of the young man and broached the question of his daughter's marriage to the young man. With his death, Ruth lacked that good counsel and so it became her duty to negotiate marriage arrangements with the parents of each young man. Ultimately she completed arrangements with the family and upon reaching an agreement, the marriage took place between her daughter Ruth, or one of her sisters.

Ruth's trunks held fabric and yard goods, much of it purchased from England. She had a large quantity and a variety of textiles. Judging by the vast amount of fine cloth like India silk, silk Genet, fringe and ribbons she had, Ruth was prepared well in advance for her daughters' ultimate departure from the family. As a part of the process of finding a husband for them, she first strove to compliment their youthful assets by dressing them in the finest attire possible. The sheer volume of the inventory showed these women were active seamstresses and spinners, but the finest materials were purchased from overseas. Ruth's store held large amounts of fine fabrics, including 23 yards of silk and 31 yards of ribbons, plus sewing silk, ten yards of fringe and twelve of edging. Her tools included scissors, knitting needles, and several packets of pins, thread, six dozen coat and breast buttons and fourteen pair of children's gloves. Nestled among the yard goods were four fans and two necklaces, items purchased to compliment the gowns of silk and organdy that Ruth or her sisters would wear at genteel gatherings.

The women spent time spinning, weaving and sewing flax, or country cloth, worn every day by the family. They also had stores of corduroy and Irish linen, and wool-felt for hats either made by them or purchased from England. Ruth had a goodly supply of other cloth they purchased from abroad, like a light wool called shalloon used to line their clothing in winter, and for summer they wore cotton and organdy.

> Someone in the Davis family played the violin, probably Richard, but it may have been one of his sons. He was also better read than the average planter, however, with over a dozen books in his collection, he was an equal among his peers. He had two bibles, and also two dictionaries, the Parson's Christian Directory and Cole's Dictionary. There was also another on arithmetic and one titled *English Liberties*. Above all others, a popular magazine of the day, *The Tatler*, indicated Richard Davis was a thinker, interested in other men's ideas. The magazine was an English publication primarily read by politicians, the educated and the merchant class. Its issues covered subjects like taxation, federal power, Indian treaties, public education and colonialism. Poetry and political essays were also sometimes featured.[36]

Stored with Richard's saddle and bridle was £41 of brushed leather to make men's breeches and £26 of leather to make and repair the family's shoes. As a general aside to this part of the story, it is possible that Thomas Jacks, the cordwainer, was also shoemaker to this family. If so, perhaps young Jacob Hewitt accompanied him on a visit to the Davis household, thus meeting this family many years before he was to become a part of it. If he was introduced as . a youngster, perhaps remembering the Davis plantation led him there years later.

The kitchen was separate from the house and it was Ruth's domain. Probably a large space, it had a variety of the best utensils of the day, and was equipped with a large array of bowls, plates, glasses and pots, as well as everything else necessary to prepare, cook and serve meals for a large family. All that belied a modern kitchen were items such as fire tongs, a spit, forks for turning meat and a brass mortar and pestle. Many of the items were either brass or pewter, another status symbol. This room also held items considered a luxury in most households of the time. The most obvious was a large assortment of spices like ginger, cloves, cinnamon, nutmeg, allspice and pepper. She also possessed silver teaspoons, sugar tongs and a tea strainer to sip tea, a custom becoming popular among the gentry of that period.

In the Davis inventory were seven beds for a family of ten with six slaves. Some beds were shared and the obvious combinations suggested that the parents and some of the older children used the four feather beds. They were the best beds, regarded so because it took between forty and eighty pounds of feathers to form a proper bed. The younger children used the trundle bed and one with a sheared wool mattress. The slaves Alice and Hannah slept together on a bed in the kitchen. As there were not enough beds for all, other servants either slept on hammocks, on the floor in a bedroll, or on ticks stuffed with cattails or rushes. Ruth Davis grew up in a rural setting, but on the plantation of a prosperous planter known and respected in the community. As a child she was given all the comforts of that time, and certainly as long as her father was alive she, as the eldest daughter, received all that was her due.

Courting the Widow

The Davis home was on the Patuxent River just south of Clarksville near Highland. The property known as *Duvall's Delight* was about ten miles from the present towns of Savage, Guilford and Annapolis Junction.[37] Nearby was the *Addition to Huntingtown Quarter* where Charles Elder lived, and adjoining it the home of Caleb Davis's father-in-law, Orlando Griffith.[38] Northeast of these towns in Elk Ridge Hundred was *Jacks Peacock*[39] "on the south side of the Patapsco about one mile from the falls." Although the Jacks family held this property until 1728 when they sold the last of their plantation, they probably continued to live on the property as tenants.

In 1736 when Jacob Hewitt and his siblings came to live with them, Thomas and Elizabeth Jacks were in Anne Arundel County. What these properties had in common was their proximity to Elkridge Landing where harvested tobacco was loaded for shipment to England, and where William Hall had a store. J. D. Warfield in his book, *Founders of Anne Arundel and Howard Counties, Maryland*, said this of early Elk Ridge:

> At this northern terminus of Elk Ridge, overlooking in picturesque beauty the gorges of the Patapsco on the north and spreading out to the east in a waterway, was early erected a Port of Entry to accommodate the tobacco growers of Upper Anne Arundel. As early as 1746, it was a rival of Annapolis.

In 1763 there were 1,695 hogsheads of tobacco, more than half of the crop in Anne Arundel County [was] inspected at Elk Ridge."[40] "The great north and south road ran from Elkridge Landing southward to Laurel and Georgetown and in the opposite direction it extended to the crossing at Hammond's Ferry, where it entered Baltimore County in the direction of Baltimore Town...founded in 1729—and eventually to Philadelphia."[41]

William Hall was a well-known merchant at Elk Ridge Landing and Jacob Hewitt purchased goods from his store, but he acquired debt there also. When Hall died in 1770, those who owed his estate included nearly everyone who lived near the Landing. Among the hundreds of creditors were Jacob and his brother Edward Hewitt,[42] and, as early as 1752, Charles Elder. Perhaps one day while Jacob was at the Landing loading hogsheads on board ship, or buying tools in Hall's store, he met Ruth Davis's husband, Charles Elder. Maybe he sought work on the Davis plantation after meeting her brother Caleb Davis there, and remembering his earlier experience delivering shoes with Thomas Jacks, applied for work. The couple could have met in several ways, and most likely it was after 1752, when her husband died, up until the late spring of 1755 when Ruth became pregnant with their first child. Between those dates they grew to know each other and made a vow of partnership, one that would sustain them for the next thirty-five years.

Theirs was an odd pairing between a woman of the landed class and an orphan without land, fame or fortune. When he came into her family, he possessed little more than youth and the dream of a better life. The Hewitts' social status is unknown but it was not equal to hers, so undoubtedly this was not an arranged marriage. Whatever drew them together was a personal agreement and not necessarily one initially achieved through parental consent. Although the actual circumstances are unknown, as a widow and a mother, Ruth needed to remarry and may have had other choices than Jacob, unless she was pregnant. With a formidable mother-in-law, and a wife with several brothers who looked out for her, measured against this family, Jacob shouldered a heavy responsibility. Ruth, on the other hand, must have spent some time getting to know Jacob, assessing his virtues and strengths since land and money were not his to offer. Perhaps she saw in him the potential for a husband and partner, as well as a father for Delilah and any other children she might bear. Calming her fears, he offered to care for her and the child, and so they made an arrangement based first on need, then on hope and the trust they placed in each other.

It is not known where they lived in the first years of their union, however, by 1760, Ruth Davis Elder Hewitt no longer had possession of the land willed to her first husband. A tax record for that year confirmed that the property was back in the hands of the Elder family.[43] Other records show that before James Elder died in 1769, her former brother-in-law owned the tract initially divided between the three brothers.[44] His death also confirmed that the Elder and Davis family remained close after Charles Elder died because Ruth's brother, Caleb Davis, provided sureties for James' estate along with their cousin Samuel Riggs.[45] The elder Ruth Davis was living on the home place in 1760 when she paid taxes as the owner, and perhaps when their first child was born, Ruth and

Jacob Hewitt were living near her mother or somewhere on their plantation. The child was born on 23 Nov 1755 and they named him Robert after Jacob's father.[46] At about the same time, Thomas Jacks, who once provided a home for the Hewitt children, died sometime before October 1756 when his son Richard took charge of his estate. Jacks's administration mostly reflected his debts, and since the Hewitt orphans were not named in the estate, what impact his death had depended upon who Jacks was to them. As orphans they grew up in poverty, but they may have felt the loss if he treated them kindly, otherwise he went un-mourned. However Jacob marked the passing of Thomas Jacks, unbeknownst to him, this was the first in a series of changes that would test the bond between him and his new wife. Both 28 years of age, they were about to begin the first upheaval in their long life together.

The Early Years

The first challenge to their partnership came in the guise of a lawsuit against Jacob. His money problems began in April 1754 when he signed a bond agreeing to pay William Nicholson £10.17.3 for "valued received." Nicholson's business was at Newtown near Elkridge where Hewitt applied for credit but could not pay his bill. From that date and for the next two years matters went terribly wrong for Hewitt. In 1756 Nicholas sued Hewitt in Anne Arundel County, although Hewitt was "late of Anne Arundel County," an indication he was living elsewhere. For the next two years of continuances, Jacob's attorney Robert Davis, a relative of his wife, represented Hewitt in court. With court costs and attorney's fees, the judgment against him grew, so that he owed an additional £200 of tobacco to what Nicholson had initially sought in payment. Continuances through November 1757 brought threats of throwing Hewitt in jail.[47] Neither he, nor attorney Davis, appeared in court on the last date and presumably, the lawsuit had settled by July 1761, when Nicholson died, because Jacob was not listed among the estate debtors.[48]

Although Jacob and Ruth left tracks in Anne Arundel County as they departed, they do not lead to their destination, although Baltimore appeared to be where opportunity took them. Today it is difficult to consider that this metropolis was just a small town in the 1750's, with little reason to believe it would ever eclipse Annapolis either in size or importance, but it did. In 1752, John Moale described Baltimore saying there were…

> "25 buildings, mostly wooden homes widely spaced over the hillsides that sloped gently toward the water. Lot owners jealously regarded the growing community down-river at William Fells's point, where deeper water permitted larger vessels to berth. Ships visiting both communities took on grain from the countryside to the west and flour milled on the Jones Falls, the Patapsco River, and the Gunpowder River to the north. Though growing and the site of popular spring and fall fairs, Baltimore remained a small town."[49]

Another writer's description added to the picture with a slightly different slant:

> "In the mid-1700's, there would have been little reason to visit
> Baltimore Towne on the Norwest Branch of the Patapsco
> River. For the most part, the village was a cluster of homes on
> the edge of a marshy harbor, surrounded by miles of
> undisturbed, gently rolling hills. Baltimore was modest
> compared to Annapolis, 30 miles south on the Severn, and
> hailed as the "Athens of America." It was a working town,
> with foundries and flour milled at nearby streams...The region
> had a reputation for tolerance and acceptance of diversity.
> The free practice of religion was recognized by a 1649 law
> that prohibited discussing the religious practices of others. By
> 1752, Baltimore was home to only about 200 residents. There
> was a tobacco inspection house, St. Paul's Church, and a
> brewery. Ships brought [goods] to and from other coastal
> ports, and opened trade routes to Europe and the Caribbean.
> Huge exports of flour and tobacco allowed Baltimore to
> prosper and grow faster than any other port south of
> Philadelphia. Yet Baltimore was considered so trifling that the
> British never bothered the town during the American
> Revolution, even though the city's foundries manufactured
> cannon for Washington's armies.[50]

At about the time Nicholson sued Jacob, his brother Edward Hewitt saw
opportunity in a newly developing area in western Baltimore County. He was
25 when he patented his first property on February 1756. Perhaps newly
married, he bought a 100-acre tract and called it *Hewitt's Shrubby Hills*.[51]
Perhaps his brother's purchase, and Jacob's brush with the law, precipitated his
move to Baltimore County and a new beginning close to the city of Baltimore.
Jacob owned no land for many years, but as a farmer perhaps he rented land
from Ruth's family. Other subsidiary occupations were also possible, such as a
tobacco broker, or a miller, all livelihoods followed by his sons in later years.

More than three years after Robert was born, they welcomed a second son
called Caleb. He was born 4 Feb 1759, shortly before his mother's birthday.
Ruth and her brother Caleb Davis were about three years apart in age, she being
the older of the two. They were close, as he helped her with the estate when her
first husband died. She in turn named her second son after him. Ruth's brother
was 25 years old in 1756, and one of several young bachelors of Anne Arundel
County's Westminster Parish, where tithing records show his worth at £100-
£300. He lived at Phillip Hammond's place, a merchant who owned a
warehouse in New Town on Powder Hill near Annapolis, and Davis probably
worked for him. Soon after moving there in 1718, Hammond became a leading
import merchant who was also prominent in legislative and church affairs."[52]
While living with the Hammond family, Caleb moved within a circle of his
peers, illustrated soon after by his marriage into another prominent family of the
county. In 1759, a little before Christmas he married Lucretia Griffith, the
daughter of Orlando.[53] Alas, like his father, young Davis had a short life. When
he died in 1769, he left behind a wife and four young daughters. Not long

afterward, his widow remarried, finding in Azel Waters, not only a husband but also a stepfather for her children.[54]

On 16 Jun 1761, Jacob and Ruth's third son, Jacob, was born, and less than two years later, Elizabeth was born on 28 Dec 1762. By the summer of 1765, tax records showed the family was living in Baltimore where their son Richard was born on 28 July. Living with them but recorded separately was Delilah Elder who was probably eighteen by then. She was the eldest, and in her care were three half-brothers and a sister between the ages of three and ten years old.[55] By 1760 Baltimore had become a destination town, and in twenty years the population had grown to 9,000 citizens, a figure three times that of its size when the Hewitt family first moved there.[56]

After visiting his brother and discussing the price of land in western Baltimore County, Jacob looked for property nearby. Edward Hewitt continued to enlarge his holdings with a second purchase in 1763 that was resurveyed and combined into a total of 400 acres renamed *Sandy Bottom*, all located in present day Carroll County.[57] That May, Jacob Hewitt signed a bond with Robert Gilcresh to buy 345 acres of a larger tract called *Upper Marlborough* near Eldersburg on the Old Liberty Road, a few miles from where Edward lived.[58] The transaction was not completed then because Gilcresh died before Jacob could pay him.[59] Ruth and Jacob's family continued to grow with the birth of Eli in August 1767, and Ephraim on 17 Mar 1770. Their last child, a daughter named Ruth, was born on 30 Sep 1772.[60] Tax records showed that in 1774 the family lived in St. Paul's Parish of Baltimore's Middlesex Hundred, near Woodberry on the Old Liberty Road.

Some of Jacob and Ruth's sons were farmers but others were townsmen. Having grown up on the edges of the city, two of them became Baltimore tobacco brokers, one was a judge in Nashville, and the youngest son ran a tavern, an inn, and a dry goods business from his home. They learned these skills and interests from their parents, indicating Jacob was more than a Baltimore farmer. While raising children, he and Ruth likely increased their income by turning their house into an inn and tavern. No proof has arisen that this was an earlier occupation, but it was their middle-aged pursuit as the following chapter reveals. Geographic similarities abound between their Baltimore home and the farm in Fayette County, Pennsylvania. Both locations were on well-traveled, east-west roads used to transport large numbers of people. Families moving westward and businessmen going both ways frequented the roads, making each location ideal for an inn with a tavern. The most compelling argument is that a couple in their mid-fifties on their second venture, would continue their life's profession confident that their past experience and knowledge would support them in their new endeavor. In part, the 1774 Baltimore tax list supported the idea of a multiple enterprise dwelling. Hewitt's household had five males over sixteen including Jacob, and his son Robert not yet nineteen. His younger sons were not on the list, thus the others had to be servants or tenants. This seemed to so in 1773 when the tax list showed two unrelated men and a female slave in Jacob's household.

Revolution and Change

The years just prior to and leading up to the Revolutionary War were times of great change in America both intellectually and practically. Laws tolerated in the past quickly became unbearable to those seeking individual rights. This was true in Boston and New York and it was no less true in Maryland. A writer described what Baltimore was like on the eve of the Revolution.

> "By 1776 Baltimore had become a port town of significance with emphasis on the exporting of wheat and flour and the importing of goods for sale in Baltimore and to a lesser extent to customers on the Eastern Shore and in the Frederick region. Trade and the shipbuilding industry necessary to the continuance of that trade made the town and was the basis of its growth to this point. Manufacturing was beginning, but its importance lay in the future... but in 1776, Baltimore still had a port town character that kept its distance from most of the rest of rural Maryland even though its presence was such that politically it could not be ignored. In 1776 Baltimore had a population of approximately 6,000 people of whom as many as 850 were slaves."[61]

The English considered not only Baltimore and Annapolis, but all of Maryland one of its oldest and most successful colonies in America, and up to this time planters were unquestioningly loyal subjects of the king. Success was due in large part to the subjugation of its people in not allowing colonials to produce anything other than tobacco. Thus America was dependent on the mother country for nearly everything else. Considered by the English to be one of its best experiments, that arrangement was about to change in ways that the motherland could not imagine. Today we know that revolutionary zeal was fomenting not only in Maryland, but throughout the colonies. Much of it was over taxes, those they paid to the Crown on locally produced goods but also on all imported goods. Some were angered that England forbade competition of some manufactured goods so that the colonists had to import most products from England. They protested unfair laws, but as their dissatisfaction flowed outward it gained momentum, as singular outcries became the collective voice of a larger body. Increasingly when people assembled, their demands were potent outbursts, questioning the king's authority with phrases like "liberty for the individual!" and "freedom from tyranny!" Each citizen considered his internal protest to be an original and individual quest for liberty. Collectively it was a loud voice and that worried the king.

In Maryland public clamor followed a riotous act, and representatives of the Crown in Annapolis and Baltimore came to attention. Some of the radicals who led it were among its leading citizens. They were merchants, planters and others with both political muscle and youthful revolutionary passion. Its leaders were Rezin Hammond from Elk Ridge, Charles Ridgley a Baltimore merchant, Charles Warfield and Ephraim Howard, all men from prominent families. In 1774, the individual personal struggle became mob action causing public outcry for its audacious violence. Angered Maryland citizens began protesting Britain's imposition of the Stamp Act, an enforced tobacco inspection and fees bill enacted principally to pay for England's expenses in the French and Indian War. One day a crowd of protestors formed, and egged on by its leaders they focused on a ship newly arrived in Annapolis Harbor. The brigantine *Peggy Stewart* docked that October after paying fees on 2,000 pounds of tea it delivered to the colony. Using the owner, who was for taxation, as an example of protest, the inciters at first wanted to tar and feather the captain and burn his ship. Then a voice of reason arose above the crowd suggesting they only burn the tea. In answer, there were both cheers and jeers, but in the end, the ship and its cargo was burned. While some were appalled at the action, others considered it a moderate solution to what could have been a much more rabid outcome. "This affair gave the popular party an air of comparative moderation, and at the Continental Congress its leaders gained the same reputation. [Thereafter] the Maryland delegation played a prominent part in locating the middle ground between radicals and conservatives, between the urgent pleas of New England and the practical needs of the northern commercial and southern planting colonies."[62] The outcome also placed the Maryland colonists squarely in conflict with their colonial governors.

Perhaps there was a correlation between the riot in the harbor and the sudden appearance of James Gilcresh of Chester County, Pennsylvania in 1774. Realizing the unstable situation, he chose this time to finalize the deed to *Upper Marlborough* in western Baltimore County. Jacob Hewitt paid him £128 plus interest for the property[63] which was entered in the name of Hewitt and Tevis. Then Edward Hewitt and Peter Tevis transferred it to Jacob Hewitt. Perhaps this was done because Jacob had no land and Gilcresh required collateral, so Jacob's brother acted as a guarantor for the transaction.

In 1777 the legislature required all free males over the age of eighteen to swear loyalty to the state of Maryland by March 1778. Signed in 1778, Jacob Hewitt's name was on the list along with his son Robert, brother Edward and nephew Vachel. With his signature he declared that...

> "I do swear that I do not hold myself bound to yield any allegiance or obedience to the King of Great Britain his heirs or successors, and that I will be true and faithful to the State of Maryland and will to the utmost of my power, support, maintain, and defend the freedom and independence thereof, and the government as now established, against all open enemies, and secret and traitorous conspiracies and will use my utmost endeavors to disclose and make known to the governor, or someone of the judges or justices thereof, all treasons or traitorous conspiracies attempts, or combinations, against this state or the government thereof, which may come to my knowledge. So help me God."

The oath, which Jacob and his son signed before a county justice, was one of their last gestures before leaving the state.[64] It confirmed that Hewitt lived in Middlesex Hundred, and not on *Upper Marlborough* at the time, if ever.

Leaving Baltimore

In 1778 Jacob and Ruth Hewitt were fifty years old with a family ranging in age between six and about thirty years old. Delilah, the eldest was unmarried and likely remained at home assisting her mother with the younger children, especially the three youngest children who were all under the age of twelve. Jacob and his family began preparing to leave Baltimore just before the Revolutionary War broke out, although at least one of their children remained behind. If Delilah left Maryland with her mother, she returned to Baltimore before the war was over. She was living there in 1781 when at the age of thirty-three Henry Tunstall applied for a license on 30 June so they could be married.[65] Their union suggests that Delilah never left Baltimore but stayed behind maintaining relationships of a lifetime and eventually meeting the man she would marry. Not long afterward Delilah gave birth to a daughter they named Ruth, after her mother.

By 1778 the war was a matter of conversation in every household where there was a young man old enough to join. The Hewitts' two oldest sons, Robert, who turned twenty-three that year and Caleb who was nineteen, were of the age when so many young men united in the cause. There is no evidence that Robert volunteered but his brother Caleb did. Years later, Caleb's two surviving children, Robert Hewitt and Mary Broome, applied for bounty land awarded for their father's service.[66] Paymaster records from Washington confirmed he served in the dragoons until the end of the war. He signed up in Philadelphia on 14 Jun 1777, joining the 4th Regiment of Light Dragoons, a mounted cavalry unit in Pennsylvania's Continental Army.[67] Theirs was a small elite unit composed of only four regiments whose men rode horses and wore snappy uniforms. Easily identified as dragoons, each man wore a green outer coat over a red waistcoat and chestnut brown pants. He had high leather boots and under his coat a leather pouch that crossed his chest. Topping off the uniform was a high thick fur hat. Caleb's unit was led by Col. Stephen Moylan under whom he served throughout most of the war. However, on the day he joined it was not likely that young Caleb knew he was in for the biggest, most dangerous challenge of his life. Within days the regiment was off to Woodbridge, New Jersey where they saw their first action.

The dragoons were the guard and support for General Washington's staff and throughout the war they were in the midst of many of the tactical plans and critical decisions made by its leadership. Because portions of these units were in both the Northern and Southern Campaigns and active throughout the war, by war's end the cavalry had seen duty in nearly all of the major battles of the Revolution.[68] Almost immediately after Moylan's 4th Pennsylvania Regiment was formed it caught General Washington's notice. The first time was on 12 May 1777 just before Caleb joined the army. Washington wrote to Moylan of his concern that because our horse troops were dressed in red coats that were similar to those worn by the British mounted troops, that they were in danger of being shot by our own troops. So alarmed was he wrote saying, "I therefore desire that you will immediately fall upon means for having the colour of the coats changed, which may be done by dipping into that kind of dye that which is most proper to put upon red. I care not what it is, [just] so that the present colour be changed." Thus, their outer coats became green. The second time Moylan's troops attracted his attention was on 25 Oct 1777 when he wrote to the man in charge of all the dragoons, Count Pulaski. Without compensating them, he had allowed the troops to go out and "take horses" from those loyal to the British. Washington was so incensed by Pulaski's interpretation of his orders that he wrote,

> "I am informed that under pretence of the authority derived from me, they (the dragoons) go about the country plundering whomsoever they are pleased to denominate Tories, and converting what they get to their own private profit and emolument. This is an abuse that cannot be tolerated...You will therefore immediately make it known to your whole corps, that they are not under any pretence whatever to meddle with the horses or other property of any inhabitant whatever, on pain of the severest punishment; for they may be assured, as far as it depends upon me, that military execution will attend all those who are caught in the like practice hereafter."[69]

Because their main job was to protect the encampment, the dragoons were in and around New York and New Jersey with Washington and his troops during the bitterly cold winter of 1777 at Valley Forge. After that, and for the next three years Moylan's troops served in New York and Connecticut. They moved to Lancaster County, Pennsylvania during the latter part of 1780, in time for Caleb Hewitt who had just turned 21, to marry Christina Hartaffel.[70] A pay record for 20-22 Mar 1781 indicated he had been promoted to sergeant, and received payment of £139.14.9 for his services. In January 1781, Caleb and the regiment moved south where they fought at the battle at Cowpens, South Carolina winning a major victory there. Then in May 1781, Colonel Moylan and the regiment was ordered to join Generals Lafayette and Wayne in Virginia. All that year they engaged in battle, moving from one area to the other and back. In October 1781 Caleb's regiment was at Yorktown with the Fourth Dragoons when General Cornwallis surrendered to the Continental troops. Although peace talks had begun and the war was ending, fighting continued for another two years. In the spring of 1782 the light dragoons joined General Anthony Wayne in the re-conquest of Georgia.[71]

Caleb Hewitt served until the end of the war and the last action at Ebenezer, Georgia in June of 1782. The records were not specific about whether he participated in every battle; however, this regiment saw action in nearly every major engagement of the war from 1777 until the signing of the Treaty of Paris in September 1783. Pay records extending through 4 Nov 1783 indicated that Hewitt was associated with Moylan's Fourth Regiment of Light Cavalry until the final year of the war when, because Moylan was ill, Hewitt mustered out under the command of Captain Zebulon Pike in September 1783.[72] Caleb's release came just in time to attend his daughter Ruth's baptism at the Moravian Church at Lancaster on 25 Sept 1783.[73] Even with compelling evidence indicating he was in the county, there is no proof the man who married Miss Hartaffel was the son of Jacob Hewitt and a sergeant in Colonel Moylan's dragoons. He entered the war, a boy of eighteen, and by age twenty-two he was promoted to sergeant, his rank upon leaving when he was twenty-four. While Caleb was off serving his country, his parents moved to western Pennsylvania and bought a farm.[74]

Undoubtedly Caleb, with more memories and adventures than was common in a lifetime, went home to the bosom of his family where he remained for a time to rest, recuperate and heal. Along the way, he surely stopped to see the wife and child he left behind in Lancaster County or visited her family if they were no longer alive. Arriving at his parents' farm he found that his siblings had grown up and the family prospered in their new home. Undoubtedly they greeted him with joy and relief that he had survived the many years of war. Particularly drawn to the changes in him, they saw that the boy who left was a man, one who had seen hard times and much loss of life. Eventually stories flowed from him as he released from memory what he had seen of battle, its losses and occasional triumphs. Difficult and deadly as it was, there were also adventures that he would never have again in his lifetime. Eventually the family went back to their lives and their chores, leaving Caleb to his memories. As time has a way of doing, he hopefully reached a place of healing and was able to put those memories aside. They were forever a part of him but soon became his past. As he thought about the future Caleb did not choose the frontier where his parents had settled but instead he went back to Baltimore, perhaps taking his younger brother Eli with him. It was a place where they had friends and family who would welcome them.

Where Caleb actually lived during the three years after he mustered out in 1783 goes unrecorded. However, on 6 Jul 1786 in Baltimore a man named Caleb Hewitt married Mary Hull.[75] There is no proof he was the same man who fought in the Revolution, however there was no other man by that name living in the city at the time. Four years later in 1790 his father died, but prior to that Caleb had power of attorney to settle his father's remaining legal affairs in Baltimore.[76] When their father's will was read and they received the traditional "five shillings" bequest required by law, both Caleb and Eli were living in the city of Baltimore.[77]

The Tobacconists of Baltimore

Caleb settled in Baltimore at least by 1788 when he purchased Lot #628 on an unknown street. The following year he bought another lot on Baltimore Street.[78] Tax lists revealed that by 1798, when Caleb was thirty-nine and Eli thirty-one, that both of them were living in the city of Baltimore.[79] Their sister Delilah and her husband Henry Tunstall were living there also in 1790 when they both died leaving Ruth an orphan.

Henry made a will in Aug 1788 leaving half of his personal estate and one-third of his real estate to Delilah. To Eli Hewitt, he gave his watch. The balance of the estate went to their daughter Ruth. Delilah died on 13 Jun 1790 and

Henry followed her on 24 Nov 1790.[80] Two days later the estate went into probate. On 15 Dec 1791, Caleb Hewitt filed his final account as administrator of the estate and guardian of his niece, Ruth.[81] There is compelling circumstantial evidence that Delilah Elder Tunstall was the daughter of Ruth Davis and Charles Elder. There was also a lifetime of connections providing a preponderance of evidence that she was the daughter of Charles Elder and Ruth Davis. First, her name was placed before her siblings in the Bible, linking her to her mother, Ruth Davis Elder Hewitt, then to Jacob Hewitt as her stepfather, Henry Tunstall as her husband, and finally as the mother of Ruth Tunstall. Jacob's personal history alone would pre-suppose that he had strong feelings about rallying around a child left without parents, for his memory about being orphaned was keen. Like links on a chain, when Caleb became Ruth Tunstall's guardian, the Hewitt's familial connection to Delilah Tunstall only became stronger.

While some events in Caleb's life were concrete, others indicated that his personal life was more complex than most. This becomes particularly apparent when counting his wives. He must have married many times, perhaps four in all, beginning with Christina Hartaffel. If she was his first wife, his second was Mary Hull to whom he was married in 1786. She may have been one of the four women listed in the 1790 Baltimore city tax list, an enumeration indicating there were a large number of individuals living in Caleb's home. Aside from the women listed, there were four males over sixteen, and four males under sixteen.[82] Not counting Caleb, they were either servants or hired workers, although one of them could have been his brother, Eli, who was 23 and single. However, unaccounted for were four younger males and three or four females. Although Caleb married several times he had no children then, and it was doubtful he was running an orphanage or a refuge for the homeless. His will indicated that he rented his property or ran a hotel and those living on the premises were lodgers with children.

He continued to buy property, and in 1792 Caleb purchased Lot #509 on Liberty Street.[83] Two years later, apparently a widower again, on 15 May 1794 he married Sarah Wilkinson at the First Methodist Episcopal Church of Baltimore (formerly the Light Street Church) where he was a founding member.[84] In 1797, the Baltimore congregation worshipped at the Lovely Lane Meeting House, but soon outgrew the building and moved to the Light Street Church. A disastrous fire occurred shortly thereafter destroying it and the seminary. That year the trustees, including Caleb, paid to have it rebuilt, renaming it the New Light Street Church.[85] As a strong supporter of Methodism, in 1800 he was elected a member of the First Baltimore Conference of the Methodist Church.[86]

Caleb may have sustained permanent injuries from his service in the Revolutionary War, and in 1798, perhaps fearing he might not live much longer, he made his will. He was also financially successful and determined to leave his estate to his siblings if he died without children. A portion of it read...

> "I do hereby...appoint my friend John Brevitt, with my beloved wife if I should leave one, to execute this my last will. If it should happen that I die without a wife, then and in that case, I will and leave my estate to my child or children as the

> case may be...but if my child or children should die in their
> non-age and I leaving no wife, then and in that case I will and
> leave my estate in the following manner, that is to say, one
> part to my brother, Robert Hewitt..."

and then he went on to name all of his siblings. The will indicated that at the
time he had neither a wife nor children, leaving unanswered the question of what
happened to Christina, Mary and Sarah, if they were indeed his wives.

Although some areas of Caleb's life were clouded in ambiguity, his will,
its codicil, and the estate settlement were enlightening. Its clear identification of
his siblings was a gift to posterity. The Hewitt Family Bible was the first
source, but this corroboration confirms who of his siblings was living in 1798 as
each was named in birth order beginning with his brothers and then his sisters.
Missing was their brother Jacob born in 1761 and presumed dead.   He
remembered his niece and ward, Ruth Tunstall, whose parents had died in 1790,
and Eli's "oldest child" who was born earlier in the year.

While there were three women who may have been wives of Caleb Hewitt,
the only woman known to be his wife was Mary Morton who the *Baltimore Sun*
identified as being "both of Baltimore" when they were married Saturday, 24
August 1799, less than a year after his will was made.[87] By profession, Caleb
was a tobacconist with both a shop and a warehouse where he stored a large
quantity and a variety of tobacco. As an additional source of income he rented
space in his warehouse, and he had a house and some lots on Liberty Street,
which went to his wife as a lifetime gift.[88]

Their home was large; possibly two stories, and comfortably appointed. It
contained all the necessities and some of the luxuries a Baltimore merchant
required. Their best furniture was mahogany including the baby's cradle and
one of the children's beds. The inventory suggested they had three bedrooms
outfitted with either mahogany or poplar furniture and at least one room had a
fireplace. There were many tables and chairs, and an unusually large supply of
tableware suggesting they ran a small inn or boarding house. The dining room
was equipped with several mahogany tables, a sideboard, eighteen Windsor
chairs, plus brass andirons and chimney ornaments for the fireplace. A nearby
storage room held a large quantity of tablecloths, napkins, a set of china, plus
cups, goblets and all the other necessities to set a "nice table"—but for a large
number of people. The kitchen had two tables with the usual cooking and
pantry implements. The larder was large containing together about seven
hundred pounds of pork and beef. In the inventory the building was described
as "a lot of ground fronting on Liberty Street extending to Forest Lane on which
were erected two frame houses and a warehouse on the alley." Its value without
the contents was $3,000. Hewitt's tenant's owed house rent of between $31 and
$187. Of their two slaves, Dick got his freedom after April 1800, but Hannah
had to serve seven more years.

In their brief marriage Caleb and Polly, as she was called, had several
children but as they were little more than babies at the time of their father's
death. Their family lived comfortably as several examples indicate. They had
several mirrors, and many "pictures," placed throughout the house. Five of the
largest were upstairs, probably in the bedrooms. There were carpets throughout
the house, including the staircase furnished with a "stair and passage carpet" and

the final addition, "brass rods for the stair carpet."[89] Like his father, and later his brother Ephraim, Caleb's inventory strongly suggested he was running an inn or a boarding house in addition to his main business.

He lived a little more than five years after his marriage to Polly. Prior to his death he owed four doctors for their care during his perhaps lengthy final illness, not including his executor who was also a doctor. Perhaps the family, as well as Caleb, was ill just prior to his death. Either that or Caleb called in every doctor he knew to try to cure him of whatever illness or injury caused his death. He focused on illness and his will shows just how much. It specifically mentioned them living "beyond their nonage." There was good reason to do so it seemed. James died after his father but before the estate settlement, and his portion was divided among his siblings. The language of the will plus the number of wives he seemed to outlive was an indication of how fragile life must have been in Caleb's experience. Prior to his death, not only had he witnessed death and illness on the battlefield but it surrounded him much of his adult life. Caleb died on 21 Jan 1805 just prior to his forty-sixth birthday, and he was buried in the Methodist Burial Ground.[90] A codicil to his will, dated 1804, named a son Caleb saying that, "if he should die in his minority his share shall be equally divided between my other children, share and share alike." What he had feared came true because his namesake died on Christmas Eve of 1814.[91] The other children named in the inventory were Robert and Mary, the only two who lived beyond childhood. They claimed their father's land rights from his war service by laying claim to the bounty land due him as a cavalry officer.[92]

Polly Hewitt was recognized by a statement in the inventory that read, "current money retained by Mary Hewitt one of the accountants on account as her thirds." Caleb left her $100 in slaves, plus houses and lots on Liberty Street valued at $1,000, also bank stock and cash totaling over $2,600. His children Caleb, Robert and Mary each received about $1,600 from an overall estate valued at approximately $13,000. As guardian of his niece, Ruth Tunstall received $1,600. Three years after his death, on 7 May 1808, Caleb's widow married a man named Francis Hopkinson.[93] At the 3 October 1812 settlement she appeared as Mary Hopkinson to give the final accounting.[94]

Eli Hewitt

Caleb was not the only tobacconist in the family. Baltimore tax records began in 1798 for both Caleb and Eli and either tax or census records continued at least through 1808 for them or their families. Perhaps the brothers were partners in business, or maybe just attracted to the same profession. However, their shops were both in the Third District of Middlesex Hundred. It was where they grew up and probably lived until their parents left Maryland. The Hewitt family was attracted to this area from its beginning. In 1730, Richard Hewitt, likely related to them in some way, purchased Lot #35 on the corner of Charles and German Streets in the newly surveyed town of Baltimore.[95] He died soon after without improving the property and his family lost it. This district adjoined the city on the northwest and its eastern border cut cleanly through the middle of the city south until it touched the Middle Branch of the Patapsco River. Later that century the railroad intersected the district at several points as it entered the core of the city. Court and York Roads traversed the district as well as Liberty Road providing access to travelers going northwest. In combination, these avenues of transportation provided access in all directions for people and goods coming into and passing out of the district. On its east and west borders were Jones' and Gwynn Falls that in the mid to late 19th century provided water for the mills and factories that sprang up nearby. With its outlying farms and easy access to the city over much-traveled roads, this district was not only a thoroughfare for those bringing goods to market, it also provided access to travelers and merchants who had business in the city or were traveling in the opposite direction toward Pennsylvania.[96] For a tobacconist or an innkeeper this was an excellent spot to set up shop.

In the spring of 1797 Eli Hewitt married Martha Dennis on March 25 at St. Paul's Parish in Baltimore. Several children, including four sons, were born to them, and three were recorded at the church. The eldest was Jacob who was named for his grandfather, born 28 Oct 1798, and Rezin Davis Hewitt whose birthday was 7 Feb 1801. Then Eli was born in 1799 and baptized that year. He lived just past his second birthday, and on 24 Sep 1801 he was buried in St. Paul's Church, Baltimore.[97] Martha gave birth to a son in 1805, also named Eli, who grew and flourished.[98] The couple may have had a daughter who died young and was remembered by her tombstone inscription. She was buried in Mantua on the Coan River in Northumberland County, Virginia with this inscription, "Sacred to the memory of Elizabeth, consort of James M. Smith, and only daughter of Eli Hewitt, Esq. of Baltimore, who departed this life on the 16th of September 1827 in the 20 year of her age."[99]

As late as 1814, Eli and his family were living in the city of Baltimore. His tobacco shop was in the Third District at 232 Baltimore Street. He served on the new Community Vigilance and Safety Committee as part of the city's civilian defense. Meeting monthly, committee members selected workers among men exempt from military duty and free people of color to build up the city's defenses during the latter part of the War of 1812. Using wheelbarrows, pick axes and shovels, Eli and the committee directed the workers as they assembled dirt mounds into battlements and fences.[100] Fortunately this action was never tested, as the fighting did not enter the city.

Eli Hewitt lived two decades longer than his brother Caleb, not giving up the ghost himself until he was 60 years old. Not all of those years were particularly happy ones for the family. By 1825, Martha and Eli were divorced and since he refused to pay alimony, she sued him for $175, half of her yearly allowance.[101] About that time, Eli was admitted to a mental institution although he was soon released. He wrote a will on 2 May 1827, and when its legality was later disputed in court by his son Rezin, it became clear that Eli was alienated from more than one member of his family. Eli complied legally by giving Rezin a dollar, but otherwise cut him out of the will. He died in June 1827, and shortly after Rezin challenged the will in court, calling upon friends and neighbors to testify that his father was insane and incapable of writing a will.[102] His intent was to secure the estate for all of the survivors and to appoint a trustee for his brother Jacob who had some infirmity.

On 31 Jul 1827, the court heard depositions for both sides of the action. What clearly emerged was a picture depicting Eli Hewitt's decline.

Hewitt lived in Anne Arundel County and wrote his will in a nearby tavern, appointing Eli Junior his executor. In exchange, Eli got the 400 acre family homestead and farm, all the equipment, livestock, his father's slaves and personal property as well as two houses in Baltimore. Jacob was to have a house and ten acres during his life, but Eli Junior was responsible for his care. As the depositions began, there were few declarations supporting Eli's will, and as the evidence mounted, first one and then another witness declared Hewitt insane. Benjamin Shipley who had known Hewitt for sixteen years, said the will was written at his tavern. His testimony was contradictory in that he said he found Hewitt's mind sound at times but not at others, particularly when Martha Hewitt was mentioned, then Hewitt became violent. Shipley knew that young Eli was the major recipient of the will and that he not only wrote it for his father but was its executor as well. Shipley asked Hewitt why he left Rezin out of the estate, and his answer was that Rezin had treated him ill and he meant to make a "beggar of the damned rascal." Several others refused to to witness it because they thought Hewitt was insane, particularly some of the young men who testified that over the past two years, Hewitt periodically acted insane. Defending his own actions, Eli testified that his father was sane when he dictated his will.

Thomas Turner who signed the instrument at Shipley's Tavern said he did not know Hewitt well, but noted that Hewitt had a deep-rooted enmity toward his wife calling her "everything but a lady." He recalled that in 1825 he went to see Hewitt about a bill, which provoked Hewitt into verbal abuse of all the lawyers in Annapolis. He told Turner to "go back to that damned city and tell the judges and lawyers they were all damned rascals and liars and they ought to go to school again". Turner thought Hewitt intoxicated at the time, and left determined not to do business with him again.

Benjamin Hood was the first to mention Eli's estranged wife, Martha. He had known them about twenty years, and said that she left Eli because of his violence toward her and moved in with a neighbor. Hewitt wrote Hood several letters complaining that his wife had left him, and from the tenor of the messges, considered Hewitt insane.

Several witnesses spoke persuasively against Hewitt. The first was George Warfield, 25 years old, and Hewitt's doctor. He attended Eli for two years before he died and said that he was "under a partial derangement of mind," appearing rational except when asked about his family who he then verbally abused. Warfield said his family were"virtuous and amiable people," and that Rezin Hewitt was dutiful and affectionate toward his father during his sickness and had performed other duties for him with the same care. Warfield declared Eli incapable of making a fair disposition of his property. Two years before his death, Robert Welsh, the Anne Arundel County sheriff, went to Hewitt's house to serve him with a writ of insanity, and found him to be so dangerously insane, it was unsafe for him to be at large. A jury of his peers gathered and unanimously declared Hewitt a lunatic, commiting him to a hospital from which he was later released. Welsh said he did not understand how that happened.

Following the depositions, the court considered the case against Eli, and to no one's surprise, concluded that he was wholly incompetent to make a will. Martha refused her right to settle the estate, and so letters of administration were given to her sons, Eli and Rezin.[103]   Finally, Rezin was appointed, with Eli's consent, as Jacob's trustee and guardian.[104]   Although it took several years to settle Eli's estate, he left his family financially secure and Martha, who was about 60 years old, had peace at last.[105]   The 1830 census indicated that after their father died, the three brothers lived with their mother,[106] but that she died that year prior to 11 Aug when her will was probated.[107]

Because Eli's will was declared void, technically he died intestate, so that four years later, when money for Jacob's upkeep was needed, Rezin sought the court's permission to sell part of his inheritance. Hearings in 1831 determined that, like his father, Jacob too was insane, that the property he inherited must be sold for his upkeep, and that his guardian must be other than a family member. He was 29 when he signed his estate over to a court appointed guardian, a Dr. Goldsborough who was a neighbor, and an "uninterested party."[108]

Eli's sons lived well on their inheritance, and in 1838, Rezin and Eli Junior, as well as Dr. Goldsborough, were among the first trustees appointed to the Springfield Academy of Carroll County. At the same time, Rezin became a trustee of the Warfield Academy.[109]   While overseeing their father's estate and establishing a place in the community, two of the brothers married and began families of their own. Eli married Ann Coulter on 24 Oct 1831[110] and ten years later they were living near Carter's Crossroad in Carroll County.[111]   By 1850 they lived in nearby Freedom where farmer Eli and Ann raised eight children. A snapshot of tht years showed that Eli Junior, John and Robert, were teenagers. Their siblings, Elizabeth, William, Mary, Edward and Septimus, ranged in age from twelve to three years old old. Rezin and his wife Delia lived in Lisbon, Howard County and had property worth $12,000. Their children were Alexander, who was seventeen and twelve-year-old Agnes. Rezin was a practicing physician who had gone deaf.[112]   By 1860, Delia was a widow and Eli's wife Ann had died.[113]   Some of them were buried in Carroll County's Springfield Cemetery, including Ann Hewitt, who was about 52 when she died on 18 Jan 1859. Eli died at age 62 on 10 Apr 1868.[114]   Jacob may have died a few years earlier because in 1850 he was not living alone or with either of his brothers.

Edward Hewitt

Like his brother Jacob, Edward Hewitt moved to northern Baltimore County on the outer reaches of the city. With him were others who had begun a steady advancement westward into the north central part of the state, later called Carroll County. In 1756 when he was 25, Edward bought 100 acres of unspoiled land and called it *Shrubby Hills*, conjuring up visions of treeless undulating hills and valleys where a variety of native wildlife roamed securely in their habitat. Hewitt was on the poll tax list for St. Thomas Parish in 1763 in

Hewitt Family Bible.
This typed copy of the original Bible was made by William Buckner McGroarty in 1912.

Jacob Hewitt tombstone (9 Nov 1791-20 Jun 1850), Old Moore
Cemetery, Batavia, Ohio

Delaware Upper Hundred. He resurveyed his property that year into 400 acres known as *Sandy Bottom*, again descriptive of the area. Edward was probably in business with a neighbor Robert Tevis because in 1774 they signed a deed release recorded as "Hewitt and Tevis," on land called *Upper Marlborough* purchased by Edward's brother, Jacob. The men were neighbors, living on adjoining properties near the Old Liberty Road not far from Eldersburg.[115]

Buying land was sometimes a precursor to marriage, and if Edward was not married in 1756 he seemed to be preparing for such an event. His wife when he died was Rachel and she may have been his children's mother, but there are no records to prove it. He was married by 1763 with three children who most likely were Edward Junior, Vachel and a daughter Hannah who was born on 18 May 1760.[116] Edward Junior paid taxes in 1783 proving he was over 21, but he was not named in his father's estate in 1792 and must have died in the interim.[117] Vachel Hewitt was probably over 21 when he married Ann Redy (Rady) in 1779, so he was probably born about 1758.[118] He lived near his father and brother in the Delaware Upper Hundred and paid taxes in 1783 for five people. Twenty years later Edward Senior paid £4.13.17 in Baltimore County for two horses, eight cows and 306 acres indicating he had sold 96 acres, perhaps to one of his children. Vachel was assessed £0.36.15, while Edward Senior paid the tax bill for his son Edward, a sign that neither of the younger men owned land but lived on their father's property.

In all Edward had nine children, whether with Rachel or an earlier wife, but she was probably mother to Rachel Hewitt who married Zachariah Linsicomb on 25 Nov 1790 when she was about eighteen. Most likely she was the mother of Rebecca and Amelia who married after Rachel. The first daughter to wed was Hannah who married John Lowe on 19 Aug 1778 in Baltimore. Catherine, called Cathy, married John Marsh on 30 Apr 1784.[119] Elizabeth probably married John Triplett about 1786 and Margaret married William Cook about 1792.[120] The last siblings to marry were Rebecca to William Jordan on 4 Dec 1792[121] and Amelia Hewitt on 5 Aug 1795 to Hugh McMechan.[122]

Edward Hewitt Senior died before 7 Sep 1790 when his estate went into probate under the capable hands of his wife and Peter Tevis who did the inventory. Edward left his wife her widow's thirds of about £23, and gave his daughters' bequests in their husband's names of a little more than £5 each.[123] Rebecca and Amelia were unmarried then, but in 1804, a deed naming Edward's heirs gave the names of his children and their spouses.[124] Two were not named, Elizabeth Hewitt who married John Triplett and Vachel Hewitt, both who must have died after 1792 when the estate was settled. The last named was Robert Hewitt, probably Vachel's son, another indication his father had died.

In 1798 several of Edward Hewitt's daughters and their husbands were living on *Sandy Bottom* where they grew up. Zachariah and Rachel Linsicomb had 82 acres and John and Cathy Marsh lived on twenty. Samuel Jordan owned part of *Sandy Bottom* where William and Rebecca Jordan were living. Although rustic, the largest log house was 18 x 26 feet and each house had either a barn or a separate kitchen. Hugh and Amelia McMechan lived nearby on land owned by Edward Dorsey. Robert Hewitt, probably Vachel's son, also lived on *Sandy Bottom* on 80 acres of land that had a log cabin with a separate kitchen and a smokehouse.[125]

Perhaps Rachel Hewitt was alive in 1813 when a woman by that name paid taxes in Carroll County for 82 acres of *Sandy Bottom*.[126] If she was Edward's widow, she must have been in her mid-70s by then. Over time many changes took place around the family enclave of *Hewitt's Shrubby Hills* and *Sandy Bottom*. Long their heritage and a vital part of the family's past, the land and the farm on Hewitt's Farm Road remained visible up until the mid-1990's. When Liberty Reservoir was built the farm disappeared under water. Other lands surrounding the farm are currently in the hands of developers who are building a new community of homes and shopping malls. Quickly disappearing along with its shrubby hills and sandy bottoms are some of the last open lands in northern Maryland.[127]

Robert and Hannah Hewitt

Although the author has made an exhaustive search in tax assessments, deeds and church records of Baltimore, Carroll and Anne Arundel Counties, records for Robert Hewitt, the eldest of the orphaned children of Elizabeth and Robert Hewitt, have not been found. From the time he moved into the Jacks household in 1736, he seemed to disappear, and so did his brothers until they came of age. However, Robert never emerged as they did with clues pointing to their whereabouts throughout their adult lives. Instead, like their younger sister, he disappeared from the horizon. The most likely explanation is that he died young at a time when burial records were few. However, his name has lived on in his siblings' children and their grandchildren, as a tribute to the father of the four orphans from Anne Arundel County. Although Robert was probably not the immigrant ancestor, his was the earliest proven record for this line of the Hewitt family.

Among all the discoveries made on this journey of discovery, amid bits and pieces of history and the many lives uncovered, there was another child who has remained elusive. Also left behind without a trace was the youngest child of Elizabeth and Robert Hewitt, their only daughter Hannah, whose tiny voice was never heard above the din of historic discovery that was used to tell her brothers' story.

Chapter Four

TWO BROTHERS:
Richard and Ephraim Hewitt
Baltimore, Maryland; Fayette County, Pennsylvania (1765-1827)

Two Brothers

According to the old Bible, Richard and Ephraim Hewitt's birthdays were five years apart, one in summer, the other in late winter. Born between them was Eli, a probable companion in their youth,[1] until he returned to Baltimore to join his brother Caleb in the tobacco business.[2] Delilah remained in Baltimore where she married. Later, when the war was over, her brother Caleb joined her.[3] Their bond remained strong though they were separated into two families, and parted by many miles. Several times over the years, when an important event presented itself, a member of the family answered the call.

For reasons unknown, history linked the paths of Richard and Ephraim. Throughout their lives, events brought them together much as two broad branches of the same tree are separate but bound by trunk and roots. On 16 Oct 1795, Richard opened the Bible and recorded his siblings' names and birth dates, yet it was Ephraim's children whose births and marriages were added later, and his family who finally possessed this precious family document. It was an important day, one of significant event, perhaps precipitated by plans of leaving home. By then, as the executor of his father's estate, his duties were complete leaving him free to follow plans that may have been germinating for several years. Knowing he was going into the wilderness to lay down new roots, as he looked down upon Phebe tending their young son, Jacob, he pondered the uncertainty of the venture. Richard had just sold his inheritance, a part of the family's farm, and the idle dreams and promises he made to himself were about to be realized.[4] He and Phebe were about to embark upon a new life, but before they left some things needed to be completed while others, such as old friends, had to be left behind. If anticipation generated by its fruition prompted doubt, he pushed it aside and while pressing pen to paper he recorded the past and gave it meaning. At the same time, each stroke of the pen brought courage preparing him to move ahead into this dream and to say goodbye. That year Richard Hewitt was thirty years old, a man with a wife and child, his life was not only expanding it was turning in a new direction. Decisions he made then were to set into motion a course of events that would bind his family and Ephraim's family for all time.

This new phase of Richard's life was similar to one his parents began with their children when they left Maryland more than ten years before. Records showed the family left Maryland sometime after 1778, but their whereabouts for the next five years are unknown. It is challenging to understand why this middle-aged couple left Maryland in the first place. Both were fifty-five years old when they uprooted their children from their birthplace and moved to a western land on the outer edges of civilization. Hayes, who joined them, was over 21, but Caleb was nineteen when, rather than go west, he joined the dragoons. Elizabeth was sixteen, and Richard thirteen, but Ruth, the youngest of the children, was only six years old.

During the Revolutionary War, the Pennsylvania land office did not give out warrants, so the family may have been living in Fayette County until 1783 when they could obtain one. That year Jacob Hewitt paid taxes in Westmoreland, Pennsylvania on land in Menallen Township.[5] It was west of the Laurel Hill range in a valley several miles wide through which ran the tributaries of Redstone and Dunlap Creeks, defining the township. Their farm on the "road to Redstone" was about three miles from the county seat of Uniontown. A pioneer to the area in 1788 described it saying,

> "When they reached Fayette County, they had to cross two ridges of the Alleghenies, first, Laurel Hill and then through the valley and over Chestnut Ridge. There they crossed the Youghiogheny River; before them for miles lay a land covered with ancient forest growths of huge oak, ash, walnut, hickory and maple, with hollows, small ridges, creeks and abundant coppices, and rich, green valleys. Never had they seen such a healthy, strong green color in plants and growth." Just prior to reaching the Monongahela River the writer described the waterways he saw as an "ineffable network of winding streams–sparkling a welcome of quiet cheer to the traveler, crowned on all sides by hollows, beautifully green bushes, ancient sylvan giants–made him pause with a reassured happiness at the thought that this would always be his family's home."[6]

Perhaps Jacob and Ruth had a similar experience as they viewed their new home. Hopefully the land itself inspired them, because whatever their reasons for leaving Maryland, as they settled into this young community under the Laurel Hills, they had to know it would be their last move. In 1785, the same year he applied for a tavern license, Jacob became a township officer and an Overseer of the Poor for Menallen Township.[7] While the opportunity for office was open to anyone, the nomination had to be confirmed by a county justice. In Fayette County most of those who, like Jacob, held a lower office were merchants, landowners or tradesmen. As a landowner and tavern keeper, he qualified for this civic responsibility. Not many sought this job because its duties were disagreeable, but it offered Jacob an opportunity to serve the community. As overseer, he cared for the poor of the town and discouraged them from becoming a public nuisance. Should they wander into an adjoining county he was responsible for bringing them back, finding them work or binding them to those who needed laborers. In addition, Jacob's duty was to enforce the liquor laws and to bring charges against any man who got a girl pregnant.[8] Orphaned and poor as a child, Jacob may have had a natural empathy for those who were forced into servitude. While in some ways he might be suited for the job, he was only in that position a year. Perhaps what he saw was too close to his own experience, then again, it may be that Jacob by the nature of his personality, and his business, was not suited to be a policeman to his neighbors.

When the county was formed one of the first duties of its officers was to establish a court system that met four times each year. Common pleas court, where news was collected and disseminated, was where most lawsuits were heard. Court day was a time of hustle and bustle in town, when farmers who might otherwise be working the fields came to town. The courthouse was the center of it all, a place where neighbors met and exchanged news, conducted personal business, and discovered who was suing whom. The courtroom was packed with lawyers, litigants, witnesses and a host of onlookers. In a place of ordered chaos, the judge maintained order and made the decisions. Nearly everyone there knew a juror or someone taking the oath that day. Spotting neighbors outside the courthouse, they exchanged gossip about newly arrived or departing families, discussed their crops, shopped for bargains and visited the saddler for a new harness. Eager to get a seat before the session began, some exchanges moved into the courtroom, creating a lively and boisterous cacophony only brought to silence with the judge's gavel.

Farmers and neighbors were not hesitant to sue each other in those days. Jacob Hewitt was one who got the call, although he only appeared twice in court, each time when someone sued him. In 1786 John Collins, a Uniontown tavern keeper, was the first to bring action against Hewitt. He wanted £150 from Hewitt for loaning an indentured servant to him, suggesting that Hewitt had used the man's services for a lengthy time without paying Collins, or that he was injured while working for Hewitt, or that he ran away and Collins was seeking reparation for the remainder of his service.[9] The last lawsuit occurred that spring when another man sought £100 reparation for an unknown cause.[10]

The Tavern

A 1786 warrant described Hewitt's land as "on the Great Road that leads from Union[town] to Redstone Old Fort." Later known as the National Road, its beginnings were well established when Jacob Hewitt purchased property on it. Originally an Indian trail, it was also known as Burd's or Braddocks Road, and used by early traders and adventurers to this territory. In his first journey west in 1754, George Washington ordered its trail widened for the militia wagons heading to Redstone to build a fort. The first attempt was unsuccessful, but in 1759 Colonel James Burd completed the trail and rebuilt the fort at Redstone on the site of an earlier fortification.[11] Today Highway 40 is a part of the national highway system.[12] It was with the wisdom of middle age that Jacob chose this site along the road for his farm and tavern, a place where families could get a hot meal and a place to stable their horses for the night.

Menallen Township tax records are missing, so it is not known if Hewitt had a mill or a distillery to support the tavern that was active between 1784 and 1801. Other records indicate Jacob had a tavern license from 1784-1788,[13] and that in 1795 Ephraim took over the business and was licensed until 1801.[14] Although there are gaps in the records, the business continued for at least fifteen years on the site as a family enterprise. Its success was determined by the combined efforts of parents and children, each with chores assigned according to their skills, ages and interests. The boys, Hayes, Richard and Ephraim, probably worked the farm, but they also helped tend the horses and clean the stables. Their sisters, Elizabeth and Ruth, helped prepare and serve meals.

The 300-acre family farm included a large stock of cattle, hogs, sheep and horses. Jacob also had three slaves who worked either in the household or in the fields.[15] In the 1790's, those who could afford it hired neighbors, or got indentured servants to work in the shops and on the land. However, western Pennsylvania was a frontier and a melting pot of sorts, attracting people from the north and from southern states, bringing with them a clash of cultures. Chief among them were Virginians and pioneers from Maryland, like the Hewitt and Hall families, who were from states that practiced slavery. There was a decided difference in philosophy between those from New England and their southern neighbors determining lifestyle, marriage and choice of friends. While slavery was practiced throughout the south, Pennsylvania was not a slave-holding state, but allowed those who had slaves to bring them west. When Jacob died in 1790, he had three slaves, Esther, age 30, a mulatto boy named Ben who was eleven years old, and a man named Harry, who was 40.[16] Pennsylvania law stated that after 1780, a child born to a slave had the same status as an indentured servant and must be freed by age 28. This ruling applied to Ben who was born about 1780, although in his will Jacob gave him to his wife Ruth. Later, in 1813 he was living in Union Township, a 34-year-old man who was taxed as "Binn Hewett, a Negro forge-man."[17] The timing suggested that, if it was not Ruth who freed him, perhaps it was Ephraim who did so some time around 1807-1808.[18]

While we have no real evidence of how the Hewitt home looked, there are models for the time. A tavern along the National Road was usually placed broad side adjacent to the road, and built of logs or stone with a stone chimney on either end. Ephraim's daughter Sophia described their home, saying she was "born in a stone house at the foot of the Laurel Hills."[19] The tavern, also built of stone, was usually attached to or a part of the house. The largest room served many purposes and its fireplace was a welcome sight to guests as they sat on benches around a long table eating their evening meal. Shelves lined the room with mugs and pitchers for drinks, while tables held platters, plates and serving utensils. The kitchen, often a separate building but sometimes built onto the main room, held the other fireplace. It was large enough to hang kettles, and pots and pans of all sizes above it, while within it soups and stews were always simmering, watched over by younger children so the soup did not burn. Above the main floor were sleeping rooms and outside, a horse stable. Today's taverns smell mostly of alcohol and are bland when compared with those of yesteryear. Then, an inn combined many other scents that indeed, made a pungent mixture. Food was continually being prepared and wood smoke wafted throughout the building, mingled with the smell of dusty, sweat drenched clothing and the scent of alcohol and those who drank it. Pungent fumes wafted in from the stable creating a sharp smell recognizable to all who frequented an eighteenth century inn.[20]

While early courts regulated fees by imposing a standard charge for meals and drinks served in inns and taverns, there was no standard coinage. In 1787, being but a few years beyond the Revolution, the country was not quite a nation and each state determined its own monetary system, mostly using the English pound but also Spanish currency. In southwestern Pennsylvania, an innkeeper received a variety of coins in payment for food and lodging. Sometimes he was paid with a "fip or a levy," both Spanish coins, or in shillings, while other times he was given a U.S. minted copper penny in payment for services rendered.[21] It was not until 1787 when our leaders met in Philadelphia to revise the Articles of Confederation, the contract they lived by until then, that this matter was discussed. However, rather than revising the Articles, our founding fathers spent months in discussion and argument, and in the end forged a blueprint for a new nation known as the Constitution of the United States. One of its achievements was the standardization of the monetary system we know today.

However, prior to the revision in the monetary system, at the local level there was an enforced standard charge for food and drink. These regulations were in place in southwestern Pennsylvania, in particular in Washington County in the 1780's. Meals were large but varied, seasonal choices were vegetables, fish and game. Potatoes were a staple, as was cornbread and meat—usually pork, followed by pie and coffee. Breakfast was a hardy meal begun with tea, coffee or chocolate, followed by a choice of beefsteak, mutton chops or cold leftovers served with bread and butter. Dinner, served at noon, was the largest meal of the day, and it contained the same meats and vegetables served at breakfast except in larger proportions and offered with a small beer, cider or weak grog. The evening supper was a similar but smaller meal, and on average cost about £0.1.3 per person, with drinks at two shillings. A "good bed with clean sheets" was four pennies per person, the same as a tot of whiskey. So, if the traveler skipped that second whiskey his cost per person for a night, with hay and oats for his horse, would amount to about £0.3.6. However, with a wife and children, meals and lodging could cost considerably more, or at least a couple of "fips."[22]

For those who drank, and many a traveler imbibed, the tavern had provisions for all appetites. The most common drink was whiskey because it was plentiful and cheap. Some chose whiskey toddy for a penny, or a drink with peach or apple brandy. Meals were communal served at long tables where families dined with strangers. Men sometimes gathered separately and over a drink, sought information about the roads or inquired about a place to stay the following night. Sleeping accommodations for travelers were often much less satisfactory than were the meals and by today's standards, unacceptable.

The tavern and inn's success depended upon Jacob and Ruth's dedication as partners to attain their goals. Different by nature, they had to pull together and be creative to make it work. Jacob's curiosity and interest in others, as well as his naturally hospitable nature were important, but his ability to work with others without stepping on their toes made the difference between a well-run and a badly managed establishment. Overall, it was their eagerness to oblige and the desire to serve which made a difference to their guests. While service was intrinsic to the profession, its success was highly dependent on the resources and size of the establishment, as well as the continued good humor of the innkeeper. Since Jacob was unlikely to turn anyone away, there must have been times when the family had more people than spaces to sleep. It was not uncommon to find travelers sleeping with strangers or, on a busy night, spreading a blanket to lie on the floor. Under those circumstances privacy was not possible, so women often slept with their children while men slept separately. With the constant changing of guests, vermin was a big problem and how often bed linens were changed was up to the mistress of the tavern and her sensibilities about cleanliness. Inns were hospitable to disease and disease spread as flies moved from the stable into the dining room. The recipe for success in this business was to have a forgiving disposition, good health and immunity to most of the illnesses encountered. However, should Jacob or Ruth became ill, a family member might stand in for a time, but often enough, a tavern owner carried on regardless of influenza, rheumatism, or just a bad night's sleep.

Since their guests were often going out into the unknown, Jacob and Ruth had to be excellent communicators, both good at listening and at exchanging information. A tavern was also a place for stories and tall tales that sometimes included those of land speculators who boasted of the bounteous nature of far away lands. Often it was pure hype, embellished for quick sale of unwanted land. After sundown, men sat near the fire with their pot of beer or mug of toddy and told stories. They began as simple tales that sometimes grew into grandiose yarns, and in the retelling good qualities became stellar virtues and simple mistakes grew into foul bad luck. Beginning with one man's attempt to top a yarn just told, the night got longer, the visits to the privy pit more often, and the mugs less full. However, on most nights travelers turned in early. They arose early as well, hungry for breakfast and hungry to begin their day while the sun was still low in the sky.

The tavern was a social environment, the locus of information, and the innkeeper was the disseminator of all he learned. With his constant opportunity to meet people, Jacob heard about broken down wagons, washed out trails and accidents on the river. Occasionally he may have passed on messages from one family to another, as a kind of oral postman. There was little leisure, and even at the end of the day when guests were fed and bedded, there were preparations for the following morning. Hungry travelers awakened early, needed to eat and be on the road again. This was a selfless profession but it had its rewards in the occasional compliment, and from repeat customers who made Jacob's place his choice for the night. Many years later, Jacob's great-granddaughter Rebecca, who was in a similar profession, expressed her feelings about satisfaction for a job well done.

As a widow, Rebecca Hewitt Adams found it necessary to use her talents as a homemaker to help her family survive on the prairie near Atchison, Kansas. In 1864 at the invitation of her brother, William, she came to live once again with her family near the Big Muddy River outside of town. There, her brothers were building stables to provide "an exchange station where travelers could change horses and take meals." To support her two children Rebecca followed an earlier family tradition and began cooking and caring for travelers who passed the station. She says in her diary, "I'd moved up to the Big Muddy and my brothers began to build a larger house. People who traveled across the plains in the overland stage had to be fed and sometimes there were eight or ten who crossed in one stage stopping at our place. I had to have meals for them once a day and sometimes twice a day. I received many compliments from passengers for the unexpected meals. Some would declare they never sat down to a better meal. Others would say, 'if we could only get such coffee as that in other places. It is really the first good cup of coffee I have had.' Another traveler declared, 'That meal is worth two hundred dollars because we have only had a lunch meal elsewhere.'" Rebecca conveyed how these compliments affected her by saying, "This was some encouragement." Undoubtedly it was a hard life, and praise allowed her to persevere through long days of service to homesteaders and soldiers who traveled through the community, much as it did for her great-grandparents in their 1780's tavern on the National Road.[23]

Jacob's Will

In the last decade of the eighteenth century, the inns and taverns on the Old Road were a hub of information for surrounding farms, and it was in that atmosphere that Jacob and his neighbors felt change pervading the countryside. It was the beginning of a great movement not only in Fayette County, but also in every part of the newly expanded United States. Its momentum began at the close of the Revolution, and eight years later those families who discovered their lives were not and never would be the same again, left New Jersey, Maryland and Virginia for lands west and south of home. Their paths led many of them down the Old Road leading to Pittsburgh, and the Monongahela River where it meets the Ohio River. However, the greatest draw for those who had suffered the losses of a great war was the creation and the annexation of new territory that opened in both the west and southern territories. Western Pennsylvania was a crossroads and for many, Fayette County was only a stopping place for families moving elsewhere.

By 1790, Ruth and Jacob's children were accustomed to their Pennsylvania home, but the elder ones had begun to ponder whether they wished to remain there. The Hewitt boys witnessed what had become an exodus from the eastern states through Fayette County as families headed for Ohio and Kentucky. Privy to neighborhood talk and rumor, they sensed the restlessness around them as neighbors caught the fever, pulled up stakes and went west. What they heard at the tavern and in town enticed and enchanted the young men of the family. Abuzz with conversation, the air vibrated with an energy and excitement that stirred them, and they too, dared to dream and to plan. Some fifteen years earlier, their parents packed up their children and their belongings and moved west. Now grown, the day was approaching when they would repeat the past.

Jacob Hewitt was ill in the late spring of 1790 when he made his will, and therefore he had some time to contemplate how he wanted his legacy divided. It was witnessed by his nearest neighbors, who like him were significant landowners living on the Old Road. Hayes was 34 years old and planning to leave the county, and so he appointed Richard who was nearly 25 as executor along with his wife, Ruth. Ephraim, the youngest son, was only twenty when his father gave him the house and tavern, with a good portion of the land to support it. Caleb and Eli received five shillings each, either because Jacob had settled on them earlier, or because they did not need the money. At the age of 31, Caleb was a prosperous tobacconist and Eli, then 23, was quite successful in later years.[24] Although muted by his impending death, Jacob must have felt satisfaction while contemplating his lifelong labors, because for a boy with few financial resources, at life's end he had accomplished enough to give something of value to each of his children. In his last days as images of the past played across his closed eyes, there was reason for contentment as well.

As their father lay dying his children, while immersed in sadness, were already part of the winds of change. Even as they wept, its momentum pushed them along. Western Pennsylvania was charged with activity of all kinds during the closing years of the century and this family was in its midst as they said goodbye to friends. They listened too, as others planned to go to Pittsburgh to build a flatboat that would carry them downriver to Cincinnati or Mayslick on the Kentucky side of the river. Nearly as many remained behind as left, but two of the Hewitt brothers were already planning their adventure, and their neighbors' actions became mirrors of their own minds. That they might suffer deprivation and tragedy was a possibility, but it was the challenge for which youth is endlessly ready.

Hayes had informed his father of his plans and undoubtedly received his blessing.[25] He was married by June 1790 and planned to go downriver the following spring with his father-in-law, Phillip Shute, and others who were preparing to move into Carolina Territory, land that would later become the state of Tennessee.[26] In earnest discussions between father and son, they viewed the challenges of moving to the wilderness. Jacob also knew that Hayes' enthusiasm for the adventure would inevitably inspire his younger sons, Richard and Ephraim, to follow his lead. When he died in June 1790, Jacob left something for everyone. He thoughtfully gave Hayes and Anna, and their two-year-old son Caleb,[27] the land they were living on, plus "fifty bushels of wheat of my crop that is now growing providing he should move down the river next spring."[28] Removing this statement from its dry legal context, it speaks of a father's concern as well as his blessing on the journey his son and family were about to make. Wishing his son success, Jacob knew that after selling the land, the wheat crop would provide extra money for the trip.

Hayes Hewitt

Hayes sold his inheritance, and less than a year after his father's death moved to Davidson County, Tennessee.[29] He and Anna, their children Caleb and Elizabeth, and his father-in-law left Fayette County, Pennsylvania, in 1791 and settled just outside the town of Nashville.[30] His dreams held potential but only hard work brought them to fruition. As he thought about carving a place for his family in Tennessee, he could not have known what a high price success would demand, nor that its rewards would be met equally in tragedy. His choices differed from that of his brothers, Richard and Ephraim, but in the end, each of them became pioneers in new lands of their choosing. Anna's brother, Philip Shute, Jr., wrote in his memoirs that Hayes and his wife were married in

Pennsylvania and went to Tennessee with his father in 1790, although it was actually 1791 when they made their voyage.[31] While waiting, probably in Pittsburgh, they talked to other travelers about the trip and some of the dangers they might encounter. They also had the opportunity to see how their flatboat was built.

The builders cut trees along the river, then trimmed and floated the logs downstream to the landing where they were cut into planks or sawn in half lengthwise. The boat was assembled upside down; beginning with gunwales that were formed from two large logs placed about twenty feet apart. Next cut planks were laid side by side until they reached both sides of the gunwales. Gaps between were filled with old rope driven in by a hammer. Because a boat could be as large as nine by fifty feet, it was difficult to turn over. This was accomplished by raising one side with long poles used as levers until it stood upright, then it was gradually lowered to the ground using shorter poles with each movement. Workers put the platform on timbers secured by ropes, then it was cut and the boat slid over the timbers into the water where it was tied to the shore and finished. The boat's walls were formed by nailing planks upright around the perimeter of the platform. After a small deck was made for the crew, they built the roof and cut doors along the sides. Except for the gun holes cut out on each side, when it was finished the flatboat looked like a small house. The boat had oars to steer it, two long ones on the sides and a large one at the stern.

Once on the water, the long poles directed the boat to land or away from a sandbar and into deeper water. Inside the families set up quarters led by the women who set up housekeeping on the end that had a fireplace for cooking, eating and sleeping. The men took the end that pointed into the river where the overhead lookout was located.[32] When all was in readiness, Hayes and Anna and the families traveling with them, moved their belongings onboard and set off down the Monongahela River to where it and the Allegheny meet to form the Ohio River. With good luck, it was not a long trip, and as they made their way downriver, they glimpsed the countryside, and it was not unlike what they had left, only less populated. They passed dense forests broken occasionally by a fort, a reminder of just how dangerous it was to move into Indian territory. They were warned about continuing hostilities between tribes living near the river and the pioneers traveling down it. Travelers were relatively safe during the months when the current was swift and they could keep their boats in the middle of the river. Danger lurked during the summer when the Ohio River carried less water and boats got hung up on a sandbar. Should they get stuck for any length of time their vulnerability increased out on the open water, so men kept their guns ever ready, and women and children prepared to hide among their belongings should they be waylaid by attack.

The Mason family traveled with the Shutes and the Hewitts on their way from Pittsburgh to Nashville, Tennessee, and the perils of the journey were recorded through the eyes of a twelve-year-old boy. Abram Mason of Madison County, Tennessee was an old man in 1860 when he wrote about the trip his family made in 1791 from southwestern Pennsylvania to the Carolinas, later Tennessee. He and his father were among eighteen neighbors, some from Monongalia County, Virginia, who built a large keelboat and began the journey.

We did not start till May; we then started down the
Monongahela River. It was very troublesome times on the
Ohio River. There were no settlements from Pittsburgh to
down the mouth of the Ohio, on the north side of the river,
except forts. General St. Clair had one where Cincinnati now
stands, and one opposite Louisville [Kentucky]. It was very
dangerous traveling on the Ohio in those times; the Indians
were taking boats often on the river. We saw the Indians
crossing the river before us. We made ready for battle. The
women and children were placed in the bottom of the boat
and beds placed around them. When we came near to where
they were, a gun or two was fired, and they landed and took
to the cane and we saw them no more.

We got to the Falls of the Ohio in June, and the river got
so low we could not get the boat over the falls. We stayed in
Kentucky the balance of the summer and then tried to get her
over and stuck fast. The river took another rise and she went
off and was lost.

In September 1790, nine families out of nineteen built
pirogues, one to each family, and started down the Ohio.
There was not a settlement on either side of the river to the
mouth of the Cumberland, and none on it till we got to
Clarksville, forty miles below (above) Nashville. If the
Indians had met with us, we would have been killed or taken.
We killed some buffaloes, elk and other game. Our powder
gave out before we got up the river. We landed about the first
of October, three miles below Nashville.[33]

The Isaac Mason family reached Tennessee, as did the Hewitt and Shute
families, thus they were among those who built pirogues and reached their
destination after the flatboat sank. When they reached the Cumberland River,
they headed south following the western edge of present day Kentucky into
Tennessee where the Cumberland River flowed southeast into Davidson County
and the frontier town of Nashville. Upon reaching Tennessee, which was then a
part of Carolina Territory, Philip Shute, the Hewitt and Mason families,
"...settled at Mansker's Station near present day Goodlettsville [Tennessee].
After about a year Shute moved to Richland Creek, also known as the
Chickasaw Trace. On land purchased from Peter Turney, he built his own
station, known as 'Shute's Fort', where he lived and died."[34] In 1797, Shute was
living there when he sold Isaac Mason 61 acres adjacent to his land.[35] Sometime
after 1794, on 100 acres Shute sold to Hewitt, Hayes and Anna built a home on
Richland Creek described as a "red brick manse."[36] A drawing, made from a
photograph of the house, known as "Belfield," showed a two-story brick house,
longer than it was tall, with a fireplace at either end. In front were eight four-
paned windows and above the entrance a large double window. In 1794 the
size, the kind of construction and number of windows a house contained was a
standard for wealth and comfort. Someone who once lived there described the
house.

The twelve-room structure faced toward Richland Creek with many lofty trees surrounding it. At one time the plain façade contained two large columns supporting a small balcony on the second floor and a marble entrance porch on the ground level. The columns and porch were said to have been torn down by the Yankees during the Civil War. A crack in the rear of the house was caused by a striking cannon ball shot from Federal gunboats on the Cumberland River. After the war the columns were not replaced nor the balcony rebuilt.

On both floors of the house were large stair halls containing a massive, oak staircase said to have been beautifully hand carved. The floors were made of wide white poplar boards set together with pegs. Stretched across the rear of the house was a long ell porch and a double door led to a cellar of three huge rooms with dirt floors. Separate from the main residence was a two-room stone house probably originally used as a kitchen or perhaps a gin house. Located between the two buildings was a cistern while a barn was situated northwest of the brick structure. A graveyard was reported located at the rear of the back porch.

By 1794 Hayes and Anna had three children, Caleb, Elizabeth and Hazael, called Hayes, who was born 3 Mar 1793. Their large house was suited to a family that continued to grow until by 1809 they were a family of ten. While undoubtedly they shared many good times, they also had an unusually large number of tragedies that paralleled Hayes' rise as a civil servant. In 1799 at age 44 he was appointed a justice of peace. He continued serving the justice system, until in 1828 he was appointed Chairman of the Court of Pleas and Quarter Sessions for Davidson County.[37]

The Hewitts' large family was common for the times, and as was often the case, not all children survived childhood. Two of Hayes and Anna's children died before they were eight years old, and the stark truth of each circumstance was recorded in their Bible. Elizabeth, named after her grandmother, Elizabeth Waller Shute, was little more than five years old when she drowned in her Grandfather Shute's spring—probably a tributary of Richland Creek next to where they lived. When she died, Caleb was six years old and Hazael, named after his father, was little more than a year old. Robert Junior was born in 1796, followed by Matilda in late 1797. Their sister Emily was born in 1800, and only three years old when the second tragedy struck their family. On 22 Sep 1803, Robert was seven years old when he "burned to death in a gin house," and although the Bible does not say so, there was one on their property. Anna had two children after Robert died, Mary born in December 1805 and Caroline in 1809. She lived long enough to see her youngest daughter turn five before she died in 1814. Hayes remained a widower for the remainder of his life, but death's toll continued to ring for his family.

In 1816, Caleb Hewitt was 27 years old and in his first term as sheriff of Nashville. One day, as he was serving a suspect with an arrest warrant, the man struck him with an adze—a tool similar to a hatchet, seriously wounding him. Caleb was brought home and tenderly nursed, but his wound was grievous, and he died four days later.[38] This time, Hayes was left to bear the sorrow without his wife's support. Death visited the family for the fifth time in 1824 when Mary, called Polly, died unmarried at the age of eighteen, cause unknown.[39]

Those children who lived, Hayes Junior, Matilda, Emily and Caroline, grew up, married and added substantially to the community on Richland Pike. Matilda married William Watkins, a widower, on 20 Oct 1819. Hayes Jr. married a local girl, Caroline Newsome in 1820, but later moved to a county near the Mississippi border. Before they were married, his sisters brightened their father's later years, and when Emily married Edwin Childress in 1832, he bought the family manse from his father-in-law.[40] Eventually Hayes went to live with Caroline and her husband Joseph Wharton where in the early spring of 1837 he died at the age of 81. Ed Childress continued to live on the land he bought from his father-in-law even after Caroline died. In 1850 he was 59 and probably remarried, but the census confirmed his success as a cotton planter, indicating he had real estate worth $12,500, and 27 slaves to run it.[41] Hayes Hewitt Junior left Nashville and moved to Madison County, Tennessee where he was said to have a 1,000-acre plantation.[42] There cotton was grown almost exclusively and the 1850 census showed his land was worth $20,000, a very large sum for the time. Hayes too was a slaveholder, with 70 men, women and children, most of whom were field hands rather than house slaves.[43]

The old homestead on the Charlotte Pike at 51st Avenue had served several generations of the Hewitt family before it passed out of their hands. Eventually it was sold but it remained a landmark until 1924 when it was torn down and a home for orphans and wayward children was built on the property. By 1964 that building had become a fire hazard, so it too was razed and replaced by cottages and outbuildings known today as Richland Village where a counseling and emergency shelter is maintained for needy youths of Davidson County.[44]

A Child is Born

The spring of 1790 was a sad time for Ruth Hewitt. While in mourning for her husband, it was probably through the post that she learned that her daughter Delilah had died in Baltimore. Delilah Elder Tunstall was about forty years old[45] and when the news arrived, Ruth was too old to travel and Maryland was a long way from the Pennsylvania frontier. It was a familiar story once distance separated families. Sometimes parents heard from their children once each year, and sometimes not ever again. Ruth and Delilah may not have seen each other for years creating a sadly poignant ending for Ruth, and as she sought to maintain a balance between two losses, their repercussions must have echoed painfully. In November that year Ruth learned of a third death, that of her son-in-law Henry Tunstall,[46] leaving her granddaughter and namesake, Ruth Tunstall, an orphan. Among so many losses, perhaps it was some consolation to Ruth that upon Henry's death, her son Caleb stepped in to manage his estate and agreed to act as guardian for his niece, Ruth.

As so often happens when an elder dies, a child is born soon after. Jacob's arrival on 11 Nov 1791 was a momentous event, as he was not only Richard's first child, but he was the first grandchild born into the Pennsylvania branch of the family.[47] Although welcomed by all, he was a special gift to his grandmother. His name and his presence became a soothing balm placed upon the wound of her losses. At the time, Richard was settling his father's estate and because he lived nearby the family felt the baby's presence. Now that she and Richard were joined through the child's birth, his wife was welcomed into the energetic lifestyle of the larger family, one always grateful for another helping hand.[48]

It was a time of endings and new beginnings for Richard, but there was a perceptional shift as well. He had lost his father but gained a wife and a son, and perhaps for a time he was content to continue tending to the farm and the needs of his new family. However, with the death of the patriarch authority shifted, not to the next in line, because by 1791 Hayes had moved to Tennessee, but instead Richard essentially became the head of the family. He was 25 when he became his father's executor and had to decide whether to keep the tavern open before 1795 when Ephraim applied for a license and took over the job.

Although burdened by family duties, by 1793 Richard's concerns broadened outward into the community at large. Southwestern Pennsylvania had become a hotbed of political activity that had begun two years before when Congress passed a bill adding an excise tax on locally distilled whiskey. The citizens of Fayette and neighboring Washington County were incensed at the injustice, and some of the more vocal citizens made inflammatory speeches against it. By 1793, the backlash caused riots and the local militia was called in. It continued until in 1794, unable to quell the violence, President Washington sent federal troops to Fayette County to fend off the hysteria historically known as the "Whiskey Rebellion."

He ordered four states to provide 15,000 troops equipped and ready to march on a moment's notice. In command was Governor Henry Lee of Virginia, known as "Light Horse Harry." Under him was a division of 2,300 men from Maryland.[49] One of them was Thomas, the son of Ruth Davis Hewitt's first cousin, Ephraim Davis.[50] Whether young Thomas stopped to pay his respects to his Aunt Ruth is unknown, and maybe the gesture would have been antagonistic to his purpose for being there. If not, perhaps he met his cousins, and they spent a few hours at the tavern exchanging anecdotes about their mutual Maryland family, before they waved him off after a hearty meal, never to see him again. Although the opportunity was certainly presented, it may never have happened.

The presence of a large encampment in their little town was an incentive to restore order because it impacted everyone, particularly the Hewitt family. Their tavern was an important source of income and so increased taxes concerned them, but like everyone else, they wanted the army to leave. Although they probably reacted in some way, they were not insurrectionists, nor did they go to jail. While others rebelled, they were not fined for rioting or generally being obnoxious toward the troops or their neighbors.[51]

However, some of those events may have precipitated Richard's decision to leave the state. After Hayes, he was the next to sell his property in Fayette County and move away. He began in 1792 by patenting his 100-acre inheritance in Menallen Township, north of but adjoining Ephraim's land. In April 1793 he sold *Springfield* to a neighbor, John Craig, and he and Phebe left Fayette County and moved to Kentucky.[52] He was twenty-eight and his adventurous spirit had blossomed until he was ready to tackle another set of challenges. The couple knew instinctively that success was dependent on their merits and the ability to face an unknown future with courage, but as they stepped out of the boundary of the familiar, even their imagination could not take them where this adventure would go.

Hall's Bold Adventure

Jacob Hewitt and John Hall were alike, at least in one way. When the storm clouds of revolution blew an ill wind across their doorways, separately they made plans to move west. Both eventually moved to western Pennsylvania, and although their paths toward that end were very different, each was motivated by a desire for a place with fewer restrictions and less government. Hewitt left Baltimore before the Revolutionary War, but Hall remained in Loudoun County, Virginia until it ended. However, Hall was out scouting land prior to its beginning, and in 1776 he obtained warrants in Westmoreland County on several properties. His intent was to move the family there, but the land office closed when war began, and he was forced to wait until it opened again in 1783. John and Elizabeth arrived in Pennsylvania with seven children ranging in age from Margaret who was about twenty-three to her younger sisters, Sarah and Rose who were probably ten and thirteen respectively. Thomas, the eldest son, was about twenty-one and John was a couple of years younger.[53] Hugh was the youngest son, and he and Elizabeth were both about seventeen years old, perhaps twins, because separate family Bibles indicated both were born in 1766.

Hall was a man who knew his way around. Prior to 1784, Pennsylvania prohibited an owner from purchasing more than 600 acres, but he wanted more, and was not averse to bending the rules to buy the property he wanted. While he was not the first to circumvent this law, Hall did it his way. On April 15, 1776 he applied for two warrants in Westmoreland County (later Fayette County). The first was 200 acres in Dunbar Township called *The Gulph*, made in the name of George Wood,[54] a Bedford County, Pennsylvania surveyor and associate judge.[55] The same day he received a warrant for 200 acres in Franklin Township using his daughter Margaret's name, indicating she must have been at least sixteen, the legal age for women at the time. The third warrant, for 216 acres in Franklin Township was in his name, and he called it *Bold Adventure*, perhaps an indication of how he felt about his plan.[56] However, war was just over the horizon halting any plans he might have had to move his family to Pennsylvania.

The Halls of Virginia

John Hall was from an old Virginia family, old in that they had lived in Northern Virginia for perhaps as many as four generations before moving to western Pennsylvania. The land where the Hall family lived was part of an original five million acre grant made by King Charles II to several English noblemen in 1649. Known as the Fairfax Proprietary, it covered all the land between the Potomac and Rappahannock Rivers. Originally it was a vast acreage called Westmoreland County that over the years was carved up into smaller, more manageable tracts beginning with Stafford County in 1664. The next boundary realignment formed Fairfax County, then Prince William and finally Loudoun County in 1757. However, few settlers came to the Northern Neck of Virginia until 1722 when the Treaty of Albany banished the American Indian nations west of the Blue Ridge Mountains making it safer to move into northwestern Virginia. Between 1725 and 1730 their numbers increased dramatically as settlers began arriving from Pennsylvania, New Jersey and Maryland, but also from other parts of Virginia. The Hall family settled in lower Loudoun east of the Bull Run Mountains where several tidewater Virginians owned huge tracts of Fairfax Proprietary lands that they broke into smaller properties and sold to settlers like Hall who were eager for good agricultural land where tobacco grew easily.[57]

The Hall family may have settled first in Stafford County, Virginia around 1665, and within a generation or two moved northwest into Loudoun County around 1731. That year William Hall, the first known ancestor of this family, bought 1,241 acres in Prince William County along a tributary of the Little River called Howser's Branch.[58] Ten years later he bought an additional 351 acres on the branches of the Beaverdam of Goose Creek increasing his holdings to nearly 1,600 acres. One of the chain carriers for the survey was William Hall, Junior, establishing that he had a son by that name.[59]

William's wife was named Jane and they had at least two sons, Thomas and William. In 1746 the eldest son, Thomas, was living in Truro Parish when he sold land his father had given him. That same year, William Senior and his wife transferred 200 acres to William Junior bordering property the elder Hall owned and some he previously sold to his neighbor William West.[60] Hall died before September 1750 when William West and Elisha Hall, who was perhaps a relative, inventoried his estate.[61] By then William Junior was about forty years old and married. Fortunately he owned the land he lived on, because in Virginia until 1786 the law of primogeniture ruled the colony, and if a man died without a will, the eldest son inherited everything.[62] Mary was William's wife, and their children were Thomas, John, Mary and Susanna.[63]

John Hall was at least twenty-one years old in 1760 when family responsibility fell upon his shoulders. His elder brother Thomas had moved from the state and on 14 May 1760, with the assistance of William West, John took over his father's estate. In court that day, they made a £500 bond guaranteeing John's ability to care for his sisters who as minors had chosen him as their guardian. By 1765 when he became constable, John and Elizabeth had been married five or more years and had three children. Nothing is known about Betty's family, although she was probably the daughter of one of her husband's neighbors. As constable, he covered the area "from the Little River to Cub Run and the Ox Road to the County Line, a fairly broad area within which he lived.[64] John's family was expanding and that year he had both the money and the opportunity to make a significant purchase from a neighbor's sale. He bought several items to make life easier for Betty, but he also purchased a horse, a man's saddle and bridle, plus farm stock and equipment including a plough and seven pigs.[65]

John was at least twenty-one years old in 1760 when he was taxed on 150 acres that probably came into his possession when his father died, and on which he paid annually until he left the state.[66] Over the years there were many interactions between the Hall and West families indicating they were not only neighbors but friends as well. As an example, when William West, Junior made his will in 1763, Hall was both a witness and an appraiser for the estate. When his father, William West Senior, died sometime prior to 1769, both John and Betty Hall witnessed his will. She was also named in her husband's will of 1791 suggesting that Betty was John's only wife and the mother of each of his children. She was, however, at least the mother of his four youngest children, including Hugh and Elizabeth, who was named after her mother.

Hall was nearing forty years old in 1777 during the brutal winter when Washington and his troops were at Valley Forge, and although he was not a soldier or an officer in the war, he served his country in a rather remarkable way. The people of Loudoun County were strong supporters of the war and of their fellow Virginian, George Washington. When the cry for support came, donations from Loudoun's citizens was so overwhelmingly generous to the Continental Army that it became known as the "Breadbasket of the Revolution." Their provisions of food and equipment fed Washington's troops in Valley Forge but also supplied the armies in New Jersey and Pennsylvania too. Although Hall may have given throughout the war, the only surviving record for him was in 1782 when he provided 100 pounds of mutton and 320 pounds of beef to the cause. Later that year he gave another 60 pounds of mutton, 60 pounds of Indian meal, salt, 100 pounds of hay, and a bushel of Indian corn.[67]

As the war drew to a close, Hall was anxious to return to his earlier plan to move to western Pennsylvania. They began in earnest on 7 Jun 1782 when he sold three properties totaling 202 acres to Joseph Lacey, a neighbor who ran a tavern previously owned by William West. The complexity of the sale was increased by the inclusion of the former owners, but it also defined Hall's neighbors and friends as those who witnessed his deeds as he did theirs.[68] Many years later Lacey's property, formerly Hall's land, was on a map showing that it intersected Braddock's Road and the Carolina Road just north of Haymarket Road.[69] Called West's Ordinary or Lacey's Tavern, it is clearly marked on contemporary historical maps at that location using both names.[70] If one was to take the Carolina Road, now called the James Monroe Highway, south from Gilbert's Corner about one mile and look to the right just after crossing Braddock's Road, it might be hard to imagine there was once a tavern where for many years, people met, exchanged pleasantries and did business. Nearby is the farmland John Hall sold to Lacey where, at the time, it was meaningful to describe it as "being on Rogers Spring Branch near the new road and on the first fork of Bull Run where it crosses the new road." Perhaps it was meaningful then, but it is lost today in a highway that criss-crosses between green fields that have grown up around old rotting timbers that once formed a house.

A New Home

Shortly thereafter, the Hall family moved to what was then Westmoreland County, Pennsylvania, but in 1783, with border changes it became Fayette County. There were other changes on the frontier that affected them also. By 1784 the law limiting the number of acres per individual was struck off, so Margaret Hall signed the property affected by it over to her father.[71] The following year he got a warrant for 327 acres in North Union Township just outside the county seat of Uniontown, where the family finally settled. By 1785 Hall had warrants for nearly a thousand acres spread over three townships.[72]

By county standards he was a man of wealth. Statistics for Fayette County in 1796 indicated the largest landowners had between 400 and 4,200 acres. Statistically only about half of those who lived in the county owned land. Of those who did, the average in the 1780's was about 209 acres, and ten years later, it had decreased to 177 acres per family. Statewide statistics showed that of the 4,500 tracts surveyed during the early 1780's, the average landholder again held about 200 acres, a statistic partially skewed by the law of maximum ownership. Hall's neighbor in the adjoining township, Jacob Hewitt, had the legal limit of 300 acres. The tax records where these two families lived are gone, so the value of their livestock and outbuildings cannot be included as a source of wealth.

Slaves were considered property and therefore an additional means of wealth. It was a means to determine a family's origin because Pennsylvania required that all slaves born after 1783 had to be registered or they must be set free. Children born to a slave were not considered slaves, but indentured servants, and when they reached twenty-eight, they were freed. In the years between 1785 and 1793, about forty percent of those living near a river in Fayette County had between one and three slaves. Statistically John Hall and Jacob Hewitt fell within these parameters. While there were no tobacco plantations in Pennsylvania as there were in Maryland and Virginia, most slaves worked either in the fields or in the house as domestics. Both men were above average in wealth, and although Hall had three times more land, Hewitt had an additional income from the tavern. Philosophically and socially they were compatible because of their southern upbringing and this being so, Jacob's son Ephraim was a suitable match for Elizabeth, the daughter of John Hall.[73]

The young couple could have met in several ways. Philip Shute and John Hall certainly knew each other, as both settled early in Fayette County, Shute by 1769 when he got a warrant in North Union Township for *Thorn Bottom*, and his neighbors benefited when he built the first tub mill in the county. Both men owned land in this township and were actively involved in county improvements, so they were bound to run into each other from time to time. Although they may have known each other before, Hewitt and Hall's paths crossed in 1786 when each man was summoned separately to court.[74] Their children intermarried, and it was probably business combined with geographic proximity that brought their fathers together.[75] The Hewitt and Shute families intermarried first, and then about six years later the Hewitts joined the Hall family when Ephraim wed Elizabeth Hall about 1792.[76]

John and Betty's children were grown and had begun to marry, and as he was growing older, it was time to secure their future by thoughtfully planning their legacies even before he made his will. He had nearly a thousand acres to divide between his children. Thomas was born before his brother John, and when John died holding 98 acres in Dunbar Township, according to law because he died in testate, it reverted back to the eldest son, who was Thomas.[77] Hugh owned the remainder of it and in 1790 sold it to Thomas. Then in 1787, John Senior sold Hugh a 200-acre tract called *The Gulph*.[78] In his will, he left land to three of his four daughters. Elizabeth and Rose got property in Franklin Township of about 300 acres valued at nearly £1,700.[79] The following year Elizabeth married Ephraim Hewitt, and Rose eventually married as well. Sarah Hall Boyle received land in the will, but not so his daughter, Margaret, whose sisters were directed to give her the choice of £100 in stock or produce within five years. In a gift similar to Jacob Hewitt's bequest, after his mother died, Hugh, who was the youngest son, got the homestead and its property. Perhaps John Hall began a family tradition in giving as generously to his daughters as he did his sons, and it was unusual that he did so because most women received bedding and tableware or other assorted personal goods. He gave his daughters land and a slave each, as well as annually collected rent bonds. He settled all his personal property and household furnishings on his wife but asked her to give the children what she did not want.[80]

The Youngest Son

In planning how his family would get along after he died, Jacob had many things to consider. Since he was an orphan he had no traditions to uphold, thus fairness and good judgment were his guides. His will, which not all men made, indicated his thoughtful consideration, but also awareness that his children were planning their lives even before his ended. He probably sat with Ephraim and asked if he was willing to stay and run the farm and tavern, but also to care for Ruth. Although only twenty his parents must have seen qualities in Ephraim that led his father to give him the larger part of the family legacy. A few years after their father died, Richard sold his land and left Fayette County but Ephraim stayed there for nearly twenty years. His father's will directed that "my wife, Ruth, should enjoy the whole of my dwelling plantation during her natural life." It was a standard provision for one's wife, but one that increased the bond between mother and son because in essence her care was in Ephraim's hands. She was 62 when her husband passed on to his reward, and her trust was in Jacob's wisdom that Ephraim would treat her thoughtfully during the remainder of her life. By 1810 Ruth Hewitt was probably no longer living, but in 1800 the census indicated a female over 45 was living with Ephraim in 1800, either his mother or his mother-in-law, both of whom were widows by then.[81] Ruth probably died between 1800 and 1810, and as was the custom in the early days, she was buried next to Jacob in a family cemetery somewhere on the Hewitt farm.

Ephraim grew up quickly after his father's death. When Richard moved away, he was only twenty-three but he had begun to shoulder responsibility even before then. He probably knew most of the men in the neighborhood and even some in Uniontown, the county seat, where records show that shortly after he turned twenty-one, he served as a juror.[82] He also married Elizabeth Hall about that time because in 1793 their first child, a daughter Nancy, was born.[83] By the time he was twenty-six years old, Ephraim had stepped up to the grand jury— the difference being that this was a criminal rather than a civil panel. In 1798, he received a two-year appointment as constable for Menallen Township, an assignment comparable to that of the justice of the peace or sheriff.[84] Some of his duties were to levy taxes, to help conduct and maintain order during elections, and when court was in session, he reported offenses used to initiate a trial.[85] By 1797, Ephraim was generally known in the community, and financially able to sign a bond on a man's estate, an act that in itself was not notable except that Ephraim was a young man of only twenty-seven years.[86]

Serving as constable, also gave him a chance to move about the community looking for property investment opportunities. He began his first venture a month before the birth of his fourth child, Ruth, who was named after her grandmother. It was a complicated sale involving John Hall's dowry gift to his daughters, in which Ephraim and Peter Johnson, Rose's husband, sold the land to a neighbor for $4,500. The brothers-in-law agreed to pay cash, less the value of land in Harrison County, Virginia that the purchaser had bought from Peter, but had not yet paid him.[87] Ephraim continued to buy land, one purchase was $25 for a lot in nearby Middletown that he later sold for $375, a substantial gain on his investment.[88]

By 1800, farmer Ephraim was also a tavern keeper, a land investor and an active county citizen. Sometimes business led him to court because he had accumulated too much debt. Between 1798 and 1800, he was a defendant in several lawsuits. The first to sue was his brother-in-law, Hugh Hall, whom he owed money on an investment loan. Then a man sued both of them for £120. Next Ephraim borrowed money from Isaac Wood, an extended family member, who sued him for £200.[89] The latter relationship was through Ephraim's sister, Elizabeth, who was married to Isaac's brother John. There were two more lawsuits, one for return of property and the last for debt, and then the tables turned. From 1802 through 1804 Ephraim initiated legal proceedings, winning several judgments of $75-$300, one in which he sued for the return of a horse held as collateral.[90] By 1800 when he was thirty, Ephraim and Elizabeth had five children.[91] Until then, court records showed he struggled to earn a living while attempting to stay ahead of his creditors, a feat not always accomplished in a timely manner. After 1802 he initiated the lawsuits, indicating perhaps he had a financial turnaround.

The family continued to expand so that by 1810 there were ten children; nine of them were girls. Daily life was long and arduous for this couple, particularly for Elizabeth. Ephraim had business and civic responsibilities, and was not always at home or at the tavern. His activities supported their livelihood and fed a growing family, therefore she depended on her older daughter, Nancy who was seventeen, to help at home and in the tavern. Ephraim accepted two other responsibilities in 1809, one as a tax collector for Menallen Township,[92] and then as guardian for the children of a near neighbor.[93] Over the years, and certainly by age forty, Ephraim had become a responsible man and a trusted friend to others. Although his family's welfare was his main duty, he was respected in the community, otherwise he would not have been asked to manage the affairs of orphaned children.

Several events happened in 1813 that precipitated and probably accelerated Ephraim's efforts to leave Fayette County. His mother probably died about 1812 releasing him from the obligation to remain in the state. In February 1813, he advertised his farm and several properties in the local newspaper,[94] and then in July he borrowed money from his brother in Baltimore, using the farm as security. It came at a heavy price because Eli charged him $500 interest, although Ephraim paid the loan in full a year later.[95] Ephraim's intent was unstated but it may have been a business loan to finance a dry goods business, which he began after his move to Ohio. However, that November John Wood died, perhaps escalating Ephraim's attempt to leave the area.[96]

Wood, who was married to Ephraim's sister Elizabeth, lived in Uniontown where he was a saddler and harness-maker. He also had a dry goods store in town advertised by the local newspaper, and the advertisement read, "...just received from Philadelphia at the well known Corner Stand in Uniontown, formerly occupied by John Wood, Esq. an extensive and elegant assortment of the newest and most fashionable summer and fall goods." The goods ranged from ladies black cotton hose to English and domestic linen and cotton, and from parasols to beaver gloves and "smelling water." Ephraim Hewitt may have been in business with Wood, or purchased some of the items from his estate for his future business.[97]

John Wood, moved to Pennsylvania from England with his brothers. Clement settled near Philadelphia while Isaac and John moved to Uniontown. In 1784 John was elected to the county's Supreme Executive Council, and after becoming a justice of the peace, he was elected to the state legislature. His son William took over the Uniontown saddlery when he died and it continued in all for 112 years and three generations of the Wood family. Undoubtedly, travelers who stopped at the Hewitt tavern and needed their equipment repaired were sent to see John Wood who was known as the "the horse doctor" because he knew so much about them.

After paying his brother, and buying off pieces of nearby land, including some from John and Elizabeth Wood, Ephraim sold the farm. A neighbor bought it for $4,000, indicating what a valuable property it had become.[98] Then after saying farewell to friends, Ephraim and Elizabeth prepared to leave. With much sadness they left the widowed Elizabeth Wood in her son's care. She lived until 1843 but never remarried, and shortly after her eightieth birthday died, and was buried beside her husband in Uniontown's Methodist Episcopal Cemetery.[99] When they pulled away from the community, Ephraim may have also left behind his sister Ruth. After 1798 when she was named in her brother's will, nothing more is known about her, and so she may have died or married and disappeared into a new name. Without Ruth, Elizabeth was the last of the Hewitt family to remain in Fayette County.

Perhaps Ephraim came to Ohio at Richard's urging, convinced by his brother that the community needed his services and the goods he had to offer. More than twenty years before, Richard left Pennsylvania and moved to Ohio Territory with his wife's family. He longed to have a sibling nearby, and although it may have been many years since the two brothers had seen each other, Ephraim was willing to make the move and uprooted his family to do so. Each, for reasons of his own, came to southern Ohio to begin a new life in a place along the Ohio River just emerging from the wilderness.

MAP OF SOUTHWESTERN OHIO, NORTHERN KENTUCKY
Including these counties:

Adams, Brown, Clermont and
Hamilton Counties, Ohio

Bracken, Campbell, Fleming. Kenton,
Mason and Pendleton Counties, Kentucky

HOME OF THE
Ackerman
Cochran
Fisher
Durham
Hall
Hewitt
Kenny
Kyle
Morrison
Schmidt
Terhune
Williamson Families

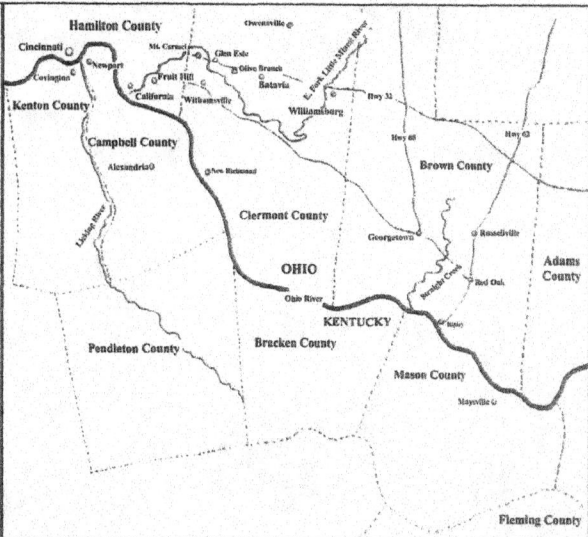

Hamilton County

Cincinnati

Owensville

Mt. Carmel
Glen Este

Newport
Covington

Fruit Hill
Olive Branch
Batavia

E. Fork Little Miami River

Kenton County
California
Wilbamsville
Williamsburg

Hwy 32

Hwy 68
Hwy 62

Campbell County

Brown County

Alexandria
New Richmond

Clermont County

Georgetown
Rossellville

OHIO
Adams County

Red Oak

Ohio River
Bracken Creek

KENTUCKY
Ripley

Pendleton County
Bracken County

Mason County

Licking River

Maysville

Fleming County

Chapter Five

TAMING THE WILDERNESS:
Richard Hewitt
Mason County, Kentucky; Brown County, Ohio (1793-1827)

Phebe Hall

In 1793 Phebe Hall Hewitt placed her mark next to her husband's name on a deed ending their Pennsylvania life. She and Richard were about to depart Fayette County for northern Kentucky, a part of Virginia's western frontier. If Richard paused to remember the last time he moved, he realized he was little more than ten years old when the Revolutionary War began and his family left Baltimore for an unknown western frontier. Although no stranger to change, he was nearly 28 years old and a family man; his father's estate was settled and he was eager to depart. In a state of anticipation and excitement, he and Phebe signed away their claim to the 104 acres called *Springfield* that was his inheritance. Then with £130 in their pockets, they departed full of hope. As if in response, spring itself was bursting from the earth and with it, all the promise and expectation of renewal and a new life.[1]

Most of their lives Richard and Phebe lived only a few miles apart in the same township, and perhaps they knew each other growing up. Although education in the early days was unorganized, they may have been schoolmates, or attended the same church. Phebe's father was Edward Hall, and Richard's brother later married Elizabeth Hall, possibly a distant cousin of Phebe, and another possible source of introduction. Elizabeth's father, John Hall, was from Loudoun County, Virginia where several generations of his family lived including a neighbor named Edward Hall who paid taxes there through 1769.[2] If he was Phebe's father, there was a gap of fourteen years between records, until in 1783 a man by that name applied for a land warrant in Fayette County. His property was in Upper Middletown (Plumsock), a 300-acre tract straddling Redstone Creek and bordering settlers Jeremiah Pierce and Hugh Thompson.[3]

Phebe was the eldest daughter in a family of six children, corroborated by the 1790 census that indicated they were a family of nine with three men above sixteen, one under sixteen and five females.[4] An 1820 Brown County deed further corroborated the family makeup, naming Edward's children and their spouses but not his wife, who must have died.[5] The deed and other records suggested the children were born between 1770 and 1780, and that Phebe was the eldest daughter, born about 1770. Elijah and Charles were born next and John was her youngest brother, born between 1776 and 1778. Anna and Mary, called Polly, were probably born on either side of John.

Edward Hall's presence in his community was quietly understated. He paid his taxes, served as a juror when called and generally took care of his family without fanfare. Twice however, he was compelled to file suit for money owed to him. He was a good friend too. In 1790 Elijah Barkley was putting his affairs in order and asked Hall to assist his wife with the administration. Hall followed up on that promise the following year appearing in court with Rachel Mooney—formerly Barkley, who had married since her husband's death. Together they reported on the moneys due and owed by the estate. In 1791, another neighbor, William Sparks, in nearby Franklin Township asked Hall to assist his family. Sparks asked Hall to be guardian of his fourteen-year-old daughter, to which he agreed.[6] Whether the families were interrelated is unknown, but in 1810 Hall's son, Charles, married a woman named Rachel Mooney suggesting there was at least, an ongoing relationship with the Mooney family.[7] A few months later he purchased 276 acres in Brown County, Ohio, which he and Rachel immediately transferred to his brother Elijah Hall. One of the witnesses to the transaction was Elijah's brother John Hall.[8]

There are no records to suggest that Richard and Phebe were formally married. There were some churches in Fayette County in 1790, but many young people formally tied the knot only after a circuit-riding preacher passed through the county to bless their union. These ministers traveled widely and so came infrequently to these sparsely populated communities. When they did, they not only brought the Word to those seeking it, but also baptized the children and sanctified the unions of those living together without benefit of ceremony. Richard and Phebe may have gone elsewhere to marry, but likely their marital estate was blessed by a minister who afterwards rode away on his horse, leaving no record of his visit to their community.

Jacob Hewitt was born 9 Nov 1791 but there is no proof that Phebe was his mother.[9] She probably was, given the circumstances of their journey, although if she was not his mother, she was duty bound as Richard's wife to accompany him and bring his child with her. Thus, only circumstantial evidence binds her as the mother of Richard Hewitt's eldest child.

Leaving Home

The last decade of the eighteenth century was for many families a transitional time when men and women sold their farms and moved into the western unknown. Therefore it was no coincidence that when Edward Hall put his "X" on the deed to his land, it was within days of when Richard and Phebe Hewitt sold their property.[10] They probably departed together, either that fall or the following spring, and after saying goodbye to friends and family they placed their belongings on a flatboat and headed down the river.

It was a perilous journey so people traveled in groups. Richard was personally aware of the risks because of the near disaster that waylaid his brother Hayes and the Shute family on their voyage to Tennessee, and so they proceeded with caution. Their companions, among others, were Phebe's father and her siblings. Then, the Ohio was unlike today's river, and timing was everything during a water venture. Now it is a broader, deeper river created by dams and canals, but then the river was low in the summer and in winter before the snows melted. At times it was so shallow in places that it was possible to wade across. In early spring, other than the fear of Indian attack, drifting ice was another danger to the river traveler. Fast and uneventful trips usually happened in the rainy months of spring and fall when it rained and the river rose high enough to move safely over the sandbars without being grounded.

In 1793, Ohio was too dangerous for a man to bring his family. Instead, Edward Hall and Richard Hewitt's destination was Maysville in Mason County, Kentucky, across the river from Ohio. It was not much safer there because the influx of new settlers agitated the native population, and caused continued raids on frontier forts. The problems became so serious that the following year Kentucky's governor employed spies to be on the lookout for Indian raids. Although the territory was wild and sparsely populated, unlike Ohio, Kentucky had walled enclosures like Fort Washington to protect the settlers. Standing alone in the wilderness, these sturdily built structures held many families who banded together to tend their families and keep watch. In the meantime, farmers plowed their fields, the first jail and courthouse was built in 1790, and a ferry was established in 1794. In 1793, after Gen. Anthony Wayne defeated the Indians at the Battle of Fallen Timbers, where thy had gone seeking British protection from Wayne's troops, England and the U.S. made peace. When news finally reached the settlement, rejoicing broke out on the frontier. The conflict had ended but memories of what the frontiersmen endured up until 1795 lingered much longer. It would take many more years before that part of Kentucky's northern border was no longer remembered as that "Dark and Bloody Ground."[11]

That same year Edward and Elijah Hall arrived in Mason County, Kentucky. Richard Hewitt was probably there as well but he was not taxed until 1794 when all three men were on the District One list. In 1794 and 1795 the lists for Edward's family indicated his sons' approximate ages, and thereby their birth dates. Three of them were between 16-20 years old in 1794 and a fourth was added the next year, indicating that John was born in 1779 while Elijah, the eldest, was born before 1773, and Charles, birthday was between those dates.[12] Richard and Phebe Hewitt did not own property in Mason County but paid taxes from 1794 through 1797 for their horses and cattle only.[13]

Pioneers began flocking to the Ohio Territory well before it was safe to settle upon the lands they purchased, so it was imperative to make peace with the native population. By August 1795, hostilities ceased and peace was made in the form of the Greenville Treaty, an agreement in which amity was exchanged for land. As representative for the settlers, Gen. Anthony Wayne negotiated the settlement with the Indian tribes of the Ohio Territories promising that if they allowed a peaceable settlement their established hunting and fishing privileges would be honored. Thereafter boundaries were redrawn giving the various tribes land north of a line stretching vertically from Fort McIntosh in Pennsylvania, west to a line just below the Wabash River in present day Indiana. Promised also was that a government reservation would be established on the new lands, and that forts would be built for trade and stations established to make payments to the tribes in reparation for land they relinquished.[14]

Like other early Ohio pioneers, Hewitt and Hall purchased land well before they could live on it, and both families stayed in Mason County well after the treaty was signed. It was not until after 1797 that they ventured across the river to Brown County to begin negotiations with the owners of Crawford's Survey

#664. Because none of them received clear title until many years later, court documents contained a great deal of information about the relationships between the families and the original purchasers.[15]

With peace assured and promises of unencumbered land, those families who had been awaiting word made their move. After 1795 families began pouring into the Ohio territory, and with even more arriving in 1796 they spread across the land. Amidst the flood of land-seekers were Richard and Phebe Hewitt who because they arrived early were able to get choice land. In 1797 they bought 100 acres on Straight Creek in Pleasant Township and soon began to make their home. What greeted their eyes as they looked across the river from Maysville were dense woodlands of primeval beauty. Their uncut luxuriance undulated over the land as it melted into varying shades of green. A raft or small boat got them across the shallow river quickly and easily so they could explore. Once across, Richard paddled up Straight Creek to inspect the land. Looking around and up he saw that the old growth forests were tall and thick providing a verdant canopy that shielded the forest floor from sunlight. Leaving the boat, he was able to walk the land because, unlike today's forests that stretch from the top of the hills down to the river's edge, these forests had fewer shrubs and bushes and were more easily accessible. Looking at the horizon he saw that the land was a mixture of gently rolling hills and large flat areas that over time could be turned into fields of corn, wheat and tobacco. Known as burley tobacco, the latter grows well in Brown County and small fields of it still dot farmlands today.

Richard tramped the land by Indian footpaths, discovering along the way that the woods held a variety of deciduous trees and the meadows were full of wild lilies and roses. Once he had the land, he cut back some of the magnificent walnut and oak groves, the remainder would be used later. He began by removing bushes and small trees with his scythe and replaced them with crops. Sycamore and elm grew along Straight Creek and on higher ground there were sugar maple trees. Wild animals roamed at will through the woods and streams, and a bounty was paid on some of them. Bear, wolves, panther and wildcats were among the most dangerous, as well as poisonous snakes that ruled the waters and the earth beneath the trees, including rattlesnake, moccasin and copperhead. Food was easy to find as there was a great variety of edible fowl and game roaming through the forest, including large numbers of red deer and wild turkey.[16]

At some point, either in his negotiations for land or after he began clearing it, Richard brought Phebe to see it. With a keen gaze and a good imagination he might have envisioned the landscape bereft of trees, revealing the earth beneath it so that he was able to describe for her where the farm would be someday. First he showed her where the cabin would be, then as they walked about he checked the soil for drainage and content, deciding the best place to grow the corn, wheat and oats that would become a staple of this farm. This was good land, he knew that, and not just because it had a low survey number. Originally eight hundred acres, Survey #664 was on a creek[17] and in a county where the numbers were as high #12569, it was among the best land available.[18]

Richard Junior who was born in Kentucky on 22 Sep 1794 has been well documented through Mormon Church records, including his parents' names[19] and his birth date.[20] His descendants agree that he was born in Kentucky where tax records show his parents were living.[21] A petition sent to the territorial governor, Arthur St. Clair on 10 Jan 1799, proved that the Hewitt family did not settle immediately on their Ohio lands. At the time a group of settlers who lived "between the waters of Eagle and Straight Creeks" petitioned the Governor of the Northwest Territory, imploring him to appoint a justice of the peace and militia officers to restore order to the area. Richard Hewitt's name was not on the list confirming that he was still in Mason County.[22]

Community responsibilities placed him firmly in Ohio in 1801, a thirty-six-year-old man with a growing family. His children's names were not in the family Bible, suggesting that at least until 1815 it was in Fayette County with Ephraim. However, his will named them apparently in the order of their birth. If so, then William and John were born after Richard Junior while the family was in Kentucky. Eli was the youngest son, born about 1803 in Virginia (Kentucky) says a census record, but more likely in Ohio.[23] However, Phebe might have remained there with some of her family until Richard was born, since it was a safer place for her confinement.[24]

Taming the Wilderness

Clearing land in a virgin forest was backbreaking work, but Richard was not alone. His in-laws' land was nearby and they helped each other. However, to get along in this wild land it was also necessary to meet and enlist their neighbors' support. Using their collective wits and skills it was possible to turn unspoiled country into a pastoral landscape, and with the assistance and willingness of others they succeeded. Neighbors assisted each other in the harshness of the early years through an exchange of labor and by sharing particular skills that made each man a unique part of the venture. It took teamwork to build a town and friendship was the key not only to its continuation, but also for its growth and prosperity.

In a place like this, it might take a man working alone nearly seven years to clear enough land for a small farm and a second house. Although not always working alone, Richard spent intervals between 1796 and 1801, when he officially joined the ranks of Brown County residents, clearing farmland and assisting the Hall family in the same efforts. To begin, brush was cleared away, then small trees were cut down and others trimmed. Larger trees were felled by chipping around the circumference with an axe and leaving them to die. The ka-thunk of the axe against wood in an otherwise silent forest was often an announcement to others that someone new had moved in. A neighbor, at first curious, might tramp over the footpaths or ride on horseback to meet the newcomer then remain to help.

After clearing some of the area, the following spring Hewitt chopped down the dead trees and removed the stumps so he could build a cabin and plant the first corn crop. With his immediate needs met, he was able to remain for longer periods clearing land and planting crops. The first cabin built was usually small and made of round logs notched at the end. The gaps between each log were filled with bits of wool mixed with clay. Its roof was clapboard and the floor, if there was one, was made of planks split from logs. A primitive fireplace was formed from split sticks covered over with clay. The cabin door was also of clapboard, hung on wooden hinges and fastened with a wooden latch. The window was covered with oiled paper that allowed some light inside. Early cabins were primitive and nearly all furnishings, from tables and benches to sitting stools and shelves, were made by hand. A couple felt fortunate if among the handmade furniture they had a good bedstead, and their bedding arrived undamaged. Other necessities included a spinning wheel for flax and one for wool, a mortar and pestle for grinding corn and some cooking utensils. Initially a man's most important possessions besides his axe were a flintlock rifle, powder horn and a pouch for bullets.[25] Another indispensable but little remembered tool was a frow, used to split boards for shingles, it was combined with a drawing knife to make clapboards and floorboards.[26]

For several years after Hewitt bought land, county boundaries were assigned and reassigned. Original tax records showed he lived in Adams County until a boundary reorganization placed him in Pleasant Township in Clermont County. A final redefinition fixed his farm firmly within Franklin Township in Brown County. He was a resident by 1801 when he was elected a supervisor of the roads for Pleasant Township.[27] By then many more families had moved to Brown County, increasing the safety of those who had built a permanent abode. Some of the same families who lived in Fayette County in 1782 were Hewitt's neighbors in Pleasant and Franklin Townships. Among them were Uriah Springer, Isaac Prickett and Edward Hall, suggesting that some of those who later settled in Ohio were already acquainted.[28]

Frontier Town

Life in Maysville, or Limestone as it was called, was like most any small town. A militia was formed, a post office opened and court was organized. Couples married when a traveling preacher passed by and babies were born regardless of timing. Some men made a will before they died, and to that end Edward Hall, ever a reliable friend, was there to serve his neighbors. He witnessed a will in 1793 and again in October 1794, signing each time with an "X" as he had in the past. In 1808 his sons, John and Charles, were mentioned in an estate inventory suggesting either that the deceased owned property on both sides of the river or Edward's sons were still living in Mason County.[29]

Records suggest that Elijah and the Hall family moved to Straight Creek at about the same time. Edward Hall left Maysville after 1797 and settled in Pleasant Township. Brief records follow him for a few years; first in 1802 when he became a supervisor for the highway in his township. Then in 1806 he was on the county jury.[30] By then, Elijah and John lived in Brown County on Survey #664 where Phebe and Richard Hewitt made their home.[31] A county history named Hall as one of the early settlers, along with the Calvin, Woods and Prickett families who married into the Hewitt family in the next generation. Fielding Martin who married Edward Hall's daughter, Anna, also lived on this claim.[32] It was Martin, who in 1820 brought a lawsuit against his father-in-law to settle a land dispute, naming each of Hall's children and their spouses. After living on the land more than twenty years, Edward Hall died before the dispute was over, sometime in 1820 between May 12 and May 22.[33]

Settling the Wilderness

Initially those families who formed Brown County arrived principally from Virginia, Maryland and Pennsylvania via the Ohio River, stopping once they reached the fort at Limestone, Kentucky. Others migrated deeper into Kentucky while some went further south and settled Carolina Territory. However, those pioneers who crossed the river and stepped upon Ohio shores, joined other men and women who were about to transform the wilderness into an organized system of interconnected towns and villages from whence its cities sprung. A citation from Beers' 1883 *History of Brown County, Ohio* aptly described them.

> The early emigrants to Brown County may be described as a bold and resolute, rather than a cultivated people. It has been laid down as a general truth that a population made up of immigrants will contain the hardy and vigorous elements of character in a far greater proportion than the same number of persons born upon the soil and accustomed to tread in the footsteps of their fathers. It required enterprise and resolution to sever the ties that bound them to the place of their birth, and upon their arrival in the new country, the stern face of nature and the necessities of their condition made them bold and energetic. The absence of old familiar customs, family alliances and the restraint of old social organizations fostered individuality.
>
> The early settlers of Brown County were plain men and women of good sense, without the refinements which luxury brings, and with great contempt for all shams and mere pretense. A majority of the early settlers belonged to the middle class. Few were by affluence, placed above the necessity of labor with their hands, and few were so poor that they could not become the owners of small farms. The mass of settlers were owners in fee simple of at least a small farm.

By 1801 Richard Hewitt had built a cabin and cleared enough land to support his growing family. However, outbuildings were needed, so next he built a barn, then storage sheds. Inside the house Phebe's never-ending tasks went more smoothly when set to the tempo of her husband's axe thudding on wood. As she moved about the cabin stirring the cook-pot, feeding the babes and sweeping the ever-present dirt out of the cabin she ticked away the daily chores that kept her busy until it was too dark to see. After a long day, with the children fed and tucked into bed she and Richard warmed themselves by the fire and began the evening chores. Most nights she spun either flax or wool to make into winter hats and sweaters, while Richard repaired a bridle or cleaned his rifle. In the spring and early summer when days were pleasant, Phebe scrubbed their clothing outdoors laying them on the bushes to dry. Then after weeding her kitchen garden she picked vegetables to be chopped and added to the stewpot along with the meat that had been simmering since she arose that morning. Around her the children played, fought, and tumbled, as much a part of her world as the sunshine outside the window. Sometimes she paused a moment from her outdoor chores to stand up and relieve her back, and while doing so she marked the day, as she had so many others, by the height of the corn crop in the nearest field. Daily she worked, often not far from her husband and in bearing and raising his children she marked the years as they passed.

Aside from their relatives, some of the men and women on neighboring farms became their friends, bonding with the Hewitt and Hall families and supporting them when in need. In time they joined the family as their children married each other. Sometimes they blended by virtue of proximity, or because of economic arrangement, but other times marriages happened through natural inclination. Those who lived nearby were the Stephen (Calvin) Colvin, and the James Woods families from Washington County, Pennsylvania who moved to Pleasant Township in 1800-1805. Jacob Slack lived on nearby Camp Run and Fielding Martin was a neighbor and an in-law. There was James Prickett, and the Abbotts, Joseph and his son John. Down the road were James Dunn from Virginia and Joseph and David Newman. A stranger who visited this young community in 1808 described his first impressions. After embarking at Maysville and crossing the Ohio River he described what he saw there.

> I was employed in rambling about the woods, exploring and
> examining a tract of land of 1,000 acres, in the state of Ohio,
> which I had purchased when in Europe last year, and which
> had been the principal cause of my present tour. As it was
> only six miles from Maysville, I crossed the Ohio and went
> to it on foot. I had expected to have found a mere wilderness,
> as soon as I should quit the high road, but to my agreeable
> surprise, I found my land surrounded on every side by fine
> farms, some of them ten years settled and the land itself both
> in quality and situation not exceeded by any in this fine
> country. The population was also astonishing for the time of
> the settlement, which a muster of militia while I was there
> gave me an opportunity of knowing, there being reviewed a
> battalion of upward of 500 effective men, most expert in the
> use of the rifle, belonging to the district of ten miles square.
> And now I experienced among these honest and friendly
> farmers real hospitality for they vied with each other in
> lodging me at their houses, and in giving me a hearty and
> generous welcome to their best fare...These were farmers,
> and had not contracted habits which I have observed to
> prevail very generally amongst the traders in this part of the
> world. (See next footnote)

Initially the roads in Brown County were Indian paths replaced by horse trails but once the county was organized it was imperative to upgrade them to wagon roads. The highway supervisor was responsible for organizing a work crew in his township to broaden the roads and to create entrances at each farm. Today, the roads closest to Hewitt's property, and which in 1801 he helped to make, are Day Hill Road running north and south and Camp Run Road that abuts horizontally the northern edge of Pleasant Township. Later state funds were used to broaden the road near Charles Abbott's farm, because it was the township's main-east west corridor. Hewitt was probably supervisor for a year or two, or until his father-in-law took over the position in 1804.[34]

Richard and Phebe had seven children in all, but some of their birth dates are unknown. William and John were probably born in Kentucky between 1796 and 1800. Eli was born in 1803, and in 1807 Elizabeth was born.[35] Seven years later Letty Ann was born in 1814, suggesting there may have been one or even two children born between her and Elizabeth.[36] His eldest son, Jacob, turned 23 during the fall of the year Letty was born. The family lived on their original property as tax records show,[37] but in 1811 Richard bought 50 acres on an adjacent tract bringing the total to 150 acres.[38]

The War of 1812

Once it became a state in 1803, Ohio was required to form a militia. Officers were chosen, a regiment was formed, and then all able-bodied men over twenty-one were required to serve. They mustered regularly for drill and practice at arms, and since nearly everyone had a brother, cousin or father in the militia, practice days became splendid entertainment for country folk. Farmers left their fields, and merchants their shops to line up on main street and cheer as young men practiced their maneuvers to the beat of a drum. Lingering memories of Indian troubles in the Northwest Territory caused Ohio to respond to the War of 1812 rapidly and in significant numbers. They blamed the English for fomenting and supporting Indian hostilities in the western territories, so that this was known as the "second war for independence." It began when American soldiers invaded Canada and tried to subdue British troops stationed there. The U.S. weakness was revealed within months as England allied with Native American warriors to capture three posts on the Great Lakes. Although the campaign was directed against the British, when General Harrison was defeated by the Shawnee chief Tecumseh, the nation's dream of creating a confederacy south of the Great Lakes was halted. It was also the beginning of a long war between an older nation and the army of the youthful United States.[39]

True to the call, Jacob and Richard Hewitt signed up to fight along with their friends. As sharpshooters who used guns since boyhood, they learned how to fight as a unit. Richard was twenty when he signed up with a mounted infantry battalion. He served as a private between September-December 1814. Jacob was twenty-one in 1812 and marched with Captain Shepherd's Company from Brown County. He had two short tours of duty; the first was September-October 1812, and the other July-August 1813.[40] Captain Shepherd stopped at

Laycock's tavern in Eagle Township just prior to leaving the county where he "halted and refreshed his men with Laycock's brandy while on the march to Sandusky and Detroit in 1812."[41]   Shepherd's company "probably marched north by the Scioto to General Harrison's headquarters at Franklinton, by the mouth of the Olentangy."[42]   Therefore, if Captain Shepherd was present on 5 Oct 1812 when Harrison's troops retaliated by killing Tecumseh and defeating the British near Detroit, then Jacob Hewitt was also a part of that campaign.[43] Like Jacob, many men served for sixty days and then re-enlisted. Whether they helped construct a blockhouse, cut a road or fight in battle, when they returned they gathered at the tavern to recall their experiences and trade war stories. John Hall was married to Ephraim Hewitt's daughter, Nancy, and he kept a tavern east of Georgetown that reportedly was a "well known rendezvous for military men during the war of 1812...where they met at the place and held many a carousal."[44]   Jacob was an apparent participant in one of the war's storied battles, and perhaps he frequented his uncle's tavern afterward with the companions who served with him.

The War of 1812 was fought on three different fronts and it attracted several branches of the Hewitt family. While Richard and Jacob followed their regiments into the campaigns in northern Ohio, their cousin from Nashville, Hazael Hewitt, son of Robert, enlisted in the West Tennessee Mounted Volunteers.[45]   When President Madison asked Tennessee to help defend the country, men offered their services en masse, thus earning the name, the "Volunteer State."   By 1814 the northern campaign was drawing to a close, while in the south, it was heating up. In service for sixty days, "Hayes" Hewitt from Davidson County was among other young, green volunteers who went to Fort Strother to fill the ranks of Andrew Jackson's depleted troops. In January 1814, while Jackson and his troops were away on maneuvers, some of the fiercest fighting in the south occurred when Indians attacked the fort with such ferocity, that upon his return, Jackson retaliated by ordering a Creek Indian village burned. Still vengeful, two months later Jackson sent his troops agains the Creek Nation and defeated them at the Battle of Horseshoe Bend. He went on in 1815 to beat the British at the last battle of the war in New Orleans.[46]   By war's end Hayes who had turned 21, had long since returned to his family. Memories lingered for him and his cousins, as each of them had seen more of war and death than they ever hoped to again. Some years later he married a Nashville girl, Caroline Newsome, and they moved to Madison County, Tennessee.[47]

On another arena, the war in Maryland was directly related to old problems that brought the U.S. into conflict with England in the first place. They began in Europe ten years prior to 1812 when Britain and France, while fighting each other, began stopping American ships on the high seas. Then Britain set up a blockade stopping U.S. trade with other European nations, and both France and England began impressing American sailors into war service.   Although provoked, the U.S. took no action. However, when Americans were killed as Britain forcefully boarded the USS *Chesapeake*, President Jefferson created the Embargo Act, halting U.S. trade with foreign ports. Disastrous to American trade, it was repealed and replaced by a law allowing trade with nations other than Great Britain and France. Reluctantly in 1812, James Madison declared war against the British when one of their ships in New York harbor fired on an American vessel that refused to stop. The Americans fired back, sinking the ship and the war began.

In August 1814 British forces landed on the shores of Chesapeake Bay, marched into the nation's capital and burned the Capitol and the White House. Flushed with victory they surrounded Baltimore expecting to take it also. Out in the harbor the British zeroed in on Fort McHenry. All during the night of September 14 they poured shot into the fort and still those within held firm. So inspired was he by the courage of men who would not give up that Francis Scott Key, who was a witness to that night, felt compelled to write about it. As the bombs lit up the night skies around the harbor he penned the words to the anthem that would become *The Star Spangled Banner.*[48]

Among those defending the city that night was Eli Hewitt, the uncle of Jacob and Richard. As a superintendent for the Committee of Vigilance and Safety, he was one of eight men charged with helping his district prepare for attack. Hewitt, who was 47, was responding personally as well because he had a tobacco shop in the Third District at 232 Baltimore Street. Prior to that night, and in preparation for what they viewed as an inevitable attack by the British, his men gathered to defend their city. On 30 Aug 1814, citizens exempt from militia duty and free people of color showed up at Washington Square with axes and shovels to build a fort around the city. Hewitt directed them to fill the wheelbarrows and deposit their loads at the town's perimeter next to those men who were building the defenses. Those dirt fortifications were all the city had to guard the town against an impending British invasion, but because the men at Fort McHenry fought so valiantly the British gave up and fortunately the hastily built defenses were never tested against attack.[49]

When Richard Hewitt Junior returned from Detroit, he arrived to find that his Uncle Ephraim and Aunt Elizabeth had brought his cousins to live in Brown County. He may have met his uncle on an earlier visit, but perhaps not his many cousins. The two families were of all ages, beginning with Letty Ann who was a year old, to Nancy Hewitt Hall who was 21 years old. Whether they all came together as a boisterous mélange, or were quietly curious, it was an occasion for comparisons, a search for similarities but also some cousinly competition. However, it was also a time for these young people to discover that while they were complete strangers they also shared many attributes.

Two Brothers

No one knows how long it had been since Richard and Ephraim had seen each other. Ephraim probably inspected the land before he bought it, so there was an initial visit, probably in late 1813. With years of separation there was much to talk about during the initial visit. Richard's family had grown, with young Elizabeth nearly six years old, and Phebe was pregnant again. Ephraim shared Fayette County news while they tramped the land. Richard entertained his brother with settlement stories, all the while waxing poetically about the wonderful potential that was before them. Ephraim's plans for the future fostered plans and dreams about what could be accomplished when their families were reunited. Ephraim mused silently to himself, thinking how like Richard to make his way wherever he landed, but he too was hooked. Sometime during the visit they put up a cabin large enough to hold Ephraim's large family when they arrived.

The following year in midwinter, Ephraim sold the farm in Fayette County and since spring was the best time to leave, they packed up their belongings and he brought the family to Ohio in April or May 1814. Arriving with them were their beds and dishes, pots and pans, tables and chairs but also, the beginnings of a small dry goods business.[50] Ephraim's property near Straight Creek abutted his brother's land, and was not far from where some of Phebe's siblings lived. In an effort to prepare for the winter to come, that summer they made the cabin comfortable, planted corn and put in a vegetable garden. The entire family was invited to a wedding on 1 Jan 1815 when Ephraim and Elizabeth's eldest daughter Nancy was married to John Hall.[51] He was Phebe's youngest brother and about fourteen years older than his bride who was 21 years old.[52]

Unbeknownst to all, the clock was ticking down, and there was little time to accustom themselves before tragedy struck. Less than a year later Ephraim's plans for a new life ended abruptly. In January 1815 he was on a business trip to Fayette County when he died suddenly, either by accident or because of a brief illness. It was announced there in the local newspaper, saying that "on Wednesday last, Ephraim Hewitt of Adams County, Ohio, late of Menallen Township, Fayette County, Pennsylvania [died] in the 45th year of his age."[53] Perhaps he had been buying new shawls or calico for the store, or something special for Elizabeth or one of his daughters. The suddenness of the event becomes more poignant when viewed through the auction and the items sold to pay off his debts. The list of dry goods established his business intent and the personal assets provided entree into their lives before leaving Pennsylvania. Much of the inventory was ladies clothing and accessories that included purses, shoes, handkerchiefs, shawls, and yards and yards of fabric.

For Elizabeth and her children, the loss was devastating. For his brother, Richard, all plans they might have made together ended that day. Perhaps his grief was too raw or the sudden loss of one who had only just re-entered his life was too great, but after the initial property appraisal, Richard had no other involvement in the estate. If the brothers were close it seemed likely that he would have assisted the widow to aright her life. However, later events indicated there was some animosity between Elizabeth and her brother-in-law and perhaps Ephraim's death was where it all began.

In whatever way the message was delivered to her, Elizabeth Hewitt was expecting to meet her husband that day, not a flatboat carrying his body or a messenger announcing his death. What she learned has been lost to time but not so the repercussions of that terrible occasion. After his death Elizabeth turned to Nancy and John Hall for support and guidance. Perhaps they helped her make the difficult decision about whether her husband's body should be transported to Ohio for burial or laid to rest in Fayette County where he died and where he had lived for thirty years. Elizabeth was allowed two months' respite to mourn her husband before she had decisions to make. Then in March 1815 she and Hall took charge of the estate. Within a month his brother Richard and two neighbors appraised his personal estate, and Elizabeth was given a year's maintenance of eighty dollars to care for her family.

Ephraim's sudden death left his widow with extraordinary debts. Unable to pay them, the court ordered an estate sale to wipe out some of the liability. It netted $870 but not everything sold, including many of their finer possessions. Settlers on the raw frontier had little need for silver teaspoons or even a "looking glass." Passed over too, were their Windsor chairs and fancy cooking items such as brass kettles, a three-legged frying pan and a Dutch oven. These items were impractical luxury items to many people who instead bought farm equipment; axes, pitchforks, mattocks and shovels or a singletree—a wooden cross bar to hitch a horse. One man paid a dollar for a froe, an iron wedge used to make shingles. Another needed a grindstone badly enough to pay two dollars more than its worth. The inventory had a sizeable variety and quantity of goods and tools that was unusual at a time when most people were content with a stew pot and a frying pan.[54] The Hewitts were a family of twelve but even so, there were more dishes, fancy cookware and utensils than even they needed. It is evident that much of the inventory was from the Fayette County tavern and was brought to Ohio, perhaps for a similar purpose. Among the kitchen items were two twelve gallon kettles, a five gallon pot, two brass kettles, three Dutch ovens, a baker and three frying pans as well as smaller pots and kettles, many of which were specialty items not found on the frontier or in an ordinary household. Among the items that were not sold was an array of dishes, several coffee and teapots, a tea canister, a pewter ladle and dish, a china mug, candlesticks and two clocks. Also not purchased were crockery bowls, cups, saucers and dishes, some drinking glasses, a saltcellar and pepperbox, and a spice mortar and pestle. Among the livestock that supported their livelihood were a goodly quantity of sheep, pigs and geese. Richard Hewitt bought a white-faced yearling heifer and John Hall purchased a steer, but the family kept the remainder of the livestock. Nancy was enthusiastic about the box of glass her husband bought to lighten their home. Three of Ephraim's horses sold, but the best one, a bay valued at fifty dollars, remained with the family. They also kept seven beds, two of them trundle beds for the children. The family's relative prosperity was revealed in the number and kind of furniture they used. It was common to use a trestle table that sat against the wall around which trunks were arranged for seating during meals. This family had nine Windsor chairs that were styled with broad-seats, spindle backs and narrow curved arms. They had a carpet and two drop-leaf tables that could be pulled out from the wall for meals and folded back to provide more living space. It was evident that the family had achieved some measure of comfort, reached through hard work and an enterprising spirit.[55]

One of Elizabeth Hewitt's problems was that she was debt encumbered. Ephraim bought the land for $2,000, but he still owed money on it when he died. She could not get a clear title until it was paid, and so the administration continued for several years. On 27 Aug 1817 it reached an impasse. Although it was overwhelmingly apparent to everyone else that the property must be sold, Elizabeth did not want to do it, so she and John Hall were relieved of their duties. Next William White became the court-appointed administrator, along with two new appraisers who assisted the already appointed Stephen Colvin (Calvin) to evaluate the remainder of the estate.[56] Fortunately Elizabeth had other assets in the form of payments by Hugh Thompson of Uniontown, and later his widow, to whom Hewitt had sold his 500-acre farm. Thompson's payments were $333 yearly and continued through 1818. However, expenses were eating up the income. As an example, in one of the accounts, the estate was charged $120 for "time and expenses on going up to Pennsylvania to settle up the estate there" and $25 to go to the local county seat five times. In gratitude for his help during those difficult days, Elizabeth gave her husband's silver watch to her son-in-law, John Hall.

While dry court documents do not tell the real story of the family dilemma, it was clear why Elizabeth refused to sell the farm. Not only would her income shrink, but it meant she had to sell her children's inheritance. This she resisted with all her might. However, once it was taken out of her hands, the following year, White sold 148 of the 230-acre tract "sufficient to discharge the debts." This property, on Crawford's Survey #664, adjoined that of her brother-in-law, Richard Hewitt, and in preparing its sale, White had to secure the deed from the sellers. It became a long and laborious effort made more difficult because the original owner was dead, and signatures had to be obtained from his heirs who were six separate families living in four counties. When this was finally accomplished Elizabeth received only her dower right of 81 acres. On 3 Mar 1818 John Abbott was the highest bidder at the auction, paying $14.10 per acre or $1,986.80 total for the land. A new deed was drawn in 1819 to confirm the sale and Ephraim's heirs relinquished their rights to John Abbott for one dollar.

Several documents were drawn up to complete this transaction providing valuable information on this family. The heirs were named, as were the married daughter's spouses. The 2 Sep 1818 deed named Nancy and her husband John Hall; Jacob Hewitt and Elizabeth Hewitt, his wife and first cousin; Ruth and her husband James Woods; Clarissa and her husband Luther Calvin. Under age and single were Sophia, Ephraim, Harriet and Hannah Hewitt. Both deeds named neighbors who bordered the property. Richard Hewitt's name was not part of the larger property sold. It appeared only in the 81 acres that went to Elizabeth, indicating they lived near each other.[57]

Widow's Weeds

Elizabeth took on the black gown of grief and wore it like a badge. After the initial shock she had to gather courage and help her family survive their loss. Abandoned in a place that was not home, and in reduced circumstances, the younger children needed her guidance. While deep in shock herself, she reached deep within for the necessary reserves to build a future for them. Ephraim's death had changed their lives drastically, and it was painful to sell the land but debt had swallowed their assets so that there was no other choice. Most of all it was embarrassing that their personal lives had been laid bare at a public auction. Gone were all of the shawls and shoes and calico and with it the dry goods business. All was gone except for her widow's portion which they could not take from her. Elizabeth was forty-nine years old, away from friends and family, and she had seven children under the ages of eighteen, all daughters but one. Initially she turned to Nancy and Elizabeth and their husbands for help, but after a while she pieced her life together again, and as was the duty of a mother, found husbands for her daughters. Eventually she asked for and found the courage not only to survive but to flourish. That she was honored and respected by her children was evident in that of the six daughters whose children's names are known, all but one named a child after her.

Amongst the tears and the murmurs of sympathy, along with dark dresses and whispers on the doorstep, a romance had blossomed. Named after her mother and grandmother, Elizabeth was their second eldest child and twenty years old when her father died. Over the generations a story was passed down in the family that "she was engaged to marry and when her sweetheart asked for her hand in front of her, in a fit of pique she married her cousin," Part of the story is true, she did marry her first cousin Jacob Hewitt, son of Richard. No formal record of their union was found and oddly, she was the only one of Ephraim's children who did not have one. They sealed their bond with the birth of a son on 10 Nov 1815. Named Richard Davis Hewitt, he carried the name of two grandfathers, and that of his great-grandmother, Ruth Davis.[58]

Theirs was also a marriage between two families who shared a bond of grief, one that might have bridged the growing gap between Richard and his sister-in-law, Elizabeth. Or perhaps Ephraim's death caused ill feelings between them, some that finally reached the point of high drama. The negative undercurrent between them was apparent to the family, and soon after it became public knowledge. Some questions arise naturally about why Richard was so uninvolved in his brother's estate. Although time has hidden the details, several incidents set the scene. After living apart for twenty years the two brothers were reunited, only to be wrenched apart a few months later. Left to pick up the pieces were the two who loved him the most. To complicate matters, Elizabeth and Richard were newly bound by their children's marriage, and perhaps therein lies the cause of their discord. Within two years after Ephraim died, the relationship between them deteriorated to the point that they ended up in a court of law. Two events happened at about the same time.

Richard was strong-willed, temperamental, and never reluctant to express himself, while Elizabeth was impulsive and sometimes let her emotions get the better of her. Their clash came sometime before Aug 1817 when Elizabeth sued him for slander. At that point, William White took over her duties as the estate administrator. How Richard offended his sister-in-law is unknown, but she went to court asking for $1,000 in damages. He did not show up, so a special jury was convened and by default she was awarded $583. While blaming his non-appearance on "the pressure of business," he was probably stalling because he did not have the money. However, he took the action seriously. By that December he had hired an attorney who asked that the case be reopened and the judge agreed. On 3 Feb 1818, a month before their court date, he was feeling desperate. He appealed to a William Hewitt, relationship unknown, for a loan of $500, and a lien was placed on 50 acres he owned.[59] Three weeks later he went to court again and swore that he had delivered a "case of drawers" to William as a good faith gesture toward the loan of another $800. With the second loan, a lien was placed against his house, livestock, farming implements, furniture and household goods, everything but the land on Straight Creek.[60] In less than a month Richard Hewitt had mortgaged nearly everything he had for the enormous sum of $1,300. In March 1818, the feuding Hewitt in-laws had their lawyers appear before the judge, who upon hearing the argument dismissed the case and the previously awarded damages.[61] Court records relayed the action and the reaction, but what cannot be explained in this way was how Richard had offended Elizabeth, and what brought them to such a state of animosity that they made their argument public.

The Hall and the Hewitt families were tied to one another in many ways, and a rift between them caused ripples throughout the family. Elizabeth Hall was Richard's sister-in-law, but Phebe Hewitt was John Hall's sister, and he was married to Elizabeth's eldest daughter, Nancy. Whatever happened in one household rocked the other family. In many ways Phebe was the woman in the middle, but it was her husband who had to repair the damages. Elizabeth was publicly humbled when the case was dismissed making it seem frivolous and vindictive. Their sorrows were caused by Ephraim's death, and anger was their weapon. They had counted on his presence in their future, and each had their hopes and dreams shattered in a minute. What seemed clear was that Elizabeth's heightened emotions evoked an all-encompassing need to protect herself and her loved ones whatever the cost.

Elizabeth never remarried. Perhaps no one could replace Ephraim in her heart. The more practical view was that she had too many daughters who needed husbands and no dowry to give them. Her assets were limited to an 80-acre farm and all the responsibilities inherent within. With few choices, she relied on tenacity and resourcefulness to see her through, becoming yet another example of the strength of pioneer women facing impossible odds. On 24 Jun 1826, Elizabeth signed her property over to Elizabeth and Jacob Hewitt for their use during her lifetime.[62] By 1833 she was 67 years old, and with the marriage of all but her youngest daughter Hannah, to men from the neighborhood, her duties as a mother were nearly complete. New to the community in 1815, the tragedy that befell the family eighteen years earlier strengthened the bonds between this mother and her children, so that in the years following they supported and comforted each other as only those who suffered loss at a critical juncture in their lives would understand. Elizabeth probably died in early 1833, because on 18 April 1833 Jacob Hewitt passed the land to another family member, William Masterson, for a dollar.[63]

The land Ephraim and Elizabeth chose for their home also had an historical context. Not long after Elizabeth sold it to John Abbott, the land was initially selected in 1818 as the county seat. However, at the same time there was a campaign to have Ripley named instead. It was the largest town in Brown County and thought to be a better choice although it was not centrally located while the Hewitt/Abbott property was. At least one term of court was held there before the honor was given to Ripley and this small piece of Brown County history faded into oblivion. A county historian described the spot as "a place on the east side of Straight Creek near where the state road from West Union to Cincinnati crossed that creek."[64] Another writer described it this way.

> The Pleasant Township portion was just south of where
> Straight Creek enters the township, on the Charles Abbott
> place. Bridgewater was the name given to the embryo city,

comprising one hundred acres of land, forested, but platted and staked. A term of court was held here in the solitude, in a hewed-log house; a deserted cabin, which had stood on the Fielding Martin place, a half-mile to the westward, had been hastily torn down and removed to the seat of justice one Saturday, roofed on Sunday, and the following morning, was in readiness for the tribunal that issued its mandates of law from the midst of most dismal surroundings. But one term of court is said to have been held here...and the virgin forests, preserved intact, bore no evidence that this locality had once been the seat of justice of a populous and wealthy county. (*See footnote 66*)

Because of that long ago decision, this township has retained its rural splendor. It would have been vastly different had it become the seat of commerce for the county. Some of the property remained with Hewitt descendants for a number of years according to Godfrey Bohrer and his cousin William McGroarty, both Hewitt progeny. A statement referring to it stated that "Dr. Godfrey Bohrer, [is] our next to the oldest living relative at this time, and who was born and reared on the Ephraim Hewitt farm. To this day the site of the Ephraim Hewitt farm is known as 'The Old County Seat.'"[65] After moving it to Ripley and building a courthouse in 1820 the search for a permanent site for the county seat continued. Finally after much debate and many offers to donate land it was moved to Georgetown. On 12 May 1821, James Woods offered the county ten and one half acres, "reserving a half acre to surround my house that is on said land." From the proceeds received through that sale and the donated land of two others, a permanent courthouse was built at Georgetown in 1824.[66]

The Trials of Richard Hewitt

In the years following the death of his brother, Richard Hewitt had a downturn of his own. Elizabeth's lawsuit, although dropped, reverberated through both lives and may have altered their relationship forever. Perhaps he wandered in an undiminished void for a while, frozen in time as the years made their inevitable march forward. At some point he awoke deep in financial trouble or at least in need of a large sum of money. He often appeared in the common pleas court with relatives either bailing him out of debt or suing him for money he owed them. However, one of his long series of court appearances was made to secure a clear title to his farm. It was his greatest and most valuable asset although he laid it on the line several times as collateral for a loan. Just after his sister-in-law received the deed to her portion of that property, Richard began the long and laborious process of securing a deed to his original 100-acre purchase on Crawford's Survey #664.

Edward Hall and the two Hewitt families all settled on land to which they had no clear title. Property is often lost that way but they were more fortunate than others and eventually received a clear title to the land. However, it was not gotten easily, and what ensued was a series of lawsuits seeking general warranty for those who had property on John Crawford's Survey #664. After twenty years some of the original, as well as the second owners had died, so it was a long process. However, information about family relationships that could not be obtained elsewhere was revealed in these documents. When Richard Hewitt went to court on 16 Jul 1819, he explained that when he bought it in 1797 from Stephen Colvin and Bernard Thompson, they had not transferred the title from John Crawford, for whom it was surveyed, and that both men died before doing so. By 1818 the land was further divided amongst their heirs who held the title. Hewitt needed a lawyer to untie this Gordian knot, and he hired a man to find the heirs and get a general warrantee to the property.

It was a costly and lengthy procedure, lasting more than a year. Repeatedly Hewitt's attorney went to court while the sheriff reported that the heir had eluded him, and each time a sheriff turned up empty-handed the judge threatened the non-appearing defendant with a $1,000 fine. After visits by the sheriffs in five counties, an heir was finally found. In June 1820 John Colvin admitted in court that his father sold land to Hewitt and was paid for it. Colvin never gave Hewitt a warrant, and his defense was that before he could do it, Thompson died. On 26 Oct 1820, Colvin the son, promised to make Hewitt a valid deed by the following January. He was assessed court costs and Hewitt's lengthy search for justice was over.

Phebe Hewitt was probably not a silent partner to her husband's activities, but he handled their affairs, and since he did no more than mortgage their property, her consent was not required. She was, however, linked with him in her family's efforts to secure a deed to their land, also on Crawford's Survey near Straight Creek. During the process of seeking quiet title to the land her father, Edward Hall, died. Because several documents were filed at around the same time, his death can be pinpointed to between 12 and 20 May 1820. Phebe died after June 1821, when when she was named in her father's deed, but before March 1827 when her husband wrote his will and did not name her as his wife. She probably rests in a family graveyard on their farm where Richard joined her shortly thereafter. If it was fenced and marked at the time, it has not survived the years.

Perhaps when Hewitt borrowed money it was for improvements on the 90 acres he had under cultivation, or for equipment to run the farm. His land was near a creek and it had a mill seat, a structure about twenty feet square erected to designate its future use as a mill.[67] An 1827 newspaper advertisement described his farm, saying that 60 acres was uncleared but lay on well-timbered land with excellent soil. The land where he lived had "three-hundred apple trees and a variety of other fruit trees, a good barn, an excellent log house and kitchen, and a never-failing spring."[68] The farm was too large for one man to run, and it probably included crops other than his orchards. His sons lived on the land as adults and undoubtedly they all worked together to plant and harvest crops. His will disclosed that Richard Junior lived on the farm after he married and was cultivating part of it.[69] Between court visits Richard continued serving as a township officer and as a supervisor of the highway. His reports to the county in 1823 and 1825 survived and they revealed that for his services he received fifty cents.[70]

On 12 Feb 1824, Hewitt put a notice in the local newspaper saying, "The public are hereby cautioned from taking by assignment or otherwise, a note signed by me in favor of W[illiam] Hewitt for $260 as the said note was fraudulently obtained from me. I am determined not to pay the same unless compelled by law, Richard Hewitt, Senior."[71] Perhaps it was in addition to what he borrowed in 1818 during his sister-in-law's slander suit. Regardless of the reason, on 7 Feb 1824 Richard returned $500 to William Hewitt on a loan made six years before, and the lien against his property was removed.[72] Possibly the lesser amount was deemed uncollectible and William was satisfied with payment on the earlier loan, because he forgave the later debt responding that "With consent of Richard Hewitt, Senior I dissolve and revoke and make void every contract which I have made with him as he has given me satisfactory consideration."[73]

Not a month passed and Richard was again looking for money. In March 1824 he went to Warren County with his youngest son, Eli, to ask John and Nancy Hall for $100, again using land as collateral.[74] Hewitt continued to borrow against his property but managed to pay off the mortgages, borrowing only once from each lender. Looking for money, he hit up family members but also his neighbors, as he did in 1825 when he sought a loan of more than $100 from two neighbors.[75] Both mortgages occurred on the same day and each man witnessed the other's transaction.[76]

The Dark Doorway

Whether by insight or design, two brothers changed their family's destiny by bringing them to the Ohio Territory. Because of parental decisions, two sets of cousins grew to depend upon each other, first because of relationship and physical proximity, but then because of marriages to neighbors and to each other. Just as Richard and Elizabeth's disagreements after Ephraim's death caused reverberations throughout their families, when their children grew up their relational entanglement continued to affect them in powerful ways. As the first day of 1827 dawned on Richard Hewitt's family, they were oblivious to the impact the year would have on them. As events took hold an old memory surfaced of the year Ephraim died. When it came, change was sudden and swift, and life turned on its axis, only this time in multiples. Pivotal to the co-mingling of bloodlines between the Hewitt and Hall families were Jacob and Elizabeth Hewitt, a child of each brother, who married and carried their lines forward near the heart of the family. Richard's eldest son Jacob was 35 and his brother Richard was 32 when the year began. Richard Junior was the first to feel the sudden shock of death when his wife died suddenly. The obituary said,

> "Departed this life on 6th [Feb 1827] at 6 o'clock a.m., Edy Hewitt, consort of Richard Hewitt Junior on Red Oak, in the 27th year of her age, after a painful illness of only fourteen hours, supposed to have been a *congestive inflammation of the brain.* She has left a husband and five small children to feel and mourn the irreparable loss of a companion and

> Mother…A funeral sermon will be delivered …by Elder
> Matthew Gardner, on the first Friday in March at the house
> of Richard Hewitt, Senior on Straight Creek at 12 o'clock."[77]

The sudden onset and description of Edy's illness suggested either encephalitis or meningitis. She and Richard married ten years before on 4 Aug 1817 when she was seventeen.[78] Their children, all under age ten were Phebe, Sally Ann, Sophia and Buckner, and one whose name is unknown.[79] Witnessing his son's encounter with death, Richard Senior saw darkness closing around him from another direction. The week after Edy died, he put an ad in the newspaper to sell his personal property including "horses, cattle, sheep, all kinds of farming utensils, household and kitchen furniture, beds and bedding and many more articles too tedious to enumerate." A week later he advertised his farm, noting that it came with an indisputable title.[80] For years, he had mortgaged his land, but this was an outright sale. What brought him to this dark doorway was illness, sadness and debt, but it was a rash decision nevertheless.

At the same time, far too much was happening to Richard Junior. One week he was a father and a husband, the next week he was a widower with five small children. Lost in grief and shock, perhaps he was not thinking about the strange way in which events were unfolding. Beginning on March 2 the family attended memorial services for Edy at his father's house, the next Thursday the house and all its contents was scheduled for sale. In the meantime, his father, very unwell, was writing his will. How Richard reacted to Edy's death was not immediately known but his father's state of mind can be deduced by the structure and number of codicils the will contained. He began writing it on the day of his daughter-in-law's funeral, and when interpreted as a linear document, his muddled thinking was apparent. First, he remembered his sons Jacob, William, John, and Elizabeth, his eldest daughter, who each received a dollar. Richard got his clothing and the profits from the part of the farm where he lived. The two youngest, Eli and Letty Ann, fared best. Eli, the executor, got the farm and all its contents. Philip Buckner, the other executor, who was married to Ephraim's daughter Sophia declined to serve.

Family turmoil was apparent from newspaper advertisements and Richard's will. On 12 Feb 1827 he put his estate up for auction. On March 2, he signed his will with an "X", indicating a literate man who was too weak to write his name. On 5 March, unable to write, he asked his brother-in-law Fielding Martin to sign for him and witness the codicil instructing Eli to give his brother John the bedstead, bed and bedding for his two young sons. In a non-disposable society, clothing was often handed down between generations, and a dispute arose over why Richard Junior got all of his father's clothing. Seeking peace, on March 8, Richard wrote another codicil clarifying a bequest over a black pelisse (spelled perlise) coat belonging to Eli, saying Richard was to have all his other clothing.[81] Then he apologized saying, "I had no right to them when I made my will." On 9 March he wrote an addendum explaining that after he had made his will, his personal property was sold at public auction but that the proceeds were to go to Eli regardless. Over the years, Richard and his sister-in-law Elizabeth probably made peace, because the witnesses were her sons-in-law.[82] He died about 15 March because a memorial service was scheduled on March 20.[83] On Friday 13 April, Reverend Gardner, pastor of the "New Light"

Christian Church in Russellville preached a sermon at Hewitt's home. As Richard was eulogized, the tears and sighs of those in attendance were a final farewell to brother, father, uncle and friend.[84]

Southwestern Ohio where the Hall and Hewitt family settled was called the "Crossroads of the Nation." There beside a crooked little waterway known as Straight Creek, men and women were drawn to sweat and toil as they bent nature's chaos into some sort of order. The creek meanders southward to empty into the Ohio River, but when Hewitt and Hall chose this land in 1797, this small tributary was significant to their success. It pleased the children and grandchildren too, because those who inherited the land remained to care for it, and so reaped the bounty of the rich farmlands fed by this brook so wisely chosen by Edward Hall, his children and his son-in-law, Richard Hewitt.

Chapter Six

COUSINS BY THE DOZENS
Siblings of Jacob Hewitt and Eizabeth Hewitt (1794-1850)

Richard Hewitt and Jarusha Parker
William Hewitt and Dorothy Prickett
John Hewitt and Loramey Curtis

In 1820 Jacob and Elizabeth Hewitt were living in Clark Township, Brown County, with two children. Richard, known as Davis, was five and his little sister Emeline was about a year old. Living two doors away were Luther or "Luke" Calvin, who married Elizabeth's sister Clarissa in 1817, and their son, probably age two. Living in Pleasant Township was another of Elizabeth's sisters, Ruth, who married James Woods in 1816, and their three children, Elizabeth, John and Hannah.[1] Jacob's brother Richard and his wife of about three years, Edy, also lived in Pleasant Township with their two children.[2] By that date, Elizabeth's eldest sister, Nancy Hall, was living in Warren County with her husband John. In all, Richard and Ephraim Hewitt's offspring numbered sixteen cousins, of whom six were married and among them had nine children.

The events of 1827 were life changing for Richard Hewitt Junior who, like his father, was named after his great-grandfather, Richard Davis. In March his father died, but even more shattering, a few weeks earlier his wife died suddenly leaving him a widower with five young children. Edy may have been the youngest daughter of John Welch who had five other children, all named in an 1826 chancery court record.[3] Richard and Edy's children were, not necessarily in birth order, John, Phebe, Sally Ann, Sophia and Eli Buckner Hewitt. Although the pall of sorrow lingered, Richard had a family to support and needed a good woman to help him meet their needs. A family story revealed that after her death "he escorted wagons or freight trains from Cincinnati, Ohio, to Tennessee. While in Cincinnati Richard attended preaching services of the Latter Day Saints and at the services he became acquainted with a 'spinster' and dressmaker, Miss Jarusha Parker."[4]

When she married at age twenty-eight, Jarusha was a spinster although younger than her husband by about six years. With no other prospects barring the way, their courtship was short and they married on 24 Feb 1828.[5] Once again the children had a mother who fixed porridge in the morning and in the evening silenced the darkness as she sang them to sleep. When New Year's Day dawned in 1830, Richard and Jarusha welcomed into the family their first daughter, Mary Jane.[6] Three years later Leah was born. Not long afterward, perhaps as a prelude to leaving Ohio, Jarusha and other members of the Parker family sold a lot in the town of Batavia.[7] Within months they left the county to follow the Mormon enclave to Cleveland where, in 1834, William was born.

The family's migration patterns followed a torturous route as they sought freedom to practice their beliefs in a society that disdained their existence. Because of it, they were not only religious pioneers but also western pathfinders whose lives can be traced in the places they fled and died in pursuit of spiritual freedom.

Richard and Jarusha were among a group of Mormons who went to Missouri in the 1830s but they were destined to continue moving and seeking a place to call home. They were in Jackson County, Missouri, in 1831, but they were driven away two years later. From there they moved to Clay County (now Caldwell), Missouri where they lived until 1838, when they were again forced from their homes and were again on the move. Their names were on a list of Hancock County, Illinois citizens in 1843, indicating they were there when the Mormons were forcibly expelled from the state for their religious beliefs. Next they sought refuge in Nauvoo, Illinois where a petition was written by church elders seeking to redress the "injuries to persons and properties" of those Mormons who were living in Missouri prior to their expulsion. Four members of the Hewitt family were on the 1843 list including Richard and Jarusha, and two of his children from his former marriage. They were Sophia and Eli Buckner Hewitt.[8] Buckner, as the family called him, was listed as a private in the 1846 Illinois State Militia, also known as the Mormon Battalion.[9]

By 1840 when Rebecca Mariah was born, the family was in Fountain County, Indiana.[10] The two youngest children were born in Illinois: Richard in 1844, near Nauvoo, and Letty Ann about 1846.[11] The family moved to Travis County, Texas in 1847 but traveled back and forth between Texas and Oklahoma several times. According to Rebecca, to keep the family together her father worked a variety of jobs other than farming. Sometimes he was a teamster driving oxen; he also helped his neighbors put up hay and he worked in a sawmill cutting timber to build houses.[12]

Sally Ann Hewitt went to Fountain County, Indiana with her father, and in 1841 she married Bailey Robinson.[13] About a year later a daughter, Elizabeth, was born. The following year they moved to Warren County in western Illinois where John was born. Two daughters, Sarah Jane and Alcy Ann, were also born in Illinois.[14] Meanwhile Richard and Jarusha moved to Texas where they were living in 1850. He was fifty-six and Jarusha was fifty years old. Enumerated in the census within three houses were his elder children, Buckner and Sophia, and both were married. Buckner's wife was Elizabeth and Sophia's husband was Enoc Hacksaw, a native of England who was a cooper. Living between Richard and his son was James Welch, who was 48 and probably a relative of Richard's first wife, Edy.[15] In 1852 the family moved to McCoy's Prairie in Oklahoma Territory, where on the busy byroad they rented property to run a transit hotel and cattle corral. The following year after a fall in the river Richard took a chill and was soon seriously ill. He desperately fought a severe cold and fever but alas, he did not recover. Death came on 15 Sep 1853 surrounded by his family who laid him to rest on the Oklahoma prairie near the town of Tahlequah.[16]

William Hewitt, a son of Richard and Phebe, received a dollar in his father's will.[17] Years later he married Dorothy Prickett on 8 May 1836.[18] Three years later, in March 1839, both of them signed a deed to sell two lots in Higginsport, Ohio. Dorothy signed with an "X." and Jesse Prickett, perhaps her brother, signed as one of the witnesses. The other signatory was Jesse R. Grant, the mayor of Georgetown and father of Ulysses S. Grant.[19] When the 1840 census was taken, Dorothy was enumerated without her husband as head of the household, and living with her was a man 20-30 years old, one too young to be her husband. She was between 30-40 years old and lived between the houses of her Hewitt in-laws, James Woods and Eli Hewitt, in Franklin Township.[20] It must be assumed that William died soon after selling the property, as there are no records for him after that date.

In 1824 there was once again a match between the Hewitt and the Hall families when on 19 August Loramey Curtis married as her second husband, John Hewitt, the son of Richard Hewitt and Phebe Hall.[21] Loruhama, as she was also known, was the daughter of Phebe Martin and Uriah Curtis of Brown County. Her grandparents were Fielding Martin and Anna Hall. By her first husband, George Jones, whom she divorced on 10 Feb 1824, she had a daughter Elsa.[22] Thus, with the marriage of Loramey and John, two great-grandchildren of Edward Hall were linked. Standing in as a witness to her union was her brother Gardner Curtis.[23] Two of their children, Eli and Richard, are known through Richard Hewitt's will, because he left his bed and bedding to his grandsons.[24] The couple lived in Pleasant Township through 1830 but were gone by 1840[25] when they followed the Mormons to Nauvoo, Illinois. Perhaps they all left together, Loramey and John, his brother and sister-in-law, Richard and Jarusha, and Loramey's brother, Joseph Curtis. Loramey's father and several of her brothers were on the 1842 Nauvoo tax list,[26] and it is known that John, Loramey and their children were also part of that group.[27]

Eli Hewitt and Mary Masterson
Elizabeth Hewitt and William Masterson
Letty Ann Hewitt and William A. Williamson

Among some of the earliest settlers in Franklin Township, even before the Hewitts moved there, were James and John Prickett and Joseph Abbott. Abbott married Rhoda Masterson in 1805 in Kentucky, where her family lived,[28] and she then moved to his farm in Franklin Township.[29] The Abbotts lived near Richard Hewitt and, as the elder sister of William Masterson, Rhoda's siblings must have visited often enough to get to know their next-door neighbors and thus William and his younger sister, Polly Masterson, had the opportunity to meet their future spouses. With her brother, Eli, posting bond and serving as a witness, Elizabeth married William Masterson on 17 Jan 1826[30] when she was eighteen. Three years later, on 18 May 1829, Eli married William's sister, Mary, or Polly as she as called. William and Elizabeth Masterson lived in Franklin Township near their families in 1830.[31] She was however, not destined for a long life nor to see her children grow up. In 1838, less than a year after the birth of their sixth child, Viola Jane, she died at the age of thirty. Census records indicated that Jane, as she was known, was born in Indiana and it was probably where her mother died.[32] The eldest child, Charles, was then eleven years old[33] and perhaps their father brought them back to Brown County to live for a while with his sisters, Rhoda Abbott and Polly Hewitt, or with a member of the Hewitt family. In 1840 William Masterson lived in Spencer County, Indiana, but ten years later he was not in any state census, and may have died.[34] In 1850 his children, John and Jane Masterson, were living with their aunt and uncle, Letty and William Williamson, in Brown County and may have been with them soon after their mother died.[35]

Richard Hewitt's will showed deference to his two youngest children not accorded to their elder siblings. Eli, the executor, received the bulk of the estate including the farm and land. Letty Ann, just thirteen when her father died, got all the household furniture, but even in his concern was that she was well-married, his fondness for his youngest child shown through the document's legal language.

> "...and to my youngest daughter, Letty Ann Hewitt I give all
> my household furniture, also as much of the rents of the farm,
> from year to year as will board and clothe her genteelly and
> educate her, until she is eighteen years of age, at which time I
> require of Eli Hewitt to pay to her a horse, saddle and bridle
> worth $100, one cow and calf, twelve head of sheep, a sow
> and pigs, a silk dress and other articles, suitable to make out a
> full suit of the best ladies clothes and a genteel suit of clothes
> each year she remains single, and in case he fails to comply
> with the above injunction, she, Letty Ann Hewitt, shall hold
> at her disposal such part of the Land as will make that
> sum."[36]

Letty was the last to marry but she was not in a hurry to do so. On 6 Oct 1840, when she was about twenty-six, she married William Ann Williamson, son of William and Ann Terhune Williamson of Fleming County, Kentucky.[37] Once again it seemed that extended family members provided the opportunity for these two young people to meet. When William Williamson, father of the above-mentioned young man, moved from Kentucky to Illinois to live with another son, he left William behind in Ripley, Ohio, in the care of his sister and brother, Mary and Samuel Williamson, who lived together with their parents,[38] William and Halena Williamson.[39] They all lived in Franklin Township, as did Eli and Polly Masterson.

Although separated by distance, a repeated theme in the Williamson letters was their effort to maintain close family ties. Another was an ongoing search for good farmland that for some of them was a greater struggle than for others. The earliest letters were written prior to William and Letty's marriage, but they established his father's arrival in Illinois to live with a younger son. The first one was composed on 3 Dec 1837 and it began, "Dear Son." He says,

> We have moved from where we did live to Meredosia, a small
> town on the Illinois River six miles above the town where I
> tended ferry.... Seems long since I heard from you and let me
> hear from all my brothers and sisters and particularly from
> your grandmother and direct your letter to Meredosia, Morgan
> County, Illinois. No more at present but remain your
> affectionate father. William Williamson.

The reference to "your grandmother" was to Halena Williamson. The envelope from the next letter written a couple of months later read, "Meredosia, March 4th, Mr. William A. Williamson, Ripley, Brown County, Ohio." The name "S. Williamson" was stamped three times by the post office on the envelope and referred to his Uncle Samuel at whose residence he lived. It began, "February 18, 1838. Your letter of the 12th of January we received the 28th which informed us that you were all in good health." While unsigned, portions referred to William's brother and sister saying, "Richard [Mullins] and Ann [Williamson Mullins] went to see Samuel [Williamson, Ann and William's brother] about two weeks ago. He was then well but Syntha [Samuel's wife] was not very well and expects an increase in their family before you will receive another letter."

The last letter was from Cass County, Illinois. Written many years later on 20 Apr 1862, it was addressed to A. J. Hartman and Mary Williamson, who was William's cousin, the daughter of Margaret (Williamson) Steele and Albert Hartman. The letter spoke of several members of the family:

> Jane Masterson is in Sangamon County teaching school. She gets $20 per month. She has taught the winter term and then came home one week and M. E. [Mary Ellen] and Eli is gone to take her back. She commences the summer school tomorrow morning for which she gets the same wages and I think she has the next winter term engaged. Eli is still at home and helps me to farm. He is very stout and heavy. His common weight is 190 lbs. He is not fleshy but rawboned. Mary E. is tolerable fleshy and as near the build of Uncle John's Mary as anybody I can compare her to. Letty Ann still has the "dispepsy" though not so bad as she used to. I have never been to say sick one hour since I have been in Illinois.[40]

Jane Masterson referred to in the letter was Letty's niece, child of her sister Elizabeth who died when Jane was about a year old. Before moving to Illinois, in 1850 the Williamsons lived in Batavia, Ohio, on a farm owned by Letty's brother Jacob. Living with them was their son Samuel who was nine, Mary Ellen aged six years and Letty's nephew and niece, John Masterson who was seventeen, and his sister Viola J[ane] Masterson, eleven years old. As indicated by the 1860 census, Jane was twenty-one but she continued living with her aunt and uncle until she married. Within a few months of the above letter Jane got married to William Boyd on 17 Jul 1862 in Cass County, Illinois.[41]

As the youngest children in a large family, Eli Hewitt, Elizabeth Masterson and Letty Williamson seemed close. It was particularly true of the sisters, because even though it was a common occurrence to split children among the family when a parent died, it was also the proof of devoted siblings. They were also favored children whose father significantly rewarded them in his will, because when it came time to divide the wealth, he did not. Instead he gave it all to Letty and Eli, legalizing his bequest by giving the others a dollar each. However, lest he be considered unfair or infirm in his old age, there were likely good reasons for this decision. First, the elder children could have received their fair portions in a cash gift as they married. More importantly, Hewitt knew that dividing the land would diminish its value greatly, particularly with so many children. In choosing to give Eli the farm, he seemed to be repeating his father's wisdom in leaving the farm and tavern to his youngest son, Ephraim.

If Richard Hewitt helped his sons acquire land it would explain why he mortgaged his property so often, but that is unproved. However, his responsibility showed through in his daughter's bequest, and he was likely as concerned for his sons. Not long after he died the children began separating. Perhaps it was youthful stretching, but these children of pioneers shared the same adventurous spirit that brought their parents and grandparents to Ohio. Like their ancestors before them, they were searching for that elusive better life as they directed their feet and hearts toward the western sunset. With their siblings' departures, left behind were Jacob and Eli, the eldest and youngest sons of Richard and Phebe Hewitt. It was left to them to fulfill the remnants of the dream that had brought their parents to Ohio some thirty years before.

ELIZABETH HEWITT'S SIBLINGS:

Nancy Hewitt and John Hall

Elizabeth's elder sister was Nancy Hewitt. She and her husband, John Hall, lived in Pleasant Township where he had a distillery, a "horse-mill" for grinding corn and a small store.[42] When Ephraim died, Hall owed his father-in-law thirty dollars, so he may have become a merchant by default because he bought most of the dry goods from Ephraim Hewitt's estate sale. However, because of this purchase at least part of his shop had ladies shoes and practical fabrics like calico, apron check or buckram that ladies wore under their skirts to make them full. He also had ladies' cotton shawls for daily wear and fancy evening shawls of silk, and some with overall patterning or fringe all around. For his personal use he bought a silk handkerchief and some hand brushes.[43] Not long after Ephraim's estate was settled the couple left Brown County and moved to Turtle Creek Township in nearby Warren County, Ohio.

John and Nancy Hewitt Hall had a unique place in the family, a double relationship in which Nancy was Richard Hewitt's niece by birth but became his sister-in-law when she married his wife's brother. When Ephraim Hewitt died a month after their marriage, their complex relationship was soon apparent. After his brother died, Richard began fighting with his sister-in-law placing the newly married couple in an awkward position because John was an estate administrator. He relinquished that duty, and by 1816 he and Nancy were living in Turtle Creek Township where Nicholas Devore moved about a year later. In 1817, Devore and his wife Mary Hall, who was John's sister, sold prime real estate on on Straight Creek for $1,000 and moved to Warren County.[44] Although both couples lived in Warren County, their circumstances were not the same. John farmed there between 1816 and 1826, but by 1820, Devore was a widower without property, living in a nearby Shaker community.[45]

In April 1821, John Hall went to court to seek clear title for 100 acres he owned on Smith's Survey #685 in Pleasant Township adjoining Fielding Martin and Nicholas Devore, husbands of his sisters Anna and Polly. The court ruled for Hall giving the original owners three months to produce a general warrant. Following that was Devore's action.[46] Later that year in July, Fielding Martin sought a warrant for his portion of the same tract. Mentioned within were John Hall and Devore's children, each identified as the heirs of Edward Hall. In 1823 Hall sold 173 acres he owned in Brown County.[47]

John was about forty-seven when he wrote his will on 24 Feb 1826. A few months later he died, on 22 May 1826, leaving everything he owned to Nancy and their daughter, Louisa Ann. His Turtle Creek neighbors served as witnesses and administrators of the will. Jacob Longstreth assisted Nancy as executor, and because Hall owned land in Brown and Warren Counties, his will was recorded in both places. However, the Brown County property did not have a clear title so it went into litigation.[48] Furthermore, in November 1827 Joel Martin filed suit against the estate claiming that in 1811 and 1812 Hall sold him 200 acres but never gave him title. Hall had also been involved in a bounty land sale of individuals from Prince William and Loudoun County, Virginia, who owned land in Ohio. That sale was declared invalid because the agents were unauthorized to make the sale, thus Martin sued Hall's estate either for a title or for monies he had previously paid. Eight pages later the judge declared that since the title could not be secured, Martin should be reimbursed from the estate for the purchase price.[49] Then his widow, who had to pay Martin, went after the original owners for reimbursement.[50] Aside from the Brown County land, tax records show Hall owned 92 acres in Turtle Creek Township.[51]

Perhaps Nancy moved back home again after John died so that Louisa could be near her cousins. Sometime in the early twentieth century, a descendant interviewed family members about Nancy Hewitt Hall and learned that she married again a few years later. Her second husband was John Holmes whom she married in Brown County on 9 Sep 1829 then went to live with him in Lemon Township, Butler County, Ohio.[52] Holmes was both older than she and appeared to have a family, so probably both were marrying for the second time.[53] Probably about 1842 Nancy's daughter Louisa married a man from Lemon Township, John Dickey, who was about sixteen years older than Louisa Ann who in 1850 was thirty-two years old. Among their several children in 1850 was a five-year-old daughter who was named after her grandmother, Nancy Hewitt.[54]

Ruth Hewitt and James Woods
Maria Hewitt and James Woods
Clarissa Hewitt and Luther Calvin
Harriet Hewitt and Charles Ewing
Hannah Hewitt and Harvey King

Ruth Hewitt's husband, James Woods, came to Brown County as a boy in about 1803 and settled with his family near Georgetown. In the ensuing years his father, Allen, purchased land on Lawson's Survey #2523, cleared it of timber and underbrush, and in 1819 laid out the north end of town into lots. The following year Allen built a brick home that was enlarged over the years, and in

1880 became the American Hotel. Following his father's lead, in 1820 James and a partner extended Main Street by adding more lots bringing the total to 138. After donating land to the town, Allen Woods opened a tavern on Main Street with provisions that included a school and a church. Town officers were elected and authorized to sell lots, but progress was slow, at least to Woods' son-in-law, Peter Wilson, who said that when he first moved to Georgetown in 1821-1822, few people lived there and that of the five or six houses begun, including the one built by Allen Woods, none of them were completed.[55]

On 11 Feb 1816, James Woods married Ruth Hewitt in Clermont County.[56] In 1822 they were raising a family in a small log cabin in Georgetown, and when her mother died in the late summer of that year, Elizabeth, the eldest, was eight years old.[57] Six months afterward, with four children to care for, James married her younger sister Maria on 17 Mar 1825.[58] Not yet twenty years old, along with the promise to love and obey, she also agreed to raise her sister's children.[59] Together, she and James brought seven children into this world and raised eleven. In 1840 the couple had seven children living at home,[60] and among them were Hannah, Carey and John, children of the first marriage.[61] Elizabeth married George Bohrer in 1832 and in 1840 their home was just a few doors away from where her father lived.[62]

Clarissa Hewitt and Luther "Luke" Calvin married in 1817 and remained in Brown County for about ten years. They owned 100 acres in Pleasant Township not far from where her sister Ruth and James Woods lived. On 13 Apr 1827, they sold 34 acres to Clarissa's brother Ephraim Hewitt and the rest to a neighbor.[63] With over $600 to buy new land, they packed their belongings and accompanied by Luke's brothers, moved to Johnson County, Indiana. They lived briefly in Nineveh Township before settling in Brown County, Indiana, near Spearsville in 1831. While living in Ohio the couple had two children, James and John, and in Indiana four more were born, Sophia, Maria, Jackson and Greenlee. After Clarissa died on 9 Jan 1870, Luke went to live with his eldest son, James.[64] He died shortly thereafter on 16 Sep 1870 and was laid beside his wife in the Calvin Cemetery near Spearsville.[65]

Harriet Hewitt's marriage to Charles Ewing, on Tuesday, 27 Mar 1827 was announced in the local newspaper.[66] Upon marrying into this family, she became part of the Masterson family as well. Charles's mother was Rachel Masterson, who married Samuel Ewing. What his relationship was to Rhoda, Mary and William Masterson has not been determined but Rachel was probably born to an earlier generation. The Ewings remained in Brown County, raising seven children near the town of Ripley. Their birth dates are unknown, but a descendant of Harriet's daughter Louranah, remembered their names as Elizabeth, Jonathan, Louisa, Hannah, Martha and Jennie.[67] Harriet Ewing was 61 years on 1 Nov 1868, and when she died she was buried in Ripley's Maplewood Cemetery.[68]

On 14 Feb 1828 Ephraim Hewitt sold the land he bought from Luke Calvin to Joel Martin for what he paid for it, indicating he was his assisting his sister's move to Indiana.[69] These deeds are the only records that show Ephraim Hewitt lived in Brown County. Another descendant who interviewed family members noted that Ephraim never married and that eventually he left Ohio and died in

Arkansas.[70] This was confirmed in a January 1836 notification that a letter to him lay unclaimed at the post office in Georgetown.[71]

Hannah was Ephraim and Elizabeth Hewitt's youngest child. When her father died she was six years old and did not marry until she was more than thirty.[72] On 15 Dec 1840 she chose as her husband a lawyer named James Harvey King by whom she had two children, William and Elizabeth.[73] An old-timer who was recollecting the subscription schools of that community said his most vivid memory was of a teacher born in 1801 called, "Uncle" Harvey King.[74] "[He was] a very learned and scholarly man [who taught] in the basement of the Methodist church." He recalled that the room had no desks, so the students brought their own chairs and put their books on the floor. Harvey King was the principal of the public school for many years and lived just outside the town limits of Georgetown on the brow of the hill facing State Street. It has been said that the couple left Ohio and moved to Baldwin, Kansas, but when or where either Harvey or Hannah died is unknown at this time.[75]

Life in a Frontier Town

On 8 Aug 1822, when Sophia Hewitt was twenty, she married Philip Buckner, the first doctor to practice in Georgetown.[76] The following year he built a large brick house and wanted to put a large stone by his front door. After asking several people who tried but failed at the task, he found a young man who accepted the job and succeeded. Using a combination of agility and forethought, he moved a three-by-nine-foot rock from the creek and placed it at Buckner's front door. In time he became famous, not for physical strength but for much greater accomplishments. Today the rock and his name, Ulysses S. Grant, are on a commemorative plaque that stands at the gateway to the Confidence Cemetery in Brown County in tribute to the man, the general and the eighteenth President of the United States.[77]

Dr. Buckner was the grandson of a pioneering family from Augusta, Virginia. His grandfather, Captain Philip Buckner, established a town in Bracken County, Kentucky, from a bounty land warrant he received for Revolutionary War service.[78] Dr. Buckner began his medical practice in Brown County but later moved to Hamilton County where he became an esteemed Cincinnati surgeon. However, some statements made about him, as well as incidents in which he was involved, provide insight into the man, his relationships to others, and the difficulties of being a frontier doctor. Examples from the town newspaper were especially enlightening. In *The Castigator*, Dr. Buckner was referred to as "a surgeon of skill and daring unprecedented in that day." Another statement claimed, "he had a remarkable record for performing major operations which he described in lectures before the Ohio Medical Association." He was evidently a man of passion as well, having given vent to it one day, and consequently he was charged with assault. Buckner went to court on 24 Feb 1824 and both parties to the fisticuffs were found guilty and fined.[79]

Buckner was a physician and surgeon in the Pleasant, Franklin and Clark townships but his patients did not always pay on time. In December 1826 his troubles were described in the newspaper where he demanded that all bills due him had to be paid or payment attempted by Christmas. Pleading considerable debt of his own, he complained that should bills not be paid, his property was "liable to be sacrificed." Like other professionals in the community he accepted barter for services and agreed to accept payment in produce or livestock, adding that anyone who did so would be doing him a kindness. However, he added that if not paid he was compelled to enlist the law to enforce collection. A year later he put up another notice to his patients, this time with a softer tone. He ended it by saying, "Necessity alone compels me to the above course; it is not to distress my customers but to enable me to pay my indulgent creditors. I am willing still to take country produce, such as can be agreed on mutually."[80]

P. J. Buckner was a man of many interests and, following in a family tradition, he had a large farm from which he annually shipped products to market at Natchez and New Orleans. This enterprise enhanced his medical practice, enabling him and his wife Sophia to live comfortably. It also benefited him when his patients paid with livestock because it could be sold at market and the produce could be eaten on the way. To prepare for a trip down the Mississippi, he had boats built on Straight Creek onto which he loaded wagons and when ready they moved down the creek from Ripley to the Ohio River where they were launched.[81]

Dr. Buckner's character, and his appearance to others was questioned because of a disagreement with local attorney, Thomas Hamer. Their dispute went from the streets to the editorial pages of the newspaper, so that those neighbors who did not know him well before, soon learned more then the wanted to know about each man. It began in late summer when Buckner wrote an editorial regarding something boiling and roiling inside him for a while. When Hamer responded, it was with a combination of broad humor and the "slings and arrows" representative of the day's popular language. Then as now, some local "rags" used editorials more to sell newspapers than to bring a measured response to community concerns, or to resolve neighborly disputes.

Hamer didn't build up slowly but ripped into Buckner with raucous abandon, beginning by addressing him as "your worship." His physical description of Buckner set a cartoonish tone as he accused him of swelling up with pride, "putting on airs and trying to ape the gentleman, cocking your hat on one side, brushing your large whiskers forward, looking big and assuming a terrible aspect and thundering voice." Then, dripping with condescension, Hamer continued his diatribe by addressing the issues. First he responded to being called "two faced" by saying they might still be friends if Buckner possessed more common sense and less vanity, then revoked that statement by saying that friendship never existed between them. He blessed Buckner with his insight by saying, "friends are scarce with you and me both in this country but you have not the sense to distinguish between friendship and intimacy. You think every man who does not throw brickbats at you in the street …who converses freely and treats you with politeness and attention, is a friend and must consequently be blind and dumb to all your follies, weaknesses and frailties." After that blast he fueled the fire by bringing up fifty dollars that

Buckner owed him and went on to describe how he had to turn the debt over for collection. Hamer then answered Buckner's attack on how he was currently handling a court case and about money he owed James Woods, who was the doctor's brother-in-law. Hamer responded by saying, "this is a pitiful attempt on your part to create difficulty between me and Woods but it has failed." Then he fired back with "Why don't you pay James Woods what you owe him yourself and not trouble me about my dealings with him? I suspect you owe him $300 from what I know of your contracts."

Hamer sometimes put an anonymous column in the newspaper called the "Spy." He wrote, "Spy has called you a fool and a bankrupt and charged you with being in debt, you say. The first two you do not deny, and I shall not do it for you for fear I shall not be believed by those who know you." He continued,

> Spy did not name your indebtedness as an objection to your being a commissioner. He charged you with want of judgment, with buying things you did not really want, with extravagance, with making foolish bargains and thereby involving yourself in debt. He doubted your fitness and capacity of making contracts and to disburse money for the county from the manner in which you manage your own concerns.

Not content with an attack on his financial problems, Hamer sought to bring Buckner to his knees by attacking him in his profession, saying,

> "If you would attend to your practice; read and endeavor to qualify yourself for it, and lay by a great deal of your vanity and some of your supercilious airs; learn to tell the truth on all occasions and remember that there are some others in the world as good as you are, and a few who know nearly as much, you might in time become a tolerably decent fellow."

Hamer then sought to finish off his opponent with a final thrust of the sword again aimed at his profession by warning,

> "rest assured sir that whenever I hear of your giving 150 or 200 grains of calomel to a patient [with] typhus fever in twenty four hours I will denounce it as dangerous and an unauthorized mode of practice." Then, "when I hear you saying about the time your patient is expiring that you had given him mercury enough to salivate a horse, I will remark that if some other physician had attended on him...the poor fellow might still have been alive."[82]

At the time of this rejoinder Hamer was twenty-six years old and a recent appointee to the state legislature for Brown County. Elected again in 1829, he was chosen speaker of the House of Representatives. Buckner was about five years older and an established physician in the county. Both men were destined to serve their communities in an important capacity. As contemporaries they were probably intellectually well matched but were, however, not temperamentally suited to be friends.

This form of expression was a nineteenth century example of the term "freedom of the press" and of the rollicking days of early newspapers in Ohio. It was also an example of why so many of our ancestors ended up before a judge defending their actions. Finally it is an illustration of how members of two of the highest professions in town—one a lawyer and future congressman and the other a surgeon—rather than brawling in the streets, instead brandished words like swords in the press. Swaggering in front of each other while letting the public in on the display, they did it—not with fisticuffs but with words—sniping and carping at each other until one or the other gave up and called it off.

Sophia and Philip Buckner remained in Brown County until about 1847 but then moved to Cincinnati where he was a professor of obstetrics at a medical college in the city. Their daughter, Matilda, first attended school in Georgetown and later in Cincinnati where prior to her marriage she studied at Wesleyan Female College. When she married Robert Higgins she returned to Brown County where she and her husband raised eight children. Matilda's parents stayed in Cincinnati, where sometime prior to 1853 Dr. Buckner was appointed an associate professor of surgery at the College of Medicine. He died that year and was buried in Cincinnati's Spring Grove Cemetery. Beside him also rests his wife of many years, Sophia Hewitt Buckner.[83]

Thomas Hamer and P. J. Buckner were responsible, leading citizens of the community but in one way they were not unlike their neighbors. Most of the early settlers were plain men and women of good sense who had little more than a practical education. Some, especially the women, were adept at the spinning wheel or behind the plow, but could not sign their names. They worked hard but their lives included few intellectual and cultural refinements to soften their brows. Even basic reading materials were scarce in the earliest days, although nearly every household claimed a Bible. For those who could read, the local newspaper sufficed as their weekly brush with literature. The county papers were bereft of much more than local politics, wars in Europe and sales by the sheriff of delinquent properties. Any musical entertainment available was provided from within the home should the man of the house play the fiddle or a harp. Lacking finer entertainment, "men engaged in rude, coarse and sometimes brutal amusements. Public gatherings were often marred by scenes of drunken disorder and fighting." They had ready access to rye or corn whiskey, the common man's drink, and every neighborhood had a still. Some neighborhoods had more than others as relayed in an account stating that at one time there were more than twenty-four distilleries in the Georgetown area. Whiskey "was kept in the cupboard or on the shelf of almost every family and sold at all the licensed taverns…The early merchants advertised that good rye whiskey, at 40 cents a gallon, would be taken in exchange for goods [and when] houses and lots were offered for sale [that] flour or whiskey [was] taken in full payment. It was hospitable to offer the bottle to a visitor." In no other place in this early history were the sorrows of drinking more evident than through court records. Although the language was formal, scenes from revelry to brutality were played out in words and consequential punishment was described. Names familiar to this family history were listed along with a variety of insults and assaults they foisted upon one another.[84] As an example in 1818 Clarissa and Ruth Hewitt's husbands, Luther Calvin and James Woods, got into a fight and ended up in court. Calvin lost and was charged with assault. The following year, a man was indicted twice, once for assaulting Richard Hewitt, and then for "engaging in fisticuffs" with John Woods three weeks later. A year later another man was indicted for selling whiskey without a license to William Hewitt.

In 1820 one unfortunate man was indicted for betting at cards with James Woods, and winning. The offense was paid off in whiskey, which Woods probably then sold in his tavern. Woods got in trouble several times between 1818 and 1822. His first offense was assault for once again fighting with his brother-in-law, Luke Calvin. It appeared that neither James nor his father, Allen, kept up their tavern licenses because both were indicted at different times for selling whiskey without one. Perhaps James mended his ways for a few years because he stayed out of court until 1834, when he was charged with playing and betting at poker but was found not guilty. However, in 1840 he was charged with assaulting and shooting at George Bohrer, his son-in-law, but again was found not guilty and the case was discharged. Bohrer must have been on a tear because a few months later he was accused of shooting a man with intent to kill although later he was found not guilty of the charge.[85] The accusations and offenses presented here were those which happened between the Hewitt family and their in-laws and they represented only those instances of committed violence that were brought before the courts. Much more occurred behind closed doors and never reached the magistrate. In the words of a county historian, "The backwoods age was not a golden age."

Elizabeth Hall Hewitt

After purchasing Elizabeth Hewitt's farm in 1818, John Abbott brought her into court twice again, in 1819 and then in 1823, to ensure that the deed was valid. As has been shown previously, the widow Hewitt stood up for herself. In 1826 she sued her son-in-law and nephew, Jacob Hewitt, for the use of Luther Calvin, also her son-in-law, claiming damages of $200. Jacob's father paid the debt plus damages, perhaps because he had once faced the wrath of his sister-in-law himself. After that the ladies got involved when the executors of John Hall's estate sued Elizabeth Hewitt for $600 in debt and damages—that is, Elizabeth's daughter Nancy sued her mother. Represented by their attorneys, Elizabeth lost the suit and had to pay half the court costs. Not to be undercut by her daughter, she filed for an appeal.[86]

Most of the events detailed above were in the year and in the days leading up to significant changes in the various Hewitt households, a warning perhaps that thunder was rumbling both in the heavens above and below on the ground. On one tumultuous day in particular, 5 March 1827, two activities played out simultaneously through a will and a deed. That day as Richard Hewitt was writing his will, William Masterson, newly married to Richard's daughter, Elizabeth, paid $100 for a quitclaim deed to Elizabeth Hewitt's property, the same property allowed her as dower right after Ephraim's death in 1815. Some but not all of her children signed the deed. Those who did were Luke and Clarissa Calvin, Ephraim Hewitt, and James Woods, who signed for both his deceased wife, Ruth, and his current wife, Maria Hewitt Woods.[87] Those who did not sign were Nancy Hall and Sophia Hewitt Buckner, and Elizabeth, wife of Jacob Hewitt. Although, both were over twenty-one, Elizabeth's two youngest daughters, Harriet and Hannah Hewitt, also did not sign the release in 1827. Their signatures appeared several years later on 6 Jun 1832, when as married women they signed a quitclaim deed and Masterson gave each couple $25. The names on that deed were Elizabeth and Jacob Hewitt, Harriet and Charles Ewing and Hannah Hewitt.[88] A final transaction was signed on 17 Apr 1833, and Jacob Hewitt turned the property over to William and Elizabeth Masterson for one dollar, thereby nullifying the transaction made between Jacob and his mother-in-law in 1826.[89]

What significance there was between the two acts has been clouded by family intrigue as well as time. Court documents did not reveal what was happening but, based on later events, there may be a simple explanation. Presumably Elizabeth Hewitt died about that time, and some of her children were entertaining a desire to move away from home. To bring their plans to fruition they had to relinquish their claim on the last remaining property the family owned. Masterson had the money and so he purchased the property, thus keeping it in the family for a while longer. Nancy Hall and Sophia Hewitt Buckner, wife of Philip did not sign and perhaps it was not necessary for them to do so as neither left the state. Their sister Elizabeth also remained in Ohio although not long afterward, she and Jacob moved to Clermont County where they settled on farmland just outside the town of Batavia.[90] Perhaps in a time of change for everyone, the protagonists of the two Hewitt families died about the same time restoring peace to a family fraught with drama that began shortly after Ephraim and Elizabeth settled on Straight Creek next to the farm of Richard and Phebe Hewitt.

The Family Farm

As Richard's eldest son, Jacob was aware of his father's ongoing search for cash. If not directly involved he at least overheard conversations about the difficulties that ensued each time his father mortgaged a property. Perhaps he also assisted his father in managing the farm while searching for other means to make money. Having grown up hearing tales of life within the family's tavern in Fayette County may have prompted Jacob to follow suit, but he had his own approach. In April 1826 he applied for a license to sell liquor in his home and the judge approved it pending payment of a six-dollar fee. Four months later and still not paid, the court fined him a dollar three different times for operating a tavern in his house without a license.[91] Perhaps it made better business sense to pay court costs that were half as much as a yearly license, however, the business may have been more trouble than profit because he never reapplied for a license, nor was he ever again fined. Instead, after his father died, he and Elizabeth moved to the next county. Whatever the relationship between father and son, Jacob experienced his father's death with a painful finality, as did all of his children. Whether passionate or compassionate, measured or undisciplined,

Richard Hewitt was a force to be reckoned with in their lives. While he was alive, it was usually in flux and so it remained until he drew his last breath. Even in his will, Richard's influence lived on after his death.

When he was twenty-four, Eli inherited a large and prosperous farm. This may have been a surprising blow to Richard's other sons, or perhaps they had known their father's wishes for many years. However, shortly before he died Richard's behavior was erratic, putting the farm up for auction, and then giving away what he had already sold. Maybe he was grandstanding because his children reacted negatively to his bequests. If so, it was up to Eli and his sense of diplomacy to mend fences with his siblings. Neither court records nor newspaper articles have been found revealing how the farm was saved from his father's intent. The several codicils to his will were indications of an unsettled and confused mind, and of the infighting between siblings over the pickings of his personal estate.

Nevertheless, Eli got an impressive spread. He followed in his father's footsteps as supervisor of the roads when he took over for William Masterson in 1831.[92] A few years after that, in 1838 Hewitt and his neighbors engaged in a few business deals. Eli wanted to expand his farm and so purchased 79 acres from neighbors David and Eliza Brown, paying them $900. The land was adjacent to Brown's as described in the deed, "beginning at a beech, corner to Richard Hewitt."[93] In 1832, George Bohrer, who was married to Eli's second cousin Elizabeth Woods, built a steam sawmill and a horse mill on the run below his house so that he could grind corn and wheat. In 1838 he bought four acres from Eli Hewitt, and on the property built a brick house and a freestanding still house.[94] Around 1847 Bohrer sold his interest in the sawmill and the following year bought more property from Eli Hewitt.

A historian writing in 1883 described the land in Franklin Township as fertile and level, except along the streams, but said that much of it was worn by being "corned to death." Originally it was forested land with a large variety of trees. When Eli's father chose it in 1796, it was timbered in white oak, beech, hickory and maple trees. Near Straight Creek were walnut, poplar and ash as well as elm and wild cherry trees. The streams were lines with limestone which when crushed and used to surface the roads. The principal crops in the early years were corn, wheat, oats and hay, and for many, burley tobacco. Until 1850 tobacco was second only to corn as a cash crop in the county. While the average yield was 1,000 pounds per farm, in 1850, Eli's tobacco crop was twice that amount.[95] In corn, he had 800 bushels and 150 in oats. The third largest food crop was wheat, yielding 100 bushels. The remainder of the land was given over to potatoes, both sweet and Irish, peas, beans and buckwheat. Eli produced six tons of hay and had ten cows and calves that produced 200 pounds of butter.

His livestock was worth $350 including five horses. He had fourteen pigs and seventeen sheep that produced thirty pounds of wool. The land consisted of 150 acres in crops, and the balance of it, 61 acres, was unimproved land. There was no evidence in 1850 of the numerous apple orchards his father had in the 1820s. In its entirety, the farm was 211 acres, valued at $5,000 and the machinery an additional $150. Of the forty surrounding farms, only three were worth more. Next door lived Silas Abbott who had 3,700 acres in tobacco and

600 in corn bringing its worth to $9,500. Of the other thirty-six farms of lesser value, the least productive was 26 acres with a $700 yield.[96]

Eli and Polly Hewitt were charter members of the New Light Christian Church in Russellville. Its minister, Elder Matthew Gardner, began preaching in Georgetown in about 1822. In his autobiography he remarked that, "There was much opposition from the Methodists and Presbyterians. They did not like to see the Christians taking a start with the town. But this did not prevent the people receiving that religion which has the Bible for its only rule of faith and practice to the exclusion of all sectarian creeds."[97] Officially organized in 1827, the church numbered among its members several of Eli's neighbors, including the families of David Newman and John Abbot. Their first meeting place was a log structure, but eventually the congregation contributed enough materials to erect a brick building. Its interior was truly rustic as the "church was first heated by huge iron kettles filled with burning charcoal," and the "first seats were benches made of tree trunks with wooden pins for legs." To buy the supplies to build it the women in the congregation "traded eggs, butter, carpet rags and other home commodities for nails and hardware."[98] As a member of the congregation, Eli was eulogized similarly to the manner in which his father had been mourned many years before when the church was first organized.

In 1853 Eli Hewitt was about fifty years old. All of his siblings were gone in one way or another. He had outlived his eldest brother Jacob, and Richard who was out west, would die within the year in Oklahoma Territory. William was probably long dead, and John, if alive, did not live in Ohio. His sister Elizabeth had died years before and Letty Ann had left home to live in Illinois with the Williamsons. Except for his wife and children, Eli was alone with the land. He wrote his will on 23 April 1853 and shortly after he died in May it was admitted to probate. He left specific instructions that the farm on Crawford and Smith surveys of about 200 acres was to go to his wife, Polly, the executor for three years. Thereafter, she could live on the western half where the house was, but he wanted her to sell the property on the east side. After her death he wanted the land sold at auction, and his debts paid through the sale of his personal estate or property if needed. Finally, when the farm was sold he wanted it divided equally among his children, who were not named.[99] His decision broke with two generations of tradition, that of giving the farm to the youngest son. Perhaps there was a lesson in it for him that he did not wish to repeat with his own children.

Today the land that Richard Hewitt bought and farmed so many years ago remains the mostly rural farmland it was 200 years ago. Tobacco still grows but not in large quantities, and soybeans have replaced other crops. The summer of 2001 was rainy in Ohio and in late August it was readily apparent. Among the well-kept barns and farmhouses were abundant fields bursting with various shades of green. Purple flowers poked their heads above tall grasses growing along the roadside, and everywhere was the rasp of insects as they went about their business. Lofty trees appeared in the distance surrounding the lush greenness that defined the flow of the creek as it snaked its way across the land. Wildflowers still grow in profusion over fallow ground, waving their heads at the passing breeze, and at passers-by in cars. They waved also at a descendant of the original owner who was walking beside the road looking back in time.

Chapter Seven

JACOB AND ELIZABETH HEWITT
Brown and Clermont Counties, Ohio (1791-1879)

The Blue Shawl

On 3 May 1815, Ephraim Hewitt's personal estate was sold at the home of his widow, Elizabeth. On that spring day, aside from the bereaved family, a crowd of at least thirty-five people gathered at their home—curiosity seekers and bargain hunters alike. Milling among the prospective buyers was her nephew Jacob Hewitt, aged twenty-four and the eldest son of Richard Hewitt who was there also. He got to know his aunt's family when they moved from Fayette County, Pennsylvania a year before, and he was there to console them when his uncle died. Looking around, Jacob noticed that aside from the Hewitt family, the bidders were neighbors, people he had grown up knowing. As the sale got under way, his father made several purchases, buying a heifer then a waffle iron for less than its $2.50 value. Jacob mostly bought practical things, a couple of hoes and a saw, but he also bid on an item that was completely frivolous. It undoubtedly struck his fancy because he paid too much for it, suggesting there was another bidder who also wanted a ladies blue shawl. Bought on a whim, it was for his bride, Elizabeth, who probably stood beside him as he upped the ante for the object of his desire. Upon raising his hand to claim the prize, with a little knowing smile upon his face he looked into her eyes as he wrapped it around her shoulders. By then he was aware she was carrying their first child due to be born in November near his birthday.[1]

When Elizabeth Hewitt and her cousin Jacob met in 1814, he was back from service in the War of 1812 and she had not yet turned twenty. He was the eldest of seventeen cousins and she was second eldest in her family. It was an erratic but exciting time as the two families came together in one place for the first time and it was inevitable that these two would become friends. What their families were not prepared for were the consequences that followed, when after her father died they sought comfort in each other. A diligent search for their marriage record proved fruitless, and was particularly puzzling since their were records for Jacob's siblings and for all of Elizabeth's sisters, including Ruth who married less than four months after Elizabeth's first child was born.

Theirs appeared to be a singular instance of first cousin marriage in the family. Prior to 1850 there were no laws against unions of close degree, although today in Ohio it is prohibited. At some point this couple had to "jump the broom" because of the impending birth of their child. Richard may have faulted his sister-in-law for a lack of attention during her bereavement resulting in her daughter's pregnancy, and it may have been why she charged him with slander and they ended up in court. However, it may have been something else altogether. One advantage in their co-mingling was that each had prior and intimate knowledge of the other's family.   Another was that comparable characteristics and genetic similarities created the attraction but sharing the same goals and philosophy fostered compatibility.

On 10 Nov 1815, the promise of their commitment arrived when Elizabeth gave birth to a son they named Richard Davis Hewitt, in honor of their mutual grandmother, Ruth Davis Hewitt. Not long thereafter, Elizabeth's sisters Ruth and Clarissa married, as did Jacob's brother, Richard.[2] Soon new cousins arrived to greet young Davis, and by 1827, when Jacob's father died, all but the youngest of the Hewitt cousins were married.

The Early Years

As a child, Jacob's life was chaotic but Elizabeth lived with a constant stream of people, strangers mostly, stopping by her home on the way to somewhere else. Her father was a farmer who ran a tavern and inn about three miles from town, and whether gregarious by nature, she was accustomed to the constant blending of family and guests where structured change was the norm. Elizabeth's first big adjustment came when she left her Wood cousins and lifelong friends to move to Ohio. Jacob experienced change much earlier when, propelled by the adventurous spirit of his parents, he moved with them to the Kentucky wilderness before his third birthday. By the age of ten he was living in Ohio, a seasoned veteran of change. Perhaps adventure really was not his style, because until the end of his days he lived within a few miles of the home on Straight Creek where he had spent most of his youth.

When young Davis was five years old his family lived in Clark Township in Brown County, but they moved west into the next county near Batavia shortly after his father died. They remained near enough to visit but had distance enough to build a life away from family scrutiny. Jacob seemed to be on good terms with his mother-in-law because on 24 Jun 1826 he gave her $165 in exchange for the 81 acres where she lived. It was probably a loan secured by the property that Jacob and his siblings eventually inherited. Between 1827 and 1831 he had two lots in North Georgetown worth between $30-$35, and another 60 acres on Straight Creek valued at $139. In 1834 he paid taxes on 40 acres worth $93, so prior to that date he sold twenty acres.[3]

Jacob Spreads His Wings

Batavia Township lies in the middle of the county, and while the town was platted in its flattest area, the outlying areas surrounding it rise into rugged hills of verdant greenery. Running diagonally through the township from southeast to northwest is the East Fork of the Little Miami River, essentially the farmers' source for water but also used as a recreational resource. While much of the soil is clay, the streams that flow into the river continually enrich the topsoil supporting the many well-tilled farms in its bottomlands. The township's first cabins were built between 1797 and 1805, and soon after several sawmills and gristmills were erected to support the community. By 1815, a formal township had been organized from parts of Williamsburg and Ohio townships. Ten years later when the town of Batavia was sectioned and laid out into lots, it had become a community well established in agriculture and commerce.[4] Transportation between villages improved dramatically after road crews constructed a turnpike across the county linking Brown County on the east to Batavia and from there west to Cincinnati.

On 8 Feb 1827, Jacob Hewitt paid $123.64 toward the $300 purchase price of 130 acres of good farmland in Clermont County near the town of Batavia. He was thirty five years old and life there began modestly with a forty-dollar horse and an eight-dollar cow.[5] Davis was eleven years old by then and had four sisters. Emeline was about eight, her sisters Ann and Nancy were five and two years old and Harriet was a baby. Elizabeth bore two other children by 1830, Eliza Jane and then Jacob, named for his father and great-grandfather.[6]

Life in Batavia started out with as many bumps in life as there were in the road to town. Just after buying the farm, Jacob's father died. Then he had a struggle getting clear title to the land, an experience similar to his father's, and just as difficult. He hired an attorney to prove he had paid for the land and thus fulfilled his side of the contract, but that the owner had not produced a deed nor appeared in court to answer a subpoena.[7] The case continued from November 1829 until July 1832 when the owner finally appeared to answer charges, and admitted that Hewitt had paid him, but denied repeated requests for a title. In dispute, however, was fifteen acres Hewitt claimed the defendant sold him but which he denied. In August 1832 the judge ruled that court costs should be split equally, and that the former owner had to produce a warranty for 118 acres and pay Hewitt $38.64 plus interest on the fifteen acres originally agreed to but which he did not receive. For Jacob and his family, on 9 Nov 1832 the dispute was over and the long awaited title was theirs. It was a time to celebrate not only that victory, but on the following day Davis's seventeenth birthday and the day after, Jacob's forty-first birthday.

While seeking legal title to the farm and working the land to feed his family, Jacob also entered into county political life. In 1831, he received a two-year appointment as coroner for Clermont County, a job where he worked in tandem with the sheriff and one wielding the same power. In those formative years of the state's criminal justice system, Jacob's main duty was to hold an inquest over anyone believed to have died by criminal violence and to report his findings to the clerk of Courts of Common Pleas.[8] Records indicated he served in that position in 1831-1832 and again in 1834, and that his counterpart William Curry the sheriff, lived only a mile or two from the Hewitt farm.[9]

Two events occurred marking 1832 as a year the Hewitt family would remember for as long as they lived, but it was a significant year for the community at large. First was the February flood. Over time, the Ohio River near Cincinnati had many destructive floods but the 1832 deluge was recorded in the newspapers as it happened. The river forms where the Allegheny and Monongahela Rivers merge near Pittsburgh, and in those days during the summer months it became lazy and shallow. Sometimes late winter rains or a sudden snowmelt from the mountains coupled with warm temperatures caused the waters to rise dramatically. Occasionally all of these factors occurred at once combining conditions that brought a flood of great significance. A record flood occurred on 18 Feb 1832[10] and the Hewitt family who lived near the Little Miami River was affected but in a less dramatic way. Among the many local newspaper records of the destruction wrought on the city of Cincinnati was that of a young attorney living in the city who documented what he saw. This is a portion of his journal written when the flood reached its peak.

> After reaching its ordinary height (50 feet) when reckoned at full flood, the noble stream as if satisfied with that display of strength, flowed steadily on for a while, without increase or abatement...the Cincinnati Hotel at Broadway and Front Street and the Broadway Hotel, Broadway and Second Street...had 20 inches of water in their bar-rooms...I saw the water pouring into the fourth story of a steam mill reckoning from the top. Newport and Covington were both in a measure flooded...a great part of the former being under water...The Ohio, now swelled to an immense flood, more than a mile from shore to shore and 70 feet in depth, rushed almost without a ripple. The whole quay, lately so dry, was now covered with steamers riding majestically on the bosom of the water, crowded together in close neighborhood...The boats were receiving and discharging their cargo directly on the sidewalk, being lashed, for the first time, I suppose, to the trees which had been planted to shade it...It was sublime. It was a power mighty terrible yet unostentatious. It was simple grandeur, a calm putting forth of gigantic energy.[11]

The second event occurred about six months later when cholera broke out locally bringing death in large numbers. While today it has been wiped out in the United States, in the nineteenth century everyone feared the scourge of cholera. The many deaths in Cincinnati and surrounding areas brought the disease to epidemic proportions, and in an attempt to gain control doctors in Georgetown, among them Philip Buckner, Elizabeth Hewitt's brother-in-law, published its symptoms in the local newspaper. Healing remedies and preventive methods were described in detail to help families cope with the dread disease. Its onset was much like a severe intestinal flu followed by muscle cramping throughout the body. When a patient had expelled most of his bodily fluids, he was rubbed with camphor, or a mustard plaster was applied to his wrists and ankles. Personal cleanliness was prescribed along with fresh air and moderate food and fluids. Patients were encouraged to avoid strong drink since it was supposed to be a "powerful predisposing cause of the disease." These attempts to control cholera seem futile and torturous today, but then it was all that doctors could do for its victims. A point of reality was that one either recovered from it, or passed on as death's chill reached the body's extremities and crept toward the heart. As a counter method to these remedies, it helped to drain stagnant ponds, clean the streets and spread them with quicklime. The newspaper did not give statistics for Brown County, but in nearby Cincinnati at the epidemic's peak there were between fifteen and twenty deaths each day.[12]

Jacob's family appeared to have weathered both the flood and the cholera epidemic without casualties,[13] and because life goes on, that December he purchased two lots in Batavia for forty-five dollars.[14]

The Late Years

In 1834 Jacob paid $500 to enlarge his farm by 36 acres, bringing it to a total of 154 acres.[15] Several years later during a lawsuit the house where they probably lived was described as being a "frame dwelling house on the west side of the road leading from Batavia to Williamsburg about three miles from Batavia." For several years, as he could afford it and others could not pay their taxes, Jacob continued buying lots in town. Each year the newspaper announced the names of those who had not paid taxes for the prior year, often in January, and for several weeks prior to a sale an announcement appeared in the newspaper. One had only to show up at the courthouse doors on those days before the sheriff began the bidding. Many men took advantage of others' bad luck and Hewitt appeared on several occasions looking for a bargain. By 1835 he began turning a profit by selling them. He made $90 that year selling six properties, a gain of nearly three times what he originally paid for them.[16] 1836 tax records provided an estimate of Hewitt's worth, and as indicated he owned ten lots in town valued at between eight and forty-three dollars each, or $326 for all of them.[17] In 1837 the original 118-acre farm was worth $350.[18] Counting it and the additional acreage plus the lots in Batavia, Hewitt's property in Clermont County was worth about $1,100. About ten years later he began selling some of the lots, beginning in May 1846 when he sold a lot that two of his children, Davis and Harriet, witnessed. She signed for a second time on a lot he sold in 1847.[19]

Of all the land he bought, one sale would haunt Jacob Hewitt years after its purchase. When he bought 36 acres to enlarge his farm in 1834, the deed seemed valid. It was purchased from William Parker, whose sister Jarusha was married to his brother, Richard Hewitt. However, a dispute occurred when, Leah Parker, the widow of the original owner, and William and Jarusha's mother, challenged Jacob's right to it. The deed stated that the survey belonged to "James Parker, deceased, laid off for Enoch Patterson and Richard Hewitt," who were married to Parker's daughters, Rebecca and Jarusha. Their claim against the property in 1844 was that one of the heirs had died and his children had not received their share. Hewitt's counter claim was that the grandchildren were not entitled to it because the will stated that deceased man's portion of the land went to his siblings. The judge ruled against Hewitt who tried to have the verdict overturned by a higher court. In April 1848 the Ohio Supreme Court heard the case, but ruled for the Parker family and the suit was dismissed. After paying court costs, Hewitt was ultimately obliged to return a portion of the land to the Parker heirs.[20]

Between lawsuits, Jacob and Elizabeth's children were growing up, and some were getting married. Davis married into the Williamson family, the second in his family to do so after his Aunt Letty Ann married William Ann

Williamson.[21] Jane Williamson was William's half-sister from her father's second marriage to Jane Cochran.[22] Prior to Davis and Jane's wedding on 10 May 1842 in Clermont County[23] they both lived in Batavia.[24] By 1850 the couple had moved to Jackson Township about five miles north of Davis's parents and had four children.[25] Their children, all under age ten, were Samuel who was seven, Ann aged five and Louisa, a year old. John Hewitt was less than a month old and was nameless in the census.

Two of Davis's sisters were married by a justice of the peace within a few years of his nuptials. Dressed in their finest on that special day, Nancy and Eliza Jane probably followed established family customs rather than the formal structure of a church wedding. Weddings were happily attended by relatives who could get there as well as by friends in the neighborhood. A Hewitt wedding in that generation must have been a large affair, since between them Jacob and Elizabeth had eight siblings plus nearby offspring. Nancy wed William Wheeler on 30 Mar 1845, and two years later on 15 Jul 1847, Eliza Jane married George Carter.[26] Those living in either Cincinnati or Brown County might take the stage-line to the wedding as it ran three times a week between Georgetown and Cincinnati, stopping along the way in Batavia.[27] Probable attendees by train were Elizabeth's sister, Sophia Buckner, and her husband, Philip, who by that time were probably living in Cincinnati. Most of Jacob and Elizabeth's siblings lived in Brown County and could have traveled together, whether by carriage or bus. His sister Letty Ann and her husband lived on one of Jacob's farms and probably hosted some of the family during the celebration.[28]

Preceding the event was a flurry of sewing between Elizabeth and her daughters, beginning with a gown commensurate for the occasion. If resources permitted they made other dresses and accessories suitable for the first year of marriage. In addition to fashioning attire for the occasion, they baked, dried, stored and cooked food for the occasion. As the day approached, the air hummed with the flurry of preparations and in the midst of it all guests arrived. Those who came early were undoubtedly put to work, attending to last-minute details. Amidst the washing, sewing and cooking chores there was ample opportunity to exchange family news and anecdotes. In the evening over a little whiskey the men gathered separately to talk about farming, the weather, land for sale or other business interests. With the addition of friends and family of the bride and groom, the house was bursting with celebration. With so many guests around, Davis, Nancy and Eliza Jane and their spouses were feted well into the night before they slipped away. The wedding day belonged to the bride and her family, but the traditional infair on the day after, was celebrated at the groom's home. Richard and Eliza's weddings were in May and June so the event could be held out of doors as they feasted on turkey, roasted pig, salads and homemade condiments followed by puddings, cakes and pies. Later, whiskey was passed around while others played games and danced to the fiddler's tunes, and another day of merriment lasted well into the night.[29] Having come a long way, guests often stayed for both nights and those with extra room put up as many of their relatives as possible, often with cousins sleeping two to three in a bed, while those who could afford it stayed at a hotel in town.

Two of Jacob and Elizabeth's daughters married away from home. On 2 Aug 1848, when Emeline was about twenty-nine, she married Robert Giffin in Butler County, where she may have been living.[30] By 1850 they had moved to Clinton County, Indiana, and in 1860 may have been living there ten years. By that date, Emeline who was forty-one years old had five children, Eliza, who was eleven, then Lucinda, John, Samuel and the baby Thomas who was born in 1859.[31]

Perhaps Jacob Hewitt's move into town coincided with the state of the lawsuit against the Parker heirs, but it also seemed to coincide with a desire to broaden his community role. At a meeting in 1846 the Batavia Township officers appointed him town marshall. Several members of the council lived near Hewitt, including Isaac Worstell, a blacksmith, and Shadrack Lane, a painter. That year James Carter was elected mayor. Other trustees appointed that year had mixed occupations. There was a farmer, a merchant, a shoemaker, a clerk of the court and a surveyor.[32] Hewitt may have taken the responsibility of town marshall so that the lawsuit would not consume him, but it dragged on. Perhaps it was an inappropriate time to embark on civic affairs, because he did not accept a reappointment beyond that first year nor did he accept another position. Two years later it was filled by his son-in-law, William Wheeler, who the following year became Batavia's mayor.[33]

A major disruption to Hewitt and all of those living along the Ohio River in 1847 was another devastating flood, which occurred in December that year. Along with the one in 1832, it was considered to be among the five most destructive floods in the Cincinnati area through the year 1890. While those who lived along the Ohio River grew to expect periodic floods, for two of them to occur within fifteen years of each other must have seemed to Jacob, Elizabeth and their neighbors as if the destructiveness of nature was seeking them out for the most cruel punishment. Waters from the second flood reached sixty-three feet, seven inches, short of the height of the 1832 flood but devastating to the community nonetheless.[34]

In 1850 Hewitt was fifty-nine years old, and according to the census he was a laborer who owned land valued at $3,500. While the facts appear to be at odds with each other, perhaps by that age Jacob had slowed down and was doing odd jobs for his neighbors, picking and choosing as it suited him. A somewhat diminished working schedule would have been possible because he owned farmland he rented out, plus he had income from some of more than a dozen lots he owned in the village of Batavia. Hewitt appeared to have been a conservative man who purchased land, acquiring it over time when there was a bargain in the offing. He sometimes acquired property at sheriff's sales, where it was sold for a fair price but could often be purchased for less than its actual value.

When his father died in 1827 Hewitt, not yet forty years old, had farmland in Brown County as well as town lots in Georgetown. However, once the family moved to Clermont County, they bought land just outside the village of Batavia. An additional purchase of thirty-six acres in 1834 gave Hewitt a farm of a little over 150 acres. Land was the source of his livelihood and his income, but this farm was also the source of much agitation and bewilderment over the years. It must have been worth the effort it cost in money and time, lawsuits and counter-suits, because he never sold it. The cloud that hung over this land became evident within a year of its purchase, and the initial lawsuit in 1828 was not settled until four years later. The family then entered into a period of peaceful existence for nearly fifteen years until the final suit hit them. Hewitt fought like a man possessed to retain the farm in its entirety without having to split it or sell any part of it. Upon losing the suit, he must have paid the plaintiffs in cash because at least until 1850 the family retained the farm in its entirety.

Three of Jacob Hewitt's neighbors on Gray's Survey #1116 in 1840 were Jacob Duckwall, Hezekiah Mount and Charles A. Moore who married into the Parker family that sued Hewitt.[35] By 1850 the township had grown to 734 individuals, giving a clearer definition of their nearest neighbors, but also indicating that Jacob and Elizabeth were living on one of their lots in town. The 1850 census confirmed that Mount and Duckwall had not moved in the ten years between the censuses, but Hewitt, while still within the township, was listed more than twenty pages away in another part of it. His neighbors, rather than listing their profession as "farmer," were a constable, two wagon makers, a shoemaker, a painter and a carpenter, professions that townsmen of Batavia were more likely to pursue. There were three unmarried children living at home with their parents: Ann, who was twenty-eight; Harriet, twenty-four years old; and Jacob, aged nineteen, who was a chair maker. He worked either in Batavia or in the neighboring township of Mt. Carmel where there was an important chair-making industry employing about 30 factory workers.[36] Occasionally, the census-taker counted an individual more than once in the same year, and it happened to Jacob Hewitt Junior. Listed first in his father's house in Batavia, he was counted once more in November 1850 in Union Township living with his sister Eliza Jane and her husband George Carter who worked in the Mt. Carmel chair factory. By then Jacob had turned twenty.[37] The event that caused him to be counted twice changed him from a child into a man overnight.

Dark Waters

On the evening of 20 June 1850, Jacob Hewitt went fishing on the Little Miami River with his son and some neighborhood friends. It was getting dark by nine o'clock, and somewhat separated from their friends, Jacob and his son decided to cross the river in a flatboat to retrieve a skiff on the other side. As they started back across the river, Jacob in the boat and his son in the skiff, the young man heard the sound of something heavy falling into the water accompanied by a slight gurgling noise. He looked around, saw the overturned boat, but could not see his father. He called to their friends for help, but they were too far away to hear. Eventually he reached them, and they frantically called for Jacob. They wanted to help the distraught young man, but it had become too dark to see and he did not answer, so the search was abandoned until the following morning. The newspaper reported the accident but did not name his son, so it may have been Davis but it was more likely his younger brother Jacob who was single. Davis lived several miles away in Stonelick with his wife and four children, one less than two months old so it was not likely that spent the evening fishing with his father and his friends. Whether it was the man or the boy, he was obliged that evening, after much frantic searching, to go to his mother's house and tell her, in the deepest sense of pain and loss, that her husband was drowned and that his body was still in the river.

Someone, perhaps William Williamson, went to Jackson Township that evening to tell Davis about the accident, and then took him to the river to await morning's light. While William informed his sister and his brother-in-law, his wife Letty Ann probably stayed with Elizabeth during the nightmare hours before dawn. At the first sign of light they gathered, family and friends, at the edge of the river watching and hoping while the men dredged its bottom. About noon that day Jacob's body was recovered from about twenty feet of water. Because of severe bruising on his face it was determined that after he and his son started across the river, at some point he fell overboard, and when he tried to get back in the boat he overturned it, striking himself in the head. He was probably unconscious from the blow and unable to call for help, and so he drowned. His son, upon realizing that his father had gone under, may have turned his boat around in time to see his father's craft capsize but was too late to rescue him before he went under the final time.[38]

This was the second time Elizabeth Hewitt's life had spun out of control. She was a young woman the first time that sudden death shifted life's perspective. Then it was her father, this time it was her husband of thirty-five years who was accidentally but irretrievably taken from her life. Enlarging her grief was the pain carried by her son who was unable to save his father that night.

Family history says that Jacob received a Masonic funeral, but there are no records of his service. In August 2001 his grave was discovered in a small private cemetery outside the town of Batavia. Unnamed, and mostly unnoticed, locally it is called the Moore Cemetery, but in 1882 it was known as the "ancient village burying ground," described as "a small enclosure now grown up with brambles and briars, weeds and grass with the untrimmed trees adding to the dingy somberness of the site."[39] More than a century later the author can report that the cemetery is in much better condition today. It is mostly hidden and probably rarely visited because it lies on the high side of the road, and most travelers are drawn instead to the river on the opposite side of the road. The headstones in the small cemetery are remarkably preserved under a canopy of trees that insulate and protect them from the weather, even though some are green with lichen from the damp. Standing guard at intervals are patches of poison ivy ready to strike at the hands and legs of unwary intruders. Summer brings tiny strawberries that weave across and over the carpet of greenery out of which the stones emerge. Walking under the trees on the carpeted floor, the stillness of it feels like a sacred place. Jacob Hewitt's stone was found on the outer edge of the cemetery near the road, lying on its face and broken in half. After turning it over and brushing off debris, the inscription could clearly be read: "Jacob Hewitt born Nov 9, 1791." The stone was severed after the word "died" and the death date obscured. Records stated it was 20 June 1850, and that must be what was engraved on the stone. Below are the words "Aged 59 yrs, 7 mo, 11 da." Jacob's resting place was among his neighbors and friends, most of whom had died before him. Prominent among the names buried there was the Moore family, who were Jacob's neighbors, both in the village and near their farm outside of town. One of them offered their family cemetery as a place for Elizabeth to lay her husband to rest.[40]

Shortly after the funeral the widow put aside her shock and grief to handle the estate administration. Her husband, who was not yet sixty, was in the midst of life and active up to his last days, and his sudden death left business affairs in disarray. A week later Elizabeth became sole executor and Davis paid part of the $400 administration bond.[41] She sprang into action and on 3 July posted a notice requesting payment of debts owed the estate.[42] On the same day the appraisers gave her $150 to begin paying off her creditors.[43] Without cash enough to pay the bills, their personal estate was put up for auction, and once again Elizabeth's life was laid out for all to see. In a way, her married life was the period between two public sales, and it undoubtedly brought back memories of the day Jacob gave her a blue shawl. She thought about their hopes and dreams, and now so many years later, she had a deeper understanding of the wrenching event that threw her mother into widow's weeds.

As the sheriff's sale proceeded the widow was allowed to hold back items from the auction block, and in most instances a family member bought favorite items. Unmarried daughters Ann and Harriet Hewitt bought several things, as did Davis and Jacob Junior, and Eliza Jane's husband George Carter. The Wheelers did not participate in the personal sale, perhaps because they instigated the petition to claim Nancy's inheritance. Emeline may not have attended the auction because she and her husband, Robert Giffin, lived in Indiana.

The estate sale brought $252 against $400 in debts. About $165 was collected from small loans due Hewitt and from property rents paid by his tenants, but that was not enough, so much of their real estate was sold to pay remaining debts, but also to divide the remaining assets between Jacob's heirs. An examination of their personal items revealed how they had lived, what the widow valued and her future needs. While Elizabeth pared down, she had three unmarried children living at home, so took with her three beds and two bedsteads, a table, six chairs and tableware for six people. They had a lot of clothing, some of which was made at home on their spinning wheels and loom. While she sold the farm equipment and some of the horses, she kept their red and white cow, a sow and seven pigs. She held aside a tea set with cups and saucers, and servers that may have been treasured family items. Other personal items not for sale were family pictures, a few schoolbooks, a Bible and a nine-year-old cow. Her children bought two rocking chairs, a bureau with a small mirror, a clock and a tea canister. She also kept Jacob's safe. Ann bought five split-bottomed chairs, a pair of andirons, a meat and soap barrel, a washtub and an old sidesaddle. Elizabeth kept essentials, but she had lived modestly and continued to do so. Davis bought the most expensive items, including his father's horse, a two-horse wagon and two sets of harnesses. He also bought a buggy and a lame sorrel mare, spending about $80 total.[44] The event following the auction was probably the most emotional for the family because it was prompted by one of their own.

Within weeks of Jacob's demise, birds of prey began circling overhead; causing shock waves to a grieving family when there should have been room only for mourning. Except for young Jacob, his children were adults and three were married. Perhaps it was a natural progression that one of them wanted her inheritance, but not within a month of her father's death. On 9 Jul 1850 William and Nancy, nee Hewitt, Wheeler filed a petition naming the widow and her children, and demanded the immediate distribution of the estate. As an historical document, it named and verified Jacob's children as well as the spouses of those who were married.[45]

Aftermath

The family could not fairly divide the farm just beyond Batavia village, so in March 1851 the court ordered a sale and the proceeds divided. The real estate, including the lots, was worth about $3,500, and most of it was sold at public auction, in the same way that Jacob had acquired it in the first place. Since it could not be sold for less than two-thirds of its value, when the 118 acres farm (worth eighteen dollars) sold for twelve dollars per acre, it was a fair price bringing $1,426 for the heirs. The balance of land, mostly lots in Batavia, was either sold or divided between the heirs, with Elizabeth receiving eight lots as her dower right. Davis Hewitt got ten acres near town and two lots in Batavia.[46] The widow's distribution of a block of lots supports the premise they were living in town when Jacob died, but further proof comes from a list of Batavia dwellers as compared to the 1850 census showing that fifty-five individuals match both lists.[47] If Elizabeth remained in town, it was not for long as her children called out for her to join them in Mt. Carmel.

In the aftermath of the tragedy, young Jacob who was twenty had a guardian appointed to oversee his welfare during the estate division.[48] At the personal property sale he bought his father's most valuable horse, a wood bed for the wagon, a rocking chair, a stand and several cups and saucers, items to set up housekeeping—or to leave home.[49] A family history written by William McGroarty says that he "went to Oregon in his youth and was never heard from [again]."[50] The statement was probably true, and it supports the theory that it was he, not his older brother, who went fishing with his father on that fateful night; that he left home in order to recover, and to begin life anew in a place far away from his memories. The 1860 census corroborates family lore. Jacob lived in a farming and mining community in Josephine County, Oregon near Grants Pass, and not far from Roseburg. He was a chair-maker, unmarried and lived alone.[51]

Jacob's death changed his family's lives in other ways too. Although Elizabeth did not go to live with her daughter, she bought a place near Eliza Jane Carter and her family in Mt. Carmel. She was fifty-seven years old in 1851 when she paid $575 for a small lot on "Mud Corner" at the elbow of the Batavia Turnpike.[52] Next door lived a woman who was a weaver, another neighbor was a widowed seamstress, and further down the block were two carpenters, a milliner and a wagon maker.

An 1870 village atlas indicated that Elizabeth had about a quarter of an acre on an elbow of the turnpike. Her house faced the road on the narrow side, but the property deepened toward the back, enough for a small garden plot and some shade trees. Directly across the pike was a hotel. The Carters lived a few houses north on the turnpike and they had three children: Nancy, who was eighteen; and sons Henry, aged six, and Richard, a year old.[53]   By 1860 Elizabeth had been living on the turnpike for about nine years. She valued her house at $500 and claimed a personal estate of $100. Ann, who was thirty-eight, lived with her mother, as did Nancy Wheeler, aged thirty-five, and all three worked as seamstresses.[54] Nancy had filed for divorce from William Wheeler in 1852, citing adultery, marriage with another without benefit of divorce and drunkenness, and went to live with her mother. Ten years later Elizabeth was not faring much better, as her home was worth less while her personal estate had doubled.[55] She did not advertise in the town directory, so business must have come from the community based on work she had done for others. She and her daughters may have advertised their business by leaving a card across the street at the hotel, where they picked up sewing from guests passing through and from those living at the hotel.

Harriet lived with her mother for a while after her father died, but then went to Indiana where her sister Emeline lived. On 20 Jul 1854 she married Martin Pittsenbarger at her sister's home in Clinton County. The *Clermont Sun* announcement reminded its readers she formerly lived in Mt. Carmel.[56] Davis Hewitt lived in Jackson Township, a few miles away from his mother and sisters. He and Jane had eight children; the youngest was Elizabeth who was just two months old when her mother died on 24 Sep 1859.[57] The following year Ann, who was fifteen, was no longer in school but had taken charge of the younger children who ranged in age from a year to eleven years old.[58] Knowing that his children needed a mother, within a year he remarried.

Ann Hewitt lived with her mother at least until 1873, when close to eighty years old she signed *Mud Corner* over to her daughter in exchange for five dollars. Ann was about fifty years old, and Elizabeth sensing her time was getting close needed to provide for a daughter who was probably disabled. During the Wheeler petition to divide Jacob's estate, it was specifically noted that a copy was brought to the house for Ann to sign, and that while her sisters could write, she made her mark with an "X." Whether or not giving the land to Ann was a closing gesture on her life, Elizabeth worried about her and wanted to ensure that she had a provision when her mother was no longer there to look after her.[59]

Elizabeth paid taxes in 1873 and died before they were again due.[60] However, neither death nor cemetery records have been discovered to indicate the date. A family history says she was buried next to her husband. In the Moore Cemetery, the author found that Jacob Hewitt's grave had not only a tombstone, but also a headstone and a footstone, with the initials "J.H." outlining where he was buried. Next to him there was what appeared to be another grave outlined only with two rude stones, one at the head, the other at the foot, the same distance apart as those marking Jacob's grave but without an inscription. Another grave was lightly outlined next to that one, with two more fieldstones laid at the head and foot of the grave, but otherwise without identification. This cemetery is so remote, and so unlikely to be seen from the road that any stone deliberately placed there was likely to be lying in the same place a hundred years later. Each of these graves, including Jacob Hewitt's tombstone, is on the outer edges of the cemetery next to the incline leading down to the road. If Elizabeth Hewitt was indeed buried beside her husband, perhaps the other stone was for Ann, the unmarried daughter who, ever her mother's shadow, was laid to rest next to her.

There is a list of those buried in this cemetery, naming not only Jacob, but also his granddaughter Lorah. Next to his, there are two tombstones carved for her. One was discarded and found lying up against the fence near his grave. The corrected one was for Jacob and Elizabeth's granddaughter, Lorah Carter, child of George and Eliza Jane. The last burial in this cemetery was in 1855 sealing it for all time and thus relegating it to obscurity. It appeared however, that the family allowed the Hewitts to continue to populate the outer perimeter of this small family cemetery. If both Ann and her mother lie in this little cemetery, their gravesites are so obscurely marked that only informed intuition brought about their discovery. May they rest in peace.[61]

Sometime before February 1884, many years after her mother died, Eliza Jane Carter, as widow, followed her. As a provision for her grandchildren, and for her minor children, Richard and Henry Carter, a petition was filed to sell her estate. Their elder sister Nancy had married but died leaving two children, who were living in an orphans' home. Eliza Jane owned about half an acre on Mt. Carmel turnpike worth little more than $178 in debts she left behind.[62] Eliza's daughter was buried in the Moore Cemetery and her mother may be buried there. Clearly, there was no money for a funeral or tombstone to mark her passing from this world.

After her mother died, Ann worked as a domestic servant. In 1880 she lived in Brown County near the original family homestead in Pleasant Township where her parents once lived,[63] in the home of Elizabeth Woods Crosby. When Elizabeth's first husband, George Bohrer, died she married John Crosby. Ann was fifty-seven years old at the time and Elizabeth was sixty-two years old. They were cousins, Ephraim Hewitt's granddaughters, and in their small way, by living together these two elderly women reformed the family circle in the place where their mothers, Ruth and Elizabeth, had lived and married so many years before.[64]

Chapter Eight

RICHARD DAVIS HEWITT
Clermont County, Ohio (1815-1903)

Davis as a Youth

By late 1814, the country was at peace. The bitter conflict that for a second time drew this nation into war with its mother country had ended, and men were home from the War of 1812 in time to celebrate the holidays. All was well in Georgetown and Ripley, as the last troops made their way home in time to spend Christmas with their families. Toasts were raised across the countryside for the safe return of fathers, brothers and husbands, and because restored peace brought hope that life would settle into its normal stride once again.

The following November, when the harvest was in and the land lay fallow once again, the small community surrounding Georgetown settled in for the approaching winter. Once the first snow of the season had fallen, quiet settled over the land, muffling all but the most prominent sounds. Breaking the silence across the land one brisk day was the lusty cry of a newborn babe and the first child of Jacob and Elizabeth Hewitt. Richard Davis Hewitt announced himself to the world on 15 November 1815, and it would be a long time before anyone heard the last of him. Whether he entered this life with health and vigor cannot be said, but if he bore childhood frailties, he soon outgrew them.

Known to friends and family as Davis, their son must have been a robust man in body as well as in spirit, for he lived a long time. A photograph taken of him in old age showed a lean and lanky man who was perhaps tall. His sons were like him in that way. Sporting the full beard common at the turn of the century, he sat erect in a chair, next to him a cane. His hands were large with the long, thick fingers of one who worked the fields most of his life, but his carriage was upright and alert for a man of his years. At least that was a writer's opinion who worked for *The Clermont Sun* newspaper when, after having been gone a few years, Hewitt paid a visit to his hometown in 1899. The reporter remarked, "Mr. Hewitt in his 84th year was well preserved for a man of his age."[1] As the offspring of a double Hewitt alliance, he lived more than eighty-seven years, outlasting most of his siblings including one of his sons. In a span of more than fifty years, Davis married four times, buried three wives, and divorced the last one in 1894. He fathered a dozen children and ruled over them as well. During his long life, Davis Hewitt showed he was capable of both passion and compassion, and this is his story.

One of Davis's early memories may have been the death of his grandfather, for whom he was named. He was eleven in 1827 when Richard Hewitt died and his parents moved to a farm just outside Batavia village west of the county where he was born. However, to a young boy who was the eldest of four children, the move to a new town must have seemed like the beginning of an adventure. Davis probably attended a Batavia school until he was about fifteen or so. Certainly his sisters attended, since their mother was literate and would have wished it. A schoolteacher of that day often had other professions as well, and this was true of those who taught the Hewitt children and their neighbors. One teacher was John Hill, a surveyor who taught math to the village. Years later, one of Davis's children married into his family. There were so many distractions for a teenage boy, that he was probably only peripherally aware of his father's ongoing efforts to obtain a clear title to their farm. However, the flood in Feb 1832, when he was nearly seventeen years old was something he would remember always. He had witnessed its destruction and if curious, read the newspaper reports.

Six months later Clermont and its surrounding counties experienced a cholera epidemic that must have passed over the Hewitt doorstep without stopping. Davis, who spent time with his relatives in Brown County, may have heard a first-hand account from his uncle Philip Buckner, a doctor in the county who wrote about preventive measures for the local newspaper. He spent some time with his Hewitt cousins because a descendant who interviewed the family, mentioned, "There was living in Georgetown, Ohio, in 1837 a youth known as Davis Hewitt. He was the son of Sophia [Hewitt] Buckner's sister Elizabeth, who had married her cousin Jacob Hewitt."[2] Davis was about twenty-two years old when he took a trip to New Orleans with his uncle. It was perhaps not the first they shared, nor the last, but Dr. Buckner recorded this trip in his journal.

Although a doctor in Georgetown, Buckner was a practical man who had to supplement his medical practice. River journeys were fraught with peril at times but they fulfilled his passion for boating on the Mississippi while visiting friends and family from childhood. He was also a farmer and an entrepreneur, adept at making money in various ways. Annually he transported the fruits of his neighbors' harvest to a ready market at Natchez and New Orleans. One day he asked his nephew Davis Hewitt to accompany him, knowing what an enriching experience it would be for a young provincial man who might never again have the opportunity of boating on two of the nation's mightiest rivers. Because travel in 1837 was difficult, most farmers had no opportunity to sell their produce except in the local market. Those like Buckner who knew of ways to expand their business beyond county borders took their goods south to New Orleans. Careful planning was necessary, as it was a long and arduous trip, sometimes taking up to six months to get there and back. Propelled only by oars and poles, the flatboats they used were cumbersome. They could not be taken home, and so were sold at the point of delivery. From New Orleans, a man either walked or rode a horse north taking trails that led back to Ohio.[3]

Davis traveled to New Orleans on a "Kentucky Boat." Built to drift with the current, it was large and sturdy with a partial roof for shelter, and had a wide sweeping oar attached to the stern to maneuver it through turbulent and dangerous waters. Dr. Buckner lived near Straight Creek where his boats were constructed for the annual trip south. When completed they were loaded with produce from his large farm then guided down the creek to the Ohio River, where the trip began. The boat Davis took was built to carry heavy cargo, but it also had edible goods, and what was not consumed during the trip was sold along the way and new goods were brought aboard.

Buckner had more than one boat on this trip, one for the crew and a couple of others for the horses and cargo. As the horses commanded a fair price, it was no sacrifice to leave one behind when they offloaded their cargo. The boats were in great demand in the South, and once sold their new owners disassembled them and sold the lumber to build houses and warehouses. Charles Ewing, who was married to Davis's Aunt Harriet Hewitt, was also on the 1837 trip. Several hired crewmen accompanied them as they began their journey on 21 Nov 1837. Davis had just turned twenty-two years old.

The first entry in Buckner's diary indicated it took until Nov 25 to leave Straight Creek, and after a stop and layover, they got to Cincinnati on Nov 28. From there they went west down the Ohio River. During the night, only five miles beyond Cincinnati, they were badly frightened when foggy weather almost caused their boat to get hung up on a snag. As they made their way down the Ohio, Buckner logged each juncture of the trip, documenting the towns and rivers and marking on which side of the riverbank their boat passed. On an ever-changing river, his log became a valuable record for future trips. Two days and 100 miles later on the Madison, Indiana, side of the river, foggy weather hindered their journey, so they lay over until the next morning. By December 3 the company of men had traveled about 200 miles when hard winds and rain caused them to stop again. Dr. Buckner used the delay to buy a quart of milk. A few miles before reaching Evansville, Indiana, his coat needed mending so the crew stopped to buy a skein of silk and needles so he could fix it. One man bought a violin at the next stop so they had music for the remainder of the journey. Except for the two times they nearly ran into dangerous snags, the trip proved uneventful for the first 300 miles. However, Buckner noted that just after leaving Evansville a steamboat "liked to run into us."

A notation just after that says, "one mile above the head of this island caught a wild turkey swimming in the river; Ewing went out and shot one. I went out on the island and walked two miles through a canebrake; found horses, hogs and cattle on it. The island is two miles wide and four long." Having come nearly 400 miles down the Ohio River, they were not far from the Mississippi but stopped first at Hurricane Island, where Buckner bought 50 bushels of corn. The boat landed so hard against the bank that the bow of the horse boat sprung a leak, causing water to pour in. The men unloaded and repaired it by caulking the hold with hemp and tar. The log noted that during the early part of the trip they stopped to get a hay boat, indicating that with the horse boat, the crew was guiding not one, but several boats down this river.

While still on the Ohio they had another bad scare at Dog Island. The crew was again navigating at night in the fog trying to get past a stone dam that was built to lead boats from one island to another. Buckner's words describe what happened:

> Here, being lost in the fog we ran broadside over this dam
> before day; the water roaring almost like the falls. But as God
> would have it, we either hit the gap made by the channel or
> else the water was high enough to take us over safe. (All
> hands badly scared.) We ran on without being able to tell

which course whether side, bow or stern [was] foremost. Near
the foot of [it there were] two boats stuck the night before.

They left thankful to have come through safely. A few miles further down
the river their chimney caught fire and they had to tear it down and rebuild it.
To reach the Mississippi on December 5; it had taken fourteen days, including
two days of lost time, from the time they left Straight Creek. Buckner noted
they had passed forty-five towns and traveled 483 miles. He also noted that the
Mississippi was high and had backed up onto the Ohio for several miles, so that
to move forward they had to row against the wind and tide about six miles.
Surrounding them as they made their way onto the Mississippi were twenty-one
other flat boats leaving the mouth of the Ohio River. Once they began
navigating the Mississippi River, log notations became even more critical with
many more references about the locations of snags and sandbars. Several times
they had layovers and would spend the time taking the horses on land for
exercise. Upon passing the banks of New Madrid, Missouri, Buckner noted a
now famous earthquake saying, "Here the banks still show the sinks in the earth
produced by the heavy earth quakes of 1811." The boats landed at Memphis,
Tennessee, on 15 December and remained there three days, while the men
transacted business: "Sold all Cahal's pork and lard. Saw sights among the fair
sex. Saw one Chickasaw Indian had him on the boat and sold him a rifle gun for
$15. Bought some sugar and a pair of pants at $6 as mine were getting a little
open at the stern. Took out horses again to rest."

Upon leaving Memphis the weather turned stormy, with hard rain and
heavy winds that hampered progress on the river, so they laid over more often
than before. About 300 miles from where the Ohio meets the Mississippi River,
near Helena, Mississippi, the crew stopped for a while. Buckner said, "At the
foot of [Horseshoe Bend we] went to shore and bought some bear meat, six fine
skins hung out on the trees and a smoke house full of meat." Then, "Lay here
for wind—here I took the steam boat *Glasgow* and went on to Vicksburg, where
I waited four days for the boats. Hired a horse at $2.50 per day and went out to
Blanchard's on Big Black [River]. [On] Christmas day S. Blanchard came to
Vicksburg with me and stayed two days and nights. The boats arrived at this
place. Got stable and lot and rested my horses ten days. Sold seven head and
one died."

On 9 Jan 1838 the company landed at Grand Gulf, just south of Vicksburg.
Dr. Buckner reports, "Here discharged four hands more and left hay boat in
charge of Solomon Bingerman. Landed at Rodney on the tenth. Sold one horse
and had offers for four or five others. Davis Hewitt lay sick from the fifth to this
time (the tenth), quite sick—but today think him better for the first time." The
diary did not end there, but the remaining journal including the trip back home
has been lost. It would have indicated whether the company rode horseback or
walked, taking the Natchez Trace as Buckner's grandfather had done many
years before. Davis recovered, and he was no doubt grateful to have been in the
company of a family member who was a doctor.[4]

Perhaps the trip to New Orleans explains why Davis Hewitt was neither in
the 1840 census in either Brown or Clermont County, nor anywhere in Ohio or
neighboring states. He was probably missed by a census taker, who apparently
only operated on *terra firma*. Perhaps the previous experience whetted his

appetite for adventure and he was on another escapade with his Uncle Philip somewhere down the mighty Mississippi waiting to experience whatever surprise was around the bend.

Davis and Jane

By 1842 Davis seemed to have gotten his fill of river travel, or possibly he was simply preparing for an adventure of another kind. At that time he lived near Batavia, where his parents moved some years before. In the spring of that year, amongst a profusion of the glorious pinks and whites of the season, he was about to step through the bower and begin the walk down a new path. As announced in the local newspaper on 10 May 1842, Davis stood in front of a justice of the peace in his hometown ready to accept the responsibilities of a married man. He was twenty-six years old and Jane Williamson his bride was twenty.[5] As the first among his siblings to marry, on that day Davis took a right angle into another life. Emotionally the trip would be a journey through hills and valleys, across swollen streams, hidden sand bars and snags—a trip not unlike the one he made a few years earlier with his Uncle Philip. Standing next to the young woman who had just promised to be his wife, their future was a blank canvas, waiting to be filled with the brilliant hues and somber colors that would illustrate their union, a unique portrait created as they lived each day one upon another. On the first day, after the official gave his blessing and upon joining their families in celebration, they walked blithely into the future.

Nine months later began the second phase of their journey, when on 11 Feb 1843 their first child, Samuel, was born. Following in the tradition of the Hewitt family, his middle name was Davis[6] and first name after Jane's great-grandfather, Samuel Williamson.[7] Shortly after his first birthday, Jane and Davis purchased 25 acres in Fleming County from her sister and brother. This land was a legacy left to the children by their grandfather, John Cochran. They did not want to live in Kentucky, so to gain full possession of the land, Davis had to buy their portion then sell it to buy other land. Using part of the proceeds they bought a 52-acre parcel in Jackson Township on Mountjoy Survey #4448 near the town of Monterey in Clermont County.[8] By then Ann was a little over a year old and Sam was nearly three.

Clutching hands and hungry mouths surrounded Jane while Davis tended the farm and expanded their estate. Between 1845 and 1847, he bought several pieces northeast of Batavia, also in Jackson Township, one a fifteen-acre parcel by their farm.[9] He bought a third property of 42 acres in January 1847 in Jackson Township,[10] but the census showed they lived in Batavia, probably on a lot owned by his father. By then he had about 110 acres in Jackson Township that he rented out in the same way his father did with property he owned.

Following Samuel's birth, the children arrived in quick succession, with Ann on 15 Aug 1844, followed by Thomas, who was born in September 1847. Two months later in December, the second great flood of Davis Hewitt's life inundated the county and surrounding countryside. In 1832 he was seventeen when he experienced the Ohio River's wrath, and like everyone felt awe-struck upon seeing its power for the first time. When a second flood devastated the area fifteen years later, he was a thirty-two-year-old husband and father, seeing its destruction from a different viewpoint, that of his family's protector but also as a landowner for the first time. The Little Miami River bordered the town of Batavia, probably causing major flooding at home, and his family's protection was Davis's major focus at that time.

They came safely through the flood but fared less well during the next event, when as parents they experienced the fragility of life when their son Thomas died on 9 Aug 1849. Perhaps that year's cholera epidemic carried him away as it did so many of the young and vulnerable.[11] Born 5 Sep 1847, he was not yet two years old when they laid him to rest in the Old Owensville Cemetery in Stonelick Township.[12] Thomas's death was followed four months later by Louisa's birth on 16 Dec 1848, an early Christmas present for a grieving family. A year later, John Holmes Hewitt was born on 22 Apr 1850. A snapshot of their life in 1850 shows they had four children, the youngest John, an infant, at the time not yet named or so someone told the census taker. Farmer Hewitt, who lived between two other farmers valued his real estate at $620, somewhat more than what he had paid for it. Samuel, who was seven, was in school that year, and sisters, Ann and Louisa, were five and one year old.

That spring the circus came to town and for the townspeople, the excitement began building weeks prior to its opening in May 1850. Fueling their excitement, were newspaper reports informing everyone of the mammoth pavilion hall being built in Batavia to house all the events. Billed as "Crane & Company's Great Oriental Circus," the hall boasted the ability to accommodate 5,000 spectators and was in all likelihood the biggest event in the county that spring. Jane could not go because of the ritual of "lying-in" observed by women of that day, and so baby John who was less than a month old, stayed home with his mother and sister Louisa, while Davis took Ann and Samuel away in the wagon to see the sights. Stepping up to pay an admission fee of twenty-five cents, plus fifteen cents for each of the children, the Hewitts entered the big top, where the little ones gasped at the contortionist and the "aerobatic artists." Excitement rose even higher upon seeing the "twelve diminutive ponies" and all cheered at the pageantry of the chariots. Exited from the spectacle on their return home, the children spilled over with delight as they described the clowns, the jugglers and the "dragon chariot drawn by ten camels," and for days afterward they regaled their mother with the wonderful sights they saw.[13] While scenes from the day played across the closed eyes of the children as they fell asleep, it was not long afterward that another event drew their parents' full attention.

A little more than a month after the circus left town, Davis's father died suddenly. One evening while fishing with friends, Jacob accidentally drowned in the Little Miami River. One of his sons was with him at the time, most likely his younger brother, Jacob, who was nineteen and unmarried. Sometime afterward Jacob left home and Ohio and went to Oregon, and as his aunt remarked, was never heard from again. Perhaps the message in Jacob's disappearance was that he felt unbearable grief that he could not save his father, and if he remained there the river was a constant reminder of failure, and so he left. His mother also left Batavia after the event and settled in the next township, perhaps because she too could never again look at the river as it flowed through town without thinking of her husband.

Jacob's elder brother guided the family through the repercussions of his father's death. The accident must have brought untold pain to Davis, but more stunning to the family was the demand by Davis's sister Nancy and her husband, William Wheeler, for an immediate partition of their father's estate. While still mourning the death of his child, Davis, the eldest in the family, was further burdened with his sister's petition to divide the real estate, and the need to sell it to pay his father's debts. His mother, Elizabeth, seemed to handle much of those responsibilities herself, particularly since Davis had a wife and growing family to look after. Signaling one more abrupt change in her life, Elizabeth Hewitt, who had been living in Batavia village, moved to Union Township to be closer to her children. While embroiled in the division of family property, Davis tended his farm, purchased more property and once again became a father. William Jacob was born on 10 Sep 1851, and he was named in honor of his grandfathers on both sides of the family.

As indicated by the 1850 census, some time after 1847, when he and Jane were living in Batavia, they moved onto their Jackson Township property. As his children multiplied, so did his property. Davis learned from his father, and guided by the principle of gradual accession, he began buying 40 or 50 acres here and there, and adding adjacent land when it became available. In 1848 Davis added ten acres to the Jackson Township property and increased the farm to about 75 acres.[14] Not long after the estate was settled, in December 1851, he and Jane sold the two lots in Batavia he received from the partition.[15] A few days later he bought ten acres, bringing the farm to 87 acres by year's end.[16]

There was a space of nearly three years after William's birth, and the birth of the twins. Mary was born on 28 Jun 1854 and lived to a very old age, but her unnamed brother did not. Jane's last two children were James, born on 22 Oct 1856 and Elizabeth, called Lizzie, whose birthday was 6 May 1859, and this rounded the family to ten children who were born to this couple in sixteen years. Although two of them died, eight children was still a large family, even for the times. Jane seemed to hold sway in naming their children, in particularly their sons Samuel, John and William, whose names commemorated members of her family, but even Ann and Mary Jane bear the names of her Cochran and Williamson ancestors. Although Davis deferred to his wife's choices, he named his youngest child after his mother. However, the manner in which this couple sometimes merged names so that the child bore the name of an ancestor from each one may be an indication of the unity and partnership in their marriage.

If Davis had a close relationship with any of his sisters, it is not readily apparent and the fifteen years' difference between him and his younger brother may have precluded an alliance. Harriet moved to Indiana, as did their sister Emeline who was a widow in 1880 living with four of her children in the town of Warren. Harriet married Martin Pittsenbarger in Clinton County but by 1880 they were in McLean, Illinois, where they lived with their son Jacob and nephew Richard Carter, the son of her sister Eliza Jane.[17] Three of Davis's sisters lived in Clermont County, and like he, were closely concentrated in Union Township. Eliza Jane Carter and her husband George lived next door to their mother, Elizabeth. After divorcing her husband William Wheeler, Nancy moved in with her mother and sister Ann. The county newspaper did not indicate cross-town visits between Davis and Jane to see his sisters or his mother, so perhaps he was not close to them. They, however, all appeared to be devoted to each other.

In 1858 Davis and Jane joined a new congregation organized in Jackson Township by the Reverend T. F. Cortelyou. They were without a church the first year and so services were privately held. The following year a committee was formed of church trustees, and Hewitt was among those who raised $600 to build a church. The first services in the new Monterey Presbyterian Church were held in 1859, shortly after Davis's daughter Lizzie was born.[18] While Jane was a member of the church, she was probably too weak, and perhaps not allowed the first month after giving birth, to attend church services. She was thirty-eight years old when Elizabeth, her tenth child, was born, not yet a middle-aged woman, but ill, her body depleted from pregnancy and her energy spent. Jane had dropsy, now called congestive heart failure, which becomes life threatening as fluids collect in the tissues and organs, causing undue stress on the heart. Pregnancy taxed her heart even more, and because she was ill for four months, it is known that the decline began during her pregnancy.[19] She lingered throughout the heat of summer, unable to recover. Having given her all to bear the child, on 24 Sep 1859 she relinquished her spirit. They had named the baby Elizabeth Helena after a grandmother on either side of the family, much as they had done in naming her brother William. Lizzie lived a long life, well beyond that of her parents and a few of her siblings.[20]

Reverend Cortelyou presided over the services held for Jane Williamson Hewitt. Then he accompanied Davis, the congregation and the family to the little cemetery where Jane was laid next to their son Thomas who was buried there ten years before. Upon visiting in 1996, the author found the two stones together and photographed them. The smaller marker for Thomas was no longer on his grave but was resting against his mother's stone facing out over her plot. This visit proved to be most propitious because two summers later, upon once again stopping by this small but well-tended cemetery, the author was unable to locate Jane's tombstone anywhere. Thomas's marker remained and had been kindly placed against the stone of an unrelated family. A photograph and the efforts in 1952 of the Beech Forest Chapter of the D.A.R. are all that stand as proof that Jane Williamson Hewitt was buried near the intersection of two streets in the little village of Owensville, Ohio.[21]

A Second Marriage

After Jane died, Davis struggled to meet the needs of a family of eight children, including a baby a few months old. He was forty-four years old and doing well financially; but he needed a partner to support him in the challenges ahead, and a woman to mother his children. Hard work gave him a measure of modest success, so that by 1860 his worth was $2,500 including a personal estate of $500. In some ways it made him an attractive prospect for marriage, but in his search for a wife, he also came burdened with a large family. Not all of his children were dependent; Samuel was sixteen and helped his father on the farm while Ann, who was fifteen when their mother died, undoubtedly cared for the younger children. She was still a girl, and could not be expected to meet the needs of childcare, cooking, cleaning and mending forever.

When the insulating numbness subsided and the need to care for his family overtook his grief, Davis knew what to do. In seeking a suitable wife, he again looked within the Williamson family and found another Jane. With the marriage to his first wife's cousin, it would be the third time an alliance was struck between the Hewitt and the Williamson families. Davis's Aunt Letty was the first to marry a Williamson. Her husband, William Williamson, was his first wife's brother. A year and a half after Jane's death, on 30 May 1861, Davis married Jane Williamson, a single woman of thirty-seven years. He could not have known that this second marriage was about to take another right-angled turn into unexplored territory.[22] While his expectations are unknown, it was not possible to bring his wife back by marrying her cousin, so he focused on keeping the family intact by seeking a mother for his children. And while Jane could not replace her cousin, she could care for their children and this she did. Their fathers were brothers, born a year apart in age, and because they did not live in the same village the families made an extra effort to get together. When they met, Davis's first wife was probably living with her brother William who lived on one of Jacob Hewitt's rental properties. After their marriage she and Davis sometimes went to Brown County to see this family and her cousin Jane.[23] So there is the likelihood that Davis knew his second wife for many years prior to their marriage.

Their first child was born on 29 Jul 1862, a son named Richard after his father and great-grandfather. Then on 1 Feb 1865, a second son was born to the couple and they called him Benjamin after Jane's father. Both children were partially disabled, either at birth or possibly a childhood illness like polio that left them both "partially paralyzed," as was stated in the 1880 census.[24] Later records indicated that they could not read or write.

Within the first two years of their marriage, Davis began selling the Jackson Township property he had acquired over the years. In January 1863 he sold more than 100 acres originally purchased for about $800, but which he sold for $3,400.[25] Two months later Hewitt paid $4,500 for 112 acres in Union Township.[26] After retaining about twenty acres, two years later he then sold 93 acres of it for $5,400.[27] The final purchase of his buying spree was made a month after Benjamin was born, when he bought a combination of Darby's Survey #2058 and Stephen's Survey #3877 of 84 acres for about $5,000.[28] It bordered Union and Batavia Townships just south of the Batavia Turnpike, across which meandered two branches of Shaler's Run, their paths outlined by trees that snaked across the landscape. Referred to in this history as the "Hewitt Farm," Davis eventually sold it to his children. Thereafter they rented the property to tenant farmers, but kept it in the family into the twentieth century.

Shortly after their marriage, the threat of war once again entered into the daily lives of the community. This unprecedented conflict was even more disturbing because it pitted sections of the nation against each other for the first time, separating families and dividing friends because of fractured alliances and beliefs. Cousins and sometimes brothers lined up on opposite sides in a war that not only divided the nation geographically but also separated it economically and philosophically. As the conflict's counter truths divided the nation, it demanded that individuals choose between the blue and the gray uniform. This stratification reached a point of tension causing the southern states to secede from the union, and declaring Montgomery, Alabama, as the new capital with its own president, Jefferson Davis. Young men listened as their fathers heatedly discussed the issues, and while they were distracted by talk their sons walked away to answer the call to arms. Some joined with their friends while other young men showed up alone after a long night's struggle with their conscience. In the end the youth of America left the fields and went to war not knowing whether they would return. Sam Hewitt was of age to join and may have done so although records of his enlistment have not been found.

Whether returning from war or not, in the winter of 1867 Samuel Hewitt got married. That day, 11 Feb 1867, was also his twenty-fourth birthday, and in celebration he married Louisa Duckett, whose family lived on Taylor Road in Olive Branch.[29] Although he was the first to marry, his sisters Ann and Louisa at nineteen and twenty-three were of marriageable age and probably annoyingly excited about the details of their brother's celebration. Since they were underfoot, their girlish excitement was put to good use in preparation for the arrival of their cousins and aunts and uncles. John and his brother Will, in their teens, were likely bored by it all and stayed out of the way until dragged in at the last minute to get scrubbed up for the event. All available hands were needed around the house during this time to assist Jane Hewitt. Help was especially important with the two youngest children, who were four and two years old and, and being disabled, needed extra care.[30]

Jane did not live long after Samuel's marriage. Whether she suffered from a chronic disease or was swiftly and suddenly carried away, the cause of her death is unknown. Married only six years, Davis buried his wife in Olive Branch Cemetery. On her headstone is a simple message: "Jane, wife of R. D. Hewitt, d. Sep 20, 1867, aged 43 years, 9m, 15d." As her stone differs from others belonging to the family, it may have been placed there immediately after her death. She was the first in the family to be buried in that cemetery, but eventually other members of the Hewitt family surrounded her on a hill overlooking a peaceful landscape where so many buried in that cemetery came to rest.[31]

Davis and Louisa

Davis Hewitt toiled on alone for several years. He and his children lived near the Batavia Pike outside of Olive Branch village.[32] In 1870, William who was nineteen, and James, fifteen, worked with their father on the 87-acre farm he bought in 1865. John and his sister Mary both worked outside the home for wages but lived at home. He was twenty-one and a laborer on a neighbor's farm, while she worked as a local domestic. Ann, who was twenty-six, and Louisa, twenty-two, were the mainstays in caring for their younger siblings, Richard and Benjamin.[33] Lizzie, the youngest child, was in primary school, but sometimes stayed at her grandmother's house in Mt. Carmel.[34] After Jane died, and up until 1870 they managed somehow, with most of the children either helping at home or on the farm. Samuel, who three years before had married Louisa Duckett, left home to begin a family but remained nearby.[35]

In 1871, ten years after he wed Jane Williamson and four years after her death, Davis Hewitt ventured down the path once again. He was fifty-five years old and his bride-to-be, who gave her age as forty, was Miss Maria L. Evans, who was called Louisa. As they stood before the magistrate that autumn day on 24 October and promised to love and honor each other, Davis was placing a great deal of faith in the woman he had asked to be his third wife. She, in promising to love, honor and obey, was taking on a large responsibility as well.[36] Whether she was forty or forty-four as her tombstone indicates, Louisa was beyond childbearing years. So that on the day she walked through the door of his house a married woman, Louisa also became the mother of Davis's three youngest children who were between six and twelve years old, and into a family of mostly grown children living at home. However, she had arrived to take charge of the most vulnerable of them. Davis's elder daughters must have struggled to run the household and care for their younger siblings after Jane's death, and with a new wife, the family was once again in transition. Louisa's elevation from single woman one day, to mother of a large brood the next was a challenge, particularly the care of the two youngest boys. She had to maintain a delicate balance in a family consisting primarily of adults, and if she was wise, she won over Davis's daughters by not challenging their previous management of the family unit.

If the tenor of Louisa's position in their family can be perceived so many years later, perhaps it is most apparent in the placement of her memorial in Olive Branch Cemetery, and an indication of Louisa's eventual significance to this family. Several tombstones, now crumbling, were erected side-by-side on the hill. On either side of Davis's headstone are two of his wives, Jane and Louisa. Strategically placed in front of them is a four-foot monument with inscriptions on two sides, one for Davis and the other for Louisa. On either side of the monument are footstones marked with the inscriptions, "Father and "Mother." Louisa raised the two youngest boys, Richard and Benjamin, who probably regarded her as their mother, as they are buried closer to her than to Jane, the woman who bore them.

Maria Louisa Evans grew up near Georgetown in Brown County, and Davis Hewitt had a number of aunts, uncles and cousins in the county, and from time to time he visited them, sometimes spending more than just a day or two. Louisa, as she was called, lived in Pleasant Township, as did Eli and Mary Hewitt, so there was ample opportunity over the years for them to meet. It seemed that when things went awry, Davis turned to the core family for answers, and in each case he was rewarded, this time, like the last, it was to search for a wife. How Louisa and Davis came to an agreement about marriage is unknown, but perhaps it was in the renewal of an old friendship, or maybe one of his relatives suggested she would make a good wife. Louisa had family in Olive Branch who lived just north of the Hewitt farm on the Batavia Pike, and others related to his son Samuel's in-laws, thus their courtship may have begun in a number of ways. It was a small neighborhood surrounded by farms, and folks knew each other and visited frequently on business or on a Sunday afternoon, just two of the many avenues in which Davis might find a wife.[37]

Like the Hewitts, Louisa's relatives were pioneers in Brown County, Ohio. Her grandfather, Robert Curry, moved from Rockingham County, Virginia, to Ohio in 1801. As the daughter of Lucinda Curry and Elijah Evans, she was one of ten children, thus in marrying Davis, she had intimate knowledge of what it was like to live within the bosom of a large family.[38]   Shortly after their marriage, Davis joined the Olive Branch Huston Lodge of the I.O.O.F, the "Odd Fellows." Although new to the neighborhood, this fraternal organization was originally European, probably originating in England in the eighteenth century, and brought to Baltimore in 1819 where it was founded in this country. Symbolized by three linked chains, its precepts are not complex, they are to visit the sick, relieve the distressed, bury the dead and educate the orphan.[39]   In 1871 Hewitt, along with fifteen other men living in the Olive Branch area, was initiated into its fold. Appointed as a trustee that year, his son John who was 23 also joined. Within two years Davis became grand noble, the fifth man to hold that position. Originally they met in a church, but in 1874 it was remodeled and enlarged so that by 1880, when the organization had sixty-two members, there was ample space for all to meet.[40]

The next ten years were an ongoing parade of changes and transitions for Davis and Louisa. Some of his children got married, and others moved out, so that by 1880 none of them except the two youngest boys were living at home. The second in his family to marry, William was twenty-two when he wed seventeen years old Rachel Hill on 4 Dec 1873. The following spring Louisa, then twenty-five, became the wife of Thomas Mitchell on 10 May 1874.[41] Several years later on 22 Apr 1880, John Hewitt married Lizzie Belle Morrison, who lived in Mt. Carmel with her parents and brother, Otto.[42]   Shortly afterward they moved next door to her parents, Perry and Eliza Morrison, on property her father owned.[43]   By 1880 James had left home and was living in Morgan County, Illinois.[44]

After the children moved out, sometime prior to 1880, Davis and Louisa moved into a small house near town and rented the farm on the Batavia Pike. It probably took place in the spring of 1875, just after Davis purchased two properties on the Batavia Pike of about eighteen acres; one of them was eight acres in the village where they made their home.[45]   In December that year the house on Davis's farm burned down. It was insured for $500, half of its worth, so it was not a total loss and the tenant got out safely.[46]

Six months after the election of 1878, on 16 Apr 1879, a grumbling letter appeared in *The Clermont Sun* about the election of Orin Temple as a justice of the peace in Batavia Township. The complainant said that he voted for Mr. Temple not because of political affinity but as a personal favor because the man had recently lost his wife and was in a financially embarrassing situation.[47]   Mr. Temple's finances had become an issue prior to the appearance of the news item when Davis Hewitt, in a similar circumstance, sued him to foreclose on a mortgage. Temple's intent was to purchase ten acres owned by Louisa Hewitt, but he was unable to pay the promissory note. The court ruled for the plaintiff and Temple was ordered to pay damages of $145 plus the mortgage of $201 owed to Louisa Hewitt. It is not clear whether she brought this property to the marriage, but in the ensuing years, she and Davis placed liens against it equal to its value.[48] To move matters forward the judge ordered a sale and it brought $40 per acre or $420 at the sale on 7 Feb 1880.[49]

In 1880 the family no longer lived on a farm but they maintained seven acres partially in crops, with the remainder given over to pasture their animals. Davis's two youngest boys—Richard, who was seventeen, and Benjamin, fifteen—had always lived at home, and their ability to assist their father was impeded by their physical handicap, if they were able to help him at all. This meant that Davis, who was sixty-four, took care of the property himself, a small enterprise valued at $1,325 including farming equipment and livestock. With Louisa's help he fed and cared for the animals that included five pigs, two calves and two cows that produced 200 pounds of butter. His twelve chickens were less productive, dropping only fifty eggs that year. Davis grew no grains or corn, but his apple orchard of 100 trees produced 25 bushels of apples. Clearly it was a struggle for him to care for his family and make the most of the land. This was particularly apparent when compared to his neighbor next door who, with half as many trees, produced twice as many apples. The balance of Davis's land in production was given over to sweet and Irish potatoes, although he grew barely enough to get through the year. Whether the low productivity was due to poor soil, illness, impending old age, lack of outside help or all of these factors combined, times were hard for Davis's family. Their other resources were rental income from the farm on Shaler's Run and perhaps two or three other small properties. However, measured against his earlier more fruitful years, Davis struggled financially at that time, sometimes mortgaging property when finances got too tight.[50]

1880 was an election year, and leading up to the November vote were months of bombast and posturing by the candidates that were enthusiastically reported in the county's two opposing newspapers. *The Clermont Sun*, a decidedly Democratic paper, kept its readers entertained with election news in the form of editorials and sidebars, and readers were fed a diet of rhetoric long after the candidates threw their last brickbats at each other. A year later *The Sun* was still going strong with post-election smears against the Republican Party, accusing the candidates of buying votes. Sidebars offered barbs such as,

> "It is wonderful how many people knew just how the election was going to turn out weeks ago, and how remarkably quiet they kept it all the time." Or, "If election laws were enforced very few of the Republican candidates could hold their offices and a large number of 'influential' gentlemen who sold their votes and 'influence' would wear for a period the striped livery of the State." The final arrow pointed toward "two or three drizzling idiots about Batavia who have been placed in office by the Democratic party, and who now much of the time keep their skins saturated with bad whisky...to hide their perfidious conduct at the late election. In their recent bacchanalian fights they have given away themselves and their co-conspirators."

Such was the oratory that accompanied the 1880 election in Clermont County, and perhaps campaigns then were usually fought with reckless abandon, or perhaps this one was unusual for its disturbing accusations. Voters on the streets of Batavia were particularly contentious, and the male population spoke loudly when they were liquored up, some with their fists and others with money. That year Davis Hewitt was a part of it, and his antics got him arrested. It took nearly a year to bring the ruffians to justice, but in October 1881 the courthouse was filled for four days while the judge examined 125 witnesses. When brought into court, the complaints against the offending rabble centered on the sale of alcohol on Election Day, assault with intent to wound, burglary, obtaining money on false pretenses and other similar offenses. Davis Hewitt must have gotten pretty tanked that day because he was brought in on two counts of assault and battery. He pled guilty and paid a fine of five dollars plus costs.[51]

A month after his day in court, Davis's youngest daughter, twenty-one-year-old Lizzie, was married in Cincinnati to Edgar Bratton on 8 Nov 1881.[52] The following year, while the countryside was all in bloom, on 7 May 1882, Mary Hewitt wed Joseph Gehres, a man from Waverly, Ohio, she met while teaching school in that community.[53] Rounding out the close of the year, Davis and Louisa attended a neighborhood celebration of friends on Thanksgiving Day. They were part of a group of nearly 100 guests who were there to celebrate the twenty-fifth wedding anniversary of their neighbors, Mr. and Mrs. J. H. Avey. Gifts were many and varied and some, like the Hewitts, gave silver coins rather than a butter dish or sugar castor.[54]

Mounting debt plagued Davis Hewitt as he grew older. Moving from the farm to a smaller place may have been a good decision, but when the farmhouse burned, the conflagration was like a sentinel announcing his troubles. At some point he must have rebuilt it so that he could rent the property, but he also tried other means to resolve his problems. In March 1882, two contracts took place at the Batavia courthouse intended to relieve some of the burden. First Davis sold the property he lived on for $1,600, and then the buyer sold it back to Louisa Hewitt for the same amount.[55] She may have brought this property to the marriage as her dowry, and the second transaction made it her asset rather than Davis's. Although unclear, it is one explanation of why he was excluded from the release of claim against the house and property, which was put exclusively into his wife's name. Next, they sold the 88-acre farm to Davis's children for $3,000.[56] These transactions essentially prohibited him from incurring any more debt, since he apparently no longer owned any property.

Eventually that year rolled into the events of 1883 and 1884, a disastrous time for the people of Clermont County and its surrounding neighborhoods, including Cincinnati. It began the first week of February 1883 with rain. It continued as rains swelled the Ohio River until it overran its banks, and still the river rose. By Saturday, the tenth of the month, it briefly came to a standstill at fifty-nine feet in the channels but continued to rise until later in the day it reached sixty-six feet, surpassing previous benchmarks reached in 1832 and 1847. Warehouses, factories and homes in Cincinnati were filled with water and some were submerged. Thousands of people were engaged in saving theirs and others' property using boats and rafts, anything that would float, to haul away goods and people. The railroads were flooded and trains weren't running. The

Cincinnati gasworks was flooded and people resorted to using candles. Mills and manufactories on the Kentucky side of the river in Newport and Covington were as deeply submerged as their neighbors were on the opposite of the river.

In Clermont County, New Richmond was the low spot along the river, and it was so severely flooded that people left their homes for fear of losing their lives. When the post office's first floor flooded they moved services upstairs. Some townships were better off than others but sections of the county had difficulty estimating the damage because most buildings were damaged. In Batavia, through the efforts of a citizens' committee, money was raised to aid recovery, and the town bakers were ordered to provide 1,000 loaves of bread to feed the newly homeless. While severe damage was reported throughout the community, no one died as a direct result of the flood. One report seemed to say it all: "There are no boats, no mails, and no communication with the outer world save by accident of visitors whom we persuade to act as messengers."

Months after the flood, when the mud was cleared away and damaged structures repaired, Davis's daughter, Mary, came to visit from her home in Waverly about fifty-five miles away.[57] On this auspicious occasion in October, she introduced her son, Hewitt Gehres, who was born in March 1883, to his grandfather.[58] As the year ended, many were grateful to have survived and overcome another great flood, and when Thanksgiving arrived that year, the people living along the banks of the Ohio celebrated and gave thanks. At Christmas they visited family, bringing gifts and cheerful greetings as they turned once again to the normal cadence of life. The new year began with hope and one winter evening in January a group of young people went out for a sleigh ride and, perhaps traveling too fast, they overturned on the pike near Davis's house. No one was hurt and after dusting off the snow they continued on their way. The writer retells the event in a wistful way, suggesting he would like to have been a part of their adventure on that winter's evening. The story was also a refreshing transition from the aftermath of the flood that so occupied everyone just two months earlier. Another reporter described a similar evening of simple pleasures spent with friends that reflected on that period of youthful innocence that in a rural community may last a bit longer than usual. In part it said:

> One of the most delightful gatherings of the season was at the hospitable residence of W. W. Hulick, one of Clermont's successful and generous husbandmen, on Tuesday evening of last week. A score or more of the belles and beaux of Batavia, taking advantage of the fine sleighing made a call on Miss Emma, the charming and accomplished daughter, who is the light of the home. Although the assembling was rather impromptu, it was no surprise to the young hostess, who is always "at home" to her large circle of friends. The evening was enlivened by vocal and instrumental music, interspersed with social topics of conversation. A spread of good things, sufficient to gratify the most exacting epicure was provided, and at a seasonal hour the gay and happy party dispersed feeling that they had spent a most delightful evening.[59]

Then February 1884 arrived and it began to rain again. Everyone watched and waited, fearful but hopeful too. This could not happen again. But it did, only bigger and higher this time. Terrible headlines counted the feet and inches as the waters rose steadily at about three-quarters of an inch every hour. This was a flood of vast proportions, causing widespread damage east of Cincinnati all the way to Wheeling, West Virginia, and Pittsburgh, where estimates were pegged at four million dollars. Buildings in Cincinnati closest to the river were fully submerged and water reached further inland, causing broader destruction than the previous year. Damage to property within the city was less because the water rose more slowly and citizens were alerted to remove their goods from warehouses and buildings near the water. Once again, in Cincinnati, the trains stopped running because in places the tracks were under three feet of water. The waterworks quit pumping, so no water or gas was provided to homes in the city for days. The story was much the same as the previous year, only the river rose higher, peaking on 14 Feb at seventy-one feet. It was not only the greatest flood of the century; it was Ohio's worst flood in history.

This was a catastrophe of historic proportions, calling for a quick response and the endurance to subdue an elusive foe. It was a disastrous time for some but difficult for all, and spontaneous acts of kindness, and in some cases actual heroism, helped its citizens through a terrible time. Batavia, Clermont's county seat was on high ground so it became the staging area for relief in the county. Once again, money and food were collected and delivered by volunteers wherever it was needed. Reporters visited small towns around the county and gave vivid descriptions of individual plight in the newspapers, so that although they could not get out, if they had a newspaper, they were informed about friends and family. In Olive Branch friends reached out to help John Nichols, whose tobacco business in New Richmond was in danger of being lost in the waters. Enlisting several friends, including Davis Hewitt, he made ready to go there and remove it. Many people like Davis were experiencing the fourth major flood of their lifetime and they were eager to help. Working together, in a matter of hours six men built a boat, placed it on a wagon and headed toward New Richmond. It was pouring rain when they got there and began removing 5,000 pounds of tobacco, and a large amount of stock and machinery. They accomplished the task and brought it all back to Olive Branch. Sometime later, Nichols pondered whether to move his business to a less perilous place.

Eventually the waters subsided and the people of the county hitched up their suspenders and went back to work. With resilience and determination they assessed the damages and either repaired, rebuilt, or tore down their property and began anew. Eventually order returned to the city and its surrounding villages and life went on. In early spring, a group from Olive Branch gathered at the Methodist Episcopal Church to discuss measures to open a road from the pike to the nearby railroad station. A committee of three that included Davis Hewitt was appointed to make a decision, and upon agreeing to meet the following evening, they adjourned.[60] Indeed, rural life or at least life the nineteenth century, was less purposefully chaotic than it is today. Individuals not only had the time, but also the desire to convene often, sometimes more than once a week if necessary. Wedding bells in the community were another indication that life had gotten back on track. This time they rang for Davis's daughter Ann, who had just turned forty and was marrying for the first time. Her husband, Marion McClellan, called Mel, was from Clermont County where they probably met and married on 24 Jul 1884.[61]

Sometime in early winter of 1885, her Olive Branch neighbors learned that Louisa Hewitt was very ill.[62] It was the beginning of a long fight against cancer.[63] She spent her final days under the care of a New Richmond doctor where she died after a long and painful illness of about four years.[64] She was sixty-one years old on 29 Nov 1888,[65] and she and Davis had been partners for seventeen years. Although they had no children together, Louisa entered the household when his two youngest boys, Benjamin and Richard, were six and nine years old, and she was essentially their mother for most of their lives.

Actions and Reactions

When Louisa died, Davis immediately became her estate executor. Six months later, in July, a newspaper ad announced he was selling his personal goods on 2 Aug 1889. It listed nearly everything he owned, his horses, farm implements, corn, oats, bees, household, even the kitchen furniture. For the next couple of years, Hewitt's whereabouts and activities were tracked through a series of newspaper articles. Shortly after selling his land, he left for Nashville and went to live with his son William. He returned the following February, stopped by *The Sun* office to visit with the staff, saying, "He drove through [from Nashville] and was just one week in making the journey." Most of those who knew him were probably surprised when less than a month after his return, he married again. Both *The Sun* and the *Clermont Courier* announced this startling news. Moreover, it was remarkable, because Davis was approaching the grand old age of seventy-five when it was announced that he had wed Mrs. Mary J. Smith on 25 Mar 1890.[66] Where they lived is unknown, but Davis was about to go through another calamitous period in his life.

Wherever he was, Davis was up to his armpits in his late wife's estate settlement. In May 1891 he posted $1,200 bond as administrator of Louisa's $600 estate, all of it in real estate, which she left to her husband and several siblings. The debts against the estate ate up most of the assets because of liens against their property of $325, plus Davis's claim against it for bills he had paid.[67] To clear their debts he settled the estate with a private sale rather than a public auction.[68] A few days later he took action on a difficult decision, and what drove him to it may be better understood by later events. In 1891 he was an old man, three times a widower but with a new wife, and so that spring he placed his sons, Ben, aged twenty-seven, and Richard, two years older, in an institution.[69] Presumably, until the day they were admitted to the infirmary, they had always lived with their father. Only under the direst of circumstances were individuals admitted by family to the "county home." Usually it was because of indigence, homelessness, mental illness or a physical incapacity of some kind. In their case it was probably the latter reason and because Davis had simply become too old to meet their needs any longer.

One day in May, and with a heavy heart, Davis brought his sons to the infirmary. Many years later, the three-story building was still physically imposing, surrounded by the few acres left of what was once a substantial farm of 120 acres. Most of the property was in crops used to feed the inmates, as they were called, through the fruits of their own labor. On average, fifty to eighty individuals lived there at any one time.[70] While the admittance record for both men shows they entered in May, a record further down the page says they were "returned" on 23 Sep 1891, four months later. Perhaps their father relented and brought them home for a while. The fact that they were taken to the institution, only to return home, and then were brought back again later, indicated turmoil existed about their being taken there in the first place.

The institution was self-sufficient as 1880 records show. Of its 136 acres, ninety were in crops and thirty acres were pasture. They had forty pigs, twenty-two cows or calves that produced 600 pounds of butter, and seventy-two chickens producing 300 eggs. The harvest yield was 1,400 bushels of corn, 200 bushels of wheat and 220 gallons of sorghum, a sugar product. Four acres produced 370 bushels of Irish and sweet potatoes and they had 200 apple trees that gave 150 bushels of product.[71] Few records exist about the individuals who lived there, but in 2001, just before the infirmary was demolished, the author examined what remained of their records. Among them was a book of personal information, one individual per page, which showed individual charges for clothing and shoes. Ben and Richard were in room six from 1914 through 1920, and some of Richard's charges were two dollars for a pair of shoes, ten cents for socks and forty-two cents for a shirt. That winter he paid for another shirt and a kerchief. Ben's bill was approximately the same. In 1915 Richard needed a shirt in February and a hat in March. Throughout the summer and fall, he was issued one pair of shoes and two shirts, and in 1918, both men received standard issue shoes at $1.90 each. Although both men's records are similar, Richard's showed that he sometimes received shoes twice each year, an indication that the paralysis afflicting him may not have been in his feet. In Nov 1919 Ben was issued an outside shirt and Richard a pair of shoes, and in the summer a shirt, so perhaps he remained indoors most of the time. The last entry for room number six was Richard's in 1920, when he received a pair of socks for fifteen cents.

A few months after Benjamin and Richard were admitted, a reporter from *The Clermont Sun* gave an account to his readers of conditions at the home. He informed them that most of the farm was under cultivation but the institution remained indebted to the public for other expenses. Ranging in age from five to eighty years old, the eighty-nine individuals who lived there were mostly in good health and tended to live a long time. Daily, their activities were regulated by the clock, arising for breakfast at 6:00 a.m., coming in for dinner at 11:30, then summoned for supper before 5:00. Lights were turned out by 9:00 p.m. in preparation for an early day. If it was requested, individuals were given a pass to visit family and few abused the privilege. In describing their quarters *The Sun* noted that the kitchen was in the basement, along with the dining room, storage cellars and boiler room. The larger rooms in the front of the building on the first two floors were reserved for the superintendent's private residence, while the back of the building held sleeping quarters for everyone else. Rooms were small, ten by twelve feet, and the reporter noted that few of the residents "undertake even the simplest forms of decoration or ornamentation of their rooms. They take the goods that the gods give them and are content." Each floor had one bathroom and part of the third floor was used as a classroom. The journalist concluded that "taken as a whole the infirmary is a model one."[72]

The author's visit in the summer of 2001 left a somewhat different impression of how Ben and Richard might have fared during the years they lived there. While probably well fed because of the bounty of the farm, there was central heat only in the superintendent's rooms. Institutional records show that consistently over the years the brothers were assigned room number six on the first floor, which upon examination does not seem to be altered in any way. Standing in the doorway looking in, the ten-by-twelve-foot room appeared even smaller, and it was difficult to imagine how two adults managed together in such tight quarters. Perhaps as the article reported they spent most of the day separately at some task and used the room only to sleep at night. Rooms on all three floors were of different sizes and may have been altered when the infirmary was closed and the county transformed the building into offices. Those living on the first floor, like the Hewitt brothers, were better protected than some, warmer in the winter, and they likely benefited in other ways by close proximity to the superintendent's quarters. Viewing this massive building from outside, the eye is drawn toward the tiny windows on the top floor. It must have been impossible to sleep on an August night of 100 years ago with hardly a breeze to stir the air. With only the glow of sweat to cool one, the steaming heat of an Ohio summer was unyielding for anyone lying on a cot in one of those tiny rooms. Ben and Richard may have been fortunate to share room number six on the first floor where there was the possibility of an occasional night breeze.

Those were the conditions under which Davis's sons lived. Having spent time on a farm as youths, they adapted to their new roles. Gone forever though was the feeling of waking up in bed at home. No longer could they simply sit across the table and eat a meal with their father. Therefore, on that day with promises of home visits, a sad father left behind his two grown children—men they were in age, but they were boys in spirit. Richard and Ben remained in the county home for the rest of their lives; with occasional visits home as long as their father was alive. Richard died of a stroke on 21 Mar 1931 at the age of sixty-eight.[73] Discharge papers from the infirmary show Ben died during the winter nearly ten years later on 15 Feb 1941, when he was seventy-six, which recalls the statement by the reporter some fifty years earlier that those living at the infirmary "tend to longevity."[74] The brothers were reunited with their parents again in death, at the Olive Branch Cemetery near the farm where they grew up. Standing tall and to the right of the single stone marking their graves is a monument dedicated to Davis and Louisa Evans Hewitt. To the right of it is the gravestone of the woman who bore them, Jane Williamson Hewitt. The placement of the graves and their markers indicate their two mothers, Jane who gave them life, and Louisa who raised them.

The newspaper announced the next hint of trouble in Davis's household. A front-page article began, "Gleanings from in and about the Courts," while a second caption trumpeted, "Rapid Decline of Marital Bliss" and at last shouted, "The Divorce Mill is Grinding at a Rapid Rate. Five Decrees Granted During the Past Week upon the Grounds of Willful Absence and Failure to Provide."

Among them on 7 March 1894 was a statement that Richard D. Hewitt was awarded a divorce from Mary J. Hewitt on the grounds of willful absence.[75] More was learned from court records. Davis's petition stated that Eliza J. Smith, who was mistakenly referred to in all previous announcements as Mary J. Smith, had deserted her husband three years before the proceedings. This meant that about a year after their marriage and probably prior to Davis's sons' admission to the infirmary, Eliza left his bed and board and did not return.[76] In her counter suit to the divorce, she asked that the property she brought to the marriage, approximately 37 acres in Jackson Township, be returned to her, and it was granted.[77]

The court documents clearly show not only the dissatisfaction of both parties, but also a misrepresentation or lack of understanding of what was promised upon their marriage. Davis likely wanted a wife to take care of him and his sons. She apparently refused or was overwhelmed by the added responsibility of caring for three grown men and perhaps demanded they live elsewhere, to which Davis responded by sending his sons to the infirmary. But she left him anyway, unable to accept the obligation of caring for an old man and his sons. And thus began the decline of Davis's final years.

Latter Days

A little more than a year later, in June 1895, Hewitt once again sold his personal property at public auction, consisting of a plow, a buggy, a bay mare and a lot of lumber, an indication he had little left to sell.[78] He also sold his home as indicated by a deed entry in the Clermont County books that year.[79] While few personal memories of Davis have come down to the present, the following story by his great-granddaughter is an enlightening peek into his latter days. The memory must have stood out for Ruth Violett Ungethuem, Samuel Hewitt's granddaughter, because she passed it on. She grew up in Olive Branch, in the bosom of family memories, and wrote fondly to her cousin, George Schmidt, who as a young man left Hamilton County, Ohio, to settle in the west. He was the grandson of John Hewitt, Samuel's brother. The story was of a trip Davis made to Waverly, Ohio, to see his daughter, Mary Gehres. The contents of the letter indicated it might have happened shortly after the 1895 advertisement of personal property sale. Dated 5 May 1977, the letter accompanied a large brass milk pail and a serving dish that had belonged to Davis Hewitt, which Ruth gifted to her cousin. It began with some background saying he had a farm in the early 1800s in Olive Branch and was buried in the cemetery outside the village. After his wife, Louisa, died Davis sold the property where he lived. Ruth goes on to say that,

> being of advanced age [he] packed this glass dish together
> with other personal possessions in a cherry wood chest of
> drawers, tied it on a two wheel cart, hitched his milk cow to it
> and proceeded to walk with it to Waverly, Ohio, Pike County,
> a distance east of at least 100 miles then (over roads that were
> gravel in my recollection but have been cut to 85-90 miles

now). He lived off the cow the best he could until he got there. Being village folks her boys didn't appreciate having to milk the cow twice a day until after he passed on. It is quite possible that it, the dish, belonged to his mother and father [who are] buried in an abandoned cemetery on the outskirts of Batavia, Ohio.[80]

The letter included several interesting insights into the family but the most important was the reference to the "abandoned cemetery," now identified as the private burying ground of the Moore family on Riverview Drive, where Jacob Hewitt's tombstone was discovered in August 2001. The indication that Jacob's wife, Elizabeth, was also buried there lends credence to the evidence that next to Jacob is the outline of a grave with two stones seemingly placed to mark it.

Over the years, Davis lived with several of his children and he visited those he did not. In 1899, after traveling to Ohio from his home in Nashville, he visited Waverly, Ohio. Their newspaper, *The Courier Watchman* reported the visit to his daughter, Mary Gehres, accompanied by his grandson, Hewitt Mitchell, of Norwood, Ohio.[81] Not only was Davis glad to have Hewitt's company, he also needed it by then, as he was blind.[82]

By 1902 Davis was living in the Cincinnati suburb of Norwood with his daughter Lou Mitchell and her family. However, he continued to travel between families, visiting first one and then another. The Olive Branch news was that "Davis Hewitt of Norwood is visiting at the home of his daughter [in-law] Mrs. Louisa Hewitt," the widow of Samuel.[83] There are many indications that in his old age, and especially after he was blind, the family worked together to care for their father. Their training began early when their mother died, followed by their stepmother, Jane. The children cared for each other during the periods of their father's bereavement and long afterward, and when he was in need, they banded together to care for him. At different times, several of his children gave their father a home, and when he grew restless, or they needed a break, another one offered to give him a home. And so he lived until the end, always safe within the bosom of his family.

Davis was 87 years old when he made his will on 4 Mar 1903. Shortly after signing it, the family alerted out-of-state siblings about his imminent passing. Ever the vigilant watchdog, two days after he died, *The Clermont Sun*, wrote that this long-time resident of Olive Branch had died at his home in Norwood on Sunday, March 22, of old age.[84] His funeral held at the Baptist Church in Olive Branch was apparently elaborate. Attending were not only his children and grandchildren but also those Olive Branch neighbors who had known him for nearly forty years. Among them most likely, was someone from the *Sun* who walked among the mourners listening to stories about Davis while they marked his passing into another life.

It was clear from Hewitt's signature on his will that he was weak and without sight, but he was clear about his responsibility. His concerns were for several of his children, but mostly for his sons living at the Clermont County Infirmary. Mel McClellan, a son-in-law, was the executor who he instructed to pay the bills and divide the balance between four of his children, Ann McClellan, Lizzie Bratton, Richard and Benjamin Hewitt. Mary Gehres accepted the responsibility for disbursing monies for her brothers' maintenance and support.[85] Five of his children were not mentioned, Louisa Mitchell, John, William and James, nor Samuel's daughters. It must be assumed that those who received a bequest needed it most. However, when the will was admitted to probate, the names of all of Davis's children or their descendants were included. Samuel's daughters, Almedia McCullough and Bertha Violett were named, and Louisa Mitchell received a legacy for her father's board during his last years, that reduced the $400 note he held on their house. Since he sold the farm to his children and he lived with them, Hewitt had few assets. After expenses, including $103 for the funeral, his children received about seventy dollars each.[86]

Davis was laid to rest near some of the earliest citizens of the village of Olive Branch, where at the top of the hill they mark the oldest part of the cemetery, their outlines gathered in death as they were in life, as a small community of friends and neighbors. The author noted also that among the grouping of Hewitt tombstones, Davis Hewitt's strong personality commanded his family in death as he did in life, his monument standing tall among the smaller crumbling stones. Richard and Benjamin's names are on one stone, united in death as they were together in life. Nearby headstones reflected the names of Davis's neighbors, but buried miles away in another cemetery was his first wife, Jane Williamson, mother of all but his last two children. Her absence from this place created the impression of two separate families, the latter one united by the man for whom the monument was built. Jane seemed to be forgotten, except that surely all of his life Davis must have seen her presence etched upon his children's faces and in their eyes when they looked up at him.

Thomas Hewitt tombstone (1847-1849), son of R. D. and Jane Hewitt,
Old Owensville Cemetery, Owensville, Ohio.

Olive Branch Cemetery, Olive Branch, Ohio,
showing a line of Hewitt tombstones

The Hewitt Monument

R. D. (Richard Davis) Hewitt,
10 Nov 1815-22 Mar 1903

Mariah L. (Evans) Hewitt
wife of R. D. Hewitt
(8 Jul 1827-29 Apr 1888)

Jane Williamson
wife of R. D. Hewitt
(Dec 1823-20 Sep 1867)

Benjamin Hewitt (1864-1941) and Richard Hewitt (1862-1931)

Clermont County Infirmary, Batavia, Ohio, where
Benjamin and Richard Hewitt lived after 1891. It was torn down in 2001.

Probably Almedia Hewitt (1878-), Samuel Hewitt (1843-1892), and
Bertha Hewitt (1872-1937), photograph ca. 1892

Samuel D. Hewitt (1843-1892) and Louisa Duckett Hewitt (1837-1903),
tombstone, Olive Branch Cemetery, Olive Branch, Ohio

John Holmes Hewitt (1850-1930), photograph ca. 1900

Chapter Nine

JOHN HOLMES HEWITT
Clermont and Hamilton Counties, Ohio; Nashville, Tennessee (1850-1930)

John and His Siblings

It rains a lot in southern Ohio during the spring and the year 1850 was no exception. April's response to the moisture was that buds popped out everywhere, dressing the hills along the rivers and streams in their new green coats. Into the hope of the season Davis and Jane welcomed their third son, John Holmes Hewitt on 22 April. He was born less than a year after two-year old Thomas died and in this new babe was the promise of healing. Named for Jane's grandfather, John Cochran, the choice of his middle name is unknown. Curious about the new arrival were his sisters, Ann and Louisa, but also Samuel who was seven years old.

Following close on the heels of John's birth, Davis had another life-changing event thrust upon him when his father drowned in the Little Miami River while fishing with friends one evening. Whatever brief happiness he felt over his son's birth was replaced by numbing grief and the responsibility he shouldered as the eldest son. Too soon, he was compelled to cast aside his feelings and assist in his father's estate administration. By July the muggy summer turned lethal as cholera was discovered in the county and nearby Cincinnati. Having felt its power the previous year, when death entered their neighborhood, the Hewitt family was spared another loss. When the census-taker appeared at Hewitt's doorway in 1850, he documented the summer's particular chaos when he was told that the child just born had not been named. As he grew, John eventually found his name and in a noisy, busy household learned to answer to it.

The following spring and summer was in sharp contrast to the previous year, because a bit of frivolity was in the air. Style was on young ladies' minds in 1851, and a new fad soon overtook the nation, spreading rapidly outward from the cities into the surrounding countryside. Many of Clermont County's young women began wearing an outrageous new fashion—bloomers. Although considered vulgar and unladylike to some, the trend was enthusiastically accepted by young women everywhere, even in conservative rural areas. As fashion does, it caught the media's attention providing fodder for so much scorn that the woman who named them, Amelia Bloomer, had to defend this new trend. It was outrageous for the times, but women liked it because for the first time they could move about easily. The outfit had a shorter skirt than was usual, with full pants underneath that dropped to the hem of the skirt. To encourage its acceptance, a doctor's opinion accompanied one newspaper endorsement claiming that long dresses led to consumption and caused injury to the muscular, nervous and circulatory systems of women who wore them. If that support was not sufficiently acceptable, the doctor also claimed that long dresses adversely affected the spine and frequently induced lumbar abscesses in women. Once there was backing from the medical community for this newfound freedom, there was no holding back America's youth. So many young women showed their daring at Fourth of July celebrations across the country that the trend quickly gained acceptance.[1] Once the boundaries were broken, women found the courage to try other scandalous new fangled things. The older long-skirted crowd was shocked once again when they saw young women riding astride on a bicycle…

Jane had no time for such fads, and her children were too young to test her resolve in such areas. Her days were filled to overflowing with cold hands needing mittens and hungry mouths seeking porridge. John was about eighteen months old when his brother, William Jacob Hewitt, entered the world on 10 September 1851. Jane had a break of about three years before the twins were born on 28 Jun 1854, Mary lived but her brother, unnamed, did not survive. Two more children followed quickly thereafter beginning with James who arrived on 22 Oct 1856. They were a family of eight children, evenly divided between boys and girls when Elizabeth was born on 6 May 1859. Four months later, when John was just over nine years old, his mother died.

Theirs was a large and noisy family with John somewhere in the middle, too old to be coddled but too young to understand the feelings he held inside. Sam's reaction was his key to understanding death, but John was more a boy than a man in his struggle to accept the unthinkable, and for a while he was lost in a morass of confusion and anger. Rather than going to school that fall, he was old enough to help with the harvest, and through hard work he made peace with the world. Davis's burden was heavy but it was also hard for Ann and Louisa, who cared for the four youngest children. Desperate for help, he may have asked one of his sisters to take the youngest ones for a while.

John was eleven when his father married Jane Williamson in 1861. Older now, he viewed life a little differently than he had just two years before. Will was a year younger and probably John's ally in his efforts to understand a world so fraught with change. With no one to monitor them for two years until Jane appeared, each had gained a certain measure of freedom they would not easily relinquish because there was a woman in the household once again. His sisters probably gained the most from their father's marriage since they no longer had to carry full responsibility for the younger children. Annie was seventeen and Louisa thirteen when Aunt Jane joined the family and began to run the household. Within a year though, she had a child of her own they called Richard, and two years later Benjamin was born. Both children had physical challenges defined as "paralysis" in the census. Neither learned to read and write, an indication they had other disabilities. For the girls, Annie, Lou and even Mary, after the boys were born, rather than alleviating their duties their father's marriage brought added responsibility.

1867 was another pivotal year in John's life. It began on 11 February when Sam got married. The event shifted the family dynamic because suddenly John at age seventeen was elevated to older son. Years later he and his brother were friends, but Sam's marriage created distance particularly because John was still a teenager and changing daily. When his Aunt Jane died late that summer, it demanded from John a maturity that was untested. Sam was no longer at home to guide his reaction, so he was on his own to work through another loss.

By 1870 John was twenty and no longer worked with his brothers on the farm. Although he lived at home, he worked locally as a farm laborer. Somewhat separated from the family by his job, when his father married in late 1871 he may not have been as affected by it as his younger siblings. Louisa Evans was Davis's third wife and she had come to care for him and the younger children. One by one as she settled in, the elder children married or left home, beginning with Will in 1873. The following year Lou got married, leaving Mary, who was sixteen, to care for her brothers. She was both working and attending school; likely the only one of her family to receive a high school diploma, it was at great cost to her. Her father was a country farmer with Victorian principles who probably did not encourage her education even though he allowed her to attend high school. He tolerated her ambitions as long as she took Richard and Ben to school with her. Mornings were an ordeal because in order to arrive on time, she had to "get the boys dressed, pack a lunch and drag them off to school with her."[2] A young woman of determination and focus, she somehow found a way to complete her schooling. Her granddaughter, Mary Ann Gehres, was the president of a local chapter of the *American Association of University Women*, and she wrote an article using her grandmother as an example of a woman who rose from humble beginnings to achieve a rich and satisfying life, while noting that she was also "the most steadfast feminist I have known." She wrote that Mary's mother died when she was young leaving her without a strong female role model, and in contrast, "her father dominated the surviving family in true Victorian fashion." The author related that somehow "my grandmother was inspired to cast off the confining yoke, win a scholarship to normal school, and prepare to be a teacher."[3] A photograph of her in the summer of 1875 when Mary was at the Normal School in Lebanon Ohio showed a young woman who managed to appear both serious and compassionate at the same time. In April 1877, along with forty-two others from Clermont County, she took the teacher's examination where her knowledge of math, grammar, geography, orthography and theory and practice was tested.[4] She passed her exams and then, "On her own she took a train and stagecoach more than 200 miles to her first job in southern Ohio. There she presided over a one-room school for several years. We still have the wooden geometric shapes she [used and] had a carpenter make for her students–an advanced teaching aid for the time."[5]

In contrast to his sister, John Hewitt remained within the nearby embrace of the family searching for the niche that would suit his dreams and aspirations. He visited his grandmother in Mt. Carmel until her death in 1873, and was close to his aunts who lived with her. By 1879 he must have lived there because that year he and Clark Thompson offered their threshing machine services to farmers in Glen Este.[6] As partners, Hewitt may have lived with Thompson and his wife who lived about two or three miles east of Mt. Carmel on the Batavia Pike.[7]

John had a friend, Idelbert, who was twenty-four years old and the son of Robert and Lucy Kyle who lived near Mt. Carmel.[8] In midsummer 1879, he died and John became the estate administrator, posting bond and filing the inventory.[9] What may have been a simple act of kindness to the family turned into a complex affair, trying John's patience as he trekked back and forth to Batavia on estate matters including several continuances followed by a lawsuit and a judgment. To complicate matters, over time one defendant died, and another was charged with fraud for selling the deceased man's real estate. The outcome occurred nearly three years later, when in January 1882 the property was sold to pay Kyle's debts.[10] During that time John learned a thing or two about the ins and outs of the justice system that were helpful to him years later.[11]

While John was otherwise involved with court affairs, his youngest sister Lizzie married Edgar Bratton in November 1881.[12] By then only Richard and Benjamin lived at home while their siblings' families expanded. Sam and Louisa lived near her relatives in Batavia Township with their two daughters, Bertha eight years old, and Almedia who was four in 1880. He sold fresh produce locally from a wagon, his horse alerting potential customers to his presence by the clanging bell around its neck. The huckster's visit was a time when a farmer in his field or his wife hanging wash on the line, stopped work to visit with Sam and see what he had to sell that day. He brokered deals with his customers, taking excess produce of their hands to sell to another.[13] Perhaps Sam's route was as far as Stonelick Township where his sister Lou lived with her husband Tom Mitchell and their son Hewitt, three years old. Tom worked locally as a day laborer and they lived next door to his family.[14]

Sometime between late 1880 and February of 1881 while still deeply involved in Idlebert Kyle's estate, John Hewitt accepted another task. His aunt Eliza Jane Carter who lived in Mt. Carmel died sometime before February 1881, and John became guardian for her two minor children, Richard and Henry Carter.[15] Because their father was ill with consumption,[16] Richard went almost immediately to live in McLean County, Illinois with John's aunt, Harriet, and her husband Martin Pittsenbarger.[17] His name was not in the census, but Henry also went to live with a relative.

The Courtship of Lizzie Belle Morrison

There is a bend in the Batavia Pike as it enters the little village of Mt. Carmel called Mud Corner, so named because after a rain the water drains toward that low point. For twenty years Elizabeth Hewitt and her daughter Ann lived there, and by 1870 Nancy, who was divorced, went to live with her mother and sister. Each was employed as a seamstress, including Elizabeth who was sixty-two years old. The village was a craftsman's enclave, with shops of all kinds hugging the bend along the pike. Near the Hewitt house was a master carpenter and a wagon-maker, while some of their neighbors worked in the local chair factory. The village had a painter whose specialty ranged from house décor to sign painting, also an auctioneer, two fruit farmers and a doctor. Its public buildings included a Unitarian church, a school, an Odd Fellows Hall serving several purposes, plus a hotel with a stable. Somewhat off the main road and away from the village lived the Morrison family on a 132-acre farm.[18]

Lizzie Belle Morrison was eighteen years old in 1870, and she lived with her parents, Perry and Eliza, and her brother Otto who was fourteen. Her father bought the farm when she was a toddler, improving it over the years until in 1860, at its high point it was worth $10,000.[19] Twenty years later its value dropped to $7,000. Otto worked with his father growing potatoes and corn on 50 acres, and on the remaining 30 acres, oats, wheat and apples.[20] It was a small community and they were well acquainted, thus Lizzie Belle grew up knowing John Hewitt's aunts and his grandmother. She and her mother were likely customers of the ladies who lived on Mud Corner, so it is easy to imagine that one day when Lizzie was there for a fitting with Nancy or Eliza Jane, John Hewitt popped in to visit his aunts, and their paths crossed. Then again, he may have known her brother or father first as both were active in the community. In 1876 the county held a "narrow-gauge ball" in nearby Batavia. Otto Morrison, then twenty, was on the invitation committee for Mt. Carmel. Equally involved locally was Lizzie Belle's father, a democrat, who in late 1876 served on the Committee of Resolution for Union Township. His appointment by the party's executive committee was in preparation for the convention in January to select delegates for the Ohio State Convention in Columbus. Whether John and Lizzie Belle were drawn together at a ball, the county fair, through a family member, or had been acquainted for years, one day they began courting.

On 30 Apr 1879, Lizzie Belle and John Hewitt attended a twenty-fifth wedding anniversary in Jackson Township where John had lived when he was young, and so knew the celebrants. Their attendance was noted, and so they probably arrived together. Several days later the local wag covering the event included a cryptic message meant to entice and tease the reader as well as the couple it targeted. It began, "Here and there were groups with happy hearts and smiling faces, and one might imagine some were planning their future wedding." Up to that point the message fit any number of young folk enjoying spring's blessing, but then the arrow found it's target saying, "Tis whispered—ere long, and we will not fault her, Miss M—will be lead to the hymeneal altar. How is it John?" Someone let the cat out of the bag, or maybe they let it slip. The odds are that Cupid's message was aimed directly at them, even though they were not married for another year.[21]

Idelbert Kyle was Lizzie Belle's cousin, and John's diligence on the estate helped to win her heart. As the newspaper suggested, they were probably engaged by November 1879.[22] They married on 22 Apr 1880, which coincidentally was John's thirtieth birthday. Three days before when they applied for a marriage license, for reasons known only to each other, neither gave their true age. The scene before the judge can be imagined all too easily, as John, when asked his age, shaved off two years saying he was twenty-eight. Quickly thinking that two could play that game, she replied that she was twenty-three, dropping nearly five years off her age.[23]

John and Lizzie Belle

Their first home was near her parents, probably in a house Perry Morrison owned[24] and where Bertha Pearl, who was called Birchie, was born on 22 Jul 1882.[25] Elsie was born on 14 Apr 1885, died four months later on 20 August, and was buried at Mt. Moriah Cemetery.[26] During these years, John farmed and may have worked for his father-in-law, or continued in business with his friend Clark Thompson, whom they visited in the late summer of 1886, bringing Birchie with them.[27] She was nearly five when her brother, William Otto Hewitt, was born on 17 Mar 1887[28] at Cherry Grove in rural Hamilton County. The family was in transition, because in 1888 they were living on a rented farm in another area of the county.[29] In 1891 they settled for while in Mt. Summit where for several years John continued farming.[30]

When he married into the Morrison family, John became part of a large extended Union Township family that included kin from Mt. Carmel south to Withamsville and the county line. Lizzie's mother, Frances Eliza Kyle Morrison, was from a pioneer family who settled the township nearly 100 years before, and who over the years, married into neighboring families including the much smaller Morrison clan. John probably knew most of her family prior to their wedding, including Robert Kyle who was Idelbert's father. Surrounded by her family, there was ample opportunity to meet more relatives, as the Kyles were a vigorous bunch. However, by 1882 several of them were elderly. Robert Kyle was the family's founder in Ohio, and Lizzie Belle's grandfather, so it was not surprising when he died on 30 Jan 1882 at the age of eighty-nine years. Not long after, a petition required the estate to be divided amongst his heirs. As one of Robert's seven children, Lizzie Belle's mother received 33 acres in Union Township, a portion of a larger tract. The next one to pass on was Mary Kyle, wife of John, and sister-in-law of Robert, who died in 1882 when she was eighty-four years old. On 12 Aug 1887, a third member of that generation died, Lizzie's great-uncle, Zacheus Kyle, who was eighty-nine years old and Robert's younger brother.[31]

The Grim Reaper had not yet completed his visit to the Kyle family. On 16 Mar 1888 he entered the Morrison house and claimed Frances. Her death at fifty-seven from liver disease was perhaps the result of a long illness, yet none was prepared for that end, her husband least of all.[32] With immense effort, he gathered his children together for her funeral at the Universalist Church the following Sunday, attended by at least two of Frances' siblings, Prudence Manning and John Kyle. Soon after Perry erected a final tribute to his wife of nearly forty years, to which someone responded that it was the finest monument in the Union Township (Mt. Moriah) cemetery. A year later on 10 Nov 1889, Frances' brother Jefferson Kyle died and again the family was called to the Mt. Carmel Universalist Church to say goodbye to one of their own.[33]

As so often happens, when one soul leaves the earth they cross paths with another, and so it was Lizzie Belle's turn to announce the good news that Francese Vesta was born on 9 Nov 1889. In remembering her sister years later, Birchie called her the "sweet one," known as Vesta, whose first name honored her grandmother. By 1891 John Hewitt had three children and he was looking for suitable ways to support them. He looked for work that would pay the bills but also jobs appropriate to his skills. That year he bought a lot in nearby Summerside[34] and opened a store near their home in Mt. Summit.[35] The following year he placed the lot in Lizzie Belle's name, perhaps because financially she was a better risk.[36] While living in Mt. Summit in 1891-1892, Birchie attended the fourth and fifth grades at Mt. Carmel Primary School. At the time, students in rural areas went to school only about five or six months of the year because their parents needed their help during planting and harvest seasons. This was particularly true of the boys and of older students, some of whom did not attend school beyond the eighth grade.[37]

Sam Hewitt

In 1887, John's brother Sam Hewitt was forty-four years old, and he had lived long enough to know that what he had been given in life was enough, and was grateful for it. He and Louisa lived near Olive Branch village on Taylor Road next door to her relative Thirza Duckett.[38] His peddler's cart was known throughout the neighborhood and beyond. Probably gregarious and outgoing, Sam was also generous to his neighbors as one public declaration of appreciation indicated. At harvest season one year he brought vegetables to the newspaper office in Batavia, and his reward was a bit of free advertising, boasting that he had the largest beets and potatoes of the season. His daughters, Almedia, called Media, and Bertha were nine and fifteen years old. In late fall Media was ill with acute inflammatory rheumatism, an affliction causing pain in one or more of the joints but usually in the outer extremities.[39] It was not the first time she had known illness; when she was four years old she had scarletina, a rash caused by a strep germ gone wild that sometimes causes rheumatic fever. She recovered from both illnesses although whether they caused complications later in life is unknown.

When John's brother James Hewitt moved to Oregon, several photographs were given to him so that he could stay abreast of their growing family in Ohio and Tennessee. The author was given copies, and in one of them is a thin older man with a receding hairline and a long white beard, who must be Samuel. White hair by age fifty must have been a Hewitt trait on the male side as photographs of his brothers Will and John indicated. Standing on either side of his rocking chair in the dandelion dusted grass of the front yard are two young women wearing dark dresses, one a teen and the other somewhat older looking. Behind them stands a two-story farmhouse with a long walk leading to the street. In 1892 Sam Hewitt had two daughters, aged fourteen and twenty, a profile that fits no one else in the family. Surely the picture was of him and his daughters, taken by his wife when he was forty-nine years old, a few months before he died in October 1892.[40]

Samuel probably was ill for a year or more, but by late 1892 consumption was taking its toll and he began failing. Sensing this, he sold his personal property on 6 Oct that year, and ten days later, not yet fifty years old, he died at his home in Olive Branch. He was the eldest, the first to marry and the first to die, leaving his siblings vulnerable for the first time to feelings of personal mortality. Sam had been a member of the village Baptist Church for ten years, and an officer of the Synod when he died. Whoever wrote his obituary recognized his mother's influence in his faith, repeating that he "tried to live the life of a Christian—the principles being instilled into his character by the influence of his mother who died when he was but sixteen years of age." The article emphasized his illness noting that his "sufferings have been intense at times for the past year but all summer he has expressed himself ready to go whenever the Master called him." After the church services, the minister and the entourage of family and friends moved to Olive Branch Cemetery to conclude the ceremony.[41] Samuel's grave is within view of his father's headstone, and his wife and daughter Media surround him in death. Upon visiting the cemetery in 1998, the author observed flowers laid next to his headstone, an indication that even today someone visits his grave.

Bertha Hewitt was twenty years old and in the midst of wedding plans during her father's last illness, but he did not live to see her marry Charles Violett at home in late December 1892. As a young married woman, she plunged into neighborhood activities, including as an officer of the newly established Epworth League of the Methodist-Episcopal Church, responsible for the church's Sunday evening social programs. Media Hewitt was fifteen and boarded in town when she attended Batavia High School. She was home in April 1893, and throughout the summer their home was open to friends of mother and daughters. As the heat and humidity of southern Ohio rose that year, the village of Olive Branch cooled off with an ice cream social attended by Media, her sister and brother-in-law. Then in September she went back to school while Bertha and Charles Violett went to Columbus to take in the state fair.

Throughout the spring and into the fall of the year following Sam's death, his siblings came to console his widow, Louisa. His sister Annie and her husband, Mel McClellan visited that year in August. Their brother John Hewitt visited in May and again in October just after the first anniversary of his brother's death. Sam and John were close in age and they did not live far from one another, so it was probably an established habit once both were married, that their families came together for Sunday visits, and because music was important to them, it was a source of entertainment for all. Even after she married, Vesta was in touch with her cousin Bertha, who because she was seventeen years older acted as a surrogate mother to her younger cousin.[42]

Media Hewitt graduated in May 1896, one of six young women and five men to participate in the fifteenth annual commencement services of Batavia High School. An orchestra played as ceremonies began at the Batavia Opera House, and the graduates paraded their talents. Among the readings, speeches and performances of her peers, Media played a piano solo, *Fatime* by Kalfka, while her family and the community looked on and listened. Sometime after graduation she moved to Huron County, Ohio near Sandusky on Lake Erie where she met John Spearing. They were married at her mother's house on 19 Dec 1900 then left for their home in Gringage, Ohio. They were not married long, because when Media visited her mother in the summer of 1902, she was referred to as Mrs. McCullough.

Louisa Hewitt had tuberculosis and during her long illness, Bertha alone cared for her because Media lived far away. As she approached her last days, however, both daughters were with her. Louisa was sixty-six years old when she died on 26 May 1903. Her daughters made the journey to the old cemetery on the hill where they laid her body beside their father.[43]

Ann, James and Louisa Hewitt

Ann married at age forty, beyond the time when she could bear children. Her husband, Marion, or Mel, was nine years younger than his bride when they wed on 24 Jul 1884.[44] Although the McClellans had no children of their own, they were part of an early social service placement program for orphaned children. In 1900 they became foster parents to a nineteen-year-old girl named Lydia whose parents were born in Germany.[45] In 1901 in conjunction with the Cincinnati Children's Home, the couple again brought a foster child to live with them in Maywood, a part of Batavia in Union Township.[46] Later the couple moved to Oregon to be near Ann's brother, James Hewitt, who lived in Roseburg. Both lived and worked on a ranch near Roseburg for a number of years, until Annie became ill, probably with complications of diabetes that had plagued her for years. She died on 20 Mar 1911 and was buried at Roseburg Memorial Gardens.[47] Shortly thereafter Mel returned to Ohio.

Like his brother John, James Hewitt was nearly thirty years old when he married Mollie Brady in Jacksonville, Illinois. Many years later her granddaughter relayed the story of how Mollie and her mother, Mary Ann Brady, were abandoned in St. Louis by her father, Jonathan. For several years after, mother and daughter lived in a convent where the nuns provided them with food and shelter, and where Mollie learned to sew. A pieced quilt she made at age nine is a treasured memento of her granddaughter, Mollie, who is named after her. In 1880, James was single and twenty-five years old, working on a farm outside of Jacksonville where he boarded.[48] He became acquainted with Mollie Brady and they married on 3 May 1886. They brought Mary with them when they moved to Oregon two years later to live with Mollie's aunt in the Camas Valley. In 1889 James found farmland just north of Roseburg where they settled. Oregon was agreeable to James and Mollie, and it was where they raised eight children, several of whom lived to a very great age. With a home at last, Mary Ann Brady helped raise her grandchildren, sometimes cooking for them, but always listening as only a grandmother can, while she dried their tears and watched them grow into men and women. Hewitt had a well-developed farm, with many fruit trees, a large vegetable garden along with the requisite cows, pigs and chickens. Emulating his elder brother, Sam, as an additional source of income, he gathered the extra produce and sold it to his neighbors. James was also a carpenter and many of the fine homes in and around Roseburg bear the stamp of his craftsmanship. James had a massive stroke when he was seventy-one years old and he died a few days later on 31 May 1928.[49]

In 1880 John Hewitt's sister Lou Mitchell and her husband Tom lived in Clermont County's Stonelick Township, but by 1900 they had moved west into Hamilton County. Their home was in the Cincinnati suburb of Norwood on Wesley Avenue. Tom was a painter and their son Hewitt, who was twenty-three, worked as a mail clerk for the railroad and lived at home with his parents.[50] A portrait taken about ten years earlier captured the family in a studio pose, showing a slender woman of piercing gaze sitting erectly on an overstuffed chair. Behind her on either side, were Tom and Hewitt who was about ten years old, dating the photograph to about 1886 when Lou was thirty-six years old.[51]

Will and Mary Hewitt

By 1881, Will Hewitt and his wife Rachel Hill had moved to Davidson County, Tennessee where they owned a large grocery store in downtown Nashville. It stood at the corner of 13 Chestnut and Maple Streets, and a photograph taken about 1900 depicts a substantial brick building placed firmly on a corner lot that extended half a block in each direction.[52] Parked in front, on the snow-encrusted street were horse-drawn delivery wagons, whose drivers and animals were bundled against the cold. Displayed prominently on the building and the wagons was *W. J. Hewitt, Dealer in Groceries & Produce Fruits & Vegetables a Specialty*. His store was in a mixed-use area, both commercial and residential, and the family lived just around the corner. Will and Rachel married in Clermont County in 1873, and by 1896 had seven children. In 1900 his father, Davis, who was eighty-four years old and blind, lived with them. Will's eldest son John was eighteen and worked in the store while the other children attended school. It was clearly a family business as their sons, Carl, John, Harry, Amos and William Jr. all clerked in the store and lived at home.[53]

In July of 1881 Mary Hewitt must have been on summer break from teaching school because she went to visit her brother in Nashville for a month. Returning home she stopped at Olive Branch to bring news to her family before returning home to Waverly Ohio.[54] A descendant tells the story about how she came to marry Joe Gehres. One day she was standing by a window and saw him walking down the street. She asked who he was and when told, responded, "That is the man I'm going to marry," and she did.[55] The following year Mary relinquished her role as a teacher, married Joe who was a lumber dealer, and never looked back. Within three years she bore two sons, Hewitt then Loyd; Mary was born in 1890 and Irma in 1892 to complete their family.[56] Over the next few years, the children grew and the business that Joe shared with his brother expanded. The Gehres Brothers lumberyard was their main business, but they also built homes, some of them experimental. In 1897 they departed from the typical southern Ohio architecture and began using contemporary eastern designs that were quite successful in revamping the town.

In 1897, Tennessee celebrated its centennial with an international exposition similar to the Columbian Exposition held in 1893. Although not as spectacular as its predecessor, that July the world's fair attracted Mary and Joe who went there to visit Will and Rachel, and to see the sights.

As her children became more self-reliant, Mary began moving out into the community to help where there was need. Her volunteer work and public obligations became very important to her and for the remainder of her life she was heavily involved both locally and nationally. In 1900, she was the secretary of the Board of County Visitors for Pike County, one of five individuals who

Rachel Hill Hewitt and William Jacob Hewitt (1851-1928)
Nashville, Tennessee, photograph ca. 1900

W. J. Hewitt Grocery Store, Nashville, Tennessee, ca. 1900

Hewitt Family photograph, ca. 1897 Will and Rachel Hewitt's yard in Nashville, Tennessee.
Back Row: unknown, unknown, Joe Gehres, unknown, unknown, Mary Jane (Jen) Gehres, Hewitt Mitchell, unknown, Ann Hewitt McClellan, Harry Hewitt.
On the porch, Mary Hewitt Gehres, Richard Davis Hewitt.
Middle Row: Rachel Hill Hewitt, Louisa Hewitt Mitchell, unknown, Tom Mitchell, Will Hewitt, John Hewitt.
Front row, William Hewitt Jr., Hattie Hewitt, Mary Gehres, Lillian Hewitt, Ruth Hewitt, unknown, unknown.

Mitchell Family photograph, Cincinnati, Ohio, ca. 1885.
Hewitt Mitchell (1876), Louisa Hewitt Mitchell (1848-1911),
Tom Mitchell (1846).

Mary Jane Hewitt (1854-1950)
photograph, summer 1875

Mary Hewitt Gehres (1854-1950) and Joseph Gehres
Photograph, Waverly, Ohio, ca. 1910

James Hewitt (far right back row), Mollie Brady Hewitt (far left front row) and family, Roseburg, Oregon, ca. 1914

visited and reported to the board of health on the vitality of the county infirmary, the children's home and the county jail.[57]

Will was three years older than his sister Mary, and perhaps they were drawn together from childhood. As adults they had similar interests and both families liked to travel. They visited each other often, particularly after their father went to live with Will in Nashville. Fond memories of their trip to the Tennessee Centennial a few years earlier may have drawn them together again, but the second time they got together, Joe drove the family's Cadillac touring car.[58] In July 1901, the world's fair was held in Buffalo, New York. It was known as the Pan-American Exposition, so called because it featured the industry and culture of both continents. Just as before, the fair presented the latest trends, developments and technical accomplishments of this country presented under Spanish Colonial architecture. Called the Rainbow City, electric lights splashed the buildings nightly with multi-colored hues. By day, visitors were treated to such delights on the Midway as Cleopatra's temple, African and Eskimo villages and a fantasy trip to the moon. Other replicas of exotic places featured a Japanese village and a taste of Venice. There was a Wild West show and one attraction featuring an upside down castle with its entrance from the top.[59] The two families left the fair full of memories of another extraordinary visit to the wonders of their world, but rather than go directly back to Nashville, Will agreed to detour east and bring his family to Clermont County to see their cousins.[60] Later, the Hewitt and Gehres families had reason to be grateful they were in New York in July, rather than in September when President McKinley and his wife visited the Exposition for the first time. They went first to Niagara Falls and then to the Exposition where the president attended a reception. While standing in a line greeting people a man concealing a gun under his handkerchief walked up and shot the President. McKinley was whisked off to a private residence nearby where he lingered for several days. In the early hours of 13 Sep 1901, McKinley died, and in a simple ceremony later that afternoon, Theodore Roosevelt was sworn in as America's twenty-sixth president.[61]

Mary Gehres was politically active throughout her life. She was a Republican, mostly because she thought the Democratic Party was corrupt and paternalistic, and in mid-life she became the party's county chairwoman. Her granddaughter, Mary Ann Gehres, wrote in a tribute "grandmother remained a teacher all her life, instructing Bible classes, founding literary societies and speaking on a wealth of topics."[62] Her heroines were Susan B. Anthony and Carrie Nation in whose honor she worked for women's suffrage, and to improve race relations as a member of the WCTU. Her enthusiasm in promoting her suffragette and temperance beliefs at rallies was welcomed by others, but it embarrassed her children. When Mary first voted in 1920 at the age of sixty-six, it was a supremely happy moment for her. Then because she was so interested in the education of Waverly's children, she organized a chapter of Junior American Citizens, and continued in that endeavor until she was ninety-five. One cold night in March of 1950, she had a chapter meeting to attend and a friend was going to pick her up. She waited outside, and when her ride did not appear she started walking but became disoriented and wandered onto the farm of a relative. After being outside for hours she was found but had taken a chill from the cold. Never one to give up easily, Mary fought to survive but when she developed uremic poisoning, her body betrayed her and she died on 24 Mar 1950, a few months before her ninety-sixth birthday.[63]

Elizabeth Hewitt

By 1910 there occurred a distinct geographic shift within the Hewitt family and it took place in Davidson County, Tennessee in and around Nashville. When Hayes Hewitt and his wife Anna Shute moved there nearly 100 years before, the city was a small frontier town on the edge of the Carolina wilderness, and that branch of the family continued living in the area, mostly bearing names other than Hewitt. Will and Rachel may have moved there with members of the Hill family, yet they may have chosen it because his cousins were there. Will was, however, the first member of the Ohio branch of the family to make Nashville his home, and it may be why Lizzie Hewitt Bratton moved there too. She wed Edgar Bratton on 8 Nov 1881 when she was twenty-two years old, but nothing else is known about their marriage.[64] An undocumented source indicated Lizzie moved to Nashville after Edgar's death, and that she married Rachel's brother, Amos Hill. About 1910 their brother, John Hewitt, also moved to Nashville. When Will Hewitt died on 2 Jun 1928, his obituary named his siblings as, J. H. Hewitt of Madison Tennessee, Mrs. Joe Gehres of Waverly, Ohio and Mrs. A. K. Hill of Nashville, verifying that two of them still lived in the Nashville area.[65] Amos Hill's first wife Ellen died in 1919, and he married Lizzie after 1920 when he was a widower, but before 1928 when her brother died. In 1930 the couple lived on South Springs Road near the Murphreesboro Pike in Davidson County. By then Lizzie Hill was seventy-one years old, and Amos who was seventy-six, was actively farming. His son, Ed Hill, who lived with him ten years before, was next door living on part of the farm, which when valued together was worth $11,500, substantially more than their neighbors'.[66] When Amos died on 24 Nov 1941, Lizzie was eighty-two years old and only she and Mary Gehres, of the original family were still living.[67]

Richard and Ben Hewitt

In 1892 John and Lizzie sold 33 acres she inherited from her mother, then in February 1893, after John's father had placed Richard and Ben in the Infirmary, he bought their portion of the family farm for $200.[68] In May that year, Lizzie Belle paid $675 for three acres in the Summerside neighborhood.[69] Clearly they were trying to get ahead, by working to establish John in a business, and by buying land as income property.

John's father, Davis Hewitt, was seventy-seven years in 1892, aging and going blind. A year earlier he placed his two youngest sons in an infirmary because he could no longer care for them, either physically or financially. He was in debt with liens against the farm, and no means to pay if off. He was no longer able to pay his bills because ten years before he sold the farm to his children to rid himself of debt. In June 1893, John brought a lawsuit against his siblings to pay off the debt so the farm would be free and clear. Perhaps he took the lead because with the death of his brother, Sam, he was now the eldest son. Whatever his motives, he seemed unable to enlist his siblings' cooperation on a plan to save it, so he sued for partition of the farm. When John purchased his brothers' portions three months earlier, he became the major owner, and so he was thus more interested in paying off the debt. When he filed for a partition of the premises, his father filed a cross petition. The court settled the matter by determining that although the liens had to be eradicated, splitting the land between them would reduce its value. To free the title, Davis's children, or their heirs, were ordered to pay their father fifty dollars annually until the debt was paid in full. Because most of them had married and some had died, there were twenty owners. Named in the petition was Sam's widow, Louisa, and their two children, Media Hewitt and Bertha Hewitt Violett. It also confirmed the marriages of all of John's sisters. Finally the order declared that Davis Hewitt was entitled to all the firewood necessary for his private use on that portion of land owned by his son John.[70]

From time to time members of the Hewitt family gathered for family events, sometimes in Nashville. One such gathering was photographed about 1897, and passed on to the family in Oregon who were not present. Gathered outside on the lawn in the summer sun was a large group of varying ages. The number on the house leading to the verandah corresponded to that of Will and Rachel Hewitt who lived at 118 Maple, and so the group was probably gathered in their Nashville back yard. Because the young ladies among them had light colored dresses, and a few of the youngsters were barefoot, it was probably high summer. In contrast, their mothers wore dark everyday dresses and the men had on either suits or working clothes. An elderly man with a cane who was sitting on the porch in a rocking chair was probably Davis Hewitt, who in 1897 was living with Will and Rachel. Next to him was Mary Gehres who was about 43 years old. That summer Joe and Mary, and his sister Dollie Gehres, went to Nashville to see Will Hewitt and his family, probably traveling by train. Thus, the families were probably photographed sometime during their visit to see the Tennessee Centennial Exposition. Will, who was their host, was seated in the middle row of adults next to his brother-in-law Tom Mitchell. To his right sat his wife Rachel, and next to her, Will's sister Lou Mitchell. Standing behind Will and one of his sons was probably Lizzie Bratton. The younger Gehres children sat on the lawn with their Hewitt cousins, while the older cousins stood in the back row of the photograph. Missing was Sam Hewitt, who died in 1892, James to whom the photo was sent, but also John Hewitt and Annie McClellan, who lived in the Cincinnati area and did not make the trip to Nashville.[71]

A Shift in Perspective

Perhaps Perry Morrison considered it an omen when one of his houses burned in May 1889.[72] The blaze, caused by a defective flue in the exhaust system, burned the house to the ground and although the furniture was saved, without insurance it was a total loss of $1,500. Shortly thereafter he signed his property over to his children. Otto got the most valuable land, the 132-acre Mt. Carmel farm, and Lizzie Belle Hewitt received a small 65-acre farm on Rumpke Road in Union Township.[73] The only property not signed over to them was what his wife inherited from her father. When he was about 70 years old, Morrison made some thoughtful choices about how he wanted his family remembered. After Eliza died he had a large monument installed in Mt. Carmel cemetery that would someday include all of their names; he freed himself of debt; and gave his real property to his children. He was not exceptionally old, and his health may have declined because of Eliza's death, so it was important to put his affairs in order.

An incident reported in the newspaper in spring 1892 was a precursor to other events that unfolded shortly thereafter, and which eventually became public. The headline began with the word *Missing*. In fairness to Otto, all that is known is what was reported. It said:

> The mysterious disappearance of Amos O. Morrison, a wealthy farmer, under circumstances that give rise to a suspicion of foul play, which has caused considerable excitement in the vicinity of Mt. Carmel. Morrison who is 36 years old, lives with his invalid father...in Mt. Carmel, Ohio. He is very wealthy, owning all of Turkey Bottoms, east of Columbia, a very valuable farm and stable full of horses. He left home for Cincinnati last Tuesday driving a two-horse team and leading another horse which he had decided to sell. He put up his team and wagon at Packer's stable on Second near Ludlow, and started for the Fifth Street stables with the other horse. He was a well-known figure at the auction stables but none of the men there remember seeing Morrison on that day. He has not been seen since. Meredith Johnson, one of Morrison's neighbors, went to town Saturday and reported the matter to Lieutenant Fisher. He says that the stable is locked and that the horses are starving, not having been fed since last Tuesday. He wanted to know what to do, and Fisher told him to get some more of the neighbors, break in the barn and feed the animals. Johnson fears that Morrison has met with foul play. He always carried a lot of money, a valuable gold watch and chain and elegant jewelry. The police of all the districts have been notified and are on the lookout for the missing man.[74]

He did not meet with foul play and eventually came home. What really happened did not reach the newspapers but from the neighbor's concern it appeared that his behavior was unusual. The article indicated that Perry was quite ill and Johnson seemed to know better than to consult him about the problem and instead turned it over to the authorities. The elder Morrison's health continued to decline and on 22 Sep 1892 he died from the strain on his heart caused by dropsy.[75] Perry was 72 years old and he left no will, probably because everything of importance was distributed prior to his death. There was no obituary to notify the neighbors of his passing, and most of his family died when he was young man, so his funeral was small and private. Left to mourn were Otto and Lizzie who laid him to rest in Mt. Moriah Cemetery next to their mother for whom he had erected the monument.

In the long parade of deaths within the Kyle family including their mother, and then father, Lizzie Belle and Otto were left with gaping holes where their hearts had been nourished before. Surrounded by the Kyle family since childhood they felt alone, orphaned by the deaths of their parents. At the end of the day they were left with one another. Lizzie Belle had an advantage over her brother in that she had a husband and three children to fill her arms and with them the opportunity to mend her heart. Not so, Otto. As expected, he was the estate administrator and began his duties almost immediately, with the assistance of his neighbor Merritt Johnson, and others who helped appraise the property. Perry left behind cash and securities of nearly $6,000 plus other bonds and notes payable to him bringing his assets, aside from the land he had previously given his children, to about $7,000.[76]

Most of the administration was complete by early February 1893, and within a month Otto was dead. Both county newspapers reported his ending but one of them blew the lid off a family tragedy. *The Clermont Sun* reported it this way, "Very sudden were the deaths of William Prickett and A. O. Morrison of Mt. Carmel. The citizens of Mt. Carmel and vicinity have been caused to mourn the loss of two of their prominent and well-known citizens. Both died on the same day near the same locality and without any immediate previous sickness, but from different causes." The article then went on to describe how Prickett, who was 67 years old, probably died of a stroke. He was well known to the Morrison family as he appraised Perry's estate just a few months before his death. The other newspaper, *The Clermont Courier* began the article with the headline "His Last Freak." This is what it revealed.

> A. O. Morrison of Mt. Carmel, who for many years has been a resident of that place, where he owned two fine farms, a large amount of stock, a fine home and all the accessories that go to make a home comfortable, with the exception of a wife, was found dead in his kitchen at four o'clock last Sunday evening. Morrison has for a long time lived alone having neither wife, housekeeper or acquaintance to share with him the comforts of his wealth, or relieve the monotony of his life. In the dearth of other associations he has for a long time cultivated the companionship of the bottle, and it was by this treacherous friend that he was done to death. The neighbor who discovered his condition had ventured on the premises on some errand, and receiving no response to his knock, and knowing that Morrison was at home, made bold to enter. He found him lying on the floor quite dead, but notwithstanding this, hastily summoned a physician, and later a messenger rode into Batavia for Justice Nichols, by whom an inquest was held Saturday evening.

The deceased was found lying on his face on the kitchen floor. The fire was out in the stove, and the kitchen presented a scene of the greatest discomfort. The room was unkempt and unswept and the table contained an array of empty bottles, jugs and dingy glasses, a pitcher half-filled with water, a sugar bowl bearing the traces of acquaintance with moistened spoons, a number of which were scattered about, having evidently been long in use without washing. The bed in the sleeping apartment was almost squalid, and all the surroundings gave evidence of the most slovenly neglect of everything except the business of drinking.

The expert testimony taken before Squire Nichols, acting as coroner, disclosed the fact that Morrison had met his death from asphyxia, the result of excessive alcohol drinking and the verdict was to this effect. Deceased was 37 years old, unmarried, and for several years has been indulging in the use of the fiery liquids that destroyed his life. Some months ago it will be remembered, the *Courier* contained an account of a visit of deceased to Cincinnati, leaving his stock locked up, the poor animals becoming almost frantic with starvation before his return. His nearest relative is a Mrs. Hewitt, who keeps a store at Summerside and is in comfortable circumstances. It is not known if Morrison left any will. His estate is estimated to be worth about $25,000.

Morrison's funeral was held in Summerside the Tuesday following the inquest and some of those who attended the services, probably family, lived in nearby Glen Este.[77]   Afterward an engraver carved his name on the tall monument in Mt. Moriah Cemetery, leaving Lizzie Belle the last remaining member of that family. Her father's final illness and the unexpected death of her brother left her heir to everything the family owned, farm, land, bonds and personal possessions. She was also heir to the loss of her family and as such, immediately after her brother's funeral she plunged into the administration of his holdings and debts as well as accounting for whatever remained of her father's estate. The official announcement was 29 Mar 1893, but the combined estates were not settled for another year and a half.[78]

Otto owned three horses worth $285 that he raced in Cincinnati, but most of the estate he inherited from his father. Perry's wealth was in securities, the largest a $5,000 bank bond. Between Otto and his father they had a personal inventory of $1,200, and with notes, bonds and cash from the land sale, the overall estate was worth nearly $8,000. Not included were the several properties, including a valuable working farm, all of which in 1894 was owned by Lizzie Belle Hewitt and her husband, John.

On one hand, she was a smalltown heiress, but on the other she had lost her entire family in five years. Land could not replace a father's smile or a mother's touch, and land was all that remained. With nothing but sad endings behind them, it was perhaps with clouded vision that Lizzie and John made their next decisions. Their private response to Otto's death and the embarrassment from public exposure took its toll. Some of their activities in the years following the estate settlement indicated they were unfocussed, but also naïve about contractual agreements they made. When things really soured and why it happened only they would know, but outwardly they seemed to be reacting to mounting debt. The first crack in the egg appeared in April 1894 when John's half-brothers, Richard and Benjamin, sued him for $200 he owed them as their part of the family farm.[79]

Freefall

Cincinnati was expanding in the years leading up to the twentieth century, with new subdivisions opening and housing developments popping up all around the city. Opportunity was there if you had the money, and John and Lizzie Belle had land that could be turned into cash. 1896 became a pivotal year, because in October they sold the land her father gave her, a 65-acre farm on Rumpke Road. They made $2,400 on the deal, each signing separately, and with separate witnesses, signifying they were not signing as a couple.[80] Next, they bought two lots in Norwood near the center of the city, and purchased land in the Bofinger and Hopkins Subdivision of Millcreek Township. Their troubles began soon after and Lizzie Belle mortgaged one of the lots for $320.[81]

By 1897 the family had moved from Mt. Summit on the Clough Pike to Fruit Hill, a rural area near Cincinnati in Anderson Township. Their home was not far from the boarding and livery stable at 236 East Second Street that John managed in an industrial section of Cincinnati.[82] John also owned property near Withamsville, and they probably used part of the mortgage money to pay back taxes on that land.[83] However, tax bills were only a minor blot on the landscape of their overwhelming debts. In early February of 1897, a petition by her creditors was filed against Lizzie Belle, and she was forced to file bankruptcy. At stake was the land left by her father and brother when they died.

To bring the problem to its final resolution, she appeared at the Hamilton County's Court of Insolvency on 19 Feb 1897. That day she and John signed over three properties. First, the 132-acre farm appraised at $4,800 (less than half of what her father had paid for it.) Then they released for sale three acres John bought to setup a store in Summerside. Last to go was a Bofinger and Hopkins lot adjacent to the one she mortgaged earlier.[84] However, the landslide was not yet over. A few days later, another of John's properties was foreclosed,[85] and Lizzie Belle paid the mortgage on the Norwood lot. Bankruptcy is always difficult, but they were at the mercy of the Torrens Act, "a land registration system which, upon the owner's application, the court may issue a certificate of title. However, it is the registration of a title as distinguished from the recording of evidence of a title."[86] Why the Torrens system was used is unknown but it was costly to John and Lizzie Belle, and so unusual that both Cincinnati newspapers wrote articles decrying its use. The *Enquirer* said, "A petition was filed in the Insolvency Court yesterday by the assignee of Lizzie B. Hewitt asking for the sale of the real estate which has been appraised at $48,487. It was estimated that the expense of taking it through the Torrens system of titles when the sale is made, will be from $750 to $1,000. It will have to be so taken through, if the Supreme Court holds that the law is constitutional. The liabilities of the assignor in this case are returned at $21,671."[87]

When it was over, their hopes and dreams were shattered, and their assets depleted. Perhaps they still owned the Norwood lot and 33 acres in Union Township that Lizzie Belle inherited from her mother, but the story continued. After moving to Sutton Avenue in Mt. Washington, in 1898 and 1899 John ran a livery and boarding stables in the city but opened another in Fruit Hill.[88] Swirling around the turmoil were the couple's three children who were aware of their parents financial problems, but as school children, did their homework while seeking amusement apart from their parents. While dealing with life's stickier issues, John and Lizzie continued the children's music lessons, and Birchie who was seventeen and a violinist, was for the first time listed in the city's directory as a musician. Her next move was to marry and leave home.

By 1900 the family operation moved into the heart of Cincinnati, that is John, Lizzie Belle, William who was thirteen and Vesta aged ten years. Economic necessity probably drove them to the industrial section of Cincinnati near the livery stable, and where in 1900 John ran a saloon. Used to a quieter rural life, they were unaccustomed to the noise and bustle of the city, and some of the unpleasant sights that greeted their eyes and ears whenever they ventured into the streets. The census provided a look into the neighborhood that year.

Life in Cincinnati

To make ends meet, John rented a house on 216 Sycamore Street, which Vesta and Will shared with their parents and two boarders in their twenties, one was a baker, the other a servant. The latter was a woman known to the family before they moved to the city, because three years before she witnessed the sale of the farm on Rumpke Road. Will was in high school and Vesta went to a nearby grade school. New friends were as close as the children next door whose father was a baker. Other neighbors were craftsmen and laborers of varying descriptions, a tanner, a janitor and a foreman of some kind. Some worked in restaurants as waiters or cooks. Their nearest neighbor was a stable hand, who may have worked for John. Most of their neighbors worked in service related industries, including a painter, a barber, an ironworker and a bookbinder. Several men, like Hewitt, were hostlers indicating that most city business was conducted by horse-drawn wagons.[89]

The children found new sights, sounds and smells in the city. For a young boy and girl it was stimulating and exciting to the senses. The Cincinnati telephone book provided a vivid description of the kinds of business that lined Sycamore Street in 1889 on either side of Hewitt's stable and saloon. It was heavily industrial and probably colorful too. Among the many manufactories was a glass works and carriage manufacturer, and a seller of patent medicines, soda water and ginger ale. There were wagon companies, a brass foundry, a packinghouse, lithographers and a number of markets carrying wholesale food. Carpenters and builders in the area had ready access to materials supplied by nearby lumber dealers. Access was only blocks away for a company providing packing boxes for another one that sold axles, bolts, and plumbing supplies. Above all else, there were plenty of breweries, wine companies and wholesale liquor dealers. Not surprisingly, there were a good number of doctors and undertakers in the neighborhood too.

Although the family moved twice after their initial entry into the city, Hewitt's livery stable remained at the same location. They lived at two locations on Sycamore, then in 1902 they moved to 103 East Pearl Street where they lived for two or three years.[90] The move into the city was an adjustment, but more consuming to them was Will's health. Early in their marriage, they lost a daughter and now their son was ill. With pressing need they sought a cure for the ravages of consumption that was sapping his young life.

It all began in 1901 when Otto began Woodward High School. During the school year he caught a cold from which he never fully recovered, although there was brief hope when he revived the following summer. After a downturn in the fall of 1902 he was diagnosed with tuberculosis. The cure then was to send the patient for a sanatorium rest cure, and the early twentieth century there were such hospitals in the New Mexico, Colorado and North Carolina mountains. With high hopes, his parents sent Otto to New Mexico where he remained until March 1903. Finally, with great sadness, John brought his son home on the train so that in the end he could be with his family. Otto died a week later on 22 Mar 1903, but death and tears were not yet over for this family. In a strange twist of fate, Otto's grandfather Davis Hewitt who was 84 years old, also died that day. Their obituaries appeared on the front page of the local newspaper, marking their passing but not their relationship to each other.[91] Davis's funeral was on Tuesday, and Otto's on Wednesday at the Universalist Church in Mt. Carmel where relatives and family friends gathered for their second funeral that week. They gathered that day at Mt. Moriah Cemetery where Otto Hewitt was laid to rest near both his grandfather Perry Morrison and his sister Elsie.

It was a sad time for John and Lizzie and for their daughters. Stripped from them within twenty-four hours was a parent, a child, a sibling and a grandparent, producing an overflow of emotion that hurled those grieving into a foggy vacuum for a time. That was where Lizzie found herself in the aftermath of death, and she did not recover. A month before Otto died, she caught "la grippe" and was sick for two months. Grief and illness fought a dance for her life, one she did not win. The death knell counted three when she surrendered on 24 Apr 1903 and that is where it ended. With Lizzie's death, another relationship was added to their losses, that of mother and wife. Whoever wrote her obituary, either her daughters or her husband, wanted assurance that her lineage and family history was known to all.[92] Three times within a month, family and friends attended a funeral. Watching John, a daughter on either side as they sat, or clutching his arm as they emerged from the carriage at the cemetery, those attending must have wondered how this family, now reduced by two would survive. At that moment, they wondered themselves, but as Lizzie Belle was laid next to the freshly dug grave of her son Otto, they prayed for her soul. Others prayed for John and Birchie and for Vesta.

The Family Regroups

Vesta was thirteen when her mother died, and when she and her father returned from the funeral to the house on Sycamore Street they were alone in a house with voices that echoed of loved ones now gone, where every room brought memories of those who would not return. Sometime afterward, John gave up the house and the business, and moved with his daughter away from their house of sadness. By 1905, they were living in Spencer Township just east of the city where he rented a place on New Richmond Pike and took up farming again. Vesta was fifteen and for the next two years, the city's directory listed her as a vocalist. In 1908, driven away by the sadness pervading their lives, she left her father's home at seventeen and escaped into marriage.[93] John condoned it by accompanying her across the Ohio River to marry George Schmidt in Newport Kentucky on 17 Apr 1907.

With both daughters married and safely in their husbands' care, John left Cincinnati and Ohio in search of a new life. It began with a visit, but soon he was living near Nashville. In 1909 he wrote to his niece, Bertha Violett and her husband Charley who lived in Olive Branch. What he told Sam Hewitt's daughter was an indication of his state of mind and his health at the time.

> Nashville, Tennessee. Dec 12 '09, My dear Niece Bertha & Charles. I have often thought of writing to you but just never got at it. That didn't stop me from thinking of you. How are you anyhow? I hope it will find you with a multitude of turkies for the holidays. They are bringing 18 and 20 cents per pound alive here and scarce. Write and tell me all the news you know of. Got a letter from Vesta and Birchie last week. Vesta is feeling much better. Birchie is well also. You don't know how I would like to see all of them and all of the folks. Those little boys I am crazy to see them but it will be a long time before I will I expect. I am in an awful shape. Have been doctoring for two months. Have got so poor I can't make a shadow when out in the sun. I feel sometimes like I would be starting for Mt. Moriah (the cemetery) soon. I can go around but don't feel like I could do anything.
>
> I am going to meet some parties tomorrow to see about taking a large farm to superintend it for them. There is 150 acres of orchard on it. There is 350 acres in the farm. I think I will get it. John Hill is one of the parties. He is going to have them meet me. If I get it I will have to get me a housekeeper...It is up in a mountainous country that will be good for me to get out of town. Then I will have my goods shipped to me. Then you can come and see me.
>
> Well Bertha I haven't seen a well day since I came home from my trip west but I'm feeling better since the cold weather has come. It was 8 above zero here last week. You had it some cooler I suppose. I like warm weather the best.

Charley (Violett) is still carpentering I suppose. It is dull here and no wages. If you could get work $1.50 to $1.75 a day [is] the best. I made some last summer contracting but there is nothing here for a mechanic of any kind. Well I will have to close as it is almost mail time and news is scarce. I heard from Oregon (James Hewitt) some time ago. They were all well and Uncle Will's folks (Will Hewitt) is all well. They send you their best wishes and [for] a happy Christmas. I will send you a card and save 1 cent. Wishing you well and a Merry Christmas. Write soon and let me hear from you both. Yours Lovingly, Uncle John.

Hewitt had probably been living in Nashville at least since the summer of 1909. Perhaps he never got the superintendent's job in the mountains, and while he may have been looking for a housekeeper, instead he found a wife. John was 60 years old when he remarried on 3 Feb 1910, less than two months after his letter to Bertha Violett.[94] His second wife was Jessie Miller, a forty-year-old widow with an eighteen-year-old daughter. By April, they were living on a fruit farm outside Nashville, perhaps the one he mentioned in his letter.[95]

John's letter referred to his trip out west to a convalescent sanatorium in Boulder Colorado where Vesta was hospitalized with tuberculosis. Feeling better, she returned to Cincinnati where she and George lived, but soon she was ill again, and sent to North Carolina, to recuperate. Vesta died there, alone and far from her family. Her body was shipped to Cincinnati for burial and lovingly placed in the Hewitt family plot at Mt. Moriah Cemetery near her mother. Buried a few yards away was her grandmother, Frances Eliza Kyle, after whom she was named. Her father's lament about not seeing his grandsons may have been an unspoken cry for his daughter who was no longer within his reach. Only Birchie survived from his first family, and living far away, John soon became fully absorbed in a new life. His siblings lived nearby and in the spring he was a father again when Jessie gave birth to their son John on 20 May 1912.

The couple eventually moved to Madison, Tennessee, outside the city of Nashville, where they spent their remaining days. John died from bronchial pneumonia in 1930 on 15 March, a few days short of his eightieth birthday, and was buried at Spring Hill Cemetery in Nashville. Jessie lived another eight years, until she was seventy-two, then on 5 Mar 1938 she died and was buried near her husband. When his mother died, young John was approaching his twenty-sixth birthday.

Francese Vesta Hewitt (1889-1910) ca. 1909

Chapter Ten

FRANCESE VESTA HEWITT
Francese Vesta Hewitt, George C. Schmidt, and George O. Schmidt
Clermont and Hamilton Counties, Ohio (1889-1930)

The Youngest Child

In preparation for another day of rain, the leaden skies of November lay heavy upon the southern Ohio landscape. However, no one in the Hewitt household took notice of the weather, as John and Lizzie Belle's focus was the daughter born to them that day. She arrived on 9 Nov 1889, joining a brother Otto who was two and a sister Birchie who was seven years old. The family lived in Cherry Grove, a small village straddling the Hamilton and Clermont County border, not far from where Lizzie Belle grew up and where less than a year before her mother had died. As a tribute to Frances Eliza Kyle Morrison, they named her Francese Vesta although everyone called her Vesta.

She was two years old when her grandfather Morrison and her uncle Otto died. When their estates were settled, her parents were initially flush with money and investment opportunities. Maybe it was a bad business decision, bad luck, or a combination of both, but for several years thereafter, the family floundered through a series of financial ups-and-downs. John and Lizzie Belle bought into a suburban housing development project that went awry, followed by a flurry of lawsuits that eventually caused them to declare bankruptcy. Perhaps the children were aware of a certain underlying tension between their parents, but youngsters have their own interests to block out reality and the woes of adults. In 1897, Otto was about ten, two years older than Vesta was, when their lives veered seriously off track. They were probably playmates and companions, whose playful antics diverted their attention away from family problems. Their elder sister Birchie was a violinist, and since practice must follow lessons, she worked to master her instrument, while her younger sister who was too young to appreciate her sister's talents, listened for a while before running off to play, oblivious to all that was falling down around her.[1]

The family remained in the Mt. Carmel-Mt. Summit area at least through 1892, where Birchie, then aged nine, attended Mt. Carmel Primary School. Her mother had attended the four-room school on the turnpike as a youth, and statistics from a later date described its organization. It was a typical rural school in Clermont County, with an eight-month schedule allowing its pupils to be at home during the planting and harvesting seasons. In 1879, it had about 140 students but only three teachers who earned about $400 a year teaching primary through high school grades. The divisional breakdown showed there were 42 children in primary class, 38 pupils in intermediate classes and 25 students in high school. It appeared that since fewer students attended high school than the primary grades, education much beyond grade school was neither encouraged nor considered necessary for children living in a farming community. This was particularly true for girls at that time.

School was a resource for students, but the rural village church was not only a place for worship, it was the center of neighborhood social events. The Universalist Church at Mt. Carmel was such a gathering place. It came into being in 1867 when the Odd Fellows needed a new hall to hold meetings. When it was finished, the main floor was used for church services while the men used the upper floor for meetings. By 1880 the church had 100 members, among them the Morrison and Kyle families.[2] John Hewitt's religious affiliation is unknown, but by virtue of marriage, he became a member, as did his children. While primarily a source of religious instruction, musical entertainment was a regular feature. Yearly at Christmas they presented a cantata and on other occasions plays containing strong moral messages that served as adult behavioral guides. An example of their programming, and a big hit, was held in January 1880 when the church presented *Ten Nights in a Bar Room*, and made fifty dollars for their Sunday School.

When word got around that a musical event was scheduled using local talent, it brought everyone together, parents, friends and neighbors. Farmers left their fields and merchants their shops to exchange pleasantries and support the young folk. Afterward, at the social, men talked business, while the womenfolk spread the word about weddings, and babies, anniversaries and the inevitable death in the family. Best of all it encouraged the young folks in their musical endeavors, and when Vesta was a toddler their church had an evening event her family probably attended. Sponsored by the Women's Missionary Alliance, and directed by Professor Eugene Dial, the church presented a program of vocal and instrumental music featuring youthful musicians ably assisted by more accomplished players from the community. Birchie, who was nine, may have been among the children who played that evening. The following Christmas they put on a cantata, *The New Year's Mistake*. Several years later in 1894, while the Hewitt family was still living in the neighborhood, the Sunday School presented a cantata called *Santa Claus and the Children*. Vesta was too young to participate but she was old enough to watch Birchie, who was twelve years old, play the violin to the delight of her parents and their friends.[3]

Music had an important role in the Hewitt family, but how it began and which parent fostered their children's talents is unknown. It may have been John who recognized his children's abilities, but more likely it was Lizzie Belle who nurtured her children's musical talents and provided lessons for them. Although both girls chose to master a demanding instrument, Vesta who played the clarinet, was so much younger than her sister that it took years to equal Birchie's accomplishments on the violin. Vesta also had a lovely voice and later as a teenager she addressed herself professionally as a singer. Music held a special place in the family and may have been a blessing for the children during hard times. Birchie turned fifteen in 1897, and she may have drawn her siblings more deeply into music as a way to divert their attention from a household spiraling out of control. Birchie played professionally as a young woman so she may have been oblivious to her siblings, spending much of her youth thoroughly engrossed in music and the mastery of her instrument.[4]

In 1899, Professor Dial, who once taught school in Union Township, organized a ladies band in Cincinnati. Begun as early as 1897, the *Tuxedo Ladies Band and Orchestra* had fourteen young women who toured Hamilton, Clermont and Brown Counties giving concerts during the summer months.[5] That year the Hewitts lived in Cincinnati at 4th and Sycamore Streets where the band maintained its headquarters. Not only did they practice nearby, but the family knew Professor Dial from the Mt. Carmel Universalist Church where he had been its musical director.[6] Family tradition says that the daughters played in a traveling band, and perhaps this was Birchie's introduction to a musical career, which was how she listed herself in 1899. Opportunity and motivation were there, although not for Vesta, who was nine years old at the time.[7]

Swept Away

In 1900 the family moved to downtown Cincinnati where Otto, who was thirteen, attended Woodward High School. During the fall of 1901 he caught a cold that turned into a lingering illness from which he never fully recovered. His health improved in the summer of 1902, but he was again ill that fall and finally diagnosed with tuberculosis. Vesta was twelve when her parents took Will to a sanatorium in New Mexico in hopes of a cure, but the dry air, plentiful food and overall healthy environment did not bring him back to health. Instead he grew weaker and in March his father brought him home to die. They did everything possible but he was losing his grasp on life, and on 22 Mar 1903, Otto slipped away while at home. Gathering at the Mt. Carmel Universalist Church friends and family mourned his passing and then journeyed to Mt. Moriah Cemetery to say a final goodbye. The next day there was another funeral. This one was for Vesta's grandfather, Davis Hewitt, who also died that day. It is not known whether John and Lizzie Belle attended.

Birchie was not at home to share the latter events with her family, because by 1901 she was married to a musician and they had set up house together. Harry (Heinrich) Damm was a violinist, born in Denver, Colorado, who had traveled and studied extensively in Europe before settling in the Cincinnati area. He played in nearly every one of Cincinnati's theater orchestras during his lifetime, and perhaps that was how he met Birchie.[8] In later life he had his own theater orchestra, but well before then Birchie gave up playing professionally to raise their son, Henry, who was born 2 Oct 1901.[9] She remained actively involved in her husband's profession from the sidelines although she did not rejoin him as a musician even after Henry grew up.[10]

Witnessing her parents' desperate efforts to heal their son was a singular experience for Vesta, but it grew more frightening when her mother became ill. Lizzie had a severe chest cold that only grew worse, and when Vesta looked into her father's eyes for answers, she did not like what she saw. With Otto gone and her sister married, she was more vulnerable than before, because without the sounds of her siblings, the pall that hung over their house grew in the silence. Lizzie Belle never recovered from Otto's death, and she grew weaker day by day until on 24 Apr 1903 she died. In little more than a month, three members of their family died, wielding a wrenching blow to the serenity of its last three members. Either John or Birchie wrote Lizzie Belle's obituary, saying "the mental strain caused by her late son Otto's illness and death" brought about her own demise. "There left to mourn her loss are a loving husband, and two daughters Vesta and Birchie."

Vesta was thirteen when her mother died, and dependent upon a grieving father for financial and emotional support at a time when he must have been bereft of solace. Their loss was extraordinary and it was swift. In a day John was deprived of son and father, then his wife. Vesta lost her playmate and then her mother was suddenly swept away. Somehow, she kept her balance after these sudden changes, perhaps because of an angel in the guise of a cousin. Throughout the years, John and Sam Hewitt remained close, until he passed on. His daughter, Bertha Violett was well acquainted with her cousins. Although she was seventeen years older than Vesta, she knew the loss of both parents, so she was able to support her cousin after her mother's death.

Between 1903 and 1905, John and Vesta moved to East Columbia Township in Hamilton County where he rented a place on the New Richmond Pike for the next three years. In 1905 her father farmed and used a business address at Station C in Cincinnati, and Vesta at age seventeen was a vocalist by profession. As the family story goes, she met her future husband George Schmidt while ice-skating on a neighbor's pond, and there is little reason to dispute the story.[11] His family lived in Anderson Township, a community East of Cincinnati in Hamilton County, not far from where the Hewitt family lived for many years. George's parents, Conrad and Anna Schmidt, lived in California, a village west of Fruit Hill on Kellogg Avenue near the New Richmond Pike. Vesta and her father lived on Gwendolen Drive very near Kellogg Avenue, and undoubtedly somewhere nearby was a skating pond where George and Vesta met and took a few spins on the ice together. On another day they chased each other across the wide expanse then landed breathless on the bank to rest, and he, noting that her skates needed tightening knelt down to tie them, and then stretched out his hand to help her up. Skating away they held hands—only to keep their balance, and smiling shyly at one another glided away into their future. Whether quickly or slowly, at some point a romance blossomed and on 17 Apr 1907 in Newport, Kentucky, John Hewitt gave permission for his seventeen-year-old daughter to marry this young man.[12]

Shortly after their marriage the couple moved into a small house on Kellogg Avenue built for them by George's family, and not long afterward their first child was born. Named to honor his paternal great-grandfather and his mother's brother, George Otto Schmidt was born 21 Jan 1908. In an autobiography he began as a young man, George talked about the difficulties of his birth. His mother was not only young but unwell during her pregnancy and he was not vigorously strong at birth.[13] Both parents worried about George's health but Vesta soon became aware that she had health concerns of her own. The exact circumstances of her illness are not clear. Perhaps she was ailing prior to her marriage, or pregnancy and childbirth weakened her already delicate constitution. However, within a year after George's birth, she became seriously ill and by midyear of 1909, Vesta was diagnosed with active tuberculosis. The disease was not unknown to her. A few years before she saw its incipient effect on her brother as he struggled in vain to live. The chilling truth was that before she had been a witness, this time the Great White Plague was making a personal visitation. While Vesta probably knew little of its history, she was very familiar with its look. The mirror told the truth and it was all about her.

The Great White Plague

Tuberculosis has an odd history. Prior to the 1870s it was considered by some to be a highly spiritual affliction, romanticized in novels and sometimes celebrated among writers and artists as a source of inspiration. Because it piqued the novelist's interest, its physical manifestations and the languorous decline of its victims were often recorded in eighteenth and nineteenth century literature. The very people who were its victims sometimes described the ravages of the disease; Robert Lewis Stevenson was one example. Other authors used friends or family to illustrate its effects, which in many cases were enhanced by drugs such as laudanum, a remedy thought to help cure the patient, but instead rendered him more or less comatose. Some considered tuberculosis a moral failing and God's way of weeding out the sinners from the saints. Known as pulmonary consumption, it was a disease of many moods and phases. The truth beyond the novel was a much sadder story. Initially an individual lost weight and felt generally weak. As the disease progressed the victim took to the couch or bed, growing weaker still. Weight loss enhanced the cheekbones and fever made them pink. Fever also brought an unnatural luminosity to the eyes, and dilated pupils made them appear larger than normal, giving its victims an appearance particularly associated with consumption. Another peculiarity of the disease was that a patient sometimes had a sudden burst of energy and optimism, lasting only long enough to complete a project before his spirit plummeted again. Within hours, this momentary upswing was followed by weakness and depression matching in intensity the initial high. Creative people with the disease used a sudden energy surge to write, compose or paint, and many well-known works were accomplished during the fervor of these periods. As more was discovered about the disease, the once romantic image disappeared and it was finally recognized as the physically ravaging killer that it is.[14]

In earlier times, before the Victorians romanticized it, tuberculosis was a scourge on the land, plucking those living in crowded cities more often than in rural areas. Even with this evidence before them, doctors did not discourage patients with active tuberculosis from living with and eating at table with their families. It took many years to understand that the disease spread in close quarters. Consumption peaked in the mid-nineteenth century but time elapsed before a real decline occurred in the numbers of new patients. Even then this decrease was sometimes attributed to the disease nearing the end of its natural cycle, when it was actually the advent of the sanatorium and its belief in fresh air and cleanliness that brought about the reduced numbers of victims.

Antibiotics were in evidence in the 1940s but it was not until mid-century that they were used to cure tuberculosis. Until then the sanatorium cure was the method most often used to restore lost health. It was an extreme method of bringing the disease to its knees, used only when all other methods failed. These rest hospitals were mostly built in mountainous parts of the United States. Many were out west and treatment began with the "hardening process" most effectively implemented in cold climates. Most sanatoriums were designed on a similar plan with a specially built, screened porch surrounding two or three sides of a central building. Another plan consisted of cottages scattered around a central hospital. Regardless of the style, the regimen of the hospitals was the same. Those who came for the cure spent some part of each day outside or on an enclosed porch. In the summer it might be all day and night. During the winter the patient was bundled with blankets and rugs and remained on the porch five or six hours each day. Those opposed to the sanatorium cure claimed patients died at the same rate as those who remained at home, but they just looked better.

The cure was implemented by a rigorously controlled day. Upon entering the hospital an individual received explicit instructions about eating, dressing, sleeping, bathing and every other aspect of his stay while at the institution. Thus Vesta's temperature was regularly checked, her sputum reported and weight noted. Control extended even to the regulation of her breathing.[15] When the response to treatment was poor and the disease progressed, these wellness checks were particularly dreaded by a patient who was not doing well. The measures implemented by the sanatorium system were not meant to be cruel; they were simply a means to harness a monster that killed thousands of people yearly. While the vast number of cases of tuberculosis peaked in 1840, it remained the number one killer for nearly a century until the 1930's when it was edged out of that spot by cancer.[16]

A closer look at part of the daily regimen shows the excesses of the treatment. This was what Vesta endured during her several stays at sanatoria in 1909-1910. She got lots of fresh cold air, considered optimal at 65-68 degrees. This was part of the hardening process. However, some methods bordered on cruelty. Freezing cold showers were *de rigueur*. Another barbaric treatment used to lower the sufferer's temperature was to drape her in a cold wet sheet beginning at 90 degrees then lowering the temperature gradually until it reached between 60-70 degrees. More sensible remedies included a healthy diet and mild exercise. Once it was understood how the disease spread, cleanliness became a prime component of the cure. It was important to the treatment to keep her quiet and calm so she and her companions were encouraged to relax by reading authors like Mark Twain and Jane Austin or by playing non-stimulating board games.[17]

In the early twentieth century when the diseased had peaked and there was hope for permanent relief, doctors and patients became more open to remedies that might eradicate the disease. In 1899, after a meeting of the American Medical Association in Columbus, Ohio, the report of its finding appeared in *The Clermont Sun* newspaper. The talk was about a new therapy promoted by a widely known chemist in Paris whose treatment was quite radical for the times. It required the patient to breathe formaldehyde vapor as it was transported directly into the tissues by the aid of "light tension static electricity."[18] Reportedly, some doctors at the meeting were skeptical of its application and with good reason; it did not work. Not long after Vesta's brother died, there was a special dispatch to the *Cincinnati Enquirer* in 1903 that reflected more about contemporary thinking on the disease, and perhaps John Hewitt read the newspaper that day. It came from the State Tuberculosis Commission and stated clearly that tuberculosis was the most destructive of all infectious diseases, and then gave statistics to back it up. The facts were that in Ohio, one in nine deaths was from the disease, and annually 6,000 deaths were caused by tuberculosis. Because of experience, he may not have agreed with the next part, which said that if caught early and treated in a sanatorium, tuberculosis was curable. The article ended with a recommendation to the legislature for an appropriation of $200,000 to build an instate hospital. Plans called for a facility housing up to 200 patients for a maximum stay of six months.[19]

Colorado was well known for healing, and thousands flocked there in the early twentieth century looking for a magic cure, all the while realizing it was a place of last resort for very ill patients. By the summer of 1909, Vesta was actively infected with the disease and her family sought the treatment recommended at the time, that of rest in a quiet environment, preferably in a high mountain climate. Leaving baby George with her sister Birchie, Vesta and George went to Boulder, Colorado, where she entered a sanatorium to begin convalescence. With her husband beside her she got better.[20] She spent Christmas there and in a holiday card sent to her cousin Bertha Violett, she lamented not being with them for the holidays.[21] Not only was she ill with tuberculosis, Vesta was also five months pregnant with her second child. She wrote to her father and he in turn sent a card to Bertha in December 1909, saying he had heard from Vesta the previous week and that she was feeling much better. John Hewitt also alluded to a trip he had taken a few months earlier where he went "out west" which could only mean he had been to see his daughter in Boulder that fall.[22]

Vesta also missed her family and with her advancing pregnancy, she wanted to see her son and give birth at home. Katheryn Eleanor Schmidt was born 27 Apr 1910, probably in Cincinnati, but her birth left Vesta weaker than before. Soon she was back in the mountains for another rest cure, this time in North Carolina. They began with hope she would recover from childbirth and the disease that sapped her strength. Not long after she arrived, she got a message that the baby, less than three months old, had died on 8 Jul 1910. With her mother far away, Katheryn was buried at Mt. Moriah Cemetery near her maternal grandmother.

Tryon, North Carolina, is fox hunting country in the Blue Ridge Mountains. It was never a large town although it is quite historic, so that what once was a tuberculosis sanatorium was easily identified. Listed on the National Register of Historic Places, one of its cottages dates to 1760, but the current facility was built in 1900. Seventeen years later it was converted into a retreat, and today it is an outstanding resort called the Pine Crest Inn. The inn used to be a hospital and of the surrounding thirty-five cottages, one of them was where Vesta lived for a short time.[23] While she grew weaker her son, who was living with his father in Cincinnati, gained in fitness daily. It was partly good health that prodded him to take young George to see his mother in North Carolina. He was about two and a half years old in the summer of 1910 but distinctly remembered the trip albeit with the fuzzy impressions of a toddler. He began by saying that...

> "His father decided to go to his wife in Carolina and take the son thinking it would cheer his wife and he was very anxious to see her for it had been months since she had gone South...The son was told...about the trip and why they were going. [He] was very young but a vivid picture formed in his mind of two things...The first was the great emptiness below when going over High Bridge Kentucky and [the second] when his mother met them at the door."[24]

When she first saw her little boy's face, it must have been with extreme restraint that she did not fling her arms around him. Longing to hold him, she dared not lest she pass her illness on to him. The visit was short and especially painful, because Vesta knew the disease had advanced toward its final progression. So too did her husband. Young George never saw his mother again but carried the memory of her image in the doorway with him for the remainder of his life.

Vesta died in the sanatorium on 1 Sep 1910, without husband or family to witness her passing. Her remains were shipped by train to Cincinnati, where after the service at the Methodist Episcopal Church at California, she was buried next to her daughter in Mt. Moriah Cemetery.[25] Viewed in the summer of 1996, the author observed that initially the burials were planned so that John could be buried beside Lizzie Belle, but fate played a role in who was and who was not buried there. The Morrison and Hewitt plots are next to each other in the cemetery, and each is marked by a large monument. Below the Hewitt name, Lizzie Belle's grave is in the middle of the first row with Otto and Elsie on one side, and Vesta's grave in front of Elsie's and below her mother. Birchie was buried next to her mother, with her husband, Harry on the other side. Their graves took the place of John Hewitt, who was buried in Nashville. Standing tall and to the right of the Hewitt monument is that of the Morrison family, Lizzie Belle's parents and brother. With the exception of John Hewitt, in death each of them eventually returned home to family, community and the tradition in which they grew up.

The author has an unmarked photograph taken perhaps after Vesta's funeral. It is a rural backyard setting with three people seated on a hammock. One is Birchie Damm and her father, John Hewitt. Next to him is one of his sisters, probably Lizzie Bratton Hill who lived in Nashville and accompanied her brother on the journey to bury his daughter. Two couples are standing behind the hammock, each about the same age as Birchie. Likely they are her cousins, Bertha and Media and their husbands, Richard Violett and John McCullough. Corn stands tall in the background suggesting late summer, near harvest time when Vesta died. Except for Birchie who was dressed in silk, each of them wore dark formal clothing, too warm for the season. Their faces are exceptionally serious, suggesting a solemn occasion. Vesta's absence from a family portrait lends the strongest evidence the picture was taken after the funeral, in a private gathering at her dear cousin Bertha's home in Olive Branch, where the family would have felt at home. More importantly, Birchie gave this photograph to Vesta's son George, one that commemorated an occasion that was only slightly more meaningful to him than it was to her.[26]

Young George

He was born in January, a sometimes-cruel month in the midst of winter. Sickly and struggling for life, his strong spirit overcame the physical weaknesses he inherited. When his mother died he went to live with his grandparents, Anna and Conrad Schmidt, and on Saturday nights his father visited. His most vivid memory of those times was when his dad appeared bringing with him a large bag of fruit from which George, standing on the dining room table, was allowed to have first choice.

His father did not remain a widower long and in the fall of 1912 he married Minnie Dorothy Rech and George went to live with them on a farm adjoining his birthplace. The following spring brought torrential rains to southern Ohio and with it severe flooding. To be safe, he and his stepmother went to stay with her parents. When it was time to leave, rather than returning to live with his father, he was brought to his grandparents' house to live. His father, after remarrying, no longer wanted the home where he and Vesta lived so briefly, so he sold it to his parents.[27] Conrad owned a lot zoned for commercial use that he bought from his father, and behind it was a small house where George lived with his grandparents. He joined the family in May 1913, and found it was a lively place with three children still living there. He was happy with them and enjoyed his aunts, Zetta, Lydia and Olive, none of whom were known by their correct names. His favorites were Ted the eldest and the youngest known as Dot. She was eight years older than her five-year old nephew but easily joined him in rough and tumble games. Bud, as they called him, liked Babe the middle daughter but thought she was too strict. Although he was never given a reason why he went to live with them, he learned to love them well, especially his grandmother Anna, who grew close to her grandson. When he talked about his grandmother, George always smiled upon telling others that she would tell him "he was more trouble than all of her children put together." It was not long before he began calling her "Mom" and said he thought of her more that way than as a grandmother.[28]

George Schmidt and His Descendants

European emigration to the United States began to surge around 1850 and among the largest group leaving the continent were those from the German states. They left their homeland for several reasons; two of them were political unrest and poverty. It began in 1846 with a sinking economy and crop failures provoking desperation among the general population.[29] A peasant revolt in 1848, while bringing reform that guaranteed them the right to own property, did not guarantee there was land to buy or that if it could be found, it was affordable. Because Germany was a collection of states and principalities, it had no cohesive government and thus remained politically unsettled and regionally distinct. For those and other reasons, its leaders were unable to either unite their people or bring about real change. It would take years, until 1871, before what is now Germany would emerge as a country, and only after a war. Called the Franco-Prussian War, it was decisively won by the German states, and with a treaty orchestrated by Otto von Bismarck, at last the mélange of disparate federations commenced in the unification of Germany as a nation.[30]

In the nineteenth century, Hesse was a mid-sized German state located between its larger neighbors, Prussia and Westphalia in Western Germany. Its boundaries fluctuated over time but it retained importance as a major crossroads for the Prussian military. For this reason and others, it was in a constant state of political and economic flux. When George Schmidt emigrated in 1858 or 1859 from Hessen-Kassel, in the northern district of West Germany, like much of the rest of the country, it was "known chiefly for its poverty, its archaic agrarian structure, and its acrimonious constitutional politics."[31] Along with neighbors and strangers alike, he was one of thousands who bought passage to America at the peak of emigration. Statistics collected by the United States government show that in the course of twenty years, between 1847 and 1867, nearly two million people emigrated from Germany to the United States.[32]

Schmidt was between twenty and twenty-one when he arrived in this country and made his way to the Cincinnati area. He apparently arrived without his parents or at least they were not living nearby in 1860.[33] However, records indicated that both he and his parents were born in Hessen-Kassel.[34] George's son, Conrad Schmidt, indicated in census records that both of his parents were born in Saxony, so that in combination it suggested that they later moved to the area of Hesse.[35] George may have arrived with relatives, or to ease the transition, met upon debarkation those who had arrived earlier. He married prior to 1860 a woman eight years older than he, named Katherine Ackerman.[36] They settled in Anderson Township east of Cincinnati on Tompkins' survey #365 called California, the first village to be established.[37] George was a shoemaker, and although a man by that name worked in downtown Cincinnati, it is more likely he pursued his occupation in his home village.[38] In later years he took up farming.

California is about eight miles east of downtown Cincinnati, bordered on that side by Kellogg Avenue, which runs parallel to the Ohio River on its western boundary. It is a sleepy little village formally laid out at its inception with few boundary changes over the years. In all, the village is about five blocks deep and seven blocks wide. Small by any standards, it is mostly residential with some houses and buildings dating as far back as 1865. The village is well known because on its south side is an amusement center once known as Coney Island, but now called Riverstar Park.[39] An old map marks the place of a foundry where many of the town's citizens worked. Called the Molder's Union Foundry, it was a cooperative founded by striking stove molders from Cincinnati and in 1880 it gave many of the 375 people who lived there a living wage, among them George's seventeen-year-old son, Conrad. Probably his first job, it was hard work for a young man but gave him a wage, some of which he probably took to the bank.[40]

Although he lived in a neighborhood with many other German-born residents, Schmidt may have Anglicized his name when he arrived in the United States. Even when his neighbors retained the German spelling of their names, in the U.S. census he was listed consistently as Smith from 1860 on until 1900 when it was spelled correctly. Upon arrival in his newly adopted country, George may have thought he had left turmoil and war behind, but he was mistaken. In 1863 this nation became engaged in a civil war and he was eager to prove his loyalty. He was twenty-six years old and married, with a newborn son, but he did not hesitate to pick up arms and defend this land. According to family oral history, George served in the heavy artillery and mustered out at Camp Dennison. This branch of the army had fewer men than the infantry or the cavalry, and Ohio had but two units in the Civil War, so there was a relatively short list of soldiers who served in this capacity. However, this did not lessen the difficulty of finding a man named George who may have served either as Schmidt or as Smith. There were several records for men by that name but none that can be proven conclusively as an ancestor. George's wife Katherine died before him, thus eliminating the widow's pension as another means of tracing his service in the war.

The lack of a service record does not disprove his service in the Civil War, especially with other evidence, including cemetery records, that reiterate his service.[41] The physical evidence of Schmidt's service in the Civil War is a U.S. Army issue sword that was passed down from father to son over four generations and is currently in the possession of the author. However, it is not a heavy artillery sword, but rather an embellished saber worn by an officer in the cavalry.[42] To date there is no proof he served in that branch of the service, although a man from Ohio by that name did serve in the cavalry. If George Schmidt was in the heavy artillery, the Ohio engagements of the first and second regiments of that branch of the army are well documented. However, what he witnessed during his term of service will go untold until his records are found. Memories of his experiences or stories of injury were not passed along, and so it must be assumed that he left the war physically unscathed only to live many more years beyond its end. When the war ended, the turmoil George experienced during his youth causing him to leave home, may have helped him to slip quietly back into family life as the village shoemaker, much as he had done before it all began.

Others from the same region in Germany where they were born provided support in a new land for George and Katherine, and sharing similar origins and customs helped change a strange land into a community of peers. By 1870, the couple had three children, the youngest a daughter also named Katharine, who was two years old. Her brother Conrad was seven and went to school while George, who was four years old, remained at home with his parents. The family grew and seemed to prosper. Property values over a dozen years between emigration and the next census showed their real estate had risen in value from $250 in 1860 to $1,500 in 1870. Both were literate and saw that their eldest son attended school. They found their small community was supportive of their origins but it was also personally enriched by their family. John Ackerman, Katherine's father lived with them in 1870. He was seventy-two, worked in the foundry, and like the others, was from Hessen-Kassel.[43] A widower, ten years earlier he lived with his son Alex and daughter-in-law Katherine.[44] The 1880 census indicated that "George Smith" was forty-seven and a shoemaker; his wife Katherine was fifty-four, and both were from Hessen-Kassel as were their parents. Their three children were all born in Ohio, and the two youngest were in school while Conrad worked as a stove molder and lived at home. They had two servants or maybe tenants, one who worked as a farm laborer and the other as a domestic. Katherine's younger brother Alex who was fifty-two, continued to live nearby and worked at the foundry. Records from Mt. Washington Cemetery where he was buried in 1907 indicated he was born about 1828 and died when he was seventy-nine years old.[45]

By 1900 the census reported Katherine was a senior citizen aged seventy-four while George was a sixty-two-year-old farmer. For the first time their names were correctly spelled in the census, perhaps prompted by their adult children to support their heritage. Katharine revealed to the enumerator that she had two children who died in childhood. Her first child was born when she was thirty-eight and the last at age forty-two, so those who died were probably born after 1867.[46] They lived in California village, but George also had property in the Newtown area valued at $250 and a personal estate of $1,500. About 1880 he purchased six lots in California,[47] and in 1889 a lot on Third Street not far from the foundry. Three months later he sold it to Conrad along with six lots he bought previously.[48] Most of them were part of Rogers Addition on 8th Street between Rensler and Rohde Avenue,[49] while the others were on 5th Street, a part of Murdock's subdivision.[50] However, the couple probably lived on 3rd Street, now Panama Street near the Ohio River.[51]

Eventually their children grew up, married and left home. Katharine, called Kate, wed George Dickhart and moved to Pickaway, Ohio, where he worked for the Favorite Stove Company. George, the youngest son, married Anna Perry. Their elder brother, Conrad, married Anna Sturm, daughter of George Sturm and Margaret who lived in Lawrenceburg, Indiana. Anna was born there in 1862 and had five siblings, several who were younger than she was.[52] Her father owned a cooperage business in the town and he made whiskey barrels for the Schenley Distillery until his livelihood went downriver in the 1884 flood. As a young man, Conrad Schmidt worked and traveled with a fair. Perhaps it was during a stopover in Lawrenceburg that he met his future wife, Anna Sturm.[53] They married sometime before 12 Jan 1886 when their first child was born. He was aptly named after both grandfathers, George Conrad Schmidt.[54]

Conrad and Anna also lived in California, Ohio, and all of their children were born there. After George, a son John was born in 1887 called Hontas, then a daughter Zetta who was born in 1891. To round out a family of five children, Anna gave birth to daughters, Lydia who was born in 1893 and Olive in 1900.[55] Once Conrad's parents divested themselves of their property, the census indicated they continued to live separately from their children in the home where they had lived for many years. Katharine was eighty-two when she died in 1907. George lived about two years longer and died in 1909 at age seventy-two. They were buried in Mt. Washington Cemetery, a large, old and well-maintained cemetery where also lie many of the pioneer families of Anderson Township and its neighborhoods. Along a tree-lined lane in the cemetery, the family purchased a plot, and a large monument honoring George and Katharine. It was placed there by their children and grandchildren to honor the immigrant ancestors of this line of the Schmidt family. In the end they spent many more good years in this part of rural, southern Ohio than in the land of their birth. For their descendants it was a fortunate choice.

For many years Conrad and Anna had a small grocery store on the west side of Kellogg Avenue across the street from where they lived. They must have rented the property because it was not listed among the lots they owned in the town. Sometime between 1900 and 1910, when he was between forty and forty-seven years old, Conrad gave it up and went to work for the Cincinnati Water Works as a boiler man. The census indicated that Anna, who was a year older than her husband, continued to run the grocery store.[56] On 17 April 1907 their eldest son George married Vesta Hewitt and not long after, George Otto Schmidt was born, on 21 Jan 1908.

Along the way Conrad and Anna lost three of their family. First, their daughter-in-law Vesta Hewitt Schmidt died in North Carolina on 1 Sep 1910 after a long bout with tuberculosis. Then Lydia, called Babe, caught a chill while working on a Christmas program at the church and became very ill. In a weakened condition she developed tuberculosis and her husband, Lou Glasbrenner, took her to Denver for recovery, but to no avail. Ted and Dot brought their mother to see Babe prior to her death in 1917 at the age of twenty-four. Eventually, Zetta married Babe's husband, Lou Glasbrenner and they had two children. Dot married Andy Vettle who built and operated rollercoasters for local amusement parks. She too became ill and died in 1925 at age twenty-five. Young George remembered Dot's struggle because he lived with the family and worked at a gas station across the street from his grandparents' house. In this way he grew to know his father's family more intimately than most children do, so that the generation between them melted into one. Thus the deaths of his aunts, Babe and Dot, were to him as if he had lost his sisters. The memory of death remained in George's mind, beginning with his mother, then his aunts, and each time death appeared he learned anew the fragility of life.[57]

The year 1939 changed the lives of the Schmidt family. On 3 March Conrad died, and perhaps his children were anticipating it.[58] They did not expect their mother would follow him just ten days later. Suddenly the family was in deep mourning, including Anna's grandson for whom she was the only mother he knew. In keeping with all they had shared in life for more than 50 years, the couple was placed in Mt. Washington Cemetery beneath a single headstone, separate and apart from his parents.[59]

Estate records indicated all of their children lived in the neighborhood. George Senior and Zetta lived in Mt. Washington, and John Schmidt bought the property where his parents lived.[60] John and his wife Mabel Crosley Schmidt had five children together, and according to his grandnephew, "Hontas" was a good ball player who the St. Louis Cardinals tried to recruit as a pitcher, but he turned them down, choosing to be a family man instead.[61]

Hewitt Monument, Mt. Moriah Cemetery, Mt. Carmel, Ohio

Francese Vesta Hewitt Schmidt
(9 Nov 1889-1 Sep 1910)

Lizzie B. (Morrison) Hewitt
(26 Jun 1852-24 Apr 1903)

Birchie Hewitt Damm
(22 Jul 1882-30 Oct 1952)

Schmidt Family, California, Ohio.
Back row, Zetta Schmidt, George Conrad Schmidt, Lydia Schmidt;
front row, Olive Schmidt, George Otto Schmidt, neighbor, ca. 1910

Schmidt Monument, Mt. Washington Cemetery, Mt. Washington, Ohio.
George Schmidt (5 Nov 1837-11 Apr 1909)
Katherine Ackerman (10 Nov 1825-15 Nov 1907).

Conrand Schmidt (1863-1939) and Anna (Sturm) Schmidt (1862-1939)

Hewitt Family photograph, probably Olive Branch, Ohio, September 1910, after Vesta's funeral. Back row, Charles Violett, Bertha Hewitt Violett, Unknown, Unknown; Front row, Bertha "Birchie" Hewitt Damm, John H. Hewitt, probably Ann Hewitt McClellan.

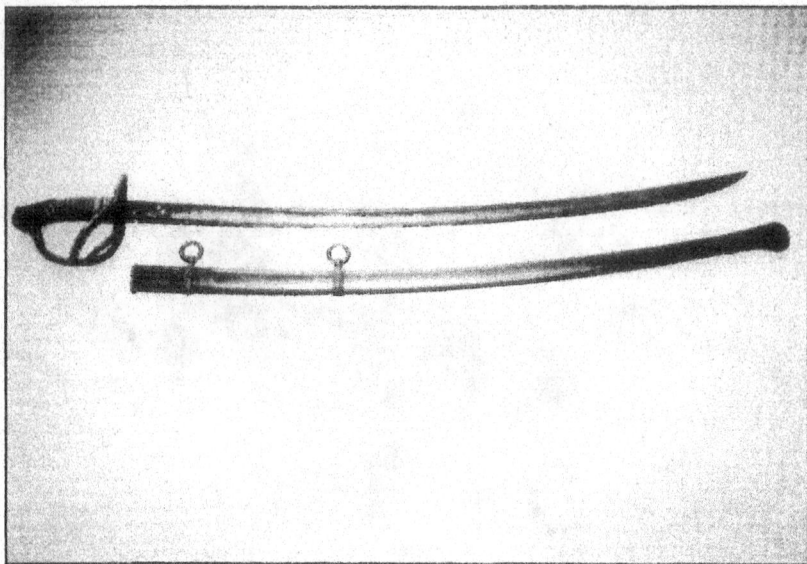

Model 1840 Civil War Cavalry Officer's Saber,
maker P. D. Luneschloss & Companie, Solingen, Prussia; sword and scabbard.

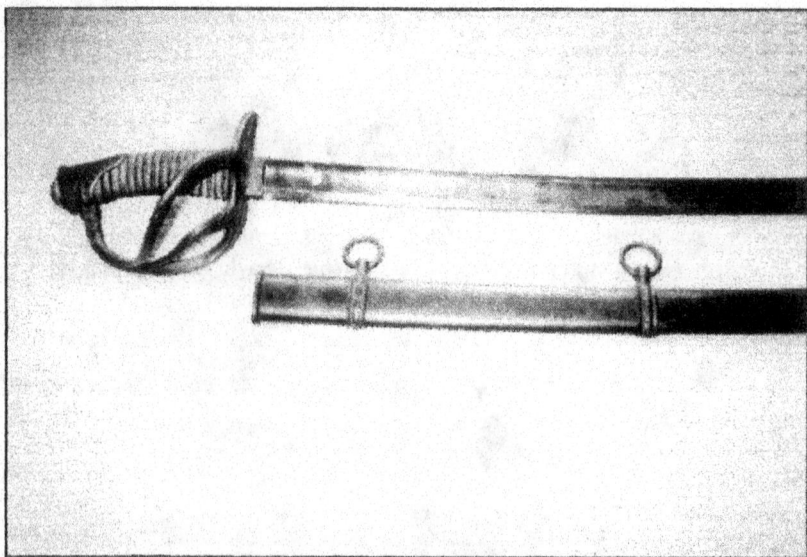

Close up view of sword and scabbard

Conrad Schmidt (1863-1939) and Anna Sturm Schmidt (1862-1939)
California, Ohio, ca. 1928

A Rural Childhood

Winter in the Midwest was often brutal but in 1917-1918 it was exceptionally bad in Cincinnati. George was living with his grandparents when one night the temperature dropped to twelve degrees below zero, the wind blew the transom over the front door open and the radiators froze, then one broke spreading water all over the floor. It took about a week to replace the heat, and in the meantime, their only warmth was from the kitchen stove and a small kerosene heater upstairs in one of the bedrooms. The day after George went to the store for his grandmother, and to keep warm he put on every coat he owned. Out on the street he noticed that few people ventured out, it was just too cold. He remembered two other things about 1918 when he was ten years old. The war was over, and in December he became dangerously ill with pneumonia followed by scarlet fever. It began after he took a hot bath then went outside to ride his bike with his friends. They rode downtown and were gone long enough that he got chilled, became very ill and was in bed for Christmas. The doctor told his family he was teetering on the brink, but he passed through a critical period when his recovery was in doubt, and gradually George fully regained his health.

Like most young boys he spent a lot of time outside with his friends. Fortunately he left a record of how country boys amused themselves in the early twentieth century. In general they liked to play the same games as kids today, with baseball and soccer among their favorite sports. They also played quieter games of skill like tops and marbles. Other games such as Mumble-de-peg, Go Sheepy Go, Fox and Hound, Boulder On and Boulder Off have disappeared into history and even in mid-century were games of the past. However, kite flying, skating, sledding and swimming remain as alive today as then. In writing his autobiography, George told many stories. One summer evening as he and Dot were playing hide and seek in the neighbors' summer garden, Ted interrupted their play, and not wanting to leave their fun they protested, but soon gave in and left. Within half an hour a cyclone struck causing widespread destruction to property all over. In their neighborhood alone trees, power poles and lines were down so that they were without lights that night. At Coney Island, an amusement park nearby, people left in droves but found it difficult to get around the downed trees and ripped electric lines that were sparking all around them.

Nature provided great entertainment for the children of the neighborhood. The woods abounded with trees untouched by timbering. Several creeks ran north and south feeding into the Ohio River on the southern border of Anderson Township and to the west was the Little Miami River. Within its thick mantle were wild grapevines, some thick enough to hold a boy ready for an adventurous swing. One summer George and his friends cut the vines near the ravine and like Tarzan swung across it from side to side, screaming at the top of their lungs as they did. Occasionally the vines broke and the fall into the ravine broke a boy's arm or leg but the game was so much fun they decided to improve it. One day upon finding a steel streetcar cable line that broke, the boys dragged it to the woods and substituted it for the grapevine swing.

One boy or another was always testing his invincibility against death, and George remembered one boy who brought some .22 caliber bullets to school one day. He lined them up on a rock and began hitting each one with an axe until it exploded and the lead hit the fence. Disaster happened when a shell casing went the wrong way and hit the boy in the knee. It took several operations to restore his leg and the boy never fully recovered and walked with a limp for the rest of his life. Seeing him always brought back memories of that day.

At the first sign of spring George and his friends spilled out of their houses. As it grew warmer they swam in the creeks but by mid-summer they had abandoned their clothes to go "skinny dipping." When the creeks dried up they swam in the rivers grown tolerable with the summer's heat. There were two reservoirs nearby good for fishing and George and a pal often went there. In the evening he brought his catch home to his grandmother who fried it for his supper. On a good day he brought home enough perch for the family's meal.

The neighborhood boys were always looking for mobility, and one summer they made scooters from discarded materials. Using a twelve-bottle beer case, they nailed a board to one end and a broomstick across the other end. For wheels, they used a disassembled roller skate and fastened each half to an end of the board, thus a scooter was born.

Kids rolled hoops in those days that they got from barrels and wagon wheels. They devised games of skill and coordination that involved contests to see who could roll his hoop the longest or who could make the most figure eights before the hoop fell over.

It rained often during the winter, affording the children unasked-for entertainment. One winter after the river escaped its banks and the backwater froze, George donned his skates and went in search of his friends. Sometimes they played a crude game of hockey called Shinny on the Ice. The boys had many days of pleasure by using a small tree with a hooked root for the stick and a small milk can for a puck. Just for fun they sometimes played more dangerous games on the ice. One great cold day George and one of his pals went in search of adventure, finding it where the river had backed up the creek. Before them was untouched ice as slick as glass. However, it was not frozen around the edges so they had to find a way to get into the middle of it. Finding a tree that leaned out over the ice they donned their skates, shinnied up the tree and climbed out on a limb as far as possible, then dropped down on the ice. Tired after a day of skating they then had to figure a way to get off the ice without falling into the water near the edge. After some discussion they decided to skate as fast as possible toward the bank then jump across the water and scramble onto the surrounding bank. It worked and they went home with the knowledge that it had been a rare day.

When George was a kid, Halloween was a favored time for youngster's pranks. They looked forward to this yearly event by dreaming up tricks to play on adults. One year when he was fourteen or fifteen, "the gang" went looking for a man who had a lawn swing in his front yard. It was a process, and first they had to get him primed, so shortly before Halloween George let the man know they were watching his swing. That night as they walked by looking for trouble, he was out in his yard with a bushel basket full of pears that he threw at the boys when they came too close. He was a ballplayer with an expert arm and the pears hurt so the boys left. Not to be defeated so easily in their prank, they spotted some little kids and got them to distract the man so they could carry away his swing. It worked and they began disassembling it piece by piece leaving parts along the street. Two blocks away they left the frame on top of a shed, went another block and left the seat on a light pole. They continued to disburse parts until they were many blocks from the man's home. The next day the man saw George on the streetcar and confronted him, but he denied having anything to do with the disappearance of the lawn swing. Somehow, later that fall, all the pieces were found and the swing came back to its owner.

George had his share of chores, and as a young boy it was his job to keep the coal bucket in the kitchen filled for his grandmother. He split kindling for the morning fire, hauled the trash to the dump and the ashes to the lower end of town where his grandparents owned a vacant lot. He fed the chickens, gathered their eggs and cleaned the chicken house. At one time he had a bunch of rabbits but they always got out of their cages and he had to catch them. One day he decided they were too much trouble so he opened their cages and chased them all away.

The city waterworks owned several properties adjacent to his house and one year they tore down the farmhouses and barns leaving behind a glorious array of fruit trees, fruit-bearing bushes and many flowers. Growing in luxurious abandonment were pear, crabapple and plum trees as well cherry trees and berries of all kinds. Nuts fell from the trees and he gathered them by the sack full. George often brought home walnuts, butternuts and hickory nuts. As the blackberries ripened he went out daily, picked a gallon and brought them home to his grandmother so she could make jam for the winter. When his grandpa came home from work, after dinner the two of them would go berry picking together. They each took a gallon pail and filled them with elderberries which they brought back and poured into crocks that were set aside to ferment. Every year they were able to collect enough berries to make between twenty and thirty gallons of wine.

When George was fourteen he entered East High School, now called Withrow High. He liked shop classes and signed up for mechanical drawing, wood shop and pattern making. His other courses included sheet metal training, foundry, forging and machine shop. Obligatory classes included algebra, science and English. All went well the first year until he broke his right arm and missed six weeks of school. It was hard to catch up when he returned, but he persisted and completed that and his sophomore year with no further problems. During the summer, he worked with his father who was a produce broker, but did not return for his junior year of school. On weekends they worked the small farm and the following spring he plowed for his father. One evening his father stopped by the house after work and told George he sold the business and was going to work for Swift and Company. He liked working for his father but now he was out of a job. Rather than return to school George worked odd jobs, but nothing challenging for a young man. About 1927, when he was nearly twenty he caught a chill while out hunting and came down with the flu. It turned into pneumonia but he seemed to recover and went back to work. In his words this is what happened next.

> One morning my grandmother asked me why I was breathing
> so hard, I said, "I don't know." She said, "You are not going
> to work, you are going to the doctor." The X-ray showed my

left lung was two-thirds filled with water. The doctor thought
it was in the lung cavity and not in the lung, but he was wrong.
He treated me with medication for some time and then tried to
draw the fluid out with a long needle and syringe. [There was]
no fluid. By that time it was early spring. He would not let
me go out of the house on cloudy, cold days. He would not let
me work. Around the first of May 1928, Dad came to the
house to see how I was doing. He said, "Why don't you buy a
car and spend the summer just driving around the country."
That sounded like a good idea. I bought a model T-Ford
coupe, got a gasoline stove, some pots and pans, a bedroll and
started out on the 29th of May. My first stop was
Indianapolis, Indiana [where] my cousin, Henry Damm had an
office. I had planned on going to the Indy races on the 30th,
the next day.

The weather was dark and terrible that day and the streetlights were on
well into the morning. Henry talked him out of going to the races and he left to
continue his journey, noticing that a few miles outside the city it was clear and
bright. He later heard that the races were called off at about 250 miles.

George continued west taking his time while observing the changing
landscape. He remembered stopping in Manhattan, Kansas, where it rained for
several days. There were no interstates and the drive across Kansas was wet and
muddy, challenging his ability to stay in the two ruts called a road. Passing a
car, wagon or truck was an even greater feat. The drive across the prarie was so
difficult and the roads so bad, that when he left Manhattan he drove only 98
miles in eight hours. When he reached Denver he stopped because his father
had given him the names of two men to contact for a job in the city. One he
found shortly after his arrival and was hired to work for Swift and Company.
George did not look back nor did he return to Cincinnati except to visit.
Denver's arid climate was good for a young man with but one healthy lung. It
was not far from where his mother lived for a short time, and in Denver he
somehow felt closer to her, and there he lived until the end of his days.[62]

Chapter Eleven

WILLIAMSON AND COCHRAN FAMILIES
New Jersey, Pennsylvania, Kentucky and Ohio (1637-1859)

Williamsons of Gravesend

Willem Gerritsen and his wife Mary arrived in the New World in 1659 with their children, Willem who was eight years old and his brother Cornelis who was three.[1] The town of New Amersfoort as the Dutch called it, or Flatlands as it was later known, had been formally laid out by then, its magistrates appointed and its streets patrolled by militia officers. Its current orientation to New York City is the southeastern area of the borough of Brooklyn. Claimed by the Dutch as part of the New Netherland settlement, the decade between 1655 and 1665 was a time of tension between them and Manhattan Island's English settlers. The Dutch cried out to their homeland for assistance but were met with silence, thus when the English invaded in 1664 claiming the island as English territory they were hopelessly outnumbered and were met with little resistance from the first settlers. Without troops or financial aid, Peter Stuyvesant surrendered New Amsterdam to the victorious English in less than a month of fighting. Following the Dutch surrender, English settlers moved to the island in such numbers that the original scattering of farms at its western tip was overwhelmed by the steady expansion eastward as more colonists arrived, until its boundaries included all of Long Island.[2] The English were eager to make their mark, and soon the Dutch influence disappeared as the city of New York was born. However, remnants of their presence linger on in street names and in the names of the boroughs, so that today although it is no longer spelled Brueckelen, it is still Brooklyn.[3]

Willem and Mary, whose last name is unknown, were married in Bermuda in 1650. She was fourteen years old and a native of the island, probably of English descent. He was probably Dutch, but why he was living in Bermuda at that time is unknown. What little is known about them comes from Bible records, written in Dutch by Mary's son Samuel, who painstakingly wrote the bare bones of his family's history in this book. From names, dates and events, a chronological picture of their lives emerged.[4] Mary gave birth to Willem in 1651 and Cornelis in 1656, while they lived in Bermuda. Within a few years they set sail for New Amersfoort where Sarah was born in 1660, then Hannah two years later. In 1662 Mary was about twenty-five years old when life took an abrupt turn and Willem died leaving her with four children under the ages of twelve. He was probably buried in the little village where, so full of expectations and hope for a new life, the couple had moved only three years earlier.

Alone with young children who needed a father, it was necessary for Mary to find a husband and provider for them. Mary was probably not Dutch, based

Map of Mary Remmersen's property, Chelsea Farm,
Chelsea, New York City, New York, ca. 1680.
Reprinted from I. N. Stokes, *Iconography of Manhattan Island*
(New York: R. H. Dodd, 1928)

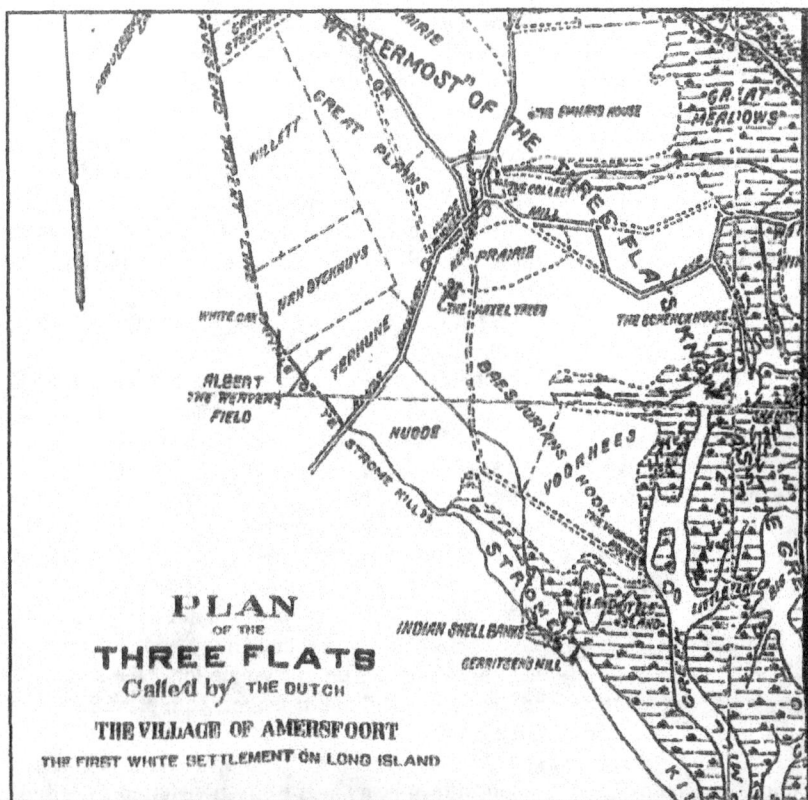

Map, Long Island, Kings County, New York,
Keskachauge or The First White Settlement on Long Island,
Frederick Van Wyck, G. P. Putnam's Sons, New York, 1924

on the names she gave her daughters, but she lived in a Dutch community, so when she married again she sought a man of similar background to Willem. Her second husband, Gerrit Remmersen, was twenty-nine years old in 1663 and she was twenty-six when they married. A child they named Anna was born the following year. Between 1667 and 1675 four more children were born and named Rem, Samuel, Maria, and Rachel. Gerrit and Mary sought change in 1678 and "removed out of the bay of York Island to a hamlet named Sapochkanika," located in Manhattan at about Mid Town on partly wooded land fed by a stream called Minetta Brook. When the British took over the island much of it was renamed, as in Greenwich or "green village," called today Greenwich Village. The early settlers subdivided the land into large lots and through diligent effort; prosperous farms grew sprinkled across the landscape. Less than a year after they arrived, Gerrit died at the age of forty-four, once again leaving Mary a widow. In December 1678 she buried her husband, this time in Stuyvesant's Church in Greenwich Village. Mary and her children lived for another seven years on land she owned a little north of Greenwich called Chelsea Farm around which was the larger "Chelsea Village," on property that currently is the area of Manhattan known as Chelsea.[5]

In 1685 when she was about forty-nine years old, Mary and her children left Chelsea and moved back to Brooklyn, settling in Gravesend near today's Coney Island. It was a good choice for her because her eldest son lived there, but it had another distinction as well. Originally settled by the English who came there as dissenters from the Church of England, it was also the only town in Kings County founded by the English.[6] Their origins were plainly seen in the earliest inhabitants of the town, families with names like Holmes, Spicer, Hubbard and Wilkins. When first settled, Gravesend's planners laid it out as a square divided through the middle into four parts from which ran streets leading out from the center, today called McDonald Avenue and Gravesend Neck Road. Originally, there were less than thirty families on thirty-nine lots,[7] the larger of them on the outer perimeter of the square, laid out in spokes, with provisions for a town hall and a cemetery in the middle.[8]

In 1689, William Wilkins of Gravesend sold his property, naming Mary Remmersen as a neighbor. About fifteen years later Mary transferred a deed to her son Samuel Gerritsen giving him the property right for eight lots. The same names as in Wilkins' earlier deed were named as neighbors, including the Widow Remmersen as well as Jonathan Griggs, Jr., the Widow Strycker and Kryne Janse, familiar names in succeeding generations.[9] Mary lived more than twenty-five years in this community watching her children grow up, marry and begin families of their own. Based on longevity alone, she was a woman of formidable energy and determination, but clearly she possessed other strengths as well. Hers was a long life and well lived, and thus on a Wednesday evening in spring just after midnight when Mary closed her eyes forever, it may well have been with a sigh of peace. On 24 May 1721 she died, for burial she was taken to the Gravesend Churchyard where she lies among the unmarked stones. Mary was eighty-five years old when she died, a remarkable feat in an age when youth was lost swiftly and often. Her children followed that pattern, and most lived to about seventy-seven years, a greater lifespan than the average person of that or of any age. As the mother of all the Willemsen and Gerritsen children, Mary passed that genetic stamp on to her many descendants.

Mary's son Willem Willemsen was about twenty-five years old in 1676 when he was taxed for land his father had originally purchased in Gravesend.[10] He remained there when his mother and Gerrit moved to Manhattan, because in 1670 at a town meeting where tillable land was meted out, Willem received an allocation given only to Gravesend residents who owned property. He received Lot #32 on Johnson's Island, the easternmost of three small islands near the present Coney Island in Gravesend. His nearest neighbors, according to the lot assignments, were John Lake, Ann Wilkins, John Emans and Ralph Cardell. His brother Cornelis also lived in Gravesend, and in 1685 he purchased several lots that he sold the following year before leaving with his wife, Magtel, for the Hempstead-Jamaica community.[11] It was a mixed community east of Gravesend also composed of English and Dutch families.[12] It was there, when he was about eighty-two years old, that Cornelis died on 10 May 1738.[13]

Willem Willemsen and Mayken Wyckoff

Although Willem Willemsen owned land in Gravesend, in 1676 he also had property in Flatlands where he paid taxes, and perhaps where he met Mayken Pieterse Wyckoff whom he married about 1677.[14] She was the daughter of Pieter Claesen Wyckoff and Grietje Cornelis Van Ness of Flatlands. Mayken was baptized 19 October 1653 in New Amsterdam and was about twenty-four when she wed Willem.[15] How Judith Stuyvesant, the granddaughter of Governor Peter Stuyvesant, became a witness to Mayken's baptism is a story that began with her father's arrival in this country.[16]

Pieter Claesen Wyckoff was aboard the *Rensselaerwick* when it left Amsterdam Holland on 25 Sep 1636. He arrived at Fort Orange, now Albany, on 7 April 1637, a young man, perhaps seventeen and unable to read or write.[17] He worked on the Van Rensselaer estate to pay his passage, and his specific duties were described in a colonial record dated 10 Jul 1655. "Peter Claesen agreed to fodder and winter, according to custom, all the cattle which Petrus Stuyvesant has at present in his bowery at Amersfoort; also to sow all the land that is fit for sowing, provided that he deduct from the rent the grain sown thereon. For said service [he will be paid] the sum of 325 gilders; [he is] to leave the manure of his own and the general's in the bowery."[18] He must have been free to marry by 1645 when he wed Grietje Van Ness, the daughter of Cornelis Van Ness and Mayken Van Der Burchgraeff, his first wife.[19] The Van Ness family lived in Rensselaerwyck, and in 1650 Cornelis leased a farm in Greenbush and opened a brewery. His political rise was gradual, beginning in 1652 when he was appointed Counselor of Rensselaerwyck, a capacity he filled until 1663. On 23 May 1659 he purchased fifty morgens of land in Flatlands where he settled, and where his daughter Grietje and her husband also lived. Cornelis Van Ness remained there until his wife Mayken died sometime prior to 1664, and then he moved to Schenectady where he purchased more land and

Map, Gravesend, Long Island, Kings County, New York,
Atlas of Long Island, New York, map from actual surveys,
Beers, Comstock and Cline, New York, 1873

1934 photograph of Pieter Wyckoff home,
Brooklyn, New York, built ca. 1650.
(Library of Congress, Prints and Photographs Division, Historic American
Buildings Survey, Reproduction Number HABS, NY, 24-BROK, 32-1.)

Wyckoff home and museum, Brooklyn, New York, after 1981 restoration.
Courtesy of Wyckoff House and Association.

married the widow Maritje Damen. She died in 1681 and sometime after November 1684, Cornelis too, died.[20]

By 1646, Pieter no long worked for Peter Stuyvesant and he had moved his family from Rensselaerswyck to Flatlands, where about that time Nicholas, thought to be their first child, was born. Like his father-in-law, Pieter Wyckoff was also politically active and in 1655, he was appointed a magistrate of Flatlands, a duty he performed until 1664.[21]

Over the years Grietje and Pieter had ten children although only a few of them had documented baptismal records. Perhaps born next was Grietje, then Ann and Mayken who was born in 1653. Their other children were Cornelis, Hendrick, Geertje, Willemptje, Garret and Marten. As Europeans, the Dutch did not use last names, instead adopting as their second name, that of their father, hence Pieter was called Pieter Claes because his father was named Nicholas or Claes. Pieter did not use the name Wyckoff, and while there are theories, there are no reliable explanations about why future generations used the name Wyckoff. However, the English were accustomed to a first and last name and eventually, although Pieter did not use it, his family adopted the name Wyckoff. In 1654 he was a founder of the Flatlands Dutch Reformed Church, originally an octagonal building overlaid with spruce shingles, but when rebuilt more than a century later, it was replaced by traditional rectangular white clapboard structure.[22] Pieter died on 30 Jun 1694 and after a ceremonious goodbye, his body was buried beneath the church's pulpit.[23]

The land Grietje Van Ness' father purchased for her eventually became the Wyckoff homestead and remained in their family until the twentieth century. Now restored as a museum, it is an oasis of colonial history in the city of Brooklyn reflecting both its early beginnings and the architecture brought by the Dutch to this country. The museum's website described the house in this way:

> Once a stone's throw from salt marshes and clam beds, the Pieter Claesen Wyckoff House Museum is probably the oldest home in New York City. The house, built around 1652, became the City's first landmark in 1965. Pieter Claesen Wyckoff's life is an American success story. In 1637, he arrived in America, an illiterate indentured servant. He eventually became a magistrate, successful farmer and the wealthiest citizen of New Amersfoort, which later became the town of Flatlands. The father of 11 children, Wyckoff settled a tract of land once inhabited by the Canarsie Indians. His descendants lived in the house until 1901. The Wyckoff House Foundation bought back the house in 1961 and donated it to the City in 1969. Saved from ruin, it was restored in 1982.
>
> A modest house, with wide pine floorboards, shingled walls and a gable roof with flared "spring" eaves; it is typical of its time. The oldest section, the kitchen, has a low, seven-foot ceiling designed to retain heat in the winter. An east wing was added between 1730 and 1750, and a central hall was created in 1819, when the roof was raised to enlarge the rear of the house. In several areas, exposed walls show the original construction; the walls were filled with handmade brick and

mud for insulation and covered with plaster. The home's furnishings reflect its Dutch heritage. On display are a large wooden kas, or cupboard, a spinning wheel, old cooking tools and original mauve and white ceramic fireplace titles imported from Holland in the late 1600s. Artifacts include a document affirming Wyckoff's allegiance to the King of England, a 17th-century pistol and a hand-sewn initialed stocking worn in the 19th century by Cornelius Waldron Wyckoff. In the surrounding one-and-a-half acre park, daffodils and tulips bloom in the spring, and a kitchen garden grows herbs and medicines used in colonial times.[24]

Willem and Mayken Willemsen had eight children, of which three were baptized at Gravesend. Willem's will named all of his living children, and the first was Nicholas to whom he later sold all of his Gravesend land. Named next, perhaps in birth order, was Pieter who was baptized 16 Apr 1682 at the Reformed Dutch Church at Flatbush.[25] After them were probably the younger sons, Willem, Jacobus and Cornelis. His daughters and their husbands were named last, Annetje, baptized 29 May 1695 in the Brooklyn Reformed Dutch Church,[26] and Marritje baptized 12 Apr 1685. Gretje, for whom there was no christening record, may have been their youngest child.[27] The 1698 tax rolls for Gravesend confirmed Willem had a wife and eight children. It also named some of their neighbors who were John Lake, Abraham Emans, James Hubbard, John Marsh, Nicholas Stillwill and the Widow Strycker, names familiar from records and deeds signed by Willem's mother and his half-brother Samuel Gerritsen. It was into some of those families that Willem and Mayken's children married.[28]

Willem and his sister Hannah Willemse both married into the Wyckoff family. Her husband was Marten Peterse Wyckoff, Mayken's brother, and they exchanged vows on 27 May 1683 at the Reformed Dutch Church at Flatbush.[29] At baptisms over the years, the siblings became godparents to each other's children.[30] Marten Wyckoff made his will on 27 Sep 1697 and died sometime between then and February 1707 when it was proved.[31] Hannah's brother Willem was one of the executors but refused to serve so the administration was turned over to his widow, Hannah. She married between February and 22 May 1707 when the estate was inventoried, signing her name as Hannah Hubbard. Her second husband was Samuel Hubbard, a man several years younger than his wife and without property. However, upon marrying he essentially became the owner of all the lands formerly owned by Marten Wyckoff, perhaps the reason why her brother Willem declined to be part of the settlement.[32]

In 1687, when he was fifty years old, Willem Willemsen took an Oath of Allegiance that as a citizen of Gravesend he had been a loyal subject of the king for thirty years. English residents were not required to take the oath, thus his signature defined him more probably as Dutch.[33] Additional proof of his origins was his use of the Dutch patronymic in naming his children, that is Willemse(n), and in the method in which he and Mayken named their children.

Willem was about seventy years old when he made his will, and probably a widower since no provision was made for his wife. Dated 2 Feb 1722, it was witnessed by his half-brother, Samuel Gerritsen, his brother-in-law Samuel Hubbard and John Lake, a near neighbor. Besides his sons, Willem named his daughters and their husbands, who were Annetje married to John Griggs, Jr., Marritje wed to Bartholomew Marsh and Gretje's husband who was Abraham Emans. Also described were the terms for Nicholas' purchase in 1717 of his father's property. Annually he paid £20 toward the £600 debt, which at the time his father died was £454. The will stipulated he divide the balance due by eight and pay his siblings for their part of the legacy, keeping an eighth part for himself. Willem named his sons, probably by birth rank after Nicholas, as Pieter, Willem, Jacobus and Cornelis.[34] Although she died first, Willem and Mayken probably rest under unmarked stones in Gravesend Cemetery, one of the smallest in New York City, dating back to 1643 when it was the final resting place of many of its earliest citizens.

Cornelis and Willem Willemsen

By the early 1700s, a number of families living in Gravesend and Flatlands, at Long Island's western end, began moving into middle New Jersey. Initially families allied through marriage moved together settling in what is now Somerset, Middlesex and Hunterdon Counties. One group who moved to New Jersey was the Willemsen, Wyckoff and Gulick families. Cornelis Willemsen was named last in his father's will, and was probably Willem and Mayken's youngest son. About 1709, before departing for New Jersey, he and Margarietje "Grietje" Gulick were married, likely in New York. Their siblings Willem Willemsen and Catalyntje Gulick married at about the same time. Neither union was found among church records, but other documents proved a long-standing relationship between their families. One was the 1697 will of Marten Wyckoff, who was Cornelis and Willem's uncle. His executors, Jochem Gulick and Willem Willemsen, were the fathers of the four young people. The other record was from 17 Dec 1711 when Grietje and Catalyntje's father, Jochem, made his will asking Willem Willemsen and Samuel Gerritsen to protect and guard the interests of his wife and children. Again, one man was Willem and Cornelis' father and the other, Samuel Gerritsen, was their uncle.

Willem and Cornelis Willemsen, were probably the third and fifth sons of Willem and Mayken, and since their brother Nicholas bought the Gravesend farm, with their share of the legacy, they were free to move elsewhere. Thus released they sought their fortunes and a place to raise their families in New Jersey. Both brothers were married by 1710 as indicated by their children's baptismal records. The Gulick sisters were also from Gravesend, and the 1698 census for the town indicated they had six siblings.[35] Jochem's will of 1711 proved this, but amongst his daughters he named Catalyntje and Grietie, as well as his four sons.[36] Two of them, Hendrick and Jochem, also moved to New Jersey, and in 1717 they were living at Three-Mile Run in Somerset County just down the road from where their sisters lived.[37]

Willem and Catalyntje Willemsen probably lived in New York when their son Jochem was baptized at the Flatbush Reformed Dutch Church on 18 Sep 1709. Sponsors were his grandfather after whom he was named, and Catalyntje's sister, Geertruy Gulick.[38] It must be presumed that Cornelis

Willemsen and Grietje Gulick were married prior to 8 Aug 1710, the date when their son Samuel was baptized at the Six-Mile Run Church in Somerset County, and when their siblings, Willem and Catalyntje, were witnesses and probably sponsors for their son. Cornelis and Grietje's son Johannis was baptized at this church on 23 Oct 1711, this time clarifying the double marriage between the Gulick and Willemsen siblings by calling her Cattelyntye Gulick.[39] Samuel may have died young because there are no later records for him.

This couple also had a son Willem who was probably born about 1705 although no baptismal records have been found for him. Proof of his lineage was found in his children's baptismal records and in the will he wrote many years later. The elder Willem left no will and it is unknown when either he or Catalyntje died. Some say he was the Willem who lived at the Raritan Landing and in 1739 either he, or his son by that name, left after a major flood did too much damage. Their property was sold and the family moved from the flats to higher ground further west up the Old Road.[40]

The younger Willem married Jannitje Van Nest and they had a son Jacob born about 1725 who was mentioned in his father's will. Their daughter Catalyntje was born and baptized on 30 May 1731 at the New Brunswick First Reformed Church.[41] Sometime after 4 Sep 1767 when he wrote his will, Willem Junior died. He mentioned his wife although not by name, and left bequests of £400 each to his daughters Catalyntje, married to George Van Nest, and Jannitje whose husband was John Piatt. Willem also endowed his grandchildren by his son Jacob who died about eight years before.[42] Willem, the eldest son and executor of his estate, got half of the land, and his wife the other half until she married again. His will was probated in 1780 when William the executor died, a man many called "The Captain" because of his Revolutionary War service.[43]

A survey map shows others who settled along the "old path" in Somerset County, including brothers of Grietje and Jacomentje Gulick. Common to all of the maps was the road running through it which had many names, the Old Indian Path and the York Road are but two of them. Grietje and Cornelis Willemsen lived along it at the western boundary near Kingston. Her brother, Pieter Gulick's, house was between Six Mile and Ten Mile Run, near Willem Willemsen's tavern and the home of Cornelius DeHart.[44] Neither Willem nor his brother Cornelis left a will, thus the map and other records must suffice to flesh out the events of their lives. However, the greatest proof lies in kinship, with the double marriages between siblings creating an alliance and an unbreakable bond that in succeeding generations remained as a thread of kinship strengthened by their origins in Gravesend and the transition to New Jersey. The brothers and their wives, and then their children over the generations lived near each other and some, like Samuel Williamson, returned to his origins near Six Mile Run when he married. These collateral ties bound them as their children married and gave birth and a generation later, it kept them together as cousins followed each other into war.

On 25 Mar 1718 Cornelis and Grietje baptized their daughter Jacomentje at the New Brunswick Dutch Reformed Church. She was named for her maternal grandmother and the sponsors and witnesses to the event were Grietje's siblings, Pieter and Jacomentje Gulick.[45] According to the 1727 will of Isaac Van Dike of Middlesex County, Cornelis Willemsen lived there near its border with

Somerset where Van Dike and neighbors Teunis Quick and Thomas Yates, who were his witnesses, lived.[46] Several years later, in 1735, Cornelis and his neighbors were listed on the Franklin Township, Somerset County tax list—a change in the county boundaries rather than a move by the individuals who lived there. In the order of visitation his nearest neighbors were Thomas Yates who owned 200 acres, then Cornelis who had fifty acres and next to him, Teunis Quick with 100 acres. After that were Cornelius De Hart and Peter Gulick.[47] Living four houses on the other side of Thomas Yates was Willem Willemsen, probably Cornelis' brother or his nephew who had a tavern at Ten Mile Run. The records showed that the tax collector followed the same route as that of the 1766 survey map that clearly indicated each residence and owner on the road from New Brunswick to Kingston.[48] Cornelis' property was more closely pinpointed in a 1740 Somerset County road book that gave the names and locations of his neighbors, saying they lived between Rocky Hill and Kingston near the "Dirty Brook."[49] A contemporary Somerset County map showed that the brook is a small branch of the Millstone River between the Higgins Farm on Washington Street and Kingston Road. Cornelius' neighbor was Jediah Higgins, an indication that the property remained in his family long after the Williamson name was no longer associated with the area. Although he may have lived several years beyond that date, the last known record for Cornelis was a 1745 Somerset County tax list.[50] Perhaps Grietje outlived him but eventually they were both buried somewhere in Somerset County in a family graveyard whose markings were obliterated over time.

Willem Willemsen, son of Cornelis and Grietje was born about 1715, and probably baptized at Six Mile Run where Samuel was christened earlier. Without a will or probate records to link Cornelis and Willem, who was named after his grandfather, proof of the relationship must be established by other means. One is the Dutch naming system, which can be relied upon when marriage and baptismal records are unavailable, as is the case with this family. The patronymic method linked a child to his grandparents through a highly structured order of naming that was a consistent and predominantly used source at the time.[51] Willem surely did exist and he carried as proof his will and a deed to the property he left his children, plus the will of his father-in-law stating their relationship. Had the records for the Six Mile Run Church survived between 1711 and 1743, undoubtedly Willem's baptism would have been among them. Lacking that evidence, the link between Cornelis and his son will be established through William's children.[52]

William Williamson and Patience Hull

Cornelis and his brother Willem had unusually close ties because of their marriages and the extended family that came with them, but they were also connected socially to the larger community in three counties. That said, it takes a leap of faith plus documentation to prove that a deed made in 1735, was for Cornelis' son Willem. He bought a 290-acre tract in Hunterdon County, New Jersey, on 12 May 1735 that encompassed the Plum Branch of the Wickecheoke

Creek and established where he lived. First, his neighbors bore the same last names as those families who lived near his grandfather Willem Willemsen in Gravesend, an area of New Jersey largely settled by those same Gravesend families. Of mixed Dutch and English blood, they were widely intermarried on Long Island, and when they moved to New Jersey they settled into similar groups of mixed ancestry. With an already established pattern of marriage, it is not surprising that William Williamson married a woman of English background named Patience Hull. Once again, marriage records have not survived but proof lies in the will of her father, Samuel Hull of Amwell Township.

Samuel Hull's grandfather was the Reverend Joseph Hull of Crewkerne, Somersetshire, England. Born in 1595, he was educated at Oxford and took his degree at the age of seventeen. He was appointed the rector of Northleigh in 1621 and remained in that capacity for eleven years. Philosophically he was a moderate and a conformist to the old religion, his view amidst a growing religious revolution did not fit with the times and so he resigned his post in 1632 and moved back to Somersetshire where he began preparation for a move to the New World. When the Hull family set sail for New England on 20 Mar 1635 with fifteen other families, Joseph was 40 years old and his wife Agnes 25. Arriving in Boston that May with seven children they proceeded toward their assignment.[53] The Reverend settled uneasily into the Weymouth, Massachusetts community because as a moderate, his ministry was antagonistic to that of the Puritans who made up the majority; and in both religion and politics, he opposed Winthrop, the colony's governor. The family remained there only a short time before moving on to Hingham, then to Barnstable and Yarmouth, finally settling in York, Maine, in 1643. Throughout his ten years in New England, Reverend Hull struggled for his beliefs and thus was often in trouble with the religious authority of the colony. After a time he was relieved of his duties in York and he moved back to England. Not long after, Reverend Hull returned to New England and went to New Hampshire to live with one of his sons where on 19 Nov 1665 he died. A researcher who had spent a good deal of time studying Reverend Hull described him as a man possessing three characteristics, "in habit he was scholarly, in temperament religious, and in spirit contentious."[54]

When Joseph and Agnes Hull left Somersetshire in 1635, their son Samuel was not yet born. He was probably the youngest child, born in York, Maine, sometime between 1645 and 1649. Several of Reverend Hull's children moved to Piscataway, New Jersey, around 1668, including Samuel, although the most historically notable of them were his elder brothers, Hopewell and Benjamin.[55] On 16 Nov 1677, Samuel Hull married Mary Manning at Piscataway.[56] He first owned land next to John Martin in 1682[57] and on 10 May 1688 he purchased 80 acres on Doty's Brook,[58] which is just east of Bound Brook and northeast of New Brunswick. The youngest of Mary and Samuel's seven children was born in Piscataway on 20 Jul 1678 and they named him Samuel.[59] Evidence that the elder Samuel remained in Piscataway until his death came from town records describing the marks each man gave his cattle. The first one was recorded in 1686 but the most distinctive was from 1703, described as "a half penny on the underside of the left ear and a slit in the half penny." Samuel died sometime prior to 7 Apr 1706 when Joseph Drake was assigned to his mark.[60] Drake was undoubtedly a neighbor as was his brother, Samuel Drake, who married Elizabeth, a daughter of Samuel and Mary Hull on 10 Sep 1700.[61]

Prior to that date, probably in about 1701, Samuel Hull, Jr. married Margaret, whose last name is unknown. They had eight children, and between the probate of Samuel's will in 1761 and that of his wife Margaret seven years later, Patience's siblings were clearly identified, as were some of their spouses. Moses was their eldest son, followed by Gersham, John and Daniel. Patience was likely the eldest daughter as she was named first among her sisters, Margaret, Mary Ann and Joanna. Samuel Hull Sr. died after 6 Jul 1761 and his will not only named his daughter Patience but also her husband William Williamson, Samuel's executor, as his son-in-law. The term "dearly beloved wife" appeared to be a true description of his affection for Margaret. He not only gave her the two best rooms in the house, but also offered her a choice of furniture, a yearly stipend, a garden and an orchard plus a horse and cattle. Their son Daniel was required to supply and deliver to his mother as much firewood as she wanted and to see that she had a "suitable diet for such an old person."[62] She outlived her husband by several years and when she wrote her will on 1 Feb 1768 she was nearly eighty-five, and probably died soon thereafter.[63]

William Williamson married Samuel's daughter around 1735. Patience Hull was born about 1715 and would have been at least twenty years old at the time of their marriage and when her husband first purchased land. Hull's name was among the freeholders taxed in Amwell Township, Hunterdon County in 1741, as was his son-in-law, William Williamson. The term freeholder presupposes that Hull owned at least 100 acres.[64] By 1741 William and Patience had two or three children, Cornelius the eldest son was followed by Samuel and then William.[65] Using the Dutch naming pattern, this branch of the Williamson family named in each generation a son Cornelius and William. Samuel was also an ancestral name, used by Mary Gerritsen to name her first son by Gerrit Remmersen. In turn, Samuel Gerritsen, named a son Samuel, as did his cousin Cornelius Williamson. In the fourth generation William and Patience took the name from both sides of the family. Their younger sons were John and Abraham and daughters they named Margaret and Mayeke for ancestors on both sides of the family, as Margrietje translates to Margaret and Mayeke to Mary.

Seldom mentioned outside of the two properties he bought, William Williamson busied himself with his farm, clearing land, raising crops and in general minding his own business. His children grew up and some of them married into local families. Margaret, probably their eldest daughter, left some of the more traceable records in the family. She married Daniel Larue who left a will in 1762.[66] When he died Margaret married John Hull who died in 1794 also leaving a will.[67] She died in 1816 fulfilling Hull's wishes that their grandson have the house and land.[68] Their eldest son Cornelius married, and although his children's names are well documented, his wife's name is unknown.

Samuel Williamson and Margaret DeHart

Samuel was William and Patience's second son, born between 1735 and 1738. He grew up on his father's farm in Hunterdon County among an extended family that lived in neighboring counties, and when Samuel came of age he extended his reach to those areas just beyond the borders of his home. As a youth he went with his parents to visit his Williamson cousins who lived along the road bordering Somerset and Middlesex Counties. Perhaps he knew Margaret DeHart, a daughter of Cornelius and Moica DeHart since they lived near John Piatt and the tavern owned by Samuel's uncle, William Williamson, on the Ten Mile Run. The Wyckoff, Gulick, DeHart and Williamson families settled early near Kingston where Samuel's grandparents Cornelius Williamson and Grietje Gulick lived, and where his father William grew up.[69] These children of the second generation, that is, their Gulick cousins and the DeHart children, knew each other from both family and church gatherings, as the DeHart's were members of the Six Mile Run Reformed Dutch Church. The couple was probably married there about 1758, but proof of their union comes from Cornelius DeHart's will wherein he named Samuel Williamson as the husband of his daughter Margaret.[70]

The first of the DeHart family to settle along the Old Road was Gysbert (Gilbert) DeHart and his wife Antye Wynants who in 1710 were members of the Six Mile Run Church in Middlesex County.[71] In 1720 their son Cornelius bought 210 acres on the Ten Mile Run not far from Kingston.[72] He married Moike, sometime before 1734 and their son Gysbert was baptized on 2 Aug 1747, at the New Brunswick First Reformed Church. A daughter, Sarah, was baptized there also.[73] After 1751, their children were christened at the Six Mile Run Church.[74] Margrietje, or Margaret, was one of their older children, probably born about 1740 and probably baptized in the same church as her younger siblings.

When they married Samuel and Margaret probably lived near her parents in Middlesex County and may have always lived there. When their union began, Samuel was about 21 and his wife was about eighteen, thus she was born about 1740. Their eldest child, William, was born 6 Apr 1759 and baptized a month later. Cornelius was born in 1761 followed by Peter whose birthday was 24 Jul 1763.[75] Then they had two daughters, Mayeke and Antje whose baptisms were in 1766 and 1768. Jacob was born in 1771 and the last child, John, was baptized in 1777.[76] All of the children, with the exception of Jacob, were baptized at the Six Mile Run Church, an indication they lived close to the Somerset County border. Further corroboration was found in a 1772 newspaper advertisement when Samuel, who was living in New Brunswick, offered a reward for the return of a horse.[77] He was taxed there in 1779 and 1780 in the North Ward where his cousin William Williamson lived.[78]

Prior to 1768, Margaret's father, Cornelius DeHart, and some of his children were named in the account books for Jacob Piatt who was the cobbler for the Three Mile Run District of Somerset County from 1765 to 1772. Piatt's records named Cornelius, his wife, and their children, Abraham, Antye, Cornelius, Gisbert, Sarah and William. Margaret and Samuel Williamson lived nearby and the list included their children as well two elderly individuals who were probably Margaret's grandmother and her uncle Jacob, because after Cornelius Dehart's father died, his mother, Antje, married Jan Vandeventer and had several children, one named Jacob.[79] Cornelius DeHart wrote his will in 1768 naming among his children, "Margaret, the wife of Samuel Williamson."[80] He died soon after and was buried in the Ten Mile Run cemetery. His gravestone is a simple brownstone marker with the message, "CDH 1769." Beside him a companion stone reads "MDH 1769," most certainly that of his wife Moike.[81]

Living nearby on the Old Road was Samuel's uncle, William Williamson, and aunt, Jannitje Van Nest who ran the tavern at Ten Mile Run. Sam was about the same age as his cousin William, born in 1739.[82] He married Angenietye or Agnes and their son William who was born in 1757 died young. Isaac was born in 1759 and called the eldest son in his father's will.[83] Named next in the will was William, born in 1762, a confirmation of the death of his sibling by that name. Samuel and William's children were cousins of the fourth generation and each had in common, Gulick and Williamson grandparents. Although they lived near each other and shared the same first names, their descendants, all cousins, can be distinguished from one another by wills and baptismal records.[84] When Jannetje's husband, William Williamson, made his will in 1767 their children were grown and so their daughter's spouses were named. Catalyntye was married to George Van Nest, and Jannitje's husband was John Piatt the cobbler. Between 1765 and 1772 the elder couple lived with their son William and his wife Agnes, whose children were identified as Billy, George, John and Isaac. A daughter Jenny was named, as were several slaves.[85] They were all baptized in the Six Mile Run Church and are thus doubly identified as the children of William and Agnes Williamson.[86]

The Revolutionary War in New Jersey

By fall of 1776 the colonies were so thoroughly immersed in the battle for freedom that every man, woman and child in New Jersey knew that the fighting was all violence, privation and patriotism. During the fall of 1777 and into early 1778 the Revolutionary War had entirely enveloped those living in western New Jersey, and it was especially focused on those living on or near the Old Road leading from New Brunswick to Trenton where the Williamson family lived. In an effort to gain control of strategic areas like New York, Staten Island and Long Island became the sites of major battles. However, to save New York, New Jersey became a battleground. In 1776, troops retreating from Manhattan used established settlement routes to get through the narrows of New Jersey encompassing Somerset and Middlesex counties. The Continental troops marched through these lands to get to the Delaware River in Pennsylvania. Invariably following closely on their heels was the vastly superior British army taking needed supplies as they passed through.[87] The path between New York and their Pennsylvania destination went right through Hunterdon County, and as a result three major battles took place there between December 1776 and January 1777, the first two near Trenton and the last at Princeton. The siege of

New Jersey began in April 1776 at the narrows separating Long Island from Elizabethtown, but it ended with skirmishes there and at New Brunswick in February 1782. Throughout the war, New Jersey was savaged again and again.[88]

In times of peace and war, every able-bodied man in New Jersey over the age of eighteen was required to serve in the militia. By mid-1776 Washington had less than a few thousand Continental troops to cover all bases and he desperately needed the militia, a group of mostly untrained youth guided by elder brothers and uncles. Consequently, men with only slight military experience found themselves serving as substitutes for trained soldiers. Out of desperation, young, poorly armed men were hastily trained on the village green, then sent to war against disciplined British and Hessian troops. Samuel and Margaret Williamson had four sons who were born before the war began, the youngest, Jacob, only five years old. William, the eldest child was seventeen and Cornelius was fifteen, both too young to join the militia in 1776, as was their brother Peter who was thirteen. Samuel was about forty years old, and his brother Cornelius a couple of years older when they went to Bridgewater on 24 Feb 1776, to join those who signed up with Captain Jacob Ten Eyck's First Battalion of militia at Somerset. All served in Colonel John Neilson's Regiment of State Troops including Captain William Williamson from Middlesex who was cousin to Samuel Williamson.[89]

The battles at Trenton and Princeton in late 1776 and January 1777 demanded fierce patriotism, as well as patience and understanding from those who lived there. At Trenton, Washington's troops overwhelmed the Hessians, taking more than 900 prisoners. Then as the British charged through New Jersey toward Princeton the following January, Washington's troops defeated a superior British army. The tiny hamlets through which they marched became the stage for, not only some of the major battles of the war, but for smaller skirmishes that took place in farmer's yards, in their cornfields and on the roads as they went to market. Ordinary citizens were interrupted on their way to court, when they went to church to pray, but above all, the war around them was a reminder of why they also had to bury their sons and brothers. In the chaos of it all and not knowing when and how it would end, people were not only fighting for their country, they were literally fighting for their homes, their lands and their possessions. Although Washington was victorious in New Jersey, those who lived there paid a high price for freedom. To add insult to their privations, when the British swept through their lands, they took whatever provisions they needed for their troops and animals, including housing, food, bedding, wagons and livestock, and the most vulnerable were those living along the main roads. Their losses were sometimes overwhelming.

Samuel Williamson's family was directly affected by the swath of destruction left by the British army as they cut through town. His claim for reimbursement of damages during the war was a vivid example of the disruption that ordinary families suffered. When his claims were multiplied by those of his neighbors, the entire community was disrupted Samuel testified that he knew of the "enemies taking and destroying almost all of the above articles" which suggested that he was there when his home was invaded. He claimed damages of £129.13 of goods taken in a six-month period between December 1776 and June 1777, including the loss of $48 in silver. The enemy ravaged his livestock, taking his cattle, sheep and hogs, then went into the barn and took fifty bushels of wheat and two tons of hay. They destroyed or stole 100 panels of fencing and rails. Also taken were two muskets and bayonets, his wagon harnesses and two horses. The loss of a looking glass, a Bible and a pewter teapot suggested their home was forcibly entered. Other items taken also suggested thievery—the loss of a new notebook and pocket book as well as silk handkerchiefs and ladies petticoats. Also stolen were linen sheets, quilts and tablecloths plus a dozen shirts and stockings and a greatcoat, probably the best clothing he and Margaret owned.[90] In 1777 she was pregnant with their youngest child while all around her ebbed and flowed marching troops and the swirl of war. As their young men and boys went off to fight, the British army was stealing their livestock and looting crops. Although Samuel's son Peter was quite young, his father allowed him to take his place as a substitute, maybe because he feared losing everything the family owned. A descendant of Peter Williamson tells a different story. When he filed for a pension for war service he stated, "his father could not leave his mother who was very ill with consumption," and thus Samuel remained behind while Peter took his place in the militia.[91] He served as Samuel's substitute from January to July 1777, probably the reason why Samuel could make a verifiable report on what had been taken by the British. Then with chaos surrounding them, Margaret gave birth to their son John, some time prior to 20 Jul 1777, when he was baptized.

Years later in his application for a Revolutionary War pension, Peter Williamson made some surprising revelations about his service as a youth. He lived in Amwell since the war ended and in 1833 when he was sixty-nine years old he told the remarkable story of how at the age of twelve he joined the Flying Camp or minutemen troops as a volunteer. For several months in 1776 he moved with the troops between Staten Island and Long Island in the fight to keep New York from British possession. During the battle of Long Island in 1776, he served with a man who taught him to be a fifer. When he re-enlisted it was not as a fifer which he quite obviously detested, saying he would not return to it because he "could not stand it, [and] that his constitution would not permit it." In his second stint, Peter was a private in the militia, again as a substitute for his father, and was present at the Battle of Princeton. Three times he substituted for Samuel, the last time in May 1777 when he went to Elizabethtown under the watchful eye of his uncle, Captain William Williamson. He was present when Burgoyne surrendered to General Gates at Saratoga on 17 Oct 1777. Overall Peter spent six years either in the Flying Camp or the regular militia, leaving the service when he was nineteen. Initially his pension was rejected because no one could believe that a youngster of "but 12 years of age when he entered the service...[could] be considered as having been capable of the performance of military duty at that age." He persisted by enlisting friends and family to prove he served, including his cousin Isaac Williamson, the son of Captain Williamson, who stated that he had known the Peter since boyhood. Not long afterward, in 1833 Peter got his pension.

The Williamson boys may have seemed older than their ages, and according to Peter's application he was considered "stout for his age and he recollects attracting the attention of Colonel Neilson on his first trip as a private who spoke in terms of commendation of his ability and willingness for duty at such an age."[92] Peter was not the only one of Samuel's sons who joined the war effort before he was eighteen. According to his application, William the eldest son was born in Middlesex County and joined the war effort in 1775 when he was just sixteen. Most of that time he served as a militia guard in under the eye of his uncle, Captain Williamson, in the regiment commanded by Colonel Nielson. Perhaps once or twice the brothers, Peter and William, served together but most of the time they were on duty at different times and places.[93] They were youngsters, teenagers still, when they were hurled into history like flotsam on the crest of a wave. When it was over, having served his country, William began thinking about his future, one that would ultimately lead him to seek a suitable young woman and ask for her hand in marriage.

William Williamson and Halena Terhune

In 1780 Albert Terhune was taxed for 200 acres in New Brunswick's North Ward, the neighborhood where the Williamson family lived and probably where William met Albert's daughter, Halena.[94] The Terhunes moved to New Jersey around 1750 from Flatlands, some forty years and a generation removed from when the Williamson family left New York. Albert was named after his great-great grandfather, Albert Albertse Terhunen, the immigrant ancestor of all of the New York and New Jersey families by that name. He was a ribbon weaver married to a woman named Geertje Pieters and they came to New Amsterdam sometime prior to 1654. Albert had land in New Utrecht and in Flatlands, but in 1664 he sold the Utrecht plantation and bought more property in Flatlands where he and Geertje eventually settled. There in 1675 he was assessed for 29 morgens (about fifty acres) of land plus five horses, nine cows and ten sheep. Albert's last transaction was in 1685 when he and several associates obtained a patent from Governor Carteret for 5,000 acres in New Jersey on the Passaic River. As members of the Reformed Dutch Church of Flatlands in 1677, it was probably where their son Jan was baptized around 1750.[95]

Jan was in his thirties when he married a young woman named Annetje, the daughter of Roelof Martense Schenck, on 1 Jul 1683 in Flatbush. Their son Albert who was born in 1684 died young.[96] A second son was born in 1688, and again named Albert.[97] Annetje died on 25 Mar 1688, perhaps in childbirth, and her husband purchased a burial plot from the church at Flatlands. Their children were named in Roelof Schenck's 1705 will gifting "to ye two children of my daughter Anneke, deceased, by name Roeloft and Albert, each ten pounds in money."[98] On 6 Jun 1691 Albert Terhune married a young woman from Flatlands named Margrietie Van Siegelen. It was she who raised Annetje's sons and the children she and Albert had together.

Albert Terhune, born in 1688, was living in New Amersfoort or Flatlands on 17 Oct 1708 when he married Altje Voorhees.[99] She was the daughter of Steven Coert Van Voorhees and Eva Janse Van Dyck of Flatlands, born 4 Oct 1685.[100] Albert's will, probated on 11 Apr 1721, left Altje the estate in Flatlands where they lived, and then it went to John who was directed to sell the land in Princeton, New Jersey, to pay all debts. In his will Albert described the relationships to him of his executors, which determined he had married twice, both times to women named Altje. He was married to Altje, the daughter of Peter Nevius when he wrote his will. He identified Roelof Terhune as his brother, but more importantly, he called Coert Voorhees his brother-in-law, that is, he was the brother of Albert's first wife Altje Voorhees.[101]

Based on when his parents married, John Terhune was born in Flatbush about 1709/10 where he grew up. He married Neltje Duryea, the daughter of Abraham, about 1732.[102] John's will of 1780 named Albert as his first-born followed by Gerrit to whom he left all his land.[103] John and Neltje's son Albert was born September 1733, the same year his father became a deacon of the Reformed Dutch Church at Flatlands.[104] John and Neltje left Flatbush and moved to Middlesex County, New Jersey, before 25 August 1751 when their son Jan was baptized in the Six Mile Run Church.[105] John died soon after he wrote his will in April 1786. In it he mentioned his wife, Ellener, (Neltje) and his son Albert to whom he gave £5 as his birthright, an assumption that he was provided for at an earlier date. A witness was Isaac, brother of the former Marya Selover who had married his son Albert.[106] Marya who married Albert Terhune was a younger daughter of Daniel Selover and Helena Schermerhorn. She was baptized shortly after her birth in 1739 at the Readington Reformed Dutch Church and so was probably no more than eighteen when they married. They wed in late 1756, perhaps around Christmas, because their first child, Jan, was baptized on 4 Sep 1757 at the Six Mile Run Church.[107]

Halena Terhune, or Lena as she was called by her family, grew up in Middlesex County, a middle child in a family of nine, and the eldest daughter of Albert Terhune and Marya Selover, born in 1763. She was probably well acquainted with the young man she married because her siblings were baptized in the church at Six Mile Run, and they parallel in time those of the Williamson children who were also christened there.[108] It was 13 Jun 1784, a fine spring Sunday when Lena and William Williamson exchanged vows at the Cranbury Presbyterian Church in Middlesex County. After they married, William carefully wrote the date of their marriage in the Bible, and continued with their birthdays, as well as those of all their children. Their first child, Samuel, was born at Kingston in late November 1785. They left New Jersey and moved to Allegany County, Maryland where their next three children, John, Mary and William, were born between 1787 and 1792. They returned to Amwell, where Lena gave birth to Albert in 1795 and Daniel in 1797. Abraham and Margaret were children of the new century, born in 1800 and 1803, both in Amwell. In his pension application, William stated he had lived in Middlesex County for 31 years. No mention was made about the five years he lived in Maryland, why he left or the reason for their return to Amwell in 1795.[109]

The Williamson and Terhune families probably went to the same school and church. Along the way, friendships grew among them and the result was that three children from each family intermarried. Lena and William were married first in 1784, then her brother Abraham married Mayeke Williamson about 1786, and Daniel Terhune married Antje Williamson the following year.[110] Some of their families attended Kingston Presbyterian Church in Somerset, a county formed as early as 1723. The village was even older because when the Williamsons came to New Jersey around 1710, Cornelius Williamson was the first of his family to settle in Kingston. Then, his nearest neighbors were Cornelius DeHart and some members of the Gulick family.

Samuel Williamson and Eleanor Williamson Gulick

William Williamson, father of Samuel and Cornelius, died in 1764 naming them the executors of an estate that included the farm where they were raised. With her husband's death, Patience took charge of the estate and kept it intact until she died in December 1787. Cornelius lived on the property with his mother and remained there afterward. The land was 260 acres his father bought in 1735 and an additional 30 acres purchased in 1742. William left explicit instructions in his will that the land was to be sold within two years after Patience died and the proceeds divided among his children.[111]

In the years between the death of his parents, Samuel Williamson and Grietje DeHart lived in Middlesex County. Of the few surviving tax lists was one for New Brunswick's North Ward in April 1779 and June 1780. A comparison of the two records indicated that the Revolutionary War wrought changes in the lives of cousins William and Samuel Williamson. William, a captain in the militia during the War, served actively for several years, at least through the fall of 1778 when Samuel's son William served in the captain's unit. Sometime after that he fell ill, and in September 1779 William wrote a will naming Agnes, his wife, and eldest son Isaac the estate executors. Using tax lists, the date William died can be narrowed even more. He paid taxes in April 1779 for 435 acres, livestock, a riding chair and £200 out at interest. But in June 1780 it was his widow who was taxed for 400 acres and £2,500 out at interest, indicating he died sometime between September 1779 and June 1780.[112]

The same tax list indicated Samuel Williamson was also in the midst of changes, and perhaps of endings too. He paid taxes in New Brunswick's North Ward on April 1779 for 300 acres, six horses, three cows, seven pigs, a riding chair, and a declaration of £200 loaned out at interest. The following year he was not on this list but a William Williamson, probably his eldest son, was taxed in the same district for 250 acres (50 acres was probably sold), five cows, eight pigs, an orchard and £400 loaned out at interest. 1780 may have been when Samuel's wife Grietje died. Of their children, the younger ones were under ten years old, and older ones were unmarried and living at home, including William who was 21. Samuel may have left William in charge of the property in Brunswick and moved to Hunterdon County to take charge of the family farm in Amwell Township. This appeared to be corroborated by his brother's tax assessments for the same years. In 1779, Cornelius paid taxes on the family farm of 440 acres, but in 1780 he was assessed for 280 acres, the approximate size of the family property where he had been living with his mother. However, Samuel's name did not appear on either list.

Two years later, when Samuel Williamson was about 55 years old he married again and moved in with his wife Eleanor Williamson Gulick, the widow of Gilbert Gulick. They wed on 12 March 1782 when she was about 40 years old.[113] Her parents were Elizabeth and Cornelius Williamson of Amwell,

Hunterdon County, and when her father died early in 1767, her husband Gilbert, and her mother refused to be administrators of the estate.[114] Eleanor had six children by Gulick, her youngest merely four years old, and Samuel brought seven children to their marriage.[115] At the time of this union, some of Samuel's children were of a marriageable age and within two years they began assembling families of their own. One of them was Cornelius, his second eldest son who married Staintje Demott, the daughter of Michael who lived in Reading Township.[116] The marriage between Samuel and Eleanor was a legal bond, but it was probably also fraternal because they were both Williamsons by birth, so it is reasonable to assume they were also cousins in some degree.[117] In 1784 the Gordian knot of relationship was pulled even tighter when Samuel's son Peter and her daughter Charity (Gitty) Gulick married, thereby increasing their degree of relatedness to include in-law as well as step-parent but also possibly cousins. With the births of their daughters Margaret, Elizabeth and Ellenor between 1783 and 1788, Samuel and Eleanor were jointly the parents of sixteen children.[118] The land he paid taxes on in Hunterdon County in 1784 and 1785 may have been land Eleanor brought to the marriage. Samuel was active in the Amwell community in 1785 when he was elected township constable. How long he served is unknown but a notice in 1795 called him the "late constable" so it was less than ten years. Then in 1797, when he was approaching sixty years old he was appointed an overseer of the roads for Amwell.[119]

The Dark Years

Samuel's troubles ratcheted up sharply in July 1810 when he found himself in court embroiled in family troubles, defending himself against charges brought by the heirs of his brother Cornelius. The brothers were the executors of their father's will, Cornelius the elder was named first, then Samuel but because his brother "refused and neglected" to do so, Samuel proved the will in 1774. Cornelius and his family lived with his mother on the farm, then on 11 Mar 1789 two years after her death, Samuel took possession of it, and in his testimony described how it happened. He held a public auction at Cornelius house where Samuel claimed he urged his brother to bid, saying that since he lived on the land it would suit him better than someone else to own it; but Cornelius declined saying that the land had little value. Others bid, but evidently they were low or the terms were not to Samuel's liking. He urged his son, Cornelius, to bid but the 42 shillings per acre he offered was too low, and so the auction was struck without a sale. Samuel left it at that saying that if anyone offered more he would sell it.[120] For a time nothing more happened, and then in 1807 Cornelius died, seemingly without resolution of the issue. However, he addressed it in his will saying there was a "dispute about an over-plus of land between my brother, Samuel Williamson, and me and if said dispute is settled in my children's favor then sons William and Cornelius, are each to have $133.33 and the residue to be divided amongst all my children."[121] However, this meant his children had to take their uncle to court to get satisfaction and so they did.

Court records defined the familial relationships that included the names of Samuel and Cornelius' children and their spouses. The dispute against Samuel was long and rancorous and likely gave impetus to the departure from New Jersey of some of his siblings as well as his children. Much was percolating between Samuel and his brother's children between 1789 and 1812 when it spilled over into a lawsuit nearly 45 years after the death of William Williamson, father or grandfather of those involved. It seemed that what Samuel initially revealed was not the entire story. The plaintiffs charged that beginning in 1789 when Samuel put the property up for sale it was worth £6 per acre, which he denied, saying it was closer to £2.2 per acre the same as nearby land. Even so, it was more than Cornelius would give for it. Samuel made no other attempts to sell the land, so on 9 Aug 1792 he sold both properties to his son, Cornelius for £613. Then Cornelius immediately sold the land back to his father. That became a big issue with the plaintiffs who brought charges of fraud against their uncle.[122] According to Samuel's testimony, most of the trouble between the siblings stemmed from Cornelius' belief that when the family farm was resurveyed showing an over-plus of approximately 70 acres, he thought it should have been given to him. Apparently Samuel disagreed, saying that since it had not been surveyed prior to the sale, he was unaware at the time that there was any over-plus, and that it was not until a subsequent survey was done that the over-plus was discovered. Samuel also claimed he offered to pay his brother his share of the larger property as well as his one-fourth part of the over-plus land. Over the years as the lawsuit languished in court other issues evolved, namely that William's will directed his executors to sell the land and distribute the proceeds, and that neither Cornelius nor Samuel had done so.

On 20 Mar 1808, after Cornelius' death, Samuel wrote up a years lease for $86.66 on 150 acres of the farm where William Williamson, presumably his son, had been living. It was witnessed by Abraham Terhune, his son-in-law. Cornelius' heirs were represented in court on 24 Oct 1812 by his son Asher Williamson, a man who was relentless in his pursuit of justice for his siblings. He claimed that his Uncle Samuel owed them a portion of the rents on property he had leased out between 1789 and 1812. He also claimed that Samuel and his tenants damaged the property and its value by cutting timber. Both the plaintiff and the defendant had character witnesses. Samuel's witness, James Larew, said he lived nearby and had seen much improvement on the farm since Samuel had taken charge of it.[123] That Samuel had repaired fences and outbuildings and cut away an overabundance of timber, which he used to build a large barn in 1790. Then in 1793 he built an addition to the house, erected a wagon house and other buildings, which improved the land greatly. He cited as an example of improvement, that while Samuel's son William was living on the place, he had cleared away some five acres of woodland as was customary so that he could plant wheat. While the court may have agreed that the land was improved, it also ruled that the plaintiffs were owed £45 rent for each year claimed, and that a total of £1,035 or $2,760 must be paid and divided between the plaintiffs. Another witness who was a tenant on the property described it further saying there was a log weaver's shop on the west side of the house but that a kitchen at the east end of the house was torn down when the addition was built.

From Samuel's point of view, the lawsuit was a dispute over the land value including Cornelius' claim for his part of the over-plus of property discovered in the resurvey. Samuel claimed that by 1810 he paid his brothers William and John their share of both the main property and the over-plus. The court, in complete disagreement with Samuel, deemed it improper that as acting testator of the will, he purchased land he was instructed to sell. That it was also wrong to reject a higher bid for the property because he did not like the terms, only to sell it to his son for less. The deeds between Samuel and his son were declared fraudulent and ordered cancelled. Under supervision he was instructed to sell the land and turn the proceeds over to the court. Thus on 31 Mar 1812 Samuel sold 396 acres, including an over-plus of 106 acres, to his neighbors Alexander Bonnell, Nelly Quick and Thomas Gordon for $7,923 or $20 per acre. In all, the value of the sales and the rents owed to the plaintiffs was over $10,000.

Yet, that was not the end of it. Asher Williamson continued his quest taking it in 1818 to the Supreme Court in Trenton. There he sued Samuel for $2,400 for his deceased Uncle Abraham's share of the estate. By 1819 Samuel was incapacitated in some way. During his active life he was a businessman, making deals, loaning money and signing his name on a variety of documents over the years. However, he revoked a letter on 11 Jun 1819 giving his son Peter legal power of attorney. That was important because Samuel, who was literate, signed his name with an "X" indicating he was very ill, although still in command mentally. Abraham and Mayeke Terhune, who were caring for Samuel, witnessed the paper, recorded in January 1820. Asher and his Uncle John Williamson apparently got no response from Samuel, so in March 1821 they brought an injunction against him in the Supreme Court, claiming he owed John about $1,300 for his share of the original estate.[124] Asher appeared for Abraham Williamson making a similar claim. The sheriff summoned Samuel to answer the charges or have his property confiscated. All that remained was a lot in Amwell that was seized and put up for sale. No one bid, and finally Asher offered $200 and the sheriff sold it to him. In May 1821 Asher, this time acting for Samuel's brother William who had died in Kentucky, sued Samuel for another share of the estate. Knowing by then Samuel was insolvent, Asher petitioned the court to sue the bondsman for $5,000 Samuel had posted years before when he was ordered to sell the estate. However, by that date Samuel had himself died without a will, having nothing left to leave his family.[125]

John Terhune, the son of Abraham Terhune and Moike Williamson assisted his Grandfather Williamson with his legal affairs during the last two years of his life.[126] Subsequently, his expenses in attending to Samuel's business revealed the larger picture. Sometime in the winter of 1820, Samuel moved from his home in Flemington to John's parents' house some seventeen miles away. He signed over to his son-in-law, Abraham Terhune, the last of his assets in a note for $800, to be used in exchange for lodging and care in his last days. John testified that Samuel's illness lasted two years, during which his grandfather was given the best room in the house, the family sitting room. He described his grandfather's illness as of the "most loathsome nature," saying that after he was moved to their home, he never left his bed. However, while the ailing man may have had the best room, his family charged him $20 per month for board and care.[127] Samuel died sometime before 14 May 1821 when Asher

Williamson filed the last claim against the estate. That August Abraham Sutphin was appointed administrator of Samuel's estate, one that was bereft of assets but complicated by the continued lawsuits against the deceased.

The final act that would lay Nellie and Samuel Williamson to rest forever occurred several years later on 26 Oct 1825. At that time Abram Gulick, the youngest son of Nellie and Gilbert Gulick, acquired from his mother's heirs the property left from her father's estate, part of which belonged to the children of Gilbert Gulick and the remainder to the three youngest children of Samuel Williamson who had married Gulick's widow. There was a total of 194 acres when Cornelius Williamson died in 1767 and Gilbert wanted the land so he paid off all of the heirs.[128] Because the estate settlement occurred many years after some of them were dead, their heirs were named so that a great deal of history was gleaned about Samuel's marriage to Nellie Gulick, everything except for that elusive detail that could have defined their degree of cousinship.

When the war ended, many stayed behind to rebuild a landscape pockmarked by damages sustained during the long siege for independence. Others lacked the heart to rebuild, and thus began a major exodus from New Jersey. Losses and destruction were the reasons why many Jerseymen sold their property, kissed their parents goodbye, and moved west in search of untouched lands. Three of Samuel's children from his first marriage remained in Hunterdon County until the end of their days, raising their children and attending to their farms. They were Mary, who had cared for her father, and Peter, who served in his stead during the Revolutionary War. Cornelius kept in touch with his brother William through letters, sharing vicariously in his adventures when William moved to Fleming County, Kentucky. Cornelius died in 1818 but William lived on for many years. Of their brothers, John and Jacob, nothing more is known about them and perhaps they too moved away, as did William and their sister Antje who married Daniel Terhune.

Sweet Home Kentucky

Many who went west were looking for the paradise promised in hometown newspapers goaded on by the hyperbole about the vast opportunities available in Ohio's Northwest Territory. Whatever their expectations, if northern Kentucky was their destination, they ended their journey in Maysville, Kentucky. To protect themselves from sporadic Indian attacks, the earliest pioneers, like Albert Terhune, initially lived in forts when they first arrived. About a year after he arrived he married Nancy Carter in February 1798.[129] By 1799 they were living on the North Fork of the Licking River, but as Albert did not own property they may have lived with his bride's family.[130]

By 1811 when William and Lena Williamson arrived, the territory had changed from a lawless frontier to a series of formally laid out villages, with courts and appointed magistrates. It was still a frontier, but it had taken on a formality and an order that was not there when Albert Terhune arrived. New Jersey was home to William; it was where he had always lived, where he married and the only place his children knew. When he left home for the challenges of the Kentucky wilderness, perhaps it was to be free of the past and the turmoil surrounding the lawsuit his cousins had brought against his father. He had a destination, because Lena's brother Albert Terhune had been living in Kentucky since 1797. When they arrived with their children, William was a little over fifty years and his wife a few years younger. Their family was all ages, from Samuel who was twenty-five and not married, to Margaret, their youngest, who was eight years old. John, their second eldest son, was accompanied by his wife, Jemimah Dalrymple, whom he had married in 18 Oct 1809 prior to leaving New Jersey.[131]

Daniel Terhune and his wife Ann Williamson (Lena and William's siblings) probably arrived in Kentucky before the others, perhaps as early as 1807. It seemed that when he left he broke contact with their Jersey family, or at least this was the complaint of his brother Abraham Terhune who remained there. Seeking verification on his Revolutionary War service in 1832, he complained, "he was unable to procure the testimony of Daniel Terhune...who is supposed to reside in the state of Kentucky. That he has not seen him in 25 years –has never received a letter from him during that period." A story attributed to Abraham was that prior to painting the famous work of art known as *Washington's Crossing the Delaware*, he had a conversation with the painter, Emanuel Leutze, about that historic night. Abraham told him that during the war, when he was twenty years old he had been one of Washington's bodyguards at Valley Forge on Christmas in 1776 when Washington crossed the Delaware River to surprise the enemy at Trenton. Upon hearing his story, it is said that the artist painted Abraham in the position he held in the boat that night, and that he is the young man pulling the starboard bow oar, nearest the viewer.[132] It could be a true story because when Abraham petitioned the government for a pension he testified that he served six months as a guard in the New Jersey state militia, beginning in May of 1776, and that "one of the regular officers who were with the troops when he served was General Washington."[133]

The Williamson-Terhune families were taxed in Mason County until boundary changes placed them in Fleming County. Albert and Marya Terhune accompanied their children to Kentucky, probably in 1797 when Daniel arrived but most certainly by 1810 when their son Isaac lived within shouting distance of them.[134] Albert Terhune Senior had survived a revolution and the beginnings of a new life in Kentucky by 1816 when he drew up his will. A widower, he was destined to be separated from about half of his family, and his will reflected the loss. Those he named probably lived in Kentucky, and those he referred to as "the rest of my sons not mentioned" did not. He gave land to Gerrit, Stephen, mentioned Halena, and his son-in-law William Williamson, who with his son Isaac were in charge of his final bequest.[135]

William's pension application stated he moved to Kentucky in 1811, although the Mason County census placed him there in 1810.[136] About that time a notice was posted in the December 1811 issue of a Lexington Kentucky newspaper, stating there was a search for the heirs of William Williamson of Hunterdon County. Specifically the search was for William, Samuel, Abraham, and Richard Williamson who had left New Jersey and were possibly living in Kentucky. The family in Jersey also had lost track of Cornelius Williamson who left his family in Fayette County, Pennsylvania, to visit friends in Kentucky and had not been heard from in a year.[137] Abraham Terhune's pension application and the plea in a frontier newspaper speak volumes about the repercussions of war and how its aftermath not only broke up farmland but families too, leaving breeches in their relationships that were never mended. Distance engenders a void, and in a desire to forget and move on, families sometimes broke up and dissolved without ever meaning to do so.

In contrast, William Williamson maintained strong ties to his New Jersey roots after he moved to Kentucky. His efforts and the good fortune of time have preserved some of their exchanges. About five years after William left New Jersey, in early 1815, Cornelius Williamson in Hunterdon County wrote to his brother to share how their hometown celebrated the ending of the War of 1812. He described the joy felt throughout the countryside. That even in the little village of Flemington where he lived, the bell rang nearly all day at news of the truce, and the night was lit by celebratory fires. That day and the next, folks ventured into the cold winter's air, some riding into town on sleds, others on horseback to see and greet neighbors who had already arrived. As day changed into night crowds cheered as tar barrels were lit and sent down the street on a sled. From the barrel, bystanders lit sheaves of straw holding the flames high in the air as they waved to the throngs lining the streets. The air came alive with fire and smoke and the excited shouting of celebrants overjoyed that peace was restored to the nation. Cornelius also relayed news of the family, mentioning his wife Staintje and son Abraham who attended Flemington Academy and was going to college the following year. In contrast to his Abraham, Richard had a difficult time with school and so worked on the farm. Cornelius asked to be remembered to their sister, Ann, and ended his letter by alluding to hardships William may have been having, saying that life in New Jersey was more plentiful for him than it was at the time for his brother in Kentucky.[138]

Three years later Cornelius died and William's childhood connection was broken. His son Abraham maintained the link with his Kentucky family and a letter dated 19 Apr 1824 was from him. By then he had graduated from college and was a pastor in a small community in Morris County. Part of the letter alluded to the departure from the New Light Church in Kentucky of the Terhune and Williamson families to a church across the river in Brown County, Ohio. Abraham relayed to his uncle the difficulties in administering his father's estate, claiming that his brother Cornelius was draining the estate assets while Abraham took the loss, a familiar story no doubt to William.[139]

Being part of a congregation of faith was important to William and Lena and the reason that shortly after her father died, they were among the founding members of the New Hope Presbyterian Church in Flemingsburg. Church records indicated that all of the Williamson family belonged to the congregation and that in 1818 Daniel Terhune was a ruling elder. Those who joined the church between 1816 and 1819 were John and Jemima Williamson, Margaret Williamson and her brothers William and Daniel. Albert Williamson and his wife Aramina Dalrymple were members of the church, and were probably married there on 21 Dec 1818. Two years later, Daniel Williamson married Nancy Money on 30 Sep 1820, and his brother Abraham married Keziah Smith on 25 Feb 1825.[140] The Williamson family's dismissal from the church was recorded on 22 Jun 1827 and soon thereafter they joined the New Light Church at New Hope.[141] Being a part of the congregation of faith provided them, not only a relationship of belief but was a source of friendship in a new and sometimes hostile environment.

Most of this combined Williamson-Terhune family settled in Fleming County in Poplar Plains along Locust Creek. All that is, except for Daniel Terhune who lived on the northern side of Flemingsburg. In 1820 the grouping included the three Williamson brothers, William, Albert and John, who were married and living separately. It also included one unit of nine individuals living with a "Miss Williamson" who was probably Mary, the eldest daughter, then thirty years old. It included two adults over forty-five years old, suggesting that Lena and William lived with her as well as her unmarried siblings. These categories fit the ages of her eldest brother, Sam, who was not married, her younger brothers, Albert, Daniel, Abraham and their youngest sister Margaret.[142] The tax list in 1822 provided information about their economic conditions showing that William and his sons, Albert, John, Daniel and William Junior leased rather than owned farmland. William Senior's taxable property was worth $500 while his sons' was between $100 and $150, except for William Junior who had three horses and property valued at $210. William's parents lived with him but Albert and Daniel Williamson lived somewhat outside the family compound.[143] By 1830 the larger group of thirteen people lived with William Junior who was 38, and his father William who was over 70 years old.[144]

By 1730 most of the children were married, Daniel Williamson to Nancy Money on 30 Sep 1820 and Abraham married Keziah Smith 1 Mar 1825. The last to tie the knot was Margaret who wed Joseph Steele on 10 Feb 1829 when she was 25 years old.[145] In an undated letter, probably written in 1831, Margaret and Joseph wrote to her father William in Mason County announcing their daughter's birth on June 29, and to ask if Mary would come and help her for a few weeks while she recovered her strength. It was also the chance for sisters to spend time together as Mary, who was thirteen years older than Margaret was, was probably more like a mother to her youngest sibling than otherwise.[146]

When he went to the Brown County, Ohio courthouse to file for a pension in March 1835, William Williamson Senior was nearing his 76th birthday. His application was quickly approved, and he was awarded an annual payment of $35 for his service as a private in the militia during the Revolutionary War. Perhaps he realized his time of departure was near because he and Lena had been in Brown County for just a year when he began putting his affairs in order.[147] A few days after Christmas in 1835, Margaret Steele wrote to her father. Knowing he was very ill and had asked to see her, she hoped to cheer him by her letter because she had no way of getting across the river from Kentucky during the winter to see him. She promised that if it got colder and the mud froze, she would surely come to him, yet fearing she might not make it in time, she said farewell in her letter.[148] Sadly, on the day she wrote, it was already too late, as her father had passed on a week before, on 22 Dec 1835.[149]

William Williamson left eight children, numerous grandchildren and many experiences behind him when he died. As a boy of seventeen he discovered what he was willing to do for freedom and when it was over, how high the price. Later, with his family in disarray over the lawsuit, life at home looked even better from a distance. Whether he regretted the move to Kentucky is unknown although there were hints of privation in his letters to his brother Cornelius, but starting over gave him hope for his children's future. He believed in community including that of his faith but he also trusted in family and in its survival even across the separation of miles and this he taught to his children. Encouraged by him, they and their grandchildren stayed connected down through the generations, and the reward to his descendants was in the treasure of letters left behind. In the simple gesture of reaching out to one another, their imprint reached well beyond their time, touching anyone who read about their struggles and triumphs. What seeped through the writing was how ordinary they were, but how in living a day at a time, putting one foot before the other, they made their way through extraordinary times.

Echoing the actions of his father, when William Williamson Jr. was twenty-four years old, he too married into the Terhune family on 23 Mar 1815.[150] He and his bride, Ann Terhune, were the same ages as his parents were when they wed. The difference was that Ann, who was twenty-one, was the daughter of Daniel Terhune and Ann Williamson, thus she and William shared the same grandparents making them double first cousins.[151] As bondsman, her father Daniel permitted the marriage to William on 23 Mar 1815 in Fleming County, Kentucky, where both families lived. Their son William Ann Williamson was born sometime prior to 2 Jan 1816 when Ann died, perhaps from compications of childbirth.[152] The following year on 3 Mar 1817, William married Jane Cochran, the daughter of Jane Fisher Cochran of Fleming County, Kentucky.[153] Her name appeared with William's in the Flemingsburg Presbyterian Church records showing her birth date as 25 Jun 1798, and that she joined the church on 28 Feb 1818, about a year after they were married.[154]

Jane was nearly twenty when she married William, a twenty-five-year old farmer, and a widower with a namesake son who was ten years old. He and Jane named their first child Ann, perhaps after the Dutch custom of calling a child after a deceased first wife.[155] They had two more children, Samuel, who was born about 1821 and named after his great-grandfathers Fisher and Williamson. Their daughter Jane was the youngest child, born 22 Jan 1822 and named for her Fisher grandmothers. A week after Jane's birth, on 2 Feb 1822, Jane Williamson died, probably from complications of childbirth. A widower for the second time in six years, William had four children including an infant who needed both a father and a mother. After a year of mourning, he married again on 11 Sep 1823 to Isabel, the daughter of Samuel Henry. Many years earlier Henry had inventoried Robert Cochran's estate, an indication of a close knit group of neighbors who helped each other during the county's settlement. Upon marrying William at the age of twenty, Isabel became mother to his children ranging in age from Jane, who was a year old, to William, then aged eight. Samuel Henry died in 1826, and his will recognized Isabel Williamson as one of his children.[156] Over the next eight years Isabel had six children, bringing William's family to ten children, none of whom were married in 1834 when Isabel died in mid-summer. She was 30 years old when he laid his third wife to rest, and William, who had just turned 42, did not marry again.[157]

The Cochran and Fisher Families of Pennsylvania

William Williamson's second wife, Jane Cochran, was born in Kentucky on 25 June 1797, the only daughter of Robert and Jane Fisher Cochran. When she married William, her mother was living but her father was not. He died between February 1797 when he signed a bond for his sister's marriage and 27 June 1797 when his wife Jane paid taxes on four horses, and nothing else. Where the tax sheet was marked, "males above the age of 21" the space was left significantly blank.[158] Young Jane never knew her father, but those who did inventoried his estate on 6 Sep 1797. They were the administrator George Glass who would impact young Jane's life, and Samuel Henry who would influence her children.

Cochran's estate was worth £106, and his most valuable assets livestock consisting of cattle, hogs, a few sheep and some horses. A third of his estate was the usual farming equipment plus two riding saddles and bridles. Their personal property was minimal, the collection of a young couple yet to acquire more than life's necessities. They included a rifle, a greatcoat, two jackets, a silver watch and a case of razors. They had the necessary furniture, a bed and frame, a clothes box, dresser furniture, a table and three chairs. Shared between them was a mirror. Jane made some of their woolen clothing, weaving it on her loom. Robert was literate as seen from his signature on a bond, and the inclusion of a couple of books and a Bible among his personal items. He and Jane had an elder son named Thomas who was about three years old when his father died. Several years later their grandfather, John Cochran, sought custody of both Thomas and Jane, and when it was not readily granted he went to court. On 8 Nov 1802 the judge ruled against Cochran without explanation and he was denied custody. Instead he appointed George Glass, Cochran's administrator, as the children's guardian, aided by Samuel Henry who posted £500 security against the estate.[159] It was settled on 20 Oct 1803 with the widow Jane awarded £26, leaving £53 to be divided between the children.[160]

The Cochrans probably arrived in Fleming County about 1788 and had been living there less than ten years when Jane Fisher Cochran's husband died. Both families came from Cumberland County, Pennsylvania. The Fishers were from Sherman's Valley in Tyrone Township and the Cochran family lived nearby. Tax records for 1768 showed Samuel Fisher had 300 acres, although he probably settled there earlier.[161] Robert Cochran, father of John and grandfather of Robert arrived in the county even earlier. He and his kin were in Cumberland County by 1756, before land had been cleared for crops, and when most settlers lived protectively within a stockade, and those who ventured beyond its walls did so at their peril. The Cochran family learned all of this on one fateful day. There are two versions about what happened. The first story was passed down in the Cochran family and it tells how John Cochran, grandfather of Thomas and Jane, survived the great massacre of 1756.

"John Cochran, the great-grandfather of William Cochran and sisters, was captured by the Indians, and was held a prisoner for fifteen years. During this period he is said to have 'run the gauntlet,' and returned unhurt. After this he was liberated, and he returned to his family in Fleming County, Kentucky. After remaining with his family for about twelve months he left and never again returned. The supposition is that he had become so accustomed to their ways and habits that he deserted his family and led "a wild life among his Indian friends...John Cochran had a son named Robert..." The other account of what happened during the raid was a very different story.[162]

Robert Cochran and his wife Jane were among the early Scots-Irish emigrants who entered the Tuscarora Valley of Pennsylvania and may have been among those who settled without a warrant. Essentially squatters, they were living near or at Fort Bingham, a small stockade about twelve miles from Mifflintown in that part Cumberland County called Tuscarora Township which later became Juniata County. A historical marker near Spruce Hill describes its historical significance. The stockade was built on the Traders' Path leading from the Conococheague settlement up through Sterrett's Gap (also called Croghan's Gap) into Sherman's Valley then west to Fort Bingham and on to Fort Robinson. Wilderness living was precarious because, while these early pioneers were encroaching on settled Indian lands, their attitude was that there was room for all. However, as more European families entered their lands and proposed to stay, hostilities erupted between the two groups. In 1754 Samuel Bingham was one of the first settlers, and he built the fort with the assistance of two other families. Living as a group within the fort they had some protection. However, there were times when the men left to work on the land that surrounded it.

The day began much like any other June day in the valley. By sunset the horror of its memory would remain forever in the minds of those who survived. Most of the men were tending the fields, leaving their wives and children in the stockade to prepare for the evening meal and their return. The Indians watching from the distance observed this, and when the men left, they quietly moved in and attacked the fort taking it by surprise. Unprepared for the onslaught, those inside succumbed to their attackers. Their assailants then moved into the fields and slew the men. The chilling story of what happened quickly reached the larger world. The army post at Carlisle Pennsylvania was one of the first to report the incident. The headline began, "On Friday night, 11 Jun 1756, Captain Bingham's Fort in the Tuscarora Valley was destroyed by the Indians...it is said that all that were in it are either killed or carried off; and that a woman, big with child, was found dead and scalped near the fort, and mangled in a most shocking manner." The *Pennsylvania Gazette* provided the names of fifteen who were missing and of the several killed were "Robert Cochran and Thomas McKinney found dead, scalped." Also "Jane Cochran and two children missed."[163] Those two children were John and his sister Margaret, whose parents were the above-mentioned Robert and Jane Cochran. Sometime later it was discovered that by a stroke of luck the children were not at the fort that day, but were instead at the farm of a maternal uncle. Thus both escaped being carried off with their mother, or murdered as their father had been. More than two years later in November 1758, it was reported that Jane Cochran was sighted about 100 miles west of the Ohio River but she was not seen again, thus dashing her children's hopes that she would return and take them home. They remained with their uncle and continued in his care at least until 1765 when Margaret, called Mollie, was fourteen and her brother a year or so older.[164]

Mollie Cochran probably married John Corbin around 1772 when she was twenty-one years old. He took up soldiering when the Revolutionary War began, joining the First Pennsylvania Artillery. They had no children and Mollie refused to be left behind while her husband marched off to war, so she joined him, traveling with the troops as other women did, working as laundresses or cooks for the regiment. She was with him on 16 Nov 1776 when his company was ordered to New York and where the American troops fought against the British and Hessians as they mounted an attack on Fort Washington. During a fierce fight in northern Manhattan, John Corbin was killed by a musket ball and when the officer commanded that his cannon be withdrawn, his wife stepped up to take his place. At the moment she first began loading cannon Mollie entered the pages of history. Later called "Captain Mollie" Corbin, she fired cannon with such skill and vigor that she caught the attention of the company officers who considered her one of the deadliest gunners of the day. To her detriment, her aim and accuracy brought the attention of the Hessians who turned their guns on her, wounding her severely. Yet she fought on, and hers was the last American gun to be silenced that day. Defeated, the Continental army was driven back, apparently leaving their wounded where they fell, because it was British doctors who found Mollie alive, but barely. Grapeshot and three musket balls found their mark nearly severing her left arm, mangling her chest and lacerating her jaw. It was a miracle she lived to be transported to an army hospital in Philadelphia where she underwent surgery and remained to convalesce. For her service and bravery on that day Mollie Corbin was declared the first woman soldier in the American army. It was a high price to pay for the honor because Mollie never fully recovered from her wounds and was unable to use her injured arm again. Initially the State of Pennsylvania made some provisions for her support, but in 1779 the state's Supreme Executive Council recognized that she had been inadequately compensated for her severe disabilities and they awarded her half of a soldier's monthly pay for the remainder of her life.[165]

Some years later the Philadelphia Society of Women wanted to erect a monument to Mollie and so they went to visit her at West Point where she lived. Surprised upon discovering that their heroine was a "hard drinking impoverished veteran," they cancelled their memorial. Later reports described the toll the war had taken on her, saying that she "had a lot of trouble integrating into the community. She was rebuffed by the ladies of the town because of her uncleanness and disagreeable temper. It was also her habit to spend most days at the post smoking her pipe and finding companionship among the soldiers. In 1800 Mollie died in obscurity and was buried in the highlands above the Hudson River. Her grave had a crude stone marker." Well over a century later, in 1926, after verifying her service records, the New York State Society of the Daughters of the American Revolution found her grave, had her body exhumed and proved her identity through her wounds. Then on 14 Apr 1926 she was buried again, this time with full military honors at the cemetery of the U.S. Military Academy at West Point. A plaque was erected in Fort Tryon Park commemorating the Battle of Fort Washington, and finally giving acknowledgment to Mollie Cochran Corbin's heroism during the War of Independence.[166]

John Cochran married earlier than his sister Mollie and may have been older than she was. His vows were sealed before the Reverend John Bucher of Cumberland County when he married Jane Fisher on 2 Dec 1768.[167] She was the daughter of Samuel Fisher of Cumberland County as described in his 1775 will. In it, Fisher named his executors first as wife Mary and son James. Next was Samuel Junior, Thomas and William. His daughters and their husbands were identified as Margaret married to James Morrow, Jane who was married to John Coughran and Elizabeth whose husband was Robert Scott. Near the end of his will Samuel referred to his grandson Hugh Sharron, whom he had raised, and willed him to make restitution by serving his wife during her lifetime. More than a servant, Samuel wanted Hugh to be educated in reading, writing and casting accounts, however should his grandmother die before he was twenty-one, then James was to give him £10 and his freedom papers.[168]

Hugh Sharron was Jane Fisher's son, born prior to her marriage to John Cochran. In 1767 Jane, "a spinster" was indicted in Cumberland County court "for fornication and bastardy with Hugh Sharron. It happened in mid-February at the house of Robert McWhinney of Carlisle. Her father is Samuel Fisher of Sherman's Valley." The testator was Mary Fisher, presumably her mother. Jane was probably no more than twenty at the time she bore Hugh who was named after his father.[169] After their marriage, she and John had four children all born in Pennsylvania. The eldest was Robert born about 1770, followed by Jane about 1775, and then John Junior who was born around 1777. Mary, called Polly, was born about 1780.[170] Because of Samuel Fisher's directive, it is doubtful that John Cochran raised his wife's first child Hugh Sharron. They probably moved to Kentucky with Jane's brothers about 1788 when Robert was about eighteen and their youngest was about eight years old. John bought property in Mason County (now Fleming County) in 1796.[171] The following year he paid taxes for ten horses and 555 acres on Mill Creek. In 1798 he was taxed for 500 acres, but over the years it varied between 500-550 acres, most of it unimproved land of which about 50 acres was in crops.[172]

Within a few years John and Jane's children began to marry, and Robert was probably the first to wed. Polly wed James Finney on 6 Feb 1797 and her brother signed the bond, as she was perhaps seventeen at the time.[173] Court records showed that John Junior's wife was named Elizabeth, and that their sister Jane married Benjamin Hutton.[174] Jane Fisher Cochran died sometime between 1810, when the census indicated she was living, and late 1813 when her husband remarried.[175] On 28 Jan 1813, John Cochran wed Rachel Reed who was perhaps a widow, and like John, had grown children, leaving the two of them with the singular responsibility of caring for each other.[176]

Robert Cochran was a farmer and about twenty-seven years old when he died, leaving Jane to provide for their two young children. They were cousins, as Jane was the daughter of Thomas and Margaret Fisher and the granddaughter of Samuel and Mary Fisher. Just as Robert's parents were identified through Samuel Fisher's will, so Jane Fisher was linked as Thomas Fisher's daughter by his 1788 will. It reiterated the earlier will by identifying James and Samuel Fisher as Thomas' brothers and calling Robert Scott his brother-in-law. The order of naming, presumably by ages was Samuel, John, Thomas, Mary, Jane, Elizabeth, Margaret and Sarah. More importantly, the will provided an approximate date that Thomas' wife and their children were planning a move to Kentucky.[177]

Once they reached Kentucky, records linked Jane as Thomas Fisher's daughter but also confirmed she married her cousin Robert Cochran. She was about twelve years old in 1788 and about eighteen in 1793 when she married Robert Cochran. Within a year their first child Thomas was born and named after her father, followed three years later by Jane who was born shortly after Robert's death. She was perhaps twenty-seven and widowed about five years by the time Robert's estate was settled on 20 Oct 1803. Within a few days Samuel Henry served as bondsman when she married Alexander Armstrong on 16 Nov 1803.[178] Confirmation that she was Thomas Fisher's daughter comes from a deed where "Alexander Armstrong and wife Jane" sold her inheritance to her three brothers. Her sisters, Elizabeth, the wife of Henry Armstrong, and Polly who married Joseph Santee, signed similar deeds.[179] Other actions lending weight to this conclusion are the timing of her second marriage just after Cochran's estate was settled, and in naming her first child Thomas. The evidence leads to the conclusion that she was not only Thomas' daughter but that Robert Cochran was her first cousin.

In 1810 there were five children in Alexander Armstrong's household, and two of them were a boy and girl between the ages of ten and sixteen. Since Jane and Alexander were married less than seven years the two elder children were probably her son and daughter, Thomas and Jane Cochran.[180] He was the subject of an 1812 court record. Although she remarried, George Glass remained her children's guardian and when Thomas Cochran was about seventeen, Glass apprenticed him to Jane's brother Samuel Fisher, to learn to be a millwright. His term was four years, or until he was twenty-one, and pending that time Fisher agreed to provide Thomas with room, board, and schooling for at least eight months each year. When his apprenticeship ended Fisher was obligated to give Thomas a complete set of bench tools and new clothing or forty dollars to begin his trade.[181] George Glass remained in charge of Jane Armstrong's children in 1817 when he gave his consent for Jane Cochran to wed William Williamson.

John Cochran was over seventy in 1821 when he died and his estate went into probate early the following year. He had been through hard times and bad times, first as a young boy when he was orphaned during an Indian attack on his home. Then several years after he married he brought his family to live on the Kentucky frontier. Once settled he farmed his land near Mill Creek and watched his children grew, but losses followed with the death of Robert and then his wife Jane. However, grandchildren multiplied his wealth and they seemed to mean a great deal to him. Cochran did not have a will and his administrator, Benjamin Hutton, also his son-in-law, sold his personal property. With whiskey to loosen up the crowd, the sale on a brisk January in 1822 brought in £776. But Cochran also owned valuable property, some of which was improved by his son Robert's heirs, increasing its assessment by £138. With land and his personal inventory, he was a man of moderate wealth who lived modestly. Prior to his death, the yield for his fields of wheat, oats and corn plus some tobacco and flax was £140. His livestock of pigs, cows and sheep was worth even more at £200. Most of the remainder of his personal estate was in cash or money and crops owed him equaling £175. Of greatest value were two mares worth more than £125 including saddles and bags. The rest of his personal property was household furniture, clothing and farming tools. His son John bought many of the items including his father's clothing, a chest, and some woolen cloth. His son-in-law and administrator, Benjamin Hutton bought farming tools, and Alexander Armstrong and William Williamson each bought a saddle.[182] The estate was settled in April 1829, but in September 1830, John Cochran Junior sued the administrator, claiming he gave Hutton land to care for his wife and children, and that Hutton sold it, so Cochran sued for a portion of the proceeds.[183]

When Jane's brother Thomas Cochran was about seventeen years old he went to live in Fayette County, Kentucky with his uncle, Samuel Fisher. Then on 25 Nov 1817, when he was about twenty-three, he married Ruth Carrick.[184] They had a son named William Carrick Cochran who was born about a year later, followed by several daughters born between 1821 and 28 Oct 1828, when Ruth died.[185] Thomas married again in Fleming County, Kentucky, on 16 Aug 1829.[186] His second wife was also his first cousin, Mary Cochran, daughter of John Cochran Junior; their grandfather was John Cochran Senior who died in 1822.[187] At some point Thomas and Mary moved to Indiana, near Indianapolis where they lived for a time. He was a widower when he died there on 6 Nov 1836, leaving William and his four sisters orphans. The children returned to Fayette County, Kentucky, where they probably lived with relatives until they were grown. Later, after William's sisters married, they scattered in different directions, even other states than their brother who lived in Boone County, Kentucky and later in Carroll County, Kentucky where he died on 6 Nov 1836.[188] William Cochran was the great-grandson of John Cochran of Cumberland County, Pennsylvania. Although some of the stories attributed to his grandfather were fanciful, the blood of early Pennsylvania and Kentucky pioneers flowed through William, thanks to John Cochran's sheer luck in not being home the day his father was scalped and killed and his mother taken hostage at Fort Bingham.

Williamson: Separation and Change

In Kentucky William Williamson had fathered ten children and buried three wives. He was surrounded by the memory of loss, yet for his children's sake he had to move on. Whether it was William or his brother Abraham who thought of the solution, it was resolved that they would move to Illinois where land was plentiful, cheap and fertile. While unknown, Abraham and his wife Keziah probably traveled with William and his children. Two children, William and Jane, remained behind in Brown County, Ohio, with their Aunt Mary and Uncle Samuel, while young Samuel, who was about seventeen, accompanied his father as did Ann who was a year older. The transition to a new land and a new life was documented in letters exchanged between William and his family back home. Written between August 1836 and February 1838, six letters survived that document his struggles to support his family, while homesickness was also a strong theme. In contrast, his children wanted news about their siblings, and their letters were a part of that exchange.

William's first letter was from Morgan County, Illinois, where he taught school. The pay was not enough to support his family, and not knowing where to turn, he was at a very low point when he wrote saying, "I have kept the family together and wish to do so, but I sometimes fear that we cannot stay together much longer for we have so much difficulty getting wood and the grinding done that I almost despair of trying to keep house much longer, and all for the want of a team. If we had that I do believe we could do better here...than we ever have done anywhere." In debt to his brother Abraham, he complained to Samuel that "Abraham has never yet been left with a family of little children to support by himself and he does not know the difficulties we have to undergo," but then countered his lament saying, "I suppose everyone thinks their own necessities are the greatest." To William, Jane and his sister Mary he wrote that "you cannot conceive [of] how much I want to see and converse with [you] and how lonesome and bad I feel at this time. The children is all gone out of the house to hunt some blackberries and I am left alone." He asked after his mother, and hoped that William and Jane were not troubling their aunt. He wrote a message for Samuel, explaining he was not literate enough to do so himself, then turned the pen over to Ann who wanted to know if any neighbor girls were getting married, then ended by asking her brother to write.

The letters document that by April 1837, William had moved to Exeter, about twenty miles from Beardstown, and taken a job as a ferryman. The salary was $500 a year allowing him to buy a team of horses for farming. Samuel, who was about seventeen but "stout and strong," helped him run the ferry. William found a house about seven miles from the river but was concerned about whether Ann could care for the six younger children by herself, as Samuel came home only every few days, and William not at all. Samuel had other interests since he had met Syntha Mullins whose family had lived with the Williamsons the previous year. He wanted to marry but William was adamant that he was too young and tried to dissuade him. Lonely for his family in Kentucky, William complained that he had not heard from his youngest sister, Margaret Steele, or from Isabel's family in Kentucky. Correspondence between Illinois and Ohio was regular, because about the time Abraham thought it was time for a letter from home he showed up at William's house to hear the news.

By August Samuel had married Syntha, moved fifteen miles away, and could no longer help his father. Ferry traffic was busy and William had to hire a helper, which reduced his income. Unable to get home to his family, he quit that business. After getting a new job, he told William, "I work now about a mile from home digging stone coal but I come home every night." In a note to Jane he told her that the younger children missed her very much, and then reflecting on ways in which her sister had changed he wrote, "if you could see Ann you could see your mother (Jane) both in likeness and manners." Ann then wrote to Jane saying that none of the family had been to Samuel's wedding, and she agreed with their father that Samuel should have waited longer to marry. She asked Jane if she had a beau, and hinted to her sister that she might get married soon. Speaking for Samuel, Ann told William that Syntha was the prettiest girl around and if William wanted one like her, he should come to Illinois.

A few weeks before Christmas William wrote from Meredosia, a town in Morgan County on the Wabash River, where he had a job as a laborer earning $1 a day, but enough to pay his house rent of $3.33 monthly. He announced that on 27 Oct 1837, Ann had married Richard Mullins, a cousin of Samuel's wife. With that event, he felt that since two of his children by Jane Cochran had wed it was time they claimed their inheritance from their grandfather Robert Cochran, if Jane, who was not married, agreed. William was clearly homesick, saying he missed his brothers and sisters, but more than anything, he wanted to hear about his mother. Ann and her husband were living temporarily with him, but knowing they would be leaving soon, he tried coaxing Jane to move out to Illinois.

Although undated, the next letter was from Ann to Jane. She said she regretted getting married when she did but in their youthful minds, both she and Samuel thought it was for the family's greater good. They knew how overwhelmed their father was in caring for his family, but what they were unable to understand was that they lightened his burden more than they added to it. By February 1838, William had begun taking in boarders and had five men who paid him two dollars per week for food and lodging. Yet he still struggled to feed and clothe his family. His daughters helped with cooking and cleaning, but he lamented that his house was overrun by people unrelated to him.[189]

By 1860 William was living with Samuel, Syntha and their six children on a farm in Morgan County. Samuel owned the farm worth $10,000 and he had other assets of $2,550.[190] William Junior and his wife Letty Ann remained in Ohio until after 1850, but by 1860 they too were living in Morgan County, Illinois with their children Eli and Mary and Jane Masterson, daughter of her sister Elizabeth who had died many years before.[191]

Ten years later the elder William was living with his son James, Amanda his wife, and their two children. By then a retired farmer and teacher, William's initial years had been difficult, but he succeeded in bringing his family to Illinois where they prospered, undoubtedly better off than if they had remained in Kentucky or even Ohio.[192] The letters probably continued for many years, until 1874 when he died in Illinois at the age of 82 years.[193]

Williamson-Hewitt Alliances

Samuel and Mary Williamson lived in the village of Arnheim, Ohio, in 1840 with their niece and nephew, Jane and William Williamson. Their home was just south of Pleasant Township where siblings Letty Ann and Eli Hewitt lived.[194] Letty's cousin Davis Hewitt lived near Batavia but sometimes visited his relatives in the Georgetown area not far from Arnheim. They included Philip Buckner, the town doctor, with whom he made a trip to New Orleans in 1838, but also Uncle Eli, and Aunt Letty. Two marriages five months apart proved that the two families knew each other. The first wedding was on 10 May 1842 when Jane Williamson married Davis Hewitt. Four months later on October 6, her brother William married Letty Ann Hewitt, Davis's aunt.[195] True to her family's tradition, Jane undoubtedly wrote her father sometime in

February 1843 when Samuel was born. Named after a grandfather on either side of their family, the honors went to Jane's Uncle Samuel who had given her a home when she most needed one. In 1850 he and Mary lived in Williamsburg with their thirteen-year-old niece Margaret Steele.[196] Many years later Margaret married Albert Hartman and when Uncle Samuel died on 22 Oct 1857, he was buried in the Hartman Cemetery in Clermont County with a citation on his tombstone for his service during the War of 1812.[197]

Davis and Jane were married seventeen years in 1859 when she died, leaving a family of eight children; three who were under age five. They needed a mother, and less than two years later Davis married as his second wife a woman named Jane Williamson. She was Daniel Williamson and Nancy Money's daughter, born in Kentucky on December 1823 and first cousin to Davis's first wife. Ten years before in 1850, when she was twenty-five years old, she lived in Pleasant Township with her father and siblings. Her father Daniel was fifty-two, a widower and farmer, with eight children most of them teens or older. His sons were John and Benjamin who helped on the farm while his daughters kept house.[198] When Daniel died in 1855 his sons became guardians of the younger children.[199] Benjamin left Brown County with his siblings, including Jane, and by 1860 they were living in Jackson Township in Clermont County.[200] The following year when she was thirty-eight years old, Jane left her brother's household to marry Davis Hewitt who lived near Olive Branch village. They had two sons, the elder named Richard after his father and the other Benjamin, after her brother. Jane was forty-four when she died in the spring of 1888 from unknown causes, and Davis was once again a widower. Once again, out of need he married but there would be no more children. In all, the Hewitt and Williamson families intermarried three times, and the blending of characteristics produced fifteen children, ten of them between Davis and his wives named Jane but also five children born to his cousin Letty Ann and her husband William Williamson.

Chapter Twelve

MORRISON AND DURHAM FAMILIES
Maryland, Pennsylvania and Ohio (1697-1903)

Ancestors of Lizzie Belle Morrison

In 1840, William Perry Morrison and his brother Harrison, or Reece as his family called him, lived together in Anderson Township near the Clermont County border.[1] Reece was a widower with a young son named John, and Perry was twenty-one and a single man. His house was on Survey #608 owned by Daniel Durham, their grandfather, and nearby were the Bennett, Fagin, Durham and Kyle families; some were neighbors, others kin.[2] Their sister Lucinda, her husband John Moore and two young children lived a few doors away.[3] By 1850, all of their families had increased. Lucinda was thirty-eight years old and she and John Moore had five children, Samuel, Mary Ann, William, Eliza and Susan.

Frances Eliza Kyle had a large extended family, and when she married Perry Morrison on 28 Apr 1850, it was probably a well-attended affair.[4] About two years later Lizzie Belle was born on 26 Jun 1852 at Mt. Summit, a small village east of Cincinnati Ohio near Cherry Grove. Within two years of her birth, Perry had the means to buy a place of his own. The farm he purchased was 132 acres in Clermont County near Mt. Carmel, away from their parents, but conveniently near enough to visit. They were firmly established on the land where they would raise their family by the time Amos Otto Morrison was born on 12 Oct 1856.

Samuel was the oldest of the Morrison clan, born between 1813 and 1815, and in 1850 he was about 35 years old. He lived in Clermont County with his wife Julia, and their three children, Lucinda, Hiram and James.[5] In late fall, Julia gave birth to Sarah Jane who was born on 5 December 1850.[6] Two years before, Reece married as his second wife, Eliza Gowdy, on 5 Mar 1848 and by 1850 their son William was a year old.[7] Perry was the youngest, and the last to marry, and when he and Eliza wed, they moved into the house he had long shared with Reece, but sadly she moved into a house in mourning.[8]

In the decade from 1850 to 1860, the Morrison family faced difficult challenges and some came swiftly. On 12 Mar 1850, a little more than a month before Perry's marriage, his brother Reece died from tuberculosis at the age of 35, leaving two children.[9] The eldest, John, who lost his mother Rebecca Kyle when he was three years old, and was orphaned at seven,[10] was raised by his grandparents, John and Mary Kyle.[11] Reece's story and that of his two wives was revealed in a private cemetery on Nine Mile Road. This cemetery in Union Township was where several members of the Kyle family were buried, including Rebecca. She was 21 when she died on 23 May 1846. Her husband's headstone is adjacent to hers, and next to it is Reece's second wife Eliza Ann, who died about a year after her husband, on 8 Mar 1851.[12] Surrounding the three headstones are smaller ones engraved only with first names, likely those of their children who died as infants.[13] Some of the smaller stones have been washed clean, so it is not known whether William lived beyond infancy, but Reece's eldest son John Morrison lived to marry Elizabeth Witham on 15 May 1866.[14] In 1870 they lived in Union Township with their three-year-old daughter.[15]

By 1860 Lucinda Moore was a forty-seven-year old widow living in Withamsville with her children, Samuel, William, Eliza and Susan. John died sometime after 1850 and their daughter Mary Ann who was not living at home was likely married by then. Her brother Samuel lived in nearby Mt. Carmel with Julia and their two daughters, Lucinda who was eighteen and Sarah Jane ten years old.[16] Beginning in 1859 Sam's family began to mirror his brother Reece with repeated tragic losses, that in the end helped Sam make his own no less fateful decision. One by one, over a period of six years all of the family, including Samuel, slipped away from the earth. His death was war related, but how his wife and children died is unknown. James Morrison was fifteen and the first to die in September 1859. Something else was amiss as well, because just prior to Christmas that year, Sam and Julia sold their 141-acre farm to a neighbor, Andrew Fagin, for $9,000.[17] The following April, after witnessing the sale, Hiram, who was eighteen, died. Julia was pregnant in 1861 and that spring Ida was born and died within a few months. Swiftly following the baby was Julia who died on 30 Jun 1861 at the age of thirty-six. She and Samuel were married for more than twenty years, and then suddenly she was gone.[18] In less than two years four loved ones had died, leaving his world reeling and forever torn asunder. Perhaps there was only one solution to his sorrow, or so he thought on 23 Sep 1861 when he went to the recruitment office and enlisted for a three-year stint in the Union Army. He was about forty-seven when he mustered out from Camp Dennison in Hamilton County, and because he was older than most of the volunteers he was made a captain. Soon afterward his company, a part of the 57th Regular Ohio Volunteer Infantry, was sent south where they quickly became engulfed in the brutal conflict known as the Civil War.

The troops were trained at Camp Chase and in February 1862, Capt. Sam Morrison's troops of Company D left the camp and headed south into Kentucky. Accompanying him was Andrew J. Banks, a first lieutenant in the infantry, who was probably his brother-in-law. Undoubtedly they signed up together but neither could possibly have known of the perils that lay ahead of them or if they would ever return to their families. In Paducah, Kentucky, they joined the Fifth Division of the Army of the Tennessee, sometimes under the command of General William Tecumseh Sherman. Ahead of them were some of the most significant battles of the war, fought in towns that would later evoke chilling reminders of courage and death, places called Shiloh and Vicksburg, or Mission Ridge, Tennessee, all places of heavy losses. Upon leaving Mission Ridge in November 1863, Morrison's regiment went on furlough to Chattanooga, but by mid-December they were on their way to Alabama. By then the men had been on the road and away from home for two years and "the regiment was almost exhausted by fatigue, privation, hunger and exposure. The men were hatless, shoeless, and half naked."[19] After minor engagements in the South, in February

1864 the regiment headed north to Cincinnati where they furloughed again for a month. In mid-March the troops headed back to Tennessee, arriving in Chattanooga in early May at the beginning of the campaign for Atlanta.[20] When they reached Georgia in mid-May, Sam Morrison, who until then had been physically sound and fit, became gravely ill with dysentery. He was transferred to the 15th Army Corp Hospital in Marietta, Georgia, where he remained for two months. Nights were long and fever-drenched, filled with moans and tears, sometimes his own. Death was all around him, had been around him since his son James died nearly five years before. Drifting in and out of fever in the sultry Georgia spring there was time to think about Julia and time to mourn her death and that of their children, if only in delirious dreams. Only a miracle could have brought Samuel back to health since he had lost everyone he loved. He never recovered, and on 14 Jul 1864 death came from "chronic dysentery and flux," the war's second most common cause of death outside of gunshot wounds. He was buried in Marietta but honored at home in Ohio. His brother Perry, who cherished him, erected a monument in Mt. Washington Cemetery where generations to come would remember him and the life he gave in service to his country.

Much of the information about Samuel's war service and domestic situation was in the pension application that Perry Morrison made on behalf of Samuel's daughter Sarah Jane, who was thirteen when he died and probably the last living member of the family. Perry filed for guardianship on 23 Sep 1864 and his cousins, John and Samuel Durham, vouched for his character saying they had known him for twenty-five years.[21] Sarah must have been ill during that time because she died the following first of May 1865. After 1860 nothing more is known about her elder sister Lucinda, who would have been twenty-three when Sarah died. The Morrison line ended with this generation unless Reece's son John had a male child, because Perry's son, Amos, did not marry.

Alexander Morrison

Alexander and Elizabeth Morrison must have been in Ohio in 1810 when Samuel was born, and public records prove they lived in Anderson Township, east of Cincinnati by 1820.[22] Some of their neighbors were George Fagin, John Silver and Joseph Kyle, but Elizabeth's parents, Daniel and Jane Durham, and Daniel's father, Joshua Durham, also lived there.[23] By 1820 there was a family enclave including Alexander and Elizabeth's five children, and a son who was born after Perry. In 1830 the configuration of adults to children was the same, but Daniel's daughters, Ellen and Elizabeth and their husbands, lived so near him that they were undoubtedly occupying his property.[24] Alexander entered county records only once, in an 1822-1823 dispute between his father-in-law and the estate administrator for Durham's deceased son-in-law. Alexander was one of the appraisers and Durham provided the bond to complete probate.

Alexander died prior to 2 Sep 1834 when his administrator John Moore, who was his son-in-law, began probate of his estate. John Gwaltney and John Silver produced the bond and his appraisers were Thomas Banks, George Fagin and Zacheus Kyle. They were his neighbors and three of them, Moore, Banks and Kyle, had children who within fifteen years married into his family.[25] His wife relinquished her dowry rights at the time, but she could not have been Elizabeth Durham Morrison because the prior year, on 2 Jul 1833, when her father gave 50 acres each to her and Ellen Martin,[26] the deed was to the "heirs of Elizabeth Morrison, deceased." The property bordered the state road and Hamilton County and was probably where she and Alexander were living all along.[27] Thirteen years later the property was sold by her heirs and it was in this second deed of 2 Oct 1846 that the names of Alexander and Elizabeth's children and their spouses were learned. George Fagin's property bordered theirs, and in 1846 he paid $1,500 to Elizabeth Durham Morrison's heirs, who were Samuel and his wife Julia (Banks) Morrison, John and Lucinda (Morrison) Moore, Harrison Morrison and William Perry Morrison.[28] By then the Durham family had been living in Hamilton County nearly fifty years, but their story began much earlier and in another place. They came to Maryland several generations prior to the Revolutionary War, and afterward Daniel Durham, a descendant, left Maryland with his father, Joshua, and moved to Ohio.

Durham Family of Maryland

John Durham, the earliest known ancestor of this line, was in Baltimore County, Maryland on 2 Sep 1673 when he claimed land in exchange for service to Mathew Ward.[29] In 1680 he was a testator for the estate of William Choice of Baltimore County and by 1682 had married his widow, Jane, who was the administrator and sole heir of her husband's estate, a legacy that included 82 acres on the Bush River.[30] In less than fifteen years Durham acquired a small fortune in cash and property, and when his will of 1694 was read, John the executor and named first in the will, received 125 acres on the Bush River near Winters Run called *Bilbury Hall*, plus £1,700 in trust so that he could build a house on the property. Son Samuel got *Levy's Tribe* and *Levy's Addition*, tracts that were also on the Bush River in Broad Neck. Francis Durham received land called *Choice Trips* near Samuel's property. The will disclosed that his widow had two children from her first marriage who received maintenance from the estate. To daughters, Mary and Elizabeth, he willed livestock.[31] In all, Durham's estate had a value in tobacco of £11,967.[32] A few years later Jane Choice Durham married John Boone, one of the testators of her husband's will.[33]

John Durham, son of John, was probably the eldest child, born about 1670 before his father moved to Baltimore. He had to be over twenty-one years of age when he paid property taxes in 1692 on the north side of Gunpowder Hundred where his father also lived.[34] Another indicator that he was of legal age came two years later when he became sole executor of his father's will. Jane Choice was not his mother because John Junior was about twelve years old when she married his father. The younger man was married by 1699 when he and his wife Sarah sold a portion of his inheritance. The deed showed that Durham, a planter who signed with an "X," lived in St. Johns Parish in Baltimore County and that he sold land on Winters Run for £4000 of tobacco.[35]

A year later his brother Samuel willed him 50 acres of *Levy's Addition* on the Bush River, a legacy to Samuel in their father's will.[36]

Durham died young. He was probably no more than thirty-nine years old in March 1709 when Matthew Green, his half-sister Mary's husband, became administrator for the estate.[37] Her parents were John Durham Senior and Jane Choice, and prior to 1715, when he would have been twenty-one years old, Mary petitioned the court to have her half-brother Samuel bound to her, explaining that since his birth, he had been partly supported by her mother and partly by her late husband, Matthew. To help pay for Samuel's keep while in Mary's care, Jane Choice Durham and her third husband John Boone sold Samuel's inheritance, *Levy's Tribe*, to Matthew Green.[38]

Before he died, John Durham arranged for his wife Sarah to have the property his brother gave him to support her and Samuel, perhaps her son as well.[39] Perhaps she lived on for a number of years but whether she remarried is unknown. Samuel was born about 1695-1698, but he produced no public records until he married eighteen-year old Eleanor Smithson at St. John's Parish on 15 Jan 1723.[40] He was between twenty-five and twenty-eight years old when he married the eldest daughter of Thomas Smithson and Ann Scott who was baptized on 24 May 1704. A few months later on 25 Jun 1723 Samuel purchased 100 acres of *Bynum Branch* on the Bush River for £4,500 of tobacco. In 1726 the 50 acres of *Levy's Tribe* passed down over three generations, from John Durham to his grandson Samuel, was sold on 9 Jan 1726 for £2,500 of tobacco.[41] The Durhams probably lived near the Bush River because records indicate he was a carpenter, and according to family history he was a ships' carpenter who worked in the Baltimore shipyards, a distance of twenty-five miles away from home.[42]

Eleanor and Samuel's first child was born 8 Jan 1723 and named John.[43] About two years later Sarah was born, and then Samuel. Joshua was born in 1733 and after him were four brothers, Mordecai, James, Daniel and John. A daughter Hannah was born in 1740 and after her, sons David and Aquila, the youngest child, who was born in 1746.[44] Thomas Smithson made his will in 1731 and in it he named his daughter Eleanor, saying she was the wife of Samuel Durham. He left land to his sons and personal items to his two youngest daughters. Then he stated, "and further my will is that none of my four daughters that are now married shall ever have any part of my estate more than what I have already given them," a not unusual pronouncement, but one so provocatively stated that it begs the question of its stern language.[45]

In 1744 Samuel purchased 400 acres of *Ewing's Contrivance*, and over the years he added nearly as much land to his holdings as he did children to his household. By 1754 when he was in his mid-fifties he had substantially increased his father and grandfather's original purchases. Besides the 400 acres, he added in total three additions to *Bilbury Hall*. He owned 100 acres of *Edmund's Camp* where he and his family lived, as well as a tract called *Friend's Advise*.[46] Joshua was Samuel's second eldest son and on 10 Jan 1754, when he was twenty-eight years old, he married Sarah Thompson in St. John's Parish, Baltimore.[47] Her parents were Andrew and Elizabeth Thompson who lived along Bynum's Run.[48] The Bush River Lower Hundred where the Durham family lived encompassed Joppa, a town where many men had enterprises and conducted their business. In 1768, some of them wanted to move the county seat from Joppa to the growing town of Baltimore. Before it was being put to a vote, notices were posted on churches throughout the county, so that everyone had a chance to voice their opinion. Joshua Durham saw the notice on the doors of St. John's Parish in Baltimore County, and not surprisingly those who lived near Joppa, like he and his brothers, voted against the petition.[49]

On 31 Aug 1772 when Samuel drew his will, he was more than seventy years old, an old man for the times. It was the end of an era, and a proper time to bid farewell to a country that was changing in ways he may never have understood. Revolution was in the air and on the lips of many. He died on the cusp of a new age when its citizenry was ripe with discontent and moments away from demanding social change. He was not there to hear the watchword of the times, a call for freedom that became a roar, but his children would be. Samuel died at a time when the old ways were still intact, when his countrymen owed their rights to a foreign government and where men were enslaved and made to toil endlessly on other men's farms, and that included his. Samuel's directives and the contents of his will provided a window into his time and the circumstances of his relative wealth, which was land and tobacco, the currency of the times. He was specific in his bequests and democratic in its distribution. He required division without administration and asked Samuel to manage it as the sole executor. He distributed it equally among his children, including his daughters. Some of his sons got land but those who did not received a corresponding inheritance from his personal estate including money on loan, and other property including slaves, of which there were about ten. The specificity of the devise evokes a poignancy that touches the past with understanding, such as in the statement, "I give and bequeath unto my daughter Hannah Durham...the bed whereon I now lay with all the furniture." Apart from her thirds to which she was entitled, Samuel left his wife a most detailed bequest, probably in keeping with the way he provided for her throughout their marriage. He gave to...

> "my dear and loving wife, Eleanor Durham, one Negro as a
> legacy and she to take her choice of my Negroes as also my
> clock, my large chest of drawers, her sitting chair, one feather
> bed and furniture, her riding chair and furniture, one horse,
> one cow and calf, her crop of tobacco and her ready cash that
> she may have by her at my death, and my still and utensils
> thereunto belonging. And I allow her to take her choice in the
> articles I have bequeathed to her."

Samuel divided his estate in such a way that all benefited equally, but it was up to his children to make it happen.[50]

Joshua Durham was given 200 acres of *Ewing's Contrivance* in his father's will, land where he and Sarah probably raised their children. A family story was repeated in a history book saying that, "at the age of 21, Joshua... was given a plantation with slaves to work it, but he declined it, believing that it was not right to own slaves."[51] There may be some truth to the story because in the Baltimore County census taken at the beginning of the Revolutionary War, everyone in a family, or anyone living with a family was named including their ages. Joshua Durham's family was counted on 15 Aug 1776 in the Bush River Lower Hundred on land he got from his father. He and Sarah were each forty-three years old with eight children ranging in age from Hannah, who was three, to John, twenty-one years of age. Their son Daniel was sixteen, born on 3 Jan 1760.[52] They also had a twenty-year-old servant. Joshua's mother, Eleanor Durham aged seventy-three, lived nearby with several of her sons, a daughter Hannah and ten slaves.[53] Joshua was not unique among his neighbors in that he did not have slaves, although he was surrounded by many who did.

The Durhams were patriots and Joshua as well as several of his brothers served in the Maryland militia. His eldest son John as well as his brothers Samuel, Aquila and Mordecai was in Capt. Jacob Bond's Company No. 11.[54] In 1776 Joshua and his brothers signed a petition of the Association of Freemen, men who had a growing desire to separate from England and make their destiny as a nation.[55] While there is proof that he was in the Maryland Militia, nothing has been found to indicate his son Daniel served.

In 1783 most of the family lived in the Bush River Lower Hundred. Joshua and Sarah Durham lived near his mother who was nearly eighty years old. Aquila, their youngest son had celebrated his fourth birthday, and sons Daniel and John, who were single, lived near their Uncle Aquila Durham who was also single.[56] When the Revolutionary War ended in 1783 the nation's struggle ceased but the turmoil caused by the conflict left many families in a state of flux. Should they stay and rebuild their lives, or move on to the new frontiers that were being avidly touted in local newspapers? Joshua and Sarah Durham decided to sell their land and move west eventually settling in southern Ohio. Public records hint at the challenges faced by the Durham family in their quest for a new home, but the story, likely told by a family member to a historian, gives the more colorful side to their adventure. It began when Joshua sold his land.

> "In 1783 he sold his farm, receiving $42,000 in Continental money. He then started westward over the mountains, but being delayed by bad roads and storms he was compelled to winter in the mountains. The Continental money depreciated until it was scarcely of any value. He bought a small place for $2,000 on the Monongahela River, and started to make himself a new home, but found that he had a bad title to his property and lost it all. He moved back to the Susquehanna River, and in 1795 started for the Ohio territory, landing at the mouth of the Little Miami River on the 13th day of May, 1796...He went up the Little Miami River and built a cabin at a place near where the union bridge now stands. Here he remained until the next spring [when his son] Aquila prevailed upon his father to buy some land on the top of the hills back of Newtown."[57]

The land that Joshua paid $2,000 for and then lost was called Beach Bottom near Wheeling, West Virginia. From there he moved on in 1795, settling in Ohio near the Little Miami River not far from where Daniel had moved the year before. Sarah did not live long after their arrival in Ohio, and when she died in 1800 she was buried in the family cemetery. Joshua lived on, and when he died in 1829 he had been a citizen of Hamilton County for thirty-three years, twenty of them as a widower. Daniel shared both the early adventure and the hardships encountered by his parents as they traversed Pennsylvania several times before eventually settling in southern Ohio. However, he was a young man when they set out and his challenges were met with the zeal of youth.[58]

In 1783, the date when his father probably sold the farm, he was twenty-three years old and a taxpayer, who with his brother John, was living somewhere within the family compound on the Bush River Lower Hundred. Of marriageable age and with his inheritance, Daniel was probably married when he left Maryland about 1783. He probably traveled with his father in the beginning, and thus experienced some of Joshua's travails, but by 1790 Daniel and his wife Jane were in western Pennsylvania, living along the Monongahela River in Luzerne Township of Fayette County. No marriage records have been found for them, but she was probably Jane Hartshorn, a daughter of John and Margaret Hartshorn of Susquehanna Hundred in Harford County, Maryland. A census of the neighborhood in 1776 gave Jane's age as fifteen, the eldest of their children, she was born in 1761 and thus a year younger than her husband.[59]

Daniel and Jane were in Fayette County in 1790 with four children, two sons and two daughters. Other records identified the eldest children as Joshua and Samuel and their sisters Sarah and Ellen.[60] Daniel's parents lived nearby, but were on the west side of the Monongahela River in Washington County. With them were six of Daniel's siblings, two brothers and four sisters.[61] Those children known to have come west with their parents were Benjamin and Aquila, and sisters, Alazanah and Martha. Two other sisters, Priscilla and Hannah, died sometime after the census but before the family reached Ohio.[62]

Durham Family in Ohio

Daniel's family left Fayette County about 1794 and settled in Clermont County, Ohio, near the Little Miami River, where he worked as a cooper while building their cabin.[63] In 1800 he paid two dollars per acre for 300 acres where the family made their home in what is now the village of Tobasco.[64] Then in 1816 he bought 142 acres of James Taylor's Survey 608 on Five Mile Creek.[65] He continued to buy land when he could until eventually he owned 800 acres on five surveys, some in Clermont and other land in Hamilton County.[66] In Hamilton County, he was first taxed in 1808, then again in 1808.[67] A local history declared that he was the first man to produce wheat in the area. It was an arduous and primitive process in which first he "beat [it] out on a sheet with clubs, blowing the chaff out by throwing it up in the wind, and then ground it on an old coffee-mill, running it through a coarse meal-sieve, mixing it with water," after which it was ready to be made into bread and baked.

Daniel's eldest son Joshua married Elizabeth Woodruff and they settled in Cherry Grove near the Hamilton County border on Nine Mile Creek. Still living when the story of how he built his cabin was written up in a local history book, he might have personally contributed the information. It was a three-day process, on the first day he cut and prepared the logs, the next day he put up the walls, and on the third, he moved in. It was crude abode, with a clapboard door hung on wooden hinges, a window cut into the rear of the house and for lack of glass, greased paper tacked over it to allow light. Joshua cleared enough land for a larger cabin and to plant crops. The passage to and from his dwelling was no more than a bridle path blazed through the woods from his house to the Columbia settlement where the larger population lived. In those early years, their family lived mostly on game and domestic meat, and occasionally they had bread. Pork was so plentiful that a large hog sold for a dollar and so many wild turkeys abounded in the woods that they fell to the bottom of the list of desirable meat. Although food was plentiful, hunting was dangerous because so many wild animals roamed the forest. There were bear and panther in the woods, and wolves were plentiful, but because they killed the livestock, they were considered more annoying than threatening. Joshua Durham was more than exasperated when wolves killed and devoured the three dogs he bought to rid himself of those pests.[68]

Daniel's children grew up in a semi-wilderness near the border of Clermont and Hamilton Counties, on land that even today is sparsely populated. His children married into neighborhood families; the eldest daughter Sarah married Jonathan Frazee and Ellen married Joseph Martin. Elizabeth was a younger daughter and she married Alexander Morrison. Son Samuel married Susan Ayer and settled near Tobasco.[69]

Daniel was nearly seventy years old when his father Joshua died in 1829 at ninety-six years. His mother Sarah had been buried at Newtown many years earlier in the Durham Family Cemetery near the current streets of Koszo Lane and Nordyke Road. That is where they laid Joshua, although years later their remains were moved and re-interred in other cemeteries.[70] There are no cemetery records for Daniel's wife Jane who died well before her husband. He married again on 23 Sep 1834 to Catherine Clark, and until illness took his life, she nursed him.[71] Although it had been long and productive, in comparison to his father, he was a mere eighty-six years old when he died in 1846. However, events in those last years transpired in such a way that Daniel did not leave this world peacefully.

Controversy surrounded his will, but his third and final testament made shortly before he died, provoked family hostility that permeated the atmosphere in his last days, and ultimately compelled them to contest the will. Although the cause of his last illness is unknown, Daniel was bedridden only a short time before he died. It is, however, the testimony about his mental stability given by neighbors and friends that provided rich details about how others perceived him. Depositions from those who knew him clarified that his mind was unsound and had been deteriorating for some time. The nineteenth century lacked a term for it, but today it might be called dementia or Alzheimer's. The bitter taste for him was that lying just beneath the surface of his deteriorating mind was an iron will accustomed to having its way. Because he had a firm hold on his family, when they ventured into deep waters by grumbling about his will, they suffered the wrath of his anger, at first not realizing it was compounded by a confused mind.

Eventually what was unleashed could not be put back in the box, and provocations escalated on both sides. His children were unhappy with his will and they expressed it to each other and to him. Some visited individually, others in groups to speak their minds. He, on the other hand felt that giving 900 acres to his children, 200 each to his sons, and 50 acres each to several daughters, was fair. The real cause of his children's ire was the bequest to his wife. Daniel and Catharine were married about twelve years and because she was a good and faithful wife, he planned to reward her generously. He intended to give her the house and about 60 acres where they lived, $500 in cash, plus the household furnishings, livestock and everything else except for a farm of about 112 acres. This he directed her to sell and divide the proceeds between his children. The problem was that it was the second will. The first will reportedly gave his wife $500, the use of the house, property during her lifetime, then it was to be sold, and the proceeds divided among his children. Daniel was so angry with his kids that in the final will he gave each of them $10 cash and no more, and everything else went to his wife. His children were probably livid at the thought that so much of their father's accumulated wealth should go to a woman who was not their mother, and so they took their anger to court and sued for what they felt was their rightful legacy.[72]

In those last days when Daniel Durham was holding court from his bed and keeping his family at bay with his anger, many people came to see him. Some were friends, one was a young man who nursed him; others were his lawyers, both current and former. His eldest son Joshua was probably the leader, but among others who came to complain was his grandson Reece Morrison, son of Elizabeth Durham Morrison who died thirteen years earlier. His complaint was that the new will deprived him of his mother's portion of the $500 that was to be divided between him and his siblings, Perry, Samuel and Lucinda.

The deposition given by a Cincinnati hardware proprietor was insightful in that it indicated just how stretched Daniel's thinking was in that last year. A former schoolteacher, he had known Daniel for about ten years but when Durham walked into his store one day he did not recognize the teacher even though some of his former pupils had boarded at the Durham house. Daniel was there to buy andirons. He found a pair, liked them and placed them apart from the others so that his wife, who he expected shortly, could see what he had picked out. He talked to the proprietor for a while and then told him he had come to the store to pick out andirons and set aside another pair for his wife to see when she came in. Again he talked to the storekeeper and for the third time said that he had come in to pick out andirons, at which point his wife arrived. She said, "Pop, have you got those andirons picked out yet?" He said he did not, and went looking for them. At that point the storekeeper reminded him that he had already picked out several pair, but Daniel denied that he had looked at any at all. He then let his wife choose one and handed the man a dollar asking him to take it out of the bill. It was not enough money so the proprietor handed it back to Durham, who turned to his wife and asked her to pay for it.

Most of the other depositions agreed with this one, saying in particular that Daniel could no longer calculate money or remember what he had just said. The escalating confusion was in sharp contrast to his former mental acuity, which was compared by someone who had known Daniel for more than forty years.

He described the man he once knew, saying he was as "firm [of] mind as I ever saw, a close seeing dealer who looked sharply after his own interests...Anybody who thought he could make anything off the old man in any commerce [or] trade at that time should have found himself mistaken...I always considered him a very firm man, a man who would listen to reason ...but I never knew that he acted under the direction of anyone. He always went by his own mind." When asked to describe Daniel's mind when he made his wills, his attorney said, "I should not consider it a strong or sound mind as I had known him previously. It was shattered and disturbed." Somehow, although his final days were physically painful and he was angry until he drew his last breath, Daniel Durham still held everyone in the palm of his hand.

Morrison Monument, Mt. Moriah
Cemetery, Mt. Carmel, Ohio

W. P. Morrison
(23 Jan 1819-22 Sep 1892),
Frances E. (Kyle) Morrison
(14 Feb 1831-16 Mar 1888)

Chapter Thirteen

KYLE, PIERSOL and KENNY FAMILIES
Pennsylvania, Kentucky and Ohio (1660-1880)

Kyle in America

When Perry Morrison married Eliza Kyle, he united with one of the original pioneer families of Kentucky and southern Ohio. On 15 Aug 1796, her grandfather purchased 1,000 acres in Clermont County's Union Township.[1] He was Robert Kyle and upon moving from Pennsylvania in 1791, he settled in Campbell County, Kentucky on the Ohio River. Just across the river was Losantiville, a dot on the map that would become the city of Cincinnati. Robert and his wife Sally came to Kentucky with her siblings, their mother Dinah Kennedy and her second husband Thomas Kennedy. They crossed the Allegheny Mountains on their journey and near Pittsburgh secured a flatboat that brought them down the Ohio River to Cincinnati. Soon after landing, Kennedy bought 200 acres on the Kentucky side of the Ohio River where the Licking River joins it, and there he built a log cabin. At the rivers' juncture, in 1792 he established the first commercial ferry on the Ohio River, while on the opposite side a relative, Francis Kennedy, ran the ferry from Cincinnati. Beside the ferry, which was quite successful, in 1794 Thomas secured a license to run a tavern from his home. That same year he was elected to the first Campbell County Court.

In 1812 Kennedy was a large landowner and a successful businessman. That year he sold some of his land to city officials for $50,000, and three years later, it became the town of Covington. At some point Thomas replaced the log cabin with a large two-story house known as "The Point" located on today's Riverside Drive. There he and Dinah raised their children, and it is where she died on 21 Mar 1821, aged eighty-six. Thomas lived a few more months, and on 1 Aug 1821, he was buried beside his wife in nearby Linden Grove Cemetery.[2] The house was a landmark, lasting into the middle of the 20th century before it was torn down and the site made into a small park. A plaque with an image of the house marks where it once stood amid three blocks of large and graceful homes overlooking the Ohio River. In contrast to the air of quiet country gentility on the Kentucky side, on the far side is the bustling city of Cincinnati, in dramatic contrast to the early days when Kennedy's ferry ruled the river.[3]

Robert and Sally Kyle probably lived with Dinah and Thomas Kennedy after they arrived in Kentucky. However, by 1796 Kyle paid £50 for property on Ninth Street and in 1798 he built the first house in Covington. Although it has since been torn down, when it was photographed in 1929, it typified an eighteenth-century log cabin. It was two stories, built of hand-cut logs, probably two rooms deep with a smaller extra room on one side. It had a shingled roof and two windows, one on each floor, at the end of the house near the door. The house was more than 100 years old when it was photographed and it had seen better days, although it was probably quite sturdy and livable when it was new.[4]

Although Robert Kyle never lived in Ohio, he bought land as an investment. It became his children's legacy after he died. He and Sally had nine children, five sons and four daughters. Their daughters married and most of them remained in Kentucky, but their sons settled the Ohio property, a vast acreage in Clermont County that stretched from Mt. Carmel to Tobasco. Each of them married and produced several children who joined matrimonially with nearby families, so that the Kyle name multiplied exponentially, even as their bloodlines circulated invisibly through their daughter's children. Prior to moving west, Kyle was a well-known name in eastern Pennsylvania where the family settled early in the previous century. The Kyles and other Scots-Irish families came to this country from Ulster where they had lived for three generations, until restrictions imposed on them during the reign of England's Queen Anne forced them to leave. It was a far different situation than what had brought them to Northern Ireland in the first place.

County Ayr is in the lowlands on the west coast of Scotland, no more than twenty miles across the Irish Sea to the nearest point in Northern Ireland. Kyle was an old name there long before they were born, but at some point they felt they could no longer remain in the land of their fathers, and some of them crossed the waters and settled in Ulster. Northern Ireland was always attractive to the Scots but it was only after James I, a Scotsman who was also the English king, quelled a rebellion there in 1606 that the island became Scots dominated. As a reward to those who helped him put down the uprising, the king gave them land. However, it wasn't vacant land. First he had to uproot the Irish land barons who lived there, and then he gave away their land. The Scots were rewarded once again in 1649 by helping Oliver Cromwell uphold Protestantism in Ireland. After he drove out the Irish Catholics with the aid of the Scots, he rewarded the soldiers with land grants in Tyrone and nearby counties.

The Ulster Kyles

Historically most of those named Kyle were from southwestern Scotland, and the County of Ayr, so named because of the river that flows through its middle. One of Ayr's three districts is Kyle and the name dates as back as far as 1250 A.D. when an ancient map showed it as Cola. The county is steeped in the history of Scottish kings, the most famous of them, Robert the Bruce, who it is said came from Ayr. Another of its more famous citizens was the poet Robert Burns who in his "Farewell Song to the Banks of Ayr," referred to the family using the name's ancient form, Coile. The poem goes, "Farewell, old Coila's hills and dales...Her heathy moors and winding vales." Many, including Burns, thought that the nursery rhyme, "Old King Cole" referred to Coilus, King of the Picts and was the old form of the name that became Coil and eventually Kyle.

When the Kyle family left Scotland for Northern Ireland it was because Scottish Presbyterians were being persecuted for refusing to convert to the official Anglican Church. The Scots were an independent people, both proud and brave, but also firm in their beliefs. Discriminated against initially by England's Charles I and later his son Charles II, they eventually fled the country for Northern Ireland where earlier, England had encouraged Scottish colonization as a buffer against the Irish population who were Catholic. One Kyle tradition states that in 1675 James, John and Robert Kyle, all brothers, arrived in Ulster with two of them settling in Tyrone County, James Kyle in Mournebeg and John in Brackey. There are both physical traces and actual records indicating the family lived in the area. In 1759, John Kyle erected a monument to his brother Robert that and placed it in the wall of the Castlederg Church ten miles outside of Mournebeg. Another artifact showing a family presence is at Mournebeg House where the Kyle coat-of-arms was carved on a stone and placed there proving that, if nothing else, the Kyle family held sway there for a time. However, tax rolls from the Belfast chancery records prove John and Robert Kyle lived there prior to 1683 although not before 1660.

During the reign of England's Catholic Queen Anne (1704-1714) it was difficult to be a Scot and a Presbyterian in Ireland. Among their many restrictions, they could not hold public office, nor could they marry except in the Catholic Church. If a couple was married by a Presbyterian minister, any children were declared illegitimate. The crown raised property rents and taxes on Irish woolens and linens produced throughout the country. When that did not halt production, the English forbade the Scots and the Irish to weave cloth for their own use. At some point the restrictions became intolerable and James Kyle left Northern Ireland with three of his children. They boarded a ship in Belfast and came to America where they arrived at New Castle, Delaware, about 1720.[5]

Some might think that when the Scots-Irish arrived in America there were any number of choices of where they could settle, however given their clannish ways, their Calvinist beliefs and a desire for farmland much like they left behind, their choices were limited because unlike others...

> In making plans for the emigration, they hardly considered the southern colonies, since they were quite undeveloped and the already impoverished Ulsterman could see no hope in a slave-owning region of large plantations. Maryland offered no great inducement, since it too had a plantation economy, accompanied by a large number of Roman Catholics, and a firmly established Church of England. New York was known to be hard on dissenters. Eliminating these, there was left only the middle colonies and New England. Reports from Penn's settlements were good. Those who had landed in Boston had unexpected difficulties and found a reception that lacked warmth. Those who entered America by the Delaware River, on the other hand found a land of their hearts desire. The praise of the early settlers led others to follow."[6]

The Kyle Family of Pennsylvania

James Kyle was middle aged when he came to Pennsylvania, and probably a widower. In 1722 he was taxed on land he bought in newly settled East Donegal Township, then a part of Chester County.[7] He brought with him three children, John who was probably the eldest, Mary who became the wife of Judge Andrew Galbraith, and James who married Mary MacArthur. Kyle had been living with his daughter Mary and her husband when he died in 1735 leaving a small estate of about £20. In little more than a dozen years since leaving his Ulster home, he saw his family established in a new land and lived to see some of his children married into leading local families.[8]

John Kyle was about 38 years old and married with three children when he came to America with his father and siblings. He and his wife Ann Kyle, who may have been his cousin, had three daughters. They were Barbara who married Andrew Galbraith, Jr., Isabel married to Andrew Work and Elizabeth whose husband was named Ramsey. Their son Samuel was born about 1715, and was quite young when he accompanied his parents on the voyage across the seas. John, perhaps James' eldest son, established himself early in Chester County (later Lancaster) when he bought one thousand acres in 1723/4. By 1731 Kyle had paid his mortgage in full and added substantially to his original purchase.[9] Eventually his lands extended over much of old Sadsbury (later Bart, then Eden Township) in Quarryville. He was active in the community, serving on the grand jury in 1730, then he was elected to the state legislature from Lancaster County in 1731 and re-elected in 1733. In 1738 he was commissioned a justice of the peace at Chestnut Level, an office he held for about twenty years.[10] He had been a citizen of Lancaster County more than 35 years when he died on 7 Aug 1759, aged 75 years. He and Ann were buried in the Middle Octoraro Churchyard in Quarryville, where what remains of her tombstone reads, "Aug 17." If she died before or after her husband the proof has been washed away in time.[11] Although John left no will, Samuel was his father's executor when the estate was settled in 1765, leaving legacies of about £18 each to his sisters, Hazel (or Isabel) Work and Elizabeth Ramsey, late Elizabeth Kyle.[12]

Samuel Kyle grew up on his father's lands and remained there into his thirties. In 1740 farmers in Sadsbury Township filed a petition to lay a road in their area. Two of those appointed to supervise the task were Samuel Kyle and his brother-in-law Andrew Work, husband of Isabel.[13] It was likely that year, when he was thirty-five years old, that Samuel married Jean Bell, a neighbor although her parents' names are unknown. When he was about thirty years old, his father divided his lands between Samuel and his sister Isabel's husband, Andrew Work. Then because his sister Mary and her husband Judge Andrew Galbraith were moving west, Samuel bought their farm, and sold it sometime after 1758, probably in 1759 when his father died. By then Samuel and Jean were no longer living in Lancaster County, but had moved their family west of the Susquehanna River into what was then western Cumberland County.[14]

Records are not clear about when Kyle settled in Mercersburg on land known as Clifton Hall, but it may have been as early as 1751 when he was listed as a taxpayer in Cumberland (now Franklin) County. He did not give the land its name because it was called Clifton Hall in 1736 before he applied for a warrant from an original squatter's grant of 349 acres. His warrant was dated 7 Apr 1769, and on 29 Oct 1771 Kyle patented the land. Prior to that grant, in 1762 he bought 150 acres in Bart Township,[15] and on 2 Jan 1763, 250 acres in Montgomery Township.[16] His and Jean's children are known from his will, which gave his daughter's married names. They were Ann Kyle Fleming married to Robert, and Mary Kyle Wilson whose husband was John.[17] The youngest, Isabella Kyle was about seventeen on 15 Mar 1770 when she married James Garrison.[18] His sons were John Kyle, born in 1742 who married Hannah Wilson. Named next was Samuel, then Joseph born in 1749 who married Catherine Chambers, a daughter of Rowland Chambers who founded Mercersburg. Robert who was born in 1751 was named next and then James. The last was Thomas who was baptized on 6 Feb 1756, and who married Elizabeth Chambers, probably a sister of Catherine.[19]

The family was strongly patriotic and all of Samuel and Jean's sons served in some capacity during the Revolutionary War. Four of them, James, Samuel, Joseph and Robert, were in Captain William Huston's company of militia under the command of Colonel Culbertson's Sixth Battalion. Just as Huston's company was about to march out for the first time, a Presbyterian minister gave a stirring sendoff to the boys. It was a long speech but the highlights touched upon persecution and injustice, old resentments bringing the blood to boil in any Scotsman with a historical memory. At its conclusion, boys and men marched away to war filled with conviction and thoroughly committed to the cause.[20]

Robert Kyle was a single man when he marched off with his brothers, serving first in 1776 under Captain Robert McCoy as an ensign, then from 1777 to 1780 under William Huston in the 5th Company, 4th Battalion of the Cumberland County militia, and finally from 1780 until 1781.[21] Sometime before war ended, probably in 1781, Robert married Sally Piersol. On 23 Apr 1782 their first child, whom they named Samuel Bell Kyle for both families, was baptized in Mercersburg's Presbyterian Church. On 28 Nov 1784, daughter Jean was baptized there, as was Thomas on 3 Aug 1788.[22]

Years of conflict had changed everyone's lives regardless of age or circumstance, but peace brought with it a sense of restlessness particularly among those boys who returned home as men. Robert's father lived to see his sons called to serve their country and he was there when they returned safely home each time they were called out. Not long afterward, Samuel Kyle began putting his affairs in order in preparation for his departure from this world. He was not a literate man as he signed his name with an "X" but his long will was specific in its bequests, and fair and generous to all. Written in 1784, he gave specific gifts to his grandchildren and land to his sons who had none, including Robert whose portion was part of the property where he and his father lived. Samuel directed his executors, Thomas and Samuel, to sell most of his personal estate, so that the neediest of his children would have some relief. James, one of the youngest children, apparently had some disability and much of the specific language dealt with how Thomas should care for his brother. Thomas Kennedy, who was a witness, was related by marriage to the family, as he was Sally Piersol Kyle's stepfather.[23] Samuel died on 3 May 1784, the year his will was probated, and laid to rest next to his wife Jean Bell Kyle who died eight years earlier on 4 Apr 1777.[24]

By 1790 Robert and Sally had five children. It had been several years since their father died, and restlessness had settled deeply within Robert's siblings. Most of them were making plans to move west, some to leave Pennsylvania.[25] By 12 Jan 1793, Robert sold the 100 acres his father left him and prepared for the journey to Kentucky. He was not the first of his brothers to leave, but most of them headed for Ohio where eventually three of his siblings settled. Joseph moved to Kentucky in 1784 then to Ohio, followed by Samuel and Thomas. Two moved further west but remained in Pennsylvania; one of them was Mary Kyle Wilson, formerly Orbison, who moved to Westmoreland County. Robert's eldest brother, John, married Hannah Wilson and they settled at Elizabethtown in Allegheny County, Pennsylvania, where they raised a large family.[26] Their daughter Ann married John Cochran whose daughter Mary became the wife of Zacheus Kyle, her first cousin once removed.[27]

Just as most pioneers traveled with family and friends, Robert and Sally headed for Kentucky with Dinah and Thomas Kennedy. Accompanying them was Sally's sister Mary, and if he was still living, her husband James Scott.[28] Kennedy was an adventurer and a romantic of sorts, perhaps impetuous and strong willed, or at least the story of how he came to marry Dinah Davis Piersol began in a way that made him seem so. Related to the Kyles by marriage, he was a fully integrated member of the family by 1784 when he witnessed Samuel Kyle's will. However, his and Dinah's story began much earlier.

Davis and Edwards Families of Pennsylvania

Dinah was the third child and the eldest daughter of Zacheus Davis and his wife Joanna. Her mother remains a bit of a mystery. Research indicates that Joanna was either the daughter of Thomas Edwards, a large landowner and a presiding justice for Lancaster County, or the daughter of Thomas Morgan who in 1733 died without a will, leaving a widow and seven children barely able to support themselves The complexity in deciphering Joanna's background is a result of the intermarriages of a handful of Welsh emigrants who were among the earliest settlers of Earl Township in Lancaster County. They were Welsh among Welsh, but different in that originally Quaker, they renounced the sect to become a cluster of Anglican worshippers amongst their Quaker neighbors. These families as well as the majority of their neighbors came to Pennsylvania beginning in 1682 at the behest of William Penn who with letters of patent from King Charles II, was sent to establish a colony in the new world. At some point Quakers, also known as the Society of Friends, approached Penn about setting aside a large tract where they could live and practice their religion in peace. He agreed and their lands became that part of Chester and Philadelphia Counties that encircled New Castle County, Delaware. It was a mixed group and because of the preponderance of settlers from Wales in Radnor, Tredyffryn and Haverford townships, that part of Chester County was known as the Welsh Tract. Many of those pioneers came from Wales as Friends but left their faith during the schism that occurred around 1692 and joined the Baptists, or reverted to Anglicanism. Others left Chester County, and of those who did, some were second generation Welsh who upon leaving Radnor, settled in Earl Township in the newly created county of Lancaster.[29]

One of them was Thomas Edwards who was born in 1673, probably in Wales and moved with his parents to the Welsh Tract in Chester County in the late 1680's. He married Mary, whose last name was probably Thomas, about 1704 and in 1705 their first child Margaret was born. She later married Rees Morgan who lived nearby. Like others who were no longer comfortable in the Quaker confines of Radnor, Thomas and Mary moved to the new frontier. In 1719, after their children were born, they sold their plantation and were among the first to settle in western Chester County. Thomas bought 1,000 acres in Earl Township at Spring Grove. One of his nearest and only neighbors at the time was Jenkin Davies. They knew each other from Radnor, as both men were early members of St. David's Episcopal Church. Edwards was an intelligent and fairly educated man, but he was no farmer. Upon realizing this, in 1735 he borrowed money for a patent and divided the property between his sons, John, Edward, Evan and Thomas. When Mary died is unknown, but it was sometime after they left Radnor and Thomas married a woman named Elizabeth.

For Thomas, the move created new opportunities and early on, he established himself as a leader in this new community. By 1728 the population had grown substantially but their farms were spread out over such a large area that no one had a close neighbor. It was a long and arduous trip of 50-80 miles for the settlers to go to market, trade goods or go to court, and after listening to his neighbor's complaints and agreeing with them, Edwards took action. He and another man wrote a petition and collected signatures from the citizens of the Conestoga region, asking for the formation of a new county out of western Chester County. He brought the petition to the lieutenant governor and with the help of 182 signatures it was quickly approved. The legislature appointed Edwards to meet with the surveyor to select a county seat and arrange for the construction of a courthouse and jail. He was appointed one of seven county justices of the peace in 1729, initially for Earl and three other townships. That same year he became a representative from Lancaster to the provincial state legislature, a position he held for about ten years. Then in 1741 he was appointed the presiding justice for the county, a position from which he retired in 1757 at the age of eighty-four.[30] It is related of Thomas that when he left home, seventeen miles from the county seat, he walked barefoot to Lancaster where he sat shoeless until the court adjourned. Analyzed once by a historian using his handwriting as a guide, it was said that if it "is any indication of character, he was uncouth, blunt, but accurate, exacting, commanding respect more by superiority of mind than appearance. His position of justice came from the Governor and Council, but his friends and neighbors had the same appreciation of his worth." Thomas' wife Elizabeth died in 1754 when she was seventy-six, but he lived another ten years, until 8 May 1764, reaching the remarkable age of ninety-one years, but then it seemed that Thomas Edwards was a remarkable man in many ways. He was buried in the Old Welsh Graveyard next to his daughter Margaret Morgan, wife of Rees whose stone is on her opposite side. Elizabeth Edwards was placed on the other side near him, if not next to him. There appeared to be an unmarked space between Elizabeth and Thomas just large enough for Mary, first wife and the mother of his children, to find a place of rest.

Thomas Edwards' neighbor, Jenkin David, was from County Cardigan in Wales, born about 1670 in the hamlet of Cilcennin on the Welsh coast of the Irish Sea.[31] A Bible record strongly suggested he was the son of Jenkin, who came from Wales bringing his wife and four children with him to Pennsylvania. They settled in Chester County in Uwchlan Township before 1715, even as early as 1702, the date that Jenkin David's name was entered into the Welsh Bible he carried with him to Pennsylvania. If it was given to him upon leaving Wales, he made it a tradition by passing it down to his son Jenkin. The second inscription in it says, "Jenkin Davies his Bible 1726," suggesting his father gave it to him shortly before he died. Surrounded by the Welsh language, the names of the younger man's children and dates of their birth were written across several pages wherever there was a blank space. The elder Jenkin died sometime after 8 Sep 1727 when he wrote his will. Martha (Edwards) his wife was the executor, and he named his brothers-in-law, Evan Edwards and Thomas Edwards as guardians of his children, David, Evan and Martha. Jenkin was not named, which does not preclude him as a son, but suggested instead that he was provided for in other ways.[32] Jenkin Junior was not landless. When the Welsh gradually began moving west into Lancaster County around 1720, he had been living in Radnor. Around then he bought 1,000 acres in Earl Township along Conestoga Creek at the mouth of Muddy Creek, making him one of the earliest settlers in the Conestoga valley. His near neighbor and a family friend, Thomas Edwards, had also purchased 1,000 acres at Spring Grove in the valley the year before.[33]

Jenkin and his wife Mary probably continued living in Radnor for several years, renting out their Lancaster property, until about 1729 when he and most of his children, except for Evan who stayed in Radnor, moved to Earl Township. His will suggested this was true. It was made on 12 Feb 1747 and to Evan, the eldest son, he left the property in Radnor and some land in Earl Township. John and Zacheus each received about 400 acres in Earl Township where they lived. He left his wife the property he owned in Wales and made a provision for it to remain in their family thereafter. Mary was the executor with her son John, and Rees Morgan and Thomas Edwards were two of the witnesses. The will named their daughters, Catherine who was married to Rees David and Sarah whose husband was John Edwards.[34] Not mentioned was their eldest daughter Jean who died years before in 1738 and was buried in the Welsh Graveyard.

Jenkins's son Zacheus married Joanna who may have been the daughter of Thomas Edwards. All that is really known about her is that she was born in 1710 and died in 1768, information that comes from her tombstone in the Welsh Cemetery. Although a man of high standing in the community, Thomas Edwards did not leave a will that might have mentioned Joanna. His son John married Sarah Davis, a daughter of Jenkin and Mary, and his daughter Margaret married Rees Morgan, the son of Thomas Morgan, all members of the community and each with family who were buried in the Welsh Graveyard. Joanna likely married into one or the other of these two families, but which one is unclear. Sometimes children's naming patterns provide clues to ancestry, but Joanna's children were equally weighted between Morgan and Edwards given names. The Old Welsh Graveyard near Terre Hill where Joanna and Zacheus were buried was another possible source of verification, but it too provoked more questions than answers because the preponderance of burials are those of the Davis family and those who married into that family. However, the first one buried on land owned by Rees Morgan was his father, Thomas Morgan, who died in 1733. Rees was laid to rest in 1769; just five years after a patent established it permanently as a cemetery. While those early burials were mostly of the Morgan family, they buried Elizabeth Edwards there in 1754 and next to her ten years later, her husband Thomas.

In a statement made after Thomas Morgan died in 1733, Thomas Edwards, perhaps in his official role as a county justice, stated that of the seven children he [Morgan] left, "some of them [are] not able to get their living." Later in Oct 1738, Edwards wrote "about seven years ago (Rees) Morgan's father died and left a widow and seven children...his father [Thomas] and several others of the deceased of the neighborhood had been buried on ye vacancy (the Welsh Graveyard)...joining his mother's place and Jenkin Jenkin's lands," indicating that the Morgan family lived in the general neighborhood of Thomas Edwards and Jenkin Davis's property. In 1740, Thomas Morgan's widow, Gwyn purchased a lot on Water Street in the town of Lancaster where perhaps she went to live, leaving the land to one of her sons. She wrote a will in 1746 naming among her seven children, daughters named Joanna Davis and Elizabeth Davis, providing the first clue that the woman buried in the Welsh Graveyard next to her husband Zacheus Davis was probably Joan[na] Morgan who was born in 1710 and died on 21 Jan 1768.[35] Joanna's parents may never be known but the evidence is strong that her father was buried near her, whoever he may be.

Zacheus Davis's name was plainly written in his father's Welsh Bible, "Zacheus born in ye year 1710 week of February ye 21, moon age." He was the youngest son in a family of seven children who were born in Radnor but who grew up in Earl Township. There he met and married Joanna, probably the daughter of Thomas and Gwyn Morgan. She and Zacheus may have had other children, but seven were named in his will, although probably not in birth order, since Zacheus Junior was named first. After him was Jenkin, followed by daughters Dinah, Sarah, Ann, Elizabeth and Hannah.

He was a farmer but he also built a gristmill on the land his father left him. An additional source of income came from a fullering mill used to extract clay from the soil and when added to raw wool it removed the oils. Zacheus was also community minded and politically active, and in 1756 when he was 46 years old, he was elected commissioner of Lancaster County. In 1761 he was appointed Justice of the Peace for Lancaster County, and when Thomas Edwards retired in 1757, he succeeded him as Justice of the Court of Common Pleas, a position he held until 1788. He and Joanna were members of Bangor church where Zacheus was a vestryman from 1756 to 1774.[36] As his help mate and wife of many years Joanna had a busy life raising and caring for their large family while also looking after the needs of her husband. When she died during the winter of 1768 on 21 January she was but 58 years old, and sometime in the spring, like others of her family, she was borne to the Welsh Graveyard for burial. Later that year as if making a concession for the loss of his wife and the changes it brought about, Zacheus sold half of his land, 206 acres for £2,600, but held on to that part containing his home and mills.[37]

He was the epitome of success, a wealthy man with valuable, productive land from two mills, but also a public servant who remained consistently in service to the people of the county. Zacheus lived another twenty years after Joanna's death; years of resistance and change and in the end, war. His brother John died in 1774, prior to the Revolutionary War, but Zacheus was quietly rebellious and did his part to provoke and escalate our country's inevitable separation from the motherland.[38] He was elected to the colonial legislature in 1774 and 1775, and all through his first term attended sessions in what is known today as Independence Hall. Because he served from Philadelphia, the heart of the country at the time, he heard the same protests in the city as he heard from his neighbors in Lancaster's countryside. The injustice of the laws imposed by England so it could maintain control over its rebel colony in America had surpassed all moderation. The citizens were not only complaining, but they were rebelling too. Zacheus may have been too old to go to war, but to voice his concerns he joined the Committee of Observation and Inspection. As a secret body, its purpose was to disrupt English control over the colonies by boycotting English goods and in general dislocating their long imposed order. It was a dangerous role for him because if discovered, he would have suffered financially and been subject to arrest and seizure of his assets. His name and those of his conspirators became publicly known only after the war was over and freedom won.[39] Zacheus continued serving the citizens of the county as justice until he died on 25 Mar 1788. In the Welsh Graveyard, he and his brother John were buried all in a row next to their wives. Between the four tombstones is an unmarked space just large enough for two more graves. Some say their parents were buried between them although any fieldstones are long gone. But so it seems. Those empty spaces seem protectively flanked by other graves where once upon a time, the families who buried their loved ones knew exactly where Jenkin and Mary Davis were located.

Dinah Davis and John Piersol

Dinah Davis was born about midnight under a full moon on the twelfth day of October 1735. It may have been an omen had anyone noticed at the time. Then again, maybe the light of that heavenly body provided her with a special strength, one that would carry her through the several twists and turns of fate that were to become a part of her destiny. On that night, however, probably all that Zacheus and Joanna considered was that as a new day dawned their first daughter was born.[40]

Growing up, Dinah lived in Earl Township near Earltown or New Holland with brothers Jenkin and Zacheus, and her five younger sisters. Less than ten miles away in Chester County lived several generations of the Piersol family of Nantmeal Township near Honey Brook. Her father, Zacheus Davis, was well known in the county, a successful man but also one who gave back to the community where he lived. He and Joanna married their children into well-established local families, one of them, daughter Ann who married her second cousin Willis Davis. Two of their daughters, Elizabeth and Mary, married Thomas Carter and Joseph Parke, both from East Bradford Township. Offspring Jenkin and Sarah also married but his namesake, Zacheus, did not.

Dinah was about twenty-five when she married John Piersol, a farmer from East Nantmeal who was about the same age. How they met is unknown, and although they lived in separate counties, their homes were only about ten miles from each other. The Davises belonged to the Bangor Church, which was Episcopalian and attended mostly by Welsh settlers. Nothing indicates that John's family was associated with a particular religion but they may also have been Episcopalian because the Piersol family was originally from England. As unalike as this couple was, both were third generation Pennsylvanians and on the same social footing, and perhaps that was what brought them together. Their marriage date is unknown, but it was about 1759. Soon after their first child, probably Mary, was born, followed by Sarah who was born about 1762, and Zacheus, named for Dinah's father, who was born in 1764.[41]

Like the Davises of Lancaster County, John Piersol's family was one of the original settlers in Chester County at a time when the borders between Maryland and Pennsylvania were blurred and the land was a backwoods. Although new to the area around Brandywine Creek in 1680, theirs was an old name in the colony. They were known in Nassau County, New York, on Kent Island in Maryland, and in parts of New Jersey. One branch moved to North Carolina and the other, from whom John Piersol descended, settled in West Nantmeal Township in the area of today's Honey Brook.

The Staffordshire branch of the Piersol family was reportedly the first to sail for America. Living near the border of Wales, this family had a long and illustrious history as attendants, knights and servants to the kings of England. Established first in Normandy they reached prominence over several centuries after arriving first as Norwegian conquerors in the tenth century. Prior to their conquest of western Europe Vikings had lived for centuries in Norway. Over time as the family moved from Normandy to Staffordshire in western England, their name changed as well. Beginning as dePechel it changed to Parshall, then to Pearsall or Piersol as this particular branch of the family spelled it. There is currently some dispute about the correct line of descent of this family at the time they made the transition from England to the colony of New York in the 1600s. Therefore, it is unclear whether the Chester County branch of the family can claim the illustrious pedigree of the Staffordshire Pearsall family or whether they are from a more humble origin.

There is little actual documentation to support the beginnings of the Piersol family's settlement in Pennsylvania because at its earliest settlement, they were living in a wilderness, and there was a proprietary dispute between Maryland and Pennsylvania over which had legal rights to the territory. While Lord Baltimore and William Penn fought over the lands, Welshmen, Swedes and some Dutch families, as well as the English settled it. George Pearsall was probably the first member of this family to move to New York. Records show he lived in Hellgate Neck and Middleburg or at Pearsall, names used for the same places on Long Island. Pearsall left Hellgate Neck in 1667 after selling his property and under a charter moved to Elizabeth, New Jersey, where he lived for a time.   When a neighbor began promoting land on the upper Delaware Peninsula Pearsall was eager to settle there. Thinking that the land was part of Maryland he and his associates settled there at the base of Welsh Mountain sometime after 1678 where they acquired Indian titles to their property. This land at the head of the Brandywine Creek is today in Chester and Lancaster counties in Pennsylvania, but at the time it was part of the disputed territory claimed by both Maryland and Pennsylvania. George and his wife, whose name is unknown, settled there with two children, John and Jeremiah. Shortly after he staked his claim, George died. His son John continued living on the land, and through two marriages had sons, John and Jeremiah, each said to be born of a different mother. His first wife is unknown but thought to be John Junior's mother. John Senior's second wife was Mary Jarman the mother of Jeremiah Pearsall. She outlived John and three other husbands, and in her will of September 1741 proved Jeremiah was her son by calling a grandchild "the daughter of Mary Peirsal and Jeremiah Peirsal her husband."[42]

When John the son of George died about 1680, his sons took up the cause and held on to the land. Eventually William Penn brought a large number of Welsh settlers to one side of Pearsall's land while Scots settled on the other side. With newcomers encroaching, the earliest settlers tried blazing the trees with tomahawks to mark the boundaries of their property. When that failed, they realized the only way to keep their land was to settle with the proprietors. That was in 1717 when John Pearsall, grandson of George acquired a warrant for 200 acres.   Together with his half-brother Jeremiah and Richard Piersol who was probably a cousin, they acquired a warrant on 13 Oct 1717 for a total of 500 acres. The family had held the land since John was born nearly forty years before, but it was worth every effort to make it their permanent and legal home. Its first value was as a source of rich iron mines but it was also located in a fertile valley between the Welsh Mountain and Barren Hill across which a branch of Brandywine Creek flowed.[43]   On an additional 73 acres, John was granted a deed on 16 Jun 1748 and later a patent. However, the reluctance of the proprietors of Penn's Colony to formalize Piersol's claim came through clearly in the phrase, "upon application by John Pearsoll…our Surveyor General was required to accept…the survey for the tract of land."

John Piersol, grandson of George, had a plantation of 321 acres.[44]   A nearby spring irrigated his fruit orchard, crops and pasture, but it also served his mill, which was about two miles from the Friend's Manor Meeting House. He built a two-story house using native stone with a cellar beneath, and nearby a log barn with stables at one end. Surrounding it all was woodland and meadow.[45] On this land John and his wife Alice Bishop, a daughter of Samuel,[46] raised seven children, among them sons Jeremiah, and John who married Dinah Davis.[47]

Most of our ancestors could neither read nor write, so their personal history was untold. John and Dinah Piersol's story is a rarity in family history, first because it was written at all, but even more so because of its intimate revelations. In a succinct disclosure, much was revealed about their private lives and all of it over an incident that occurred one night, a night that opened the door into their marriage. At first glance, a troubled relationship was revealed and perhaps an incompatibility between husband and wife. The date of the incident is unknown but it probably happened in the summer. Also unanswered was whether it occurred after their children were born, during a pregnancy or shortly thereafter. However, one evening probably when her children were young, and Zacheus was no more than two years old, Dinah walked out the door of her house, presumably forever. She was in despair with nowhere to turn and soon found herself heading toward the river. Foremost in her thoughts was her husband, a man from a good family but a man who was so disheartened by depression, expressed as "feelings of misfortune," that he seemed compelled to drink himself to death. They had had discussions about his wanting to end it all and if he did, what would become of her and the children? He had assured her that if he was gone, his parents would take care of them.

It was a dark and dismal night as she walked by the river, just like her thoughts, and the closer she came to the creek the more determined she was to throw herself in. She walked the narrow footpath following it down to the water, which as she came upon it was swollen by recent rain and more swift than usual. Now close to the edge her resolve held, and just as she was about to leap, a large dog or the specter of one so frightened her that she halted. Suddenly brought to her senses and frightened, she ran away in the dark until she was far from the water. She paused to collect her wits and decide where to go. She could not return home, not tonight, so instead she headed for her father's storehouse. When she got there she climbed to the upper room where no one could see her or find her, and there she stayed for the remainder of the night. Still frightened by what stopped her from leaping into the creek and by her feelings of despair, she did not sleep that night. Nevertheless, she also knew something had changed inside her. She had turned a corner there by the river and somehow knew that her life was not meant to end that way or that night. At morning light she walked back home to be with her children.[48]

It would appear that Dinah had fled her home and gone to her father's house since the barn where she stayed was on Zacheus' property rather than on her husband's land. She didn't say how long afterward it was that her husband died, but somehow she found the courage to go on for the sake of her children. Sometime after he paid taxes on his farm in 1765, John died at about 40 years old. Because his property was part of a larger estate and not his by deed, the estate did not go into probate. Had it not been that his parents lived after him and his father remembered his grandchildren in his will, John's existence would have faded into memory with little more than tax records to prove he had walked this earth at all.

When John Piersol Senior received a patent for his land, it described the property owners that bordered it, and one of them was Thomas Kennedy.[49] In 1765 the West Nantmeal tax list indicated that Kennedy's land was near that of John Piersol, Junior, thus proving that Dinah and Thomas were neighbors. Rather than John's, in the years 1766 through 1768, Dinah Piersol's name was on the tax assessment list.[50] As near neighbors, the Piersols and Kennedys knew each other and may have been friends, and thus at first it was neighborly kindness that prompted the younger Kennedy to stop by and offer his assistance to the widow. A friendship grew, and sometime during 1766, when he was 25 years old, Thomas Kennedy began courting the Widow Piersol.

Dinah and Thomas Kennedy

Thomas Kennedy Senior was a man of strong religious convictions who admired and often gave shelter to the Covenanter preacher John Cuthbertson on his visits to Chester County. He hoped his son would become a minister, and thus he did not approve of Dinah who not only was not Presbyterian, but also was a thirty-two-year-old widow with three children. He was so against the match that he contrived to send Thomas to Ireland, where the elder Kennedy was born, hoping his son would come to his senses and forget that woman. Thomas agreed to take the trip, but the couple was determined to marry and so they stole away to Philadelphia where on 28 Oct 1767 they were married.[51] Shortly thereafter, Thomas left for Ireland. He "agreed to keep the marriage secret until his return, but Dinah, to save her character during the absence of her young husband, disclosed the secret and showed the marriage license." Somehow, Dinah managed to carry out the charade for the tax assessor in 1768 because she was listed as Dinah Piersol. That year Thomas Kennedy's first child, Joseph, was born. After that her name disappeared from the tax list and the land reverted once more into the larger Piersol holdings.[52]

In all likelihood, when Thomas Kennedy Senior learned of his son's marriage somewhat after the fact, and when a child was born the following year, their relations became strained. Following Joseph's birth, Dinah had two more children, Samuel born in 1770 and Mary Hannah about 1772. Other events precipitated by the elder Kennedy may have fractured the relationship even further. He was a widower in his mid-sixties and about 1769, he married a woman named Ann Kilbreath, who in 1770 bore him a daughter they named Elizabeth.[53] If Thomas and Dinah were living in Chester County at the time they would have been present for the birth of, not only their son Samuel, but that of Thomas' half-sister Elizabeth, who was twenty-nine years his junior.

Dinah Kennedy had a good relationship with her former in-laws, and it was surely a necessity, because of her six children three of them were Piersols. When John Piersol Senior died in 1773, his wife Alice got their personal estate but his executor and son-in-law, Joseph Trego, was ordered to sell his land and divided the moneys between his children, grandchildren and his daughters-in-law, including Dinah Kennedy. Mentioned specifically were grandchildren "Sarah and Mary Pearsoll and their brother Zacheus Pearsoll, "son of my son John Pearsoll." Family relationships were quite a different story for Dinah's husband, Thomas Kennedy, who did not become a minister, but he also married against his father's will. Kennedy Senior and his wife Ann lived together nearly 20 years before he died in 1789 at the age of 85, and his will was revealing in several ways. He signed with an "X" so he was not literate. His church, and its pastor, Rev. John Cuthbertson to whom he left a small legacy, were vital to him.[54] The strained relationship between father and son was also apparent. Thomas was a man of relative wealth who left all of his real estate to his daughter Elizabeth. Margaret Gillaspy and Thomas, the children of his first marriage, each received notes collectible from those who owed money to their father's estate. Thomas' bequest was a £26 note, perhaps a final indication that his father was never pleased with his marriage to the Widow Piersol.

Sally Piersol and Robert Kyle

Thomas and Dinah probably left West Nantmeal Township sometime between 1768 when Joseph was born and 1769 when Thomas' father remarried. They moved west to Cumberland, later Franklin County, Pennsylvania, bringing Dinah's children Zacheus Piersol who was fifteen and his sisters Sarah and Mary who were between nine and twelve years old. In 1770 Thomas lived in Peters Township (later Montgomery Township), where he was taxed for a horse and cow. Living there also was Samuel Kyle, father of Robert, who had a large farm with 3 horses, 7 cows and 15 sheep. Kyle patented 250 acres of his land; an additional 300 acres was under warrant and 130 acres was cleared for farming.[55] In 1785 tax records showed both families lived in Montgomery Township where Thomas Kennedy served as the tax collector.[56] He and Dinah must have lived near the Kyle family, at least by the time the Revolutionary War began. Robert Kyle and his many brothers were in the militia, called up periodically to protect the farms in the county and to serve as guards for the regular army during the war. Sally Piersol may have known Robert Kyle while she was growing up or met him during those times when he was home on furlough from the war. Although no marriage records were found, they probably wed about about 1781, and by 1790 they had five children.

The census record was a snapshot of the moment, and it indicated that Dinah and Thomas lived in Montgomery Township and on either side of them were her daughters and their families. Robert and Sally lived on one side, and Mary Piersol and her husband James Scott who had four children in 1790, were on the other.[57] Upon selling their land near Mercersburg in 1793, Robert and Sally were in the final planning stages to move to Kentucky. They traveled as a family that included her sister Mary Scott, and Dinah and Thomas Kennedy. Sally's brother, Zacheus Piersol, was the only member of the family who did not leave Pennsylvania. He and his wife Margaret Davis, a cousin, remained in Chester County where they lived the remainder of their lives.[58] Three generations of inter-related families went to Kentucky including sixteen children. The youngest was the baby, Robert Kyle Junior, and the eldest was probably Sally's sister Mary who was about 38 years old. The real elders with courage enough to change their lives were Thomas Kennedy who was 52 and his wife Dinah who was 58 years old. It was yet another twist of fate that brought her to the Kentucky wilderness knowing she would probably never again see her son Zacheus or visit the land where she grew up. However, at some point Dinah must have looked at her daughters, Sally and Mary, and known it was the right choice. In much the same way, as Robert and Sally Kyle made their way downriver on a flatboat full of hopes and dreams for the future, they trusted fate. She looked down on her son, born the first day of January 1793, and talked to Bobby about their new home in Kentucky.

Our New Kentucky Home

Joseph Kennedy was about twenty-one years old in 1790 when his father sent him downriver from Cumberland County to see Francis Kennedy in Cincinnati. He was there to check out the land and look for business opportunities for his family in Ohio.[59] In 1789, Francis, his wife Rebecca, and their seven children moved to Losantiville, an early name for Cincinnati, where he established the first ferry directly across the river from Covington, now Kenton County, Kentucky.[60] Undoubtedly, they looked over the area now called The Point where the Licking River meets the Ohio. Upon his return, Joseph must have waxed enthusiastically about the area because shortly afterward, Thomas Kennedy moved his family to Campbell County, Kentucky, where he established a ferry on the opposite side of the river from Francis Kennedy's business. Probably related, the two men worked together for a few years until Francis fell into the river "while trying to get some cattle over in a ferryboat. He was steering the cattle [and they] got to ripping and tearing, and knocked him overboard. He was found way down where the river fell, with his hands gripping the root of a tree, covered with mud."[61] An exact date for his death was not found but it was likely in the spring of 1796. He left behind a grieving wife and family, but with mouths to feed the widow had only a short time to mourn her loss. On 30 Jun 1796 Rebecca Kennedy put a notice in the Cincinnati newspaper that she was establishing a ferry service under her name.[62]

While Thomas Kennedy was establishing his ferry business, he built a log cabin on part of the 200 acres he purchased on the Ohio River. While drumming up business, he got to know his neighbors and soon became active in the fledgling community.[63] About 1791 Kennedy replaced the log cabin with a much larger stone house, the first in the area. Built like many stone houses in Pennsylvania, it was meant to last as its "outer walls...were three feet thick. Inside...there was a broad stairway and the interior displayed beautifully detailed woodwork. The original estate included the house, a barn, a springhouse, a hen house and a smokehouse, all made of stone."[64] The Kennedys lived there until 1814 when Thomas sold the house and built another at Sixth and Greenup where he and his wife remained to the end of their days. Kennedy first paid taxes in 1795, but in the interest of business, he needed better roads. In December he was part of a team appointed to lay a road from "Thomas Kennedy's Ferry to Campbell's Tavern on the Dry Ridge."[65] At the same time he applied for a tavern license for his home, renewed yearly until 1802 when his son Joseph assumed the business. Kennedy was one of the first trustees of Newport and one of the first justices of the peace for the county. He not only helped survey the roads, ran a ferry and operated a tavern, but in 1798, he was the superintendent in charge of building a jail in Newport's public square.[66]

With several successful businesses, Thomas and Dinah grew prosperous in their new Kentucky home. He must have been a vigorous man with a compelling personality, and he was musical as well, entertaining visitors with traditional Scottish fiddle songs when they visited his home. One lodger who stayed there in 1812 told of how "before we had finished our breakfast, Mr.

Kennedy drew a fiddle from a box and struck up 'Rothemurchie's Rant.' He played in the true Highland style and I could not stop to finish my breakfast, but started up and danced Shan Trews."[67] Their home in Kentucky was a place where Kennedy's talents, business acumen and assertiveness paid off, and his family flourished. He and Dinah died in 1821, she first at the age of eighty-six and Thomas five months later when he was eighty years old. He wrote a will which was a model of inclusiveness in that his children and grandchildren were named with legacies but also Dinah's children from her first family including Peggy Piersol, the widow of Dinah's son Zacheus who remained behind in Pennsylvania to keep the home fires burning.[68]

Thomas' inventory was a revelation of more than wealth in cash and property consisting of a house and seven lots valued at more than $5,000. It indicated that he adopted a practice he had not known before moving to Kentucky. Among his many books, and amidst the silver spoons and feather beds, Kennedy also had four slaves who were probably a family. There was a woman named Maria valued at $300, a black man called Joseph worth $200 plus two children, Abby and John.[69]

Robert and Sally Kyle came to Kentucky with her mother and stepfather, and they too settled on the Licking River near the Kennedy farm. The bond between them began initially through Sally and Robert's marriage, but once they landed in Kentucky, it was also one of survival in a new land. It was apparent there was respect and trust between Thomas Kennedy and Robert Kyle that, since he was only ten years older, was probably more like brothers than father and son. Robert Kyle first stamped his presence in the community in 1795 when he paid taxes on 100 acres, two horses and ten cows.[70] Between 1797 and 1799, he helped mark new county roads, one at the behest of his father-in-law where he marked a road between his house on Kyle Lane down to Kennedy's ferry.[71] Like Kennedy, Kyle too became prominent in the community, first as a probate judge in Covington. Later in 1810 when he was almost sixty years old, he was appointed a county coroner, replacing Joseph Kennedy who was elected to the State House of Representatives.[72] Time passed and Sally and Robert's children grew up and married into Campbell County families. First among them was Dinah Kyle who was about twenty when she married John White in 1800. Jean was about seventeen when her father gave permission to marry Henry Dixon in December 1802. The following year in October, their brother Samuel married Anna McKay. From 1810 to 1817, three Kyle siblings married into the Rich family. They were John Kyle who married Sarah Rich in 1810, Thomas Kyle who married Susan Rich in 1815 and Sarah Kyle who married Joseph Rich in 1817. Their sister Molly Kyle married Robert Long on 14 Feb 1812.[73]

Robert Kyle had more than a year to think about the will he wrote prior to his death on 15 Mar 1825, one that began with a description of him as "my aged and comparatively worn out old body." A judge in Alexandria, Kentucky, said about Kyle, that he "wrote his own will, [that] he had been a Justice of the Peace in Covington Kentucky for over 20 years and was probably more capable than any one else." He also noted that Kyle had holdings of about 900 acres in and around Covington.[74] Kyle's will was explicit which was probably in character with the man who set his wishes down on 4 Nov 1823. There was every reason to be precise, because he had a large family and a lot of real estate to disburse.

While he was fair to all of his children, he also had his reasons for dividing the property as he did. Aside from the land in Kentucky he owned, he had 1,000 acres in Ohio he intended to give to his children. Kyle's debts were few as he stated, but he wanted them paid punctually. To Sarah, who he described as "my industrious partner, helpmate and affectionate wife," he left his farm, all monies due him to use as she wished, and all their personal belongings. When she died, he gave their personal items to Zacheus, but the farm and another property in Covington he wanted sold. He directed his executors to "be very careful and lay my farm off into such number of lots as will best advance the interest of my above named daughters," who were Dinah White, Jean Dixon, Molly Long and Sarah Rich. Included separately was 144 acres in Clermont County purchased from his eldest son Samuel B. Kyle, who had since died. That he wanted sold and divided among his sons, named as John, Thomas, Robert, Zacheus and Samuel's children. He also gave his sons a 1,000-acre tract in Clermont County that he had surveyed and where most of them lived. Kyle appointed his youngest son, Zacheus, his brother-in-law, Samuel Kennedy, and Alfred Sanford his executors. Joseph Kennedy and Joseph Rich posted a $15,000 bond, later raised to $30,000, as security. Both Sanford and Kennedy refused the responsibility.[75]

In 1830 when Sally Kyle was about seventy years old she lived on the Covington farm with two of her children and their spouses, Sarah and Joseph Rich and Zacheus Kyle and his wife Mary Cochran.[76] Sally Piersol Kyle died on 9 Oct 1838 and was buried beside her husband in Clermont County's Mt. Moriah Cemetery.[77] By then all of her children, except for Zacheus, had moved to Union Township. Eventually he joined his siblings who were raising their families and enjoying the benefits of their father's legacy to them.

Joseph Kennedy was about six to eight years younger than his half-sister Sally Kyle. They grew up together and although he was a single man upon arriving in Kentucky, he first married in Hamilton County, Ohio when he was twenty-six years old. On 15 Aug 1794 he wed Agnes (Nancy) Cummins[78] and they had a son born the following year. Nancy died in 1802 and the following year Joseph married Rachel Todd who died in 1805 without children. He married again the same year to Nancy Sanford and their only child died of smallpox. Joseph was a widower thrice over with a young son when he married for the fourth time on 11 Oct 1807. His wife was the widow Mary Davis Kenny who brought with her three children from her first marriage to Robert Kenny.[79] It would be many years later but eventually Sally Kyle and Joseph Kennedy, siblings by marriage, would also become in-laws when one of her children married his stepdaughter.

Robert Kenny and Polly Davis

Born in 1793, Robert Kyle Junior, known as Bobby, was a middle child in a family of nine. When he was about nineteen, he joined Porter's 16th Regiment of Kentucky Militia, the same regiment in which Joseph Kennedy was a militia officer.[80] He was twenty-seven years old and living with his parents in

Covington when on 5 Oct 1820, he married Mary Kenny, daughter of Robert Kenny and Mary Davis. His father posted bond, as did Joseph Kennedy who was Mary's stepfather.[81] How Kennedy became responsible for Mary Kenny was a story that began years earlier when history repeated itself. This sometimes happens, but not always so soon, nor in nearly the same way as the first time. Joseph's story was much like his father's courtship of his mother, Dinah Davis Piersol.

Her name was Mary Davis but she was called Polly. She married Robert Kenny, a blacksmith, who was about thirty-five years old when they wed in the First Presbyterian Church of Carlisle Pennsylvania on 14 Nov 1796.[82] Polly was no more than sixteen years when she gave birth to their first child three months later.[83] Born in February 1797, he was named James after Robert's father.

James Kenny was of age by 1752 when he first bought land in Cumberland County, so he was probably born between 1725-1731. Others by that name were in nearby Chester and Lancaster Counties much earlier, so possibly his family lived in Pennsylvania before James was married. His children's names were given in his will but the name of his wife and their mother is unknown. He probably married about 1752, because his first public record was on 10 Jul 1752 when he received a warrant for 100 acres in Middleton Township on the banks of Conodoguinet Creek.[84] He appeared frequently thereafter in county records beginning in 1753 when he paid taxes. By 1759 he had a warrant for an additional 200 acres.[85] He was also active in the community, serving on the county's grand jury in 1758 and many times as a juror over the next ten years. He was Middleton Township's overseer of the poor in 1766 and again in 1772.[86] In 1768 Kenny signed a petition for a road near his house that described where in the county he lived, "leading out of the road that comes from Croghan's Gap to Carlisle at Chamber's Mill on the mouth of Letort Springs and from there to Carlisle." Some of those who signed the petition were well known to Kenny, one signed his will, another bought land from his son, and yet another owned property bordering Kenny's land.[87] In 1769 James and Mathew Kenny were taxed in Middleton Township, James for livestock and 60 of 200 acres that was cleared. Mathew had 150 acres with 50 cleared and a similar number of livestock.[88] They may have been brothers, and since James appointed him as estate executor, they were surely related. When Mathew died in Mifflin County in 1811, he had nine children, of whom five shared the same first names as James Kenny's children, strongly suggesting close kinship.[89]

James Kenny had four children who were probably born in this order, Jane who married William McClurg, Rachel who married John Lytle, Robert Kenny born about 1762 who married Polly Davis, and Elinor born about 1765 who married Brice Smith. Each was named in their father's will of 27 Sep 1783, although only Jane and Rachel were married at the time. James Kenny was probably no more than 50 years old when he died, literate because he signed his name and traditional because he left all of his substantial landholdings to his only son, Robert. He left Elinor a dowry of £50, half of the household goods and some cattle, but also a directive that she live with her brother until she married. He gave his married daughters money indirectly through their husbands. Robert was his executor, but as he was only about twenty-one years old, he asked Mathew Kenny to serve as well. Witnesses were brothers Hugh and Brice Smith and John Waddell. Kenny's will was recorded on 21 Jul 1784, but Mathew Kenny refused to serve.[90] As a single man, Robert inherited a large and valuable estate of about 415 acres, mostly in Middleton but also 100 acres in Tyrone Township. Elinor lived with her brother until she married Brice Smith on 23 Jul 1785.[91]

Cumberland County was wild, untamed and sparsely populated before 1800. The local courts heard indictments for petty crimes and for the years between 1780 and 1799, these records have been published. However, they show that eighteenth century foibles were different from today's misdeeds in terminology only. Then, a man might be fined for keeping a "tippling house," whereas today he would be charged with selling liquor without a license. Some crimes were serious, such as case recorded about a cold February night in 1780 when five of Kenny's neighbors entered a widow's house while she was sleeping. Awakened by the sounds of voices at her door, she opened it only to be threatened by two men standing at her door, one holding a gun and the other brandishing a cutlass in her face. As she stood speechless they rushed into her house, ransacked it both upstairs and down looking for one of her relatives. Finding no one they took a rifle, and as a parting gesture set fire to the exterior of her house. As they headed off toward the barn she yelled after them not to set it on fire too. The Kenny men were as aggressive as were some of their neighbors. In 1783 a man was indicted twice for assault and battery, first on Robert and then against James Kenny. In 1788 Robert Kenny was accused of the same offense. In 1793 Robert was cited for neglect of his duty as supervisor of the highways. In his last offense, Kenny, a blacksmith, was indicted for stealing another man's anvil; the accuser was Hugh Smith, brother of Brice who was Roberts's brother-in-law.[92]

Robert Kenny lived a few miles south of the ridge of the Blue (Tuscarora) Mountains separating Cumberland from Perry County that is a part of North Middleton Township. His log house was southeast of Sterrett's (Croghan's) Gap), the path over the mountain to Carlisle Springs and from there into the town of Carlisle. His house was sixteen by twenty-five feet, built of logs, with two barns nearby on a total in 1798 of 294 acres.[93] It was still standing in 1886, and by looking through its loopholes, you could see anyone approaching it.[94] Robert Kenny enlarged his father's landholdings, first with 302 acres he bought at a sheriff's sale on 18 Jan 1786.[95] In 1798 Kenny rented some of his property but lived on the 56-acre farm where he probably grew up. The 100 acres in Tyrone Township he had surveyed and sold to his neighbor George Sanderson for £630.[96] Tax records between 1785 and 1794 show that Robert bought and sold property because at any time, he had between 200 and 300 acres under warrant, and as an example, in 1794 he received a warrant for 40 acres near his neighbors Sanderson and Lambertson.[97]

Robert Kenny married Polly Davis in November 1796 when she was six months pregnant with his child. Her parents are unknown but she was born in Pennsylvania sometime after March 1800, so she was probably a local girl, perhaps an orphan.[98] By 1800 the couple, who lived in Middleton Township, had two sons; the eldest was James who was born in 1797.[99] Kenny served in the local militia between 1790 and 1800 as did of his brother-in-law, William McClurg.[100] By late winter of 1802, Kenny began making plans to leave

Cumberland County and move to Kentucky. First, on 21 Apr 1802, he patented two properties totaling 313 acres that he and Polly sold to Philip Ziegler for $6,533 cash, paid in full on that day. They were adjoining tracts in Middleton Township, one called Monmouth was 97 acres on the Conodoguinet Creek and the other known as Dover was 216 acres.[101] The couple probably left shortly after with James who was five and baby Mary who was about a year old. In springtime the Ohio River could safely carry them downriver to Cincinnati where, when they debarked they probably met Rebecca Kennedy who ferried them across the river to Kentucky where they became acquainted with Thomas Kennedy who ran the ferry from the other side. They were certainly in Kentucky when their third child, a boy named John Jefferson Kenny was born on 5 Aug 1803 in Covington.[102]

Robert and Polly Kenny settled in Newport, on the east side of the Licking River, directly across the river from "The Point" where the Kennedy family lived. In 1804 the army had built an outpost in Kenton County at the confluence of the two rivers.[103] While they were being built and certainly afterwards, the Newport Barracks supported local industry giving a blacksmith like Kenny a lot of work. While Kenny's name appeared on Newport tax lists in 1805 and 1806 only, there is no record that he bought property in Kentucky. In 1805 he paid taxes on seven slaves, three over sixteen years and four under that age, and three horses. The following year he was only taxed for his horse.[104] In April 1805, with a partner, Kenny was granted a license to keep a tavern at his house in Newport.[105] Three months later, on 31 Jul 1805, he paid $260 to a man from Cincinnati for a mulatto slave named Grace, and while his intent is unknown, it may have been to assist Polly in the home and to work in the tavern.[106]

Jonathan Hewling was a Newport neighbor and tavern keeper in 1800. He was also Newport's jailer from 1805-1807, and apparently knew Kenny well as he and Polly lived nearby.[107] Although it is a second hand story, the word was out that Kenny did not treat his wife very well. He also did not live long after their move to Newport. Whether from illness or accident, Robert died on Saturday, 30 May 1807 without a will. His obituary called him "captain," probably because in was in the militia, but whether from Kentucky or his home in Cumberland County has not been determined. He was buried the following day in Cincinnati within the brotherhood of the Masons of Cincinnati Lodge No. 13.[108]

Polly was the estate executor, and his personal property inventory revealed much about his profession and interests. He was an active blacksmith holding 100 pounds of iron, 25 pounds of steel and blacksmith tools ready for any order. On hand was a substantial supply of iron and steel farm and kitchen tools, plus knives and axes of all sizes, He had on hand and for sale nearly every variety of tool necessary for either the house or farm. Much of what was in the inventory he made, certainly the pitchforks and shovels, a crow bar, trammels to hang pots in the fireplace, cutting and butcher knives. He also had a well-furnished house. For instance, Robert's rifle was worth $10, but the china and tableware, some of it silver, was valued at over $80. Three of their four beds were valued at $117, an indication that creature comforts were important to them.

He was not always standing over an anvil, dressed in a blacksmith's apron, because among the barrels and kegs, the shovels and tongs was an abundance of wearing apparel. Robert favored nice clothing and footwear, but for the era they lived in and considering that Kentucky was a barely cleared wilderness in 1807, Robert's variety and quantity of clothing was more than most people wore or even owned. He had two sets each of hats, boots, shoes, suit coats, close coats, pantaloons, plus an umbrella and his military uniform. His entire wardrobe was worth $115, or nearly as much as their bedding, usually the most valuable of personal property. He owned both a shotgun and a pair of pistols with holsters. Not everyone had "a tooth drawer and a case of lancets" for pulling teeth, and so he may have been a man skilled in the primitive kind of dentistry practiced at the time. Kenny was also literate and had a number of "books of different kinds" and although not otherwise identified they were valued at $57. He was musical and owned two violins, together worth $45. Kenny had no bank notes or notes on loan but held $100 in cash. He also owned a "spy glass" (a telescope) valued at $30. Worth more than anything else in his inventory was a slave valued at $233 who was probably the young girl, Grace.

His total account of household goods and tools was worth $1,265, a moderately sizeable estate for the times, although nowhere near the sum paid to him five years before by Philip Ziegler when he sold his inheritance. Kenny was a craftsman rather than a farmer and because he lived in town, the only implements he had were those tools he made for others use. He had three saddles, one was for a woman, but he had no horses or other livestock, indicating this was property he brought with the move to Kentucky. Polly may not have had a garden but instead purchased what they needed locally. As an example, the one spinning wheel in the house was of so little value that it may not have been used at all, indicating that instead they purchased their clothing or had it made for them.[109]

What happened next in Polly's life was entered into record many years later when she applied for a widow's pension, not from Kenny's service, but from that of her second husband, Joseph Kennedy. Robert's estate was probably settled quickly but as a widow with small children, she was defenseless in a place she had lived in only two years, and because she was far from home, she had no family looking after her needs. However, there was someone who recognized her vulnerability as well as her assets. Polly was a relatively young widow, only 27 when Robert died, and Jonathan Huling had an idea of who might be a suitable husband. His niece, Mary Reed, described how he rescued Polly saying, "She lived near my uncle Jonathan Huling. He used frequently to be talking with Mrs. Kenny about marrying again, and told her that Joseph Kennedy would make her a kind good husband and that he, my uncle, would recommend him to her. He did so. I have often heard my uncle say, he made the match [and] they were married."[110] Joseph Kennedy, the son of Thomas Kennedy and Dinah Davis Piersol Kennedy was born in 1768 and so he was nearly 40 years old when he and Polly Kenny were married on 11 Oct 1807.[111]

Aside from the three children Polly brought to the marriage, by 1813 she and Joseph had several children of their own. In June that year her sons, James and (John) Jefferson Kenny, appeared in court and asked that Joseph Kennedy be declared their legal guardian, and so he was.[112] Polly's daughter Mary was not mentioned although she was certainly one among the many children in their household. In 1828 when his widow sold the last of Robert Kenny's land, 56 acres in Cumberland County, to Philip Ziegler for $354, none of Polly's children lived in Kentucky. John was in Lauderdale, Alabama, James lived in Perry County, Tennessee, and Mary Kenny had married Robert Kyle and was living across the river in Clermont County, Ohio.[113] Joseph died on 22 Aug 1825, so when she assisted in the sale of her first husband's property, she was called the widow Kennedy.[114] Polly filed for a widow's pension in 1852 but never completed the paperwork prior to her death on 1 Feb 1855. She was buried next to Joseph Kennedy in Linden Grove Cemetery, Kenton County, Kentucky. James Kenny lived four years after signing the deed and died on 26 Jan 1833. He was buried in Mt. Moriah Cemetery where many generations of the Kyle family were laid to rest. Years later Mary Kenny Kyle was buried next to her brother James, and when Bobby died, he was buried between them. Mary's tombstone succinctly identifies her as "Mary Kenny, wife of Robert Kyle, Sr., died 5 Mar 1868 in the 67 year of her age."[115]

John Kenny lived in Lauderdale County, Alabama in 1828 but moved to Williamson County, Tennessee by 10 Dec 1833 where he married Jane Douglass, who lived there.[116] They remained in the area raising a large family. By trade John was a tanner and he guided his son John Junior in the craft. Years later, although trained as a doctor, Junior applied what he had learned from his father and opened a tan-yard for a brief time in Dover, Arkansas. He did not marry. When his mother Jane died on 7 Jan 1886, nine of her eleven children were living. John Senior died two years later on 4 Sep 1888, and both were probably buried near Nashville, Tennessee.[117]

Robert Kyle and Mary Kenny

The Kyle family, of which Bobby was the second generation, owned 1,000 acres in Union Township, Clermont County, Ohio. In 1815 it was all second rate uncleared land with no marketable timber, a sign that most of the family was not living there. Tax records between 1815 and 1817 showed the land had been divided between the children. The eldest, Samuel Bell Kyle had 248 acres, as did Thomas. The others, John, Bobby and Zacheus, each had 211 acres. The land was valuable, because even without improvements, their taxes of $4 and $5 were nearly twice as much as some of their neighbors paid.[118] By 1820 Samuel, John and Thomas Kyle were living on their inheritance.[119]

When Mary Kenny, daughter of Robert and Polly, was married in Campbell County on 5 Oct 1820, it was her stepfather, Joseph Kennedy, who signed and gave his permission. She was twenty and her husband Bobby, son of Robert Kyle Senior and Sarah Piersol, was twenty-seven years old. Sometime between their marriage and 1830, the couple moved to Ohio and settled on Bobby's inheritance. By that date, his sister Dinah who was married to John White was living there also. By 1830 Bobby and Mary had two sons, Jefferson and Robert, however five children were living in their household, three of them must have been the children of his deceased brother, Samuel.[120] Before he died on 26 Apr 1823, Samuel Kyle was married to Rebecca. He was ill and she was not the mother of his children, so he appointed his brother Robert guardian of his several children. To fulfill Samuel's will it was necessary to sell the land and distribute the proceeds to his heirs. The widow and second wife refused to leave the house until she received her dower rights, and filed a petition to get it. When Robert Kyle pled for the children before the court, the judge refused her request, asked her to leave the premises and ordered her to pay the court costs.[121]

Robert and Mary's son Jefferson was born 28 Jan 1823 and named after her brother. Robert Junior was born in 1827 and to distinguish himself from his father, he used the middle initial "K" likely for Kenny. Next, but long before it became a sweetheart's holiday, Frances Eliza Kyle was born on 14 Feb 1831. Two years later Nancy, called Nanny, was born. John was born in 1840, then Prudence, called Prudie in 1842. Alfred, the youngest child was born in 1845.[122]

When viewed as a family, the Kyle's personal property taxes in 1826 revealed they were typical but prosperous farmers. Of the three brothers and their nephew Joseph Kyle, they owned 21 cows and 12 horses, although not all were farm animals.[123] By 1835 Bobby Kyle had a stable of thoroughbred racehorses that he boarded with other breeders, and probably raced locally in Cincinnati. One horse was "Alexander Whip" and the other, "Sleeping Tiger," was "so well known to the public that it is deemed unnecessary to say anything in his favor here, except that he received the highest honors (a premium) at the last agricultural fair of Clermont County."[124]

Until the 1840s, packs of wolves roamed the Clermont County countryside, decimating the sheep population. The problem had not been rectified, and a story in the local newspaper indicated that someone took advantage of that knowledge. Community reinforcement was called for, and "Uncle Bobby Kyle," as many called him, was a foxhunter of local renown that had a large pack of hounds. Something was frightening the people of Afton so much that they were afraid to leave their homes at night. They became so frightened that they called in Kyle, imploring him to use his hounds to track down whatever beast was frightening them so much. He was told there were...

> "Terrible noises were heard after night in the neighborhood, especially on foggy evenings. The roaring was equal to that of an African lion in his native jungle. Timid people were afraid to step out of doors after night, and children hung on to their mother's dresses and refused to be comforted...Large animals were seen bounding about by moonlight and by starlight...More than once [Kyle's] hounds were brought over and the country was scoured thoroughly. There seemed to be two of them; one was heard in one direction and soon answered by another, perhaps half a mile away, but no trail could be found; nor could any wild animal be routed, though the bush was beat far and near."

Many months later, it was discovered that two men living near Batavia had caused the mischief using a "dumb bull," and when they tried the stunt again their plot to frighten the citizens of Batavia went awry somehow and they were caught and punished.[125]

Incidents such as these were usually the job of the town sheriff and had it happened later, Joseph Kyle would have been called in to handle it. He was a cousin of Bobby Kyle whose parents were John Kyle and Sarah Rich and in 1850 when he was thirty-nine he was elected to that office. *The Clermont Courier* reported it by saying that...

> "our new sheriff has had more than the usual labors of a term to perform but has managed to dispose of the business with great promptitude. Mr. Kyle came into office with some prejudice against him but we take pleasure in saying that no sheriff has done more in so short a time to inspire confidence among all parties. He is plain, easy and familiar in his manners and we believe is fully disposed to carry out in his official deportment the character of a frank, fearless and independent officer."[126]

In the two years following his election disaster struck, not once but repeatedly. For Joseph it began when his wife Lucretia who was thirty-three died during a cholera epidemic in Clermont County. Less than a month later their son, George, who was sixteen months old, also died. Three months after he buried his son, Kyle married Nancy Beckman who was twenty-two and a year later, she died. Six months after Nancy's death, Joseph married Alice Denison. Although he may have thrown his hat into the circle again, he served as sheriff for one term of four years only. In 1757, "Ex-Sheriff Kyle" again ran for office, this time as a state representative on the Democratic ticket, but he lost to an overwhelming Republican majority.

In the spring of 1859, men from all parts of the country were induced by various means to seek their fortunes in Colorado Territory. The term "Pike's Peak or Bust" is remembered locally today but at the time it was a slogan for those hoping to get rich quickly in the Colorado gold rush. Joseph Kyle may have lost on many levels, including a recent election, but he was never a man to give up and quit, and once again, he took a chance, this time in the West. In May 1859 he and several others from Withamsville struck out for Pike's Peak near Colorado Springs to search for gold. Not long after the newspapers, via the telegraph, began filtering back disastrous reports from the West. Headlines reported that thousands of men were leaving empty-handed, many hungry and angered because they were duped by a fraud. Some reports were exaggerated while others were complete fabrications about what really happened. For instance, "There is a report that Denver City and Aurora have been burned to ashes. The exasperated condition of those who have risked their lives...in the Pike's Peak fever, it is feared, will wreak a terrible revenge on those who have been engaged in fomenting the bubble." When the bombast was over and tempers quieted, men returned home poorer but hopefully wiser. Kyle evidently stayed in Colorado longer than others did but by November he was back in Clermont County where a brief aside in the newspaper reported that "Joseph Kyle (and his cousins) who went...to Pike's Peak last spring returned on last Friday. They are all in good health." Joseph was sixty-four years old when he succumbed at home to typhoid pneumonia on 10 Apr 1875. Among his other accomplishments was being first in the county to achieve the degree of Mark Mason, so that when he was taken to the cemetery near Tobasco he was accompanied by the brethren of the R. A. M. and buried with all due honors.

Robert Kyle 1793-1882 "The Old Fox Hunter"

Robert Kyle (1792-1882) photograph, Mt. Carmel, ca. 1850

Robert Kyle (1792-1882), Mary Kenny Kyle (1801-1868)
ca. 1850, Mt. Carmel, Ohio

Robert Kyle (1792-1882) "The Old Foxhunter"
photograph, Mt. Carmel, Ohio, ca. 1870

Robert Kyle (1 Jan 1792-30 Jan 1882)
Mt. Moriah Cemetery, Mt. Carmel, Ohio

Mary Kenny Kyle (1801-5 Mar 1868), wife of Robert Kyle
Mt. Moriah Cemetery, Mt. Carmel, Ohio

For a farmer's son he had lived on the high side of adventure, won some and lost some, but no one could say he had not tried.[127]

Every year in the fall, fairs were held across the state of Ohio. Some were countywide and others local. At harvest time everyone came together as either a visitor or a participant to celebrate the bounteous return of the land, where prizes were awarded for the biggest and the best. Prized vegetables and fruits were entered for prizes and so were flowers of every kind. Culinary awards were given for best cake, biscuits, bread, white and sponge cakes, jellies, honey and molasses. The fair was just outside the town of Batavia and the Kyle family heavily endorsed it. Newspaper articles from 1850 through the 1861 fair show just how involved they were as a family. At the third annual fair in 1851, Bobby Kyle represented Union Township, but he also won top prizes for a bull calf and his buck lambs. Kyle was at the 1857 fair at Olive Branch where, an expert with horses, he was on a committee to determine their ages. By then he took top prizes in many areas including for his cattle, pigs, sheep and ducks. In the "Blooded Horses" class he won the sweepstakes for the best colt.

By 1858 Clermont County had grown to the point that there were two annual agricultural fairs, one in Olive Branch and the other in Bantam, and there was great rivalry between them. That year while her father Bobby was a judge for the local fruit crop, Prudie Kyle, who was sixteen, was on the committee to judge floral arrangements. Again Kyle won top prizes for a stallion and for his hogs. By 1859, the *Clermont Courier* reported that even with bad weather threatening from above, crowds as large as 10,000 attended the Olive Branch fair to see more than 1,200 entries. The Floral Hall was beautifully decorated and the displays of fruits, preserves and needlework were of the finest kinds— although oil painting had fallen off in comparison to previous years. Many were there to try the new Singer sewing machines and throughout the hall an audible buzz accompanied those trying out mechanical sewing for the first time. Farmers Hall displayed the latest reaping and threshing machines, yet again Bobby Kyle took honors for his sheep and swine, and he continued to hold sway in those areas through the 1862 fair.[128]

Surrounded by Kyle cousins, Bobby and Mary's children grew up on a farm midway between Mt. Carmel and Tobasco. They were from large families with multiple children who all looked somewhat alike, and easily identified as one of those Kyle kids. Bobby and Mary were in their 40's or 50's when they sat for a photograph, and if faded memories revealed anything about them it was apparent that he was powerfully built although probably not very tall. A portrait in his youth revealed he had light hair, probably blond, light blue eyes and regular features that might be considered handsome. Mary Kenny had large pale eyes either blue or green, and even as an older woman her hair remained dark. Her assets were deep-set eyes and a well-shaped face and as a young woman she was probably pretty. With parents of very different countenances, their children were probably a wide variety of combined features as expressed through the Kyle characteristics. They attended local schools and many of them belonged to the Universalist Church. They married locally and most of them remained within a few miles of Union Township. Among the first to marry in the third generation was Jefferson Kyle who wed Catherine Vail on 15 Jan 1846.[129] On 28 Apr 1850 Eliza Kyle married Perry Morrison. Her brother Robert K. married

Lucy Witham in 1852 and Nanny Kyle married Merritt Johnson in 1855. Prudie was wed in 1861 to Cortline Manning. In 1863 John Kyle married Joanna Sweeney and the last to marry was Alfred who wed Levina Fitch in 1870.[130]

Natural curiosity, but also the need to sell newspapers, prompted a local rag in 1860 to publish land values for the wealthiest members of the county. It also provided many statistics about a narrow area. The richest was Miami Township with an average land value of $42,000, but the second wealthiest was Union Township with an average of $31,000 properties. No lands valued at less than $8,000 were listed and three properties were valued at over $230,000. The average landowner for that township owned land worth about $25,000, thus Zacheus Kyle's land at $29,000 was of above average value. Their readers enjoyed poring over their neighbors' business and some called to complain they were left off the list, so a second list was published a couple of weeks later. New names added in Union Township were Joshua Durham whose land was valued at $13,000 and Robert Kyle whose land was worth $12,500.[131]

Mary Kenny Kyle lived long enough to see all but her youngest son, Alfred, settled down and get married. She was 67 years old when she died on 5 Mar 1868. It had been Mary's fortune not to bury any of her children and most lived many years after she died, so that there were many hands to lift the coffin and carry it to its final resting place in Mt. Moriah Cemetery. Although many years after their mother died, two of her children died within a year of each other. First was Frances Eliza who died on 16 Mar 1888, and next was her brother Jefferson who died on 10 Nov 1889.[132] Most of their siblings lived another fifteen to twenty more years, and some outlived their father. On the day he died, 30 Jan 1882, Bobby Kyle was 89 years old and ready to lay his burden down. Born in Pennsylvania, he was married in Kentucky but planted his seed in Ohio and from it sprang forth a dynasty. He was one of the township's most recognizable figures, a vigorous man almost to the end, remembered most as a foxhunter who, when he was too old to get behind the plow, he mounted his horse and with his pack of hounds went into the woods to hunt. On the day of his funeral, if it was a typical January day, the bitter air penetrated deep into the flesh of the mourners, even though all were bundled in their warmest attire. Accompanying his coffin was a procession that, if composed only of family members, was a long line of wagons and buggies slowly wending their way to Mt. Moriah where he was buried. In keeping with the solemn occasion, *The Clermont Sun* produced an obituary suitable to its subject that said:

> Robert Kyle, probably the oldest and most noted pioneer of Union Township died on the old home farm near Mt. Carmel on Monday morning. At the time of his death he was 88 years of age. He came from Kentucky and settled in Union township in 1814 on the farm where he died. Until within a few years he was a man of wonderful vigor and even up until two years ago was able to engage in his favorite sport, foxhunting, riding as erect as five-sixths of the young men of the present day. The father of the deceased, Robert Kyle, Sr., and his family were originally from Pennsylvania but settled in Kentucky in 1792, and a short time after bought the Kyle tract of 1000 acres in Union township, where all his children,

including Robert, settled as they came of age. The funeral of the deceased took place on Tuesday.[133]

Among Bobby Kyle's personal effects, his attorney found a parchment patent dated 13 May 1796 that was according to a newspaper article, "signed by G. Washington, President." It was the original grant awarded to Robert Morrow for his service in Virginia's Continental army during the Revolutionary War, which his agents in the west sold to Robert Kyle on 7 May 1796.[134] About three years later the estate was settled and the land was divided among Bobby's seven children. Eliza Kyle Morrison received 33 acres in Union Township, part of a larger tract of 211 acres.[135] When she married Perry Morrison in 1852, she did not leave home because wherever she went in the narrow band between Mt. Carmel and Tobasco she was surrounded by family. The Morrison family lived nearby, and when Perry bought a farm in Mt. Carmel, it was right in the heart of Clan Kyle.

Robert Kyle (1751-15 Mar 1825)
Mt. Moriah Cemetery,
Mt. Carmel, Ohio

Sarah (Piersol) Kyle
(ca. 1760-1838) Mt. Moriah
Cemetery, Mt. Carmel, Ohio

Robert Kyle replacement tombstone honoring Revolutionary War Veterans;
Robert Kyle, Ensign, 6th PA Militia, Revolutionary War, 1751-1825

Appendix A

JACOB HEWITT FAMILY BIBLE

Hewitt Family Bible, William Buckner McGroarty, author of *Hewitt Family: The Ancestry of Mrs. Sophia Hewitt Buckner, Wife of Dr. Philip Johnson Buckner*. The author included in the manuscript the typed copy he made about 1912 of the contents of the original bible, in Sophie Higgins McTamany's possession. Her grandmother was Sophie Hewitt who married Dr. Philip Johnson Buckner. In 1786, Eli Hewitt entered the first records into the bible. On 16 Oct 1795, Richard Hewitt entered other birth dates into the bible.

Richard Davis, Sr. b. Oct 26, 1697, Ruth Davis Sr. b. Dec 28, 1700

Children of Richard Davis and Ruth Warfield:
(Ages written by Ely Hewitt in year 1786)
Thomas Davis b. 2d Sept 1722,
Richard Davis Jr., b. January 10 1724/5
John Davis, son of Richard b. Oct 6, 1726
(Ruth) Davis b. 12 January 1728/9, married Jacob Hewitt b. Aug 17, 1728
Caleb Davis, b. Sep 10, 1731
(M)ary Davis b. Apl 20, 1734
Joshua Davis b. Sept 13, 1737
Elizabeth Davis b. Apl --- 1740

Children of Jacob Hewitt and/or Ruth Davis Elder
(Written by Richard Hewitt Oct. 16, 1795)
Delila Elder, b. 17__
Rt (Robert) Hewitt, b. 23d Nov 17(57?)
Cb (Caleb) Hewitt, b. 4th Feb 17 (59?)
Jb (Jacob) Hewitt b. 16 June 17 (61?)
Eli[zabeth] Hewitt b. 28 Dec 17(63?)
Richard Hewitt born 28th July 1765
Ey (Ely) Hewitt b. Aut __, 1767
Em (Ephraim) Hewitt b. March 17, 1770, married Elizabeth Hall, b. 22 Jul 1766
Ruth Hewitt b. 30 Sept 1772

Children of Ephraim Hewitt and Elizabeth Hall:
Nancy Hewitt b. Apl 16, 1793, m. 1) Jno Hall; 2 ___ Holmes
Elizabeth Hewitt b. Sept 26, 1794, m. Wm. Masterson, in Ohio Jan 17, 1826
Eli Hewitt, b. Aug 2 1796, d. March 6 1798
Ruth Hewitt, b. March 24, 1798, m. James Woods
Clarissa Hewitt, b. Feb 23 1800, m. Luther Calvin, or Colvin
Sophia Hewitt, b. Feb 3 1802 in Pa., m. Dr. P. J. Buckner, in Ohio, Oct. 8, 1822
Ephraim Hewitt, b. 1803
Mariah Hewitt b. July 30 1805 in Pa. m. Jas Woods, March 17, 1825 in Ohio
Harriett Hewitt b. March 7 1807, m. Chas. M. Ewing in Ohio March 27, 1827
Hannah Hewitt b. ___, m. Harvey King, in Ohio

Appendix B

THOMAS DAVIS WILL

20 Jan 1743/4, I Thomas Davis Senior, of Anne Arundel County, planter, being in perfect health, thanks be to God, do make this my last Will and Testament in manner and form following; I give and bequeath unto my loving wife, Mary Davis, (after my just debts and legacies mentioned in the following will are paid) all my personal estate to be by her possessed during her widowhood; I give unto my grandson, Caleb Davis, son of Richard, all that tract of land whereon his mother now dwells being part of a tract of land called *Duvall's Delight* containing 200 acres to be possessed by him, his heirs and assigns forever; but my will is that his mother, Ruth Davis, shall possess the said tract without any interruption or molestation whatsoever during her widowhood; I give to my son Thomas, 200 acres of land called *Laswells Hopewell* to be possessed by him, his heirs and assigns forever; I give to my son John two tracts of land, the one called *Davistone* containing 240 acres, the other called *What's Left* adjoining to the said *Davistone* containing 100 acres to him his heirs and assigns forever; I give to my son Samuel two parcels of land lying in Prince Georges County, the one called *The Forest* containing 68 acres, the other called *The Same Name* containing 50 acres, adjoining to the said 68 acres; to him his heirs and assigns forever; I give to my son Robert all that parcel of land being part of a tract called *Ranter's Ridge* containing 315 acres with one Negro boy named Harry) to him the said Robert his heirs and assigns forever; I give to my son Francis two parcels of land, the one called *The Pearl* being part of a tract called *The Diamond*, containing 150 acres, the other called now *Davis' Addition* being part of a tract called *Grinestone* containing 200 acres, to him his heirs and assigns forever, and also one Negro boy named Hector, three pair of hand irons belonging to the house where I now dwell, two pair of iron ...racks, three pair of tongs and a fire shovel; it is my will and desire that whatever part of my estate my children have received hitherto, or shall receive before my death, shall not after my decease be deemed or appraised as part thereof; Lastly, I hereby constitute my loving wife, Mary, together with my son John and Francis, executors of this my last will and testament; and what shall be remaining of my personal estate in my wife's possession, my will is that after her decease it be equally divided amongst my ten children, five sons and five daughter; hereby revoking all other wills heretofore by me made, ratifying and confirming this only as my last will and testament; in testimony whereof I have hereunto set my hand and affixed my seal this 20 Jan 1743/4; Thomas Davis, seal; signed, sealed acknowledged, published and pronounced in the presence of us, Michael Hackett, John (JS his mark) Sappington, Richard Sappington; probated 24 May 1749, Book 26:138.

9 Jan 1755, account by John Davis and Francis Davis in the settlement of the estate of Thomas Davis, Senior, late of Anne Arundel County, deceased; distribution of £80 each to husbands of decedent's daughters named as John Bateman (married Sarah Davis), John Riggs (married Mary Davis), Joseph Marriott (married Elizabeth Davis), Joshua Warfield (married Ruth Davis), and Sylvanus Marriott (married Rachel Davis).

Hall of Records, Annapolis for Anne Arundel County Maryland, Accounts, Book 37:9-11.

Appendix C

WILL OF RICHARD DAVIS WILL

17 May 1743, in the name of God, amen, I Richard Davis of Anne Arundel County, planter, being of sound mind and memory do make and ordain this my last will and testament; I give and bequeath unto my son Thomas Davis his heirs and assigns forever, 194 acres of land called *Davis' Purchase* lying in the county aforesaid; I give and bequeath unto my son Richard Davis, his heirs and assigns forever, 200 acres of land being part of a tract of land called *Dear Bought* lying in Prince Georges County; I give and bequeath unto my son John Davis his heirs and assigns forever, the remaining parts of the above tract of land called *Dear Bought*, it being 58 acres of land which will be laid out on the north east side in the best manner it can so as not to detriment either of my sons, Richard and John; I further will that my two eldest sons, Thomas and Richard, in consideration they having more lands willed them then my son John, do provide for my son John when he shall arrive at the age of 21 years, 100 acres of land, warranted, cleared off, but without any costs or charges to my son John, but to be at the cost and charges of my sons Thomas and Richard equally between them; I give and bequeath unto my son, Caleb Davis, his heirs and assigns forever a tract of land called *The Reverse* containing 93 acres of land lying in Anne Arundel County; I give and bequeath unto my son Joshua Davis, his heirs and assigns forever, the remaining part of the above tract of land called *Davis Purchase* in Anne Arundel County being 50 acres, to be laid out at the north end of the said land so as not to detriment either of my sons, Thomas and Joshua; I further will that my three sons, Richard and John and Caleb, have paid them by my executor, one cow and calf to each of them when they shall arrive gradually at the age of 21 years each; I will after my just debts are paid that the remainder of my personal estate be equally divided amongst my three daughters, Ruth and Mary, Elizabeth and my youngest son, Joshua; lastly I ordain, constitute and appoint Ruth, my beloved wife, executor of this my last will and testament ratifying and confirming this and no other to be my last will and testament; in witness whereof I have hereunto set my hand and offered my seal the day and year above written, Richard Davis, Seal; signed, sealed, pronounced and declared by Richard Davis to be his last will and testament in the presence of John Waters, Joseph Penn, John Evitts and Samuel Richardson.

18 Oct 1743, at the reading of the foregoing will the following probate was thus written; then came John Waters, one of the people called Quakers, who solemnly testified and declared; and Joseph Penn, another witness to the foregoing will, being duly and solemnly sworn on the Holy Evangel of Almighty God, [who] deposeth and saith that they saw the testator, Richard Davis, sign the foregoing will and heard him publish and declare the same to be his last will and testaments; that at the time of his so doing he was to the best of their apprehension of sound and disposing mind and memory; and that they signed their respective names as witnesses to the said will in the presence of the said testator; and at his request and the said John Waters, doth further solemnly possess, testify and declare, and Joseph Penn doth further deposeth, that they saw the two other subscribers witnesses to the same will, John Evitts and Samuel Richardson, sign their respective names as witnesses to the same in the presence of the said testator and at his request; sworn before me, William. MacNamara, Deputy Commissioner.

Appendix D

RECORDS FROM ROBERT HEWITT FAMILY BIBLE

<u>Births</u>
Robert Hewitt, born 23 Nov 1755
Anna Hewitt, wife of Robert Hewitt, born 6 Mar 1767
Caleb Hewitt, born 5 Oct 1788
Elizabeth Hewitt, born 6 Feb 1791
Hazael Hewitt, born 3 Mar 1793
Robert Hewitt, Jr., born 26 Mar 1796
Matilda Hewitt, born 31 Dec 1797
Emella Hewitt, born 29 Jan 1800
Mary Hewitt, Born 6 Sep 1809

<u>Marriages</u>
Robert Hewitt and Anna Shute, married 16 Sep 1786
Joseph P. Wharton, married to Caroline Hewitt by Rev. William Hume on 21 Sep 1830.

<u>Deaths</u>
Elizabeth Hewitt, 12 May 1794, was drowned in Philip Shute's spring;
age 3 years 4 months.
Robert Hewitt, Jr., 22 Sep 1803, was burned to death in a gin house,
aged 7 years 4 months.
Caleb Hewitt, 9 Sep 1816, was murdered in Nashville
age 27 years 11 months, 4 days
Anna Hewitt, wife of R. Hewitt, 17 Oct 1814, age 47 years 7 months 10 days
Mary Hewitt, 22 Jun 1824, age 22 years, 6 months, 3 days.
Robert Hewitt, 3 Mar 1837 at the home of Joseph P. Wharton

Tennessee Records: Bible Records and Marriage Bonds, "Genealogical Records: Early Tennessee Settlers, 1700's-1900's," Jeannette Tillotson Acklen. Made from a copy which is in possession of his great-great granddaughter, Mrs. George R. Bouton, need Margaret Wharton Chambers, Lebanon Tennessee.

Appendix E

JACOB HEWITT WILL

In the name of God, amen, I Jacob Hewitt, Fayette County, Pennsylvania, farmer; being sick and weak in body but of a sound and perfect memory (praise be given to God for the same). And knowing the uncertainty of this life on earth and being desirous to settle things in order, do make this my last will and testament in the manner and form following. First and principally, I commend my soul to almighty God who gave it and my body to the earth from whence it was taken to be buried in such decent Christian manner as to my executors hereafter named shall be thought meet and convenient. I devise unto my youngest son, Ephraim Hewitt, all my tract of land where I now live containing 180 acres as laid out by warrant order, together with another parcel of land (adjoining this tract and land of Isaac Jackson, Robert Jackson and John Coale) to make up 200 acres to him and his heirs or assigns forever. But my will is that my beloved wife, Ruth Hewett, shall enjoy the whole of my dwelling plantation during her natural life. Item, I give and bequeath unto my loving wife a Negro wench named Esther, and a Negro boy named Ben together with my stock of horses, horned cattle, hogs, sheep, farming utensils and household furniture during her natural life. Item, I devise unto my son Richard Hewitt 100 acres adjoining the tract of land where I now live and adjoining lands of William Kirk and John Higinbotham to him and his heirs or assigns forever. Item, I devise unto my son Robert Hewitt all the remaining part of the tract (where [he] now lives) after laying off from it what will make 200 acres as above described to Ephraim Hewitt and 100 acres to Richard Hewitt. The remaining part, be it more or less to him, Robert Hewitt, and his heirs or assigns forever; also 50 bushels of my crop of wheat now growing providing he should move down the river next spring. Item, I give unto my daughter, Elizabeth, a mulatto boy named Harry and a young mare, three years old. Item, I give unto my daughter Ruth, £50 (cash) or property, namely stock and household furniture and a young mare colt. Item, I give unto my two sons Caleb Hewitt and Ely Hewitt, £0.05 each in cash to be levied out of my estate. Item, I give unto my executors, after my lawful debts are paid, my crops that are growing to support [my] family. Also my two daughters, Elizabeth and Ruth, to have sustenance while they continue to live at home or single. Last, I appoint my son , Richard Hewitt, with my loving wife, executors of this my last will and testament hereby revoking all other wills made by me. Ratifying and confirming this only as my last will and testament, in witness whereof I have set my hand and affixed my seal, 7 Jun 1790; signed, sealed, acknowledged & published in our presence, John Coale, Hugh Crawford, Isaac Jackson. Jacob (x) Hewitt, (seal)

Fayette County S. S; 28 Jun 1790, before me, the Register for the probate of wills and letters of administration for [the] county, personally came John Coale, Hugh Crawford & Isaac Jackson, witnesses to the last will and testament, and on their solemn oaths, being separately examined, declared they saw and heard Jacob Hewitt the testator, sign and acknowledge the foregoing writing, purporting to be his last will and testament; and at the time he appeared to them to be of sound and disposing mind and memory. That it was in his last sickness, that neither of them knew of any undue influence used over his will or pleasure in making the will nor any other disposition or will made by him, and that it was signed by them in each other's presence, and of the testator. Given under my hand the same day, Alexander McClean, Register. Memorandum; testamentary letters in common form were granted to the executrix and executor the same day. Inventory to be exhibited 28 July next, and an account calculation and reckoning on 28th June 1790, or when lawfully required; last will & testament of Jacob Hewitt proved 28 Jun 1790.

Fayette County, Pennsylvania Probate Records: Wills 1:1-3, 1784-1833, Family History Library, Salt Lake City, Microfilm #0861065, 1:14; Will Book 1, pages 58-59;True and Correct copy, Register of Wills Fayette County [PA], Donald A. Redman, October 2001.

Appendix F

JOHN HALL WILL

9 Sep 1791, I John Hall of Union Township, Fayette County Pennsylvania, yeoman, being under heavy affliction of body but of disposing mind, make and ordain this my last will and testament. First I recommend my soul to the mercy of Almighty God who gave it and my body to the earth its original source. Second, those worldly goods and estate with which it has pleased God of his mercy and goodness to endow me, I give, bequeath and devise in the following manner. I give unto my dearly beloved wife Elizabeth, my mansion plantation "that part of all the tract of land I now live on and which I have not sold to my son Hugh, to be held and enjoyed by her with its profits and advantages during her natural life." I also bequeath unto her all my household goods and furniture, to be disposed of amongst the children as her prudence and judgment may direct, reserving for her own use so much as she may think necessary. It is my further will that my Negroes shall be disposed of as follows, my dearly beloved daughter Margaret [is] to have Philis, my Negro wench to her and [her] heirs and assigns forever. My Negro wench Jude, I give to my daughter Elizabeth. My Negro boy named Sam I give unto my daughter, Rose to them and their assigns. My stock and implements of husbandry and all the residue of my personal estate, I allow to be appraised and sold as soon as convenient after my decease, and one-third of the amount I bequeath to my beloved wife, my Negro man Dick excepted, who I bequeath unto my wife during her natural life, then at her decease to be disposed of at auction, and the money from it to be equally divided amongst all my children. It is my further pleasure that my son Hugh, after his mother's decease, shall hold and enjoy the whole of the tract of land I now live on with all the buildings and improvements thereon, to him his heirs and assigns forever, he paying unto Nancy, daughter of my son Thomas Hall, when she is sixteen years £50 of property or articles of produce, stock or clothing as she may need. I give and devise my two tracts of land in Franklin Township near John Carmichael's to my two daughters Elizabeth and Rose to be held and enjoyed by their heirs and assigns forever, they paying unto my daughter Margaret or her heirs or assigns, £100 in stock or produce such as may best suit her or them, within five years from my decease. I further give and bequeath unto my daughter, Sarah Boyle, four bonds on Henry Fitz, three of which are for £11.13 each and the other for £7; also two years rent of lands in Franklin Township deducting out enough to patent it. I further order and direct that out of the estate before devised to my son Hugh, that he pay unto my son Thomas or his heirs within two years after my decease, the sum of £10 lawful money, or the value in produce which best suits him, Thomas or his assigns. I allow and direct that before distribution of the moneys from the sale of personal estate, that as much as may be necessary shall be applied to procure a patent for the land, for discharging debts, and then the residue be divided. Last, I constitute my son, Hugh Hall, executor of this my last will and testament hereby revoking all former or other wills made by me. In witness whereof I have set my hand and seal the day and year first written. Sealed, delivered, pronounced & declared in the presence of Robert Jackson and Hugh Hall. John Hall (Seal). Fayette County, 18 Oct 1791, before me, Alexander McClean Esq., Register for the probate of wills in the county, personally came Robert Jackson & Hugh Hall, the witnesses to the last will and testament, and on their solemn oath declared they saw and heard the testator acknowledge the same to be his act and deed. That to the best of their knowledge he was at the time of doing in his right mind, that they know of no undue influence used in making [it], neither had he made any other later will to their knowledge; witness Alexander McClean, Register; proved 18 Oct 1791, memo that testamentary letters were granted in common form to the executors; inventory to be exhibited 18 November, account calculation and reckoning, 18 Oct 1792. Note: The words "and discharging the debts that may appear" was entered before signing.

Register of Wills Fayette County, Donald D. Redman; proved 18 Oct 1791, will book 1, page 17.

Appendix G

RICHARD HEWITT WILL

2 Mar 1827, in the name of God amen; I Richard Hewitt Sr., Brown County Ohio, farmer, being sick and weak in body, but of sound and perfect memory, being desirous to settle my earthly affairs, make this my last Will and Testament in the following manner; first and principally, I commend my soul to Almighty God who gave it, and my body to the earth from whence it was taken to be buried in such decent Christian manner as to my Executors shall think meet and convenient; I give to my oldest son Jacob Hewitt one dollar, to my second son Richard Hewitt Jr. all my wearing apparel, to my third son William Hewitt one dollar, to my fourth son John Hewitt one dollar; I promise and give unto my youngest son Eli Hewitt all my land where I now live containing 135 acres, together with all my farming utensils, horses, cattle, hogs, sheep and geese; also the whole of the profits from the rents of the farm for the present year, except that part of the farm cultivated by my son Richard Hewitt Jr., which he is to have rent free; to my oldest daughter Elizabeth Hewitt I give one dollar to be paid in store goods, by my son Eli Hewitt, out of the proceeds of the farm, by the first day of October 1828; to my youngest daughter Letty Ann Hewitt I give all my household furniture, also as much of the rents of the farm, from year to year as will board and cloth her genteely, and educate her until she is 18 years of age; at which time I require Eli Hewitt to pay to her a horse, saddle and bridle worth $100, a cow and calf, 12 head of sheep, a sow and pigs, a silk dress and other articles suitable to make a full suit of the best ladies clothes and a genteel suit of clothes each year she remains single; and in case he fails to comply with the above injunction Letty Ann Hewitt shall hold at her disposal such part of the land as will make that sum; I also enjoin my son Eli Hewitt to pay all my just debts; lastly I constitute my son Eli Hewitt and Philip J. Buckner, executors of this my last Will and Testament hereby revoking all other wills made by me, and ratifying and confirming this only as my last Will and Testament; in testimony whereof, I set my hand and seal in the presence of James Baker and Allen Woods; signed Richard (X) Hewitt. (Marked A.)

9 Mar 1827, whereas I Richard Hewitt Sr., Brown County Ohio, did on 2 Mar instant, make, sign, seal, publish and declare my last Will and Testament by which I devised among other things to my son Eli Hewitt, all my farming utensils, horses, cattle, hogs, sheep and geese, and whereas in an advertisement published by me for that purpose, this property together with various articles of household furniture was sold at public sale on 8 March, on a credit of 12 months, and the notes given for the purchase were made payable by my order to Eli; now be it known that I, Richard Hewitt, have made this codicil to the Will for the express purpose of declaring that the sale was held by my direction for Eli's benefit; and I hereby bequeath to him the monies due on the notes, as if they had been mentioned in the will, and hereby publish, seal and declare this codicil part of my last Will and Testament, as if it was in the Will before executed; in witness whereof I set my hand and seal, Richard (X) Hewitt Sr., signed, sealed, executed, published and declared as part of his last Will and Testament in our presence and hearing; testators Allen Woods and James Baker. (Marked B).

Brown County Ohio, Court of Common Pleas, April Term 1827; appeared in open court Allen Woods and James Baker, who saith they are witnesses to papers produced here said to be the last Will and Testament of Richard Hewitt Sr., deceased, marked Codicil A and B; that they were present when they were executed; that they heard the Testator acknowledge it, that they signed as witnesses in his and in each others presence, that they believe the Testator was of sound mind and judgment and not under any legal restraint; Allen Woods and James Baker; Sworn in open Court April 19 1827, Wm. Shepherd, Clerk.

March 5, 1827, (note by Richard Hewitt Sr.), Eliah Hewitt ple[a]se to let the b[e]arer John Hewitt have my bedste[a]d bed and bed[d]ing for his two sons, Eli and Richard, after my De[a]th; and the same not to be considered in the Will, and the youngest boy a ?; Richard Hewitt Sr., Attested to by Allen Woods and Fielding Martin. (Marked C).

Appendix G

Richard Hewitt Will, part 2.

March 8, 1827. (note by Richard Hewitt Sr.), With regard to my clothing, the black coat and Pantaloons belongs to Eli and the Perlise Coat and pantaloons also is his. The balance belongs to Richard Hewitt, Jr.; I had no right to them when I made my Will; these belong to them after my De[a]th; Richard Hewitt Sr., Attested to by Fielding Martin and Allen Woods. (Marked D).

April Term 1827, Brown County Ohio Court of Common Pleas, Allen Woods came personally into open court, was sworn and said he saw and heard Richard Hewitt deceased, direct Fielding Martin to sign the decedents name to the papers herewith exhibited marked "C and D," that he signed them in the testators presence and at his request as a subscribing witness, and in the presence of Fielding Martin, also a subscribing witness; that Hewitt was of sound mind and memory when he signed and under no restraint, and that he declared it to be his Will and desire that such should be performed at or after his decease; signed Allen Woods, sworn in open Court; Fielding Martin also came personally into open court, was sworn and said he witnessed the papers marked "C and D," said to be Codicils to the last Will and Testament of Richard Hewitt, Sr., deceased; that he signed Richard Hewitt's name to both papers at his request and in his presence and that of Allen Woods; that the Testator acknowledged it as his will; that he signed it as a subscribing witness; that he believes the Testator was of sound mind and memory at the time the papers were signed and was under no legal restraint at the time; signed Fielding Martin; subscribed in open Court.

23 Apr 1827, Georgetown, Brown County Ohio, the Last Will and Testament of Richard Hewitt, Sr. was produced in court by Eli Hewitt, one of the named executors who made oath, and proven by the oaths of Allen Woods and James Baker, the subscribing witnesses to the will and codicil, ordered to be recorded together with the proof thereof; whereupon Eli Hewitt came into open court, (Philip J. Buckner declining to take upon himself the burthen of executing the will) with Stephen Calvin and David Brown as his securities, and acknowledged bond of $800 dollars; thereupon a certificate is granted to obtain probate.

Richard Hewitt, Sr. will (1827); Brown County Will Book #1HB-VR, Co: 86-90, Recorder's Office, Brown County OH.

Appendix H

RICHARD D. HEWITT WILL

In the Name of the Benevolent Father of All, I Richard D. Hewitt, do make and publish this my last Will and Testament; first it is my Will that my just debts and all charges be paid out of my estate.

Second, all the rest and residue of my estate, wherever, whether real, personal, or mixed, I give and bequeath unto Mrs. Ann McClellan, Mrs. Elisabeth Bratton, Richard Hewitt, Jr. and Benjamin F. Hewitt, to be equally divided among them, and to be to them and their heirs, forever.

Third, it is my will that the interests of Richard D. Hewitt, Jr. and Benjamin F. Hewitt be held in trust for their use and benefit by Mrs. Mary H. Gehres, of Waverly, Ohio; my executor hereinafter named is instructed to pay over and deliver to Mrs. Mary H. Gehres, the interests of Richard D. Hewitt, Jr. and Benjamin F. Hewitt; and Mrs. Mary H. Gehres is hereby instructed to pay the same to them at such times, and in such amounts, as may be required for their maintenance and support; and Mrs. Mary H. Gehres is given full power over same, with authority to convert the whole or any part thereof into money, as she may deem best.

Fourth, I do hereby nominate and appoint Mr. Marion McClellan executor of this my last Will and Testament, and desire that no bond be required to him; I desire that no advertisement and no sale of my personal property be made, and that the Court of Probate direct the omission of the same in pursuance of the statute.

I hereby revoke all former Wills made by me; in testimony hereof, I have hereunto set my hand, this 4th day of March, A. D. 1903; signed Richard D. Hewitt.

Signed and acknowledged by Richard D. Hewitt as his last Will and Testament, in our presence and signed by us in his presence; John G. Schanseil and Charles M. Caldwell; 4 Mar 1903, filed 17 Apr 1903.

Appendix I

GERRITSEN FAMILY BIBLE

In the year of our Lord 1634 my honorable father Gerrit Remmersen was born in
    Oostvrieslandt in a village named Pilsum.
In the year of our Lord 1658 my honorable father Gerrit Remmersen arrived in this land at Amersfoort.
In the year of our Lord 1636 my honorable mother was born on Bermodus.
In the year of our Lord 1650 my honorable mother married Willem Gerritsen on Bermodus.
In the year of our Lord 1651 a son was born to her named Willem.
In the year of our Lord 1656 a son was born to her named Cornelius.
In the year of our Lord 1659 my honorable mother with her husband Willem Gerritsen arrived in this land
    at Amersfoort.
In the year of our Lord 1660 a daughter was born to her named Sarah.
In the year of our Lord 1662 a daughter was born to her named Hannah
In the year of our Lord 1662 my honorable mother's first husband the honorable Willem Gerritsen fell
    asleep in the Lord.
In the year of our Lord 1663 my honorable father married my honorable mother, my father aged
    28 years and my mother aged 26 years.
In the year of our Lord 1664 a daughter was born to her named Anna.
In the year of our Lord 1667 a son was born to her named Rem.
In the year of our Lord 1671 on the first day of October o.s. a Sunday a son was born to her named
    Samuel.
In the year of our Lord 1673 a daughter was born to her named Maria.
In the year of our Lord 1675 a daughter was born to her named Rachel.
In the year of our Lord 1678 the first of May my father and my mother with her family
    removed out of the bay to York Island to a hamlet named Sapochkanika.
In the year of our Lord 1678 the 27th December my honorable father fell asleep in the Lord on a Tuesday
    in the Morning, and was buried in Stuyvesant's church aged about 44 years.
In the year of our Lord 1685 the first of May my honorable mother removed with her family at Gravesant.
In the year of our Lord 1715 the 4th day of May my brother Rem Gerritsen fell asleep in the Lord at Cape
    May aged 48 years.
In the year of our Lord 1721 the 24th day of May my honorable mother fell asleep in the Lord on a
    Wednesday just before midnight and was brought to the grave on that Saturday in Gravesants
    Churchyard aged around 85 years.
In the year of our Lord 1722 the 2nd day of February my brother Willem Willemsen fell asleep n the Lord
    on a Friday evening around seven o'clock and was brought to the grave that Tuesday aged
    around 70 years.
In the year of our Lord 1729 the 15th day of March my sister Anna fell asleep in the Lord on a Saturday
    evening and was brought to the grave that Tuesday aged 64 years.
In the year of our Lord 1730 the 25th day of February my sister Hannah fell asleep in the Lord on a
    Wednesday morning about six o'clock and was brought to the earth that Friday aged about 68
    years.
In the year of our Lord 1738 the 10th day of May my brother Cornelius Williamsen fell asleep in the Lord
    on a Wednesday morning and was brought to the earth that Friday aged about 82 years.
In the year of our Lord 1749 the 8th day of January my sister Sarah fell asleep in the Lord on a Sunday,
    and was brought to the earth on that Wednesday aged 88 years.**
The 14th of June o.s. Anno 1695 on a Friday I Samuel Gerritsen married Yda Reyder.
The 12th day of September o.s. 1751 my honorable precious wife Yda fell asleep in the Lord on a
    Thursday about five o'clock in the morning aged about a month over five and seventy years
    and was brought to the earth on that Saturday.
I, Samuel Gerritsen and my wife Yda Ryder have lived in the matrimonial state six and fifty years and
    nearly three months.
The 4th September 1763 about 12 o'clock my father Samuel Gerritsen fell asleep in the Lord and was
    brought to the earth the [ ] 4 after noon aged one [and] ninety years and ten months and twenty-
    three days.**
1671 the 1st October I Samuel Gerritsen am born.
1676 the 15th August my wife Yda was born.
1695 the 14th day of June on a Friday I Samuel Gerritsen married my honorable wife Yda Reyder.

**Some sections of the bible pertaining only to Samuel Gerritsen's family have not been included.

APPENDIX J

WILLEM WILLEMSEN WILL

1 Dec 1721, In the name of God, Amen, I Willem Willemsen of Gravesend, in Kings County, being very sick, whereas I have sold all my lands in Gravesend to my son Nicholas Willemsen for the sum of £600, to be paid to me £20 and as much more as he is able at or before the first day of May 1717, and so annually till all be paid; but if not paid at the time of my decease, then to such persons as should be set forth in my will, as may appear by an agreement dated 5 Jul 1716.

And whereas he hath paid me £143.3 and there is due £454.16, I will that he pay to my children Peter, William, Jacobus, Cornelis, Anne, wife of John Griggs, Jr.; and to the children of my daughter Mary, wife of Bartholomew Marsh; and to the children of my daughter Gretie, wife of Abraham Emans; each one-eighth; and my son Nicholas is to keep one-eighth for himself; my son Willem is to have £5 for his birthright, and I make him and my son Nicholas executors; signed Willem Willemsen.

Witnesses John Lake, Samuel Hubbard and S. Gerritsen; proved, 19 Apr 1722.

William H. Pelletreau, compiler, *Abstracts of Unrecorded Wills Prior to 1790 on File in the Surrogate's Office, City of New York, 1665-1800, Abstracts of Wills, Book 9*, (New York: New York Historical Society, 35, 1905), 245. Book 9, File 600, page 288. Willem Willemsen will of, dated 1 Dec 1721, probated 19 Apr 1722.

Appendix K

WILLIAM WILLIAMSON WILL

24 Jun 1764, in the name of God, Amen, I William Williamson of Amwell, Hunterdon County New Jersey, yeoman, calling to mind the mortality of the body, being poorly in health and weak in body but of perfect mind and memory, I now make, ordain and appoint this to be my last will and testament; first I give my soul to God that gave it and as for my body, I recommend it to the earth to be decently buried at the discretion of my executors; as for my worldly estate as it has pleased God to bestow and endow me, I give, devise and bestow it in the manner following; I will that my funeral charges and just debts be fully satisfied, contested and paid by my executors; next I will, bequeath and bestow to my beloved wife Patience Williamson £33 to be paid out of my bonds or bills three months after my death, which shall be her right and property; likewise I will that my beloved wife Patience Williamson shall have the command of my plantation, household goods, stock of creatures and farming utensils during her widowhood; I likewise will to my two beloved daughters, Margaret Larrew and Mayke Williamson, £50 each to be paid to them one year after my death out of the bonds, bills, book debts or money which is due me; as to the remainder of said money, bonds, bills and accounts, I will and bestow it equally between my beloved sons, Cornelius Williamson, Samuel Williamson, William Williamson, John Williamson and Abraham Williamson to be paid [to] them one year after my decease, and each part share or legacy shall be their right, property and estate forever; I likewise will, that whenever my beloved wife Patience Williamson shall either marry or expire, then my executors shall have full power and authority to take into their possession all my lands, stock and utensils, household goods and estate, and make available [as much] of the moveable estate as soon as can conveniently be done... those lands to (be sold) within (number) years after her decease by my executors, who shall sell the whole estate, convey the lands to the purchaser whose deed shall be lawful and valid to all intents and purposes; and out of the money from the sale of stock and lands, my executors shall pay to my two beloved daughters, Margaret Larrew and Mayke Williamson £50 each, which shall be their right, property and estate forever; and all the remainder shall be equally divided between my beloved sons, except my beloved son Abraham Williamson, who shall have £100 more than either of my [other] sons; and each ones share or legacy so willed and bequeathed shall be their right, property and estate forever; lastly I nominate and appoint my well beloved sons, Cornelius Williamson and Samuel Williamson executors of this my will and last testament; disallowing all and every will and executors before allowed, and approve of and confirm these now appointed; in witness whereof I set my hand and seal, William Williamson; witnesses Peter Rettinghousen, Garret Lake and John "X" Bilby.

Peter Rettinghousen and Garret Lake, two evidences to the will, being sworn do depose and say they saw William Williamson, the testator, sign and seal the same, heard him publish and declare this to be his last will and testament; that the testator was of sound mind and memory as far as they know and as they verily believe; that John Bilby, a subscribing evidence was present at the same time and signed his name as a witness to the will either with these deponents or in the testator's presence; Peter Rettinghousen and Garret Lake, sworn before me, William Frazer, Surrogate, 16 Jun 1774.

Samuel Williamson, one of the executors being duly sworn, did say that this is the true last will and testament of William Williamson so far as he knows, and as he believes; that he will pay first the debts of the deceased, then the specified legacies so far as the goods, chattels and credits of the deceased can extend; and he will render a just and true account when lawfully required; Samuel Williamson, sworn at Amwell before William Frazer, Surrogate; proved 16 Jun 1774.

Appendix L

SAMUEL KYLE WILL

23 Jul 1784, in the name of God amen, I Samuel Kyll of Montgomery township, Cumberland County Pennsylvania, being sick in body but of sound and perfect mind, memory and understanding, blessed be God, and calling to mind the mortality of my body and that it is appointed for all men once to die do make constitute and ordain and appoint this to be my last will and testament in manner and form following; first of all I commend my soul to the hands of Almighty God who gave it and my body to the earth to be buried in decent and Christian burial at the discretion of my executors herein after named; and as touching such worldly estate herewith it hath pleased God to bless me in this world I give bequeath and dispose of it in the following manner and way; I allow my funeral charges and just debts if any there be, to be paid and discharged by my executors without trouble or unnecessary lawsuit; I give and bequeath to my daughter Ann Fleming £5, and to her son Samuel Bell Fleming £5; I give and bequeath to my daughter Mary Willson £3 and to her daughter Jean Orbison £5; I give and bequeath to my daughter Isabella Garretson £5 and to her son Samuel Kyll Garretson £5; I give and bequeath to my son John Kyll £3 and to his son Samuel Kyll £5; I give and bequeath to my grandson Samuel Kyll, son of my son Joseph Kyll £5; I give and bequeath to my granddaughters of my son Samuel Kyll £5; those legacies to be paid in specie according to the way and method for paying them shall be by disposing of so much of my personal estate as shall enable my executors to discharge them beginning with the most needy; I give and bequeath to my son Samuel Kyll and his heirs that piece, parcel or plantation of land on which he now lives; and to my son Joseph and his heirs, that on which he now lives; and also to my son Robert and his heirs the land on which he lives; each of them to hold according as the lines are at present consentably marked; Robert's being a part of the tract on which I now dwell; I give and bequeath to my son James Kyll 60 acres of land to be laid out of the place I now live on, beginning at a corner on the line between William Shannan's land and mine, thence extending along the line between me and William Nowall as far as my line runs that way, taking sufficient breadth to make up 60 acres the same being uncultivated land to hold to him and his heirs if he shall have lawful heirs; but if he dies without heirs it is to revert back to the original tract; while he continues on the mentioned place and assists his brother Thomas in laboring the same to enjoy his share of the profits according to his labor; and if ordained that he shall be rendered unfit for labor it is my will that his brother Thomas supports him decently during his life and then buries him decently; I give and bequeath to my son Thomas Kyll and his heirs all the remaining part of my plantation on which I now live with the appurtenances, and all the remaining part of moveable or personal estate after the above mentioned legacies are paid and my just debts and funeral charges paid; it is also my will that my son Thomas have my silver watch, my rifle fun and all my unmarked silver buttons; and that my son Samuel have all my marked silver buttons; it is my will that my sons Robert and Joseph, or their heirs, pay each of them £20 in specie to my son Samuel or his heirs in 18 months after my decease' I do hereby constitute and appoint my sons Samuel and Thomas Kyll executors of this my last will and testament in order that it may be executed according to the above plan; and hereby revoke and disannul all other wills testament or testaments heretofore at any time made by me confirming this and no other as my last will and testament; in witness whereof I have hereunto set my hand and seal the day and year first above written; signed sealed and pronounced in the presence of Thomas Kennedy, Hugh Long and Joseph Shannon; Samuel (his mark) Kill.

Will Book A, page 42, Chambersburg, Franklin County Pennsylvania, recorded 1784.

Appendix M

ROBERT KYLE WILL

In the name of God Amen; I Robert Kyle Senior of Campbell County Kentucky, considering the great uncertainty of this mortal life, and knowing it is appointed for all men once to die, and being advanced in years but at this time enjoying perfect health and of sound disposing mind and memory (blessed be Almighty God for his past mercies and blessings) do make, ordain and publish this my last Will and Testament in manner and form following; first, I yield my soul to my all merciful and just maker from whom I received it, and my aged and comparatively worn out old body I return to its mother earth, to be disposed of in a decent form and Christian like burial; next as regards my earthly estate or worldly goods and possessions, I order and direct that the debts I owe (which are but few and small in number) shall be strictly and punctually paid by my executors, that debts which may be owing to me may be collected in as short and reasonable time after my decease as is practicable; to my industrious partner, helpmate and affectionate wife, Sarah Kyle, I give all and every description of debts due me or to become due me by bond, note, account, bill, mortgage or otherwise to be made use of and disposed of in any way for her benefit that she may think right and proper; to my beloved wife I give all my house and household furniture, kitchen furniture, farming tools and implements, mechanic tools, stock, horses, cattle, sheep, hogs, also my books or little library, but at her death all my books are to be given to my son Zacheus Kyle; to my beloved wife I give the whole of any farm on which I now live, both arable and wood land and all its appurtenances during her natural life; and should my wife survive me or I survive her, it is to be the same thing in the end, I will, direct, and order that the farm where I live and have lived for a number of years, shall be sold at the discretion of my executors in such way and at such credits as they deem most advisable for the interest and benefit of those to whom I shall leave the proceeds thereof; the whole proceeds and monies arising from the sale of my farm when collected, I order shall be equally and justly distributed, share and share alike, among my dutiful and affectionate daughters, Dinah White, Jane Dixon, Mary Long and Sarah Rich; and should any of my daughters die before my Will and Testament is carried into complete effect, my will is that the child(ren) of my daughter(s)shall be entitled to that part of the money arising from the sale of the farm to which the mother of the child(ren) would have been entitled had she (they) lived to see my Will and Testament carried into full and complete effect; I direct my executors to be very careful and lay my farm off into such number of lots as will best advance the interest of my daughters, requiring of every purchaser, at least two good and sufficient securities, I also invest my executors with full power and authority to convey the land so sold to the purchaser(s) by general warrantee deed immediately upon the payment of the purchase money; I purchased 144 acres in Ohio of my son Samuel B. Kyle and Jesse McKay for which I hold their bond; now if I should not sell the land during my lifetime, after my decease my executors are expressly directed to make sale of the 140 acres in any manner they may deem most suitable and advantageous, and to distribute and divide when the money is collected from the sale among my four sons, John Kyle, Thomas Kyle, Robert Kyle and Zacheus Kyle; and one equal share or fifth part to be equally divided among the children of Samuel B. Kyle deceased; to my dutiful sons, John Kyle, Robert Kyle, Thomas Kyle and Zacheus Kyle I give all that part of my 1,000 acre tract of land in Ohio each one holding respectively and forever that part of the tract in quantity and quality as surveyed and laid off to him by Jacob Fowler agreeably to my directions, and upon which land my sons above named (except my son Zacheus) have been living and are now in possession; my son Zacheus occupying his part of the land for some time and now by his tenant; that part of 1,000 acres laid off and surveyed by Fowler and occupied by my son Samuel B. Kyle (and upon which he lately died) I order shall be sold in such way and at such credits as my executors shall think best; the farm occupied by my son Samuel B. Kyle to be divided into two equal parts and sold to the highest bidder, the purchaser giving bond and security with two or more sufficient securities, the interest money arising from the sale of the land to be collected annually and loaned out at interest; after my executors have collected the monies from the sale they shall loan the same out at interest taking care not to loan to any one man more than $200, requiring bond for it with at least two good securities and collecting the interest annually; the principal and interest accrued from sale of the farm where Samuel B. Kyle lately deceased lived, I give to my grandchildren, Robert Kyle, Jacob Kyle, Joseph Kyle, George W. Kyle, Perry Kyle, Franklin Kyle, Mary Kyle, Sarah Kyle and Anne Kyle to be equally divided; to be paid to each boy when he is of age or his part can be collected; and paid to each girl when she is of age or sooner if married before that; I hereby invest my executors with full power and to convey all land they may sell by virtue of my last Will and Testament to my son Zacheus Kyle; I give the house and lot I purchased of William Porter, where my son Zacheus lives near Covington Kentucky to my beloved wife; I give and devise during her natural life the house and

Appendix M

Robert Kyle Will, part 2.

lot of four and a half acres purchased of Sylvanus Jamison; and at her death I order the house and lot sold by my executors and the money to be equally divided among my children, John Kyle, Thomas Kyle, Robert Kyle, Zacheus Kyle, Dinah White, Mary Long, Sarah Rich and June Dixon, who is not only to have an equal part of the money from the sale of the house, but she is to have $50 more than any of my other sons or daughters; I hereby nominate, constitute and appoint Alfred Sanford, Zacheus Kyle and Samuel Kennedy executors of my last will and testament hereby revoking all other wills and testaments by me heretofore made; in witness whereof I have set my hand and seal, Robert Kyle; sealed in the presence of Alexander Connelly and James G. Arnold, 4 Nov 1823.

Campbell County, June Court 1825, last Will and Testament of Robert Kyle, deceased, produced in court on 27 Jun 1825, proven by oaths of Alexander Connelly and James G. Arnold, witnesses, which was ordered to be recorded; Zacheus Kyle, one of the executors came into court, executed and acknowledged bond in the penalty of $15,000 with Thomas D. Carneal, Joseph Kennedy and Joseph Rich, his securities; Alfred Sandford and Samuel Kennedy the two other executors refused to take upon themselves the burthen and execution thereof; given under my hand 1 Jul 1825; James Taylor, Clerk.

Robert Kyle will , Campbell County Probate Court, Alexandria Kentucky, 4 Nov 1823, recorded 27 Jun 1825, will book B: 142-145.

Appendix N

HEWITT LINEAGE

1) Robert Hewitt,
b. unknown,
d. ca. 1732-1736 prob. Anne Arundel County MD
m. Elizabeth sup. *Chandler or Jacks *9 Jan 1723, Anne Arundel County MD
b. prob. Anne Arundel County MD
d. ca. 1732-1736 prob. Anne Arundel County MD

2) Jacob Hewitt
b. 17 Aug 1728 Anne Arundel County MD
d. ca. 7 Jun 1790, Fayette County PA
m. Ruth Davis Elder ca. 1755 Anne Arundel County MD
b. 13 Feb 1728 Anne Arundel County MD
d. after 1790 sup. Fayette County PA

3) Richard Hewitt
b. 28 Jul 1765 Baltimore County MD
d. ca. 9 Mar 1827 Brown County OH
m. Phebe Hall ca 1790, sup. Fayette County PA
b. ca 1774, prob. Fayette County PA
d. before 1827 Brown County OH

3) Ephraim Hewitt
b. 17 Mar 1770, Baltimore County MD
d. 25 Jan 1815, Fayette County PA
m. Elizabeth Hall ca. 1792 Fayette County PA
b. 22 Jul 1766 prob. Loudoun County VA
d. bef Apr 1833 Brown County OH

4) Jacob Hewitt
b. 11 Nov 1791 Fayette County PA
d. 20 Jun 1850 Clermont County OH
4) m. Elizabeth Hewitt ca. 1814 Brown County OH
b. 26 Sep 1794 Fayette County PA
d. after 20 May 1873 Clermont County OH

5) Richard Davis Hewitt
b. 10 Nov 1815, Brown County OH
d. 22 Mar 1903, Hamilton County OH
m. Jane Williamson 10 May 1842, Clermont County OH
b. 22 Jan 1822 Fleming County KY
d. 24 Sep 1859, Clermont County OH

6) John Holmes Hewitt
b. 22 Apr 1850 Clermont County OH
d. 5 Mar 1930 Davidson County TN
m. Lizzie Belle Morrison 22 Apr 1880 Clermont County OH
b. 26 Jun 1852 Clermont County OH
d. 24 Apr 1903 Cincinnati, Hamilton County OH

7) Francese Vesta Hewitt
b. 9 Nov 1889, Clermont County OH
d. 1 Sep 1910, Tryon, North Carolina
m. George C. Schmidt 17 Apr 1907, Newport KY
b. 12 Jan 1886 Hamilton County OH
d. 8 Dec 1962 Hamilton County OH

SOURCE NOTES
Chapter One

THE BEGINNING

[1] Will of Benjamin Lawrence, Family Archive CD #206, *Maryland Calendar of Wills, 1635-1685*, (Broderbund Software, Inc. 1998) 1:154.
"4:142. 6 Jan 1684, Benjamin Lawrence will, West River, Anne Arundel County, probated 3 Jul 1685, testators John Griffin, Henry Hewit, William Wheeler and Nicholas Rollson."

[2] Jane Baldwin Cotton, Editor, Archives of Maryland, *Proceedings of the Council of Maryland, 1694-*, (Westminster, Maryland: Family Line Publications, 1904-1928), 40.
"20:541, signed by the Military Officers of Ann Arrundell County: Henry Hewitt, et al."

[3] Charles Francis Stein, Jr., *Origin and History of Howard County, Maryland*, (Baltimore: Howard County Historical Society, 1972), 19-21.

[4] Family Archive CD #206, *Maryland Calendar of Wills, 1685-1702*, (Broderbund Software, Inc. 1998), 2:238.
"11:206, "will of William Cotter, Road River, Anne Arundel County, 21 Mar 1701/2, 21 Apr 1702, Apr 1702, testators Henry Hewitt, Richard Jones Jr. and Thomas Gassaway."

[5] Wright, *Anne Arundel County Church Records*, 6, 14.
"Henry Hewett (overseer to William Cotter or widow) buried 5 Apr 1702; William Cotter (Housekeeper of parish) buried 28 Mar 1702."

[6] Maryland State Archives, Annapolis, Maryland 29 Nov 1995, *Maryland Land Office Records*, Patent Record Book, MSA #SM2 SR 7278 (Annapolis: Hall of Records Commission, 1947) D:5: 680.
"13 Jan 1705, to Robert Huitts Baltimore County, from William Taylor Anne Arundel County; warrant 200 acres called *The Range* at head of Bush River in the woods, south line of St. Albans, Thomas Grove's *Timber Grove*, signed Henry Darnall Jr.; 1 Nov 1710 patent to Huitt."

[7] AIS *Census Index: Pre-1790, (1607-1789), Maryland*, (Genealogical Publishing Co, Inc., Baltimore), 155, 144.

[8] Maryland State Archives, *Anne Arundel County Court Judgment Records*, MSA #C91, (Annapolis: Hall of Records Commission, 1947), TB:1: 153.
"TB#1:153, January Court 1705, James Shorley vs. Robert Hewett, trespass, Thomas Marchman, gentleman attorney for defendant, wherein Shorley renders judgment against defendant, Hewitt to pay or be in custody of Sheriff of Anne Arundel County."

[9] Rosemary B. Dodd & Patricia M. Bausell, Editors, *Abstracts of Land Records, Anne Arundel County, Maryland*, 2:1703-1709, (Pasadena, Maryland: Anne Arundel Genealogical Society, 1990), WT: 2: 634.
"3 May 1708, Henry Pinckney, Anne Arundel assigned wife Sarah as attorney to recover all debts due, signed Henry Pinckney, witnesses Edward Hancox and Robert (H his mark) Hewett."

[10] Edward Moore will, Family Archive CD #206, *Maryland Calendar of Wills, 1703-1713*, (Broderbund Software, Inc.1998) 3: 157.
"12:217, 22 Aug 1709, Edward Moore will, Anne Arundel County, to wife Alice real and personal estate including 350 acres *Issabell Farm* during minority of her son John, he dying without issue, estate reverts to wife; testators Geo. Fry, Moses Adney, Robert Huit and William Bennett."

[11] Maryland State Archives, *Anne Arundel County Court Judgment Records*, MSA #C91, (Annapolis: Hall of Records Commission, 1947), TB#2: 122, 154.
"14 Mar 1709, Christopher Smiddors vs. Robert Hewitt, agreements at a court held at Annapolis for Ann Arundel County, 14 Mar 1709."

[12] Cotton, *Maryland Calendar of Wills, 1703-1713*, 3:244.

"13: 542; 7 Feb 1710, proved 8 Dec 1713, Charles Greenberry will, Anne Arundel County, to sister Anne, wife of John Hammond, cousin Henry Ridgley; wife Rachel executor; residue of estate during her life; testators Robert Boone, Thomas Bordley and Robert Huett."

[13] Maryland State Archives, *Baltimore County Court Land Records*, MSA #CM135, Roll 110-6, (Annapolis: Hall of Records Commission, 1947), TR#A: 174-175. Following is an abstract of the record. Transcribed from Liber ISN #A, p. 173-174.

"24 Dec 1711, deed from Robert Hewett, Anne Arundel County Maryland and wife Elizabeth; to Amos Garrett, Anne Arundel County, merchant; 200 acres for £12.35; signed Robert (his H mark) Hewet, Eliz (her EH mark); witnesses John Young, Edward (X) Hall, John Gray and Eliz. (X) Norwood; 16 May 1715 Amos Garret received £48 tobacco."

[14] Prerogative Court of Maryland. *Anne Arundel County Will Book Liber 19*, Maryland State Archives (Annapolis: Hall of Records Commission, 1947), TRA: 174-175.

"19: 306-330, 4 Sep 1714, Amos Garrett will, Annapolis, Ann Arundel County Maryland, merchant; my body shall be buried in Maryland near new house at Robert Hewett's plantation where he lives as overseer, (p. 311); I want a sermon preached in the house near Wyatt's Ridge on 225 acres where Robert Hewett is now overseer." (p. 317); 30 Aug 1737, Joseph Young answered interrogatories taken for William Cummin against Deborah Woodward, administrator of Amos Garrett, deceased;...that the plantation was near William McCubbins, whereon Robert Hewett did live (p.329)."

[15] Maryland State Archives, *Anne Arundel County Court Judgment Records*, MSA #C91, (Annapolis: Hall of Records Commission, 1947), TB#3: 418.

"November Court 1714, Rachel Greenberry vs. Robert Hewet, lawsuit for debt for £8.7.1."

[16] Debbie Hooper, compiler, *Abstracts of Chancery Court Records of Maryland, 1669-1782*, Book CL: 742, (Westminster, Maryland: Family Line Publications, 1996), 49.

"4 May 1722, depositions with names and ages on boundaries of tracts, *Waldridge, Broome,* and *Hoggneck* in Anne Arundel County, Richard Warfield age ca 60, Robert Hewitt age ca 60."

[17] Cotton, *Proceedings of the Council of Maryland*, 42: 59.

"Apr 1724, per Samuel Young, Treasurer of the Western Shore, Maryland; Robert Hewitts owed £86.18.23."

[18] Dodd & Bausell, *Abstracts of Land Records, Anne Arundel County, Maryland, 1709-1719*, 3: PK: 41.

"16 May 1711, deed from Charles Kilburne, Anne Arundel, gentleman, and wife Eliza; to Amos Garrett, Anne Arundel, merchant; an acre lot #15 in Annapolis and one house, for £16 sterling and £10 current money of Maryland (p.354); witnesses John Brice, Richard Huett and John Moonshott, recorded 19 May 1710."

[19] Wright, *Anne Arundel County Church Records*, St. Anne's Parish, 90.
"Married, Richard Hewit and Elisabeth Fraser, 28 Jul 1722."

[20] Robert W. Barnes, *Baltimore County Families: 1659-1759*, (Baltimore: Genealogical Publishing Company, 1989), 228; original record in *Baltimore County Court Proceedings*, Book OS#C, p. 244.

"Nov 1719 [Alexander Frazier] licensed to keep an ordinary at Whetstone Point, died by 16 Aug 1720, widow Elizabeth Frazier posted administration bond with George Walker, Thomas Taylor." Frazier's administration ended July 1721, a year before Elizabeth married Richard Hewitt.

[21] Vernon L. Skinner, Jr., *Abstracts of the Administration Accounts of the Prerogative Court of Maryland,* (Westminster, Maryland: Family Line Publications, 1996), 2:50.

"7:364, 18 Apr 1726, John Israell estate received from Philip Smith and Richard Huitt."
[22] Robert W. Barnes, *Baltimore County, Maryland Deed Abstracts, 1659-1750,* IS#H: 439, (Family Line Publications, Westminster, Maryland, 1996), 232.

"8 Jun 1727, deed to Richard Hewitt, inn holder, Baltimore County Maryland from Thomas Sheridine, gentleman and wife Tibitha, Baltimore County; lot #19 in Joppa on Church Street and Sharping Lane for £1.5, witnesses William Buckner and Thomas White."

[23] Robert Hewitt administration, Maryland State Archives, *Prerogative Court, Testamentary Proceedings, Anne Arundel County*, (Annapolis: Hall of Records Commission, 1947), MSA #SM15, 28: 432.

"19 Aug 1729, for Robert Huet, deceased, came Richard Huett, administrator with Charles Ridgely and Stephen Mason, sureties of £50sterling."

[24] Robert Hewit inventory, Maryland State Archives, *Prerogative Court Records*, Baltimore County Inventories, 1690-1736, (Annapolis: Hall of Records Commission, 1947), page unknown.

"30 Aug 1729, Robert Hewit inventory, deceased, of Anne Arundel County, personal appraisal £14.1.1, cash in hand £1.13.5, total estate £15.14.7, signed Elizabeth (EH) Huett; 26 Nov 1729, Baltimore County, Richard Huett administrator of [Robert Huett] Anne Arundel County, deceased, swore it was true inventory of the estate."

[25] Richard Hewitt will, Maryland State Archives, Prerogative Court of Maryland, *Baltimore County Wills*, (Annapolis: Hall of Records Commission, 1947), 19:904-906.

"3 Nov 1729, Richard Hewet will, Baltimore County Maryland executors, wife Elizabeth Hewett, Charles Ridgely, unless wife marries, then Ridgely is sole executor; Mary Hewett, daughter of wife Elizabeth, land and movables; my mother Elizabeth Huett shall live anywhere except wife's first choice, also mother to have suit of mourning; should Mary Huett die without legal issue, all to be divided between John Ridgely, his sister Pleasance, John Frazier and his sister Elizabeth; witnesses Christopher Gardiner, Jonathon Hanson and Francis Hinckley; 28 Feb 1729/1730."

[26] Bill and Martha Reamy, *Records of St. Paul's Parish*, (Westminster, Maryland: Family Line Publications, 1988), 1:40, 152.

"Richard Hewett d. 20 February 1729/1730; "Church Wardens and Vestrymen;" Charles Ridgely, Vestryman 1728-1730, 1736-1738; Church Warden 1732, 1735."

[27] *Baltimore County Wills*, 19: 904-906.

On the back of the will the following was written, "Feb 28 1729/1730, Elizabeth Hewet, widow of the deceased, declared she would not stand by the devise in the will but that she would have her full third part of it and the personal estate taken before."

[28] Reamy, *Records of St. Paul's Parish*, 1:163, 30.

"In 1731 those below were subscribers who financed the new church, these names [were] found in the Treasurer's Book, Elizabeth Huell (Huett). Married: Benjamin Price to Elisabeth Hewett, 22 June 1730."

[29] Harry Wright Newman, *Anne Arundel Gentry*, (Annapolis: Published by the Author, 1979), 98-99.

"Children of Charles and Rachel (Howard) Ridgely, Charles Ridgely, born 1733; Pleasance Ridgely; Achsah Ridgely; Rachel Ridgely; John Ridgely."

"Charles Ridgely, son of Charles and Deborah Dorsey Ridgely; born Prince George's County; quite young at the death of father in 1705; from grandfather [John Ridgely], received with brother [William] the plantation *White Wine and Claret* of 1,400 acres; later resurveyed into 2,145; on May 16, 1742 the brothers partitioned it, described as laying between Snowden and Middle Rivers, and both branches of the Patuxent in Howard County."

[30] Stein, *Origin and History of Howard County, Maryland*, 303-304.

"Honorable John Dorsey divided *White Wine and Claret* between his Ridgely grandsons. One of them, Charles, son of Charles and Deborah Dorsey Ridgely, moved to Baltimore County and founded the Ridgleys of Hampton."

[31] J. Thomas Scharf, *History of Baltimore City and County*, v.1, (Baltimore: Regional Publishing Company, 1971), 53.

"14 Jan 1730 the first lots were taken up...on the 16th Charles Ridgely took up No. 54 on the east side of South Lane and extending to the water...Richard Hewitt No. 35 on the west side of South Forest Street."

[32] *First Records of Baltimore Town and Jones Town, [Maryland]: 1729-1797*, (Baltimore: City Council of Baltimore, 1905), 8.
"4 Mar 1742/3, Reverend Benedict Bourdillon desired two Lotts in Baltemore town, viz No. 26 on 15 Jan 1729/30 by James Powell, and No 35 by Richard Hewitt 19 Jan 1729/30, both unbuilt upon by Powell and Hewitt, formerly taken up by Bourdillon on 15 May 1741/2."

[33] Barnes, *Baltimore County Families, 1659-1759*, 228.
"Baltimore County Court Proceedings, Book HS7: 50, "November Court 1730, with consent of mother Elizabeth Price, John and Elizabeth Frazier chose Benjamin Price as their guardian."

[34] Gloria L. Main, *Tobacco Colony: Life in Early Maryland, 1650-1720*, (Princeton: Princeton University Press, 1982), 185.
"The frequency of razors in the inventories suggests that most men shaved. Since keeping hair clean and free of lice was a continuing problem, many rich men ... solved it by having their heads shaved as well, substituting powdered wigs or colorful turbans for their troublesome hair."

[35] Richard Hewett inventory, Maryland Orphan's Court, Baltimore County, Inventories, 11 Aug 1730, 5:124-130.

[36] John Hall will, Maryland State Archives, Prerogative Court of Maryland, *Baltimore County Wills*, (Annapolis: Hall of Records Commission, 1947), 133-134.
"24 Jan 1717, John Hall, Baltimore County, planter; to my uncle, John Rawlins, to my Mother Jane Novell for her care of me; dated 24 Jan 1717; witness John (X) Hall; testators Jeremy Downes, Charles Baker, and Caleb (X) Hewitt; recorded 7 Jul 1718."

[37] William Carter, probate account, Family Archive CD #206, Genealogical Records, *Maryland Probate Records, Prerogative Court Abstracts 1731-1737, Books 11-15*, (Broderbund Software, Inc. 1998), 136.
"14:394, 11 Jun 1737, William Carter account, Kent County, Maryland, estate £33.19.1; payments to Caleb Hewett, executor David Hall."

[38] Maryland State Archives, *Anne Arundel County Judgement Records*, MSA #C91, (Annapolis: Hall of Records Commission, 1947), IB#1: 89.
"Nov 1740, ordered a list of soldiers raised for Ann Arundel County, from the records of Collector Charles Hammond the county agent at county court. The list is of soldiers paid bounty money by Hammond, 10 Sep 1740 under Capt. Thomas Addison...Richard Hewitt."

SOURCE NOTES
Chapter Two

ROBERT AND ELIZABETH HEWITT

[1] Stein, *Origin and History of Howard County Maryland*, 26.

[2] T. H. Breen, *Tobacco Culture, The Mentality of the Great Tidewater Planters on the Eve of the Revolution*, (Princeton: Princeton University Press, 1985), 47.

[3] Gloria L. Main, *Tobacco Colony: Life in Early Maryland, 1650-1720*, (Princeton, New Jersey: Princeton University Press, 1982), 22.

[4] Arthur Pierce Middleton, *Tobacco Coast: A Maritime History of Chesapeake Bay in the Colonial Era*, (Newport News, Virginia: The Mariners' Museum, 1953), 133.
[5] Breen, *Tobacco Culture*, 47.

[6] Robert J. Brugger, *Maryland: A Middle Temperament, 1634-1980*, (Baltimore: John Hopkins University Press, 1988), 75.

[7] Stein, *Origin and History of Howard County, Maryland*, 23.

[8] Lorena S. Walsh, *The Chesapeake in the Seventeenth Century, Essays on Anglo-American Society*, "Till Death Us Do Part: Marriage and Family in Seventeenth-Century Maryland," (Chapel Hill, North Carolina: The University of North Carolina Press, 1979), 150.

[9] Wright, *Anne Arundel County Church Records*, 91.
        "St. Anne's Parish, Robert Hewytt and Elisabeth Chandler m. 9 Jan 1723."

[10] Wright, *Anne Arundel County Church Records*, 113-115.
        "St. Margaret's, Westminster Parish, Robert Hewit and Elizabeth, parents of Robert Hewit, son born 2 Jul 1726; Jacob Hewett son born 17 Aug 1728; Edward Hewett son born 28 Mar 1730."

[11] Peter Wilson Coldham, *Settlers of Maryland 1679-1700*, (Baltimore: Genealogical Publishing Company, 1995), 1:29: 149.
        "Chandler, Job, gentleman, transported himself, Anne his wife and Anne his daughter and others before 1651."

[12] Rosemary B. Dodd & Patricia M. Bausell, Editors, *Abstracts of Land Records, Anne Arundel County, Maryland*, 2:1719-1724, (Pasadena, MD: Anne Arundel Genealogical Society, 1990), 515.
        "27 Feb 1721/1722, deed from William Chandler, Anne Arundel County, planter to John Worthington, Anne Arundel County, merchant; 50 acres for £13 sterling, called *Chandler's Slaughter* northwest of Ridgely's Great Run of Patuxent River; signed William (X) Chandler; witnesses Richard Warfield, Caleb Dorsey and wife Anne Chandler; recorded 10 Jul 1722."

[13] Wright, *Anne Arundel County Church Records*, 68, 74.
        "St. Anne's Parish, Robert Chandler and Elizabeth Bryon m. 5 May 1713; William Chandler and Ann Laswell m. 8 Feb 1713."

[14] Karen Mauer Green, *The Maryland Gazette 1727-1761*, (Galveston, Texas: The Frontier Press, 1989) 1-6.

[15] Dodd and. Bausell, *Abstracts of Land Records*, 4:CW1:495.
        "Robert Hewitt, Commander of the ship Catherine, now riding at anchor in South River in AA, to export tobacco from Maryland to GB on freight, does publish the rate at £7 sterling per ton, the freighters consigning their tobacco to Mr. Thomas Colmore, merchant in London, or any other person, signed 24 May 1722, Robert Hewitt."

[16] Middleton, *Tobacco Coast*, 248, 252-253, 266.

[17] Reverend Nelson Waite Rightmyer, Editor, *Parishes of the Diocese of Maryland*, (Reistertown, Maryland, Educational Research Associates, 1960), 41.
        "1692, Broad Neck (now Westminster) Parish was on the north side of the Severn River including Town Neck and Broad Neck Hundreds; 1694 land between the Severn and ridge dividing streams running into the Patapsco and the Magothy [Rivers]; 1722, extended to the south side of the Patapsco River in Baltimore County from the mouth to the Falls, to the Girdle Pines dividing Anne Arundel and Baltimore Counties, to Chesapeake Bay, then to the mouth of the Patapsco [River], taken from St. Paul's Parish and added to Westminster Parish."

[18] Middleton, *Tobacco Coast*, 99-102.

[19] Walsh, *The Chesapeake in the Seventeenth Century*, 141-143.

[20] Main, *Tobacco Colony:* "Life in Early Maryland," 33, 92, 164, 175, 182-183.
[21] Brugger, *Maryland: A Middle Temperament*, 63.

[22] Middleton, *Tobacco Coast*, 45.

[23] J.D. Warfield, *The Founders of Anne Arundel and Howard Counties, Maryland*, 121.
　　"When Annapolis had arisen in 1708 to the dignity of a city, Amos Garrett, its wealthy merchant, was its mayor. He was one of the largest landholders in the county, and though a bachelor he seemed to buy lands simply to accommodate those who needed money. His lands were later resurveyed under the title, *Providence*."

[24] Main, *Tobacco Colony*, 74-75.

[25] Brugger, *Maryland: A Middle Temperament*, 64.

[26] Main, *Tobacco Colony*, 140-149.

[27] Hewitt Children judgment, *Anne Arundel County Court Judgment Records*, Maryland State Archives, Annapolis, Maryland, #C91, August Court (1736), IB:1: 445-446.
　　"1:445, June Court 1736, Thomas Jacks brought four orphan children into court, the issue of Robert Huit deceased, so they may be bound out by this court; 1:446, August Court 1736, court binds unto Thomas Jacks and his wife Elizabeth; Robert Huit, Jacob Huit, Edward Huit and Hannah Huit, children of Robert and Elizabeth Huit deceased; until the boys are 21 and the girl 16 years old; (Robert Huit being 10 years old the 2nd day of July last; Jacob Huit being 8 years old the 17th of this instant; Edward Huit six years old the 2nd day of March last; Hannah Huit 4 years old the 10th day of October next); considering this, Thomas Jacks and his wife Elizabeth agree to find them sufficient meat, drink, washing, clothing and lodging; and to give each of them a good suit of clothes at the expiration of their servitude, and to teach them to read and write; it is considered by the Justices here that Robert, Jacob, Edward and Hannah serve Thomas Jacks and his wife Elizabeth accordingly."

[28] Wright, *Anne Arundel County Church Records*, 28.
　　"All Hallows Parish, Elisabeth, daughter of Thomas Jacks and Elizabeth, born 27 Jun 1708, baptized 2 8ber 1709."

[29] Walsh, *The Chesapeake in the Seventeenth Century*, 145.

[30] Main, *Tobacco Colony*, 111.

[31] Wright, *Anne Arundel County Church Records*, 18, 23.
　　"All Hallows Parish, Thomas Jacks & Elizabeth Walters married 9 9ber 1704;Thomas Jacks and Elizabeth, parents of Thomas Jacks, a son born 4 Aug 1706 and baptized 13 October 1706."

[32] Dodd & Bausell, *Abstracts of Land Records, Volume III, 1712-1718*, 3: IB#2: 95.
　　"13 Nov 1717, deed from Thomas Jacks, Anne Arundel County, cordwainer; to William Nicholson, Anne Arundel County, merchant, for £28; 100 acres called *Elk Thickett* on south side of South River in Anne Arundel County on Burridge Creek next to Archibald Arbuckle's land, sold first to Benjamin Williams then to Jacks."

[33] John Powell will, Family Archive CD #206, Genealogical Records: *Maryland Probate Records, Calendar of Wills, 1713-1720*, (Broderbund Software, Inc., 1998), 70.
　　"14:227, 7 Nov 1715, John Powell, son of John Powell deceased, of Anne Arundel County; to mother Eliza Jacks, 200 acres of *Powell's Inheritance* on South River during her life; if she dies then to my brother Joseph and heirs; if Joseph lacks issue, to Richard Jacks and heirs; to brothers Christopher Walters and Thomas Jacks, Jr., son and sole heir of Thomas Jacks, Sr., 200 acres of land equally divided between them; personalty to Christopher Walters; Elizabeth Jacks, daughter of Thomas Jacks; and Barbary Jacks; executors unnamed; testators William Wayger, Robert Nickols, John Nicholson Jr.; proved 6 Apr 1716."

[34] Thomas Jacks deed, *Anne Arundel County Maryland, Clerk of the Circuit Court Land Records, 1653-1850*, (Hall of Records Commission, 1947), microfilm #0013326, Family History Library, (Salt Lake City: Genealogical Society of Utah, 1947-1949).

"IS#H: 7-8; 3 Feb 1724, deed from Thomas Jacks, Baltimore County, planter and wife Elizabeth; to John Tailor, city of London, merchant; for £0.05.0, 200 acres of *Jacks Peacock* in Baltimore County on south side of Patapsco River at the falls, surveyed for Jacks, 28 Sep 1717, patented 6 Aug 1719; signed Thomas (T J) Jacks, Elizabeth (EJ); 3 Feb 1724; witnesses Lance Todd and Christopher Randale; recorded 10 Apr 1725."

[35] Barnes, *Baltimore County, Maryland, Deed Abstracts, 1659-1750*, 169.

"Book: IS#H: 276; 15 Aug 1726, deed from Joseph Powell who had no heirs, to Richard Jacks, son of Thomas Jacks and Elizabeth Jacks for 'love and affection toward my brother,' 125 acres of *Powell's Inheritance*, upon death of his brother John Powell, thus fulfilling Powell's will stating that when his mother died, that property was to go to Richard Jacks and his heirs."

[36] Brugger, *Maryland: A Middle Temperament*, 100.

[37] Thomas Jacks deed, *Anne Arundel County Maryland*, microfilm #0013211, 1728-1729, (Family History Library, Salt Lake City: Genealogical Society of Utah, 1947-1949), 101-106.

"RD#1: 101-106; 14 Nov 1728, deed from Thomas Jacks, Anne Arundel County, cordwainer, to Richard Snowden, Anne Arundel County merchant; for £60 sterling, 100 acres of *Jacks Peacock* his dwelling plantation in Anne Arundel County on the south side of Patapsco River Falls together with all houses, etc.; signed Thomas (TJ) Jacks, wife Elizabeth Jacks agreed to forego her dower rights to the land; recorded 21 Jan 1728/9."

[38] Robert J. Brugger, *Maryland: A Middle Temperament*, 101.

[39] Thomas Jacks deed, *Anne Arundel County, Maryland*, microfilm #0013211, (Family History Library, Salt Lake City: Genealogical Society of Utah, 1947-1949), 1729-1730.

"TI:1: 299-304; 16 Jul 1730, deed from Thomas Jacks, Anne Arundel County, Maryland shoemaker, to Zachariah Maccubbin, gentleman, Sheriff of Anne Arundel County, acting for Thomas Wordley and others; that Thomas Jacks (among others) is a prisoner in Anne Arundel Gaol, and shall surrender to the sheriff all his real and personal estate, either in possession or in trust, to which he has any claim; to comply with these orders Thomas Jacks will sell to Zachariah Maccubbin *Powell's Inheritance* on the south side of the South River in Anne Arundel County now in his attorney's possession, plus his houses, profits and appurtenances; to be used to pay Thomas Jacks creditors; signed Thomas (TJ) Jacks; John Welsh and Henry Ridgely delivered deed 16 Jul 1730; Thomas Jacks delivered the following goods to the sheriff: one old hammock, one old flock bed, and one iron pot left in the prison containing about three gallons; recorded 11 Aug 1730."

[40] Vernon L. Skinner, Jr., *Abstracts of the Administration Accounts of the Prerogative Court of Maryland*, (Westminster, Maryland: Family Line Publications, 1996), 1724-1731, Books 6-10, 2:133.

"10:279, 28 May 1730, the account of Jonathon Hanson, Baltimore County Maryland, estate value £278.17.9, and listed among the debtors was Thomas Jacks."

[41] Maryland State Archives, Maryland Indexes, 1783 Tax Assessment Records of Anne Arundel County Maryland, MSA S1161-1-3, 1/4/5/44: 2.

"Rezin Hammond, *Jacks Peacock*, Anne Arundel County, Elkridge Hundred."

[42] Dodd & Bausell, *Abstracts of Land Records*, 101.

"2:WT#2: 603; 6 Dec 1707, deed from Thomas Jacks, Anne Arundel County, cordwainer, and wife Elizabeth; to Amos Garrett, Anne Arundel merchant, for £22, 100 acres called *Gentle Craft*, part of a tract called *Roper Grey*."

[43] Walsh, *The Chesapeake in the Seventeenth Century*, 145-148.

[44] Katie Bradley McGoon, *The Reminiscence of Katie B. McGoon*, unpublished manuscript of the Hewitt family by the great-granddaughter of Richard Hewitt and Phebe Hall Hewitt, given to Charles C. Bair, Jr. March 1997, copied by George L. Bair, Jr. 1999 and given to the author.

"Richard Hewitt was born in the year 1793 in Kentucky. Nothing is known of his parents except that his father was an orphan, who was taken in by an uncle and given no education."

[45] Undocumented source from Anne Arundel County Court records made by LaDoris Weber, address unknown.

[46] Richard Miller, administration, Baltimore County Administration Bonds, Hall of Records, Annapolis Maryland, 1721-1735, Book 1:403-405.
"4 Jun 1767, Baltimore County Maryland, know that Philip Deaver, Anthony Musgrove and Thomas Jacks of Baltimore County...sealed and delivered in our presence; witnesses Philip Deaver, Anthony Musgrove, and Thomas "X" Jacks."

[47] Bill and Martha Reamy, *Records of St. Paul's Parish*, 1:32.
"Nicholas Peddicoat married Ann Jacks 23 Dec 1735."

[48] Wright, *Anne Arundel County Church Records*, 23.
"Christ Church, Queen Caroline Parish, Luke Mercer married Barbra Jacks 1 Aug 1738."

[49] Thomas Jacks administration, Family Archive CD #206, Genealogical Records: *Maryland Probate Records, Prerogative Court Abstracts, 1755-1763*, (Broderbund Software, Inc., 1998), 16.
"2:60; 25 Oct 1756, estate of Thomas Jacks, administrator Richard Jacks, distribution to representatives unknown to this office."

SOURCE NOTES
Chapter Three

JACOB HEWITT IN MARYLAND

[1] Hewitt Family Bible, William Buckner McGroarty, *Hewitt Family: The Ancestry of Mrs. Sophia Hewitt Buckner, Wife of Dr. Philip Johnson Buckner*, an unpublished manuscript written between 1912-1942, 1, 22.
"As a beginning in 1912, I wrote to Cousin Sophie Higgins McTamany at the old homestead in Ohio. Her mother, recently deceased, had been the last surviving child. Sophie, by rare good fortune, had the remains (rescued from a burning house) of the Hewitt family Bible, partly destroyed but with its precious records intact. However, they were only bare records of births and deaths and after so long a time (the oldest recorded date was 1697) some of the entries were confusing. As frequent reference is made to the Old Bible, I should explain that this is the one referred to which was discovered by Cousin Sophie McTamany and which I carried with me to Uniontown, Pennsylvania. I found that the records with which it compared were in Maryland. In rebinding, it was thought best to make two small volumes of it. Cousin Sophie gave me one of them. She has the one with the original records. My copy has exact copies of these records. The full history of the Old Bible is recorded and bound in each volume."

[2] Hewitt Family Bible, see Appendix A.

[3] Wright, *Anne Arundel County Church Records*, 4.
"All Hallows Parish, Thomas Davis and Mary parents of Richard Davis son born 19 Oct 1697." The Bible shows Richard Davis's birth as 26 October 1697.

[4] Harry Wright Newman, *To Maryland from Overseas*, (Baltimore, Maryland: Genealogical Publishing Company, 1985), 139.

[5] Stein, *Origin and History of Howard County Maryland*, 294.
"Henry Pierpont emigrated to Maryland in 1665 with his wife Elizabeth and five children....his sons, Amos, Jabez and Moses, and daughters, Elizabeth and Hannah. Four more children, Charles, Francis, Mary and Sarah, were born in Maryland. Henry Pierpont received two grants of land in 1665, *Pierpont's Range* of 150 acres and *Pierpont's Park* of 80 acres, both in Middle Neck Hundred, Anne Arundel County...Mary Pierpont became the wife of Thomas Davis, founder of the prominent Davis family."

[6] Jabez Pierpoint will, Family Archive CD-ROM #206, *Maryland Probate Records, 1674-1774, Calendar of Wills, 1720-1726* (Broderbund Software, Inc., 1998), 5: 48.

"16:388, 1 Oct 1720, Jabez Pierpoint will, Baltimore County...to five sisters, viz. Sidney, Eliza Dea, Mary Davis, Sarah Warfield and Eliza, £1 each; probated 24 Apr 1721."

[7] John Beverley Riggs, *The Riggs Family of Maryland* (Baltimore: Lord Baltimore Press, 1939), 61.

[8] Stein, *Origin and History of Howard County, Maryland*, map "Early Land Grants of the Severn River Area and New Providence." This map shows the part of Howard County that was originally all Anne Arundel County. Among the grants is *Pierpont's Lot*, 150 acres owned by Henry Pierpont and the date 1666, located southwest of present-day Crownsville, near Wyatt's Ridge.

[9] Wright, *Anne Arundel County Church Records*, 85, 84.

[10] Amos Pierpont, will, Maryland Calendar of Wills 1713-1720, 4: 179, *Maryland Probate Records, 1674-1774*, Family Tree Maker, CD-ROM (Novato, California: Broderbund Software Inc., 1998), Citations of Maryland Probate Records: Maryland Prerogative Court Abstracts and Maryland Calendar of Wills, Annapolis.

"14: 680, 1 Jun 1718, Amos Peirpoint, planter, Anne Arundel County, deceased, testators John Warfield, Thomas Davis, etc., probated 24 Jun 1718."

[11] John Warfield estate, *Maryland Prerogative Court Abstracts 1718-1724, Genealogical Records: Maryland Probate Records, 1674-1774*, Family Tree Maker, 13, 34.

"1: 367, 29 Jul 1718; John Warfield, Anne Arundel County, planter, estate appraisal £473.11.8; appraisers Edmond Benson and Thomas Davis, approver Alexander Warfield."

"2: 143, John Warfield, estate account, total £552.13.0; distribution to widow unnamed one-third; rest to children equally, Richard, John, Ruth, Benjamin, Elinor, Alexander, Edward, Mary and Philip; administrator Ruth Carter, (former Ruth Warfield), wife of Daniel Carter."

[12] Richard Warfield will, *Maryland Calendar of Wills 1703-1713*, 3: 28, *Genealogical Records: Maryland Probate Records, 1674-1774*, Family Tree Maker, 28.

"11: 409, 10 Jan 1703-4; Richard Warfield, Anne Arundel County deceased; to son John and heirs, *Warfield's Plains* and 180 acres of *Warfield's Forest*; to son John, Richard, Alexander and Benjamin and daughter, Ellinor, residue equally; executors sons, John and Richard; overseers, sons, Alexander and Benjamin; testators, John Howard, Thomas Rowles, William Mackubin and Charles Stevens; probated 11 Feb 1703."

[13] Harry Wright Newman, *Anne Arundel Gentry*, "Warfield Family," 1: 345-348.

[14] Stein, *Origin and History of Howard County, Maryland*, 324.

[15] Wright, *Anne Arundel County Church Records*, All Hallow's Parish, 7, 1.

[16] J. D. Warfield, *Founders of Anne Arundel and Howard Counties, Maryland*, 84.

"John [Warfield], his oldest son, lived upon 'Warfield's Plains,' the homestead of which still stands just opposite Baldwin Memorial Church, half-way between Waterbury and Indian Landing. 'Warfield's Plains' extended up to Millersville, and 'Warfield's Forest' was near Indian Landing. In 1696, John married Ruth Gaither, oldest daughter of John Gaither of South River. Their sons were Richard, John, Benjamin, Alexander, Edward and Philip, all of whom located upon the frontier out-posts in Howard. John Warfield's daughters were Ruth, wife of Richard Davis; Mary, wife of Augustine Marriott and Elinor who died a maiden."

[17] John Gaither, administration, *Prerogative Court Abstracts, 1699-1708, Books 25-28, Genealogical Records: Maryland Probate Records, 1674-1774*, Family Tree Maker, 46.

"27:13, 17 Jun 1707, John Gaither administration, Anne Arundel County, estate total £550.17.3; distribution to John Gaither, John Warfield, son Benjamin Gaither, daughter Rachel Gaither, widow unnamed, administrator Ruth Hardisty, relict, now wife of Francis Hardisty."

[18] Wright, *Anne Arundel County Church Records*, 18.

[19] Newman, *Anne Arundel Gentry*, 1: 359-363.
   About John Gaither, "He died in testate. According to the register of All Hallows Church, he was buried 12 Nov 1702. Letters of administration were issued to his widow, Ruth Gaither. The personal estate was appraised 29 May 1703 at £437. John and Benjamin Gaither approved as kinsmen. There was a large number of livestock, £97 of pewter, five Negro slaves, one white servant-man, a parcel of old books and household furniture including six high back leather chairs, a writing trunk, etc.; 17 Jun 1707, £35 paid to John Warfield who married Ruth, a daughter of the deceased. Francis Hardisty apparently became the guardian of the younger children. It was stated in June 1709 that the orphans, Edward Gaither, Rachel Gaither, Mary Gaither, Rebecca Gaither and Susannah Gaither were at Francis Hardisty's plantation, South River Hundred."

[20] Wright, *Anne Arundel County Church Records*, 142.
   "Christ Church, Queen Caroline Parish; Richard Daviss and Ruth were parents of Thomas Daviss, son born 2 Sep 1722; Richard Daviss, son born 10 Jan 1724/5; John Daviss, son born 6 Oct 1726; [Ruth] Daviss, daughter, b. 13 [Jan] 1728/9; Caleb Daviss, son born 10 Sep 1731; Mary Daviss, daughter, born 20 Apr 1734; Joshua Daviss, son born 13 Sep 1737."

[21] Henry S. Peden, Jr., *Maryland Deponents 1634-1799*, (Westminster: Family Line Publications, 1991), 48.
   "Thomas Davis of Anne Arundel County age 58 in 1726; age 71 in 1740."

[22] Peter Wilson Coldham, *Settlers of Maryland 1701-1730*, 41-42.

[23] Pierpont to Davis, land, *Anne Arundel County, Maryland, Land Records*, (Miami Beach: T.L.C. Genealogy, 1993), 9 Nov 1709, Anne Arundel Deed Book PK:107:13.

[24] Thomas Davis will, Maryland Colonical Probate Records, Prerogative Court, Book 26: 138-139.
   "20 Jan 1743/4; Thomas Davis, Sr. will, Anne Arundel County, planter; to wife Mary Davis personal estate, to grandson Caleb Davis, son of Richard, 200 acres *Duvall's Delight* where his mother dwells, but his mother Ruth Davis shall possess the tract without any interruption; to son Thomas 200 acres *Laswell's Hopewell*; to son John 240 acres *Davistone* and 100 acres *Whats Left*; to son Samuel 68 acres *The Forest* and 50 acres *The Same Name* in Prince Georges County; to son Robert 315 acres *Ranter's Ridge*; to son Francis 150 acres *The Pearl*, part of *The Diamond*, and 200 acres *Davis Addition*; after wife dies personal estate equally divided between 10 children, 5 sons and 5 daughters; wife Mary and sons John and Francis, executors; witnesses Michael Hackett, John Sappington and Richard Sappington; probated 24 May 1749."

[25] Riggs, *The Riggs Family of Maryland*, 61.
   This book cites *The Baxter's Directory*, in family hands, as the source for "early Davis records" including the dates that Mary Pierpont and Thomas Davis died.

[26] Richard Davis, will, Probate Records, Prerogative Court Wills, Maryland State Archives, MSA #SM16. SR4417, 23: 266-268.
   "17 May 1743; Richard Davis will, planter, Anne Arundel County, Maryland; to son Thomas 194 acres *Davis' Purchase*; to son Richard 200 acres *Dear Bought* in Prince Georges County; to son John Davis remainder of *Dear Bought* 58 acres, also 100 acres warrant, charges to be paid by two eldest sons; to son Caleb 93 acres *The Reserve*, Anne Arundel County; to son Joshua 50 acres, north end tracts and balance of *Davis' Purchase* in Anne Arundel County; to daughters Ruth, Mary and Elizabeth, personal property; executrix wife Ruth; testators John Waters (Quaker), Joseph Penn, Samuel Richardson and John Evitts; probated 18 Oct 1743."

[27] See Hewitt Family Bible, Appendix A.

[28] Stein, *Origin and History of Howard County, Maryland*, 46-47, 202.
   "Christ Church, Anne Arundel County, Maryland, Regulation of the Pews in the church by the Vestry as Follows: 6 Jul 1736, Mr. Richard Davis and Thomas Davis, pew number 7; Mr. John Elder and John Elder, Jr. pew number 25.

John Elder settled in Maryland in 1673 the founder of the Elder family of Howard and Anne Arundel Counties. His son, John Elder...in 1717 acquired 100 acres of *Duvall's Delight* ... in 1736 he purchased from Joshua Dorsey and Henry Ridgely, 334 acres of *Huntington Quarter*."

[29] Jane Baldwin Cotton, editor, *Maryland Calendar of Wills, 1738-1743* (Westminster, Maryland: Family Line Publications, 1988), 8: 145.

"22: 391; 29 Dec 1740, John Elder will, Anne Arundel County; to son Alexander 100 acres *Addition to Huntingtown Quarter*; to son James 100 acres dwelling plantation *Duvall's Delight* and 41 acres *Laxford*; to son Charles 100 acres *Addition to Huntingtown Quarter*; to children Alexander, James, Charles and Mary, residue of estate; executors sons Alexander and James; testators Richard Daviss, Orlando Griffith, Edward Penn, and Catharine Scott; probated 11 Mar 1740/1741."

[30] Wright, *Anne Arundel County Church Records*, 195.

[31] Charles Elder, administration, Maryland Historical Records R80, Testamentary Proceedings 1751-1752 (Anne Arundel County, Maryland), 35: 991.

"4 Nov 1751; Charles Elder his administrative bond by Ruth Elder his wife with Richard Davis and Caleb Davis her sureties in the sum of £60 sterling."

[32] Charles Elder inventory, Maryland State Archives, Prerogative Court Inventories (Anne Arundel County, Maryland: SR4348-1), 48: 241-243.

"21 Feb 1752, entered 10 Mar 1752; Charles Elder estate inventory, Anne Arundel County, deceased, personal inventory £107.01.6; appraised by James Elder, and Alexander Elder, relations; witnesses Phil Hammond and William Hall, Elk Ridge, creditors."

[33] Warfield, *The Founders of Anne Arundel and Howard Counties, Maryland*, 90, 115.

"The youngest son of Richard and Elinor (Browne) Warfield, was Benjamin. He married Elizabeth Duvall...and died in 1717 leaving his children minors...Joshua [son] of Benjamin held the homestead. By his wife, Ruth Davis, of Thomas, he had Benjamin, Joshua, Henry, Thomas, Caleb, Mary, Elizabeth and Elinor.

Richard Davis, of Thomas and Mary, was located near Highland, Howard. He married Ruth, daughter of John Warfield and Ruth Gaither. They had sons, Richard, Thomas [married] Mary Sappington; Caleb [married] Lucretia Griffith of Orlando. His inheritance was *Duvall's Delight* on the Patuxent."

[34] Gloria L. Main, *Tobacco Colony: Life in Early Maryland, 1650-1720, Middling and Affluent Planters*, (Princeton: Princeton University Press, 1982), 225.

[35] Richard Davis, account, Maryland Prerogative Court, Inventories and Accounts of Estates, (Annapolis: Hall of Records Commission, 1947), Family History Library, Salt Lake City, microfilm #0012905 (1744), #0012906 (1745), #0012907, (1750), 446-447, 99-100, 239-241.

"10 Oct 1744, Ruth Davis account, Anne Arundel County, widow and executrix of will of Richard Davis, Anne Arundel County, deceased; list of bad debts due estate, protested bills and notes of hand examined by Alexander Warfield, son of Richard.

16 Aug 1750, Ruth Davis account, asked for four tobacco hogsheads to pack the deceased's tobacco crops at £4 each=£16; expenses to roll 3 hogsheads of tobacco shipped on account.

28: 92-96, 2 Nov 1743; Richard Davis, deceased inventory appraised, valued at £511.10.00; signed Richard Snowden; Joshua Dorsey; Thomas Davis, father of the deceased; Francis Davis, brother of the deceased; John Corbett, creditor."

[36] Volunteer State Community College, Gallatin Tennessee, from a course book on communications in the 17-18th Centuries, online at <http://www2.volstate.edu/humanities/comm/cb09ps01.ppt.>

[37] Rosemary B. Dodd and Patricia M. Bausell, *Abstracts of Land Records, Anne Arundel County, Maryland 1712-1718*, IB#2: 485, (Pasadena, Maryland: Anne Arundel Genealogical Society, 199-), 102. This deed described where in Anne Arundel County *Duvall's Delight* was located.

"13 March 1717/18, deed from Charles Carroll Esq., Anne Arundel County; to John Elder, Anne Arundel County, planter; for £20 sterling, 100 acres in Anne Arundel County, part of a tract called *Duvall's Delight* on the west side of the north branch of the Patuxent River."

[38] Warfield, *The Founders of Anne Arundel and Howard Counties, Maryland*, 347.
    "Huntington, Annapolis Junction. South of Waterloo, upon the Post Road was Huntingtown on the east and Guilford on the west. Into this section came Colonel Henry Ridgely, his nephew Nicholas Dorsey, Orlando Griffith and John Worthington."

[39] 1783 Tax Assessment Records, Maryland Indexes, MSA S1437, Anne Arundel County MD MSA #S1161-1-3 Location 1/4/5/44 (Annapolis: Maryland State Archives), 2.
    "1783 Anne Arundel County Tax Assessment, Elkridge Hundred, Rezin Hammond for *Jack's Peacock.*"

[40] Warfield, *The Founders of Anne Arundel and Howard Counties, Maryland*, 338-339.

[41] Stein, *Origin and History of Howard County, Maryland*, 41.

[42] William Hall inventory, *Maryland Prerogative Court Abstracts 1767-1772, Genealogical Records, Maryland Probate Records, 1674-1774*, Family Tree Maker, 62.
    "107: 339-355; 18 Sep 1771, inventory of William Hall lists debts due his estate, Anne Arundel County; including Jacob Hewitt and Edward Hewitt."

[43] Stein, *Origin and History of Howard County, Maryland*, 347.
    "The Anne Arundel County Debt Books, a selection listing ownership mostly in Howard County circa 1760 (in acres), James Elder, *Addition to Hunting[town] Quarter*, 334 acres; Ruth Davis, *Duvall's Delight*, 200 acres."

[44] James Elder administration, Maryland Balance Books 1763-1770, Maryland Prerogative Court Abstracts 1767-1772, Genealogical Record, Maryland Probate Records, 1674-1774, *Family Tree Maker*, 84.
    "5: 222, 15 Nov 1769; Anne Arundel County Maryland, distribution of James Elder estate; sureties Caleb Davis and Samuel Riggs; administrator John Elder."

[45] Riggs, *The Riggs Family of Maryland*, 57.
    "St. Ann's Parish, Middle Neck Hundred Anne Arundel County; 16 Jan 1721, John Riggs married Mary Davis, born 9 Jan 1702, Anne Arundel County, daughter of Thomas and Mary (Pierpont) Davis; issue of John and Mary (Davis) Riggs, Samuel Riggs, born 6 Oct 1740, married Amelia Dorsey."

[46] Robert Hewitt Bible. See Appendix B.

[47] Nicholson vs. Hewitt, judgment, Anne Arundel County Court Judgment Records (Annapolis: Archives of Maryland), ISB#4: 72-73, 114, 171-172 (1-1-8-39).
    "8 Jun 1756, Robert Davis, Anne Arundel County, planter represented defendant Jacob Hewitt, late of Anne Arundel County, planter, in William Nicholson's judgment to recover debt; 14 June 1756 William Nicholson recovered £10.17.3 against Jacob Hewitt, also 209 pounds tobacco; Hewitt to pay costs."

[48] William Nicholson will, *Maryland Calendar of Wills, 1759-1764, Genealogical Records: Maryland Probate Records, 1674-1774*, Family Tree Maker, *Calendar of Wills*, 69-70.

[49] Brugger, *Maryland: A Middle Temperament, 1634-1980*, 66.

[50] *The Newsletter of the Maryland Genealogical Society, Inc.*, 25: 3, July 1997, excerpts "Baltimore's Bicentennial Commemorative Program," (Baltimore: *Baltimore Magazine*, July 1997), 4.

[51] Peter Wilson Coldham, *Settlers of Maryland 1751-1756, Baltimore County Patents 1753-1757*, SR 7503, 5: 134.
    "Hewitt, Edward of Anne Arundel County purchased in Baltimore *Hewett's Shrubby Hills*, 100 acres on 24 Feb 1756."

[52] Warfield, *Founders of Anne Arundel and Howard Counties, Maryland*, 217-218, 180, 207.

"On Easter Monday, Apr 19, 1756, at the parish church meeting of the vestry…a list of bachelors was returned …to be taxed for church support, those possessing £100 and less than £300 were Mr. Caleb Davis at Mr. Philip Hammond's. Philip Hammond, of Charles and Hannah Howard, inherited Annapolis portion of father's estate; was leading import merchant, with warerooms in *Newtown*, a recent addition to Port of Annapolis; also prominent in legislative and church affairs."

[53] *Maryland Genealogical Society Bulletin* (Baltimore: Maryland Genealogical Society, 1970), excerpts from the *Griffith Family* by Romulus Riggs Griffith, 11: 22.

"Lucretia Griffith, of Orlando Griffith, Sr. and Katherine Howard, married Caleb Davis 15 Dec 1759. Their children were Sarah, Rachel, Lucy and Elizabeth."

[54] Riggs, *The Riggs Family of Maryland*, 105.

"Orlando Griffith established his dwelling plantation in Queen Caroline Parish. He married, June 6, 1717, Katherine Howard…they had issue Lucretia, born February 5, 1739; married Caleb Davis and secondly, Azel Waters."

[55] Henry S. Peden Jr., *Inhabitants of Baltimore County, 1763-1774*, (Westminster, Maryland: Family Line Publications, 1989), 14.

"An Index of Some Baltimore Residents in 1765: Abraham Enlos, Delilah Elder, Henry Hostiter, Jacob Hewett."

[56] Author Unknown, "Bicentennial History of Maryland," *Baltimore, City of Promise* (Washington, D.C.: Department of Education, 1953), Internet copy, not numbered.

[57] Coldham, *Settlers of Maryland 1751-1756*, 5: 134.

"Hewitt, Edward of Anne Arundel County, purchased in Baltimore *Sandy Bottom*, 400 acres on 13 Jun 1763."

[58] Gilcresh to Hewitt deed, Baltimore County Deeds, Archives of Maryland, Annapolis, Maryland Historical Records, Roll 120, Ac. 4923, Book A.L#C: 362-364.

"15 May 1771, deed from James Gilcresh, Chester County, Pennsylvania, farmer, brother and heir-at-law of Robert Gilcresh, deceased, late of Baltimore County; to Jacob Huet, Baltimore County, planter; part of tract called *Marlborough* in Baltimore County, witnesses John Newman and Andrew Buchanan; recorded 16 May 1771."

[59] Robert Gilcresh will and inventory, *Maryland Calendar of Wills, 1767-1772, 14: 26; Genealogical Records, Maryland Probate Records, 1674-1772, Maryland Prerogative Court Abstracts, 1769-1772, 15*, Family Tree Maker.

"36: 265, 20 Sep 1763, Robert Gilcresh, Baltimore County, deceased; bequeath to Robert Gilcresh, son of James; wife Helen executrix; witnesses Unke Unckes, Peter Longworth and Peter Galhur; probated 7 Nov 1767. 102: 77, 11 Nov 1769, Robert Gilcrest inventory, Baltimore County, deceased; next of kin James Gillcrest, William Gillcrest; executrix Helen Gilcrest."

[60] Hewitt Family Bible, see Appendix A.

[61] Paul H. Giddens, *History of Early Baltimore*, online, <www.mdarchives.state.md.us/ecp/10/236/html/00010004.html>, data downloaded 27 Feb 1999.

[62] Brugger, *Maryland: A Middle Temperament*, 84-113.

[63] Gilcresh to Hewitt and Tevis, deed, *Baltimore County Land Records*, Maryland State Archives (Annapolis: Hall of Records Commission, 1947), MSA#CM135, AL-I: 434-440, (R123-1).

"13 Apr 1774, deed from James Gilchrist, Chester County Pennsylvania, farmer, to Jacob Hewet, Edward Hewet and Peter Tivis, Baltimore County, farmers; whereas Robert Gilchrist, late of Baltimore County died by 27 May 1765 before conveying a deed to Jacob Hewitt in fee simple for 350 acres *Upper Marlborough* in Baltimore County and payment of £128.7.6; whereas Jacob Hewet has a bond with Edward Hewet and Peter Tivis as his sureties of the sum plus interest owed to Robert Gilchrist, and collected by his brother and heir-at-law, James Gilchrist, witness."

[64] Henry C. Peden Jr., *Revolutionary Patriots of Baltimore Town and Baltimore County, Maryland, 1775-1783* (Westminster, Maryland: Family Line Publications, 1988), 127. Second source, Unpublished Sources, Revolutionary War of Maryland, v. 6, published by the Daughters of the American Revolution, Maryland Society, 1941 by Margaret R. Hodges.
"Hewit, Edward, Oath of Allegiance 1778 before Hon. John Merryman (A-2/70); Hewitt, Jacob and Hewitt, Robert, Oath of Allegiance 1778 before Hon. Richard Cromwell (A-2/46)."

[65] Rowene T. Obert, *Baltimore, Maryland, City & County Marriage Licenses, 1777-1799*, (Salt Lake City: The Genealogy Shoppe, Inc., 1975), 88.
"Henry Tonstill to Delilah Elder, 30 Jun 1781."

[66] Caleb Hewitt's bounty land application, see *Jacob Hewitt in Maryland*, Source Note #92.

[67] Thomas Lynch Montgomery, editor, *Pennsylvania Archives* (Harrisburg, Pennsylvania: Harrisburg Publishing Company, 1906), 2: 3: 838.
"Caleb Hewitt, Revolutionary War service; 'Soldiers Who Received Depreciation Pay as per cancelled certificates on file in the Division of Public Records,' Pennsylvania State Library. A return of the non-commissioned officers and privates of the 4th Regt. Light Dragoons, specifying the date of enlistment, 4th Troop, 14 June, 1777, Caleb Hewitt, Serjt."

[68] "Continental Light Dragoons Larkin Smith's Troop, Brigade of the American Revolution Unit #240," online, http://www.geocities.com/Heartland/Acres/8845.
"4th Dragoon Officers names, Index of the Washington Papers," not numbered.

[69] John C. Fitzpatrick, *The Writings of George Washington from the Original Manuscript Sources, 1745-1799*, online at "American Memory: The George Washington Papers at the Library of Congress, 1741-1799," online, http://lcweb2.loc.gov/ammen.org, 12 May 1777, 25 Oct 1777.

[70] Hewitt-Hartaffel marriage (Family Search In'l Genealogical Index), source call #1396212, online, http://www.familysearch.org, downloaded 9 Sep 2000.
"1780, Caleb Hewitt marriage to Christina Hartaffel, Lancaster Pennsylvania."

[71] Montgomery, *Pennsylvania Archives*, 5: 3: 386.
"Moylan's Cavalry, Pennsylvania Regiment of Cavalry; Col. Stephen Moylan…on 5 Jun 1776 Congress elected him quartermaster general with the rank of colonel…He then raised his cavalry regiment as an independent organization, the officers were not all from Pennsylvania, but all were raised there in spring of 1781; ranks recruited to 80 men who went southward to join Gen. Wayne."

[72] Caleb Hewitt military pay, Public Debt, Records of the Comptroller General at D.P.R, Accounts of Auditors of Depreciation Accounts, Book A: 6, Register of Depreciation Certificates, Lancaster County Pennsylvania, Pennsylvania State Archives, downloaded 14 Jul 2001, on-line from http://www.digitalarchives.state.pa.us/archive.asp.

[73] John T. Humphrey, *Pennsylvania Births, Lancaster County 1778-1800*, Records of the Moravian Church, Lancaster (Washington, D.C: Humphrey Publications, 1997), 147.

[74] Montgomery, *Pennsylvania Archives*, 3: 22: 449.
"Transcript of Property, County of Westmoreland in 1783…Jacob Hewit."

[75] Hewitt-Hull marriage, Dawn Beitler Smith, *Baltimore County Marriage Licenses, 1777-1798*, (Westminster, Maryland: Family Line Publications, 1989), 42.

[76] Deeds, 1653-1849, Baltimore County, Maryland, Clerk of Circuit Court, General Index Grantors 1787-1797 (Salt Lake City: Family History Center), not numbered.

[77] Jacob Hewitt will, see Appendix C.

[78] Deeds, 1653-1849, Baltimore County, Maryland, not numbered.

[79] Baltimore City Archives, *A Name Index to the Baltimore City Tax Records, 1798-1800.* (Baltimore: Baltimore City Archives, 1981), not numbered. Baltimore was the largest city in Maryland with a population of over 60,000 residents in 1800. This is an indexed database of the earliest existing general property tax records in the city, dating between 1798 and 1808. It gives the names, year of assessment and reference to the original city tax record.
"Hewitt, Caleb, 1798 p. 5; 1799-1800 p. 132; 1800 p. 6; 1801-1803 p. 151; 1804-1808 p. 183; Hewitt, Eli 1798, p. 4; 1799-1800 p. 131; 1800 p. 7; 1801-1803 p. 151; 1804-1808 p. 183."

[80] Bill and Martha Reamy, *Records of St. Paul's Parish,* 1: 49.

[81] Henry Tunstall will, inventory and administration, *Baltimore County Wills* (Annapolis: Hall of Records Commission, 1947), 4: 506-508, 10: 494-498; inventories, MSA CM155, MdHR Wk 1050-1061-3, 16: 233-238, 379.
"10 Aug 1788, Henry Tunstill, Baltimore, Maryland, to wife Deliah Tunsell half personal estate, one third real estate; to daughter Ruth Tunsell whole estate; except watch to Ely Hewitt; executors William Tinker and Caleb Hewitt; 26 Nov 1790, Henry Tunstill inventory, witnesses Mark Morris and Wm. Asquith;15 Dec 1791,Henry Tunstill final account by Caleb Hewitt and William Tinker executors; money retained by Caleb Hewitt as guardian of Ruth Tunstill, balance £405.6.6."

[82] Caleb Hewitt, census, Index to 1790 Census Records, online downloaded 16 Jul 1997, http://www.ancestry.com. "Ancestry Genealogy Library, Maryland Census 1790, p. 21.
"Head of family, Hewitt, Caleb with 3 free white males, 4 free white males under 16 years, 4 free white females."

[83] *Baltimore County Maryland Deeds, 1653-1849,* General Grantee-Grantor Index, not numbered.
"1792, grantee Hewitt, Caleb; grantor William Hammond; assignment, part of Lot #509 on Liberty Street, Book II: 491."

[84] Smith, *Baltimore County Marriage Licenses, 1777-1798,* 42.

[85] J. Thomas Scharf, *Chronicles of Baltimore, Being a Complete History of Baltimore Town & Baltimore City from the Earliest Period to the Present Time,* (Baltimore: Turnbull Brothers, 1874), 78-79.
"A lot was secured from Mr. Daniel Grant on the southwest corner of Light Street and Wine Alley...opposite corner to the one previously occupied. The trustees, Mr. James McCannon, Caleb Hewitt, and Philip Rogers paid for the lot $5,360...29 Oct 1797 about ten months after the loss of the first church, Bishop Asbury dedicated the new *Light Street Church.*"

[86] James Edward Armstrong, *History of the Old Baltimore Conference* (Baltimore: King Brothers Printing, 1907), Appendix C, Baltimore, not numbered.
"Appendix C, Names of Official Members in the Files of the First Conference; Journal (1801-1809), Baltimore, Caleb Hewitt."

[87] Robert Barnes, *Marriages and Deaths from Baltimore Newspapers, 1796-1816* (Baltimore: Genealogical Publishing Company, 1978), 154.

[88] Caleb Hewitt will, Baltimore County Wills; 1802-1805, will book 7: 356-357, Maryland Archives, Annapolis, Family History Library: Salt Lake City, film #001359228, Dec 1798, codicil 8 Sep 1804, probated, 26 Jan 1805.
"28 Dec 1798, Caleb Hewitt will, Baltimore City Maryland, executors, John Brevitt and wife, if I should leave one; if I die without a wife then estate to my child(ren); if child(ren) die and I leave no wife, then one part each to brothers Robert Hewitt; Richard Hewitt and Ephraim Hewitt; to sisters Elizabeth Wood, sister Ruth Hewitt, Ruth Tunstill (god-child), oldest child of brother Eli Hewitt; and one part to poor of the City of Baltimore; if wife survives and child(ren) die in their noneage, wife to have 2/3 of estate and 1/3 to those above named; slave Saul freed at age 30, Hannah at eleven years from this date; 8 Sep 1804 codicil, all property acquired since 1798 subject to above disposition; if my son Caleb should die in his minority, his share to be divided between my other children; witnesses to codicil, John

McClellan, Jr., George Thornburgh and John Powley; probate witnesses Joel M. Munson, Michael Grub and Isaac Edmondson; probated 26 Jan 1805."

[89] Caleb Hewitt estate inventory, Maryland State Archives, Annapolis, Maryland, Baltimore County Register of Wills, Inventory of Estate, MSA #CM155, WK 1063-1016-1064, 6 Feb 1805, 377-383.

[90] R. F. Hayes Jr., editor, *Baltimore City's Dead* (Baltimore: Maryland Historical and Genealogical Bulletin, 1947), 78: 2, not numbered, "Burial of Caleb Hewitt."

[91] Barnes, *Marriages and Deaths from Baltimore Newspapers*, 154.
      "Hewitt, Caleb, died 24th instant in his 18th year, *Baltimore Sun*, 29 December 1814."

[92] Caleb Hewitt bounty land application, National Archives and Records Administration, Revolutionary War Bounty Land Applications.
      "27 Mar 1828, No. 1280, land application by Robert Hewitt, Washington D.C., son and heir, of Caleb Hewitt late Baltimore County deceased; testify that Caleb Hewitt was a private, Pennsylvania Line, Continental Army, Revolutionary War and served until the close of the war; applies for land warrant due deceased and never received during his life; sworn Robert Hewitt; witness Edward W. Clark; also Mary E. Broome, Washington D. C., formerly Mary E. Hewitt, wife of Capt. Charles R. Broome, U.S. Marine Corps, and she a daughter of Caleb Hewitt, witness Abraham Broome; that they are children and only heirs of Caleb Hewitt, a private in the Pennsylvania Line, Continental Army; Moylan's Dragoons; witness Edward W. Clark."

[93] Bill and Martha Reamy, *Records of St. Paul's Parish*, 1989, 2: 55.

[94] Caleb Hewitt, administration, Maryland State Archives, Annapolis Maryland, Baltimore County Register of Wills, administration accounts, MSA #CM127, WK 1015-1016-1, 16: 521-525, 3 Oct 1812, 94.

[95] Scharf, *History of Baltimore City and County*, 53.
      "The Founding of Baltimore City; on 14 Jan 1730 the first lots were taken up, and Richard Hewitt [took up] No. 35, on the west side of South Forest Street, both of which were forfeited for non-compliance with the building provision."

[96] Scharf, *History of Baltimore City and County*, 833-834.

[97] Reamy, *Records of St. Paul's Parish,* 1: 106, 123, 134; 2: 3, 8.
      "Marriages, Eli Hewitt to Martha Dennis 25 March 1797; sons of Eli and Martha Hewitt, Jacob born 8 January, baptized 28 October 1798; Eli born 15 August, baptized 17 November 1799; Rezin, born 7 February, baptized 17 May 1801; Eli, son of Eli Hewitt buried 24 September 1801."

[98] Eli Hewet household, 1850 U.S. census, Carroll County, Maryland, District 3., dwelling 910, family 871; dated 21 Oct 1850, National Archives film #M432-289, page 229.

[99] Richard Lee Morton, editor, "Inscriptions on Old Tombstones in Westmoreland and Northumberland Counties," *William and Mary College Quarterly* (Williamsburg, Virginia: Institute of Early American History and Culture, 1827), 2: 9: 29.

[100] "Civilian Defense in Baltimore," *Maryland Historical Magazine* (Baltimore: Maryland Historical Society, 1944), 39: 07: 206-207.
      "Baltimore 27 Aug 1814, the Committee of Vigilance and Safety met and yesterday's proceedings were read, that those of the third district, (2nd, 3rd and 4th wards) assemble at Washington Square on Tuesday morning, under the superintendence of...Eli Hewit."

[101] Archives of Maryland Online, Maryland Chancery Court 1809-1832, Annapolis Maryland, 26 Jan 1831, "Hewitt's Case, volume 198, page 198, volume 201, page 185, *Blands* Reports, downloaded from http:// www.mdarchives.state.md.us/megafile/msa/.

[102] Archives of Maryland Online, Maryland Chancery Court 1809-1832, 10 Oct 1825, Hewitt vs. Hewitt, MSA S512-8776, volume 201, page 102.

[103] Eli Hewitt will, court proceedings on contested will by Rezin Davis Hewitt; 31 Jul 1827, Maryland Wills, Anne Arundel County Orphans Court (Annapolis: Genealogical Society of Utah, 1949), microfilm #0013596, (1827), 326-333.

[104] Rezin D. Hewett and Eli Hewett vs. Jacob Hewitt, Appointment of trustee for Hewett, Archives of Maryland Online, Anne Arundel County Maryland Chancery Court 1809-1832, 31 Jul 1827, MSA S512-11-8803.

[105] Eli Hewitt estate, Maryland State Archives, Maryland Indexes, Chancery Papers, Index, MSA 1828 S1432, 16 Aug 1828.
"Margaret Hewitt vs. William Finley, Rezin D. Hewitt, Eli Hewitt and Jacob Hewitt."

[106] R. D. and E. Hewitt household, 1830 Maryland Census Index, federal population schedule, District 6, Anne Arundel County Maryland, National Archives film #53, page 186.

[107] Martha Hewitt will, Anne Arundel County Maryland wills, 1780-1847, part 4; 4 Mar 1830, probated 11 Aug 1830; (Family History Library: Salt Lake City), microfilm #0013596.

[108] Appointment of trustee for Hewett, Archives of Maryland Online, Anne Arundel County Maryland Chancery Court, *Bland's Reports*, *Chancery Court 1809-1832*; 12 Feb 1831, Volume 198: 3, pages 198-200, MSA S512-11-8762.

[109] Maryland State Archives, Maryland Indexes, Chancery Papers, volume 601, page 85, chapter 82, Section 1 and 2.

[110] Hewitt to Coulter, marriage license, *Baltimore (Maryland) Marriage Licenses 1777-1846*, Baltimore County(Maryland) Clerk of Circuit Court 1828-1832, (Family History Library: Salt Lake City), microfilm #0013693, page unknown..

[111] Jesse Glass, editor, *The Witness: Slavery in Nineteenth Century Carroll County Maryland*, (Meikai, Chiba-ken, Japan: Meikai University Press and Historical Society of Carroll County Maryland, 2004), page 72.

[112] Rezin D. Hewitt household, 1850 U.S. census, Anne Arundel County, Maryland, Howard District., dwelling 1499, family 1518; dated 29 Novt 1850, National Archives film #M432-278, page 516.

[113] Eli Hewitt and Delia Hewitt households, 1860 U.S. census, Carroll County, Maryland, Freedom District., dwelling 3, family 3; dated 8 & 18 Jun 1860; and Howard County Maryland, Lisbon 4th District, dwelling 194, family 189, National Archives film #M653-471 & 477, pages 0 & 27.

[114] Hewitt in Springfield Cemetery, Carroll County Maryland, *Carroll County Cemeteries*, (Carroll County Genealogical Society: Westminster, Maryland, 1989), volume 1:page 129-130.

[115] George Horvath, Jr., map, "Eldersburg Map," Department of Assessments & Taxation, Tax Map Division (published by the author, 1979), not numbered.
The map was adapted from a tax assessor's map of the Eldersburg area showing land surrounding the town, including *Sandy Bottom*, *Tevis Chance* and *Tevis Venture*.

[116] Hannah Hewitt's date of birth was given to the author by Diane Paulson whose source was a group chart for John Lowe who married Hannah Hewitt; online, 12 Jan 1999, Sprtmm@aol.com.

[117] Robert W. Barnes and Bettie Stirling Carothers, *1783 Tax List of Baltimore County, Maryland* (Westminster, Maryland: Family Line Publications, 1978), 16, 20.

"1783 Tax List, Baltimore County Maryland, "Delaware Upper Hundred," Rachel [Vachel] Hewitt, owners: no Land named, 1 free male with total of 5 white inhabitants living with him; single men: Edward Hewit Jr., securities: Edward Hewit."

[118] Family Archive Viewer, CD-ROM 225, *Marriage Index: Maryland 1655-1850,* (The Learning Company, Inc., 2000). In public records, Vachel Hewitt's first name was spelled in various ways including sometimes as a man named "Rachel."

"Huety, Vachel, spouse Redy (Rady) Ann, married 22 Nov 1779, Baltimore County Maryland."

[119] Barnes, *Maryland Marriages,* 149.

"Baltimore Licenses returned by various Ministers, some from St. Paul's Parish; John March 3 May 1784 to Cathe [Catherine] Hewit."

[120] The proposed marriage dates for Elizabeth Hewitt and Margaret Hewitt are based on the order they were named in Edward Hewitt's probated estate.

[121] Smith, *Baltimore County Marriage Licenses,* 42.

"Rachel Hewitt to Zachariah Linthicum 25 Nov 1790; Hannah Hewit to John Low 19 Aug 1778; Rebecca Hewitt to William Jordan on 4 Dec 1792."

[122] Reamy, *Records of St. Paul's Parish,* 1: 93.

[123] Edward Hewitt estate, Maryland State Archives, Baltimore County Register of Wills, Administration Accounts, 12 May 1792, pages 59-60.

"12 May 1792, Baltimore County, Edward Hewitt deceased, final account by Rachel Hewitt, administrator; balance to Edward Hewitt's children, £72.05.11, including £23.16.05 refunded by widow's 1/3 part of deceased estate; disbursements of £05.19.01 each to Vachel Hewitt, Rebeccah Hewitt, Amelia Hewitt; to married daughters through their husbands, Zachariah Linsicomb, John Lowe, John Marsh, John Tripolet, and William Cook."

[124] John Lowe and others, deed to William Cook and others, (Salt Lake City: Family History Library) microfilm #0013379, Baltimore County Recorder, 25 May 1804, 3 pages, not numbered.

25 May 1804, deed from heirs of Edward Hewitt, late of Baltimore County deceased, John Low (wife Hannah), William Jordan (wife Rebecca), John Marsh (wife Catherine), Hugh McMechen (wife Amelia), Zachariah Linthicum (wife Rachel), and Robert Hewitt, all of Baltimore County Maryland; to William Cook for £20, 20 ½ acres of *Hewitt's Shrubby Hills;* witnesses F. Snowden and O. G. Dorsey; recorded 27 Oct 1804.

[125] George J. Horvath Jr., *The Particular Assessment Lists for Baltimore and Carroll Counties 1798* (Westminster, Maryland: Family Line Publications, 1986), 97-99, 103.

[126] Letter from George Horvath Jr., Eldersburg, Maryland to the author on 18 Apr 1998.

"By 1813, [in reference to Delaware Upper Hundred list of 1798] that part of Baltimore County was also called Election Dist. #6 where in 1813 Rachel [Vachel] Hewitt was taxed for 82 acres of 'part of *Sandy Bottom.*'"

[127] On 13 Jan 1999, a resident of Carroll County who was familiar with the area near Eldersburg and of the Hewitt farm, gave the author a description of how it looked before it became part of a housing subdivision, downloaded from Sprtmm@aol.com.

SOURCE NOTES
Chapter Four

TWO BROTHERS

[1] Hewitt Family Bible, see Appendix A.

[2] Eli Hewitt household, Maryland 1800 U.S. Federal Census Index, Federal Population Schedule, Baltimore County, Maryland, National Archives micro-publication #MD1a1552888, 229.
"1800, Baltimore Maryland, Eli Hewitt, males: 23110; females: 10010-00."

[3] Caleb Hewitt household, 1790 U.S. Census, Baltimore County, Maryland, National Archives Microfilm # M637-3, 33.
"Baltimore Town, Caleb Hewitt, FWM +16: 3; FWM-16: 4, FWF: 4."

[4] Richard Hewitt deed, 1 Apr 1793, Fayette County Pennsylvania deed book E: 202-203, Microfilm #0863551, 1802-1803, Family History Library, Salt Lake City. Following is a record abstract.
"1 Apr 1793, from Richard Hewitt, Menallen Township, Fayette County, Pennsylvania, yeoman and wife Phebe, to John Craig, Union Township, Fayette County, Pennsylvania."

[5] Thomas Lynch Montgomery, Editor, *Pennsylvania Archives* (Harrisburg, Pennsylvania: Harrisburg Publishing Company, 1906), 3: xxii, 449.
"*County of Westmoreland-1783, Transcript of Property,* "Jacob Hewit."

[6] Robert L. Johnson, *The American Heritage of James Norman Hall: Pioneering in Fayette County, Pennsylvania*, (Philadelphia: Dorrance & Company, 1969), 84-85.

[7] Jacob Hewitt township officer, *Orphans Court Docket 1783-1802 and Minutes of Court of General Quarter Sessions of the Peace 1783-1808*, Fayette County Pennsylvania Prothonotary, *Fayette County Pennsylvania Order Books*, (Salt Lake City: Family History Library), microfilm #1449107, not numbered.
"March Sessions, 1785, Township Officers for the year: Manallin, Constable, Thomas Brown; Overseers of the Poor, John Tate, Jacob Hewitt."

[8] R. Eugene Harper, *The Transformation of Western Pennsylvania, 1770-1800*, (Pittsburgh: University of Pittsburgh Press, 1991), 167.

[9] William L. Iscrupe, Editor, *LaFayette: History and Genealogy of Fayette County Pennsylvania*, (Laughlintown, Pennsylvania: Southwest Pennsylvania Genealogical Services, 1983), 3:3, 11.
"Civil Court Docket 9, June Term 1786, John Collins, for use of Hugh Gilmore vs. Jacob Hewett, summons Debt: £150."

[10] Iscrupe, *LaFayette*, page 12.
"Civil Court Docket 66, June Term 1786, Thomas Shane, assignee of Henry Hart vs. Jacob Hewett, capias debt: £100."

[11] James Veech, *The Monongahela of Old: Historical Sketches of South-Western Pennsylvania to the Year 1800*, (Pittsburgh: Privately Printed, 1910), 26-29.

[12] Thomas B. Searight, *The Old Pike: A History of the National Road*, (Uniontown, Pennsylvania: Published by the Author, 1894), 245.

[13] Jacob Hewitt, tavern keeper, *Minutes of Court of General Quarter Sessions of the Peace 1783-1808*, Family History Library, Salt Lake City, Microfilm #1449107, not numbered.
"Tavern Rates Order Books, December Session 1784 tavern keepers recommended and licensed Jacob Hewit, Manallin Township; March Sessions 1786; March Sessions 1787; March Sessions 1788."

[14] Iscrupe, *LaFayette*, Apr 1990, *9:19-30*, Tavern License Recommendations, Fayette County, 1795-1801, "September Sessions 1795, 1797, 1799, 1800, 1801: A list of persons recommended as tavern keepers in Fayette County, Ephraim Hewitt."

[15] Jacob Hewitt will, see Appendix C.

[16] *Old Westmoreland: History and Genealogy of Westmoreland County Pennsylvania,* (Laughlintown, Pennsylvania: Southwest Pennsylvania Genealogical Services), Aug 1986, # 7: 2.
    "A List of Negro and Mulatto Slaves, Westmoreland County, Pennsylvania, 1780-1782, registered to Jacob Hewitt, male not named aged 30; female Esther age 20; male Ben aged 1; registered 17 Dec 1782."

[17] Ben Hewit, 1813 Tax List, Union Township 1810-1815, Fayette County, Pennsylvania, (Salt Lake City: Family History Library), microfilm #1499319, page not known.
    "Union Township, Ben Hewit, Negro, forge man, tax £0.50."

[18] Binn Hewett, 1820 U.S. Federal Census, Pennsylvania Federal Population Schedule, Fayette County, Pennsylvania, Index, 1772-1890, ID#PAS2a585184, 153.
    "Union Township, Binn Hewett."

[19] McGroarty, *Ancestry of Mrs.Sophia Hewitt Buckner.*

[20] R. Carlyle Buley, *The Old Northwest Pioneer Period 1815-1840* (Indiana Historical Society, Indianapolis: 1950), 481-484.

[21] Searight, *The Old Pike,* 17-18.

[22] Boyd Crumrine, *The Centennial Celebration of the Organization of Washington County, Pennsylvania: Proceedings and Addresses,* (Washington, Pennsylvania: E. E. Crumrine, Publisher, 1881), page unknown.
    "Washington County Quarter Sessions, December Sessions 1783, Tavern Rates Order Books, Washington County PA."

[23] Rebecca Mariah Hewitt, *Autobiography of Rebecca Mariah Hewitt,* edited and pages numbered by the author with permission from descendant, Frank Bair, unpublished, written about 1910.

[24] Eli Hewitt will, Maryland Wills, *Baltimore County Orphans Court,* (Annapolis: Genealogical Society of Utah, 1949), Family History Library, Salt Lake City, microfilm #0013596, 326-333. Following is an abstract of the will and its dispute by Rezin Hewitt.
    "11 May 1827, Eli Hewitt will, Anne Arundel County Maryland, freedom for slaves after age 30; to son Jacob Hewitt a house and ten acres during his life, executor to provide board and lodging; to son Rezin D. Hewitt $1 and £5 sterling; to son Eli Hewitt executor, residue of estate including 400 acres in Anne Arundel County, two houses in Baltimore, all livestock, farming utensils and personal property; witnesses T. W. Turner, Benjamin Shipley, Jr., and John Marriott.
    Rezin Davis Hewitt, Anne Arundel County to Justices of the Orphans Court, Anne Arundel County, petition and libel against Eli Hewitt showing he is father of the libellant; that on 2 May 1827 Hewitt executed a will, witnessed by the above men; that Eli Hewitt died shortly thereafter, that will was exhibited in court and two witnesses testified that Eli Hewitt was of sound mind and competent to make his will; Rezin Hewitt charges that his deceased father was insane for several years before his death and he has witnesses to prove it; that when he made his will, Eli was insane and incapable of executing a valid deed or contract, cited the act of 1798 (Book 101, Chapter 1, Section 3), that the will is invalid; whereas Rezin Hewitt prays that the court refuse to admit the will for probate, and libellant requests summons of several men to testify on his behalf, per attorney W. H. Marriott for Rezin Hewitt."

[25] Jacob Hewitt will, see Appendix C.

[26] Phillip Shute, *Memoirs of Phillip Shute, Son of Phillip Shute and Elizabeth Waller,* unpublished, received by e-mail from <Rainsman13@aol.com>, Cleve Weathers of Tennessee, a descendant of Phillip Shute, downloaded 6 Feb 1998, p.2.
    "'My sister Anna married in Pennsylvania, Hayes Hewitt, and came to Tennessee with my father.' Robert Hewitt's full name was Robert Hazael Hewitt, and was likely known through his middle name as Hayes."

[27] Robert Hewitt Family Bible, see Appendix B.

[28] Robert Hewitt household, 1790 U.S. Census, Fayette County, Pennsylvania, Menallen Township, National Archives micro-publication #PAS1a17929366, 108.

[29] Hewitt to Alexander McClean, power of attorney, Fayette County Recorder, Uniontown, Pennsylvania, Salt Lake City: Family History Library microfilm #863548, deed book A: 356.

"13 Apr 1791, Robert Hewitt, Manallen Township, Fayette County, Pennsylvania; on 1 Oct 1790 Christian Wireman promised to deliver a warrant for 95 acres by 15 Jan 1791 and he did not; so Hewitt, about to leave Pennsylvania, sold the land and transferred warrant to John Wood, a Uniontown saddler, to collect the warrant; Hewitt's attorney Alexander McClean to deliver deed to Wood; witnesses Uriah Springer and John Wood; recorded 15 Oct 1791, by Isaac Mason."

[30] Sarah Foster Kelley, *West Nashville: Its People and Environs*, (Nashville: Published by the Author, 1987), 26 & 59.

"'The names of Phillip and Elizabeth (Waller) Shute's children are Anna Shute who married Robert Hewitt,' from a personal interview with Mrs. Roy Avery, Park Manor, August 1984, Nashville, by the author. 'Judge Robert Hewitt (born 1755, died 1837) married Anna Shute on September 16, 1786; their eight children were Caleb Hewitt...Elizabeth Hewitt.'"

[31] Shute, *Memoirs of Phillip Shute*.

"Being the youngest of a large generation my children...my mother died with the last child, an infant under three months old; he (Phillip Shute) left Pennsylvania for Tennessee in the year 1790 [1791], renting ground to cultivate at Manscor's Lick in Sumner County the first year. He then bought land of Pete Turney in Davidson County where he lived until he died...he paid for his land was $1.00 per acre. My mother's maiden name was...Elizabeth Waller. My sister Anna married in Pennsylvania, Hayes Hewitt, and came to Tennessee with my father."

[32] Cora Chenoweth Hiatt, *History of the Chenoweth Family*, (Winchester Publishing Co.: Winchester Indiana, 1925), 73.

[33] Abram Mason, *Letter of an Old Settler, 27 Mar 1860*, copied from the Mason Family manuscript by Naomi Lee Morrow Halley, published about 1860, pages 8-9 and 14-15. *American Historical Magazine* (New York: The Publishing Company of New York, 1898), 1:1:90. The letter was from Abram Mason to Dr. John Henry Currey.

[34] Goodspeed's, *History of Sumner, Smith, Macon and Trousdale Countie*, (Easley, South Carolina: Southern Historical Press, 1979), 918.

[35] Shute to Mason deed, *Davidson County, Tennessee, Register of Deeds 1796-1798*, Nashville Library and Archive, Strictly by Name, online www.strictlybyname.com, Roll One, D: 212.

[36] Robert Hewitt deed, Register of Deeds, Tennessee State Library and Archives, Volume C, 1792-1796, Roll 1, Nashville, Tennessee, 254.

"31 Jan 1794, deed from Philip Shute Davidson County to Robert Hewett of the same, for £100, 100 acres in Davidson County on the south side of the Cumberland River."

[37] Kelley, *West Nashville*, 58-61.

[38] Caleb Hewitt obituary, 9 Sep 1816, *Nashville Whig*, Nashville, Tennessee, call #TSM 106, 2 Sep 1812-25 Dec 1816, Tennessee State Library and Archives, page 3, column 2.

[39] Robert Hewitt Family Bible, see Appendix B.

[40] Kelley, *Children of Nashville*, 97, 137 158.

[41] Edwin Childress household, 1850 U.S. Census, Davidson County, Tennessee, population schedule, 2nd Subdivision, dwelling 750, family 750, page 320, plus slave schedule not numbered; National Archives micro-publication, roll M432-875.

[42] Jonathan K.T. Smith, *Tombstone Inscriptions in Historic Riverside Cemetery in Jackson Tennessee,* "Tombstone Inscriptions Scrapbook, Part III" (Jackson Tennessee: Published by the Author, 1992).

[43] Haze Hewitt household, 1850 U.S. Census, District 7, Madison County, Tennessee, population schedule, Second Subdivision, dwelling 839, family 839, page 275 plus slave schedule not numbered; National Archives micro-publication, roll M432-899.

[44] Kelly, *West Nashville,* 61-62.

[45] Jacob Hewitt Family Bible, see Appendix A.

[46] Reamy, *Records of St. Paul's Parish,* "Death Records," 1:49.
    "Mrs. Tunstill bur[ied] 13 June 1790; Henry Tunstall bur[ied] 24 November 1790."
[47] Moore (Moyer's), Clermont County, Ohio, Cemetery Records, *Ohio Records and Pioneer Families,* (Mansfield, Ohio: Ohio Genealogical Society, 1976), 19: 61.
    "This cemetery is on State Road #222, one mile beyond Batavia, on the left, just below the old mill: Hewitt Jacob, b. 11-11-1791, age 58."

[48] Widow Hewitt household, 1790 U.S. Federal Census, Fayette County Pennsylvania, Bullskin Township, online http://www.ancestry.com, image #582, roll:M637-8, page 46.
    "Widow Hewit, 2FWM+16, 0FWM-16, 3FWF, 0FP, 3 slaves." The census suggests that Ruth Hewitt and sons, Richard and Ephraim, were living at home; also daughters, Elizabeth and Ruth; slaves Esther, Ben and Harry. Phebe and Richard probably married in early 1791, so she was not living in their household.

[49] Franklin Ellis, editor, *History of Fayette County, Pennsylvania* (Philadelphia: L. H. Everts & Co, 1882), 157-180, 173, 166.

[50] Stein, *Origin and History of Howard County Maryland,* 191.
    "Ephraim Davis, who was seated at Greenwood, married Elizabeth, daughter of Cornelius Howard. His son was Thomas Davis. During the Whiskey Rebellion in Pennsylvania in 1794, he commanded a company of militia who marched to Pennsylvania and put down the insurrection, thereby establishing as a principle of law, that the Constitution of the United States did not guarantee the right of the citizen to make his own whiskey."

[51] Ellis, *History of Fayette County, Pennsylvania,* 158-159, 175.
    It is certain that Thomas Davis passed through Fayette County in October of 1794, because records show that the army took the route of General Braddock in 1755 to the Great Meadows. They went from there to Uniontown where General Lee and his troops encamped for a few days.

[52] Richard Hewitt, indenture, Fayette County Recorder, Uniontown, Pennsylvania, (Salt Lake City: Family History Library), microfilm #0863551, 1 Apr 1793, E: 202.

[53] The birth dates for John and Betty Hall's children were calculated from his will and from various deeds made throughout his life.

[54] George Woods to John Hall, Fayette County Recorder, Uniontown, Pennsylvania, (Salt Lake City: Family History Library), microfilm #0863548, A:194.
    "15 Apr 1776, George Woods, Bedford, Pennsylvania Esq. warrant to survey 200 acres for my use by John Hall, Westmoreland County, yeoman, who paid me £0.05.00 for his use, I discharge Hall of that trust and have sold him my rights and interest in the property; recorded 2 Sep 1780."

[55] E. Howard Blackburn & William H. Welfley, *History of Bedford, Somerset and Fulton Counties Pennsylvania,* (Evansville, Indiana: Unigraphic Inc, 1977), 208.
    "George Woods served as a member of the supreme executive council in 1778-9, September 1791 he became the first associate judge of the county; 1784 he laid out the "old military plan" of the town of Pittsburgh, and one of the streets of that city derived its name from him."

[56] John Hall deed, Fayette County Recorder, Uniontown, Pennsylvania (Family History Library, Salt Lake City), microfilm #0863548, E: 38.

"Book A: 105; 15 Apr 1776, to John Hall, 216 3/4 acres called *Bold Adventure*, on a branch of Boland's Run and Redstone Creek, on north side Franklin Twp.; surveyed 5 Mar 1784.

Book E: 3; 15 Apr 1776, deed from John Carmichael, in land dispute between Carmichael and Hall; whereas Hall's survey must be altered to conform with this survey and the one in Margaret Hall's name, formerly in James Craig's name; by Alexander McClean, Deputy to the Surveyor General."

[57] Loudoun Museum, Leesburg, Virginia, *A Brief History of Loudoun County*, downloaded 17 Apr 2004 from www.waterfordva-wca.org/history-loudoun/htm.

[58] William Hall deed, *The Library of Virginia*, Land Office Patents & Grants, Northern Neck Grants & Surveys, Prince William County Virginia, No. D, 1731-1732, p. 69 (reel 291), online at http://eagle.vsla.edu/cgi-bin.

"William Hall, grantee, 11 Nov 1731, Prince William County County, for 1,241 acres on the branches of Pohick [Creek] adjoining land of Francis Awbrey and John Mercer."

[59] Peggy Shomo Joyner, compiler, *Abstracts of Virginia's Northern Neck Warrants & Surveys, Dunmore, Shenandoah, Culpepper, Prince William, Fauquier & Stafford Counties, 1710-1780*, (Portsmouth, Virginia: P. Joyner, 1985-1987), 3:108, 113, 122, 128, 134.

"10 Aug 1739, deed to William Hall for 351 acres on fork of Beaver Dam of Goose Creek near Jeremiah Bronough; chain carriers...William Hall, Junior, surveyor, recorded 28 Mar 1740.

Thomas Owsley, no warrant, date from survey on 20 Jul 1739 for 1,449 acres on Little River of Goose Creek nrst...William Hall, Senior, recorded Aug 1739."

[60] Ruth and Sam Sparacio, *Deed Abstracts of Fairfax County, Virginia 1742-1750*, (McLean Virginia: privately printed, 1960), 69, 72, 75, Deed Book B, pages 202-203, 168-170.

"9 Feb 1746, deed from Thomas Hall, Fairfax County to Thomas Owsley, of same, for £5, south side of Little River near Carter; deed of gift to Thomas Hall from his father, William Hall Sr., land in dispute between Thomas Hall and Thomas Owsley, signed Thomas"X" Hall; witnesses Edward and John Barry, Thomas Middleton and George "X" Adams, recorded 17 Mar 1746.

19 Sep 1746, deed from William Hall and wife Jane, Fairfax County; to William Hall, Jr., of same; for love and affection, 200 acres of a larger tract granted to William Hall on 21 Aug 1731, near tract William Hall sold to William West and Hall's other land near Edward Graham; no witnesses shown, signed William "X" Hall and Jane "X" Hall, recorded 17 Mar 1746."

[61] William Hall, inventory, Fairfax County, Virginia, Will Book A, (1742-1752), Salt Lake City, Genealogical Society of Utah.

"8 May 1751, W. West, Elisha Hall & Henry Tailler, account continued and held for Fairfax County from 26 Sep 1750, this inventory and appraisal of William Hall's estate, deceased, was returned and admitted to record, John Graham, examiner."

[62] Ray Keim, *William and Mary Quarterly*, "Primogeniture and Entail in Colonial Virginia," (Williamsburg: Institute of Early American History and Culture, 1943), Series 3: 25:4:551-552.

[63] Ruth and Sam Sparacio, *Virginia County Court Records, Deed Abstracts of Loudoun County, Virginia 1757-1762*, (McLean Virginia: privately published, 1987), Book B: 50-52.

"4 Apr 1760, deed from Thomas Hail [Hall], Chester County Pennsylvania to William West, Loudoun County Virginia; for £50 land in Loudoun County near Blue Ridge Mountains, inherited by Thomas Hale [Hall] as the eldest son of William Hall, deceased in testate, acres not shown, signed Thomas Hale [Hall; witnesses William West Jr., Thomas (X) Botts, Joanna (X) Grinage, Joseph Hutchison, Benjamin Hutchison, Aaron Botts and John Hall; 11 Nov 1760 deed recorded."

[64] John T. Phillips, *The Historian's Guide to Loudoun County, Virginia, Volume 1: Colonial Laws of Virginia and County Court Orders 1757-1766*, (Leesburg, Virginia: Goose Creek Publications, 1996), Loudoun County Deed Book A: 458-459; 1:486.

"14 May 1760; Mary Hall & Susanna Hall, orphans of William Hall, deceased, both choose John Hall as their guardian; John Hall with William West as ecurity, entered bond to preserve orphans estate. The Hall family were William West's neighbors."

[65] Sparacio, *Virginia County Court Record: Loudoun County, Virginia,* 13 May 1765, D: 2: 440, 73.

[66] Marty Hiatt and Craig Roberts Scott, compilers, *Loudoun County Virginia Tithables, [1749], 1758-1786,* (Athens, Georgia: Iberian Publishing Company, 1995), 37, 74, 101, 102, 143, 144.

[67] John Hall, Patriotic Service, *Loudoun County, Virginia, Minute Book 1780-1783,* (Miami Beach: TLC Genealogy, 1990), 83.

[68] John Hall deed, 7 Jun 1782, Loudoun County Virginia Deed Book N, 1779-1784, (Salt Lake City, Genealogical Society of Utah, 1952), microfilm #0032303, N: 295-301.
    "7 Jun 1782, deed from John Hall and wife Betty, Loudoun County; to Joseph Lacey, of same, for £0.05 and a year's rent on all houses; three tracts of 202 acres where John Hall lives (72 acres sold by Wm. West to Wm Hall, Jr on 8 Feb 1748, 100 acres sold by Edward Graham Sr. to Wm. Hall Jr. on 23 Nov 1748, 30 acres sold by Samuel Wyckoff to John Hall 21- 22 Jun 1772); surveyed into one May 1782, boundaries to John Smarr, Graham's Spring Branch, Owsley's Branch, Pierce Bayley, John Hall, George Dowdle and Carter's line."

[69] Yardley Taylor, surveyor, *Southern Loudoun County Virginia near Middleburg,* from actual surveys, (Salt Lake City: Family History Library, map drawer, 1853), #975.528E7t.

[70] Eugene M. Scheel, surveyor and mapmaker, *Map of Southern Loudoun County Virginia,* (Salt Lake City, map drawer, 1972), #975.528E7s.

[71] Margaret Hall deed, Fayette County Recorder, Uniontown, Pennsylvania (Salt Lake City), microfilm #0863548, A: 38.
    "4 Mar 1784, Margaret Hall, Fayette County, Pennsylvania, young woman, my name was used for John Hall, Fayette County, yeoman for a warrant on 200 acres at his expense and use, and £0.05 paid me; I give claim to my father, John Hall, Margaret (X) Hall, witnesses John Hall, Jr. and Thomas Hall, recorded Aug 1739."

[72] John Hall, Sr., patent by Hugh Hall, Fayette County Recorder, Uniontown, Pennsylvania, (Salt Lake City), microfilm #0863553, H:5, 432.
    "27 Sep 1785, Hugh Hall paid $44.16 to John Hall, Sr., for 327 acres, Redstone Creek, survey toward warrant; John Hall Sr., deceased, gave land in will toHugh Hall, recorded 2 Mar 1807."

[73] R. Eugene Harper, *The Transformation of Western Pennsylvania 1770-1800,* (Pittsburgh: University of Pittsburgh Press, 1991), 9, 53-54, 22-25, 48.

[74] Iscrupe, *LaFayette,* Fayette County Civil Court Docket, Uniontown, Pennsylvania, Apr, 1983, 3:3, 11.
    "June Term 1786, #46 Commonwealth of Pennsylvania vs. John Hall, summons debt: £25; #9 John Collins for the use of Hugh Gilmore vs. Jacob Hewitt, summons debt: £150."

[75] William Franklin Horn, *The Horn Papers:* Volume 3, "Early Westward Movement on the Monongahela and the Upper Ohio, 1765-1795," (Scottsdale, Pennsylvania: Herald Press, 1945). Contains warrant, survey and patent maps for Fayette, Greene and Washington Counties, Pennsylvania: Fayette County, North Union Township. This map shows John Hall, Sr. with 327 acres, and Philip Shute with 201 acres.

[76] Jacob Hewit Bible was used to approximate marriage dates for both families.

[77] Thomas Hall indenture, Fayette County Recorder, Uniontown, Pennsylvania, (Salt Lake City: Family History Library), microfilm #0863551, D: 7 & 8.
    "8 Nov 1791, recorded 8 Sep 1796, deed from Thomas Hall and wife Elizabeth, Franklin Township, Fayette County Pennsylvania, to Abraham Stouffer, Tyrone Township, of same; whereas John Hall (Jr.) had land surveyed, has since died in testate, no issue; land descends by law to Thomas Hall as kin and eldest brother of John Hall."

[78] John Hall deed, Fayette County Recorder, Uniontown, Pennsylvania, (Salt Lake City: Family History Library), microfilm #0863548, A: 66.
"Recorded 15 Oct 1787, John Hall Sr. Union Township, Fayette County, on 15 Apr 1776 granted 200 acres to George Woods for survey, sells rights to Hugh Hall for £10."

[79] John Hall deed, Fayette County Recorder, Uniontown, Pennsylvania (Salt Lake City: Family History Library), microfilm #0863550, 1798, C: 1198-1199.
"Ephraim Hewitt, deed to Thomas Graham, New Geneva, Fayette County for £3.38.4; John Hall, Union Township, deceased, in his will gave daughters, Elizabeth and Rose, 282 acres, Franklin Township; Elizabeth now married to Ephraim Hewitt sells her part to Thomas Graham for $1,692."

[80] John Hall will, see Appendix D.

[81] Ephraim Hewitt household, 1800 U.S. Federal Census, Fayette County Pennsylvania, Menallen Township, online <http://www.ancestry.com>, Image #232, Roll: M32-38, page 569.

[82] Ephraim Hewitt, juror, *Minutes of Court of General Quarter Sessions of the Peace 1783-1808.* Salt Lake City: Family History Library, microfilm #1449107, not numbered.
"15 Sep 1792, Richard Waller vs. Jonathon Hill, jury called including Ephraim Hewitt.
17 Dec 1793, Commonwealth vs. Reuben Abrams, jury called including Ephraim Hewitt."

[83] Jacob Hewitt Family Bible, see Appendix A.

[84] Ephraim Hewitt, juror, constable, *Minutes of Court of General Quarter Sessions of the Peace 1783-1808.*
"Grand Inquest....Ephraim Hewitt was among nineteen others called to serve. Minutes of Court of Quarter Sessions, Union Town 4 Jun 1798, Sept 1798, Dec 1798, Mar 1799, sworn before the judge was Constable Ephraim Hewitt summoned for Manallin Township."

[85] Harper, *The Transformation of Western Pennsylvania*, 167-171.

[86] Iscrupe, *LaFayette*, "Fayette County Wills and Bonds, Administration Accounts," Apr 1981, V. 1.
"Ephraim Hewitt and John McCay guaranteed sureties of £300 for George Ireland of Menallen Township, witnesses Sam Salter and Isaac Jackson."

[87] Ephraim Hewitt and Peter Johnson deed, Fayette County Recorder, Uniontown, Pennsylvania, (Salt Lake City: Family History Library), microfilm #0863550, C: 1198-1199.
"3 Feb 1798, Ephraim Hewitt, Menallen Township Fayette County; and Peter Johnson, Linten Hundred, Washington County Maryland owe Thomas Graham, New Geneva Fayette County £3,384; whereas John Hall, late of Union Township, deceased, in his will gave daughters, Elizabeth and Rose, (now married to Hewitt and Johnson) 282 acres in Franklin Township, Fayette County that they sold for £1,692; title delivery to Graham 1 Mar1798, or to Peter Johns for lands in Harrison County Virginia that Graham sold to Johnson by bond; recorded 26 Jun 1798."

[88] Ephraim Hewitt deed, Fayette County Deeds, Fayette County Recorder, Uniontown, Pennsylvania, (Salt Lake City: Family History Library), microfilm #0863552, F: 364-365, K: 92.
"3 Nov 1801, James Morrison sold lot #12 in Middle Town, Fayette County to Ephraim Hewitt for £25. 27 Mar 1813, deed from Ephraim Hewitt and wife Elizabeth, Menallen Twp. to John Bute, Fayette County, Lot #12 Middletown for $375, recorded 12 Apr 1813."

[89] Iscrupe, *LaFayette*, Fayette County Civil Court Docket, Fayette County, Pennsylvania, Apr 1988, 4: 8-9.
"1798, Robert Cooper vs. Ephraim Hewitt and Hugh Hall, summons debt. 1799, Isaac Wood vs. Ephraim Hewitt., summons debt: £200."

[90] Ephraim Hewitt, plaintiff, *Minutes of Court of General Quarter Sessions of the Peace 1783-1808.*, Quarter Sessions March 1800, December 1802, March 1803, June 1804, March 1805.
"1)25 Mar 1800 Susanna Porter vs. Ephraim Hewitt, finds for plaintiff $24 damages; 2) Joseph Woodward vs. Ephraim Hewitt; 3)Dec 1802 Ephraim Hewitt vs. Francis Bryan, verdict $75,

horse to be delivered to defendant; 4)June 1804 Ephraim Hewitt vs. Daniel & John McClelland, debt $250, bail $500, defendant surrendered; 5) March 1805 Ephraim Hewitt vs. Henry debt $305 from Jun 1803, defendant confesses judgment."

[91] Jacob Hewitt Family Bible, see Appendix A.

[92] Ephraim Hewitt, collector, *Genius of Liberty and Fayette Advertiser,* "Receipts and Expenditures, Fayette County Pennsylvania," 4 Feb 1813. 43:7, page unknown.
　　"Debt received of Ephraim Hewitt, Collector of Menallen, for 1809 in part; credit for repairs done to the jail $43.98."

[93] Ephraim Hewitt, guardian, Fayette County Orphans Court, Probate Office, Uniontown, Pennsylvania, (Salt Lake City: Family History Library), 80.
　　"Apr 1809, court appoints Ephraim Hewit guardian over Peter, Elizabeth and Margaret Black, children of Jacob Black, late of Menallen Township, deceased; after they chose as their guardian."

[94] Ephraim Hewitt, land sale, *Genius of Liberty and Fayette Advertiser*, Uniontown, Pennsylvania (Salt Lake City: Family History Library), microfilm, 4 Feb 1813, page not shown.

[95] Fayette County Mortgage Books, Bond of Indebtedness, Fayette County Recorder, Uniontown, Pennsylvania, (Salt Lake City: Family History Library), microfilm #0863553, I: 168-169.
　　"3 Jul 1813, deed of mortgage on Ephraim Hewitt, Fayette County Pennsylvania by Eli Hewitt, Baltimore County, Maryland; who owes Eli Hewitt $1,024 with $500 interest; $1 from Eli Hewitt; on mortgage of Ephraim's land called *Eden* on branch of Redstone Creek and Great Road from Uniontown to Redstone Old Fort, Menallen Township, Fayette County."

[96] James Haddon, *History of Uniontown: the County Seat of Fayette County*, (Akron Ohio: New Werner Col, 1913), *161.*
　　"John Wood died 12 Nov 1813…age 64 years and was buried in the old Methodist Episcopal graveyard. His wife, Elizabeth Wood, died 17 May 1843 in her 81st year."

[97] John Wood, Esq., *Genius of Liberty and Fayette Advertiser*, Uniontown, Pennsylvania, (Salt Lake City: Family History Library), microfilm, 23 Aug 1815.
　　"23 Aug 1815, Have just received from Philadelphia at the well known Corner Stand in Uniontown, formerly occupied by John Wood, Esq. an extensive and elegant assortment of the newest and most fashionable summer and fall goods."

[98] Ephraim Hewitt indenture, Fayette County Recorder Uniontown, Pennsylvania, (Salt Lake City: Family History Library), microfilm #0863553, I: 248-249.
　　"12 Aug 1795, Ephraim Hewitt patented 288 acres called *Eden* on a branch of Redstone Creek; also on 18 Jul 1792, 109 acres called *Woodbury* on Dunlap's Creek granted by patent to Jacob Hewitt 18 Jul 1792; on 8 Nov 1797 Isaac Wood and wife Sarah sold to Ephraim Hewitt, 76 acres of *Woodbury* not sold to William Acken; on 16 Jan 1798 Acken sold Ephraim Hewitt 40 acres of *Woodbury* before mentioned; finally Ephraim Hewitt and wife Elizabeth sold to Hugh Thompson of Uniontown, all the above mentioned land for $4,000; recorded 18 Mar 1814."

[99] Haddon, *History of Uniontown*, 131, 160, 653, 650.

SOURCE NOTES
Chapter Five

TAMING THE WILDERNESS

[1] Richard Hewitt indenture, Fayette County Pennsylvania. See Chapter 4, *Two Brothers.*

[2] Hiatt & Scott, *Loudoun County Virginia Tithables 1758-1786,* 1:316.

[3] Horn, *The Horn Papers*, Volume 3, "Manallen Township Map," 13.
"Edward Hall, 300 acres, warrant 18 Apr 1785, survey 28 Oct 1785, patent to Hugh Thompson 14 Mar 1804."

[4] 1790 U.S. Federal Census, Fayette County Pennsylvania, Bullskin (Menallen) Township, online <http://www.ancestry.com>, image #582, Roll: M637-8, page 46.
"Edward Hall, 3 males +16, 1 male -16, 5 females, no others."

[5] Martin vs. Thompson Heirs, quiet title action and deeds, Brown County Chancery Court, Georgetown, Ohio (Salt Lake City: Family History Library), microfilm roll #1288389, 1:87-92.
"4 May 1820-Jul 1821, Fielding Martin vs. Bernard Thompson Heirs, John Colvin, et al and Edward Hall; 12 May 1820 heirs of Bernard Thompson, deceased, ordered to provide lawful title to land where Edward Hall "now lives;" 1 Aug 1820 amendment brought in Edward Hall heirs: Richard Hewitt, wife Phebe Hall; Elijah Hall; Charles Hall; John Hall; heirs of Polly Hall, deceased, wife of Nicholas Devore in dispute over 100 acres on Straight Creek purchased by Edward Hall 31 Mar 1806; 1 Aug 1820, Edward Hall described as having "departed this life in testate; deed ordered for Fielding Martin (husband of Anna Hall and heir of Edward Hall, deceased)."

[6] Iscrupe, *La Fayette*, 7:3:5 (1988); 1:3:13 (1981); 2:3:11(1982); 8:4:15 (1990); 1:3:6 (1981); 2:1:9 (1982); 2:1: 8 (1982).
1) Edward Hall appeared in Fayette County Quarter Sessions Court Sep 1784, Dec 1784, June 1785 and Mar 1790, as a juror, and to sue for debt owed. 2) Elijah Barkley will and estate, Fayette County Probate: Administration Abstracts, Uniontown PA, 25 Oct 1791. 3) William Sparks's estate, Fayette County Orphans Court, Uniontown PA, 25 Oct 1791.

[7] Hall to Mooney, *Adams County Marriage Records, 1789-1850,* Adams County Ohio GenWeb site contributed by Robert Kennard, online: http://www.scioto.org/Adams/marriage/1800-1900/html.
"31 Jul 1810, Charles Hall to Rachel Mooney, by James Parker."

[8] Gallagher to Hall, Hall to Hall deed, Clermont County Recorder, Common Pleas Court, deed book D-3: 347-349, (Salt Lake City: Family History Library), microfilm #0359400.

[9] Moore Cemetery is a private cemetery on Old South Riverside Drive, Batavia Twp., Clermont County, Ohio. The author visited the cemetery in August 2001, and the inscription on the tombstone says, "Jacob Hewitt born Nov. 9, 1791, died June 20 1850, aged 58 yrs, 7 mo[nths], 11 da[ys]."

[10] Hall to Warwick, deed, Fayette County Recorder, Uniontown, Pennsylvania, (Salt Lake City: Family History Library), microfilm #0863549, C: 416-417.

[11] G. Glenn Clift, *History of Maysville and Mason County*, "Cultural Beginnings: 1784-1795" (Lexington, Kentucky: Transylvania Print Co., 1936) pages 102, 111, 116-121.

[12] Mason County Kentucky tax lists 1790-1809, (Salt Lake City: Family History Library), microfilm #0000418, 1793-1797, 1793; William Lamb's District #2, p. 4; 1794; Whitfield Craig's District #1, p. 8; 1795; T. Marshall Jr.'s District #1, p. 12; 1797; T. Marshall Jr. District #1, p.12.

[13] Tax Lists, *Mason County Kentucky Tax Lists 1791-1810*, Kenton County Library, Covington, Kentucky, microfilm roll for 1794-1797, Book 1: 8, 10, 12, 12. Richard Hewitt was taxed only on cattle and horses.

[14] Allen and Betts, *History: USA*, p 144-145..

[15] Hewitt vs. Colvin and heirs of Bernard Thompson, quiet title action and deeds, Brown County Chancery Court, Georgetown, Common Pleas Court Terms: 16 Jul 1819, 7 Oct 1819, 8 Jan 1820, 22 May 1820, 26 Oct 1820, 1:14-21, (Salt Lake City: Family History Library), microfilm #1288389.
"16 Jul 1819, Richard Hewitt vs. Bernard Thompson Heirs, John Colvin, title dispute on 100 acres on Straight Creek, petitioner paid £200 in fee simple on 21 Nov 1796; land originally divided between Thompson heirs but did not legalize with deed to Hewitt; 4 Oct 1819 subpoena filed against Colvin and Thompson heirs for warranty deed subject to $1,000 fine; witnesses Stephen Colvin,

Elijah (X) Hall and Jane (X) Hall; 28 Jun 1820, Hamilton County Sheriff, Richard Ayres, brought in John Colvin who admitted sale and payment by Hewitt, that the property was divided, but a deed was never written during Thompson's lifetime, nor issued to Hewitt; 26 Oct 1820 Colvin agreed to give Hewitt a general warranty before 1 Jan 1821; witness John Thomason."

[16] *History of Brown County, Ohio,* (Chicago, Illinois: W. H. Beers & Co, 1883), 251-252, 265-269.

[17] D.J. Lake & B. N. Griffing, *Atlas of Brown County Ohio from Actual Surveys of D.J. Lake & B. N. Griffing,* (Philadelphia: Lake, Griffing & Stevenson, 1876), microfilm #1723592-1, (Salt Lake City: Family History Library), Franklin Township: 55.

[18] "Land and Farms in Brown County," e-mail message from Hermon Fagley of Clermont County Ohio, <hermfagley@juno.com> to author, 10 Sep 2000.

[19] Minson, Early Latter Day Saints Records, Nauvoo Church Records, Nauvoo IL, by e-mail from <RTMinson@compuserve.com> to author, 22 Feb 2000.
        "Hewett, Richard, 3 Sep 1843 (record date) *relationship to Richard Hewitt Jr.
Hewett--------------sister----Elizabeth Masterson (sister of *.)
Hewett--------------GD F----Hall -------------------(unknown grandfather of *)
No Name Given---GD F----Jacob Hewitt---------(grandfather of*)
No Name Given---GD M ---Ruth Hewitt---------(grandmother of *)
Richard Hewitt-----Father --Richard Hewitt------(father of *)
Richard Hewitt-----Mother--Phebe Hewitt -------(mother of *)
Richard Hewett----Wife-----Edy Hewitt ----------(first wife of *)
Richard Hewett----Brother--Ephraim Hewitt-----(brother of his father Richard Hewitt Sr., uncle of *)
Richard Hewett----Father---John Hewitt----------(* is the father of John)

[20] Richard Hewitt Bounty Land Application, Bell County, Texas; Richard Hewitt's War of 1812 service abstracts; by e-mail from RTMinson@compuserve.com, Aug 2000.
        "8 Dec 1851, Bell County, Texas; Richard Hewitt age 57, of Bell County Texas appeared before John W. Coleman, J.P. in land disposition; said he was private in Captain Campbell's Horse Regiment of Volunteers commanded by General McCarthy in War of 1812, from 1 Sep 1814 at Sinclairville, Ohio for 60 days, discharged at Detroit, Michigan Nov 1814; he lost his discharge."

[21] McGoon, *The Reminiscence of Katie B. McGoon.*

[22] Beers, *History of Brown County, Ohio,* 254.

[23] Eli Hewitt Household, 1850 U.S. Census, Brown County, Ohio, population schedule, 28 Sep 1850, microcopy, Denver Public Library, Denver, CO,400.

[24] Richard Hewitt will, see Appendix E.

[25] Beers, *History of Brown County, Ohio,* 260-262.

[26] Byron Williams, *History of Clermont and Brown Counties, Ohio,* (Baltimore: Gateway Press, 1987), 250.

[27] Louis H. Everts, *1795 History of Clermont County, Ohio,* (Philadelphia: J. B. Lippincott & Company,1880), 102-103.

[28] Ellis, *History of Fayette County, Pennsylvania,* 93.

[29] Jana S. Broglin, *Mason County, Kentucky, Wills and Estates Book "A" 1791-1797 and Book "B" 1798-1809,* (Indianapolis: Heritage House, 1998), B4-5, B56.

[30] Everts, *1795 History of Clermont County, Ohio,* 75, 110.

[31] Eileen M. Whitt, *Clermont County Pioneers 1798-1812*, (New Richmond, Ohio: published by the author, 1984), 65-66.

[32] Carl N. Thompson, compiler, *Historical Collections of Brown County, Ohio*, (Piqua, Ohio: Hammer Graphics, Inc., 1969), 14, 15, 28, 29.

[33] Martin vs. Thompson Heirs, Allen vs. Colvin, etc., quiet title action and deeds, Brown County Chancery Court, Georgetown, Ohio (Salt Lake City: Family History Library), microfilm #128838, 1:87-92.
  "Fielding Martin vs. Bernard Thompson Heirs…and Edward Hall, complaint filed 12 May 1820 regarding 100 acres on Straight Creek where Edward Hall lives, part of Crawford's Survey #664; Robert Allen vs. John Colvin …and the Heirs of Edward Hall, complaint filed 22 May 1820 regarding 54 acres on Straight Creek, part of Crawford's Survey #664."

[34] Beers, *History of Brown County, Ohio*, 263-264 (quote), 376-380, 539-540, 259-260 (quote), 381, 282; page 259-260 is an excerpt from *Sketches of a Tour in the Western Country* by F. Cuming that is included in this history of Brown County, Ohio.

[35] Elizabeth Hewitt Masterson, "Hewitt/Masterson" e-mail message from Richard C. Masterson <yreka@snowcrest.net> to author 29 Nov 1997.
  "If Elizabeth/Betty Hewitt is your ancestor, we are cousins. She was born 25 Dec 1807, died 21 Aug 1838; she married William Masterson born 10 Jun 1796."

[36] William Williamson household, 1850 U.S. Census, Batavia, Clermont County, Ohio, population schedule, 17 Jul 1850, District 22, p. 292, online http://www.ancestry.com, roll #M432-667."

[37] Ohio Auditor of State, *Tax Records of Ohio, 1801-1814*, Tax Records of Various Counties, Adams County Ohio, 1800-1810, 1-10, microfilm #522838-522839, 0522844, 0514124-0514129, (Salt Lake City: Filmed by the Genealogical Society of Utah, 1967).

[38] Richard Hewitt deed, Adams County, Ohio Deeds 1806-1814, film #054220, vols. 6-7, Family History Library, Salt Lake City.
  "14 Jan 1811, deed from John Graham, Richmond Virginia to Richard Hewitt, Adams County Ohio; for $75, 50 acres on Ballard Smith Survey #2448, recorded Mar 1812."

[39] Jack Allen and John L. Betts, *History: USA*, (New York: American Book Co., 1967), 168-169.

[40] Richard Hewitt and Jacob Hewitt, service, The War of 1812, *Family Tree Research Center* online at www.sierra.com/sierrahome/familytree/records/w1812/list, downloaded 23 Jan & 28 Mar 1999. *Roster of Ohio Soldiers in War of 1812, V.2, Roll of Captain Abraham Shepherd's Company*, Ohio Historical Society Online http://www.ohiohistory.org,.
  "War of 1812 Muster Rolls, Richard Hewitt, Battalion Mounted Infantry (Sep-Nov 1814), Ohio Militia; Jacob Hewett, 2nd Regiment (Safford's) Ohio Militia;" served 2 Sep-2 Oct 1812; and 29 July-22 Aug 1813, Capt. Abraham Shepherd."

[41] Beers, *History of Brown County Ohio*, 575.

[42] Williams, *History of Clermont and Brown Counties, Ohio*, 375.

[43] Allen and Betts, *History: USA*, "Foreign Entanglements and the War of 1812," 168.

[44] Beers, *History of Brown County, Ohio*, 389-390.

[45] The War of 1812, *Family Tree Research Center* online.
  "Hewett, Haz[a]el, 1st Regiment Perkins's Mounted West Tennessee Volunteers, Sergeant."

[46] War of 1812, *Regimental Histories of Tennessee Units During the War of 1812: Perkins West Tennessee Volunteers*, Tennessee State Library and Archives Online, http://www.state.tn.us/sos/statelib/pubsvs/tn1812.htm, downloaded 17 Mar 2001.

[47] Kelley, *West Nashville*, 59, 158.

[48] Allen and Betts, *History: USA*, 164-169.

[49] War of 1812, *Civilian Defense in Baltimore*, v. 39, (Baltimore: *Maryland Historical Magazine*, 1944), 206-207.

[50] Ephraim Hewitt, inventory, Clermont County Probate, Batavia, Ohio, film #5, miscellaneous documents, docket # 581 in the matter of Ephraim Hewitt.

[51] Hewitt to Hall, marriage, records of Clermont County, Ohio, Family History Library online http://www.familysearch.org, downloaded 1 Mar 2002, marriages 4 May 1820-Jul 1821.

[52] Jacob Hewitt Bible, see Appendix A.

[53] Jean R. Rentmeister, *Fayette County Newspaper Extracts, 1805-1854*, marriage and death notices extracted from the *Genius of Liberty and Fayette Advertiser*, Uniontown Pennsylvania, (Apollo, Pennsylvania: Closson Press, 1981), "1 Feb 1815, Ephraim Hewitt Obituary."

[55] Ephraim Hewitt inventory and estate sale, Clermont County Probate Court, Batavia Ohio, Miscellaneous microfilm No. 5, docket 581, 24 pages, not numbered.
     "Ephraim Hewitt deceased, inventory, 7 Apr 1815, total goods $871.47, appraisers, Stephen Calvin, Richard Hewitt and Henry Chapman, witness Robert Allen."

[56] Hewitt vs. Bernard Thompson Heirs, quiet title action and deeds, Brown County Chancery Court, Georgetown, Common Pleas Court Terms: 2 Sep 1818, A-1:289-299; May 1823, 2: 299-302 (Salt Lake City: Family History Library), microfilm #1288389.
     "2 Sep 1818, Elizabeth Hewitt, widow, and Heirs of Ephraim Hewitt, deceased vs. Heirs of Bernard Thompson, deceased; Hewitt heirs: John Hall, wife Nancy Hewitt Hall; Jacob Hewitt, wife Elizabeth Hewitt Hewitt; James Wood, wife Ruth Hewitt Woods; Luther Calvin, wife Clarissa Hewitt Calvin; Ephraim Hewitt's minor children, Sophia Hewitt; Ephraim Hewitt; Harriett Hewitt; Hannah Hewitt; all of Brown County; 3 April 1815, Amos Moore, attorney for Thompson Heirs was paid $200 for deed to 230 acres Crawford's Survey #664, by heirs of Ephraim Hewitt, deceased, and signed by Bernard Thompson's heirs; witnesses William White, Fielding Martin, and Robert Allen; recorded 2 Sep 1818.
     2 Sep 1818, Hewitt Heirs Petition vs. Abbott, Clermont (Brown) County Ohio Court of Common Pleas petition in Chancery between William White, Ephraim Hewitt's administrator vs Hewitt's heirs and John Abbott, Brown County Ohio; personal estate insufficient to pay Hewitt's debts, petition brought to sell the property and discharge debts; Stephen Calvin, Charles Campbell and Robert Allen appointed to view the land and set aside Elizabeth Hewitt's dower; Dec 1817 reported land could not be divided without injuring sale; Elizabeth Hewitt given 81 ¾ acres as dower; remainder, 148 ¼ acres valued at $1,779 ($12 per acre) sold to John Abbott for $14.10 per acre, with $278.46 down payment; witnesses Robert Allen and Fielding Martin.
     4 Oct 1819, Abbott vs. Ephraim Hewitt's Heirs; John Abbott filed complaint in chancery against minor heirs of Ephraim Hewitt, deceased: Sophia Hewitt, Ephraim Hewitt, Maria Hewitt, Harriet Hewitt and Hannah Hewitt; whereas Ephraim Hewitt purchased 230 acres on Straight Creek for $2,000 but deed was unsecured and payment not complete; title secured by Amos Moore in Clermont County, whereas William White replaced John Hall and widow Elizabeth Hewitt as estate administrator after they relinquished their duties; land sold at public auction but petitioner questioned if title was good since Hewitt was not "seized in fee of the tract," and not all heirs were of age; Abbott asked for a quit claim, that Elizabeth Hewitt, mother of the children be made guardian to defend them, that she relinquish any future claim to the property; 8 Apr 1820 court decreed law and equity was with complainant and ordered Elizabeth Hewitt to deliver clear title to Abbott."

[57] Ephraim Hewitt estate, Clermont County Minute Book, Miscellaneous Papers, August 1817 & October 1819 Terms, Probate Court, Clermont County, Ohio.

"27 Aug 1817, a note on Hugh Thompson, Uniontown, PA for $333.33 [each time] on
April 1, 1816, 1817, and 1818; payment on account in Will Book B. p. 398, Oct 1819, paid Hugh
Thompson on proven account $225.49.

Estate of Ephraim Hewitt, Clermont County Minute Book, March Term 1815, Clermont
County, Ohio, Recorder's Office, estate appraisers appointed, 355.

"7 Apr 1815, Clermont County Probate, Batavia Ohio, Ephraim Hewitt estate inventory;
Docket #581, 1-7. Appraisal and sale of Ephraim Hewitt, deceased personal property; filed 14 Jun
1815, recorded, pages not numbered.

October 1819, Ephraim Hewitt estate, Clermont County Probate, Miscellaneous Papers, Will
Book B, 398, Brown County Recorder, Georgetown, Ohio; Ephraim Hewitt heirs, deed, Clermont
County Deeds; Book B-2, 148-150, Brown County Recorder, Georgetown, Ohio; Book A-1, 289-
294 and 295-299."

[58] McGroarty, *Hewitt Family: The Ancestry of Mrs. Sophia Hewitt Buckner.*

[59] Hewitt to Hewitt deed, Brown County Recorder, Georgetown, Ohio, Deed Book A-1: 107-108.

"3 Feb 1818, deed from Richard Hewitt, Sr., Adams County Ohio to William Hewitt of same;
for $500, 50 acres Smith Survey #2448 on Straight Creek, patented to Graham 23 Oct 1809, to
Hewitt, witnesses W. C. Powell and Fielding Martin."

[60] Hewitt Family to Masterson deed, Brown County Recorder, Georgetown, Ohio, Deed Book A-1:
122-123.

"23 Feb 1818, deed from Richard Hewitt, Sr., Adams County, Ohio; to William Hewitt, same
county for $800, all horses, cattle, sheep and hogs, farming utensils, household stuff, furniture, also
every article I possess or have any claim to, including a tenement on Straight Creek, formerly
occupied by Richard Hewitt Sr., who has put William Hewitt in full possession by delivering [to
him] a case of drawers; witnesses Fielding Martin and W. V. Powell; recorded: 25 Aug 1818."

[61] Elizabeth Hewitt vs. Richard Hewitt, Clermont County Common Pleas Journal, August Term
1817, Book C, 188; December 1817, Book C, 221; March Term 1818, Book C, 345.

[62] Hewitt to Hewitt, deed, Brown County Recorder, Georgetown, Ohio, Deed Book E-5: 294-295.

"24 Jun 1826; Elizabeth Hewitt, Brown County Ohio, relict of Ephraim Hewitt, deceased to
Jacob Hewitt, of same, for $164, 81 ½ acres, her dower thirds, part of Crawford's Survey #664 on
Straight Creek; witnesses Franklin Shaler and Elisha Ross, recorded 12 Aug 1826."

[63] Hewitt Family to Masterson, deed, Brown County Recorder, Georgetown, Ohio, Deed Book K-10:
258; recorded 19 Apr 1833.

[64] Williams, *History of Clermont and Brown Counties*, Ohio, 389.

[65] McGroarty, *Hewitt Family: The Ancestry of Mrs. Sophia Hewitt Buckner.*

[66] Beers, *History of Brown County Ohio*, 284, 290, 384-385 (quote), 386.

[67] *Colvin Run Mill Historical Site*, The Origin of Colvin Run Mill: 1739-1811, online at
http://www.io.com/~curucahm/COLVIN/HISTORY/origin.html, downloaded 21 Apr 2001.

[68] Hewitt Notice, *The Benefactor*, 27 Feb 1827.

[69] Richard Hewitt's Will, see Appendix E.

[70] Beers, *History of Brown County, Ohio*, 550.

[71] Hewitt notice, *The Benefactor*, Editor T. L. Hamer, (Georgetown, Ohio), 18 Mar 1824, 4:13.

[72] Hewitt to Hewitt deed, Brown County Recorder, Georgetown, Ohio, Deed Book D-4: 23-24.

[73] Hewitt vs. Hewitt, Brown County Ohio Court, Supreme Court Chancery Records, (Salt Lake City: Family History Library), microfilm #1288396, A: 1, 6 Feb 1824.

[74] Hewitt to Hall deed, Brown County Recorder, Georgetown, Ohio, Deed Book D-4: 273-274.
"13 Mar 1824, deed from Richard Hewitt, Sr., Brown County, Ohio, to John Hall Warren County, Ohio, for $100; ten acres on Straight Creek; witnesses Eli Hewitt, Wm. V. Powell, and Joseph Newman, J.P., 2 Apr 1824."

[75] Hewitt to Abbott deed, Brown County Recorder, Georgetown, Ohio, deed book D-4: 335-336.
"6 Jan 1825, deed from Richard Hewitt Sr., Brown County Ohio to Joseph Abbott for $117.50; 11 acres, Smith's survey #685; witnesses Eli Hewitt, Joseph Newman and Thomas Clark."

[76] Hewitt to Newman, deed, Brown County Recorder, Georgetown, Ohio, deed book D-4: 491-492.
"6 Jan 1825; deed from Richard Hewitt Senior to David Newman, of Brown County Ohio; for $97, Smith's survey #2446; witnesses Joseph Newman, Joseph Abbott and Daniel Newman."

[77] Hewitt Notice, *The Benefactor*, 20 Feb 1827.

[78] Elsie Ewing Rayburn, *Early Marriage Records of Adams County, Ohio*, (West Union, Ohio, Adams County Genealogical Society: 1953-1956, (Salt Lake City: Family History Library), microfilm #317308.

[79] Richard and Edy Welch Hewitt's children, documentation from Alice Dion's 1957 manuscript describing how she descended from Mary Jane Hewitt, eldest daughter of Richard Hewitt and his second wife, Jarusha Parker Hewitt. In it she named Mary Jane's siblings; sent 19 Sep 2000 to the author by Carol Minson at <RTMinson@compuserve.com>, a descendant of William Hewitt, son of Richard and Jarusha Hewitt.

[80] Hewitt Notice, *The Benefactor*, 27 Feb 1827.

[81] A pelisse coat was an outer garment, a coat or a cloak, often without sleeves, worn first by men about 1817 and later by women. The length varied and could be either a long or a short coat often lined with fur. Downloaded Oct 2004 from http://www.regencygarterrobe.com.

[82] Richard Hewitt's Will, see Appendix E.

[83] Hewitt Memorial, *The Benefactor*, 20 March 1827.

[84] Thompson, *Historical Collections of Brown County, Ohio*, 963.

SOURCE NOTES
Chapter Six

COUSINS BY THE DOZEN

[1] Nellie (Woods) Whedon, *The James Woods Family of Pennsylvania and Ohio* (litho printed by the author in USA, 1942), 28.

[2] Richard & Jacob Hewitt, Luther Calvin & James Woods households, 1820 U.S. Census, Brown County, Ohio, population schedule, Clark Township, 381, 393, 395, on 1 Dec 1820, downloaded 15 Jan 2001, from U S GenWeb, http://www.rootsweb.com/~usgenweb/oh/brown/census/1820.
"Clark Township, Luther Calvin 1M-10, 1M 16-26, 1F 16-26, 1 agriculture; Jacob Hewett 1M-10, 1M 26-45, 1F-10, 1F 16-26, 1 agriculture; Pleasant Township, James Woods 1M-10, 1 M 26-45, 2F-10, 1 F 16-26, 1 agriculture; Richard Huett 1M-10, 1M16-26, 2M 26-45, 1F -10, 1 F 16-26, 1 agriculture, 2 commerce."

[3] Thomas Welch et al, petition, Brown County Common Pleas Court, Georgetown Ohio, Chancery Division, April Term 1827, 2: 206-212 (Salt Lake City: Family History Library). 16 Dec 1826.

[4] Letter from William N. McGoon, Laramie, Wyoming, to Mrs. Ronald Minson, Woodland Hills, California, 11 Feb 1972.

[5] Clermont County Genealogical Society, *Marriage Records of Clermont County, Ohio, 1800-1850*, (Cincinnati: Robert D. Craig, Publisher, 1963), 1: 97.
"Hewet Richard to Jarusha Parker, 24 Feb 1828 by Andrew S. McClain, M.G."

[6] Rebecca Mariah Hewitt, *Autobiography of Rebecca Mariah Hewitt*, 6. Rebecca is referring to her sister Mary Jane's impending marriage.
"Jane…was eleven years older than I was so at her marriage was about twenty-two years old."

[7] Parker to Voorhese deed, Clermont County Ohio Recorder, Batavia Ohio, Deed Book 12-33: 425-426, 23 Nov 1833.

[8] *Mormon Redress Petition*, Residents of Hancock County, Illinois, who signed the petition, Ancestry.com, online research service, <http://www.ancestry.com>, downloaded 30 Apr 2001.
"Nauvoo, 3rd Civil Ward, pages 9-25; E. B. Hewitt, Jarusha Hewitt, R.U. Hewitt, Sophia Hewitt, all in Ward 3, page 24."

[9] Sergeant Daniel Tyler, *A Concise History of the Mormon Battalion*, from the Illinois State Militia Commission Records, 1834-1855, 14:1163-1165 and 17: 39-45, *Mormon Battalion*, Ancestry.com, online research service, www.ancestry.com, downloaded 30 Apr 2001.
"Mormon Battalion, Eli B. Hewett, private, 16 Jul [18]46, company A."

[10] Hewitt, *Autobiography of Rebecca Mariah Hewitt*, not numbered.
"I was born in Fountain County, Indiana on November 22, 1840."

[11] Richard Hewitt household, 1860 U.S. Census, Travis County TX, federal population schedule, pages 137, 138, dated 2 Sep 1850, downloaded from http://www.ancestry.com, census images.

[12] Hewitt, *Autobiography of Rebecca Mariah Hewitt*, not numbered.

[13] Hewitt-Robinson marriage, Official Temple Records for Deceased Individuals, recorded 1991-1996, downloaded from http://www.family search.org on 26 May 2002.
"Fountain County, Indiana Marriages, Sally Ann Hewitt to Bailey C. Robinson, 9 Feb 1841."

[14] Bailey Robinson household, 1850 U.S. Census, Warren County, Illinois, federal population schedule, page 23, dated 17 Sep 1850, downloaded from http://www.ancestry.com census images.

[15] Eli Hewitt & Enoc Hacksaw household, 1860 U.S. Census, Travis County, Texas, federal population schedule, no township named, 137, 138, enumerated 2 Sep 1850, downloaded from <http://www.ancestry.com>, census images.

[16] Hewitt, *Autobiography of Rebecca Mariah Hewitt*.

[17] Richard Hewitt will, see appendix E.

[18] Patricia R. Donaldson, *Brown County, Ohio, Marriage Records, 1818-1850*, (Georgetown, Ohio: 1986).
"William Hewitt to Dorothy Prickett, 8 May 1836, by Thomas Mefford, J.P."

[19] Hewitt to McGrew deed, Brown County Recorder, Georgetown, Ohio, Deed Book Q-16: 302.
" 3 Mar 1839, deed from William Hewitt, wife Dorothy, Brown County, Ohio, to John McGrew of same, for $11, lots #95 & #96, Higginsport, Brown County, acquired by William Hewitt 10 Sep 1835 in deed book M; witnesses Jesse R. Grant, and Jesse J. Prickett; recorded 9 Mar 1839."

[20] Hewitt Family, 1840 U.S. Census, Brown County, Ohio, federal population schedule, 237a, ID#OH560396953, http://search.ancestry.com downloaded 7 Oct 2000.

[21] Donaldson, *Brown County Ohio Marriage Records, 1818-1850*, 62.
    "John Hewitt to Laramey Curtis, 19 Aug 1824 by Joseph Stableton, J.P., Gardner Curtis, present."

[22] Thompson, *Historical Collections of Brown County, Ohio*, 355.
    "Loramey Jones vs. George Jones divorce petition Feb 1824."

[23] Curtis family, from Kandice, kando@citynet.net, to author 28 Aug 1999, *Curtis Family*.
    "Joseph Curtis born 16 Feb 1769, married ca. 1789 Elsa Diadema Brockway; children Benjamin Gardner Curtis, born. 6 Dec 1802…Loruhima Curtis married John Hewett in 1824."

[24] Richard Hewitt will, see appendix E.

[25] John Hewett household, 1830 Ohio Census Index, federal population schedule, Brown County, Ohio, (Salt Lake City: Family History Library), National Archives film #OH560396953.

[26] Lyman Platt, *Nauvoo, Illinois Tax Index, 1842*, compiled 20 Aug 1842 (Orem, Utah: Ancestry, Inc., 1999).

[27] A history of the Curtis and Hall families of Brown County, Ohio, was relayed by e-mail to the author from descendants of Anna Hall and Fielding Martin in February and March 2002. They are Doris Harker reedor@xmission.com and Arcilee Frost arcie@uswest.net.

[28] Beers, *History of Brown County, Ohio*, 532, 540.

[29] Gail Childress, *Mason County, Kentucky, Early Marriages Through 1850*, author's file at USGenWeb Archives at http://www.rootsweb.com/~usgenweb/archives/ky/mason/marriages.
    "Eli Hewitt to Mary Masterson, 21 Nov 1826, Joseph Abbott to Rhoda Masterson, 10 Jun 1805."

[30] Donaldson, *Brown County, Ohio, Marriage Records, 1818-1850*, 96.
    "Book C: 53, William Masterson to Elizabeth Hewitt, 17 Jan 1826; oath of Eli Hewitt."

[31] William Masterson household, 1830 U.S. Census, Brown County, Ohio, Franklin Township, 478, (Salt Lake City: Family History Library), National Archives film #OH559258840.

[32] William Masterson household, 1840 U.S. Census, Spencer County IN, page 380, (Salt Lake City: Family History Library), National Archives, Roll #M19-127, Heads of Household.

[33] Elizabeth Hewitt and William Masterson children, downloaded from Masterson website at http://arbitrium.org/masterson, 27 May 2002, children were Charles H. (1827), Salathiel H. (1829), William H. (1831), John R. (1833), Jacob T. (1836), Viola J. (1838), Elizabeth (1838), Elijah (1823).

[34] William Masterson household, 1840 Indiana Census Index, federal population schedule, Spencer County, unknown township, 380, downloaded from http://search.ancestry.com, 3 Oct 2002.

[35] William Williamson household, 1850 Ohio Census Index, see Chapter 5, *Taming the Wilderness*.

[36] Richard Hewitt will, see Appendix E.

[37] Donaldson, *Brown County, Ohio, Marriage Records, 1818-1850*.
    "William A. Williamson to Letty Ann Hewitt, 6 Oct 1840 by Aaron Sargent, M.G."

[38] Samuel Williamson household, 1840 Ohio Census Index, federal population schedule, Brown County, ID#OHS4a2823446, http://search.ancestry.com downloaded 1 May 2001.

[39] G. Glenn Clift, *History of Maysville and Mason County, Kentucky, Pension Papers*, (Maysville, Kentucky: Mason County Historical Society, 1985), 305-307.

"9 Dec 1833, Mason County Kentucky, William Williamson, a soldier aged 74 appeared in court saying that he moved from New Jersey to Kentucky in 1811. That on 30 Mar 1835 he lived in Brown County, Ohio, aged 76."

[40] William Williamson's letters were transcribed by John Cykler and mailed to George Bragg of Boulder, Colorado, a descendant of William Williamson, who passed them on to the author March 1993. Bragg in a letter to a descendant explained the connection between John's wife, Virginia Cykler and the Williamson family, saying she is a "descendant of Joseph and Margaret Steele's daughter, Margaret, who was raised by Samuel and Mary Williamson, unmarried children of Wm. and Halena. The daughter married Albert G. Hartman, and their oldest son, Cary W. Hartman is the grandfather of the new researcher...Virginia was visiting her sister in Kentucky last year and brought back with her copies of very fragile letters written by Williamson."

[41] Masterson-Boyd marriage, Illinois State Archives Database, Cass County Marriage Records, online at Cass County Illinois website <http://www.iltrails.org/cass> #1575.

[42] Beers, *History of Brown County, Ohio*, 390.

[43] Ephraim Hewitt's inventory and sale, Probate Court, Clermont County, Ohio, Miscellaneous Papers of the Early Court of Clermont County, docket 581, inventory and sale of personal real estate of Ephraim Hewitt, recorded 14 Jun 1815, D. C. Bryan, Clerk pages 1-7.

[44] Devore to Calvin, deed, Clermont County Recorder, Common Pleas Court, Deed Book D-3: 319-320, (Salt Lake City: Family History Library), microfilm roll #0359400.

"21 Mar 1817 deed from Nichols Devore, wife Mary, Clermont County, Ohio, to James Calvin of same, 125 acres on Straight Creek for $1,000; witnesses Robert Allen and Susan Hall."

[45] John Hall and Nicholas Devore households, 1820 U.S. Census, Warren County, Ohio, population schedule, Turtle Creek Township, http://www.ancestry.com/oh/brown/census/1820/> p. 228b, 235b.

[46] Hall vs. Thompson Heirs, quiet title action and deeds, Brown County Chancery Court, Georgetown, Ohio (Salt Lake City: Family History Library), microfilm roll #1288389, 1:74-78.

[47] 6 Mar 1823, deed from John Hall and wife Nancy, Warren County to heirs of Abraham Calvin deceased, for $340, 173 acres in Brown County; witnesses William Powell and Stephen Reynolds.

[48] John Hall will, Brown County, Ohio Probate Court, Georgetown, Ohio, 1: 182.

"24 Feb 1826, John Hall will, Warren County Ohio, executors may sell real estate for debt; remainder to wife Nancy Hall, daughter Louisa Ann Hall; unless she dies before 18, then wife gets her share; executors Jacob Longstreth, Nancy Hall; witnesses John Wickerham and Matthias Corwin, recorded 11 Apr 1832."

[49] Martin vs. Jacob Longstreth, Nancy Hall & Louisa Hall, Brown County Chancery Court, Georgetown, Ohio (Salt Lake City: Family History Library), microfilm roll #1288389, 7 Jan 1827, 1:327-335; Common Pleas Court Nov 1827.

[50] Hall v. Spence, Triplett & Tibbs Heirs, for title and deeds, Brown County Chancery Court, 1827-1831, Georgetown, Ohio (Salt Lake City: Family History Library), microfilm roll #1288389, 20 Jul 1829, 3:242-248.

[51] John Hall taxes, Warren County, Ohio, Tax List 1816-1826, (Salt Lake City: Family History Library), microfilm roll #0514202.

"1816, 1817, John T. Hall, 92 acres, no range given; 1823, 1824 John Hall 19/4/3, 96 acres; 1826, page 97, John Hall Heirs, 4/3/19 (range, tract, survey) has 92 (or 94) acres, taxes £4.13.1."

[52] Hall to Holmes, Brown County, Ohio, Probate Court 1818-1939, marriage index, online from http://www.familysearch.org, downloaded 4 Oct 2002.

[53] John Holmes household, 1830 U.S. Census, Butler County, Ohio, population schedule, Lemon Township, undated, Roll #M19-127, 36.

[54] John Dickey household, 1850 U.S. Census, Butler County, Ohio, population schedule, Lemon Township, dwelling 184, family 1325, dated 27 Oct 1850, 460, National Archives micro publication.

[55] Beers, *History of Brown County, Ohio*, 385, 389-391.

[56] Whedon, *The James Woods Family*, 27.

[57] Ruth Wood obituary, *The Castigator*, Georgetown Ohio, 14 Sep 1824.
        "14 Sep 1824, died at Georgetown on the 10th, Mrs. Ruth Wood, consort of Mr. James Wood."

[58] Donaldson, *Brown County Ohio Marriage Records, 1818-1850*.
        "James Woods to Maria Hewitt, 17 Mar 1825, by S. G. Sperry, (late) J.P."

[59] McGroarty, *Hewitt Family: The Ancestry of Mrs. Sophia Hewitt Buckner*.

[60] James Woods household, 1840 U.S. Census, Brown County Ohio, Franklin Twp., undated, Roll #M704-379, p. 237 from www.rootsweb.com/~usgenweb/oh/brown/census/1840/0252a.gif.

[61] Whedon, *The James Woods Family*, 28, 31, 34, 37.

[62] George Bohrer household, 1840 U.S. Census, Brown County, Ohio, Franklin Township, undated, Roll #M704-379, p. 237, http://www.rootsweb.com/~usgenweb/oh/brown/census/1840/0252a.gif.

[63] Calvin to Allen deed, Brown County Recorder, Georgetown, Ohio, Deed Book F-6:287-288.
        "13 Apr 1827, deed from Luther Calvin, wife Clarissa, Brown County Ohio to Robert Allen of same, 66 acres, Pleasant Township for $420, witnesses Franklin Shaler and H. Southard.
        Deed from Luther Calvin, wife Clarissa, Brown County, to Ephraim Hewitt of same; 34 acres, Pleasant Twp. for $204, witnesses Franklin Shaler and H. Southard, deeds recorded 20 Feb 1828."
[64] Elba L. Branigin, *History of Johnson County, Indiana*, (Indianapolis: B. F. Bowen & Co., 1913), Calvin History, submitted by Steve Arnold, Trafalgar, Indiana, 1992, and admitted to the "Calvin Folder" at the Brown County Genealogical Society, Georgetown, Ohio.

[65] Ray Mathis, *A Brown County History*, (Bloomington, Indiana: PIP printing, 1993), Calvin History, submitted by Steve Arnold, Trafalgar, Indiana, 1992, and admitted to the "Calvin Folder" at the Brown County Genealogical Society, Georgetown, Ohio.

[66] Hewitt to Ewing, *The Castigator*, Georgetown, Ohio, 3 Apr 1827.

[67] McGroarty, *Hewitt Family: The Ancestry of Mrs. Sophia Hewitt Buckner*.

[68] Ruth Owen, Harriet Hewitt-Charles M. Ewing family group sheet, supplied 27 Apr 1997 by Owen (Maysville, Missouri). Included was a letter and a photograph of Harriet and Charles Ewing's tombstones in Maplewood Cemetery, Ripley, Ohio.

[69] Hewitt to Martin deed, Brown County, Ohio, Recorder, Georgetown, Ohio, Deed Book F-6: 286-287.
        "14 Feb 1828, deed from Ephraim Hewitt, to Joel Martin, both of Brown County, for $204, 34 acres; deeded by Calvin to Hewitt 13 Apr 1827; witnesses John and Wm. Shepherd, 14 Feb 1827."

[70] McGroarty, *Hewitt Family: The Ancestry of Mrs. Sophia Hewitt Buckner*.

[71] Ephraim Hewitt notice, *The Castigator and Democratic Expositor*, Georgetown, Ohio, 4 Jan 1836.

[72] Donaldson, *Brown County, Ohio, Marriage Records, 1818-1850*.

[73] McGroarty, *Hewitt Family: The Ancestry of Mrs. Sophia Hewitt Buckner.*

[74] Harvey King, *King Folder*, Brown County, Ohio, Genealogical Society, Georgetown, Ohio. Folder contains two page of undocumented history submitted to the society by descendants of John King from Duncannon, Ireland, and Brown County, Ohio, a copy was sent to the author 9 Aug 1997.

[75] Thompson, *Historical Collections of Brown County, Ohio*, 132-133.

[76] Donaldson, *Brown County, Ohio, Marriage Records 1818-1850.*

[77] Thompson, *Historical Collections of Brown County, Ohio*, 728.

[78] Richard Lee Morton, editor, *William and Mary Quarterly*, "Diary of Philip Buckner, M.D., with notes by William Buckner McGroarty," (Williamsburg, VA: Institute of Early American History and Culture, 1943), series 2: 23, 69-84.

[79] Patricia R. Donaldson, *Brown County, Ohio, Court Records: 1818-1850*, (Salt Lake City: Family History Library, 1980), 2: 66-67.

[80] Philip Buckner notice, *The Castigator*, Georgetown, Ohio, 14 Dec 1826 and 1 Jan 1828.

[81] Morton, *William and Mary Quarterly*, "Diary of Philip Buckner, M.D.," see above.

[82] Philip Buckner, from an article written about him by T. L. Hamer, *The Castigator*, Georgetown, Ohio, 28 Sep 1826.

[83] Thompson, *Historical Collections of Brown County, Ohio*, 127-128, 725-729.

[84] Beers, *History of Brown County, Ohio*, 263, 264, 389.

[85] Donaldson, *Brown County, Ohio, Court Records: 1818-1850*, 2:58, 59, 60, 62, 63, 66, 67, 78, 79.

[86] Hall executors vs. Hewitt, Brown County Common Pleas Court, Civil Minutes Journal, Georgetown, Ohio, (Salt Lake City: Family History Library), microfilm roll #1288393, 3: 110.

[87] Hewitt to Masterson, deed, Brown County Recorder, Georgetown, Ohio, Deed Book F-6: 75-77.
"5 Mar 1827, deed from James Woods, wife Maria; Luther Calvin, wife Clarissa; and Ephraim Hewitt; to William Masterson, all of Brown County Ohio; for $100, 81½ acres on Straight Creek earlier assigned to Elizabeth Hewitt, widow of Ephraim Hewitt, deceased as her right of dower; witnesses Franklin Shaler and P. L. Wilson.

[88] Hewitt to Masterson, Brown County Recorder, Georgetown, Ohio, Deed Book K-10: 18-20, 258.
"18 Apr 1833, deed from Jacob and Elizabeth Hewitt; Charles and Harriet Ewing; and Hannah Hewitt to William Masterson, 81½ acres for $75 total to each heir by William Masterson for a total of $75."

[90] Jacob Hewitt household, 1830 U.S. Census, Clermont County, Ohio, page 181, line 7, (Salt Lake City: Family History Library), National Archives roll #OH559258840; Heads of families.

[91] Brown County, Ohio, Civil Minutes Journal, Georgetown, Ohio (Salt Lake City: Family History Library), microfilm roll #1288393, 3: 64.

[92] Beers, *History of Brown County, Ohio*, 551.

[93] Brown to Hewitt deed, Brown County Recorder, Georgetown, Ohio, Deed Book P-15: 349-350.
"27 Feb 1838, deed from David Brown, wife Eliza, Brown County, Ohio, to Eli Hewitt, of same, for $900, 79 acres, witnesses James Allen and Alexander McClain; recorded 31 May 1838."

[94] Hewitt to Bohrer deed, Brown County Recorder, Georgetown, Ohio, Deed Book Q: 179-180.
   "14 Dec 1838, deed from Eli Hewitt, wife Mary; to George Bohrer, 4 acres for $49, Smith survey #2448; witnesses James Allen and Walter Egbert; recorded 19 Dec 1838."

[95] Beers, *History of Brown County, Ohio*, 531, 544, 546.

[96] Eli Hewitt farm, U.S. Agricultural census of Brown County, Ohio, Schedule 4, Franklin Township, District #13, 27 Sep 1850, page 211, line 20, National Archives micro-publication.

[97] Beers, *History of Brown County, Ohio*, 401.

[98] Thompson, *Historical Collections of Brown County, Ohio*, 963.

[99] 23 Apr 1853; Eli Hewitt will, Brown County Probate, Georgetown, Ohio, Will Book WB3: 93-94. 4 May 1853; Eli Hewitt will, Franklin Township, Brown County Ohio; to wife Mary N. Hewitt, executor, farm on west side during her life, 200 acres, part of B. Smith Survey #2448 and Crawford #664, east half to be sold at auction in three years; when wife dies remaining estate to be sold at auction; funds from both auctions to be divided among children after debts paid; personal estate, rents and profits to wife; witnesses Noah Drake and Preston W. Sellers; proved 2 May 1853.

SOURCE NOTES
Chapter Seven

JACOB AND ELIZABETH HEWITT

[1] Ephraim Hewitt Estate, see Chapter 5, *Taming the Wilderness*.

[2] Hewitt-Calvin marriage, *Ohio Marriages Recorded in County Courts Through 1820: An Index* (Mansfield, Ohio: The Ohio Genealogical Society, 1996), 001-086: 476.
   "Hewitt, Clarisey married to Colvin/Calvin, Luther 27 Feb 1817 Clermont [County, Ohio]. Hewitt, Ruth married Wood, James 11 Feb 1816, Clermont [County, Ohio]."

[3] Hewitt notice, *The Benefactor* (Georgetown, Ohio), A List of Lands and Lots in Brown County, Ohio, returned delinquent by the County Treasurer for taxes, 4 Nov 1828, 23 Oct 1832, 3 Nov 1834.
   "1827-28 Hewitt Jacob; N. Georgetown, lots 132, 133, (value $30, $35); 1831-32 Jacob Hewit, Tibbs Survey #1942, 60 acres, ($139); 1831 Jacob Hewitt, lots N. Georgetown #133, ($35)."

[4] J. L. Rockey and R. J. Bancroft, *1795 History of Clermont County, Ohio* (Philadelphia: Louis H. Everts, 1880) 243, 248-249.

[5] Jacob Hewitt taxes, Batavia Township, Clermont County, Ohio 1827 tax list, copied in 1998 from original records microfilmed at the Clermont County Library.

[6] Jacob Hewitt household, 1850 U.S. Census, Clermont County, Ohio, Batavia Township, District #22, federal population schedule, 16 Jul 1850, National Archives micro-publication, M432-667, dwelling #80, family #80, page 289.

[7] Hewitt vs. Taylor, in chancery, Clermont County Common Pleas,Chancery Division, Batavia, Ohio, August Term 1832, pages 366-370. Taylor to Hewitt deed, Clermont County Recorder, Batavia Ohio, Deed Book E2, #26: 293-294.
   "Jacob Hewitt vs. James Taylor; 8 Feb 1827 deed from James Taylor, Newport Kentucky to Jacob Hewitt, 133 acres, for $300 of which $123.64 paid, $76 due by 15 Mar 1828, balance in 18 months plus interest; Grays Survey #1116, Batavia Township; 29 Mar 1827 Jacob Hewitt paid $73, witness Zachariah Chapman, Taylor's agent; and Daniel Kidd; Hewitt claims repeated demand for deed; requests subpoena; 10 Apr 1829 Taylor subpoenaed; court continuances July 1829-30 Jul 1832; James Taylor, defendant filed with exceptions on number of acres, price; but agreed Hewitt had paid him, claimed he gave him deed and requested dismissal; 3 Aug 1832, court ruled law and

equity lies with the defendant who has legal title but land was short 15 acres of 133 acres total, estimated at $225 per acre, court ordered Taylor to make general warranty deed to Hewitt for 118 acres; that Taylor pay Hewitt $38.64 for 15 acre loss; each to pay half of court costs. 9 Nov 1832, from James Taylor, Campbell County Kentucky to Jacob Hewitt, Clermont County Ohio, for $261, 118 acres, Gray's Survey #1116, East Fork Little Miami River, signed for Taylor, James Taylor Jr.; witnesses John Hill and J. W. Robinson; recorded 8 Apr 1833."

[8] Barbara J. McCarthy, *Chancery Records of Clermont Co., Ohio 1824-1857*, (Cincinnati: printed by the author, 1994), 15, 16 21.

[9] William Curry household, 1830 U.S. Census, Clermont County, Ohio, population schedule, Batavia Township, National Archives micro-publication, roll M19-128, image #356, page 178.

[10] Harry M. Millar, *Ohio River Flood, History of Cincinnati and Hamilton County, Ohio* (Cincinnati: S. B. Nelson & Company, 1894), 82.

[11] Owen Findsen, *Infamous Floods, Samuel Chase: Eyewitness in 1832*, (Cincinnati: *Cincinnati Enquirer* 1997), 17 Mar 1997, online version: http://enquirer.com/flood_of_97/history1.html.

[12] "Cholera Epidemic," *The Castigator*, Georgetown, Ohio, 30 October 1832.

[13] Jacob Hewitt household, 1830 U.S. Census, Clermont County, Ohio, population schedule, Batavia Twp., National Archives film #M19-128, image 362, page 181; 1840 U.S. Census, Clermont County, Ohio, population schedule, Batavia Twp., National Archives film #M704-384, image 6, page 116.

[14] Dimmitt to Hewitt deed, Clermont County Recorder, Batavia, Ohio, Deed Book E29-2: 126
    "21 Dec 1832, from Ezekiel Dimmitt, Clermont County Ohio to Jacob Hewitt of same, lots #231 and #234 of ¼ acre each in town of Batavia for $45, signed Ezekiel Dimmitt, wife Phebe; witnesses Amos Bull and Hannah Bull; recorded 9 Jan 1833."

[15] Parker to Hewitt, deed, Clermont County Recorder, Batavia, Ohio, Deed Book C3, #47: 67-68.
    "27 Oct 1834, from William and Leah Parker, Clermont County, Ohio to Jacob Hewitt of same; for $500, 36 acres Gray's Survey #1116, East Fork Little Miami by Joseph Kidd, Abraham Hulick, Batavia-Williamsburg Road, and James Parker, deceased, laid off for Enoch Patterson and Richard Hewitt; witnesses William and Leah Parker, Patience (X) Parker, wife of William (X) Parker; witnesses D. C. Bryan and J. W. Kain; recorded 28 Sep 1847."

[16] Morris estate to Hewitt, Clermont County Recorder, Batavia, Ohio, Deed Book G2, #31: 261-262; Deed Book I2, #33: 118; Deed Book K2, #34: 2.
    "28 Nov 1833; Charles Fox and Samuel W. Davies, for James Morris, deceased; to sell lots in Batavia at public auction in Cincinnati to Jacob Hewitt, lots #174-177, 194, 220, 227, 233, 241, 242 total paid $64.25; witnesses Chas. D. Drake and W. A. Bageley, recorded 5 May 1834.
22 Jan 1835; from Jacob Hewitt, wife Elizabeth to Andrew Hopkins, for $40, lots #241 and #242; witnesses D. C. Bryan and John Denison, recorded 23 Jan 1835. 25 Sep 1834; from Jacob Hewitt, wife Elizabeth, Clermont County Ohio; to Robert Waddle of same; lots #174, 175, 176 and 177, town of Batavia for $50; witness David Morris, recorded 17 Apr 1835."

[17] Tax duplicates, Clermont County Assessor, Batavia, Ohio, *1836 Tax Duplicates, Town Lots, Batavia Township* (Salt Lake City: Family History Library), microfilm #0476482.
    "Hewitt, Jacob, Town of Batavia, Lot #231(value $25), #234 ($43), #243 ($8), #232 ($43), #227 ($43), #194 ($10), #197 ($43), #220 ($43), #233 ($25), #244 ($43)."

[18] Tax duplicates, County Assessor, Clermont County Ohio, *1837 Tax Duplicates, Rates of Taxation* (Salt Lake City: Family History Library), microfilm #0476483.
    "For township purposes, No. 1-Batavia, (1 mill upon the dollar), Jacob Hewitt, John Gray's Survey #1116, 118 Acres, value: $350."

[19] Hewitt to Carter deed, Clermont County Recorder, Batavia, Ohio, deed book 44: 420, 58: 329.

"25 Mar 1846; from Jacob Hewitt, wife Elizabeth, Clermont County Ohio to John Carter of same, lot #220 for $25; witnesses Richard D. Hewitt and Harriet Hewitt; recorded 13 Apr 1846."

"9 Apr 1847; from Jacob Hewitt, wife Elizabeth, Clermont County, to Thomas Boulton, same place, lot #194 for $20; witnesses Henry Bonnel and Harriet Hewitt; recorded 15 Feb 1853."

[20] Hewitt vs. Moore et al, Ohio Supreme Court, April Term 1848, Clermont County, Batavia, Ohio, (Salt Lake City: Family History Library), microfilm #1288385, G: 391-395; Common Pleas Court Journal Minutes, Clermont County, Ohio microfilm #1208383, 1849, S: 144.

"27 Mar 1845; Jacob Hewitt vs. Heirs of James Parker in title dispute over 36 acres claimed by descendants of James Parker, Sr., deceased, James Parker Jr. (died 22 Jul 1827) whose heirs are Caroline Parker (Mrs. Charles A. Moore) and Delila Parker (Mrs. John Finton), Leah Ann Parker, widow of Wm. Parker Sr., filed a bill against Hewitt for James Parker, Jr. heirs, father of petitioners who claims 1/5th of Hewitt's real estate. Hewitt charges will's provision excluded James Parker Senior's grandchildren, the complainants, that possession and partition was subject to the widow's life estate, that Hewitt's 36 acres fell to William Parker, an heir, who sold it to Hewitt on 27 Oct 1834 for $500, and executed a deed; the same day Hewitt purchased Leah Parker's life estate in the property; and took immediate possession; he denies complainants right of partition and asks for dismissal. April Term 1846, final decree favored complainants; 2 May 1846 Hewitt filed appeal; April Term 1847 Supreme Court advised law and equity is with complainants who are entitled to 1/5th part of the real estate; April Term 1848, bill of review filed by Jacob Hewitt, Clermont County, Ohio; remanded to circuit court; May Term 1848 Hamilton County Ohio court reviewed bill, ruled equity is with defendants, ordered dismissal, Hewitt pays costs, witnesses Isaac G. Burnett."

[21] Annie W. B. Bell, *Marriage Records of Fleming County, Kentucky, 1798-1851* (Frankfort: Kentucky Historical Society, 1935), not numbered.

"William Williamson to Ann Terhune, 23 Mar 1815; William Williamson to Jane Cochran, 3 Mar 1817; William Williamson to Isabella Henry, 11 Sep 1823."

[22] Williamson to Hewitt, deed, Fleming County Recorder, Flemingsburg, Kentucky, Y: [page numbers unreadable], 1844 (Salt Lake City: Family History Library), film #0343985.

"20 Jul 1844, deed from Samuel Williamson, wife Cyntha, Richard Mullins, wife Ann (Williamson), Morgan County Illinois; to Richard D. Hewitt, Clermont County Ohio, 25 acres on Mill Creek, John Cochran's land, late Fleming County, Kentucky deceased, was allotted to children and heirs of Jane (Cochran) Williamson deceased; who are Samuel Williamson; Ann Mullins, Jane Williamson, Richard D. Hewitt's wife; witnesses John Berdan and Porter Clay; Morgan County Illinois; William T. Dudley, Fleming County Kentucky, recorded 29 Sep 1845."

[23] Hewitt-Williamson marriage, Common Pleas Court, Clermont County, Ohio, Batavia Ohio, Journal (Batavia Township), 3: 288.

"Married on the tenth day of May 1842 Richard D. Hewitt to Jane Williamson, both of Batavia Township, H. Dupee, Batavia, 11 May 1842."

[24] Davis and Jacob Hewitt, Quadrennial Census 1847, Batavia Township (Batavia, Ohio: Clermont County, Ohio Genealogical Society, 1986), 82.

[25] Richard D. Hewitt household, 1850 U.S. Census, Clermont County, Ohio, Jackson Twp., dwelling 10, family 10; dated 16 Jul 1850, National Archives film #M432-667, Image 519, page 56.

[26] Hewitt-Wheeler marriage, Huett-Carter marriage, *Marriage Records of Clermont County, Ohio, 1800-1850* (Batavia Ohio: Clermont County Genealogical Society, 1979), Book 4:5: 91, 97, 107.

"30 Mar 1845, Nancy Hewitt to William Wheeler, by George S. Lee, J. P; Eliza Jane Huett to George L. Carter, 15 Jul 1847 by John S. Jenkins, J.P."

[27] Rocky and Bancroft, *1795 History of Clermont County, Ohio*, 253.

[28] William Williamson household, 1850 U.S. Census, Clermont County, Ohio, population schedule, Batavia Township District 22, 17 Jul 1850, National Archives micro-publication, page 310.

[29] Rocky and Bancroft, *1795 History of Clermont County, Ohio*, 52.

[30] Hewitt-Giffin marriage, Marriage Index: Selected Counties of Ohio, 1789-1850 (Family History Library, Salt Lake City: Family History Library), film #0355779, online www.genealogy.com, downloaded 28 May 2001.

[31] Robert Giffin household, 1860 U.S. Census, Clinton County, Indiana, federal population schedule, Warren Township, Middlefork post office, National Archives micro-publication, page 301.

[32] Batavia Township, U.S. Census, Clermont County, Ohio, federal population schedule, National Archives micro-publication, Jul 1850, 310a-313b, 289a-294a.

[33] Rocky and Bancroft, *1795 History of Clermont County, Ohio*, 256.

[34] Harry M. Millar, *Ohio River Flood, History of Cincinnati and Hamilton County, Ohio* (Cincinnati, Ohio: S. B. Nelson & Company, 1894), 82.

[35] Clermont County Delinquent Tax List, *Ohio Sun* newspaper, Batavia, Ohio, 1 Nov 1841; *Clermont Sun*, published Batavia, Ohio, 1 Dec 1853.
"Jacob Duckwall, James Gray Survey 1116, 100 acres, Delinquent List, Batavia Township, Hezekiah Mount, Gray's Survey 1116, 10 acres."

[36] Rockey and Bancroft, *1795 History of Clermont County, Ohio*, 450.

[37] George L. Carter household, 1850 U.S. Census, Clermont County, Ohio, federal population schedule, Union Township District #22, page 485, dwelling 3000, family 3023, enumerated 12 Nov 1850, National Archives micro-publication.

[38] Jacob Hewitt obituary, "Melancholy Occurrence, "*Clermont Courier*, Andrew M. Gest, editor, 27 June 1850.
"Mr. Jacob Hewitt, of this town, was drowned in the Little Miami River, a short distance below the mouth of the East Fork, on Thursday night last."

[39] "The Old Village Graveyard," *The Clermont Sun*, Batavia, Ohio, 14 Nov 1882.

[40] Jacob Hewitt tombstone, Moore Cemetery (misquoted as the Moyer's Cemetery), *The Historical and Philosophical Society of Ohio*, copied 1947 by Mr. Weine, published April 1948.

[41] Jacob Hewitt estate, Clermont County, Ohio Probate Court, Batavia, Ohio, miscellaneous records, not numbered.
"28 Jun 1850, administrators Elizabeth Hewitt, Richard D. Hewitt and J. B. Davis, Clermont County Ohio paid $400 bond, widow to return inventory in three months, sell real estate if necessary, and give an account within 18 months; witness R. W. Clark."

[42] "Jacob Hewitt estate," *Clermont Courier*, 25 Jul 1850, administrator's notice posted 3 Jul 1850.

[43] Jacob Hewitt estate, Clermont County Probate Court, Batavia Ohio, miscellaneous records, not numbered, Batavia, Ohio, 3 Jul 1850.
"Jacob Hewitt's personal property is insufficient to pay debts, Joseph Kyle, Clermont County Sheriff to give first payment of $175 from land sales to Elizabeth Hewitt, administrator; for estate debts, second payment to the widow and heirs, third payment for debt."

[44] Jacob Hewitt estate appraisal, Clermont County Probate Court, Batavia, Ohio, 3 Jul 1850
"3 Jul 1850, Jacob Hewitt, late Clermont County, deceased, personal property appraised; public sale of goods includes personal articles not appraised as assets included two spinning wheels, a loom, an old stove, a family Bible, 2 or 3 pictures, 2 or 3 school books, a spotted cow 8 or 9 years old, 3 beds and bedding, 2 bedsteads, a lot of the family's cooking utensils and clothing, six chairs, 6 knives and forks, 6 plates, 6 tea cups and saucers, a sugar dish and milk pot, a tea pot and 9 spoons; appraisers William H. Robinson, William M. Crane and David C. Bryan, witness James Perrine."

[45] Jacob Hewitt estate, petition for partition, Clermont County Probate Court, Batavia, Ohio, Case #1440, box 304: 559-567, 282, March, July August 1851.

"March Term 1851, On 9 Jul 1850, petition for partition filed by William Wheeler and wife Nancy S. (Hewitt) Wheeler, Clermont County, Ohio charging right to 1/7th part of 154 acres (118 and 36) James Grays Survey #1116,10 acres Wm. Johnson's Survey #1774, and Batavia lots #231, 232, 233, 234, 239, 243, 245, 248, 244, 197, 218, 227, and 240; petitioners are Jacob Hewitt's heirs and tenants in common with petitioners: David (Davis) Hewett; Jacob Hewett; Harriett Hewett; Caroline Hewett; George Carter, wife Eliza (Hewitt) Carter; of same; Robert Griffin, wife Emeline (Hewitt) Griffin of Indiana; that Elizabeth Hewett, Clermont County Ohio, widow of deceased, is entitled to dower rights; petitioners ask that heirs be made defendants to petition, that partition and dower assignment were demanded, that if partition can be made, widow gets money in lieu of dower, otherwise land to be sold and proceeds divided among heirs; October term 1850, Clermont County sheriff ordered real estate sold at public auction; appraisal on 36 acres $360, 118 acres $2,124, 10 acres $120, 14 lots $380 or $2,984 total; witnesses C. Smith, Lott Hulick and W. H. Robinson; March/July 1851; Civil Minutes Journal, T: 23-24, 281-282; property distribution after petition for partition, Elizabeth Hewitt, widow, in lieu of dower $450; R. D. Hewitt 10 acres, Johnson's Survey #1774, lots #239 and #240; John Carter lot #218; Ann Caroline Hewitt lot #227; George S. Carter lot #228; Elizabeth Hewitt, widow, lots #231,232, 233, 234, 243, 244, 245, 246. 21 Dec 1851, George Carter bought lot #228 for $20; 11 Jun 1852 witnesses D. Bryan and L. Leeds; 26 Jul 1852."

[47] Rockey and Bancroft, *1795 History of Clermont County, Ohio*, 255.

"The following persons owned a house, lived in Batavia village or near Jacob Hewitt in 1837 and also in 1850: Cassander Abbott, J. M. Brown, D. C. Bryan, Geo. W. Dennison, O. T. Fishback, John Hill, Benj. Hopkins, John Jamieson, Thomas Kain, J. D. Morris, Caleb Williams, Isaac Worstell, John White, Wm. Wayland, Sr. and John Weaver."

[48] Jacob Hewitt estate, Common Pleas Court, Clermont County, Batavia, Ohio, Minute Book October Term 1850, T: 336.

"William Wheeler vs. David (Davis) Hewitt et all, petition for partition; court ordered that P. J. Donham be appointed guardian for Jacob Hewitt, named in the petition and he accepted."

[49] See Jacob Hewitt estate appraisal and public auction.

[50] McGroarty, *Hewitt Family: The Ancestry of Mrs. Sophia Hewitt Buckner*, pages not numbered.

[51] Jacob B. Hewitt household, 1860 U.S. Census, Josephine County, Oregon, Williamsburg Precinct, Jacksonville P.O., dwelling 87, family 80, dated 6 Jun 1860, 226; online http://www.ancestry.com, census images.

[52] Hooker to Hewitt deed, Clermont County Recorder, Batavia, Ohio, 56: M3, not numbered.

"21 Apr 1851, John & Nancy Hooker, Hamilton County Ohio sold to Elizabeth Hewitt, Clermont County Ohio; 42 poles land for $575, on Mosley's Survey #1115, Union Twp. Clermont County, north side Batavia Turnpike called Mud Corner, witnesses A. Pindell and J. Getzendammer."

[53] George L. Carter household, 1870 U.S. Census, Clermont County, Ohio, Union Township, dwelling 61, family 61, dated 2 Jul 1870, page 331, from http://www.ancestry.com census images.

[54] Elizabeth Huit household, 1860 U.S. Census, Clermont County, Ohio, Union Twp., Mount Carmel P.O., page 50, dwelling 1164, family 1722; dated 11 Jul 1860, http://www.ancestry.com.

[55] Elizabeth Hewitt household, 1870 U.S. Census, Clermont County, Ohio, Union Township, dwelling 49, family 49, dated 2 Jul 1870; National Archives film #M393-1181 p. 331, image #665.

[56] Hewitt to Pittsenbarger marriage, *Clermont Sun*, Batavia, Ohio, 27 Jul 1854.

"July the 20th, at residence of Robt. Griffin, by the Rev. Jas. P. Wright, Martin Pittsenbarger of Clinton County Ind. to Miss Harriet Hewett, late of Mt. Carmel, Clermont Co., Ohio."

[57] Jane Hewitt, *Monument Inscriptions Prior to 1900 from Cemeteries in Clermont County, Ohio* (Williamsburg, Ohio: Beech Forest Chapter, D.A.R., 1952), Old Owensville Cemetery, 18.

"Jane consort of R. D. Hewitt d. Sept 24, 1859--37y 8m 28d."

[58] Richard D. Hewitt household, 1860 U.S. Census, Clermont County, Ohio, Jackson Twp., dwelling 516, family 517, dated 29 Jun 1860, 73, online <http://www.ancestry.com>, census images.

[59] Hewitt to Hewitt deed, Clermont County Recorder, Ohio Probate Court, Batavia Ohio, (Salt Lake City: Family History Library), miscellaneous microfilm #0333186, 97:496.

"20 May 1873, from Elizabeth Hewitt, Clermont County Ohio to Ann C. Hewitt of same, 42 3/10 poles of land for $5, witnesses Julius F. Perdrizet and Peter Anthes, recorded 20 Aug 1873."

[60] Elizabeth Hewitt tax record, Clermont County Archive Storage, Williamsburg, Ohio, 1873 Tax Book, Union Twp., Clermont County, Ohio, page number not copied, transcribed from original records of Clermont County Ohio tax records, August 2001 at the county archives.

[61] "The Moore Cemetery," *The Historical and Philosophical Society of Ohio*, 1947, by Mr. Weine, April 1948.

"Lorah B. daughter of George L. and Eliza Jane Carter, born Jun 22 1849, died Jan 30 1851, aged 2 yrs, 3 mo, 8 da."

[62] Eliza Jane Carter estate, Clermont County, Probate Court, Batavia Ohio, miscellaneous microfilm, not numbered.

"5 Feb 1884, Clermont County Ohio, Probate Court, Julius Perdrizet, administrator, Eliza J. Carter estate, plaintiff; against petition to sell real estate for dependents, Henry B. Carter living Mt. Carmel Ohio, and Richard L. Carter living McLain County Illinois, minors over fourteen; and Worth and Leroy McKitrick, minors under fourteen who live at Soldiers and Sailors Orphan Home at Xenia Ohio (children of Nancy Carter and Thomas McKitrick, both deceased); that Eliza J. Carter's debts are over $228 and has no estate except 2 lots (33 poles each) Mosely's Survey #1115, Mt. Carmel Turnpike; plaintiff asks that land be sold for minor heirs benefit, witness M. A. Wood, 5 Feb 1884."

[63] John R. Crosby, household, 1880 U.S. Census, Brown County, Ohio, Pleasant Township, dwelling 46, family 47, E. D. #12, dated 3 Jun 1880, National Archives microfilm, #T9-996, page 202A.

[64] Nellie (Woods) Whedon, *The James Woods Family of Pennsylvania and Ohio*, (Litho printed in USA: by the author, 1942), 28.

"Elizabeth Woods, daughter James and Ruth (Hewitt) Woods, born 23 Jan 1816, died 1908 near Chase, Rice County Kansas aged 92; married 16 Jul 1832 George Henry Bohrer, who died in 1843; married second John R. Crosby of Kentucky."

SOURCE NOTES
Chapter Eight

DAVIS HEWITT

[1] *The Clermont Sun*, Batavia, Ohio, 5 Jul 1899.

[2] McGroarty, *Ancestry of Mrs. Sophia Hewitt Buckner*.

[3] Beers, *History of Brown County, Ohio*, 303.

[4] Morton, "Diary of Philip Buckner, M.D.," 2: 23: 69-84.

[5] Hewitt to Williamson marriage, Clermont County Common Pleas, Batavia, Ohio, 1842, 3: 288.

"Married 10 May 1842, Richard D. Hewitt to Jane Williamson, both of Batavia Township, A. Dupel, Batavia, 11 May 1842."

[6] Mary Hewitt Gehres' D.A.R. 1918 application, National Society, Daughters of the American Revolution Lineage, #142023, 143:8. Iincluded was supporting documentation of her siblings birth

and death dates. Mrs Gehres was the daughter of Richard Davis Hewitt and his first wife, Jane Williamson; her siblings were: "Samuel Davis Hewitt (11 Feb 1843-19 Oct 1892); Ann Hewitt (15 Aug 1844-20 Mar 1911); Thomas Hewitt (5 Sep 1847-9 Mar 1849); Louisa Hewitt (16 Dec 1848-4 Mar 1911); John Holmes Hewitt (22 Apr 1850-5 Mar 1930); William Jacob Hewitt (10 Sep 1951-2 Jun 1928); Mary Jane Hewitt (28 Jun 1854-24 Mar 1950); Infant Son Hewitt (28 Jun 1854-same day); James Allen Hewitt (22 Oct 1856-3 Jun 1928); Elizabeth Helena Hewitt (6 May 1859-not shown); Children of Richard Davis Hewitt and Jane Williamson his second wife: Richard Daniel Hewitt (29 Jul 1862-21 Mar 1931); Benjamin Hewitt, (1 Feb 1865-not shown)."

[7] See Supplemental Chapter Eleven, *The Williamson Family*.

[8] Holliday to Hewitt deed, Clermont County Recorder, Batavia, Ohio, 1845, 44: 108-109.
"15 Sep 1845; deed from Thomas and Eliza Ann Holliday, Hamilton County Ohio to Richard D. Hewitt, Clermont County Ohio; 52 acres on Stonelick Creek, Mountjoy Survey #4448 for $168; witnesses Geo. S. Lee and L. Robinson, recorded 7 Nov 1845."

[9] Ely to Hewitt deed, Clermont County Recorder, Batavia, Ohio, 1846, 45: 145.
"28 Jul 1846, deed from William Ely, Clermont County Ohio to Richard D. Hewitt, of same, 15 acres, East fork Little Miami River, Mountjoy Survey #4448, for $146; witnesses James Perrine and Delos C. Coulburt; recorded 29 Jul 1846."

[10] County Auditor to Hewitt deed, Clermont County Recorder, Batavia, Ohio, 1847, 46: 301-302.
"18 Jan 1846, deed from John Ferguson, Clermont County auditor to Richard D. Hewitt, of same; 41 acres, Shields Survey #13523 and #13524, sold for non payment of taxes by John Hill for $[ ].25, witnesses Henry Bonnell and John Ellis; recorded 12 Jul 1847."

[11] Beech Acres is a social services agency in Cincinnati Ohio begun in 1849 during a nationwide cholera epidemic. Formed after the epidemic, it was first called the German General Protestant Orphan Home. Statistics show that in Cincinnati, from May through September 1849, 4,114 people died from the disease; downloaded 11 Nov 2002 from http://www.beechacres.org/history.

[12] The author viewed Thomas Hewitt's gravestone in Stonelick Twp., Owensville Ohio, August 1998, "Thomas, son of R. D. & Jane Hewitt, died Aug 9, 1849, aged 1 year, 11 months, 1 day."

[13] *The Clermont Sun*, Batavia, Ohio, 3 May 1850.

[14] Ely to Hewitt deed, Clermont County Recorder, Batavia, Ohio, 1848, 49: 364.
"18 Oct 1848, from William M. and Mary Ely, Clermont County, Ohio to Richard D. Hewitt, same county, 10 acres on East fork of Little Miami River, Mountjoy Survey #4448 for $100, signed Wm. M. Ely and Mary Ann Ely; witnesses James Perrine and Thomas Parrish; recorded 12 Dec 1848."

[15] Hewitt to Fishback deed, Clermont County Recorder, Batavia, Ohio, 1851, 58: 639. The following is an abstract of the record.
"16 Dec 1851, from Richard D. and Jane Hewitt, Clermont County, Ohio to John Fishback, same county, lots # 239 and #240, town of Batavia for $50, signed Richard D. Hewitt and Jane Hewitt; witnesses J. M. Hutchinson and David Jones; recorded 21 Apr 1853."

[16] South to Hewitt deed, Clermont County Recorder, Batavia, Ohio, 1851, 56: 492. The following is an abstract of record.
"25 Dec 1851, from Andrew Jackson and Missouri South, Clermont County Ohio, to R. Davis Hewitt, same county for $175, 10 acres on East fork of Little Miami River, Mountjoy Survey #4448, bound by John McElfresh, E. Nicholas and Philip Hoffman, signed Andre J. (X) South and Missouri A. (X) South; witnesses Walter McKinnie and William Ulrey; recorded 5 May 1852."

[17] Emeline Giffin household, 1880 U.S. Census, Clinton County, Indiana, National Archives film #T-9-270, image 0265, p. 14D; Martin Pittsenbarger household; 1880 U.S. Census, McLean, Illinois, federal population schedule, National Archives micro-publication #T-9-230, image 0625-65, page 466B.

[18] Rockey and Bancroft, *1795 History of Clermont County*, 554-555.

[19] Barbara Carmean, copier, 1860 Mortality Schedule, Jackson Township, Clermont County, Ohio (Hillsboro, Ohio: Southern Ohio Genealogical Society, 1983).

[20] William J. Hewitt obituary, *Nashville Tennessean*, Nashville, Tennessee, June 1928.

[21] Thomas Hewitt, *Monument Inscriptions prior to 1900 from Cemeteries in Clermont County*, 17, 18.
  "Thomas, son of R. D. & Jane Hewitt, d 9 Aug 1949, 1y 11m 4 d; Jane, consort of R. D. Hewitt d 24 Sep 1859, 37y 8m 4d."

[22] Hewitt to Williamson, *Clermont Courier*, Batavia, Ohio, 19 Jun 1861.
  "Married on the 20th of May by Rev. Thos. Cortelyou, Mr. R. D. Hewett and Miss Jane Williamson."

[23] See Chapter Eleven, *The Williamson Family*.

[24] Richard D. Hewitt household, 1880 U.S. Census, Batavia Township, Clermont County, Ohio, federal population schedule, National Archives film #T9-1000, image 0014, 5 Jun 1880, p. 6C.

[25] Clemons, Hance, South, McElfresh to Hewitt deeds, Clermont County Recorder, Batavia, Ohio, 29 Jan 1863, deed books: 77: 486; 77: 300; 77: 55; 77:70-71.
  "All Mountjoy Survey #4448; 29 Jan 1863, deed from John Clemmons to Richard Hewitt; (70 acres, $2,100) recorded 1863; Abram Hance, (13 acres, $405), recorded 24 May 1863; Louisa South, (4 acres, $121), recorded 16 Mar 1863; John McElfresh, (20 acres, $121, recorded 19 Mar 1863."

[26] Johnson to Hewitt deed, Clermont County Recorder, Batavia, Ohio, deed book 77, page unknown.
  "18 Mar 1863, deed from Emor and Susan Johnson to Richard D. Hewitt, 112 1/2 acres George Mathews Survey #1138 for $4,500, recorded 5 Mar 1860."

[27] Hewitt to Aloysious Paul deed, Clermont County Recorder, Batavia, Ohio, book 82: 387-388.
  "7 Mar 1865; deed from R. D. & Jane Hewitt to Aloysious Paul, 93 acres, George Mathews Survey #1138 for $5,400; recorded, 14 Aug 1865."

[28] Sweeney to Hewitt deed, Clermont County Recorder, Batavia, Ohio 5 Mar 1865, 81: 439-440.
  "5 Mar 1865, from John and Mary Ann Sweeney to Richard D. Hewitt, 84 acres, Darby's Survey #2058 and Stephen's Survey #3877 for $4,875; recorded; 12 Apr 1865."

[29] Hewitt to Duckett marriage, *Clermont County, Ohio, Marriages, 1850-1874*, Clermont County Genealogical Society, (Baltimore: Gateway Press, 1989), 228.

[30] Carmean, 1860 Mortality Schedule, Jackson Township, Clermont County, Ohio, page unknown.

[31] Jane Williamson Hewitt's tombstone, Olive Branch Cemetery, Clermont County, Ohio. A photograph taken by the author in August 1996 verifies the inscription.

[32] Aileen M. Whitt, *Clermont County, Ohio: 1870 Atlas and History, Union Township*, (New Richmond, Ohio: Published by the author, 1985), 17.

[33] Richard Hewitt household, 1870 U.S. Census, Clermont County, Ohio, Union Twp., Loveland P.O. page 344, dwelling 268, family 264, 13 Jul 1870; National Archives film #M593-1181, image #692.

[34] See Chapter Seven, *Jacob and Elizabeth Hewitt*.

[35] Samuel Hewitt and his wife Louisa Duckett Hewitt's names were not found in the 1770 Ohio census, but they were enumerated in the 1880 census.

[36] Hewitt to Evans marriage, *Clermont County, Ohio, Marriages, 1850-1874*, 228.

[37] Whitt, *Clermont County, Ohio: 1891 Atlas and History, Union Township*, (Mt. Vernon, Indiana: Windmill Publications, Inc., 2000), 29, 31.

[38] Beers, *History of Brown County* Ohio, 15, 247, 375.

[39] Odd Fellowship, Duties of the Organization, downloaded 6 Oct 201 from this website, http://norm28.hsc.usc.edu/IOOF/Books/IOOFDuty.html.

[40] Rockey and Bancroft, *History of Clermont County, Ohio*, Batavia Township, 263, 270, 448.

[41] Hewitt to Hill and Hewitt to Mitchell, *Clermont County, Ohio Marriages, 1850-1874*, 227-228.

[42] Hewitt to Morrison marriage, Clermont County Probate Court, 22 Apr 1880, marriage certification for John Hewitt and Lizzie B. Morrison on, recorded 26 Apr 1880, P. J. Nichols, Probate Judge.

[43] J. H. Hewitt household, 1880 U.S. Census, Clermont County, Ohio, Union Twp., Mt. Carmel, National Archives film #T9-1000, image #0588, 4 Jun 1880, page 293, Dwelling #76, Family #77.

[44] James Hewitt household, 1880 U.S. Census, Morgan County, Illinois, National Archives microfilm #T9-238, image #0465, 11 Jun 1880, page 231D, Dwelling #130, Family #134.

[45] Judd to Hewitt deed, Clermont County Recorder, Batavia, Ohio, 8 Jan 1875, 98: 408.
"8 Jan 1876, deed from Stephen and Mary Judd, S. A. and Aseneth Apple, W. Apple, David and Elizabeth Holter, Almira Meek and Rebecca E. Apple to Richard D. Hewitt for $700, 7 7/10 acres, Darby's Survey #2058, Overton's Survey #987; recorded 14 Jan 1875."

[46] *The Clermont Sun* newspaper, 15 Dec 1880.
"A house occupied by a tenant on the Hewitt farm near Olive Branch was destroyed by fire one night last week, loss $1,000, insurance $500 in the Home of New York."

[47] *The Clermont Sun* newspaper, Batavia, Ohio, 16 Apr 1879.

[48] Temple to Hewitt, Clermont County Court of Common Pleas, Batavia, Ohio, 23 Dec 1879, Case No. 6640, 184.

[49] *The Clermont Sun* newspaper, Batavia, Ohio, 28 Jan 1880, sheriff's sale R. D. Hewitt vs. Orin Temple, et al, Case #66401.

[50] Richard D. Hewitt, 1880 U.S. Agricultural Census, Clermont Co., Ohio, Batavia Twp., Schedule 2, Dist. #38, 4 Jun 1880, (Salt Lake City: Family History Library), film #1602378, page not shown.

[51] Ohio vs. Hewitt, *The Clermont Sun*, Batavia, Ohio, Wednesday, October 19, 1881.

[52] Jeffrey G. Herbert, *Restored Hamilton County, Ohio, Marriages, 1870-1884*, (Bowie, Maryland: Heritage Books, 1994), "Cincinnati Freie Presse," page unknown.

[53] Mary Hewitt Gehres D.A.R. application.

[54] *The Clermont Sun*, Batavia, Ohio, 5 Dec 1882.

[55] Hewitt to Hurley and Hurley to Hewitt deed, Clermont County Recorder, Batavia, Ohio 2 Mar 1882, 112: 477-478.
"2 Mar 1882, deed from Richard D. Hewitt, Olive Branch, Clermont County Ohio to George W. Hurley, Batavia, same county, 7 acres in Olive Branch Village, Batavia Township, Denton's Survey #987, originally purchased by Richard D. Hewitt from S. Judd on 8 Jan 1875, recorded 7 Jan 1875; 2nd property, 10 ½ acres, Darby's Survey #2058 near Shaler's Run purchased from Sheriff

Teasdale, recorded Book 7:185; both properties sold to Hurley for $1,600, signed Richard D. Hewitt, witnesses James McMath and Clinton Long; recorded 2 Mar 1882.

2 Mar 1882, deed from George W. Hurley, Batavia, Clermont County Ohio, to Maria L. Hewitt, Olive Branch, same county; 7 acres, Olive Branch Village, Batavia Township, Denton's Survey #987; same as above; both properties sold to Louisa Hewitt for $1,600, signed George W. Hurley, witnesses James C. McMath and Clinton Long; recorded 2 Mar 1882."

[56] Hewitt to Hewitt deed, Clermont County Recorder, Batavia, Ohio 2 Mar 1882, 112: 479.

"2 Mar 1882, from Richard D Hewitt, Olive Branch, Clermont County, Ohio for $3,000 paid to him by Samuel D. Hewitt, John H. Hewitt, William J. Hewitt, James A. Hewitt, Richard D. Hewitt Jr., Benjamin F. Hewitt, Ann Hewitt, Louisa Hewitt, Mary J Hewitt and Elizabeth H. Hewitt; sold 84 acres in Clermont County Ohio on East Fork of little Miami River, Darby's Survey #2058 and Stephens Survey #3877, signed 2 Mar 1882, R. D. Hewitt, Maria L. Hewitt; witnesses James. McMath and Clinton Ding; recorded 4 Mar 1882."

[57] *The Clermont Sun*, Batavia, Ohio, "Olive Branch News," 13 Feb 1883, page 1; 20 Feb 1883, page 1; 9 Oct 1883.

[58] Mary Hewitt Gehres' D.A.R. application.

[59] *The Clermont Sun*, Batavia, Ohio, 5 Feb 1884, "Olive Branch News."

[60] *The Clermont Sun*, "Batavia and Olive Branch News," 2 Feb 1884; 19 Feb 1884; 26 Feb 1884; 22 Apr 1884.

[61] Herbert, *Restored Hamilton County Ohio Marriages, 1870-1884*, page unknown.

"Cincinnati Freie Presse," Annie Hewitt to Marion McClelland on 24 Jul 1884."

[62] *The Clermont Sun*, Batavia Ohio, 20 Jan 1885, "Olive Branch News."

[63] Mariah L. Hewitt death record, Clermont County, Ohio, Probate Court, Record of Deaths in Clermont County, Ohio, 1885-1895, 4:113.

"Transcribed from handwritten cards, Louisa Hewitt, died 29 Nov 1888, married, aged 62 and 4 months; at Olive Branch, born Georgetown, Ohio; died of cancer."

[64] Mrs. David (Davis) Hewitt obituary, *The Clermont Sun* newspaper, Wednesday 5 Dec 1888, "Olive Branch News."

[65] Mariah L. Hewitt, Olive Branch Cemetery, Olive Branch, Ohio. A photograph of the memorial marker taken in August 1996 by the author shows the tombstone and that the inscription says, "Mariah L., wife of R. D. Hewitt, born July 8, 1827, died Nov. 29, 1888."

[66] *The Clermont* Sun newspaper, 26 Mar 1890 R. D. Hewitt marriage to Mary J. Smith; 24 Jul 1889 Sheriff's Sale R.D. Hewitt's personal estate; 26 Feb 1890, R. D. Hewitt visit to Batavia 26 Feb 1890.

[67] Mariah L. Hewitt estate, administrators bond, administration letters; Clermont County Probate Court, Batavia, Ohio, pages not numbered.

"2 May 1891, Clermont County Ohio, R. D. Hewitt swears Maria L. Hewitt lived in Batavia and died 29 Nov 1888 leaving no children, but has following heirs: R. D. Hewitt, husband, Olive Branch; Amanda Evans, sister, Georgetown, Ohio; Elizabeth Evans, sister, Georgetown, Ohio; Dewit-Clinton Evans, brother Georgetown, Ohio; India Ann Laycock, sister; Wm. Laycock, Russelville, Ohio; Mrs. McClure, deceased; Mariah Hewitt left real estate worth $600; $1,200 bond; appraisers Robert Jones, Henry Householder and Peter Brunaugh; witness T. P. Breeding."

[68] Mariah L. Hewitt estate, deed, Clermont County Probate Court, Batavia Ohio.

"15 May 1891; deed through private sale by Richard D. Hewitt, administrator; to Martha M. Willison; 10 1/2 acres Darby's Survey #2058 for $325; witnesses H. L Nichols, and George W. Goodwin; recorded 18 May 1891."

[69] Admittance Records, Clermont County Infirmary 1891, "Name of Males in Clermont County Infirmary," 1 Mar 1891, p. 89. In August 2001, the author examined the records, one of three remaining at the infirmary just prior to the building's final closing for demolition.

"Lines 19-20, Name of Pauper: Richard Hewitt age 29; Benjamin Hewitt age 27; Reception Date for both men, 16 May 189; Birth Place for both, Clermont County Ohio; Length of Residence left blank for both; Personal Habits good for both; Personal Conduct left blank for both men."

[70] Clermont County Infirmary, *The Clermont Sun*, 15 Feb 1968.

[71] Clermont County Infirmary, 1880 U.S. Census, Clermont County, Batavia Township agricultural census, Schedule 2, Enumeration District No. 38, 15 Jun 1880 (Salt Lake City: Family History Library), microfilm #1602378, page not recorded.

[72] "Report on the Clermont County Infirmary," *The Clermont Sun*, Batavia, Ohio, 25 Sep 1891.

[73] Richard D. Hewitt, Clermont County Probate Court Death Record. This card was found in a file drawer at the Clermont County Courthouse in August 2001.

"Name Richard D. Hewitt; date of death 21 May 1931, Age 69, white male; at Batavia Twp. Ohio; Father Richard Hewitt, Mother Jane Williamson; Cause of Death cerebral hemorrhage."

[74] Benjamin Hewitt, Discharge Notes, Clermont County Infirmary, Batavia, Ohio (Batavia Ohio: Clermont County Genealogical Society, 1987), 17.

[75] Richard D. Hewitt vs. Mary J. Hewitt, *The Clermont Sun*, Batavia, Ohio, 7 Mar 1894.

[76] Hewitt vs. Hewitt divorce, Minutes of Clermont County Court of Common Pleas, Batavia, Ohio, March Term 1894, Case #10086: 153.

"Richard D. Hewitt vs. Mary J. Hewitt, petition by Richard D. Hewitt against Mary J. Hewitt, aka Eliza J. Smith, for divorce; cross petition by defendant; R. D. Hewitt said he lived in Clermont County Ohio before the petition and was married to the defendant; claims M. J. Hewitt guilty of three years willful absence from plaintiff; court ordered marriage dissolved, divorce on desertion; Mary J. Hewitt was denied claim on plaintiff's real estate; he ordered to pay costs; defendant's name corrected from Mary J. Smith (on marriage license) to Eliza J. Smith."

[77] Richard D. Hewitt to Mary J. Hewitt, Clermont County Ohio Court of Common Pleas, 1 March 1894, 135: 24.

[78] Notice by R. D. Hewitt, *The Clermont Sun*, Batavia, Ohio, 26 Jun 1895.

[79] Hewitt to Emerson, Clermont County Court Recorder, Batavia Ohio, deed book, 136: 225.

"Richard D. Hewitt to James P. Emerson, 7 acres, Survey's #2058-949."

[80] Ungethuem to Schmidt, letter, 5 May 1977 from Ruth Ungethuem, Olive Branch Ohio; to George Schmidt, Evergreen Colorado, second cousins (grandchildren of Sam Hewitt and John Hewitt).

[81] Visit by R. D. Hewitt, *The Courier Watchman*, Waverly, Pike County, Ohio, 20 Jul 1899.

[82] William J. Hewitt household, 1900 U.S. Census, Davidson County, Tennessee, E. D. 102, sheet 7B, 6 Jun 1900, National Archives micro-publication.

[83] "Olive Branch, Visit by R. D. Hewitt," *The Clermont Sun* newspaper, Batavia, Ohio, 2 Apr 1902.

[84] Richard D. Hewitt obituary, *The Clermont Sun* newspaper, Batavia, Ohio, 25 Mar 1903.

[85] Richard D. Hewitt will, see Appendix F.

[86] Richard D. Hewitt estate, Clermont County Courthouse, Batavia, Ohio, Probate Court Records 1903, Roll #31, E-099, 45: 8109, 119, 146, 288, 337, 345, 380, 398, 590.

SOURCE NOTES
Chapter Nine

JOHN HOLMES HEWITT

[1] "Cholera, Bloomers," *Clermont Courier* Newspaper, 11 Jul 1850, 17 Jul 1851.

[2] 7 Jul 1997, Mary Jane McCormick, Glen Elyn Illinois, Mary Jane Hewitt wrote a letter to the author relaying events in her grandmother's life, including Gehres family photographs.

[3] Mary Ann Gehres, "President's Focus: Women's History: A Proud Narrative," *Bulletin, American Association of University Women*, Philadelphia Branch, (Philadelphia: 1988), 56:7:1-2.

[4] *The Clermont Sun* newspaper, 17Apr 1877.

[5] 7 Jul 1997 letter from Mary Jane McCormick.

[6] *The Clermont Sun* newspaper, 13 Aug 1879.

[7] Whitt, *Clermont County, Ohio, 1870: Atlas and History*, 17.

[8] Robert K. Kyle household, 1870 U.S. Census, Clermont County, Ohio, Union Township, Mt. Carmel P.O., National Archives Micro-publication, 13 Jul 1870, page 96, dwelling 286, family 282.

[9] *The Clermont Sun* newspaper, 5 Nov 1879.

[10] Idelbert D. Kyle estate, John H. Hewitt, administrator, Clermont County Court of Common Pleas, Batavia, Ohio, Civil Minutes Journal, January Term 1880-1882, E-179-2270: 163-164, 184-185, 16, 36, 46 62-64, 69, 75, 93, 119, 149-150, 171, 449, 420, 580-585. 230-254, Family History Library, Salt Lake City, Utah, microfilm #1728433.

[11] *The Clermont Sun* newspaper, 25 Jul 1882.

[12] Herbert, *Restored Hamilton County, Ohio Marriages*.

[13] Samuel Hewitt household, 1880 U.S. Census, Clermont County, Ohio, Union Twp., Olive Branch P.O., 3 Jun 1880, dwelling: 42, family: 43, National Archives film #T9-1000, #1255000, page 6.

[14] Thomas Mitchell household, 1880 U.S. Census, Clermont County, Ohio, Stonelick Twp. & P.O., 7 Jun 1880, dwelling 110, family 115, National Archives film #T9-100, LDS film #1255000, page246.

[15] *The Clermont Sun* newspaper, 16 Feb 1881.

[16] Laudene Davis household, 1880 U.S. Census, Clermont County, Ohio, 1 Jun 1880, household 11, family 11, page 289b, National Archives film #T9-100, Family History microfilm #1255000.

[17] Martin Pittsenbarger household, 1880 U.S. Census, McLean County Illinois, Empire Township, page 466b, National Archives micro-publication T9-230, Family History microfilm #1254230.

[18] Whitt, *Clermont County, Ohio 1870: Atlas and History*, 57.

[19] William Perry [Morrison] household, 1860 & 1870 U.S. Census, Clermont County, Ohio, Mt. Carmel Twp., National Archives film #M653-944 (1860), M593-1181 (1870); 11 Jul 1860, dwelling 1185, family 1143, page 256; 15 Jul 1870, household 325, family 321, page 348.

[20] William P. Morrison household, 1880 U.S. Agricultural Census, Clermont County Ohio, Union Township, Mt. Carmel P.O., Schedule 2, page 5, enumeration district #50, 4 Jun 1880, (Salt Lake City: Family History Library), microfilm #1602378, page unknown.

[21] "The Narrow Gauge Ball; 1877 Democratic Convention; Jackson Township news," *The Clermont Sun* newspaper, 8 Nov 1876, 20 Dec 1876, 7 May 1879.

[22] Photograph by the author of Idelbert Kyle's tombstone, Mt. Moriah Cemetery, Union Township, Clermont County, Ohio. It says: Idelbert D. Kyle born July 17, 1855, died Oct. 3, 1879."

[23] Hewitt to Morrison, marriage license, Clermont County Probate Court, 1880, page 518, #100.
"To the Judge of Probate Court, Clermont County, Ohio; I certify that I solemnized marriage of John Hewitt and Lizzie B. Morrison, 22 Apr 1880, J. W. Hill, J.P, recorded 26 Apr 1880."

[24] J. H. Hewitt & William P. Morrison households, 1880 U.S. Census, Clermont County Ohio, Union Twp., Mt. Carmel P.O., 4 Jun 1880, (Salt Lake City: Family History Library), microfilm #1255000, National Archives microfilm #T9-1000, image 0588, page 293a, family 77 and 81.

[25] Margie Thomas, *Barrere Funeral Home Records 1927-1953*, (Cincinnati: Hamilton County Chapter, Ohio Genealogical Society, 1994), page 33.
"Birchie Damm, born 22 Jul 1882; died 30 Oct 1952, St. Vincent Hospital, Indianapolis, IN; father: Hewitt, married to Harry Damm, mother of Henry Damm; interred at Mt. Moriah Cemetery."

[26] Hewitt monument, Mt. Moriah Cemetery, Union Twp., Clermont County Ohio. These stones next to the monument were photographed by the author, August 1996; Elsie Cleveland Hewitt, William Otto Hewitt, Francese Vesta Hewitt.

[27] "Glen Este News," *The Clermont Sun* newspaper, 26 Jul 1886.

[28] "William Otto Hewitt obituary," *Cincinnati Enquirer* newspaper, 29 Mar 1903.

[29] Mt. Carmel News, *The Clermont Sun* newspaper, 18 Apr 1888.

[30] John Hewitt household, 1887 & 1891, *The Williams Hamilton County Directory*, (Tucson Arizona: Williams Directory Company, 1974).

[31] Robert Kyle estate; Zacheus Kyle and Mary Kyle obituaries; *The Clermont Sun* newspaper, 4 Apr 1882, 21 Mar 1882, 4 Nov 1884, 17 Aug 1887, 18 Apr 1882.

[32] Frances Eliza Morrison death certificate; the author has a certified copy from the Clermont County Court of Common Pleas, Probate Division, Batavia, Ohio, 14 May 1991.

[33] Frances Eliza Kyle funeral announcement and memorial notice; Jefferson Kyle funeral announcement, *The Clermont Sun* newspaper, 28 Mar 1888, 26 Mar 1890, 27 Nov 1889.

[34] Rose to Hewitt deed, Clermont County Recorder, Batavia Ohio; 1891, book 129, page 418. The author copied the index showing deed from Minne H. Rose to John Hewitt, lot on Mathews Survey #1138, Union Township.

[35] "Summerside News," *The Clermont Sun* newspaper, 4 Feb 1891.

[36] Hewitt to Hewitt deed, Clermont County Recorder, Batavia Ohio, book 132:1.
"30 Apr 1892, deed from John Hewitt, Summerside, Clermont County Ohio, to Lizzie B. Hewitt, of same, for $750, 65 rods on Batavia Turnpike on Mathews Survey #1138; witnesses J. L. Perdrizet and Maggie Long; recorded 4 Jun 1892."

[37] Author Unknown, *Mt. Carmel Special School District, Mt. Carmel Primary School, 1891-1892*, Agnes Walker, Teacher. Among the students attending classes in 1891-1892 was Birchie Hewitt.

[38] Whitt, *Clermont County, Ohio, 1891 Atlas & History*, 31.

[39] *The Clermont Sun* newspaper, 31 Oct 1888, 7 Dec 1887.

[40] This photograph is probably of Samuel Hewitt and his daughters Media and Bertha, taken in the front yard of their Olive Branch neighborhood on Taylor Road shortly before he died in 1892.

[41] "Samuel D. Hewitt obituary," and Olive Branch News, *The Clermont Sun* newspaper, 21 Sep 1892, 6 Jun 1892, 2 Nov 1892.
"In Memoriam, Samuel D. Hewitt, born 11 Feb 1843 near Batavia, Ohio; died 16 Oct 1892, aged 49 years; life long resident of Clermont County; married Mary L. Duckett, 11 Feb 1867; two daughters; eldest of twelve children, nine of whom with the aged father survive him."

[42] Hewitt Family listings, Olive Branch News, *The Clermont Sun* newspaper, 21 Dec 1892, 26 Apr 1893, 21 Jun 1893, 5 Jul 1893, 20 Sep 1893, 24 May 1893, 9 Aug 1893, 18 Oct 1893.

[43] "Batavia High School Commencement Exercises," "Hewitt to Spearing," Olive Branch News, "Obituary of Mary Louisa Hewitt," *The Clermont Sun* newspaper, 6 May 1896, 26 Dec 1900, 19 Feb 1902, 26 Mar 1902, 27 May 1903.

[44] Herbert, *Restored Hamilton County, Ohio Marriages, 1870-1884*, page 2.

[45] Marion McClellan household, 1900 U.S. Census, Batavia Twp., Clermont County Ohio, 25 Jun 1900, copied National Archives & Records Administration, Denver Colorado, page 14B.

[46] "Children Find Homes," *The Clermont Sun* newspaper, 1 May 1901.

[47] Anna McClellan, *Oregon Death Index, 1903-1998*, online *Ancestry.com*, downloaded 1 May 2001.

[48] Marshall Green household, 1880 U.S. Federal Census, Morgan County, Illinois, Jacksonville Twp., 11 Jun 1880, dwelling 130, family 134, page 231D, online www.ancestry.com, census images.

[49] James Allen Hewitt family, in correspondence with the author, his granddaughter, Mollie Booth Walters, Roseburg Oregon, included a synopsis of James' life and information about Ann and Mel McClellan when they lived in Roseburg; dated 14 Nov 1998, 14 Jan 1999 and 3 Jan 2002.

[50] Thomas P. Mitchell household, 1900 U.S. Census, Columbia Township, Hamilton County Ohio, Jun 1900, copied at National Archives & Records Administration, Denver Colorado, page 284.

[51] The Mitchell Family, photograph. It was given to the author by Mary Jane McCormick, granddaughter of Mary Hewitt Gehres. The back said "Aunt Lou, Uncle Tom and Hewitt Mitchell."

[52] *Nashville and West Nashville City Directory*, 1895-1901, v. 31-37, (Nashville: Marshall & Bruce Company, 1895-1901).

[53] William J. Hewitt household, 1900 U.S. Census, Davidson County, Tennessee, 6 Jun 1900, copied at the National Archives and Records Administration, Denver, Colorado, page 7B.

[54] "Olive Branch News," *The Clermont Sun* newspaper, 6 Jul 1881, 3 Aug 1881.

[55] Letter to the author from Mrs. Leonard Frantz a descendant of Jacob Gehres, brother of Joseph Gehres, Ft. Myers, Florida, dated 14 Dec 1997.

[56] Joseph A. Gehres household, 1900 U.S. Census, Pike County, Ohio, Jun 1900, copied at the National Archives and Records Administration, Denver, Colorado, page 5B.

[57] *Courier Watchman* newspaper, 27 Jun 1900.

[58] *Republican Herald* newspaper, published: Waverly, Pike County Ohio, 1900, no day or month.

[59] Aaron T. Heverin, Buffalo History Works Online, *The Pan-American Exposition*, 14 Dec 1998, online at http://blw.buffnet.net/panamex/buildings/buildings.htm.

[60] *The Clermont Sun* newspaper, 17 Jul 1901.

[61] American Memory Project, *Library of Congress* online, "The Last Days of President McKinley," online from http://www.loc.gov/rr/mopic/ammen.html.

[62] L. Ruth Murray Klein, editor, *Bulletin: Americn Association of University Women, Philadelphia Branch,* "President's Focus: Women's History: A Proud Narrative," by Mary Ann Gehres, (Philadelphia: March 1988), V:56:7:1-2.

[63] 7 Jul 1997 letter from Mary Jane McCormick.

[64] Herbert, *Restored Hamilton County, Ohio Marriages.*

[65] William J. Hewitt Obituary, *Nashville Tennessean*, Nashville, Tennessee, week of 3-9 June 1928.

[66] Amos (A.K.) Hill household, 1920 & 1930 U.S. Census, Davidson County, Tennessee, district 2; 7 Jan 1920, image 800, page 4A, Murfreesboro Pike, South Springs Road, National Archives film #T625-1735; 17 Apr 1930, image, 0593, page 11B, National Archives microfilm #T626-2243.

[67] Amos Hill family, e-mail from descendant, Cecilia Bowman CBowman545@aol.com, 29 Sep 2001, who gave details about Amos Hill and Ellen Martin Van Buran Postan, who are her ancestors.

[68] Hewitt & Hewitt to Hewitt, Clermont County Recorder, Batavia Ohio, 3 Feb 1893, 131:325.
      "Deed from Richard D. Hewitt Jr. & Benjamin F. Hewitt to John H. Hewitt for $200, 1 share each of 84 acres, Darby's Survey #2058; Stephen's Survey #3877 sold to Richard D. Hewitt Sr., 5 Mar 1863, deed book 81:439; witnesses P. J. Nichols and John Latiman; recorded 18 Feb 1893."

[69] Lane to Hewitt, deed, Clermont County Recorder, Batavia Ohio, 27 May 1893, 134:176.
      "Deed from Edward & Maria Lane to Lizzie B. Hewitt for $675, 3 acres Mathews Survey #1138, witnesses A. E. Clevenger and Susan Worthington; recorded 7 Jun 1893."

[70] Hewitt vs. Hewitt, petition for partition, Clermont County Court of Common Pleas, Batavia Ohio, 26 Jun 1893, petition #9928, pages 347-352.
      "Cross petition and decree in partition, John H. Hewitt vs. James A. Hewitt et al; as defendants; (James A. Hewitt; William J. Hewitt; Louisa Mitchell, Thomas Mitchell; Ann McClellan, Mel McClelland; Mary J. Gehres, Joseph Gehres; Elizabeth Bratton, E. W. Bratton; Armeda (Almedia) Hewitt; Bertha Violett, Charles Violett; Louise Hewitt; cross-petitioner Richard D. Hewitt Sr., Richard D. Hewitt Jr. & Benjamin F. Hewitt; that Hewitt Sr. has a lien on real estate of $50 per year, that John H. Hewitt has legal rights to 3/10 of estate having bought 2/10 interests of Richard D. Hewitt Jr. and Benjamin Hewitt; that defendants are tenants in common with the plaintiff and subject to pay the lien, that each has an undivided 1/10 right; that Bertha Violett and Amanda Hewitt are subject to the dower of Louisa Hewitt widow of S. D. Hewitt (2/20th); appraisers Frank Apple, John Zurmehle and J. H. Hamilton determined premises could be divided without injury to value; that defendants give R. D. Hewitt $50 annually; that John H. Hewitt will furnish R. D. Hewitt Sr. firewood for his use; that $111.61 fees be paid by plaintiff and defendants."

[71] Hewitt Family photograph, ca. 1897. Conclusions about names and relationships of those in the photograph are those of the author, but made through correspondence with other descendants of this family. Back row: unknown Gehres, Joe Gehres, unknown, unknown, Mary Jane (Jen) Gehres, Hewitt Mitchell, unknown, Lizzie Hewitt Bratton Hill, Harry Hewitt. On the porch: Mary Hewitt Gehres, Davis Hewitt Sr. Middle Row: Beulah Hewitt , Rachel Hill Hewitt, Lou Hewitt Mitchell, unknown, Tom Mitchell, Will Hewitt, John Hewitt. Front row: William Hewitt Jr., Hattie Hewitt Irma Gehres, Lillian Hewitt, Ruth Hewitt, unknown, unknown.

[72] "Morrison House Burned," *The Clermont Sun* newspaper, 28 May 1889.

[73] Morrison to Morrison and Morrison deed, Clermont County Recorder, Batavia Ohio, deed book 129, pages 263, 264.
"Deed from Wm. P. Morrison, Union Township, Clermont County Ohio to Amos O. Morrison of the same; for $1; 132 acres, Wm. Moseley's Survey #1115, on west side of Batavia Turnpike; witnesses J. F. Perdrizet, Alice M. Perdrizet; recorded 19 Dec 1890; also deed from Wm. P. Morrison, to Lizzie B. Hewitt, of same, for $1; 65 acres, Union Township, Clermont County near Emor Johnson and Wm. Jones; witnesses J. F. and Alice M. Perdrizet; recorded 19 Dec 1890."

[74] "Amos O. Morrison Missing," *The Clermont Courier* newspaper, 6 Apr 1892.

[75] William P. Morrison death certificate, the author has a certified copy from Clermont County Court of Common Pleas, Probate Division, Batavia, Ohio.

[76] W. P. Morrison estate, Clermont County Probate, Batavia Ohio; 10 Feb 1893; A. O. Morrison administrator for W. P. Morrison deceased, docket 9, pages 12-19, administration letters, schedule F, bonds, mortgages and notes; copied for the author at the courthouse.

[77] A. O. Morrison obituary, *The Clermont Courier* newspaper, 7 Mar 1893; obituary and funeral notice, *The Clermont Sun* newspaper, 8 Mar 1893.

[78] Lizzie B. Hewitt, notice of appointment, final account, *The Clermont Sun* newspaper, 29 Mar 1893, and 26 Sep 1894.

[79] Richard & Benjamin Hewitt vs. John H Hewitt, for $200, *The Clermont Sun* newspaper, 12 Apr 1894. Also Clermont County Court of Common Pleas, Journal Minutes, Batavia Ohio, volume L-2 (1894-1895) cause #10289, page 162.
"Benjamin Hewitt et al against John H. Hewitt, waived jury by consent, John Hewitt, payment default; that day paid $200; judgment satisfied, witness Frank Davis, Judge."

[80] Hewitt to Miller deed, Hamilton County Recorder, Cincinnati Ohio, deed book 138, page 382.
"12 Oct 1896, deed from Lizzie & John Hewitt to William Miller; 65 acres, Matthews Survey #1138 for $2,400; witnesses John Nichols, Josie Foken, Nannie Haskell; recorded 18 Nov 1896."

[81] Hewitt to Nichols mortgage, Hamilton County Recorder, Cincinnati Ohio, deed book 730: 21-23.
"26 Nov 1896, deed from Lizzie B. Hewitt, Lot #1103 Bofinger and Hopkins 2nd Subdivision, Lydia Drake tract, Norwood, Ohio; to John Nichols for $320, payable in one year, 8% interest; witnesses S. B. Deal and Josie Foken; recorded 30 Nov 1896."

[82] John Hewitt residence, *Williams Cincinnati Directory*, (Cincinnati Ohio: C. S. Williams & Company, 1899), the livery stable was at 236 East Second Street, Cincinnati Ohio.

[83] "John Hewitt Taxes," *Clermont Sun*, 4 Jan 1899.

[84] Hewitt to Turner deed, Hamilton County Recorder, Cincinnati Ohio, Petition, Case #129, Hamilton County Court of Insolvency, deed book 807, p. 606-607; Hewitt to Simmons deed, Clermont County Recorder, Batavia Ohio, deed book 140, page 496; Hewitt to Mead deed, Hamilton County Recorder, Case #129, deed book 811, page 58.
"19 Feb 1897, John Nichols, attorney for Lizzie B. Hewitt's creditors; petition against Lizzie B. Hewitt, John H. Hewitt, Isaac Turner & John Clement; order to sell real estate, 132 acres, Moseley's Survey #1115, Clermont & Hamilton Counties, appraisal $4,800; to Isaac Turner for $3,250; he assigned rights to Edwin Turner; witnesses Josie Foken, S. B. Deal; recorded 2 Jun 1897; 3 acres, Matthews Survey #1138 to John Simmons for $225; witnesses Josie Focken, S. B. Deal; recorded 30 Jun 1897; Lot #1104, Bofinger and Hopkins Subdivision, Drake Tract, Norwood sold in a petition against Lizzie & John Hewitt, and Germania Building Assn. #3; to Allie B. Mead for $1,400; witnesses Geo. W. Hengst and Josie Focken; recorded 15 Jun 1897."

[85] 24 Feb 1897, Almira Hewlick vs. John Hewitt et al, mortgage foreclosure.

[86] Bryan A. Garner, editor, *Blacks Law Dictionary*, Torrens Act, (West Group, 1999), page 1489.

[87] "A Heavy Expense," *Cincinnati Enquirer*, published at Cincinnati, Ohio, 20 Feb 1897, page 16.

[88] John Hewitt Family, *Williams Cincinnati Directory*, page unknown.

[89] John H. Hewitt household, 1900 U.S. Census, Hamilton County, Ohio, population schedule, 12 Jun 1900, dwelling: 216, family: 131, pages 9006a-b, National Archives micro-publication.

[90] John Hewitt family, Cincinnati & Hamilton Co. Directories, 1901, 1902, 1903, pages unknown.

[91] "R. D. Hewitt and William Otto Hewitt obituaries," *The Clermont Sun* newspaper, 25 Mar 1903.

[92] "William Otto Hewitt and Lizzie Belle Morrison obituary," *The Cincinnati Enquirer* newspaper, 24 and 29 Mar 1903, 3 May 1903.
"Lizzie Belle Morrison, last surviving child of Wm. P. & Frances E. Morrison; born 26 Jun 1852, Mt. Summit, Hamilton County Ohio, died 24 Apr 1903; married 22 Apr 1880, John H. Hewitt, Mt. Carmel, Ohio; four children, Birchie Pearl, Elsie Cleveland, William Otto, and Francese Vesta; two of whom with her father, mother and brother preceded her; living are husband and daughters Birchie and Vesta; death from eight weeks *la grippe* and mental strain of son Otto's death."

[93] Hewitt Family, *Hamilton County and City of Cincinnati, Ohio, Directory*, 1905-1908.

[94] Hewitt to Miller, *Davidson County, Tennessee, Marriage Records*, Book 26 (9 Nov 1909 to Aug 1910), Family History Library, Salt Lake City, microfilm #0200315.
"3 Feb 1910, married by J. H. Wright, Elder, certified by W. J. Hewitt; J. H. Hewitt and W. J. Hewitt of Davidson County bond of $1,250; J. H. Hewitt has license to marry Jessie Miller; witnesses J. H. Hewitt and W. J. Hewitt, Davidson County, Tennessee."

[95] John H. Hewitt household, 1910 U.S. Census, Davidson County, Tennessee, E.D. No. 106, 27 Apr 1910, copied at the National Archives & Records Administration, Denver Colorado, page 7B.

SOURCE NOTES
Chapter Ten

FRANCESE VESTA HEWITT

[1] George Schmidt's 1980 reminiscences about his mother, Vesta Hewitt Schmidt and his aunt, Birchie Hewitt Damm, were the basis for their story, although at the time he spoke to the author, some details were unknown to him.

[2] Alma A. Smith, *Mt. Carmel and Summerside, Ohio, From 1788 to Modern Times*, (Cincinnati: privately printed, 1983), 44-46, 62-63.

[3] *The Clermont Sun* newspaper, 14 Jan 1880, 18 Mar 1891, 23 Dec 1891, 19 Dec 1894.

[4] George O. Schmidt interview.

[5] "Ladies Band Concert, & Womens Band," *The Clermont Sun*, 16 Jun 1897, 16 Aug 1899.

[6] Women's Band, *Cincinnati Post* newspaper, published Cincinnati, Ohio, 10 Aug 1899.
"Women's Band formed by Cincinnati Artists; inaugural concert Franklin Camp Meeting; 14 young women directed by Eugene Dial, bandmaster of the House of Refuge, organized as the Tuxedo Ladies' Band and Orchestra, headquarters at 526 East 4th Street; a popular band as illustrated by its retainer at the 4th annual assembly, Miami Valley Chautauqua at Franklin, Ohio."

[7] Hewitt Family, *Williams' Cincinnati Directory*, page unknown.

"1899, John H. Hewitt, northwest corner 2nd and Sycamore, livery business; at home, Sutton Avenue, Anderson Twp., Mt. Washington were Lizzie B. Hewitt, Birchie P. Hewitt, a musician."

[8] Harry Damm Obituary, *Cincinnati Times Star* newspaper, published at Cincinnati, Ohio, 21 Apr 1951, page 13:2.

[9] Social Security Death Index, online at http://www.ancestry.com, Henry J. Damm, born 2 Oct 1901, died September 1982, last known address Lucas Ohio.

[10] Harry P. Damm household, 1920 U.S. Census, Hamilton County, Ohio, Cincinnati, Volume 89, sheet 1, dwelling 3617, family 8; National Archives micro-publication #1388.

[11] George O. Schmidt interview.

[12] Hewitt to Schmidt, marriage; the author has a copy of the original certificate given to the bride and groom. 17 Apr 1907, George Conrad Schmidt, California Ohio to Frances Vesta Hewitt, Gwendolen Ohio; Campbell County Courthouse, Newport Kentucky; witnesses Herbert Van Carman, Grace Eleanor Broeg, John H. Hewitt, by J. W. Crates, Methodist Minister, 121 East 3rd Street, Newport.

[13] Autobiography of George Otto Schmidt, unpublished, begun 1930, continued 1981, pages 5, 13.

[14] Selman A. Waksman, *The Conquest of Tuberculosis*, (Berkeley: University of California Press, 1964), 14-15, 30-31, 61.

[15] Edward Otis, M.D. *The Great White Plague*, (New York: Thomas Crowell & Co., 1909), 120-124.

[16] Mark Caldwell, *The Last Crusade: War on Consumption*, (New York: Athenaeum, 1988), 75-83.

[17] Otis, *The Great White Plague*, 122-123.

[18] "A Cure for Consumption," *The Clermont Sun* newspaper, 14 Jun 1899.

[19] "Most Fatal of All Diseases," *The Cincinnati Enquirer*, 26 Apr 1903.

[20] Autobiography of George Otto Schmidt, page 5-6.

[21] A postcard from Vesta Schmidt to Mr. and Mrs. Charles Violett, R.R. #5, Batavia Ohio, postmarked, Boulder, Colorado 20 Dec 1909 is in the author's possession.

[22] A letter from John Hewitt, Nashville, Tennessee to Mrs. Bertha Violett, Olive Branch, Clermont County Ohio, postmarked 12 Dec 1909, is in the author's possession.

[23] Polk County, North Carolina Website, *Historic Sites in Polk County, North Carolina*, online at http://www.polkcounty.org/polkco/tours.html, http://www.inns.com/south/nc057.htm, and http://www.sc.edu/fitzgerald/facts/facts4html, downloaded 25 May 1998.

[24] Autobiography of George Otto Schmidt, page 7.

[25] Frances[e] Vesta Schmidt obituary, *Cincinnati Enquirer* newspaper, 4 Sep 1910.
"Schmidt--Frances Vesta Schmidt, once Hewitt, aged 20 years, 9 months, 22 days; beloved wife of George C. Schmidt, [died]at Tryon N.C. September 1; remains shipped to Cincinnati for burial; funeral at M. E. Church, California Ohio, Sunday, September 4 at 2 p.m."

[26] Hewitt Family photograph, ca. 1910 given to George Schmidt by Birchie Hewitt Damm and passed down to the author.

[27] George Schmidt will, Hamilton County Probate, Cincinnati Ohio, book 110: 2: 42-44, #64456; Family History Library: Salt Lake City), film #2196244.

"2 Jun 1909, George Schmidt, Hamilton County Ohio, to children, Conrad Schmidt, George Schmidt, Katie Dickhart; executors Conrad, George Schmidt; witnesses James J. Smiley, R. A. Powell; recorded 2 Jun 1909."

[28] Autobiography of George Otto Schmidt, pages 8-10; and George O. Schmidt interview.

[29] Peter Marschalck, *Deutsche Überseewanderung im I, Jahrhundert, Industrielle Welt* , 14 (Stuttgart: Klett, c1973), 35.

[30] Bismarck and Unification, *German Culture*, downloaded 18 May 2002, online at www.germanculture/history/bl_bismarck_unification.htm.

[31] James Chastain, *Hesse-Cassel*, downloaded 18 May 2002 online at www.ohiou.edu/~Chastain/dh/hessek.htm.

[32] *Statistical Review of Immigration, 1820-1910 / Distribution of Immigrants, 1850-1900*, reports from Immigration Commission 1 Oct 1846-31 Dec 1867, 61st Congress, 3rd Session, Senate Executive 756:3:23-29.

[33] George Smith household, 1860 U.S. Census, Hamilton County, Ohio, Anderson Twp., California P.O., page 293, dwelling 196, family 196; National Archives film #M653-981.

[34] George Schmidt household, 1870 U.S. Census, Hamilton County, Ohio, Anderson Twp., Newtown P.O., page 483, dwelling 58, family 58; National Archives film #M593-1208.

[35] Conrad Schmidt household, 1920 U.S. Census, Hamilton County, Ohio, California Village, ED 20, SD 1, sheet 3b, dwelling 16, family 78; National Archives film #T625-1388.

[36] George O. Schmidt interview.

[37] Henry A. Ford and Kate B. Ford, *A 1789 History of Hamilton County, Ohio: California*, (Cincinnati: L. A. Williams & Company, 1881), 253.

[38] *Williams 1869 Cincinnati City Directory*, (Cincinnati: Williams Directory Company, 1869), no page number, Family History Library microfilm #1606105,

[39] State of Ohio, Hamilton County Auditor website, www.hamiltoncountyauditor.org/realestate. The state of Ohio provides online property information for Hamilton County including photographs, current and former owners, address, original block, lot, subdivision or survey number. It gives the year built, size and number of rooms, improvements, and tax history.

[40] Ford, *A 1789 History of Hamilton County, Ohio*, "California," page 253.

[41] Mary H. Remler, editor, *Hamilton County, Ohio Burial Records: Volume Two Anderson Township 1800-1989, Mt. Washington Cemetery*, (Cincinnati: The Hamilton County Chapter of the Ohio Genealogical Society, 1990), 69.
      "George Schmidt, born Germany, late residence California Ohio, born 5 Nov 1837, died 11 Apr 1909, notes Civil War Veteran, section 2, grave 9, lot 79."

[42] John H. Thillmann, *Civil War Cavalry & Artillery Sabers, A Study of United States Cavalry and Artillery Sabers, 1833-1865*, Lincoln, Rhode Island: Andrew Mowbray Publishers, 2001), 266-271.
      "P. D. Luneschloss & Companie," maker Solingen, Prussia; includes a photograph and full description of P.D.L. Model 1840 Cavalry Officer's Saber, 1840 model, flat back blade, its measurements, description of the hilt, grip and scabbard."

[43] George Smith household, 1870 U.S. Census, Hamilton County, Ohio, Anderson Twp., California P.O., page 483A, dwelling 58, family 58; National Archives film #M593-1208.

[44] Alex Ecklemann household, 1860 U.S. Census, Hamilton County, Ohio, Anderson Twp., California P.O., page 294, dwelling & family 200; National Archives film #M653-981.

[45] Remler, *Hamilton County, Ohio Burial Records*, "Mt. Washington Cemetery," page 10.
"Alexander Ackerman, late residence California, Ohio, aged 79 years, born May 1907."

[46] George Schmidt household, 1900 U.S. Census, Hamilton County, Ohio, Anderson Twp., SW precinct, E.D #278, page 55, dwelling 88, family 94; National Archives film #T623:1281.

[47] Schmidt to Schmidt deed, Hamilton County Recorder, Cincinnati Ohio, deed book 819, pages 176-179.
"Deed from George Schmidt, wife Catherine, California, Hamilton County Ohio; to Conrad Schmidt of same; for $180.50, lots #99-104, Roger's Edition, 3rd Street, block #6, California, sold 10 Jan 1889 by Joseph Rogers to Thomas Fiscus and Fiscus to George Schmidt (662:321) for $90; witnesses W. N. Mathews and Angeline Mathews, recorded 12 Mar 1898.

[48] C. O. Titus, *Titus Atlas of Hamilton County Ohio*, from actual surveys by R. H. Harrison, C. E., (Philadelphia: published by the author, 1869), Anderson Twp.; Hamilton County, Ohio Auditor's Website online at http://www.hamiltoncountyauditor.org/realestate, and http://www.ancestry.com, census records 1790-1930.
These sources confirmed that from 1860-1900, George and Katharine Schmidt lived in California village. Sources included a 19th century and a contemporary map of the village that compared original and current street names; Schmidt's deeds and current tax assessment records were used to find current addresses; the census was compared against tax records by searching for Schmidt's neighbors during that time, and comparing their names to tax data as far back as the 1940's, showing descendants of the early settlers who still owned property there.

[49] 5740-5746 Linneman Street, City of Cincinnati Auditor, current taxes for lots 99-102 were found online at http://www.hamiltoncountyauditor.org/realestate. Then Rogers Addition, 8th Street between Rensler & Rohde Avenues, currently vacant land owned by the city of Cincinnati.

[50] Anna Schmidt estate, Hamilton County Probate, Cincinnati, Ohio, deed book 1847, pages 640-641, estate document #139099.
"2 Jan 1940, Anna Schmidt estate, deceased, R.R.#13, Mt. Washington, Hamilton County Ohio; died in testate 13 Mar 1939; 4 May 1939 George C. Schmidt, administrator; deceased had real estate, Roger's Addition lots # 99-104, 154; Murdock's Subdivision lots #6, 8, 14, 25, (plat book 1:69, recorded #1431:410); heirs, George C. Schmidt, son; Zetta Glasbrenner, dau., both R.R.#13, Mt. Washington Ohio; John Schmidt, son, 5806 Bryson Street, California; recorded 2 Jan 1940."

[51] A study determined the elder couple probably lived on 3rd Street (Panama Street), in California village near the Ohio River, as described in son Conrad's deed.

[52] George Sturm household, 1880 U.S. Census, Dearborn County, Indiana, Lawrenceburgh Twp., Lawrenceburgh P.O., page167A, ED #48, SD2, sheet 167a, dwelling not noted, family 181; National Archives micro-publication, roll #T9-0272.

[53] George O. Schmidt interview.

[54] Remler, *Hamilton County, Ohio Burial Records*, "Vine Hill Cemetery 1852-1977," Mt. Washington, Ohio, 1991, page not recorded.
"George C. Schmidt, husband of Minnie Rech; born 12 Jan 1886, son of Conrad Schmidt & Anna Sturm, buried: section 8, lot 227, grave 8."

[55] Conrad Schmidt household, 1900 U.S. Census, Hamilton County, Ohio, Anderson Twp., SW Precinct, page 297, dwelling 15, family 15; National Archives micro-film #T623-1281.

[56] Conrad Schmidt household, 1910 U.S. Census, Hamilton County, Ohio, Anderson Twp., SW Precinct, E.D. #278, page 55, dwelling 88, family 94; National Archives film #T623:1281.

[57] Autobiography of George Otto Schmidt, page 12.

[58] Conrad Schmidt estate, Hamilton County Probate, Cincinnati Ohio, doc. #139096, pages 582-583.
"Conrad Schmidt, R.R. #13, Mt. Washington Ohio; died testate 3 Mar 1939; will filed 27 Mar 1939; George C. Schmidt, administrator; that decedent died with real estate (see Anna Schmidt estate); in his will widow to have possession of all; Frank Bonham, probate judge; 20 Oct 1939."

[59] Remler, *Hamilton County, Ohio Burial Records*, "Mt. Washington Cemetery," page 69.
"Section 2, lots #79, 179; Katherine Schmidt, born Germany, lived California Ohio, born 10 Nov 1825, died 15 Nov 1907, John Akerman's daughter, George Schmidt's wife; Lydia Schmidt, born 1893-died 1917; Olive Schmidt born 1900-died 1925; Anna Schmidt, born 1862-died 16 Mar 1939, mother, Conrad's wife; Conrad Schmidt born 1863-died 6 Mar 1939, father, Anna's husband."

[60] Schmidt and Glasbrenner to Schmidt deed, Hamilton County Recorder, Cincinnati, Ohio, 4 Oct 1941, deed book 1929: 418-419.
"Deed from George C. Schmidt and Zetta Glasbrenner to John S. Schmidt for $1, lot #154 Roger's Edition, California, Anderson Twp., Hamilton County; sold by deed to Conrad Schmidt by George C. Schmidt, wife Frances Vesta Schmidt; dated 31 Aug 1907; recorded book #981:25, same as land sold to George C. Schmidt, Zetta Glasbrenner and John S. Schmidt from Anna Schmidt's estate #139099, recorded book #1847:640; George C. Schmidt, wife Minnie D. Schmidt, Zetta Glasbrenner, Louis Glasbrenner; witnesses Earl Whiting and Fred B. Sanders; recorded 6 Oct 1941."

[61] Autobiography of George Otto Schmidt, page 11.

SOURCE NOTES
Chapter Eleven

WILLIAMSON FAMILY

[1] Aline L. Garretson, "The Gerritsen-Willemsen Family Record, and the Williamson Family of Gravesend," *The New York Genealogical and Biographical Record*, (July 2002) 133:3:163-166. This translation of the Gerritsen Family Bible is from the original Dutch record by Rosalie Fellows Bailey and is now at the New York Genealogical and Biographical Society. See Appendix G.

[2] Harry Macy, Jr., "Before the Five-Borough City: The Old Cities, Towns, & Villages That Came Together to Form 'Greater New York,'" *New York Genealogical & Biographical Record*, (New York: Genealogical & Biographical Society, volume 129: Winter 1998), page unknown.

[3] A Virtual Tour of New Netherland, New Amersfoort (Flatlands), and Long Island, New Netherlands Project, New York State Library, Albany New York, online project downloaded 12 Oct 2002 from http://www.nnp.org/newvtour/regions/Long_Island/new_amersfoort.html.

[4] Gerritsen Family Bible, see Appendix G.

[5] I. N. Phelps Stokes, *The Iconography of Manhattan Island 1498-1909*, (New York: R.H. Dodd, 1915-1928), 6: 84B-c. A section of the map is of Manhattan from Franklin Street to 59th Street, over which were drawn the boundaries of the original grants to the Dutch by New York's first governor, Sir Edmund Andros. The map defines the approximate boundaries of two properties owned by Mary Remmersen after her husband Gerrit died. 16 Dec 1680, Andros granted to Mary Remmersen a tract laid out between 9th and 10th Avenues and 19th to 28th Streets, called "Chelsea Farm," part of the "Village of Chelsea." The other tract was between 6th and 8th Avenues and 25th to 29th Streets.

[6] Macy, "Kings County Colonial Church Records," *New York Genealogical & Biographical Record*, Volume 128: Winter 1997, page unknown.

[7] Teunis G. Bergen, *Early Settlers of Kings County, New York*, (New York: S. W. Green's Sons, 1881), 219.

[8] Map of Gravesend, "Town of Gravesend, Kings County," from the *New Netherlands Project* downloaded online at www.nnp.org/newvtour/regions/Long_Island/gravesendmap.html.

[9] Josephine C. Frost, contributor, *Long Island Source Records*, "Genealogical Gleanings from Book No. 2 of Conveyances, Brooklyn, Kings Co., New York." (Baltimore: Genealogical Publishing Company, Inc., 1987), pages 169-170, 175, 177.

"15 Apr 1698, deed from Wilkins to Van Sykelyn; deed from Remmersen to Gerretsen; 21 Jun 1698; deed from Mary Remmersen, Gravesend, widow of Gerret; to Samuel Gerretsen, house, etc. in Gravesend, near Martin Petersen; property near Capt. Stillwell and Reyneer VanSycklyn; lot near Willem Willemsen, Jonathan Griggs, Jr., widow Strycker; witnesses Henry ffilkin, and Jeremiah Stillwell; recorded 9 Sep 1698; 7 Sep 1698 Mary Remmersen to Samuel Gerretsen, same place, property near Rutt Joosten, Kryne Janse and Willem Willemsen; recorded 9 Sep 1698."

[10] Edward B. O'Callaghan, *Documentary History of the State of New York*, 1849-1851, (Albany: C. Van Benthuysen, printer, 1850), 2:489.

[11] Bergen, *Early Settlers of Kings County, New York*, 219, 388.

[12] Benjamin D. Hicks, editor, *Records of the Towns of North and South Hempstead, Long Island*, (1896-1904), (Jamaica, New York, Long Island Farmer Printer, 1896), 2:245.

[13] Gerritsen Bible, see Appendix G.

[14] Garretson, "The Gerritsen-Willemsen Family of Gravesend," page 168.

[15] Charles T. Gehring, editor, *New York Historical Manuscripts: Dutch Volumes XX-XXI*, "Delaware Papers, A Collection of Documents Pertaining to the Regulation of Affairs on the Delaware, 1664-1682." (Baltimore: Clearfield Press, 2000), "Baptisms at the Reformed Dutch Church of New Amsterdam, 1639-1730," page unknown.

"19 Oct 1653, father Pieter Claeszen, child Mayken,.witnesses Marten Jans, Judith Stuyvesant and Hendrickje Cornelis Van Ness."

[16] Phyllis Smith-Noah, *History of the Beeckman Family*, Wilhelmus Beeckman's will named his daughter Maria who married William Nicholas Stuyvesant, Governor Peter Stuyvesant's son; named also was their daughter, Judith Stuyvesant, born 1668, died unmarried before 1694; 9 Apr 2003, on line from http://freepages.genealogy.rootsweb.com/~beeckman/page6.html.

[17] The Wyckoff Association, *The Wyckoff Family in America*, 3rd edition, (Baltimore: Gateway Press, 1980), Introduction page 3.

"25 Sep 1636, Ship Rensselaerwick sailed from Amsterdam; 4 Mar 1637, arrived New Amsterdam, New Netherland; 7 Apr 1637, Fort Orange, Troy New York. There is no passenger list on this voyage, but 38 laborers were assigned to various farmers on the Rensselaer estate, including Pieter Claesen Van Norden, identified as Pieter Claesen."

[18] Rev. Frank R. Symmes, *History of Old Tennant Church*, 2nd edition, (Cranbury, New Jersey: G. W. Burroughs, printer, 1904), 421.

[19] Robert Gordon Clarke, *Hendrick Van Ness*, "Early New Netherlands Settlers" dated November 2001, a compilation of charts of descendants of early New York settlers including data on Grietje Van Ness and her father Hendrick Van Ness, f http://freepages.genealogy.rootsweb.com/~rclarke.

[20] David M. Riker, "The Van Ness Homestead," *de Halve Maen*, (New York: The Holland Society, 1982), 56:3:7.

[21] Symmes, *History of Old Tennant Church*, 421.

[22] Wyckoff, *The Wyckoff Family in America*," page vi, introduction, page 3.

[23] "Brooklyn's 17th Century Cemeteries, a website describing Flatlands Dutch Reformed Churchyard, Old Gravesend Cemetery and the Flatbush Reformed Dutch Churchyard, by PageWise, online at http://allsands.com/Travel/Places/cemeteriesbrook_arb_gn.htm.

[24] Pieter Claesen Wyckoff House Museum, Clarendon Road and Ralph Avenue, Brooklyn, New York, online at the City of New York Parks & Recreation website at www.nycgovparks.org/sub_about/parks_divisions/historic_houses/hh_pieter_claesen.html.

[25] David William Voorhees, translator and editor, *Flatbush Dutch Reformed Church Baptisms 1677-1754*, (New York: Holland Society of New York, 1998), online transcriptions of New Netherland, New York Church Records from http://www.olivetreegenealogy.com/nn/church/index/shtml, downloaded 17 Nov 2002.
　　　"16 Apr 1682, William Willemsz, Mayken Peters Wykof; Peter [Willemsz]; Pieter Claasz Wyckoff, Grietje van Ness; 12 Apr 1685, William Willemsz, Mayken Petersz Wykof of Gravesend; child: Marritje; witnesses: Martin Petersz Wykof, Hanna Willems."

[26] J. A. Van der Linde, *New York Historical Manuscripts: Dutch: Old Dutch First Reformed Church of Brooklyn, New York First Book of Records, 1660-1752*, "Marriages from Brueckelen Church Records 1662," (Syracuse: Syracuse University Press, 1983), 213.
　　　"29 May 1695, Parents Willem Willemse and Maijke Pieters, child: (Annetje), witnesses Samuel Gerritsen and Geertje Piet."

[27] Will of Willem Willemsen, see Appendix H.

[28] Carol M. Meyers, *Early New York State Census Records 1663-1772*, 2nd edition, (Gardena, California: RAM Publishers, 1965), 39.

[29] Charles Arthur Hoppin, *The Washington Ancestry and the Records of the McClain, Johnson, and Forty Other Colonial American Families*, (Greenfield, Ohio: privately printed, 1932), "William Jansen (Johnson) of Long Island and New Jersey and His Children," 3:14-22. "Flatbush Reformed Dutch Church Records, 1683 May 27, Martin Peterz to Hanna Willems."

[30] Bob Billard, compiler online of *Flatbush RDC Baptisms, 1677-1754*, downloaded 3 May 2003 from Rootsweb.com at http://homepages.rootsweb.com/~rbillard/flatbush_baptisms.htm.
　　　"Baptisms, 30 Mar 1684, parents Marten Pietersz Wykof, Hanna Willems, child Grietje, witnesses Peter Klaas Wykof, Grietie Van Nest; 12 Apr 1685, parents William Willemsz, Mayken Petersz Wykof, of Gravesend, child Marritje, witnesses Martin Petersz Wykof, Hanna Willems; 8 Jan 1688, parents Marten Petersen, Hanna Willemse, child Annetie, witnesses Cornelis Peterse Wykof, Annetie Petersen; 22 Sep 1689, parents Marten Petersen, Hanna Willemsen, child Sara, witnesses Johannes Brower, and Sara Willemsen."

[31] Pelletreau, *Abstracts of Unrecorded Wills Prior to 1790*, V.1: 454, page 449.
　　　"7 Sep 1697, Marten Peterse Wyckoff will, Gravesend, Kings County; executors Claes Wyckoff, Amersfort, William Willemsen, Johannes Guylick, Gravesend; wife Hannah, houses and lands; then to children, Grietie, Marytie, Anna, Sara, Mayake, Jannetie & Peter; witnesses John Lake, Abraham Emans; proved 26 Feb 1707/8; administrator wife, executors refused to serve."

[32] Hoppin, *The Washington Ancestry and the Records of the McClain, Johnson Families,* from New York County Surrogate Court Inventory book 5-6, p.490.
　　　"22 May 1707, Martin Peterson inventory, late Gravesend, estate taken by Hannah Hubbard, widow; appraisers John Larue and William Williamson; Total £7.19, witness Thomas Wenham."

[33] O'Callaghan, *Documentary History of the State of New York*, 3:136.

[34] Willem Willemsen will, see Appendix H.

[35] Meyers, *Early New York State Census Records 1663-1772*, 39.

[36] Jochem Guylick will, *New York City Wills, 1706-1790*, on line, http://search.ancestry.com.

"20 Dec 1711, Jochem Guylick, Gravesend, Kings County; wife Jaquimyntie houses, lands in Gravesend; son Johanes pays siblings Hendrick, Jochem, Peter, Teunis, Catalyntie, Grietje, Gertruyd, Jaquamintie £655; if Johanes dies without issue estate to Peter; executor wife; wife and children's guardians, Aert Van Pelt, William Willemsen, Samuel Gerritsen; witnesses Samuel Hubbard, John Lake, Nicholas Willemsen; proved before Gov. William Burnet 26 Aug 1723."

[37] W.H.H. Davis, *History of Bucks County, Pennsylvania*, (Chicago: Lewis Publishing Company, 1905), 288, Gulick Family.

[38] Billard, *Flatbush RDC Baptisms, 1677-1754*.
"18 Sep 1709, parents Willem Willemsz, Catalyntie Gulick, child Jochem; witnesses Jochem Gulick, Geertruy Gulick "

[39] Samuel Willemse baptism, *Baptismal and Church Records of Neshaminy and Bensalem Churches*, (Lancaster, Pennsylvania: Evangelical & Reformed Historical Society, UCC, 1986), page not shown. Surviving baptisms of Six-Mile Run on the Raritan, Somerset County, New Jersey, performed by Rev. Paulus Van Vlecq at Neshaminy, Bensalem and Germantown, Pennsylvania, from 1710-1712. There are no records between 1712 and 1740 for this church.
"8 Aug 1710, baptized Samuel, parents Kornelis Willemse, Grietye Gulick; witnesses Willem Willemse, Catelyntye Willemse; 23 Oct 1711; baptized Johannis; parents Willem Willemse, Catelyntye Gulick; witnesses John Folckersen, Angenietye Bennet."

[40] C. C. Vermeule, "Raritan Landing That Was," *Proceedings of the New Jersey Historical Society*, (Newark: New Jersey Historical Society, New Series, 1926): (April 1936) 54:2: 89, 91-95.

[41] "New Brunswick First Reformed Church Baptisms," *Proceedings New Jersey Historical Society*, (1926): 11: 401.

[42] A. Van Doren Honeyman, editor, *Archives of the State of New Jersey, Calendar of Wills, New Jersey Colonial Documents: First Series*," Calendar of New Jersey Wills 1761-1770," (New Somerville: New Jersey Historical Society, 1928), Book H: 1, V.4: 481.
"10 Aug 1761, Jacobus Williamson, Middlesex County, in-testate; administrators Peter Perrine, Somerset County, William Williamson, Jr. Middlesex County; 7 Aug 1761, renunciation by William Williamson, Garret Williamson who are Jacobus' brothers; witnesses Samuel Gerritsen, Isaac Brooks; 7 Aug 1761, inventory of Six Mile Run estate, Cornelius DeHart, Samuel Gerritsen."

[43] Honeyman, *New Jersey, Calendar of Wills, 1761-1770*, book 21:337.
"4 Sep 1767, William Williamson will, Middlesex County; daughter Catalyntye (wife, George Van Nest), £430; daughter Jannitye, (wife, John Piatt), £470, house, lot, 20 acres; grand-children Jannitje, Lucretia, Ida Williamson, £175; son William, executor, all lands after wife dies; witnesses Jacob Wicoff, Rem Gerritsen, Roeloff Voorhees; proved 18 Jan 1780."

[44] William B. Brahms, *Franklin Township, Somerset County, NJ: A History*, "Early Residents of Franklin Township Along the Main Roads From a 1766 Survey," map, (commissioned by the Franklin Township Public Library, 1998), page 96.

[45] "New Brunswick First Reformed Church Baptisms, 1717-1765, *Proceedings of the New Jersey Historical Society*, 11:206.
"Baptisms, 25 Mar 1718, parents Cornelus, Grietie Willemse, child Jakementie, witnesses Pieter Gulick, Jakementie Gulick."

[46] Isaac Van Dike will, *New Jersey Calendar of Wills*, First Series, 23:477.
"31 Mar 1727, Isaac Van Dike will, Middlesex County, age 47; wife Barber; children Thomas, Isaac, Maggary; executors brother Andress Van Dike, New Castle County, John Van Dike, Middlesex; witnesses Teunis Quick, Cornelius Williamson, Thomas Yates, proved 15 May 1727."

[47] James Snell, *History of Hunterdon & Somerset Counties New Jersey*, Franklin Twp. Tax List About 1735," (Philadelphia: Evert & Peck, 1881), page 815.

"Grace Harresen... Samuel Corneles; Willem Willemse, 100 acres, 5 cows; Hendrik Emans, Benjaman Emans, Tomas Yates, Corneles Wilmse, 50 acres, 5 cows...Teunis Quick, Corneles De Hart; Pieter Gulick; Tuenes Gulick."

[48] Brahms, *Franklin Township, Somerset County, New Jersey*, page 96.

[49] Somerset County New Jersey Public Records, *Road Books, Somerset County Courthouse, New Jersey, 1733-1776*, (Salt Lake City: Genealogical Society of Utah, 1972), film #0913006, A1: 1.
"16 Apr 1740, application for highway surveyors from Somerset County, to lay road from Rocky Hill to Kingston; beginning at New Brunswick to Princeton, opposite former land of Henry Harrison, Rocky Hill, deceased; to John Barien, to Richard Wright, Burlington; to Capt. Hendrick Emons; Benjamin Fitz-Randolph; across Dirty Brook on path leading down hill opposite Cornelius Williamson's house, then up the hill to Cornelius Williamson's gate; east to Moses Hull; to Jediah Higgins; to main road from New Brunswick to Trenton; recorded 16 Apr 1740; signed Cornelius (X) Williamson, Hendrick Vroom, Cornelius Meadock, Hendrick Van Lowe, John VanDerVeer."

[50] Snell, *History of Hunterdon and Somerset Counties, New* Jersey, "1745 Tax list of Somerset County, Franklin Township," page 815.

[51] Rosalie Fellows Bailey, "Dutch Systems in Family Naming: New York and New Jersey," *National Genealogical Society Quarterly*, (Arlington: National Genealogical Society, 1953), 41: 111-112.
"Children were almost invariably named for relatives, and it was customary to name the eldest two boys and the eldest two girls after their four grandparents...strong tendency to name the first child for a paternal grandparent...tendency to alternate, taking one child's name from the father's side of the family, the next child's name from the mother's side."

[52] Many records, including marriage and baptismal documents as well as deeds, survived until the Revolutionary War when they were destroyed during the British occupation of New Jersey. There was substantial troop movement and battles throughout New Jersey, cutting a swath of destruction through the middle of the state where the Williamson family lived. Consequently many church and civil records were destroyed. What remained were fragments of marriages and baptisms recorded by church ministers. As an example, there are documents for Six Mile Run Reformed Dutch Church from 1710-1711, with a gap until 1743. It is the years where there was a gap that Cornelius and Grietje Williamson, as well as their siblings William and Catalyntie, had their children baptized.

[53]John Ward Dean, editor, "The Coming of the Hull Company Bound for New England, Weymouth, England to Boston, MA 20 Mar 1633," *The New England Historical and Genealogical Register*, (Boston: The New England Historical Society, January 1871),V.XXC:13-15.

[54] Carolyn Hull Estes, *Hulls Heritage: A Genealogical History*, (Fort Worth: published by the author, 1986), 2-13.

[55] John Insley Coddington, (1902-1991), *The Hull Family*, an unpublished manuscript. Coddington was a Hull family researcher and descendant of Reverend Joseph Hull. Phyllis Hughes, Boulder Colorado, a Hull Family Association researcher, gave a copy of his manuscript to the author.

[56] Samuel Hull, marriage, "Piscataway, N. J. Marriage and Death Records," *New Jersey Historical Society Proceedings*, (Newark: New Jersey Historical Society, 1919), New Series: 4:36.

[57] John Martin, deed, *Calendar of New Jersey Records*, New Jersey Recorder, Trenton, 1:21:70.
"12 May 1682, John Martin, Piscataway, deed to son Joseph Martin of same, 80 acres bounded on the north by Samuel Hull."

[58] Samuel Hull, deed, *Calendar of New Jersey Records*, 1:21:128.
"10 May 1688, deed from Thomas Fitz Randolph, Piscataway; to Samuel Hull of same; 80 acres south by Dottie's Brook, west by Ambrose's Brook, north & east by un-appropriated land."

[59] Samuel Hull, birth, "Piscataway Register of Births, Marriages," *New Jersey: Proceedings of the New Jersey Historical Society*, (Paterson: Press Printing & Publishing Co., 1897), 3:2:171.

[60] Orra Eugene Monnette, *The First Settlers of Ye Plantations of Piscataway and Woodbridge, Olde East New Jersey, 1664-1714, A Period of Fifty Years*, (Los Angeles: The Leroy Carman Press, 1932), V. 1-6, "Piscataway Town Books, List of Cattle Ear Marks."

[61] Elizabeth Hull, marriage, "Piscataway, N. J. Marriage and Death Records," *New Jersey Historical Society Proceedings*: 4:37.

[62] Honeyman, *New Jersey Calendar of Wills 1761-1770*, #529J, 10:587.
"[No date], Samuel Hull, Amwell Two., Hunterdon County; wife Margrit personal estate; eldest son Moses Hull 1/4 acre, £0.40; sons Gashim and John Hull £10 each; Daniel Hull plantation, farming equipment; four daughters, Patience Williamson, Margrit Thatcher, Mary Ann Cane, Johannah South, divide moveable estate; executors son-in-law William Williamson, son Daniel Hull and Garret Williamson; witnesses Peter Hoffman, George Trout, John Ringo, recorded 6 Jul 1761."

[63] Honeyman, *New Jersey Calendar of Wills 1761-1770*, 209, book 14:37; 14:502.
"1 Feb 1768, Margaret Hull will, Amwell, Hunterdon County; daughters Patience Williamson, Margaret Thatcher, Mary Ann Cane and Johanna South, real and personal estate; sons Moses, Gershom, John and Daniel Hull, legacy; executor Joseph Thatcher; witnesses Bartholomew Thatcher, Martha Boyd, Thomas Sutton; administrator Moses Hull; proved 26 Jan 1769."

[64] Hunterdon County Freeholders 1741, *Genealogical Magazine of New Jersey* (New Brunswick: Genealogical Society of New Jersey, 1962), 2 May 1962, 37:2:49.

[65] William Williamson, will, see Appendix H.

[66] Honeyman, *New Jersey Calendar of Wills 1761-1770*, 1:4:241; book 11: 358.
"26 Jun 1762, Daniel Larew, will, Amwell, Hunterdon County; proved 11 Aug 1762."

[67] Hutchinson, *Documents Relating to the Colonial, Revolutionary and Post-Revolutionary History*, "Calendar of New Jersey Wills, Administrations, First Series, *1791-1795*," 37:190; 35: 118.
"27 Feb 1794, John Hull, Amwell Township, Hunterdon County; proved 8 May 1794; file #1682J, 26 Apr 1794; inventory, £148.8.7 by Cornelius Williamson and Peter Rockafellow."

[68] Hutchinson, *Archives of the State of New Jersey, Post-Revolutionary Documents: Calendar of Wills 1814-1817*, volume 13, (Jersey City: New Jersey Historical Society), 42:223
"31 Jan 1812; Margaret Hull, Amwell Township, Hunterdon County; grandson, John Hull Boughton; daughter Mary Dilts; children James Larue, Catharine Lake, Abraham Larue, Mary Dilts, and Moicah Boughton; executors son James Larue, Asher Williamson; witnesses Cornelius Lake, Atheniel Gordon, Robert Bonham; not proved."

[69] Brahms, *Franklin Township, Somerset County, NJ: A History*, "Early Residents of Franklin Township Along the Main Roads From a 1766 Survey," map, page 96. Cornelius DeHart lived near Ten Mile Run and William Williamson's tavern was on the road that leads south to Kingston.

[70] Hutchinson, Calendar of New Jersey Wills, administrations," volume 6, 1781-1785, 30:497.
"16 Mar 1768, Cornelius DeHart will, Middlesex County, wife Moike, lands, then to sons, Gisbert, Cornelius, William and Abraham; daughters each £70, Margaret, Samuel Williamson's wife; Antje De Hart, Sarah De Hart; executors sons Gisbert, Cornelius; witnesses Jacob Wicoff, William Williamson and Roeloff Voorhees; proved 22 Dec 1790."

[71] *Baptismal and Church Records, Churchville, Bucks County, Pennsylvania*: "Neshaminy and Bensalem (North and Southampton) 1710-1820," no page given.

[72] Snell, *History of Hunterdon and Somerset Counties, New Jersey*, "The De Hart Family," 805-806.

[73] New Brunswick First Reformed Church Baptisms 1717-1765, *New Jersey Historical Society*, Vol. 11, 402, 414.

[74] A. VanDoren Honeyman, editor, *Somerset County Historical Quarterly*, "Six Mile Run Church, Baptisms, From the Record: 1743-1805," (Plainfield, New Jersey: Somerset County Historical Society, 1919), Volume 8:126, 128, 130, 213, 216, 221, 223, 265.

[75] See Peter Williamson pension application file, # S3598 below.

[76] Honeyman, "Six Mile Run Church, Baptisms, 1743-1805," 8: 213, 215, 217, 219, 221, 227.
     "6 May 1759 Samuel & Grietje Willemse child Willem; 17 May 1761 child Cornelis; 14 Aug 1763 child Petrus; 9 Mar 1766 child Mayeke; 18 Sep 1768 child Antye; 20 Jul 1777 child John."

[77] *The Pennsylvania Gazette*, 7 May 1772, "Three Pounds Reward," *New Jersey Colonial Documents*, Series 1:28:134-135.

[78] Kenn Stryker-Rodda, "New Jersey Rateables, 1778-1780, New Brunswick, North & South Wards, April 1779, June 1780," *Genealogical Magazine of New Jersey*, Middlesex County New Jersey, (New Brunswick: Genealogical Society of New Jersey, January 1976) 51:1:28.
"New Brunswick, North Ward, Middlesex County, New Jersey; April 1779, Samuel Williamson 300 acres, 6 horses, 3 cows, 7 pigs, a riding chair, £200 out at loan; William Williamson 250 acres, 5 cows, 8 pigs, an orchard, £600 out at loan."

[79] Honeyman, "John Piatt's Cobbler's Census, 1765-1772," *Somerset County Historical Quarterly*, Volume VI, April 1917, 6:93, 95.
     "Cornelius DeHart (Wife, Abraham, Anney DeHart, Antye DeHart, Brom, Cornelius DeHart, Gisbart, Jack, Phil, Sarah DeHart, William); Samuel Williamson (Wife, Anney, Cornelius, Jacob, Moyche, Old Jacob, Peter, William, Peggy Duckworth, Antye Vandeventer)."

[80] Albert L. Stokes, "The DeHart Family," *The Genealogical Magazine of New Jersey*, Volume 40:1 (January 1965), 1-9; www.vandeventer.net/GroupSheets/gp110.htm#head1, van Deventer Genealogical Data Exchange; Cornelius DeHart's will, book 6:117.
     "Gysbert DeHart, fifth child of Simon and Geertje; wife was Antje Wynants; Gysbert died before 6 Dec 1712 when widow Antje married Jan Van Deventer; son Jacobus (James) VanDeventer baptized Middletown 18 Oct 1713; 16 Mar 1768, Cornelius DeHart will; farm to sons Gisbert, Cornelius, William, and Abraham after wife Moica's death; mentions daughter Margaret, wife of Samuel Williamson; proved 22 Dec 1790 no inventory."

[81] A photograph of Cornelius and Moike Dehart's gravestone are in the author's possession.

[82] "New Brunswick First Reformed Church Baptisms, 1717-1820,"11:2:406.
     "30 May 1731 Willem and Jannitie Willemse, child Catalyntie; 19 May 1734 child Peterius; 9 Jan 1737 child Jannetje; 22 Jul 1739 child William; 2 Mar 1743 child Johannis."

[83] Honeyman, "Six Mile Run Church, Baptisms, 1743-1805," 8:132, 213, 215, 218, 220, 222.
     "4 Dec 1757 Willem &Angenietye Willemsen, child Willem; 9 Sep 1759 child Isack; 28 Mar 1762 child Willim; 22 Jul 1764 child Johannes; 15 Feb 1767 child Jorys; 25 Feb 1770 child Antia."

[84] The New Brunswick First Reformed Church, Middlesex County, New Jersey had two Williamson families whose children were baptized in the church; each couple was named Willem and Jannetje, and between them eight children were baptized. Both couples had a child baptized in 1728 and 1737. Upon examination, it seemed these children's names fit into the naming pattern of only one family. They are William Williamson, Jannetje Covenhoven, children Patience, David and William; and William Williamson, Jannitje Van Nest, children Catalyntie, Peter, Jannetje, William, Johannis.

[85] Honeyman, "John Piatt's Cobbler's Census, 1765-1772," 6:95.
     "William Williamson (Father, Mother, Wife, Billy, George, Hartye, Honce (John), Isaac, Jeney, Netye, Phill, Quas (Jaques), Tune, Will."

[86] See William Williamson's 1767 will above.

[87] Jack Allen and John L. Betts, *History: USA*, (New York: American Publishing Company, 1967), 81, 84.

[88] John D. Alden, revised by D. Stanton Hammond, New Jersey Revolutionary War Map, *Battles and Skirmishes of the American Revolutionary War in New Jersey*, (Trenton: Bureau of Geology and Topography, 1974), maps online from Rutgers University at http://mapmaker.rutgers.edu/HISTORICALMAPS/RevolutionaryBattles.gif.

[89] William S. Stryker, Adjutant General, "Jerseymen in the Revolutionary War," *Official Register of the Officers and Men of the New Jersey in the Revolutionary War*, (Bowie, Maryland: Heritage Books, 1993), 419, 823.

[90] Archives of the State of New Jersey, (Trenton); *the following is written at the beginning of the report:* "A book register and copy of the inventory of damages done by the enemy and their adherents to the inhabitants of the county of Middlesex, taken and approved by Benjamin Manning, Joseph Olden, and Nathaniel Hunt in 1782." "Damages in Middlesex, Somerset and Hunterdon Counties," microfilm #0888699, 39. The record described damages to personal property from 1 Dec 1776 through 22 Jun 1777 including Samuel Williamson's losses.

[91] Letter from Mrs. Noah Webster Overstreet, Jackson, MS, to the Hunterdon County Historical Society, (Flemington, New Jersey), dated 7 May 1971.

[92] Peter Williamson, Revolutionary War Service pension application file #S3598, Court of Common Pleas, Hunterdon County New Jersey, micro-publication #M805, (Washington D.C.: National Archives and Records Administration), 7 May 1833, pages 224-231, 528.

[93] William Williamson file, #W4862, Revolutionary War Service Pension Application, Washington D.C., micro-publication M805, (Washington: NARA), pages 376-390.

[94] Stryker-Rodda, "New Jersey Rateables, 1778-1780, New Brunswick, North and South Wards, April 1779 and June 1780, 51:1:34.

[95] Teunis G. Bergen, *The Terhune Family: Contributions to the History of the Early Settlers of Kings County, N. Y.*, (New York: New York Genealogical & Biographical Record, 1880) 4:159-165.

[96] Billard, online, *Flatbush Marriages 1677-1757*, and *Flatbush RDC Baptisms 1677-1754*, downloaded 3 May 2003.
"1 Jul 1683, Jan Albertz, young man to Annetje Roelofs Schenck, young dame, both of New Amersfoort, 13 Apr 1684; parents Jan Albertsz and Annetje Roelofs Schenck; child Albert; sponsors Albert the Lintweever (ribbon weaver) and Geertje his wife."

[97] Charles Terhune Duncan, *A Terhune Family History and Genealogy*, (Indianapolis, Indiana: Guild Press, 1997), 33.

[98] Roelof Martense Schenck, will, recorded in the New York Surrogate's Office, Book 7:209.

[99] Billard, *Flatbush Marriages 1677-1757*.
"6 Jun 1691, Jan Albertse Terhunen, widower of Annetie Schenck married Margrietie VanSigelen, young dame, both from New Amersfoort; 17 Oct 1708, Albert Ter Huynen to Aeltie Voorhes, both of New Amersfoort."

[100] Elias W. Van Voorhis, *A Genealogy of the Van Voorhees Family in America, or the Descendants of Steven Coerte Van Voorhees of Holland and Flatbush. L.I.*, (New York: Knickerbocker Press, 1888), 1:50.

[101] Albert Terhune will, "Wills of Flatbush, Kings County New York," on line at Dutch-Colonies-L, http://www.rootsweb.com.
"11 Apr 1721, Albert Terhunen, Flatbush, Kings County New York, wife Altie houses, land in Flatbush; estate to raise children, then to eldest son for younger children's upbringing; mother

£100 annually, then to children, John, Gerrit, Arne, Willimentie and Sarah; sell land in Princeton for debts; executors wife Altie, father-in-law Peter Nevius, brother Roelof Terhunen, brother-in-law, Koert Voorhees; witnesses Peter Wyckoff, John Elbertsen and S. Gerritsen; proved 18 Dec 1721."

[102] Heyward Peck, *The Rev. Johannes Theodorus Polhemius and Some of His Descendants*, V:XC, (New York: The New York Genealogical and Biographical Record, 1959), 175, 229.

[103] Author's note. In an attempt to prove that John Terhune was the son of Aeltje Voorhees and not Aeltje Nevius, the research of Heyward Peck in his book, *The Rev. Johannes Theodorus Polhemius and Some of His Descendants* provided information. He named Neltje's ancestors indicating that, except for Aeltje who was named for John's mother, his wife Neltje named most of their daughters after her ancestors including her namesake Ellener (Neltje). Elizabeth was named for her mother, Elizabeth Polhemus; Magdalena Lefebre who married Joost Duryea was her grandmother. Children named for John's ancestors were Annetje, named for his grandmother, Annetje Schenck. Her brother Gerrit was named for John's side of the family, as was their son, Albert, for John's father.

[104] Van Voorhis, *A Genealogy of the Van Voorhees Family in America*, 1:5.

[105] Honeyman, "Six Mile Run Church, Baptisms, 1743-1805," 8:126, 129.
"25 Aug 1751, Jan & Neeltje Terheunen child Jan; 20 Apr 1755, child Magdelena."

[106] John Terhune will, New Brunswick, Middlesex County, *New Jersey Calendar of Wills 1785-1790*, Series, book 28:316.
"12 Apr 1786, John Terhune will, New Brunswick, Middlesex County New Jersey; eldest son Albert; wife Ellener annual interest on £200; son Gerrit lands; daughters Aeltje deceased, Magdalen, Ellener, Anne, Elizabeth, each £200; executors son Garret, sons-in-law Barent Johnson, Simon Relect; witnesses Frances Costegan, John Schureman, Isaac Slover; proved 19 Jul 1786."

[107] Mabel Jacques Hadler, *Selover-Slover Family*, (Long Beach California: printed by the author, 1968), 2nd edition, 6, 7, 12-13, 213-215. The original Daniel Seloover Bible written in Dutch is at the Rutgers University Library, New Brunswick, New Jersey.
"Daniel Seloover his Bible, born 12 Oct 1704 New York; Helena Schermerhoorn born 18 Aug 1704; Daniel Seloover married Helena 3 Sep 1726 at Eusopus; Daniel and Helena's children, Maria Selover, born 25 May 1739, baptized 17 Jun 1739 North Branch, Readington R. D. Church."

[108] Honeyman, "Six Mile Run Church Baptisms, 1743-1805," 8: 132, 212, 215, 217,219, 221, 222, 223, 225.
"Franklin Township, Somerset County, New Jersey, Albert & Marya Terhune's children; 4 Sep 1757, Jan; 4 Mar 1759, Daniel; 2 Aug 1761, Abraham; 30 Jul 1763, Lena; 6 Oct 1765, Albert; 20 Dec Elisabeth; 14 Jan 1770, Garret; 19 Apr 1772, Isaac; 14 Aug 1774, Jacob."

[109] William Williamson Family Bible, written in his hand and included in his Revolutionary War pension application, page 384, application #W4862.
"William Williamson, born 6 Apr 1759; Halena Terhune born 23 Jun 1763; William & Halena married Sunday at Cranberry New Jersey 13 Jun 1784; children, Samuel born Kingston New Jersey 6 Nov 1785; John born Allegany County Maryland 17 Dec 1787; Mary born Allegany County 15 Apr 1790; William Williamson Jr. born Allegany County, Friday 22 Jun 1792; Albert born Amwell New Jersey 11 Apr 1795; Daniel born Amwell 20 Nov 1797; Abraham born Amwell 21 Mar 1800; Margaret born Amwell, 27 Feb 1803."

[110] Honeyman, "Six Mile Run Church Baptisms, 1743-1805."8:266, 267, 268, 269.
"1 Apr 1787 Abraham & Mayeke Terhune child Albert; 1 Nov 1789 child Samuel; 2 Oct 1791 child Mary; 16 Nov 1788 child Margrit; 13 Nov 1791 child Mary."

[111] William Williamson will, see Appendix I.

[112] Stryker-Rodda, "New Jersey Rateables, 1778-1780, New Brunswick, North and South Wards, April 1779 and June 1780, 51:1:28.

"William Williamson 435 acres; 8 horses, 10 cows, 2 sheep, a riding chair, £200 out at loan; Widow Williamson 400 acres, 8 horses, 18 cows, 7 pigs, 2 sheep, £2,500 out at loan."

[113] *New Jersey Marriages, Colonial Era, 1665-1800*, online at http://search.ancestry.com/cgi-bin/sse.dll?&gsfn=williamson.

[114] Honeyman, *New Jersey Calendar of Wills 1761-1770*, 209, book 13: 20; 4:481.
"30 Apr 1767, Cornelius Williamson will, Amwell, Hunterdon County, in testate; administrators Jehokim Griggs, Abraham Williamson; bondsman Jacob Sutphen; 30 Apr 1767 Elizabeth Williamson renounced, Gesberd Gulick in favor of Jehokim Griggs, Abraham Williamson; 5 Oct 1767 inventory £394.18.0 by John Piatt, Jacob Sutphen; 9 Aug 1768 administrators Joachim Griggs, Abraham Williamson, paid widow Elizabeth Williamson and Bartholomew Williamson."

[115] Cornelius Williamson, his Bible; historian H. Everts made a handwritten copy of its contents, and the author has a photocopy. It passed from Cornelius to his daughter, Eleanor (Nellie) Williamson who married Gilbert Gulick and Samuel Williamson, the contents name all of Eleanor's children.
"Margaret Williamson b. 6 Feb 1783; Elizabeth Williamson b. 17 Sep 1785; Ellenor Williamson b. 29 Feb 1788."

[116] Hutchinson, *Calendar of New Jersey Wills, Administrations, etc., 1786-1790*, Book 30:366: 66.
"24 Mar 1790, Michael Demott, Reading Twp. Hunterdon Co.; wife; son Derick, daughters Sarah Decker, Stinety Williamson, Elizabeth Demott; executors son Derick, son-in-law Cornelius Williamson; witnesses Cornelius Johnson, John Kinney, Elizabeth Johnson; proved 1 Jul 1790."

[117] Samuel Williamson's grandmother was Margrietje Gulick who married Cornelius Williamson. Eleanor Williamson's husband was Gisbert Gulick, whose grandfather was Hendrick Gulick, a brother of Margrietje Gulick, thus Samuel and Gisbert were cousins. Eleanor, daughter of Elizabeth & Cornelius Williamson, Amwell, Hunterdon County who left will dated 30 Apr 1767. Samuel and Cornelius Williamson were related, but how he and Eleanor were related has not been determined.

[118] See Gulick to Gulick deed to heirs of Cornelius Williamson.

[119] *For the Township of Amwell, Book A, 1741-1798*, presented to the Hunterdon County Historical Society in 1980 by Jim Siuta who found it in an attic in Lambertville, New Jersey, not numbered.

[120] Williamson vs. Williamson, Chancery Court, Trenton, New Jersey, Decree #9, pages 135-289, filed 10 Jul 1810; William Williamson et al complainants against Samuel Williamson, George C. Maxwell, Solicitor for the Defendant and Master of Chancery, sworn 3 Jul 1810."

[121] Cornelius Williamson will, New Jersey Archives: *New Jersey Colonial Documents: Calendar of Wills 1806-1809*, (Trenton, New Jersey), File #2343J, 40:376.
"29 Oct 1807, Cornelius Williamson will, Amwell Twp., Hunterdon County; children to live on farm for 3 years, then real and personal estate to be sold and distributed to sons William and Cornelius, residue to all children William, Cornelius, Asher and Joseph; daughters Bernice Hoppock, Patience Williamson and Moyca Williamson; money to defray expenses in dispute with brother, Samuel Williamson; executors sons, William, Cornelius and Asher; witnesses Joseph Smith, John Hoppock, Jr., and Andrew Bearder; proved 20 Jan 1808."

[122] Williamson to Bonnell, Quick & Gordon deed, Hunterdon County Chancery Court, Flemington, New Jersey, 31 Mar 1812.
"31 Mar 1812, deed from Samuel Williamson, acting executor, William Williamson deceased; to Abraham Bonnell, Nelly Quick, Thomas Gordon, deed by order of decree for benefit of William, Cornelius, Asher and Joseph Williamson, Jacob and Bernice Hoppock, Patience and Moica Williamson complainants; witnesses James Linn, W. J. Bown; 21 Apr 1812, Samuel Williamson delivered the deed, recorded 22 Apr 1812, witnesses W. H. Bowne, and James Linn."

[123] In William Williamson's 1764 will, he calls Margaret Larew his daughter; her will of 1812 refers to her children by husbands James Larew and John Hull, and thus she is Samuel's sister.

[124] Williamson vs. Williamson, John Williamson plaintiff, Samuel Williamson, defendant and executor of William Williamson, deceased, New Jersey Supreme Court, Hunterdon County. (Salt Lake City: Family History Library), September Term 1815, Case #46714, filed 8 Nov 1815.

[125] Williamson vs. Williamson, Asher Williamson petitioner, administrator of William Williamson, deceased; vs. Samuel Williamson, New Jersey Supreme Court, Hunterdon County, September Term 1815. (Salt Lake City: Family History Library), Case #46714; 14 May 1821; filed 17 May 1821."

[126] "Kingston Presbyterian Church Records," *Genealogical Magazine of New Jersey*, (date unknown), 28:3.
    "John [Terhune] born 4 May 1793, parents Abraham Terhune, Moycay Williamson, baptized 10 Aug 1793."

[127] Hunterdon County Miscellaneous Records, a hand typed copy of the original record is among the miscellaneous records at the Hunterdon County Archives, and was given to the author by Margery H. Freas, Felton Pennsylvania.
    "23 Dec 1823, Samuel Williamson deceased; administration account by John Terhune, (son of Abraham Terhune and Mayeke Williamson). Last summer I called about a bill assigned by Samuel Williamson to my father, promising a copy of my father's account and the investigation in the court of Chancery. Following is a draft from memory of some of the items, viz. Moving Samuel Williamson from Flemington to his house ($10); to his house on business ($2); to Hunterdon three times on business between Asher and Samuel Williamson ($13); charges for board during his sickness, total $380; two years room rent ($40); two years firewood ($30); funeral expenses ($40); attorney's bill ($13.61); deed from Samuel Williamson to Abraham Terhune for lands sold by sheriff ($3.50); account against him, witness fees on his lawsuits ($89); John Terhune's expenses for Maxwell, Vroom and Bonnell ($70); business, attorney & service expenses expenses total ($891.11); assets of note assigned to my father $800. In Terhune's account of service to Williamson, he said that "he (Samuel) occupied their common sitting room, one of the best rooms in my father's house, which he had to himself during almost the whole of his last sickness of about 26 weeks, that he did not leave his bed; that his disease was of the most loathsome nature; that the account is correct and charges reasonable. For two years I attended to his business investigating his accounts, conducting lawsuits against Asher Williamson et al, defending suits brought against him, counseling his difficult and complex lawsuits of 10 or 15 years standing; I sometimes traveled 30 miles, and bore all the expenses; that I went 14 miles to my father's house about 20 times on Samuel's business, and several times to Somerset defending a suit against him and taking council of his attorneys. I hope this rough sketch is sufficient to convince you it is a full disclosure and I am due these compensations. There was mention of fraud and embezzlement in the bill, but without the least [hesitation I can say that] Samuel Williamson was incapable of performing the act then, or at any period of his life, and [that he] made that assignment after inspecting and pondering over it for weeks; his attorney's are convinced of this, and of the legality of the transactions, [however] I agreed to a compromise, from which one attorney dissented, that my father should pay $350, reducing the note to less than $500, or about half the account; my father was willing to allow $350 to be deducted from the note and paid to the administrator, although several lawyers who are well acquainted with the whole matter, would rather have an investigation in the Court of Chancery. Your most obliging and humble servant, John Terhune."

[128] Gulick to Gulick, heirs of Cornelius Williamson, deed, signed and recorded 26 Oct 1825. A typed copy of the deed was made by researcher, Edward H. Bennett, Belford NY 10506, under the auspices of the Hunterdon Genealogical Services, Ringoes, New Jersey (date unknown) for George Wylder, a descendant of Samuel Williamson, from Hunterdon County Deed Book 42, p. 382-387.
    "26 Oct 1825, deed from Abraham Gulick, Amwell Twp., Hunterdon County New Jersey to Henry Gulick; whereas Cornelius Williamson owned 194 acres, Amwell Twp., purchased 7 May 1750; that he died in testate leaving only heir, daughter Nelly who married Guisbert Gulick; that Elizabeth Williamson, Cornelius Williamson's widow got dower rights; 30 Apr 1767 Elizabeth sold her half to daughter Nelly and Guisbert Gulick for £103; that in Guisbert Gulick's will, 31 Jul 1779, he gave the property to his children, Abraham and Sarah Gulick; after Gulick died, Nelly Gulick married Samuel Williamson and had three daughters; Nelly died in testate and daughters Margaret, Elizabeth and Ellenor Williamson became partial heirs to property; that Abraham Gulick intended to buy all available property, but as long as Samuel Williamson lived he was a life tenant; 1818 Gulick

began buying property rights; when his sister Charity Gulick (married to Peter Williamson) died in testate he purchased her children, John and Samuel Williamson's rights; (9 Apr 1818, Hunterdon County, V.28, p. 441-443) deeds from heirs: Gilbert Williamson, Margaret Williamson, husband John Hanna (10 Feb 1819, recorded 2 Feb 1820, V.30, p.338). Gulick purchased rights from Nelly and Samuel Williamson's children: Margaret Williamson, Abraham Deats wife, (24 Dec 1823, recorded 26 Feb 1824, V. 36, p.541-542); Elizabeth Williamson, Gideon Hendrickson's wife (27 Apr 1819, recorded 2 Feb 1820); Ellenor Williamson, William West's wife (15 Apr 1820, recorded 27 Sep 1823, V. 36, p. 250; witnesses James J. Fisher, Andrew Miller, recorded 26 Oct 1825."

[129] Gail Childress and Kathy Hines, compilers and contributors, *Marriages: Marriage Book 1, 1798-1815, Mason County, Kentucky*, #520, February 1798; internet database downloaded 18 Mar 2003. http://www.rootsweb.com/~usgenweb/ky/mason/marriages/bk1groom.html

[130] *Mason County, Kentucky, 1799 Tax List*, Family History Center, Salt Lake City: Family History Library, Roll #0000418, James Wilson, enumerator; no page number or date other than year.

[131] Hiram E. Deats, *Marriage Records of Hunterdon County, New Jersey, 1795-1875*, (Flemington, New Jersey, Hunterdon County Historical Society, 1918), 2:230.

[132] Evelin Armstrong Struble, *In the Ramapos: A True Story of the Terhunes and the Little Town They Loved*, (Paterson, New Jersey: Rocco Press: 1966), 104.

[133] Abraham Terhune, pension application for Revolutionary War service, affidavit, 13 Aug 1832, National Archives and Records Administration, application number not recorded, not numbered.

[134] Albert Terhune, Senior household, 1810 U.S. Census, Fleming County, Kentucky, page 72, line 33, microfilm #M252-6, online at www.ancestry.com/search/rectype/census/main.htm.

[135] Albert Terhune will, Fleming County Probate, Flemingsburg, Kentucky, A-B 1798-1822, Book B, page 47, not numbered, microfilm #0344038.
    "15 May 1816, Albert Terhune will, Fleming County, Kentucky; sons John, Garret, Stephen Terhune, real estate; daughter Elizabeth and child their living; Garret, Elizabeth bed and bedding; to sons, daughter Hallana, personal estate; executors son Isaac Terhune, son-in-law William Williamson; witnesses Alexander Ramsey, Joseph Johnson, Charles Nalis; recorded, April 1817."

[136] William Williamson household, 1810 U.S. Census, Fleming County, Kentucky; page 87, line 31; National Archives film #M262-6:87:31.

[137] "Information Wanted," *Kentucky Gazette* newspaper, (Lexington, Kentucky), 24 Dec 1811.

[138] Cornelius Williamson, Flemington, New Jersey, letter to William Williamson, Fleming County, Kentucky; probably dated December 1814-January 1815. See Chapter Six, *Cousins by the Dozens*.

[139] In April 1824, Abraham Williamson, Flemington, New Jersey, a Presbyterian minister, Morris County, New Jersey, wrote to his Uncle Wm. Williamson, brother of Abraham's father Cornelius.

[140] Willliamson to Dalrymple, Money and Smith, marriage bonds, hand typed from the "Fleming County, Kentucky Bond Book," Fleming County Genealogy Records at the courthouse, p. 118.

[141] Author Unknown, *Communicants Role of Flemingsburg Kentucky Presbyterian Church About 1840*, sent to the author by Sandra Wamsley of Walden, Colorado, pages 2-10.

[142] Miss Williamson household, 1820 U.S. Census, Fleming County, Kentucky; page 67, line 7; National Archives micro-publication M33-21:67:7.

[143] Williamson Family, 1822 tax list, Fleming County, Kentucky, pages 74-75, (Salt Lake City: Family History Library), microfilm #0007970.

[144] William Williamson household, 1830 U.S. Census, Fleming County, Kentucky, page 225, line 17; National Archives micro-publication M19-39.

[145] William M. Talley, contributor, *Kentucky Ancestors*, "Fleming County Marriages," 1972: 8:1, page 6. Copied from minister's returns among loose papers of the Fleming County Courthouse.

[146] An undated latter, written about 1831, from Joseph and Margaret Steele of Fleming County, Kentucky to her father, William Williamson of Mason County, Kentucky.

[147] William Williamson, pension application, National Archives & Records Administration, Washington, D.C., #W4862, page 382-383, Brown County, Ohio, Common Pleas, 15 Aug 1839.

[148] Letter, 29 Dec 1835 from Margaret Steele, Hillsborough, Kentucky, to her father William Williamson, Ripley, Brown County, Ohio.

[149] Halena Williamson, widow's pension application, part of #W4862, National Archives and Records Admin. Washington, D.C., not numbered, Brown County, Ohio, Common Pleas Court, March 1835.

[150] Elizabeth P. Ellsberry, *Marriage Records of Fleming County, Kentucky, 1798-1851*, page 74.

[151] "Records of the Kingston Presbyterian Church," *The Genealogical Magazine of New Jersey*, 28 (January/April 1953) Baptisms, No. 1 & 2:3.
"10 Aug 1794, Ann [Terhune] born 7 May 1794, parents Daniel Terhune, Ann Williamson."

[152] Newton Bateman and Paul Selby, editors, *Historical Encyclopedia of Illinois*, "History of Morgan County," (Chicago: Munsell Publishing Co., 1906), 973.
"William Williamson, farmer by occupation; married 23 Mar 1815 Ann Terhune, born 7 May 1793; one child William A. Williamson, deceased; his first wife died 2 Jan 1816."

[153] Ellsberry, *Marriage Records of Fleming County, Kentucky*, 74.
"10 Jan 1817, Jane Cochran to Wm. Williamson, Wm. Williamson, Sr., bondsman; George Glass, guardian of Jane; page 106; 4 Dec 1817, Jane Colman."

[154] Author Unknown, *Communicants Role of Flemingsburg, Kentucky, Presbyterian Church About 1840*, page 6.

[155] William Williamson household, 1820 U.S. Census, Fleming County, Kentucky, page 63, line 27, National Archives micro-publication M33-21:63:27.

[156] William M. Talley, Vanceburg, Kentucky, letter to George S. Bragg, Boulder, Colorado, dated 24 Nov 1979. From an inquiry about the Williamson and Henry families of Fleming County, Kentucky, Mr. Talley made two references to Fleming County, Kentucky, Marriage Bonds.
"William Williamson Jr. to Isabella Henry, 11 Sep 1823; Samuel Henry, bondsman and father; Samuel Henry's will dated 4 Apr 1826/3 Jul 1826, recorded Fleming County Will Book C, page 278, lists among his heirs a daughter, Isabel Williamson."

[157] Bateman and Selby, "History of Morgan County," 973.
"William Williamson married Ann Terhune (born 7 May 1793) 23 Mar 1815, they had one child, William A. Williamson, deceased; Ann Williamson died 2 Jan 1816; 7 Dec 1817 William married Jane Cochran (born 25 Jun 1797); had children Anne, Samuel and Jane; Jane Williamson died 8 Feb 1822; 11 Sep 1823 Mr. Williamson married Isabella Henry of Kentucky (born 14 Nov 1803); their children, Mary, Elizabeth, Margaret, James, John, and Nancy; Isabella Williamson died 9 Aug 1834; William moved to Illinois northwest of Jacksonville; died at age 82 years."

[158] Robert Cochran assessment, 1797 Mason County, Kentucky, Tax List, District 3, J. Marshall, assessor; page 6, (Salt Lake City: Family History Library), Microfilm roll #0000418.

[159] Cochran vs. George Glass, guardianship, Mason County Court, Maysville, Kentucky, Court Order Book B: 173.

[160] Robert Cochran inventory, administration, Mason County Probate Court, Maysville, Kentucky, 6 Sep 1797, 20 Oct 1803, 12 Dec 1803, will book A: 313-315, and 5:357-358, (Salt Lake City: Family History Library), V. A-C (1792-1797), microfilm #0281822.

[161] Merri Lou Scribner Schaumann, *Tax Lists, Cumberland County, Pennsylvania, 1768, 1769, 1770*, "Peters Rates 1770," (Carlisle, Pennsylvania: published by the author, 1972), 215.

[162] J. T. Haley, editor, *Cochran Family Herald*, (Nashville: September 1897), volume 3:1.
A hundred years after Robert Cochran died in Fleming County, an article appeared in an 1897 Cochran Family newsletter published in Nashville that purported to tell the story of how John Cochran, grandfather of Thomas and Jane, had survived the great massacre of 1756. Following that was how William Cochran descended from John Cochran of Fleming County.
"John Cochran had a son named Robert, who married a Pshaw, his son was Thomas who married a Miss Ruth Carrick and had five children; William born 8 Sep 1819."
[163] Jay Gilfillan Weiser, *Report of the Commission to Locate the Site of the Frontier Forts of Pennsylvania*, "The Frontier Forts in the Cumberland and Juniata Valleys, Juniata County, Fort Bingham; Perry County, Fort Robinson, submitted by Donna Bluemink, volume 1: 586-592, 611-618, downloaded 27 Aug 2003 from http://ww.usgenweb.com/archives,

[164] William Henry Egle, *Notes and Queries of Pennsylvania, 1700-1800s*, 4th Series V. 1:264-265.

[165] William Henry Egle, *Some Pennsylvania Women During the War of the Revolution*, "Margaret Cochran Corbin, Franklin County, Pennsylvania," (Harrisburg: Harrisburg Publishing Co, 1898).

[166] James Renner, *Margaret Cochran Corbin*, online at http//hhoc.org/hist/mc_corbin.htm.; downloaded 20 Aug 2003 The plaque commemorating Margaret Cochran Corbin's service reads:
"1776 Hudson Fulton Celebration Commission, 1909; Fort Tryon was the northernmost outerwork of Fort Washington; 16 Nov 1776, its gallant defense against the Hessian troops by Maryland and Virginia Regiments was shared by Margaret Corbin, the first woman to take a soldiers place in the war for liberty; erected by the American Scenic and Historic Preservation Society."

[167] Fisher to Cochran, marriage, *John Conrad Bucher's Pastoral Record, Cumberland and Dauphin County, Pennsylvania, 1763-1769*, downloaded from http://www.ancestry.com on 6 Nov 2000.

[168] Samuel Fisher will, Cumberland Co. Probate, Carlisle, Pennsylvania, will book B, pages 230-231.
"24 Jul 1775, Samuel Fisher, Tyrone Twp., Cumberland County, wife Mary comfort & support; son Thomas land; son William cattle; daughters Margaret and Jenny married to James Morrow and John Coughran; Elizabeth married to Robert Scott; son Samuel Jr. land; son James land; grandson Hugh Sharron, brought up at my expense, under wife or son James command until 21; James to teach Hugh reading, writing and accounting, also £10 freedom dues at age 21; executors wife Mary, son James; witnesses George Douglas, James Baxter, George Robinson; codicil allowed other children to buy out Samuel or James, witness George Douglas, proved 8 Jun 1776."

[169] Merri Lou Scribner, *Indictments 1750-1800, Cumberland County, Pennsylvania*, (Dover, Pennsylvania, Cumberland County Historical Society, 1989), page unknown.
"1767, Jane Fisher, spinster indicted for fornication and bastardy with Hugh Sharron, mid-February at Robert McWhhinney's house in Carlisle; her father, Samuel Fisher, Sherman's Valley; testator, Mary Fisher."

[170] Cochran Heirs and Huddelston deed, Fleming County Recorder, Flemingsburg, Kentucky, (Salt Lake City: Family History Library), microfilm #0343981, Book R, 468-470.
"17 Sep 1833, deed from John Cochran, wife Elizabeth; Matthew Gray, wife Jane Cochran; Solomon Vantreese, wife Margaret Cochran; Hannah Cochran, Fleming County; Thomas Cochran, wife Mary Cochran, Fayette County; Harvey Gray, wife Elizabeth Cochran, Nicholas County Kentucky; to John Huddelston, Fleming County Kentucky; 50 acres, Lot 3 on Mill Creek for $600; part of the land division among the heirs of John Cochran Senior deceased; recorded 17 Sep 1833."

[171] *Mason County, Kentucky, Deed Book* A-L, 1898-1810 Abstracts, (Denver: Western Heraldry Organization, 1973), 68.
          "8 Sep 1796, from Richard Jackman, wife Mary, Lincoln County Kentucky; to John Coughran, Mason County; land in Mason County; witness Thomas Marshall, Jr."

[172] Cochran taxes, Mason County, Kentucky, Tax Lists 1790-1809, (Salt Lake City: Family History Library), microfilm #0000418, 0007969, various pages yearly in District #3.

[173] Childress and Hines, *Marriages: Marriage Book 1, 1798-1815, Mason County, Kentucky*, page 410.

[174] Cochran vs. Hutton, 26 Aug 1830, Bill in Chancery, Fleming County Circuit Court, Flemingsburg, Kentucky, Case #6412, pages not numbered.

[175] John Cochran Sr. household, 1810 U.S. Census, Fleming County, Kentucky; page 80, line 4; National Archives micro-publication #M262-6:80:4.

[176] Ellsberry, *Marriage Bonds, Fleming County, Kentucky*, 22.

[177] Thomas Fisher will, Cumberland County Probate, Carlisle, Pennsylvania, will book E, page 163-164.
          "12 Jun 1788, Thomas Fisher will, Tyrone Twp., Cumberland County, Pennsylvania; wife, Margaret; sons Samuel, John and Thomas, £140 each; daughters Mary , Jean (Jane), Elizabeth, Margaret and Sarah, £40 each; should wife and children move to Kentucky, brother James Fisher, brother-in-law Isaac Gibson shall provide children land in Kentucky; executors brother Samuel, brother-in-law Robert Scott; witnesses David McClure, William Foster, Thomas McTier; proved 27 Oct 1789."

[178] Ellsberry, *Marriage Bonds, Fleming County, Kentucky*, 22.

[179] Armstrong to Fisher deed, Fayette County, Kentucky, Recorder, deed book R, p. 600, 598, 605; 1 Jun 1818, 17 May 1818.
          "Deed from Alexander Armstrong, wife Jane, Fleming County, Kentucky for $110; Jane's share of father, Thomas Fisher's estate, to Samuel, Thomas &Wm. Fisher; Henry Armstrong, wife Elizabeth, Fleming County Kentucky; Joseph Santee, wife Polly, Scott County Kentucky made same transaction as above."

[180] Alexander Armstrong household, 1810 U.S. Census, Fleming County, Kentucky; page 73, line 16; National Archives micro-publication #M252-6:73:16.

[181] Thomas F. Cochran, apprenticeship, Fayette County, Kentucky, Court of Common Pleas, Orphans Court, Flemingsburg, Kentucky, book G: 90, recorded 5 Mar 1812.

[182] John Cochran estate, Fleming County Probate, Flemingsburg, Kentucky, December Court 1822, will book C: 33-36.

[183] See Cochran vs. Hutton, 26 Aug 1830.

[184] Cochran to Carrick, Fayette County Kentucky, "*Kentucky Marriages to 1850*, from original sources by Jordan Dodd, Provo, Utah, 1997, downloaded 6 Dec 2003 at http://www.ancestry.com.
[185] Melvin Hurst, Fayette County Genealogical Society, (Lexington, Kentucky: 1994) Vol. 9, #3, "Carrick Cemetery."

[186] Elizabeth Prather Ellsberry, compiler, *Marriage Records of Fleming County, Kentucky 1798-1851*, (Chillicothe, Missouri, privately printed. 1965).

[187] See Cochran Heirs, Huddelson, deed, Fleming County, Kentucky, in which John Cochran's property was divided among his heirs so that Thomas Cochran (son of Robert), and Mary Cochran

(daughter of John Cochran Junior) each received land portion from grandfather's estate. If Mary Cochran was merely Thomas' wife and not an heir, she would not have received a portion.

[188] William Cochran obituary, *Carrollton Democrat*, 16 Nov 1895, published Carrollton, Kentucky.

[189] 7 Aug 1836, letter from Wm. Williamson, Jacksonville Illinois to Samuel Williamson, Ripley Ohio; all other letters are from Wm. Williamson, Jr., Exeter and Meredosia, Illinois, to his son Wm. A. Williamson, Ripley, Ohio, dated 23 Apr 1837, 2 Aug 1837, 3 Dec 1837, 1837, and 18 Feb 1838.

[190] Samuel Williamson household, 1860 U.S. Census, Morgan County, Illinois, Indian Creek District, Emerald P.O., page 875, dwelling 1367, family 1354; National Archives film #M653-213.

[191] William A. Williamson household, 1860 U.S. Census, Morgan County, Illinois, Indian Creek District, Emerald P.O., page 512, dwelling 1108, family 1103; National Archives film #M653-213.

[192] James Williamson household, 1870 U.S. Census, Morgan County Illinois, Jacksonville Precinct, page 246, dwelling 281, family 282; National Archives film #M593-263.

[193] Bateman and Selby, "History of Morgan County," page 973.

[194] Samuel. Williamson household, 1840 U.S. Census, Brown County Ohio, Arnheim village, page 239, line 14; National Archives film #M704-379.

[195] Williamson to Hewitt, marriage, Brown County Marriages 1818-1843, (Salt Lake City: Family History Library), batch #M51351.

[196] Samuel Williamson household, 1850 U.S. Census, Clermont County, Ohio, Williamsburg Twp, page 330, dwelling 703, family 703; National Archives film #M432-667.

[197] Mrs. Harry Rankin, Beech Forest Chapter, D.A.R, *Monument Inscriptions prior to 1900 from Cemeteries in Clermont County, Ohio,* (Williamsburg Ohio, 1952), "Hartman Cemetery," page 1.

[198] Daniel Williamson household, 1850 U.S. Census, Brown County Ohio, Pleasant Twp, page 294, dwelling 325, family 328; National Archives film #M432-662.

[199] Daniel Williamson estate, Brown County Probate Court, Williamsburg, Ohio, Guardian Records, Case #6446, 5 Nov 1855, page unknown."

[200] Daniel Williamson household, 1860 U.S. Census, Clermont County, Ohio, population schedule, Jackson Township, Marathon P. O., page 753, dwelling 434, family 435.

SOURCE NOTES
Chapter Twelve

MORRISON AND DURHAM FAMILIES

[1] Friends called Harrison Morrison "Reece," because when James Hendy gave a deposition over Daniel Durham's disputed will, he referred to Durham's grandson Harrison as "Reece" Morrison, saying he did not know his given name.

[2] County Land Ownership Map, Ohio, "Hamilton County 1847 Wall Map, Anderson Township," Salt Lake City: Family History Library, microfiche #6079868, map 632.

[3] Harrison Morrison, John Moore households, 1840 U.S. Census, Hamilton County, Ohio, Anderson Township, page 411, lines 5 and 12; National Archives film #M704-400.

[4] Morrison to Kyle marriage, *Clermont County, Ohio Marriages 1850 Through 1874*, page 366.

[5] Samuel. Morrison household, 1850 U.S. Census, Hamilton County, Ohio, Union Twp., District 22, page 482, dwelling 2942, family 2965; National Archives film #M432-667.

[6] W. P. Morrison, guardian of Sarah J. Morrison, pension application as heir of Samuel Morrison, deceased soldier, Civil War Pension Claim Records, Samuel Morrison, deceased, National Archives & Records Administration. In the application is an affidavit by Isaac N. Thacker, M.D., who stated that he attended Julia Morrison, 5 Dec 1850 when daughter, later named Sarah Jane, was born.

[7] Morrison to Gowdy marriage, *Clermont County, Ohio Marriages, 1850 Through 1874*, page 366.
    "Harrison Morrison to Elizabeth Gowdy, marriage, 5 Mar 1848, by Aaron Sargent, M.G."

[8] W. P. Morrison household, 1850 U.S. Census, Hamilton County Ohio, Anderson Twp., page 188, dwelling 654, family 672; Samuel Morrison household, Clermont County, Ohio, Union Twp., Dist. #22, page 482, dwelling 2942, family 2965; National Archives film #M432-667.

[9] Harrison Morrison, deceased, *Ohio Mortality Records*, Hamilton County, 1850, downloaded 31 May 2003 from http://search.ancestry.com/cgi-bin.

[10] John A. Morrison, guardianship, Clermont County Ohio Guardianships Docket, Batavia, Ohio, Film G38-0970, Clermont County Probate, no page number.
    "8 Aug 1855, John W. Kyle, Robert B. Kyle, John Jenkins, $2,000 bond for John W. Kyle, guardian John Morrison, 11 years, child of Harrison Morrison, deceased; witness George Swing."

[11] John Kyle household, 1850 U.S. Census, Clermont County, Ohio, population schedule, Union township, page 481, dwelling 2936, family 2959; National Archives film #M432-667.

[12] Morrison to Kyle marriage, *Clermont County, Ohio Marriage Records, 1800-1850*, (Evansville, Indiana: Clermont County Genealogical Society, 1979), page 161.
    "8 Sep 1842, Harrison Morrison to Rebecca S. Kayle by Thomas D. Temple, J.P.;
5 Mar 1848, Harrison Morrison to Elizabeth Gowdy by Aaron Sargent, M.G."

[13] With permission from the owner of the Old Cemetery on Nine Mile Road in Union Township, Clermont County Ohio, in August 1996 the author visited and photographed the tombstones of Rebecca Kyle Morrison, Harrison Morrison and his second wife Eliza Ann (Gowdy) Morrison.

[14] Morrison to Witham, marriage, *Clermont County, Ohio Marriages, 1850 Through 1874*, page 366.

[15] John A. Morrison household, 1870 U.S. Census, Clermont County, Ohio, Union Twp., page 334b, dwelling 112, family 112; National Archives film #M593-1181, Image 669.

[16] Moore and Morrison households, Lucinda Moore household, 1860 U.S. Census, Clermont County, Ohio, Union Twp., page 504, dwelling 1195, family 1103; National Archives film #M654-944; Samuel Morrison household, 1860 U.S. Census, Hamilton County, Ohio, Anderson Twp., page 283, dwelling 52, family 52; National Archives film #M653-944.

[17] Morrison to Fagan deed, Clermont County Recorder, Batavia, Ohio, deed book BK: 257-258.
    "22 Dec 1859, deed from Samuel Morrison, wife Julia, Clermont County Ohio; to Andrew Fagan of same, for $9,000, 141 acres, Union & Anderson Twps., Mosley's Survey #1115; witnesses Moses Elstun and Hiram Morrison."

[18] Remler, *Hamilton County, Ohio Burial Records*, "Anderson Township 1800-1989, Mt Washington Cemetery," page 57.

[19] Whitelaw Reid, *Ohio in the War, Her Statesmen, Generals and Soldiers*, "Fifty-Seventh Ohio Volunteer Infantry," (Cincinnati: Moore, Wilstach & Baldwin, 1868), Vol. 2:342-347.

[20] *Roster of Ohio Soldiers 1861-1866, War of the Rebellion*, "57th Regiment Ohio Volunteer Infantry, Three Years' Service," (Cincinnati: Ohio Valley Pub. & Mfg. Co, 1866), Vol. 5:127,141.

[21] Sarah J. Morrison, minor of Samuel Morrison, Department of the Interior, Pension Office, 29 Sep 1864, Washington D. C., National Archives & Records Administration, Certification #83016, Box 32476, pages not numbered. Written on the outside, "Claim of only child under 16 year of age for pension by guardian, applicant's address, William P. Morrison, Guardian of Sarah J. Morrison, under 16 years of age, only child of Samuel Morrison, deceased, late Capt. Co. D, 57th Regiment, Ohio Volunteer Infantry, Mt. Carmel, Clermont County Ohio."

[22] Remler, *Hamilton County, Ohio Burial Records*, "Mt Washington Cemetery, Anderson Township," page 57.

[23] Alexander Morrison household, 1820 U.S. Census, Anderson Township, Hamilton County, Ohio, page 153, line 18; National Archives micro-publication #M33-87.

[24] Alexander Morrison, Daniel Durham households, 1830 U.S. Census, Anderson Township, Hamilton County, Ohio, page 146, line 16 and 21; National Archives film #M19-132.

[25] *Abstract of Book 1 and Book A, Probate Records 1791-1826*, (Cincinnati: Hamilton County Ohio Chapter, Ohio Genealogical Society, 1977), Book 1: 569, 611-612; *Abstract of Book 4, Probate Records 1834-1837*, Hamilton County Ohio, published 1985; 2 Sep 1834, page 82.

[26] Durham to Martin deed, Hamilton County Recorder, Cincinnati Ohio, 2 Jul 1833, deed book 50, page 355. This 50-acre deed, part of Survey #608, bordered land of "Elizabeth Morrison's heirs," and was given to "Eleanor Martin, a daughter of Daniel Durham."

[27] Durham to Morrison Heirs deed, Hamilton County Recorder, Cincinnati Ohio, Salt Lake City: Family History Library, microfilm #0344551, 2 Jul 1833, 11 Aug 1842, deed book 49:521-522.

[28] Morrison Heirs to Fagin deed, Hamilton County Recorder, Cincinnati Ohio, 2 Oct 1846, deed book 115, page 445-446

"Deed to George Fagin, Hamilton County Ohio, from Elizabeth Morrison heirs, Hamilton County Ohio, deceased; who are Samuel Morrison, wife Julia; John Moore, wife Lucinda; Harrison Morrison, Wm. P. Morrison; for $1,500, sold 50 acres on Five Mile Creek, lands of D. Bennett, George Fagin, Joshua Durham and J. Kyle; witnesses James McCrum and Dominicus A. Fagin."

[29] *Series of Patents and Warrants, Maryland State Archives*, Archives of Maryland Online, http://www.mdarchives.state.md.us, volume 17:512.

[30] Jane Baldwin, editor, *The Maryland Calendar of Wills, Vol 1, 1635-1685*, (Annapolis: Hall of Records, 1904), 1: 104.

"28 Oct 1680, William Choice will, wife Jane executor and sole legatee of all real estate including 82 acres on Bush River; testators James Collyer, John Duren (Durham), George Hooper; probated 1 Mar 1681."

[31] John Durham will, *Maryland Archives, Probate Records*, Annapolis Maryland, Hall of Records, will book 7:122-123.

"20 Feb 1694, John Durham will, probated 30 May 1695; testators James Maxwell, John Macke, James Cowdray and John Boone."

[32] John Durham, estate, *Maryland Probate Records, Prerogative Court Abstracts, 1685-1701*, Books 9-11b, Annapolis Maryland, Hall of Records, inventory and appraisal, Book 10:459, 11 Jun 1695.

[33] Barnes, *Baltimore County Families*, 1659-1759, page 91.

[34] *Baltimore County Maryland Court Proceedings, 1691-1693*, Book F, No. 1, pages 225-229; Book G, No. 1, 1693-1696, pages 273-274.

[35] John David Davis, *Baltimore County, Maryland, Deed Records*, (Bowie, Maryland: Heritage Books, 1996, 150.

"25 Mar 1699 John and Sarah Durham sold 125 acres, Winters Run; witnesses Mark Richardson, James Phillips."

[36] Samuel Durham will, *Maryland Probate Records, Calendar of Wills, 1703-1713*, volume 3:14.
"9 Feb 1700, Samuel Durham will, Baltimore County; brother John, *Levy's Addition*, Broad Neck, Bush River; testators John Taylor, Matthew Green, John Durham; recorded 8 Mar 1703-4."

[37] John Durham estate, *Maryland Probate Records, Prerogative Court Abstracts, 1708-1711*, Books 29-32b, 30:432.
"3 Mar 1709, John Durham estate inventory £8.8.0 cash, £200 tobacco; appraisers Charles Baker, John Armstrong; creditors Matthew Green, administrator listed as next of kin."

[38] Ella Harrison Rowe, *Clark, Rigdon, Wilson and Durham Families of Harford County, Maryland*, (Baltimore: Privately Printed, 1987), "Chapter Six: The Durham Family," page 60.

[39] Davis, *Baltimore County, Maryland Deed Records*, 2: 67.
"2 Jun 1736, James Boone stated that Samuel Durham is John Durham's son, that John Durham was Elizabeth Durham's brother, wife of John Stand, signed Nathaniel Rigbie."

[40] Durham to Smithson, marriage, *St. John's Parish Register, 1696-1788*, Baltimore County, Annapolis Hall of Records, pages 21, 54.

[41] Davis, *Baltimore County, Maryland Deed Records*, 2:288.
"25 Jun 1723, deed from William and Gillion Wright, Baltimore County; to Samuel Durham carpenter, of same, for 4,500 lbs. tobacco; 100 acres, witnesses Luke Raven, Daniel Scott Jr.; 9 Jan 1726, deed from Samuel Durham, planter, Baltimore County; to Thomas Coale, Bush River, 50 acres Levy's Tribe on Bush River; witnesses Edmond Hays and Mary Hays."

[42] Author Unknown, *John Durham's Children, Daniel Durham's Children, Benjamin Durham's Children*. This book was privately and probably locally printed in Cincinnati Ohio, by an unknown member of the Durham family. There is no printing date, page 6.

[43] Rowe, *Clark, Rigdon, Wilson and Durham Families of Harford County, Maryland*, "The Durham Family," 61.

[44] Diane Dieterle, compiler, *Thomas Smithson (1675-1732) of Baltimore County, Maryland and his Descendants*, "The Family of Hugh Franklin Smisson, Jr.," (Decorah, Iowa: Amundsen Publishing Company, 1993), 10. Names, birth dates from St. John's Parish, Baltimore County, Maryland.

[45] Thomas Smithson will, *Maryland Probate Records, Calendar of Wills*, Will Book 20: 568,
"11 Aug 1731, Thomas Smithson will probated 8 Mar 1732; testators Daniel Scott, his son Daniel, Richard Rhoads, his son Richard."

[46] Barnes, *Baltimore County, Maryland, Deed Abstracts, 1659-1750*, pages 19, 62, 67-68.

[47] Barnes, *Maryland Marriages, 1634-1777*, page 209.

[48] Maryland Probate, Calendar of Wills 1759-1764, Annapolis: Hall of Records, will book 31: 315.
"19 Dec 1760, Andrew Thompson will, Elizabeth Thompson called wife, Sarah Durham called daughter and wife of Joshua Durham."

[49] Peden, *Inhabitants of Baltimore County, 1763-1774*, pages 27, 42-43, 45.

[50] Samuel Durham will, *Baltimore County Wills, 1660-1777*, Baltimore, will book 39:15-16.
"31 Aug 1772, Samuel Durham will, probated 21 Sep 1772, witnesses Jacob Bond, a Quaker; William Bond, Charles Sigismund; Samuel Durham signed his name."

[51] *History of Cincinnati and Hamilton County*, (Cincinnati: S. B. Nelson & Co., 1894), page 532.

[52] Unknown, *John Durham's Children.*

[53] Joshua Durham household, *Colonial Census of Maryland*, [database online] (Orem Utah: Ancestry, Inc., 2000), taken from the same held by the Maryland State Archives, 1776 census, Bush River Lower Hundred families.

[54] Eugene Clements and Edward F. Wright, *The Maryland Militia in the Revolutionary War*, "Harford County," (Westminster, Maryland: Family Line Publications, 1987), 173.

[55] Henry C. Peden, Jr. *Revolutionary Patriots of Harford County, Maryland*, 1775-1783, (Bel Air, Maryland: Bel Air Copy Center, 1986), 71-72.

[56] Henry C. Peden, Jr. *Early Harford Countians*, (Westminster, Maryland: Family Line Publications, 1993), 125-127.

[57] *History of Cincinnati and Hamilton County*, page 532.

[58] Unknown, *John Durham's Children*, pages 7, 10.

[59] John Harthorn household, *Colonial Census of Maryland*, online.

[60] Daniel Durham household, 1790 U.S. Census, Fayette County, Pennsylvania, page 108, line 10; National Archives film #M637-8, Image 579.

[61] Joshua Durham household, 1790 U.S. Census, Washington County, Pennsylvania, page 201, line 70; National Archives film #M657-9, Image 112.

[62] Family group sheet from Kenny Burck, Hamilton County Ohio, a descendant of Daniel Durham and Jane Hartshorn through their daughter Cynthia Durham.

[63] Unknown, *John Durham's Children*, 8-9.

[64] Everts, *History of Clermont County, Ohio*, 48.

[65] Taylor to Durham deed, Hamilton County Recorder, Cincinnati Ohio, Salt Lake City: Family History Library, microfilm #0344519, deed books 1801-1818, deed book F, page 54-55.
"Deed from James and Keturah Taylor to Daniel Durham, recorded 9 Mar 1816."

[66] *Clermont Courier* newspaper, "Clermonter's Who Served in the Revolution, Many Familiar Family Names on the List—Heroes of By-Gone Days Whose Memory all Delight to Honor."
"19 June 1901, page 1, a sketch of Daniel Durham was part of a series of local men who served in the Revolutionary War."

[67] Daniel Durham household, 1800 United States Federal Census, [online] http://www.ancestry.com, pages 9, 11. These tax lists for Hamilton County were used as a substitute census.

[68] Everts, *History of Clermont County, Ohio*, page 444.

[69] *Clermont Courier* newspaper, "Clermonter's Who Served in the Revolution."

[70] Remler, *Hamilton County, Ohio Burial Records*, "Anderson Township, 1800-1989," page 130.

[71] Durham to Clark marriage, [online] http://www.familysearch.org, Family History Library, Salt Lake City, Batch #M859161; 1825-1834 marriages in Hamilton County Ohio.

[72] Daniel Durham will, Hamilton County Common Pleas, Cincinnati Ohio, Wills 1836-1854, will book 5-6, Salt Lake City: Family History Library, Microfilm #00355099, pages 113-116.
"Aug 1846, Civil Minutes Journal, Clermont County Common Pleas, Batavia Ohio; Daniel Durham, deceased, will proved, Hamilton County Probate Court July 1846, proceedings held on

Durham's contested will, including affidavits, depositions and testimony of those who knew him; recorded Hamilton County Ohio Probate, Cincinnati Ohio, 10 Feb 1846, pages 348-388."

SOURCE NOTES
Chapter Thirteen

KYLE, PIERSOL AND KENNY FAMILIES

[1] Alma A. Smith, *The Virginia Military Surveys of Clermont and Hamilton Counties, Ohio, 1787-1849*, (published by the author, 1985), page 96.
Robert Morrow Survey #666, 1000 acres, Military Warrant No. 638, Union and Anderson Townships, between Mt. Carmel and Tobasco, original patent from George Washington, President to James Taylor, William Lytle, assignees of Robert Morrow who had it surveyed 15 Aug 1796; Taylor and Lytle sold it for $1,720 to Robert Kyle of Campbell County, Kentucky.

[2] Allen J. Sexton and Shelby L. Meyer, Sr., compilers, *Linden Grove Cemetery of Covington, Kenton County, Kentucky*, typed unpublished manuscript, undated, page 99.

[3] Chuck Bricking, *Covington's Heritage: a Compilation of the City's Historical Houses and a Short Biography of the Inhabitants*, published and printed by the author, no date, "Kennedy," 21.

[4] *Kentucky Post* newspaper, 29 Sep 1929, "Romance of Pioneers is Linked with Cabin," front page. The photograph accompanying the article is the Greater Cincinnati Library Consortium of the Clyde N. Bowden Collection of Postcards.

[5] Orville M. Kile, *A Partial History of the Kyle, Kile, Coyle Family in America*, (Baltimore: Waverly Press, Ind., 1958), 19-34.

[6] R. G. Campbell, *Scotch-Irish Family Research Made Simple*, (Munroe Falls Ohio: Summit Publications, 1982), 10.

[7] Franklin Ellis & Samuel Evans, *History of Lancaster County, Pennsylvania*, (Philadelphia: Everts & Peck, 1883), 759.

[8] Robert Kyle McCord, Supplement to Orville M. Kile's *A Partial History of the Kyle, Kile, Coyle Family in America*, on the Revolutionary War Patriot Robert Kyle, (Baltimore: Waverly Press Inc., 1958), S5.

[9] Kile, *A Partial History of the Kyle, Kile, Coyle Family in America*, 39, 34-36.

[10] Alex Harris, *A Biographical History of Lancaster County, (Pennsylvania) Being a History of Eminent Men of the County*, (Baltimore: Genealogical Publishing Company, 1977), 357.

[11] *Southern Lancaster County Historical Society*, Quarryville Pennsylvania, transcriptions for "Middle Octoraro Presbyterian Church Cemetery, Bart Township, Lancaster County PA," online at http://rootsweb.com/paslchs/index.html.

[12] Kile, *A Partial History of the Kyle, Kile, Coyle Family in America*, S8, 35-37.

[13] Author Unknown, Book Title Unknown, "1740—Road, Craighead's (Middle Octoraro Church) to Smith's Mill," 60.

[14] Kile, *A Partial History of the Kyle, Kile, Coyle Family in America*, 39.

[15] Samuel Kyll deed, *Land Records: Bucks and Lancaster County Pennsylvania 1682-1825*, Family Treemaker CD#652, (The Learning Co.: Hiawatha Iowa, 1999).

"Samuel Kyll, residence Bart Township, on 11 Jan 1762, deed to 150 acres in Bart Township, record #42219, Book G: 325."

[16] John Graham Palmer, *The Kittochtinny Historical Society,* Papers Read Before the Society, "Clifton Hall," (Chambersburg, Pennsylvania: Kittochtinny Historical Society, 1957), 73-75.

"Book A.A, volume 13, page 171, patent 29 Oct 1771 for 349 acres, recorded Cumberland (then Lancaster) County Patent Book, Harrisburg, Pennsylvania."

[17] Samuel Kyle will, Franklin County Probate, Chambersburg, Pennsylvania, will book A, page 42. Orville Kyle transcribed the will in his book The Kyle, Kile Family History, pages 168-170.

[18] Robert M. Torrence, compiler, Pennsylvania Vital Records, volume 2, *Pennsylvania Magazine of History and Biography,* (Philadelphia: Historical Society of Pennsylvania), vol. 2:146; Marriages 1769-1811, "Records of Upper West Conococheague Presbyterian Church, Mercersburg, Franklin County, Pennsylvania,"

[19] Kile, *A Partial History of the Kyle, Kile, Coyle Family in America*, 53.

[20] Samuel P. Bates, *History of Franklin County Pennsylvania*, Part 2, (Chicago: Warner Beers & Co., 1887), 184.

[21] Jane Dickens, editor, *Pennsylvania Archives*, Fifth Series, volume 6, "Cumberland County Militia," (Harrisburg: Harrisburg Publishing Co., 1906), 270,276, 283,369, 378.

[22] Torrence, *Pennsylvania Magazine*, "Upper West Conococheague Presbyterian Church," pages 133, 135, 137.

[23] Samuel Kyle will, 23 Jul 1783, will book A, page 42, Chambersburg, Franklin County Pennsylvania Probate, recorded 1784.

"23 Jul 1784, Samuel Kyll will, Montgomery Twp., Cumberland County Pennsylvania, daughter Ann Fleming, her son Samuel Bell Fleming; daughter Mary Willson, her daughter Jean Orbison; daughter Isabella Garretson, her son Samuel Kyll Garretson; son John and his son Samuel Kyll; Samuel, son of Joseph Kyll; granddaughters of son Samuel Kyll; sell personal estate to support most needy first; son Samuel land; son Joseph land; son Robert Kyll land where I now live; son James land if he helps brother Thomas to work land or to support and bury him decently; son Thomas land; Thomas and Samuel silver buttons; executors sons Samuel and Thomas Kyll; witnesses Thomas Kennedy, Hugh Long, Joseph Shannon; Samuel (X) Kill."

[24] Etta May Kyle, unpublished manuscript, about the *Kyle Family* written prior to 1950, pages 1-2.

Miss Kyle, Youngstown Ohio, descendant of John Kyle, eldest son of Samuel and Jean Kyle through Joshua Kyle, Joshua Kyle Jr. and his son Otis W. Kyle, who was her father; Otis researched the Kyle family but died before publishing it; his collection was inadvertently destroyed, and in an attempt to recover his life work, Etta Kyle spent years recreating it through correspondence with descendants of Samuel Kyle's family throughout the U.S.; she collected family histories and organized an annual meeting of Kyle descendants in her hometown; Etta died in 1950; her manuscript is in the Mahoning County Historical Society, Youngstown, Ohio; Miss Kyle credits Virginia S. Fendrick, a Franklin County historian, Mercersburg, Pennsylvania, with research on Kyle family church and cemetery records including the "Upper West Conococheague Presbyterian Church, that has records of when Samuel Kyle and his wife Jean Bell died.

[25] Robert Kyle household, 1790 U.S. Census, Heads of Families, 1st census of the U.S., Franklin County, Pennsylvania, (Washington D.C: Government Printing Office, 1908), page 115.

[26] Kile, *A Partial History of the Kyle, Kile, Coyle Family in America*, 75-79.

[27] See end note below, deed from Jane Kyle to John Cochran dated 18 Dec 1796.

[28] John E. Burns, *A General History of Covington, Kentucky through 1865*, (Covington, Kentucky: Kenton County Historical Society, 1986), volume 1:148.

[29] William Henry Egle, *Egle's Notes and Queries Relating to Pennsylvania*, "1898 Annual," (Baltimore: Genealogical Publishing Company, 1970), 54-55.

[30] H. M. J. Klein, *Lancaster County Pennsylvania, a History*, (New York, New York: Lewis Historical Publishing Co., Inc., 1924), 1719.

[31] Egle, *Notes and Queries*, "Welsh Settlers in Earl and Caernarvon Townships, Lancaster County, Jenkin David, Davies or Davis," 1897 Annual, 224-227, 232.

[32] Jinkin (Jenkin) David will, 9 Aug 1727, proved 16 Apr 1728, will book E, page 79, Richland, Chester County PA, *Philadelphia County Pennsylvania Wills 1682-1819*, downloaded from http://www.ancestry.com/PA/wills, on 26 Jul 2003.

[33] Egle, *Notes and Queries*, "Jenkin David, Davies, or Davis," 1897 Annual, 232; Thomas Edwards, Esq., 3rd Series, volume 3, pages 232, 85-86.

[34] Jenkin Davies will, Lancaster County Probate, Lancaster Pennsylvania, will book I1, page 92, 12 Feb 1747, probated 5 Dec 1748.

[35] Gwen Morgan will, Lancaster County Probate, will book D:1:429.
    "11 Aug 1746, Given (Gwen) Morgan, eldest son Morgan Morgan; daughter Ann, Edward Thornbrough's wife; son William Morgan, not in PA; daughters Joan and Elizabeth Davis, proved 26 Sep 1746."

[36] Egle, Notes and Queries, 4:2:97, 142 and 1898 Annual, page 54.

[37] R. Thomas Mayhill, compiler, *Lancaster County, Pennsylvania Deed Abstracts & Revolutionary War Oaths of Allegiance*, (Knightstown, Indiana: The Bookmark, 1973), Book M, page 374; 185.
    "5 Apr 1768, mortgage to Philip Rode, wife Margaret, Earl Twp.; from Zacheus Davis of same; for $1,300, 180 acres, Earl Township near John Davis, Zacheus Davis; 25 acres Earl Twp., part of Jenkin Davis tract, late Earl Twp., deceased; to Zacheus Davis, 10 Aug 1747; 13 May 1768 Zacheus and Willis Davis, executors; Jenkin Davis received Rhode's payment, 3 May 1791."

[38] "The Old Welsh Cemetery," *Tri-County Heritage Society, History of Berks, Chester and Lancaster Counties in Pennsylvania*. This online site has a photograph of the gravestones in the cemetery, including plot, number and headstone inscriptions; downloaded 25 Jul 2003, at www.tchslibrary.com/local_cemeteries/old_welsh_buried.htm
    "The Plan of the Graves on the West Wall has a sandstone monument on the cemetery's eastern column with these words, "Here lies the body of Jaen/Jean/John Davis departed this life 21 Jan 1738, aged 56 years;" others are Margaret Morgan, died 20 Aug 1781, age 76; Rees Morgan died 13 Jan 1769, aged 59; tombstone #23,Thomas Edwards, Esq. died 8 May 1764, aged 91; tombstone #24 Elizabeth Edwards died 30 Nov 1754, age 76; Joanna, wife of Zacheus Davis, Esq., died 21 Jan 1768, age 58; John Davis died 21 mar 1774, age 68."

[39] G. Terry Madonna, *The Revolutionary Leadership*, (Lititz, Pennsylvania: Sutter House, 1976), part of a series, "Lancaster County During the American Revolution," page unknown.

[40] Jane Evans Best, *Journal of the Lancaster County Historical Society*, (Lancaster, Pennsylvania: Lancaster County Historical Society, 1984), "The Old Welsh Graveyard Revisited," 51, 53-55, 58-59, 71, note 15. Anecdotal information about the Morgan, Davis and Edwards family was obtained from this source as was the following Bible record.
    " Jenkin David's Bible is at St. David's Church, Radnor, Chester County Pennsylvania and has an inscription showing ownership, "Jenkin David his Book 1702," then it passed down to his son, "Jenkin Davies his Book 1726." Two inscriptions are, Dinah [Davis] born 12 Oct 1735 about 12 of ye clock at night, [a] full moon; Zacheus [Davis] born week of 28 Feb 1710–moon age."

[41] Egle, *Notes and Queries*, Annual 1898, pages 54-56; Annual 1897 page 232; 4th Series, volume 2:142; Annual 1899, volume 7:25.

"The principal members who built the church (1733) were Zacheus Davice. A list of Bangor Church' vestry with service shows, Zacheus Davis, Earltown, 1756-1774. "

[42] Clarence E. Pearsall and Hettie May Pearsall, *History and Genealogy of The Pearsall Family in England and America*, (San Francisco: H.S. Crocker Company, Inc., 1985), V. 3: 45:1:1352-1358.

[43] *Pennsylvania Colonial Records, 1600-1800*, "Early Pennsylvania Land Records, Minute Book H, Provincial Council Minutes, 1683-1775," Family Archive CD512, The Learning Company, 2003.
        "Warrant to Richard and Jeremiah Pearsal, 300 acres, Chester County at £10 payable in three months; warrant to John. Pearsal, 200 acres, same price, dated 13 Oct 1717."

[44] Estate of John Piersol, *Pennsylvania Gazette*, 23 Feb 1780, 15 Apr 1789, 24 Feb 1790, items #65111, 75720, 76525, downloaded 5 Feb 1999 from http://204.170.102.11/scripts/webhits.piersol As directed in John Piersol's will, his executor advertised Piersol's property for sale over a period of ten years, offering first 180 acres, then 200 acres and finally 250 acres.

[45] John Piersol estate, "To be Sold at Public Vendue," *The Pennsylvania Packet* newspaper, 15 Oct 1778, Item #63260; Piersol's property described ad by Trego for plantation's sale, 22 Oct 1778.

[46] Samuel Bishop will, West Caln, *Wills: Abstracts and Administrations 1713-1825: Chester County, PA*, online at http://ftp.rootsweb.com/pub/usgenweb/pa/chester/wills, will book B, page 103.
        "28 Nov 1741, Samuel Bishop will, West Caln; son Joseph; daughters Susanna, Hannah, Sarah, Alice, Lydia, Mary, Rose, Priscilla; son John, Charles; estate remainder to wife [Alice] not named who is also executrix; witnesses: Jason Clud, George Jefferis and John McNabb."

[47] John Piersol will, W. Nantmeal, *Wills: Abstracts and Administrations 1713-1825: Chester Co. PA* online at http://ftp.rootsweb.com/pub/usgenweb/pa/chester/wills, will book F, page 289-290.
        "23 Apr 1773, John Piersol will; wife Alice plantation, then sell, proceeds to daughters, Sarah Porter, Alice Trego, Rebecca Brown, Elizabeth Pearsoll; also granddaughters Sarah and Mary Pearsoll, daughters of son John Pearsoll; daughter-in-law Bathsheba Pearsoll; grandchildren Mordecai, Hannah, Peter and Mary Pearsoll; daughter-in-law Dinah Kennedy; remainder to daughters, grandson John Davis, son of Mary Davis; Zacheus Pearsoll, son of my son John Pearsoll; son-in-law David Davis; son-in-law Joseph Trego; executors wife Alice Pearsoll, Joseph Trego, Wm. Gibbons; witnesses Wm. Trego, William Smith, Samuel Thomas; recorded 11 Sep 1778."

[48] Thomas H. Kennedy, *History of the Kennedy Family*, an unpublished manuscript written in 1912 when he was 79 years old. A portion of it is a story about Dinah Davis Piersol Kennedy, written by her grandson Thomas Kennedy.

[49] Pearsall, *History and Genealogy of The Pearsall Family in England and America*, 3: 45:3:1361.

[50] William H. Egle, editor, *Pennsylvania Archives*, "Chester County Rates 1765, 1766, 1767, 1768," (Harrisburg: Pennsylvania state printer, 1894-99), Series 3, V. 11: 45, 174, 335, 338, 482, 608.

[51] John B. Linn, William H. Egle, editors, *Pennsylvania Marriages Previous to 1790*: "Names of Persons for whom Marriage Licenses Were Issued in Pennsylvania Before 1790," (Baltimore: Genealogical Publishing Co. 1976), http://search.ancestry.com/cgi=bin/sse.dll, 8 Aug 2003.

[52] Kennedy, *History of the Kennedy Family*.

[53] S. Helen Fields, *Register of Marriages and Baptisms Performed by Rev. John Cuthbertson, 1751-1791*, (Baltimore: Genealogical Publishing Co., Inc, 1983), 87.
[54] Fields, *Marriages and Baptisms performed by Rev. John Cuthbertson*, 86, 87, 162.
        Rev. Cuthbertson's diary includes stops made between 12 May 1752 and 5 Nov 1778 in Chester County at Thomas Kennedy's house on the Brandywine River.

[55] Merri Lou Scribner Schaumann, *Tax Lists – Cumberland County, Pennsylvania, 1768, 1769, 1770*, "Peters Rates – 1770," (Carlisle, Pennsylvania: published by the author, 1972), 215.

[56] Bates, *History of Franklin County, Pennsylvania*, Part 2, Chapter 6, "Franklin County Organized," page not shown.

[57] Ronald Vern Jackson, *1790 Census, Heads of Families—Pennsylvania*, "Franklin County, Montgomery and Peters Townships,"

[58] Egle, *Notes and Queries*, Annual 1899, "Old Churchyard Records, In St. John's Cemetery at Compass Pa.," Vol. 11:25.
    "Zacheus Piersol, died 18 Nov 1804 age 40; Margaret Piersol, wife of Zacheus Piersol, daughter of Gabriel and Jane Davis, born 15 Sep 1756, died 23 Apr 1829."

[59] John E. Burns, *A History of Covington, Kentucky, Through 1865*, (Covington: Kenton County Historical Society, 1986), Vol. 1:148.

[60] Margaret Strebel Hartman, *Register of the Kentucky Historical Society*, "Covington and the Covington Company," (Frankfort: Kentucky Historical Society, 1971), Vol. 69:5:128.

[61] Lyman Copeland Draper, *Draper Manuscript Collection*, State Historical Society of Wisconsin, "Kentucky Manuscripts," Series CC, volume 11:99.

[62] Rebecca Kennedy, notice, *Western Spy and Hamilton Gazette* newspaper, published Cincinnati, Ohio, 20 Jun 1796.

[63] Kennedy deed, Court Order Book, Campbell County, Alexandria Kentucky, Deed Book C: 109.

[64] Chuck Bricking, *Covington's Heritage*, (Kenton, County Kentucky: published by the author, no date), 21-22.

[65] *Kentucky Ancestors*, "Court Order book A, Campbell County, Kentucky," 7 Dec 1795 through Dec 1800, (Frankfort: Kentucky Historical Society, 1973), volume 9:1:74, 79, 206, 251.

[66] Hartman, "Covington and the Covington Company," 69:5:128-130.

[67] Sara L. Johnson, Musical Rambles Through History, "In Tune with the Times: The Ohio Boatmen," downloaded from http://members.aol.com/kitchiegal/smokepage.html.
    "Shan Trews is a traditional Scottish dance which literally translated means 'old trousers.' The dance depicts a man shedding his trousers and dancing in his kilt, and is a reference to a time in history when wearing a kilt was banned."

[68] Thomas Kennedy's will, *Kentucky Ancestors*, "Abstracts of Wills, Campbell County, Kentucky, will book A," (Alexandria Kentucky: publisher, 1972), 7:4:189, page 352.
    "14 Jul 1821,Thomas Kennedy will, Covington, Campbell County Kentucky; son Joseph; Joseph's children, Thomas, Alfred, Davis, Hannah, Eliza, Nancy and Sally; Sally Kyle; Mary Scott, James Scott's wife; Peggy Peirsol, widow Zacheus Peirsol; Jane Dixon, Henry Dixon's wife; Nancy Dixon, Henry Dixon's daughter; William Porter heirs by wife Hannah; son Samuel; Nancy Kennedy, Thomas D. Kennedy's wife; executors, sons Joseph and Samuel Kennedy, William Porter; testators Alexander Connelly, William Barns, A. P. Sanford; recorded November Court 1821."

[69] Kennedy estate inventory, Campbell County Probate Records, Inventories and Estates, Alexandria, Kentucky, 11 Jul 1821, Vol. 2:54-56 (Family History Library: Salt Lake City), microfilm #0530358.

[70] Margaret Strebel Hartman, *Register of the Kentucky Historical Society*, "Early Kentucky Tax Records: Campbell County Tax Lists 1795," (Frankfort: Kentucky Historical Society, 1984), page 7.

[71] Margaret Strebel Hartman, *Campbell County Court House Road Abstracts, 1795-1820*, in the Collection of the Kentucky Historical Society, Vol. 1:50, 83, 99, 101.

[72] Kentucky Order Books, Campbell Co., Alexandria Kentucky, Order Book 28 Aug 1809, 1;104.

[73] Stephen W. Worrell, *Campbell County Kentucky 1795-1840 Marriage Records*, (Falls Church Virginia: privately published, 1992), pages 3-16.

"7 Apr 1800 Dinah Kyle married John White; 31 Dec 1802 Jean Kyle married Henry Dixon, permission by Robert Kyle; 22 Oct 1803 Samuel Bell Kyle married Anna McKay; 8 Nov 1810 John Kyle married Sarah Rich; 8 Oct 1815 Thomas Kyle married Susan Rich; 17 Apr 1817 Sarah Kyle married Joseph Rich; 14 Feb 1812 Molly (Mary) Kyle married Robert Long."

[74] Taken from a typed copy of one of Etta Kyle's papers during a 1932 visit to the courthouse in Alexandria, Kentucky, where, while copying his will and other papers, she had a conversation with one of the judges of the probate court about Robert Kyle.

[75] Robert Kyle, will of, Campbell County Probate Court, Alexandria Kentucky, 4 Nov 1823, recorded 27 Jun 1825, will book B: 142-145.

[76] Kyle, *Kyle Family* unpublished manuscript. Given to Etta Kyle by Charles Kyle, Freeport Illinois; saying that Mary Cochran was Zacheus Kyle's wife, and her lineage is: Samuel Kyle-Jean Bell/John Kyle-Hannah Wilson/Ann Kyle-John Cochran/Mary Cochran-Zacheus Kyle. An Allegheny County Pennsylvania deed copied by Etta Kyle provides further proof of her lineage.

"18 Dec 1796, Deed book I-9: 185-186, deed from Jane Kyle, Elizabeth Twp., Allegheny County, single woman to John Cochran, same place; whereas late John Kyle, Westmoreland County purchased 300 acres in Elizabeth township, Allegheny County); that John Kyle died in testate leaving widow Hannah, lately deceased, and issue Ann Kyle who married John Cochran, and other children including Jane Kyle, who are John Kyle's heirs at law; whereas Jane Kyle is selling her share to John Cochran for £100; witness Henry Westbay; recorded 30 Sep 1799."

[77] The author read these tombstones in Mt. Moriah Cemetery, August 1996; Robert Kyle, died March 15, 1825; Sarah Kyle died October 9th, 1838; James Kenny born February 1797; died 26 Jan 1833."

[78] Kennedy to Cummins marriage, Hamilton County Ohio, downloaded from *Family Search,* Batch #8108302 on 24 Aug 2003, http://www.familysearch.org.

[79] Thomas H. Kennedy, *History of the Kennedy Family.*

Joseph Kennedy and Agnes (Nancy) Cummins had a son, "Thomas Davis Kennedy, born in September 1795, Campbell County; Nancy died 7 Aug 1802; Joseph married Rachel Todd in 1803; she died without children in 1805; Joseph married Nancy Sanford 25 Jul 1805; Joseph married 11 Oct 1807, Mary Davis Kenny, widow of Robert Kenny."

[80] *War of 1812*, Robert Kyle "16th regiment Porter's Kentucky Militia," downloaded on 23 Jan 1999 from http://www.sierra.com/sierrahome/familytree/records/w1812/list.

[81] Kyle to Kenny, *Campbell County Marriage Bonds, 1820*, Alexandria Kentucky Court Records, written on outside, M.S. Bone Commonwealth, 5 Oct 1820.

[82] *Cumberland County Pennsylvania Marriages 1761-1800*, (Philadelphia: Genealogical Society of Pennsylvania, 1983), Pennsylvania Vital Records, "First Presbyterian Church of Carlisle," 1: 612.

[83] D. Kennedy household, 1850 U.S. Census, Kenton County, Kentucky, Covington city, page 260, dwelling 727, family 747; National Archives film #M432, roll 208.

[84] Kenny, Kyle and Kennedy to Philip Zeigler deed, 15 Sep 1828, Cumberland County Recorder, Carlisle Pennsylvania, (Family History Library, Salt Lake City UT), roll #0021061.

"15 Sep 1828, deed from James Kenny, Perry County Tennessee; Robert Kyle, wife Mary Kenny, Clermont County Ohio; John Kenny, Lauderdale County Alabama; Mary Kennedy, Campbell County Kentucky, late wife Robert Kenny, deceased; to Philip Zeigler, North Middleton Township, Cumberland County; 56 acres, Middleton Twp., 100 acres tract warranted 10 Jul 1752 to James Kenny; (7 Nov 1806, 44 acres sold by Robert Kenny to Adam Cowper; recorded 15 Sep 1828); recorded 27 Dec 1884, deed book KK: 548-551.

[85] Kenny to Sanderson, mortgage, Cumberland County Recorder, Carlisle Pennsylvania, deed book K: 426-428.

[86] James Kenny, juror, *Cumberland County, Pennsylvania Quarter Session Docket 1750-1758*, (Baltimore: Clearfield Press, 2000), pages 181, 182 for the year 1772.

[87] James Kenny, petitioner, *Cumberland County Quarter Sessions Docket 1768.*
    "Jan 1768, Quarter Sessions Court, Carlisle, Cumberland County; petition of those living between Carlisle Iron Works and Croghan's Gap, North Mountain and Shearman's Valley, for a road from Croghan's Gap to Carlisle at Chamber's Mill, to mouth of Letort Spring, to Carlisle Iron Works; petitioners viewing and laying out road are (among others) Andrew McBeth, James Kenny, William Smith, John Bigham, John, George, Robert Sanderson, Samuel, John and Thomas Martin."

[88] James and Mathew Kenny, 1769 taxes, *Cumberland County Quarter Session Court Dockets*, Carlisle, Pennsylvania, from a typed copy of tax records in the Pennsylvania Archives, Series 3, from 1750-1779, not numbered.

[89] Dan McClenehan, *Mifflin County, Pennsylvania, Will Abstracts, 1789-1860*, (Reedsville Pennsylvania: privately published, 1983), Vol. 1:20, page 225.
    "13 Jun 1811, Mathew Kenny will, Union Twp., late Middleton Twp.; sons James, John, Robert; daughters Mary, Jane, Margaret, Martha, Elizabeth and Rachel; wife Elizabeth; witnesses David Wilson, John Wilson Jr. and John Wilson Sr.; recorded 20 Dec 1811."

[90] James Kenny will, Cumberland County Probate Court, Carlisle, Pennsylvania, 27 Sep 1783, recorded 21 Jul 1784, will book D: 216-217, number 142.

[91] Smith to Kenny, *Cumberland County, Pennsylvania, Marriages 1761-1800* "First Presbyterian Church of Carlisle."

[92] Merri Lou Scribner-Schaumann, *Indictments, Cumberland County Pennsylvania, 1750-1800*, (Dover, Pennsylvania, 1989), 65-66.

[93] Wilbur J. McElwain, *United States Direct Tax of 1798*, "Tax Lists for Cumberland County, Pennsylvania," (Bowie, Maryland: Heritage Books, 1994), x, 116.

[94] *History of Cumberland and Adams Counties, Pennsylvania*, (Chicago: Warner Beers & Co, 1886), 306, 501.

[95] F. Edward Wright, *Abstracts of South Central Pennsylvania Newspapers, Carlisle Gazette 1785-1800*, "Sheriff's Sale," (Westminster, MD: Family Line Publications, 1988), V. 3, (1796-1800).

[96] Kenny to Sanderson deed, Cumberland County Recorder, Carlisle Pennsylvania, (Family History Library: Salt Lake City), book K, page 426.
    "17 Apr 1793, mortgage deed from Robert Kenny, Middleton Twp., Cumberland County Pennsylvania to George Sanderson of same, 100 acres Tyrone Twp., land James Kenny bought 1 Sep 1759, and gave in will to Robert Kenny; 26 Jun 1789, Robert Kenny surveyed two warrants, 330 acres, Tyrone Twp. for £630; witnesses William Wallace and John Jordan; recorded 17 Apr 1793."

[97] Commonwealth of Pennsylvania to Kenny, Cumberland County Recorder, Carlisle Pennsylvania. deed book #K page not numbered, (Family History Library: Salt Lake City), microfilm #002105, deed books K-L 1791-1796.
    "Warrant to Robert Kenny, 40 acres near William Sanderson, James Lambertson, Middleton Twp., Cumberland County, rate 50 shillings per 100 acres, witness Thomas Mifflin, 11 Mar 1794."

[98] Robert Kyle household, 1850 U.S. Census, Clermont County, Ohio, Union Twp., page 481, dwelling 2939, family 2962; National film #M432; Robert Kyle household, 1860 census, Clermont County, Ohio, Union Twp., page 255, dwelling 1161, family 1119; National Archives film #M653.

[99] Robert Kinney household, 1800 U.S. Census, Cumberland County, Pennsylvania, page 153, line 8; National Archives micro-publication M32, roll 38.

[100] Robert Kenney, militia, *Pennsylvania Archives*, Series 5, V. 6, "Names of those in 1st Battalion, Cumberland County Militia,"Muster and Pay Rolls," (Harrisburg: Pennsylvania, 1906), p.173.
　　Robert Kenney is on the list as is his brother-in-law William McClurg, and neighbors Hugh Smith, and the Lambertson and Sanderson families.

[101] Kenny to Ziegler deed, Cumberland County Recorder, Carlisle Pennsylvania, patent book #47, page 206, 21 Apr 1802, deed book P, p. 47-48.
　　"21 Apr 1802, deed from Robert Kenny, wife Mary, Middleton Twp., Cumberland County Pennsylvania; to Philip Ziegler, Upper Sulford Twp., Montgomery County Pennsylvania; two tracts, *Monmouth* (98 acres), *Dover* (216 acres); to Ziegler for $6,533.23, paid cash on that date; witness John Delancey; recorded 21 Apr 1802."

[102] Jonathan K.T. Smith, *The Nashville Christian Advocate* newspaper, "Genealogical Abstracts from Reported Deaths, 1897-1899," (Nashville: by the author, 2002), Jan.-June 1889, page 12.
　　"John Kenney, born Covington KY 5 Aug 1803, m. Jane Douglas 1833; died 4 Sep 1888."

[103] G. M. Hopkins, *Atlas of Covington Kentucky*, "Map of Covington Kentucky," (Washington: Library of Congress, 1877). A map of eastern Covington where the Ohio and Licking Rivers meet, shows Newport, Kentucky, and that the Newport Barracks were on the west side of the Licking River.

[104] Robert Kenny taxes, Campbell County Kentucky Court Records, tax lists, (Family History Library: Salt Lake City), Tax Books 1785-1809 film #0007911, for 1805-1806, pages not recorded.

[105] Robert Kenny, tavern license, Campbell County Kentucky Order Books 1795-1805, (Family History Library: Salt Lake City), microfilm #0459976, April Court 1805, p. 359.

[106] Ritenour to Kenny deed, Campbell County Recorder, Alexandria Kentucky, deed book C, 1804-1810, p. 88-89.

[107] Jonathon Huling, tavern license, jailer, Campbell County Kentucky Order Books 1795-1805, (Family History Library: Salt Lake City), microfilm #0459976.

[108] Karen Maurer Green, *Pioneer Ohio Newspapers, 1793-1810: Genealogical & Historical Abstracts*, "Western Spy and Hamilton Gazette," (Galveston, Texas: Frontier Press, 1986), May 1799-December 1810.
　　"Obituary, Captain Robert Kenney died, Saturday 30 May 1807 at Newport, Kentucky. He was buried on Sunday in Cincinnati attended by the brethren of the Cincinnati Lodge."

[109] Robert Kenny estate, Campbell County Probate Records, Covington Kentucky, will books 1794-1816, (Family History Library, Salt Lake City), microfilm #0459976, will book A: 102-104.
　　"16 Jul 1807, appraisers David Lewis, Bernard Neal, George Porter, recorded Sept 1807."

[110] Mary Hewling Reed, "Declaration of Mary Kennedy's character," Campbell County Kentucky Probate Court, will books B-C 1820-1879, Washington D.C. Bureau of Records, (Family History Library, Salt Lake City), microfilm #0529406, page not shown.

[111] Kennedy to Kenny marriage, Campbell County Marriage Records, Alexandria, Kentucky. The author has a copy of the original marriage license from the Alexandria Kentucky courthouse.

[112] Kenny and Kennedy guardianship, Fleming County Orphan's Court Records, Flemingsburg, Kentucky, Court Minutes Book, June Court 1813, page not numbered.

[113] See Kenny, Kyle and Kennedy to Philip Zeigler, deed, 15 Sep 1828.

[114] Allen J. Sexton and Shelby L. Meyer, Sr., compilers, *Linden Grove Cemetery of Covington, Kenton County Kentucky*, (Newport, Kentucky: published by the author, 1963), 99.

[115] James Kenny and Mary Kenny (Kyle) tombstones were visited by the author in Aug 1998 at Mt. Moriah Cemetery, Union Township, Clermont County Ohio where they were photographed.

[116] Jonathan Kennon Thompson Smith, *The Nashville Christian Advocate* newspaper, "Genealogical Abstracts from Reported Deaths, 1885-1886, 1897-1899," copyright 2003, downloaded from http://www.tngenweb.org/madison/smith/nca85-01.htm, pages 77, 123.
    "Jane G. Kenney, nee Douglass, born N.C., 14 Feb 1811; moved with brother, Rev. Joseph E. Douglass, to Williamson County Tennessee; married John Kenney of Florence Alabama, 10 Dec 1833; died 7 Jan 1886; 11 children, 9 surviving her; John Kenney born Covington, Kentucky 5 Aug 1803; married Jane G. Douglass, 1833; died 4 Sep 1888."

[117] Author, *Goodspeed's Biographical & Historical Memoirs of Western Arkansas, 1891*, "Pope County: J. R. Kenney, M.D."

[118] Kyle tax records, *Clermont County Tax Duplicates, 1815-1817*, Batavia, Ohio, (Family History Library: Salt Lake City), microfilm #0476476, pages not numbered.

[119] Samuel Kyle, John Kyle and Thomas Kyle households, 1820 U.S. Census, Clermont County Ohio, Union Township, page 46-48, National Archives film #M33, roll 89.

[120] Robert Kyle, John White households, 1830 U.S. Census, Clermont County Ohio, Union Township, page 202, National Archives fil #M19, roll 128.

[121] Kyle vs. Kyle, Clermont County Chancery Court, Batavia Ohio, (Family History Library: Salt Lake City), film #1288377, April Court 1826, Robert Kyle et al vs. Rebecca Kyle, pages 70-73.

[122] Robert Kyle deceased, petition for estate division, Clermont County Probate, Common Pleas docket, Batavia Ohio, V. 22:53-54, Case #7517. The record was copied from the original.
    "22 Dec 1883, deed from Robert K. Kyle & Jennie K. Kyle; to heirs of Robert Kyle deceased; Alfred S. Kyle & Lavinia Kyle; Frances E. Morrison & Wm. P. Morrison; Nancy C. Johnson & Merritt Johnson; Prudence A. Manning & Courtland C. Manning; of Union Township, Clermont County Ohio; to Jefferson K. Kyle for $1 and an exchange of deeds on Lot #1, part of Morrow's Survey #666, Union Township, 37 acres set off to Jefferson. Kyle in farm partition; witnesses Ambrose Temple, Valllie Monjar, Rebecca Kelley, recorded 7 Mar 1884."

[123] Kyle tax records, Clermont County Ohio Tax Duplicates, Batavia, Ohio, (Family History Library: Salt Lake City), microfilm #0476477, 1825-1826, pages not numbered.

[124] *The Ohio Sun* newspaper, Batavia Ohio, 16 Mar 1835.

[125] "Big Hunters," *The Clermont Sun* newspaper, Batavia Ohio, 18 Jan 1893, Vol. 65, #34.

[126] *The Clermont Courier* newspaper, 3 May 1850.

[127] Joseph Kyle, articles referring to him in *The Clermont Courier* newspaper, 3 May 1850, 27 Aug 1857, 3 Sep 1857, 10 Sep 1857, 24 Mar 1859, 26 May 1859, 17 Nov 1859, Apr 1875.

[128] "Clermont County Agricultural Fairs," *The Clermont Courier* newspaper, published Batavia Ohio, articles from 31 Oct 1850, 21 Aug 1851, 30 Oct 1851, 27 Aug 1857, 10 Jun 1858, 6 Oct 1859, 20 Oct 1859, 25 Sep 1861, 18 Jun 1862.

[129] Kyle to Vail marriage, *Marriage Records of Clermont County, Ohio, 1800-1850*, page 125.

[130] Clermont County Genealogical Society, *Clermont County, Ohio Marriage Records 1850-1874*, (Baltimore: Gateway Press, 1989), 288; 05-154.

"28 Apr 1850 Eliza Kyle (20) to William P. Morrison (30); 28 Oct 1852 Robert Kyle (26) to Lucy Witham (24); 24 May 1855 Nancy C. Kyle (22) to Merritt Johnson (29); 24 Jan 1861 Prudia A. Kyle (19) to Cortline C. Manning (21); 18 Jan 1863 John A. Kyle (23) to Joanna Sweeney (18); 6 Jan 1870 Alfred S. Kyle (25) to Vina J. Fitch (20)."

[131] "Census of Clermont County," *The Clermont Courier* newspaper, 28 Nov 1860, 12 Dec 1860.

[132] Frances E. Morrison, Jefferson K. Kyle, obituaries, *Clermont Sun* newspaper, 21 Mar 1888, 27 Nov 1889.

"Mrs. Frances E. Morrison, age 57 died at home in Mt. Carmel last Friday morning (16 Mar 1888); funeral from the Universalist Church, Sunday at 11 a.m.; Jefferson K. Kyle, born Union Township, Clermont County Ohio, 20 Jan 1823; married Catharine Vail 20 Jan 1846; died 10 Nov 1889; an immense congregation gathered at the church on the 12th where Rev W. S. Bacon conducted the funeral services."

[133] Robert Kyle Obituary, *The Clermont Sun* newspaper, 2 Jan 1882.

[134] 9 Jun 1794, Washington to Morrow, to Taylor & Lytle, to Kyle deed, 1,000 acres Morrow's Survey #666, Union Township, Clermont County, Ohio; 9 Jun 1794 from Washington to Morrow, 7 May 1796, from Morrow to Taylor and Lytle; 15 Aug 1796, from Lytle & Taylor to Robert Kyle; recorded 20 Jun 1800, Deed Book C. Vol. 4, pages 350-351; recorded 29 Jan 1836; patented 15 Aug 1796, recorded 20 Jun 1800 by Kyle.

[135] Robert Kyle Estate, *The Clermont Sun* newspaper, 21 Mar 1882, 4 Nov 1884.

INDEX

Maiden names and former married names and nicknames are shown in (parentheses).
Nicknames and given names are shown with a forward slash.

www.ingramcontent.com/pod-product-compliance
Lightning Source LLC
Chambersburg PA
CBHW050600270326
41926CB00012B/2124